Procedures from Abstract D...

Procedures	Modules
Assign	Strings, Sets
AssignChar	Strings
AssignConst	Strings
Cardinality	Sets
Clear	Graphs, MFSETs
Close	FileSystem, Files
Combine	BTreeADT
Concat	Strings
Copy	Strings
CountQueue	QueueADT
Create	Tables, Graphs
CreateList	ListADT
CreateNode	AVLTreeADT
CreateQueue	QueueADT
CreateSet	Sets
CreateStack	Stacks
CreateTree	BinaryTreeADT, BSTreeADT
Delete	FileSystem, Strings, Files, ListADT, Tables
DeleteEdge	Graphs
DeleteElement	BTreeADT
DeleteNode	BinaryTreeADT, BSTreeADT, AVLTreeADT
DeleteTree	BinaryTreeADT, BSTreeADT
DeleteVertex	Graphs
Dequeue	QueueADT
Difference	Sets
DisplayKeys	Tables
DisplayTree	BinaryTreeADT, BSTreeADT
DisposeQueue	QueueADT
DisposeStack	Stacks
DisposeString	Strings
Empty	Stacks, Sets
Enqueue	QueueADT
EOF	Files
Equal	Sets
EqualElements	ListElements
ExchangeAndDelete	AVLTreeADT
Exclude	Sets
ExistNode	BinaryTreeADT
FetchChar	Strings
Find	MFSETs
FindVertex	Graphs

(continued on page opposite back cover)

Data Structures and Algorithms
with Modula-2

Data Structures and Algorithms

with Modula-2

Philippe J. Gabrini
Université du Québec à Montréal

Barry L. Kurtz
Louisiana Tech University

D. C. HEATH AND COMPANY
Lexington, Massachusetts   Toronto

Address editorial correspondence to:
D. C. Heath
125 Spring Street
Lexington, MA 02173

Cover: Design Ad Cetera, Inc.

Trademark acknowledgment: Sun is a registered trademark of Sun Microsystems.

Copyright © 1992 by D. C. Heath and Company.

All rights reserved. No part of this publication may be reproduced or transmitted in any form or by any means, electronic or mechanical, including photocopy, recording, or any information storage or retrieval system, without permission in writing from the publisher.

Published simultaneously in Canada.

Printed in the United States of America.

International Standard Book Number: 0-669-12304-8

Library of Congress Catalog Number: 91-72535

10 9 8 7 6 5 4 3 2 1

To all my former, current, and future students
Philippe J. Gabrini

To my mother, Ruth
Barry L. Kurtz

PREFACE

This textbook includes comprehensive coverage of enough topics in data structures and algorithms to make it appropriate for a variety of courses, including those with an emphasis in elementary or intermediate data structures, advanced programming and problem solving, or software engineering. If the data structures course comes early in the curriculum, one of its most important roles is to help the students synthesize problem solving and programming. These topics may have been covered in the first computer science course; however, students usually don't have much experience either in problem solving or in programming. To help overcome this possible deficit, we have included an appendix to cover the techniques of programming methodology. All chapters but one include a major case study illustrating the design, implementation and testing of software. You will find an emphasis on tradeoffs between alternative designs, the importance of developing testing strategies early, and the necessity of good documentation at every step in the process.

This book offers a sequential presentation of topics which can be modified to suit a particular course. **Part One: Data Structure Basics,** introduces data types and structures in Modula-2, array data structures, the analysis of algorithms illustrated by elementary searching and sorting algorithms, and abstract data types. **Part Two: Fundamental Data Structures,** covers linear lists, stacks, queues, binary trees, and binary search trees. **Part Three: Advanced Data Structures,** includes special purpose trees, advanced sorting techniques, tables, strings, generalized lists, graphs, and sets. These topics are relatively independent so the instructor can select chapters to suit the needs of a particular course.

The main features of this book are its emphases on

- abstract data types
- analysis of algorithms
- programming methodology
- comparison of implementations
- the use of complete application examples
- the use of standard Modula-2

The objectives of this book are to teach what could be called ''classic'' data structures, in a context of abstraction, specification and program construction. In the Abstract Data Type (ADT) context, these objectives naturally include the presentation of the algorithms associated with the data structures as well as some tools to measure their complexity. The Modula-2 programming language is used throughout the book but is not really part of the main objectives. Most algorithms are presented in pseudocode and could be implemented in a variety of block structured languages.

This book departs from the methods used by existing data structures books in that it presents each new data type in four steps.

First, there is a discussion of the ADT:

> abstract values
> operations with pre-conditions and post-conditions (with some informal relations between operations)

This leads to a complete specification of the ADT in the form of a Modula-2 definition module.

Second, the ADT just defined is used in various applications. This is absolutely *vital* for the students to comprehend the worth of ADTs and how such abstractions can be used in applications *without* any notion about the way they are implemented.

Third, alternative ADT implementations are considered:

> representation for the values of the type
> algorithms for the operations

The implementations are compared in an empirical manner, and, if possible, in an analytical manner. This should encourage students to design an implementation of their own and to compare it to the implementations already presented.

Fourth, a complete case study involving the data type is developed to emphasize the design and testing aspects of software development in addition to code implementation. Some case studies deal with applications while others involve alternative data structure implementations.

Part One: Data Structure Basics

This portion of the book has four chapters:

1. Data Types and Data Structures
2. Arrays
3. Searching, Sorting, and the Analysis of Algorithms
4. Abstract Data Types

One should consider Appendix A, Programming Methodology, part of this basic material if these topics have not been covered in a prior programming course. For students who have used a software engineering approach with Modula-2 in the first course, it will be possible to skip Appendix A and Chapter 1, as indicated below.

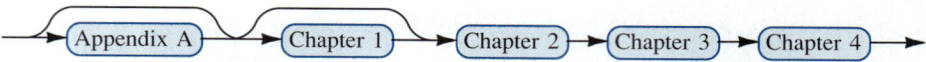

Appendix A is essentially a review that presents a six-step programming methodology based on the software life cycle. It will be used in the case studies and in the students' programming assignments. The presentation is completed by a sample case study.

Chapter 1 would be a review for those students who studied Modula-2 in their first course. Students moving from Pascal to Modula-2 should look at the material in Appendix D. Chapter 1 gives definitions and examples of the data types of Modula-2. It reviews the key data type concepts and also gives examples of corresponding data structures. The case study presents a simple application involving files.

Chapter 2 discusses a fundamental data structure, the array, and its various representations and implementations. Special cases like sparsely filled arrays are also presented with different implementations.

Chapter 3 introduces the Big-O notation for the analysis of algorithms, and applies it to a number of searching and sorting algorithms. The chapter concentrates more on algorithms than on data structures and presents most of the elementary algorithms for searching and sorting. Quicksort is presented as a more efficient sort and the case study introduces an internal MergeSort, another efficient sorting algorithm.

Chapter 4 is a very important chapter as it introduces the basic concept of an abstract data type (ADT), which is used throughout the book. This chapter also presents the realization of an ADT using Modula-2 definition and implementation modules. It introduces opaque types for information hiding and discusses the use of pointers to implement opaque types. The case study uses these techniques to develop an ADT for fractions.

Part Two: Fundamental Data Structures

This section of the text is essential for any study of data structures, as indicated by the topics in the following chapters:

5. Linear Lists
6. Stacks and Recursion
7. Queues
8. Trees
9. Binary Search Trees

These chapters should be covered in the order they are presented.

Chapter 5 covers the first fundamental ADT; the linear list, as well as the various list applications, representations, and implementations. It also presents some list related memory management techniques. The case study illustrates the implementation of a sparse matrix as a multilinked structure with embedded linear lists for rows and columns.

Chapter 6 introduces stacks and their uses, as well as their static and dynamic implementations. Using a good number of examples, the chapter also covers recursion and its implementation, the conversion of tail recursion to iteration, and the conversion of general recursion to iteration. The case study develops a nonrecursive version of Quicksort using a stack structure to save the bounds of partitions yet to be sorted.

Chapter 7 introduces an ADT for queues and uses the ADT to simulate the behavior of lines at the ticket booths of a train station. The use of queues in operating systems is discussed. After presenting both dynamic and static implementations, the case study uses the queue ADT to develop a simulation of a simple computer system.

Chapter 8 introduces trees, one of the most important, efficient, and widely used data structures. After discussing general trees, the chapter concentrates on binary trees. Applications range from expression trees to Huffman codes. Both static and dynamic implementations are discussed, but only the dynamic approach is developed in detail. the case study develops a technique important in Artificial Intelligence, the use of heuristics to search a Tic-Tac-Toe game tree.

Chapter 9 continues the development of binary trees with one of the most important applications: the binary search tree. After presenting the binary search tree ADT, it is applied to the problem of creating an index for a text. Implementations are discussed and a dynamic implementation is given in detail. The efficiency of search tree traversals motivates the case study—the development of threaded binary search trees.

Part Three: Advanced Data Structures

After covering the fundamental structures of linear lists, stacks, queues, trees, and binary search trees, the study of data structures can go many different directions. Instructors can select topics from the following chapters depending on the goals of the course.

10. Special Purpose Trees
11. Internal and External Sorting
12. Tables
13. Character Strings
14. Generalized Lists
15. Graphs
16. Sets

We have attempted to make these chapters relatively independent of one another. The presentation of materials continues at the same level as the first part of the text, so the naming of this section as "Advanced" is somewhat a misnomer. Since this text covers too much material to be included in complete detail in a one-semester course, this section presents topics that might be considered optional for a first course on data structures although all topics are fundamental to a complete study of data structures.

Chapter 10 covers specialized trees: height-balanced trees, B-trees, and partially ordered trees to implement heaps and priority queues. Height-balanced trees solve the tree balance problem on an incremental approach; the case study presents an alternative approach using global rebalancing that is invoked by a procedure call.

Elementary searching and sorting techniques were first studied in Chapter 3; more advanced techniques are presented in Chapters 11 and 12. Chapter 11 concentrates on alternative internal sorting techniques, such as shell sort and radix sort, and then studies in detail methods well suited for sorting data stored on external devices, such as disk drives and tape drives. The case study develops the tournament sort, an n log n algorithm. Chapter 12 introduces the table abstract data type, and some of its applications. It also introduces searching algorithms using the special table implementation technique known as *hashing*. The case study introduces performance analysis in the form of comparing several collision resolution strategies for hashing into a closed table.

Strings are one of the most widely used data structures: their applications are numerous. The Strings ADT is introduced in Chapter 4 and used throughout the text. Chapter 13 discusses character strings as a special kind of linear structure whose importance warrants a separate presentation. Text formatting and data encryption applications are presented, as well as several interesting pattern matching algorithms. Several alternative implementations of the string data structure are discussed in detail. The case study involves the performance analysis for four pattern matching algorithms: simple search, Knuth-Morris-Pratt, simple Boyer-Moore, and Rabin-Karp.

Chapter 14 introduces generalized lists to show that lists do not have to be necessarily linear. The main application of generalized lists is the programming language Lisp, which is briefly presented. Automatic memory management and garbage collection is also discussed. The case study presents the Schorr-Waite-Deutsch algorithm, an elegant technique for traversing and marking nodes in a generalized list structure.

Chapter 15 introduces graphs and their applications. This leads to the introduction of several representations with emphasis on the adjacency matrix and adjacency list representations. Many of the well-known graph algorithms are also presented. In the case study the performance of Dijkstra's algorithm is compared for the adjacency matrix and adjacency list representations.

Chapter 16 introduces sets and some of their applications. The implementations presented are based on built in types, lists, and trees. A special kind of sets, Merge-find sets, is also introduced and applied in a presentation of Kruskal's algorithm. In the case study alternative designs for a Merge-find sets ADT are presented and one is selected for implementation.

Other Features of This Textbook

Several appendixes cover Modula-2 syntax, ASCII character codes, and the differences between Pascal and Modula-2. All chapters in the book are followed by exercises and programming problems. Solutions to many exercises are given at the end of the text, although programming problems are not solved and can be used as assignments. An instructor's guide provides additional solutions for exercises and programming problems. A student disk provides all complete programs from the text in "soft" form. The instructor's disk includes this material plus additional programs worked out as solutions to the programming problems.

Program Disk Instructions

A program disk containing the text programs is included with each book. It is available in Macintosh, IBM 3-1/2" and IBM 5-1/4" formats. The 5-1/4" disk contains files that have been compressed using compression software. To use these files, they must be uncompressed and transferred to a larger disk. The 5-1/4" disk contains instructions on how to do this, in a file called Readme. A summary of these instructions follows:

This disk contains three files:
README   the file you are reading now
PROGRAMS.ZIP   selected program files from the text
PKUNZIP.EXE   the program you will need to uncompress the program files

The expanded files cannot fit on this disk, they need to be put on some other disk. Suppose that you want to install these programs on your C: drive in the directory Modula-2. Go to the directory C:\Modula-2. Then type A:\PKUNZIP A:PROGRAMS.ZIP. This will run the program PKUNZIP off of the A: drive, which will uncompress the file PROGRAMS.ZIP on A: and leave the resultant 138 files in the directory C:\Modula-2. If this disk is in drive B: then all of the A: above become B:. You would make similar changes if the destination drive is some drive other than C:.

Acknowledgments

We would like to acknowledge the contributions of the following reviewers:

Barbara Barkauskas, University of Wisconsin—LaCrosse; Richard C. Detmer, Northwest Missouri State University; Henry A. Etlinger, Rochester Institute of Technology; Raymond O. Folse, Nicholls State University; John Hooper, Principia College; Richard G. Hull, Lenoir-Ryne College; S. Ron Oliver, California Polytechnic State University; Richard Rink, East Kentucky State University; and R. Kenneth Walter, Weber State University.

Their critical assessments of different versions of the text certainly had a positive effect on the text. Colleagues and students have also contributed much to the text, and we want to acknowledge their contribution.

We want to thank our editors and all the D. C. Heath people without whom the book would simply not be, and the hundreds of students who endured several versions of the text. Our greatest debt is to BITNET, which accommodated innumerable chapter transfers between New Mexico and Québec, and Mircrosoft Word on the MacIntosh, which allowed for easy development and modification of text materials.

Philippe J. Gabrini
Barry L. Kurtz

CONTENTS

PART ONE
Data Structure Basics 1

1 Data Types and Data Structures 3
- **1.1 Definitions** 4
- **1.2 Scalar Types** 4
  - Modula-2 Basic Types 4
  - Enumeration and Subrange Types 6
- **1.3 Structured Types** 7
  - Arrays 7
  - Records 8
  - Sets 9
  - Procedure Types 10
- **1.4 Type Compatibility** 12
- **1.5 Files** 13
- **1.6 Case Study: Merging Two Sorted Files** 15
  - Design 15
  - Implementation 21
  - *Summary* 25
  - *Exercises* 26
  - *Programming Problems* 27

2 Arrays 29
- **2.1 Definition** 30
- **2.2 Applications** 32
  - Transpose of a Square Matrix 32
  - Matrix Multiplication 33

xiii

2.3 **Implementation of General Arrays** 33
 Lexicographic Allocation 34
 Auxiliary Vectors 37

2.4 **Implementation of Specialized Arrays** 38
 Diagonal Matrices 39
 Tridiagonal Matrices 39
 Triangular Arrays 40
 Sparse Matrices 41
 Storing Indices with Element Values 42
 Storing Elements Row by Row 42
 Using a Bit Map 43
 Using a Augmented Bit Map 44
 Linked Representation 44
 Summary 44
 Exercises 45
 Programming Problems 46

3 Searching, Sorting, and the Analysis of Algorithms 49

3.1 **Analysis of Algorithms** 50
 The Big-O Notation 50
 Common Complexity Classes 51

3.2 **Simple Searching Algorithms** 53
 Sequential Search 53
 Binary Search 55

3.3 **Simple Sorts** 56
 Selection Sort 57
 Linear Insertion Sort 61
 Bubble Sort 64

3.4 **A More Efficient Sort: Quicksort** 67

3.5 Case Study: Merge Sort   72
Design   72
Implementation   76
Summary   78
Exercises   79
Programming Problems   80

4 Abstract Data Types   83

4.1 Definitions and Formal Specifications   84
4.2 Definition Module   86
4.3 Applications   91
4.4 Implementation Module   94
A Review of Pointers   97
4.5 Case Study: An Abstract Data Type for Fractions   98
Design   98
Implementation   108
Summary   115
Exercises   116
Programming Problems   117

PART TWO
Fundamental Data Structures   119

5 Linear Lists   121

5.1 Abstraction: The Linear List   122
5.2 Applications   124
High-Precision Arithmetic   124
Polynomial Arithmetic   126

5.3 Implementation   128
Static Implementation   128
Dynamic Implementation   132
Circular Lists   139
Symmetric Lists   140
List Headers   141

5.4 Multilinked Lists   142
5.5 Linked Implementations of Arrays   143
5.6 Memory Management   149
Allocation   149
Liberation   152

5.7 Case Study: Sparse Matrices   152
Design   152
Implementation   167
Summary   175
Exercises   176
Programming Problems   178

6 Stacks and Recursion   181

6.1 Abstraction: The Stack   182
6.2 Applications   185
Infix to Postfix Conversion   185
Solving a Maze   193

6.3 Implementation   199
Static Implementation   199
Dynamic Implementation   201

6.4 Generic ADTs   203
6.5 Recursion   208
Implementing Recursion   211
Recursion and Iteration   213
Converting Tail Recursion to Iteration   217
Converting General Recursion to Iteration   219

6.6 Case Study: A Nonrecursive Version of Quicksort   224
    Design   224
    Implementation   227
    Summary   230
    Exercises   231
    Programming Problems   233

7 Queues   235

7.1 Abstraction: The Queue   236

7.2 Applications   237
    Simulation of Central Station Wickets   237
    Queues in Operating Systems   245

7.3 Implementation   246
    Static Implementation   246
    Dynamic Implementation   249

7.4 Case Study: A Computer Simulation   251
    Design   251
    Implementation   262
    Summary   276
    Exercises   277
    Programming Problems   278

8 Trees   279

8.1 Definitions   280

8.2 Abstraction   282
    Binary Tree   284

8.3 Applications   287
    Searching   287
    Expression Trees   289
    Huffman Codes   291

- **8.4 Implementation** 297
  - Dynamic Implementation 297
  - Static Implementation 304
- **8.5 Case Study: A Tic-Tac-Toe Playing Program** 307
  - Design 307
  - Implementation 314
  - *Summary* 323
  - *Exercises* 323
  - *Programming Problems* 325

9 Binary Search Trees 327

- **9.1 Abstraction: The Binary Search Tree** 328
- **9.2 Application** 330
  - Creation of an Index for a Text 330
- **9.3 Implementation** 335
- **9.4 Case Study: Threaded Binary Search Trees** 340
  - Design 340
  - Implementation 353
  - *Summary* 359
  - *Exercises* 359
  - *Programming Problems* 360

PART THREE
Advanced Data Structures 361

10 Special Purpose Trees 363

- **10.1 Height-Balanced Trees** 364
- **10.2 B-Trees** 377
  - Searching 378
  - Insertion 380

Deletion 384
Complexity 390

10.3 Optimal Search Trees 390
10.4 Heaps and Priority Queues 392
10.5 Case Study: Global Rebalancing 395
Design 395
Implementation 400
Summary 405
Exercises 406
Programming Problems 407

11 *Internal and External Sorting* 409

11.1 Internal Sorting 410
Shell Sort 410
Heapsort 412
Radix Sort 415

11.2 External Sorting 418
Merge Sort 418
Polyphase Sort 423

11.3 Case Study: Implementing the Tournament Sort 431
Design 431
Implementation 436
Summary 440
Exercises 440
Programming Problems 441

12 *Tables* 443

12.1 Abstraction: The Table 444
12.2 Applications 445
A Name Server 445

12.3 Implementations 450
Searching Tables 454

12.4 *Hash Tables*   457
    Hash Functions   458
    Collision Resolution   460

12.5 *Case Study: Collision Resolution in a Closed Hashed Table*   466
    Design   466
    Implementation   471
    Summary   475
    Exercises   476
    Programming Problems   477

13 *Character Strings*   481

13.1 *Abstraction: The String*   482

13.2 *Applications*   486
    Text Formatting   486
    Data Encryption   491

13.3 *Implementation*   496
    Static Implementation   496
    Dynamic Implementation   504

13.4 *Pattern Matching*   509
    Simple Search   509
    Knuth-Morris-Pratt Algorithm   510
    Boyer-Moore Algorithm   513
    Rabin-Karp Algorithm   515

13.5 *Case Study: Performance of Pattern-Matching Algorithms*   517
    Design   517
    Implementation   520
    Summary   529
    Exercises   530
    Programming Problems   531

14 Generalized Lists 533

14.1 Definition and Abstraction: The Generalized List 534
14.2 Application: The Lisp Programming Language 535
Definitions 536
Operations 536

14.3 Implementations 540
Lisp Representation 540
List Representations 541

14.4 Case Study: Garbage Collection 546
Design 546
Marking 549
Gathering 550
Implementation 555

14.5 Copying A List Structure 558
Summary 561
Exercises 562
Programming Problems 563

15 Graphs 565

15.1 Definitions and Abstraction 566
15.2 Applications 570
Topological Sort 570
Graph Traversal 572
Minimum-Cost Spanning Tree 576
Activity Graph 578

15.3 Implementation 581
Adjacency Matrix 581
Adjacency List 589

15.4 *Case Study: Dijkstra's Algorithm*   595
    Design   595
    Implementation   598
    Summary   604
    Exercises   604
    Programming Problems   606

16   Sets   609

16.1 *Definitions and Abstraction*   610
16.2 *Applications*   614
    Dictionary   614
    Finding a Set of Distinct Representatives   615
    Kruskal's Algorithm   618
16.3 *Implementation*   622
    Bit Vector   622
    Linked List   627
    Binary Search Tree   630
    Table   631
16.4 *Case Study: Merge-Find Sets*   632
    Design   632
    Implementation   636
    Summary   638
    Exercises   639
    Programming Problems   639

APPENDIXES

Appendix A   Programming Methodology   A1

Design   A2
Program Verification   A6

Algorithm Analysis   A7
Choice of Data Structures   A8
Implementation   A11
    Program Coding, Programming Style and Testing   A11
    Some Programming Style Guidelines   A11
    Some Debugging Guidelines   A12
    Summary of the Program Development Method   A14

Maintenance   A14
Application of the Method   A15
    Design   A15
    Implementation   A21

Summary   A32

Appendix B   Modula-2 Syntax   A33

Appendix C   ASCII Character Codes   A41

Appendix D   From Pascal to Modula-2   A54

Answers to Selected Exercises   A63

Index   A83

Data Structure Basics

CHAPTER

1 Data Types and Data Structures
2 Arrays
3 Searching, Sorting, and the Analysis of Algorithms
4 Abstract Data Types

Part One introduces the basic tools and techniques necessary for the study of data structures. Chapter 1, Data Types and Data Structures, reviews the built-in data types of Modula-2 and introduces the File type. Chapter 2, Arrays, discusses the mapping of array structures onto the linear structure of computer memory and introduces several specialized array structures. Chapter 3, Searching, Sorting, and the Analysis of Algorithms, reviews elementary techniques for searching and sorting before introducing more advanced methods. An analysis of these algorithms is presented using the Big-O notation. Modules are used to provide the data encapsulation necessary for Abstract Data Types, presented in Chapter 4. This leads to the use of the pointer type to implement information hiding. Pointers are used extensively throughout the remainder of the text.

Data Types and Data Structures

INTRODUCTION

The information that is stored and used by computer programs is called data. High-level programming languages make it possible to manipulate data after they are classified by their type. The concept of data type is very important and will be reviewed in detail in this chapter. Data are usually grouped or organized in a way that makes it easier to manipulate them. This organization of data is done through data structures, another important concept of computer science that will be reviewed in this chapter and studied in the rest of this book.

Chapter 1 Data Types and Data Structures

1.1 Definitions

A data type is the combination of a set of values and a set of operations on those values. An example of a data type is the type CARDINAL in Modula-2, combined with the basic arithmetic operations +, −, *, DIV, and MOD.

A data structure is an organized collection of data elements. A data structure can be viewed as an extension of a data type, where the values can be decomposed into component data, and where there exist relationships (structure) between the values and their components. An example of a data structure is the RECORD type in Modula-2, with the dot notation providing access to the individual fields. Another example is the ARRAY type, with indexing to provide access to individual elements.

1.2 Scalar Types

A scalar type is a type whose values (often called atomic values) cannot be decomposed. These values are simple values that can be ordered.

Modula-2 Basic Types

Modula-2 basic types are scalar types: CARDINAL, INTEGER, REAL, CHAR, and BOOLEAN, and the extended numeric types: LONGCARD, LONGINT, and LONGREAL.

CARDINAL Nonnegative integers from 0 to MAX(CARDINAL)

INTEGER Integers from MIN(INTEGER) to MAX(INTEGER)

Whatever the Modula-2 implementation, the types CARDINAL and INTEGER overlap. That is, CARDINAL and INTEGER values occupy the same space in memory (e.g., 16 bits on microcomputers, or 32 bits on larger computers). Therefore, values in the range [0..MAX(INTEGER)] are members of both the INTEGER and CARDINAL types, as illustrated in Figure 1-1.

Constants of these two types are expressed as numerals, such as 1234, −34, +456. The five basic operations that can be performed on CARDINAL and INTEGER values are represented by operators +, −, *, DIV, and MOD. Other operations include the

Figure 1-1
Integer and Cardinal Values

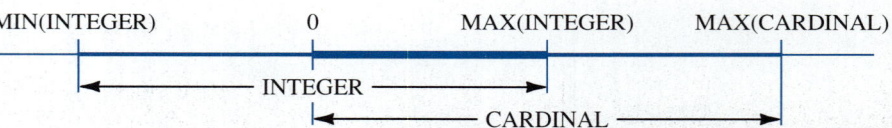

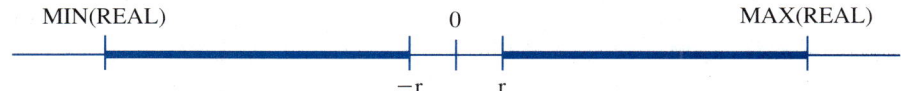

Figure 1-2 REAL Range

various comparisons, the assignment operation, and standard functions and procedures CHR, FLOAT, ODD, ORD, SIZE, DEC, INC, and VAL (a type conversion).

REAL Numbers with decimal points and an optional exponent. Limits are placed on the number of significant digits and the range of the exponent.

Constants of type REAL are expressed as an integer part followed by a decimal point (a period), followed by a fractional part, followed (or not) by the letter E and an integer exponent (power of ten). Two examples of REAL constants are: 12.345, and 765.43E − 12. The number of significant digits of a REAL and the range of the exponent are limited and are implementation dependent. As with integers, REAL values are part of an implementation-dependent range. It should also be noted that the REAL numbers **do not form a continuum,** due to the finite precision of the data representation. Values close to zero cannot be represented because of the limits on the exponent representation. As shown in Figure 1-2, the only value that can be represented between −r and r is zero. For those implementations respecting the IEEE standards, value magnitudes are limited to the approximate range 2.23E − 308 (r in Figure 1-2) and 1.79E308 (MAX(REAL) in Figure 1-2).

The four basic real arithmetic operations are denoted by the operators:

$$+ \quad - \quad * \quad /$$

Other operations include comparisons, assignment, and the standard functions ABS, SIZE, TRUNC, and VAL.

CHAR Single characters belonging to any character set; the most common of these are the ASCII set, used on most computers, and the EBCDIC set, used on IBM mainframe computers.

Constants of this type can be given as one character between quotes, or as an **octal value** followed by capital letter C. Examples are "a", "X", 40C. The operations available are comparisons, assignment, and the standard functions ORD, CAP, and VAL. Applied to a character value, function ORD returns the ordinal position of the character in an underlying character set, such as ASCII. Standard function CAP returns the corresponding uppercase letter if its parameter is a lowercase letter; otherwise it returns the parameter unchanged. Standard function CHR is the inverse of ORD: applied to a cardinal value, it returns the character occupying that position in the character set.

BOOLEAN   The values TRUE and FALSE

The operations available are NOT, OR, and AND.

The Modula-2 language includes two methods allowing programmers to construct other scalar types: enumerations and subranges.

Enumeration and Subrange Types

In an enumeration type, the programmer specifies a set of identifiers as the possible values of objects of that type. Thus:

```
TYPE Breed = (Collie, Poodle, Beagle, Greyhound, Dalmatian, Boxer);
```

defines enumeration type Breed. An object of this type can have one of the six constant values: Collie, Beagle, Poodle, Greyhound, Dalmatian, and Boxer. We can then have:

```
VAR Dog: Breed;
```

and

```
Dog := Beagle;
```

The available operations on such types are assignment and:

ORD   standard function that returns the ordinal number of the constant in the type:
ORD(Collie) = 0 and ORD(Greyhound) = 3.
VAL   standard function that performs the inverse operation of ORD:
VAL(Breed, 1) = Poodle.
MIN   standard function MIN(Breed) = Collie.
MAX   standard function MAX(Breed) = Boxer.
Comparison: Collie < Boxer is TRUE because ORD(Collie) < ORD(Boxer)

Input and output of enumeration values cannot be done directly. Rather, the programmer must write procedures to produce the desired input and output operations depending on the application.

For any scalar type other than REAL, it is possible to define a new type as a subrange of its values. Such subrange types represent subsets of the values of the base type.

```
TYPE UpperType = ['A'..'Z'];        (* a subrange of CHAR *)
     DayType = [0..31];             (* a subrange of CARDINAL *)
     ShortHaired = [Beagle..Boxer]; (* a subrange of Breed *)
```

The operations possible on the values of a subrange are inherited from the subrange base type.

1.3 Structured Types

Structured data types (also called composite types) have values made of components. This means that the values of structured types can be decomposed and the operations on the data type might act not only on the values, but also on the component elements of the values. Notice that this definition is very similar to that of a data structure.

The only structured type predefined in Modula-2 is type BITSET. However, there are three structures in Modula-2—array, record, and set—which can be used by the programmer to define his or her own structured data types.

Arrays

In Modula-2, an array is a named ordered collection of components of the same type. An array is characterized by a component type and one or more index types. For instance, in the following declarations:

```
TYPE VectorType = ARRAY [1..Max] OF REAL;
VAR  Vector: VectorType;
```

the subrange [1..Max] is the index type, and REAL is the component type. The index type specifies two things. First, the number of values in the index type indicates the number of components in the array. Second, the values of the index type are the component's positions, 1, 2, 3, . . . , Max in our example above. The index type must be one of CHAR, BOOLEAN, an enumeration type, or a subrange type, while the component type may be any type (including another array type).

An array may be assigned as a whole, or its components can be processed independently, as Vector[1], Vector[2], . . . , Vector[Max] in our example. To refer to a component of an array, the component position or subscript is enclosed in brackets following the array name.

Arrays may be multidimensional, since the components of a one-dimensional array may themselves be arrays. Multidimensional array types can be declared in two ways:

```
TYPE MatrixType = ARRAY Breed OF
                  ARRAY [1..100] OF REAL;
```

or

```
TYPE MatrixType = ARRAY Breed, [1..100] OF REAL;
```

If Mat is a variable of type MatrixType, then access to components uses the square bracket notation, as in Mat[Collie][2] or Mat[Collie, 2]. The number of dimensions of an array is not limited.

For operations on arrays, only assignments with entire arrays of the same type are permitted. The standard procedure HIGH returns the largest index value in a one-dimensional array. Operations that are allowed on array components are those that apply to the component type.

In Modula-2, string constants (that is, sequences of characters enclosed between quotation marks) are defined to be of type ARRAY [0..N] OF CHAR if they have N characters (the last character is always an end-of-string character 0C). Standard input/output modules provide operations ReadString and WriteString for such types. However, strings are so important in computer science applications, that most Modula-2 implementations include a Strings module. We will define such a module in Chapter 4 and study alternative implementations in Chapter 13.

Records

In Modula-2, a record is a named collection of components that are not necessarily of the same type. Arrays are collections of homogeneous components, whereas records are usually collections of heterogeneous components. Components of a record type are called fields and are identified by names.

```
TYPE DateType =    RECORD
                   Month:  [1..12];
                   Day:    [1..31];
                   Year:   [1990..1999];
                   END;
     Id = ARRAY [0..20] OF CHAR;
     EmployeeType = RECORD
                    LastName, FirstName: Id;
                    Address: ARRAY [1..5] OF Id;
                    BirthDate, HiredDate: DateType;
                    Salary: CARDINAL;
                    Sex: (male, female);
                    END;
VAR  Empl: EmployeeType;
```

Access to components of records is done by using the field names that are appended with a period to the record variable name. For example:

Empl.Salary	a CARDINAL value
Empl.BirthDate.Day	a cardinal value in [1..31]
Empl.Address[1]	a string of 20 characters
Empl.Address[1][9]	tenth character of first line of address
Empl.FirstName[0]	first character in employee first name

Field names must be unique within the record but can be the same as other identifiers declared outside that record. As the above example shows, components of records can themselves be structures.

The only operation available for complete records is assignment; the operations applicable to record components are defined by the component type.

It is possible to define records with two or more alternative structures using variants. A variant in a record description is introduced by a CASE construct, where the choice of the structure is indicated by the value of a tag field, which is automatically a component of the record.

```
TYPE Category = (Car, Truck, Bus);
     BusType = (School, Tourism);
     FuelType = (Gasoline, Diesel, Liquified, Other);
     VehicleType = RECORD
                    Serial, Owner: Id;
                    License: ARRAY [0..6] OF CHAR;
                    Cylinders: CARDINAL;
                    Fuel: FuelType;
                    Year, Weight: CARDINAL;
                    CASE Class: Category OF
                      Car:
                    | Truck: Wheels, DGVW: CARDINAL;
                    | Bus: Type: BusType;
                           Wheels, Passengers: CARDINAL;
                    END; (* Class variant *)
                    Date: DateType;
                  END; (* VehicleType record *)
```

An object of type VehicleType has seven fixed fields, followed by a variant field based on tag field Class. There may be added no field, two fields, or three fields to the record, depending on the variant used. The variant fields are followed by another fixed field.

Variant records are a powerful feature of Modula-2 that is often overlooked. They are not only valuable for conserving memory space by allowing overlapping variants, but they also allow a relaxation of the strong typing of Modula-2. There can be as many variants as desired within a record. Variant records can be untagged; in this case the tag name does not appear. Even when a tag is specified, its value is not checked when manipulating the variant. The selection of the variant is determined entirely by the field name, which must be unique among the variants. So, variant records are used for specific applications, as a means of achieving field equivalences. For example, one can do arithmetic on pointers (memory addresses) by using variant records. However, **variant records are to be used with caution;** they are not always safe to use, since they make it possible to bypass Modula-2's strong type checking.

Sets

A set is an unordered collection of values taken from a base type. The base type must be a subrange or an enumeration type, and the number of components of a set is limited and implementation dependent. Modula-2 includes a predefined set type called BITSET:

```
TYPE BITSET = SET OF [0..W-1];
```

where W is the memory word length in bits.

Constants of this type are expressed by listing the set members between braces, as {1, 2, 3}, {2, 3, 1}, {2, 1, 2, 3, 1}, which are all equivalent. Other set type constants must be preceded by the type name, as in the following example:

```
TYPE Hotel = (GrandHotel, Ritz, Waldorf);
     PickupSet = SET OF Hotel;

VAR  Pickup: PickupSet;
```

Here variable Pickup represents the hotels where people are waiting to be picked up by the airport shuttle. The type PickupSet has eight values:

PickupSet{ }	PickupSet{GrandHotel, Ritz}
PickupSet{GrandHotel}	PickupSet{GrandHotel, Waldorf}
PickupSet{Ritz}	PickupSet{Ritz, Waldorf}
PickupSet{Waldorf}	PickupSet{GrandHotel, Ritz, Waldorf}

In general, if the base type of a set has n values, then the set has 2^n values.
Operations applicable to sets are:

union (+)	{1, 2} + {2, 3, 4} → {1, 2, 3, 4}
difference (−)	{1, 2, 3} − {1, 4, 6} → {2, 3}
intersection (*)	{1, 2, 3} * {2, 4, 6} → {2}
symmetric difference (/)	{1, 2, 3}/{2, 3, 4} → {1, 4}
relational operators: =, #, <= ("is contained in"), >= ("contains")	
membership (IN)	2 IN {1, 2, 3}

Although operators < and > cannot be used, proper subsets can be tested with expressions like: (S1 <= S2) AND (S1 # S2).

Two standard procedures add and remove a member from a set:

INCL(s, m)	includes value m in set s
EXCL(s, m)	excludes value m from set s

The scalar types and structured types we have seen here represent the data types available in Modula-2. To these we must add the pointer type, which will be reviewed briefly in Chapter 5. A pointer indicates the address of a variable in memory. We will use pointer types extensively in the study of data structures.

Procedure Types

A procedure type is declared by a specific type declaration whose format is:

TYPE name = PROCEDURE([type] {, type}) [: type]

where square brackets indicate optional elements, and braces indicate a possible repetition (zero or more times) of the enclosed elements. For instance:

```
TYPE CompareProc = PROCEDURE(EmployeeType, EmployeeType): BOOLEAN
```

declares a type of function procedure with two parameters, where EmployeeType is defined as in the section on Records on page 8. Variables of a given procedure type may be assigned procedure values and may be passed as procedure parameters. For example, given the following declarations:

```
PROCEDURE PaidMore(Employee1, Employee2: EmployeeType): BOOLEAN;
 (* returns TRUE if Employee1 has a higher salary than Employee2 *)
BEGIN
  RETURN Employee1.Salary > Employee2.Salary;
END PaidMore;

PROCEDURE ComesBefore(Date1, Date2: Date): BOOLEAN;
 (* returns TRUE if Date1 comes before Date2 *)
BEGIN
  IF Date1.Year < Date2.Year THEN
    RETURN TRUE;
  ELSIF Date1.Year > Date2.Year THEN
    RETURN FALSE;
  ELSIF Date1.Month < Date2.Month THEN    (* hired same year *)
    RETURN TRUE;
  ELSIF Date1.Month > Date2.Month THEN
    RETURN FALSE;
  ELSE                              (* hired same year and month *)
    RETURN Date1.Day < Date2.Day;
  END; (* IF *)
END ComesBefore;

PROCEDURE HiredFirst(Employee1, Employee2: EmployeeType): BOOLEAN;
 (* returns TRUE if Employee1 was hired before Employee2 *)
BEGIN
  RETURN ComesBefore(Employee1.HiredDate, Employee2.HiredDate);
END HiredFirst;

PROCEDURE PrintComparison(Employee1, Employee2: EmployeeType;
                         Compare: CompareProc; Msg: ARRAY OF CHAR);
BEGIN
  IF Compare(Employee1, Employee2) THEN
    WriteString(Employee1.LastName); WriteString(Msg);
    WriteString(Employee2.LastName);
  ELSE
    WriteString(Employee2.LastName); WriteString(Msg);
    WriteString(Employee1.LastName);
  END; (* IF *)
  Write("."); WriteLn;
END PrintComparison;

VAR EmpCompare: CompareProc;
    Emp1, Emp2: EmployeeType;
    Message: STRING;
```

if the following statements have been executed:

```
EmpCompare := PaidMore;
Message := " is paid more than ";
```

then the call:

```
PrintComparison(Emp1, Emp2, EmpCompare, Message);
```

is equivalent to:

```
PrintComparison(Emp1, Emp2, PaidMore, " is paid more than ");
```

After executing the following statements:

```
EmpCompare := HiredFirst;
Message := " is senior to ";
```

the same call:

```
PrintComparison(Emp1, Emp2, EmpCompare, Message);
```

is now equivalent to:

```
PrintComparison(Emp1, Emp2, HiredFirst, " is senior to ");
```

In any case, PrintComparison would print the appropriate message based on the current values of Emp1 and Emp2.

We will find procedure types and procedure variables to be very valuable for searching (where a procedure will specify how to test for equality) and for sorting (where a procedure will specify how to compare two items). Many applications involving numeric computations will also use procedure types, such as a numeric integration function that will be passed to the function to be integrated.

1.4 Type Compatibility

Modula-2 is a strongly typed language. This means that there is strict type checking in Modula-2 and that objects of different types are usually incompatible. Two types are said to be *compatible* if any of the following is true:

(a) They are declared as equal to each other. For instance, if we have:

```
TYPE Vector1 = ARRAY [1..100] OF REAL;
     Vector2 = ARRAY [1..100] OF REAL;
     TypeThree = Vector1;
```

then TypeThree and Vector1 are compatible, whereas Vector1 and Vector2 are not compatible even though they have the same structure.

(b) One is a subrange of the other. Thus, in the following type:

```
TYPE Animal = (Cat, Dog, Cow, Goat, Sheep, Chicken, Goose, Duck);
     Feathered = [Chicken..Duck];
```

Animal and Feathered are compatible.

(c) Both are subranges of the same base type.

```
TYPE YearType = [1990..1999];
     MonthType = [1..12];
     HousePet = [Cat..Dog];
```

YearType, MonthType, and CARDINAL are compatible, as well as Animal, HousePet, and Feathered.

Furthermore, two types are said to be *assignment compatible* if they are either:

compatible

or

INTEGER, CARDINAL, or subranges with base type INTEGER or CARDINAL.

In the latter case, one should avoid assigning a negative integer to a cardinal, as this may result in an erroneous positive value.

1.5 Files

A file is a collection of data in secondary storage. Secondary storage can be considered to be a larger, cheaper, and nonvolatile extension of main memory. On secondary storage devices, files are usually grouped in directories; each file has a unique file name.

In order for file operations to be efficient, file organization is based on the characteristics of secondary storage devices. Files are structured types, as their values are sequences of elements. File components are usually records. Files are not standard types in Modula-2, and each implementation must define its own file type, file organization, and file operations.

Modula-2 implementations usually contain a FileSystem module, with all the available file operations. A minimum set of operations for sequential files would include: open a file, close a file, delete a file, rename a file, read a word (sequentially), append a word to the end of the file, read a character (sequentially), append a character to the end of the file.

Here is an example of such a FileSystem module.

```
DEFINITION MODULE FileSystem;
FROM SYSTEM IMPORT WORD;

CONST MaxSize = 1024;
```

Chapter 1 Data Types and Data Structures

```
TYPE Response = (done, notdone);
     File = RECORD
              refNum,
              volRef:     INTEGER;
              firstPos,
              lastPos,
              curPos:     LONGINT;
              res:        Response;
              eof:        BOOLEAN;
              dirty:      BOOLEAN;
              nameString:ARRAY [0..31] OF CHAR;
              buffer:     ARRAY [0..MaxSize-1] OF CHAR;
           END;
PROCEDURE Lookup(VAR f: File; filename: ARRAY OF CHAR;
                 new: BOOLEAN);
(* Look for the actual file with the given file name. If the file
   exists, it is connected to f (opened). If the requested file is
   not found or new is TRUE, a permanent file is created with the
   given name. After the call
   f.res = done       if file f is connected
   f.res = notdone    if the file does not exist or some error
                      occurred  *)

PROCEDURE Close(VAR f: File);
(* Terminate any actual input or output operation on file f and
   disconnect the variable f from the actual file. *)

PROCEDURE Delete(VAR f: File);
(* Terminate any actual input or output operation on file f and
   disconnect the variable f from the actual file. The actual file
   is then deleted. *)

PROCEDURE Rename(VAR f: File; filename: ARRAY OF CHAR);
(* Change the name of file f to filename. After the call
   f.res = done       if file f is renamed
   f.res = notdone    if a file with filename already exists, or some
                      error occurred *)

PROCEDURE ReadWord(VAR f: File; VAR w: WORD);
(* Read the next word from file f and assign it to w. If ReadWord
   has been called without success, 0 is assigned to w;
   f.eof implies w = 0. However, the opposite is not true:
   w = 0 does not imply f.eof. After the call
   f.eof = FALSE     w has been read
   f.eof = TRUE      read operation was not successful
   If f.eof is TRUE:
      f.res = done      end of file has been reached
      f.res = notdone   some error occurred *)

PROCEDURE WriteWord(VAR f: File; w: WORD);
(* Append word w to file f. *)
```

```
PROCEDURE ReadChar(VAR f: File; VAR ch: CHAR);
(* Read the next character from file f and assign it to ch.
   If ReadChar has been called without success, ch = 0C;
   f.eof implies ch = 0C. However, the opposite is not true:
   ch = 0C does not imply f.eof. After the call
     f.eof = FALSE     ch has been read
     f.eof = TRUE      read operation was not successful
   If f.eof is TRUE
     f.res = done      end of file has been reached
     f.res = notdone   some error occurred *)
PROCEDURE WriteChar(VAR f: File; ch: CHAR);
(* Append character ch to file f. *)
END FileSystem.
```

Input/output standard modules InOut and RealInOut make it possible to access files in a limited way, using input or output redirection.

As an example, we will now turn to the development of a program to merge two sorted files into a new file.

1.6 Case Study: Merging Two Sorted Files

In computer applications involving files, it is often necessary to merge two sorted files in order to produce a third sorted file. We will design a procedure to merge two sorted files into a third file, and we will use the methodology developed in Appendix A to design and implement our solution.

Design

Define the Problem We want to accept as input two sorted files of records, where each record has a key field that is used for sorting. The two input files will be sorted in ascending order on that key field. Our program must produce an output file comprising all the elements of the two input files sorted in ascending order.

The two input files are products from previous processing and contain only validated data, thus relieving us from having to validate input data. Input records are defined as comprising 60 characters each, with the first 10 characters being the key used for sorting the records.

Design a Solution We will need to use the tools available to handle files on our system. In Modula-2, such tools are not standard, but all implementations contain a module to handle files. In our case we will use the FileSystem module presented earlier.

Since we know in advance those tools that are available to us for file handling, we can decompose our solution (see Appendix A) in a top-down fashion. It seems clear

Figure 1-3
MergeFiles
Structure Chart

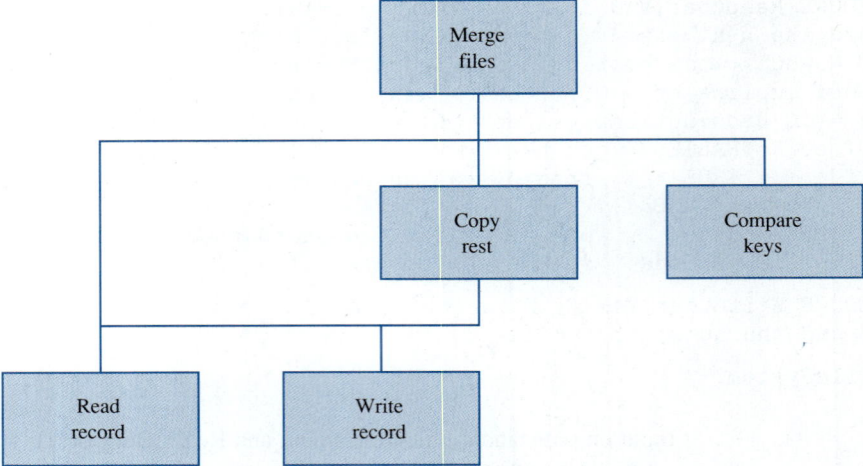

that we will need a procedure to read a record from an input file, a procedure to write a record to the output file, a function to compare record keys, and, in the case a file is larger than the other, a procedure to copy the rest of an input file to the output file. This leads us to the structure chart of Figure 1-3. The procedures ReadRecord and WriteRecord are utility routines used in several places.

In addition to Figure 1-3, which gives the structure of our MergeFiles procedure, we will also need a main program to test this procedure. Based on that, we can also start defining our modular design chart in Figure 1-4.

Our ReadRecord and WriteRecord procedures will use elements from the FileSystem module, but we do not know yet exactly what elements. The modular design chart will be completed after the next step.

Figure 1-4
Modular Design
Chart for
MergeFilesTest

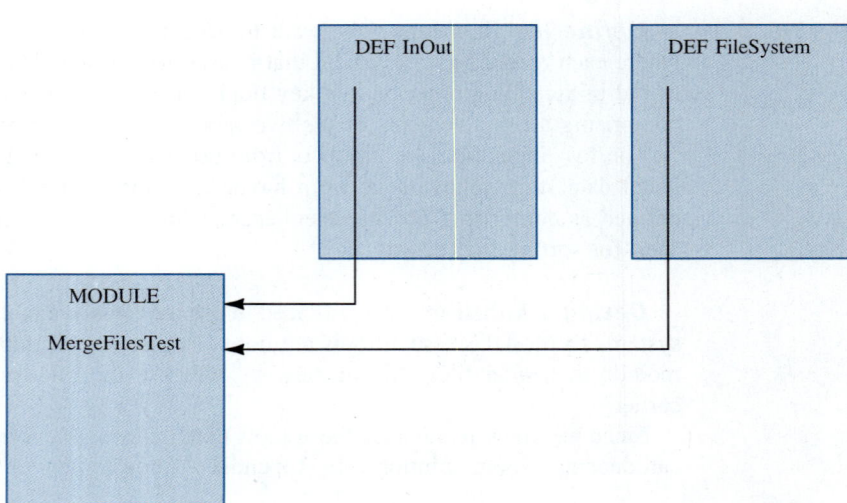

Figure 1-5
The Merge Process

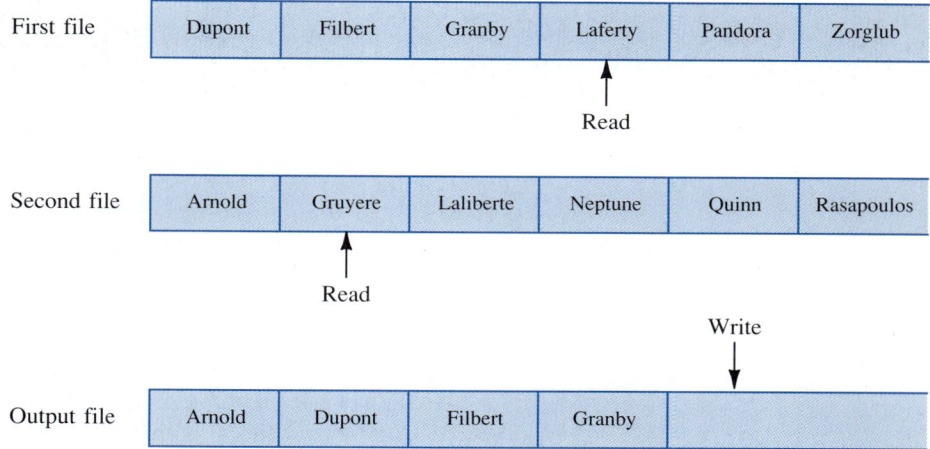

Refine the Solution Our structured design has indicated the various parts of our solution, and we must now define the algorithms we will use. In particular, we must define the merging algorithm, and to do this we will consider the operations we would use to merge the files manually. We read the first record of each input file, and write the record with the smallest key to the output file. Then we consider the next record from the input file whose record was output and compare it to the old record from the other input file. We write the record with the smallest key to the output file. We repeat these operations (reading, comparing, writing) until one of the input files is exhausted. Then, we simply copy the remaining records of the other input file to the output file and stop. This process is illustrated in Figure 1-5.

We will have to recognize the end of an input file, but our FileSystem module provides us with the means to do just that. We already know we will have four cases to consider:

1. general case—not the end of file 1 or file 2
2. end of file 1, but not end of file 2
3. end of file 2, but not end of file 1
4. end of file 1 and end of file 2

It is easy to see that case 4 indicates the end of our algorithm. Cases 2 and 3 call for the same action, i.e., copying the rest of the unfinished file to the output file. Case 1 is the general case, where we must compare records, write one to the output file, and read a new record to replace it. Each time we read a new record, we have to check if we reached the end of the file. We can now write our pseudocode solution.

Merge Files
   Read record from first file
   Read record from second file
   If not end of first file
      If not end of second file { not end of first and second files }
         Merge Both Files
      Else { not end of first file but end of second file }
         Write record from first file to output file
         Copy rest of first file to output file
      End if
   Else { end of first file }
      If not end of second file
         { end of first file but not end of second file }
         Write record from second file to output file
         Copy rest of second file to output file
      End if
   End if { end of first file and end of second file }
End Merge Files

Merge Both Files
   Loop
      { not end of first file and not end of second file }
      If record from first file < record from second file
         Write record from first file to output file
         Read record from first file
         If end of first file
            { end of first file and not end of second file }
            Write record from second file to output file
            Copy rest of second file to output file
            Exit loop
         End if
      Else
         Write record from second file to output file
         Read record from second file
         If end of second file
            { not end of first file but end of second file }
            Write record from first file to output file
            Copy rest of first file to output file
            Exit loop
         End if
      End if
      { not end of first file and not end of second file }
   End loop
End Merge Both Files

Copy Rest
  Loop
    Read record from input file
    Exit loop if end of input file
    Write record to output file
  End loop
End Copy Rest

Read record
  Read record key from input file
  If end of input file Return
  Read record info from input file
End Read record

Write record
  Write record key to output file
  Write record info to output file
End Write record

Less
  Set character index to first character
  While not end of keys and both keys have equal characters
    Increment character index
  End while

  If character index is beyond end of key
    Return false
  Else
    Return character of first key is $<$ character of second key
      Return true
    Else
      Return false
    End if
  End if
End Less

The program to test procedure MergeFiles is very simple and we choose not to develop its pseudocode solution, leaving it as an exercise for the reader. We are now able to complete our modular design chart, as shown in Figure 1-6.

Develop a Testing Strategy We will assume that input files are valid ordered sequences of records. Then the possible cases are:

1. F1 and F2 non empty → F3 = all records from F1 and F2
   (a) no relation between the elements of F1 and F2
   (b) all records of F1 are less than all records of F2
   (c) all records of F2 are less than all records of F1

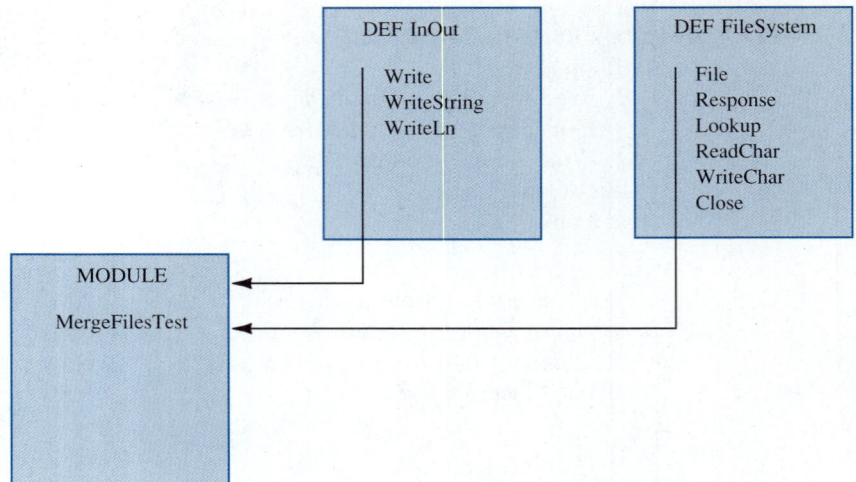

Figure 1-6
Modular Design Chart for MergeFilesTest

    (d) F1 shorter than F2, and last elements of F2 greater than the rest
    (e) F2 shorter than F1, and last elements of F1 greater than the rest
2. F1 nonempty, F2 empty → F3 = F1
3. F1 empty, F2 nonempty → F3 = F2
4. F1 and F2 empty → F3 empty

Using the same data as in our earlier example shown in Figure 1-5, we obtain test data to cover all cases.

1. (a) F1: Dupont, Filbert, Granby, Laferty, Pandora, Zorglub
       F2: Arnold, Gruyere, Laliberte, Neptune, Quinn, Rasapoulos, Simon, Sorel, Tremblay, Vuong
       F3: Arnold, Dupont, Filbert, Granby, Gruyere, Laferty, Laliberte, Neptune, Pandora, Quinn, Rasapoulos, Simon, Sorel, Tremblay, Vuong, Zorglub
  (b) F1: Arnold, Dupont, Filbert, Granby, Gruyere, Laferty, Laliberte
       F2: Neptune, Pandora, Quinn, Rasapoulos, Simon, Sorel, Tremblay, Vuong, Zorglub
       F3: Arnold, Dupont, Filbert, Granby, Gruyere, Laferty, Laliberte, Neptune, Pandora, Quinn, Rasapoulos, Simon, Sorel, Tremblay, Vuong, Zorglub
  (c) Same as in part b above, with F1 and F2 exchanged
  (d) F1: Dupont, Filbert, Granby, Laferty, Pandora
       F2: Arnold, Gruyere, Laliberte, Neptune, Quinn, Rasapoulos, Simon, Sorel, Tremblay, Vuong, Zorglub
       F3: Arnold, Dupont, Filbert, Granby, Gruyere, Laferty, Laliberte, Neptune, Pandora, Quinn, Rasapoulos, Simon, Sorel, Tremblay, Vuong, Zorglub
  (e) Same as in d above, with F1 and F2 exchanged

2. F1: Arnold, Dupont, Filbert, Granby, Gruyere, Laferty, Laliberte, Neptune, Pandora, Quinn, Rasapoulos, Simon, Sorel, Tremblay, Vuong, Zorglub
   F2: Empty file
   F3: Arnold, Dupont, Filbert, Granby, Gruyere, Laferty, Laliberte, Neptune, Pandora, Quinn, Rasapoulos, Simon, Sorel, Tremblay, Vuong, Zorglub
3. Same as in 2 above, with F1 and F2 exchanged
4. Empty files

Implementation

Code and Test the Program Using the pseudocode, we produce the following solution, which includes a test program for procedure MergeFiles.

```
MODULE MergeFilesTest;
(* Test of the MergeFiles procedure. File1.dat and File2.dat
   must be input files that have been previously created and
   sorted. File3.dat is the output file and is created by the
   program.
                          Ph. Gabrini    November 1991 *)
FROM FileSystem IMPORT File, Lookup, Close, ReadChar, WriteChar,
                      Response;
FROM InOut IMPORT WriteString, Write, WriteLn;

CONST KeyLength = 10;
      InfoLength = 50;
      RecordLength = KeyLength + InfoLength;

TYPE Item = RECORD
              Key:  ARRAY [1..KeyLength] OF CHAR;
              Info: ARRAY [1..InfoLength] OF CHAR;
            END;

     ReadProc    = PROCEDURE (VAR File, VAR Item);
     WriteProc   = PROCEDURE (VAR File, Item);
     CompareProc = PROCEDURE (Item, Item): BOOLEAN;

(***********Utility procedures for test program **********)

PROCEDURE ReadRecord(VAR F: File; VAR Rec: Item);
(* Read a record from file F. Quit if end of file *)
VAR Ch: CHAR;
    Index: CARDINAL;
BEGIN
  FOR Index := 1 TO KeyLength DO
    ReadChar(F, Ch);
    IF F.eof THEN RETURN END; (* IF *)
    Rec.Key[Index] := Ch;
  END; (* FOR *)
```

```
    FOR Index := 1 TO InfoLength DO
      ReadChar(F, Rec.Info[Index]);
      IF F.eof THEN RETURN END; (* IF *)
    END; (* FOR *)
END ReadRecord;

PROCEDURE WriteRecord(VAR F: File; Rec: Item);
(* Write record Rec to file F *)
VAR Index: CARDINAL;
BEGIN
  FOR Index := 1 TO KeyLength DO
    WriteChar(F, Rec.Key[Index]);
  END; (* FOR *)
  FOR Index := 1 TO InfoLength DO
    WriteChar(F, Rec.Info[Index]);
  END (* FOR *)
END WriteRecord;

PROCEDURE Smaller(Rec1, Rec2: Item): BOOLEAN;
(* Comparison of keys of two records. Return Rec1.Key < Rec2.Key *)
VAR Index: CARDINAL;
BEGIN
  Index := 1;
  WHILE (Index <= KeyLength) AND (Rec1.Key[Index] = Rec2.Key[Index]) DO
    INC(Index);
  END; (* WHILE *)
  IF Index <= KeyLength THEN
    RETURN Rec1.Key[Index] < Rec2.Key[Index];
  ELSE
    RETURN FALSE;
  END; (* IF *)
END Smaller;


PROCEDURE MergeFiles(VAR File1, File2, File3: File;
                     Input: ReadProc; Output: WriteProc;
                     Less: CompareProc);
(* Merge File1 and File2 into File3. File1 and File2 should be
   files of Item in ascending order of Key field *)

PROCEDURE CopyRest(VAR InFile, OutFile: File);
(* Write the remaining elements of InFile to OutFile *)
VAR Rec: Item;
BEGIN
  LOOP
    Input(InFile, Rec);
    IF InFile.eof THEN
      EXIT;
    END; (* IF *)
    Output( OutFile, Rec);
  END; (* LOOP *)
END CopyRest;
```

```
    VAR Rec1, Rec2: Item;
BEGIN (* MergeFiles *)
  Input(File1, Rec1);
  IF File1.eof THEN
    Input(File2, Rec2);
    IF NOT File2.eof THEN (* File1.eof AND NOT File2.eof *)
      Output(File3, Rec2);
      CopyRest(File2, File3);
    END; (* IF *)
  ELSE (* NOT File1.eof *)
    Input(File2, Rec2);
    IF File2.eof THEN (* NOT File1.eof AND File2.eof *)
      Output(File3, Rec1);
      CopyRest(File1, File3);
    ELSE
      LOOP
        (* NOT File1.eof AND NOT File2.eof *)
        IF Less(Rec1, Rec2) THEN
          Output(File3, Rec1);
          Input(File1, Rec1);
          IF File1.eof THEN (* File1.eof AND NOT File2.eof *)
            Output(File3, Rec2);
            CopyRest(File2, File3);
            EXIT;
          END; (* IF *)
        ELSE
          Output(File3, Rec2);
          Input(File2, Rec2);
          IF File2.eof THEN (* NOT File1.eof AND File2.eof *)
            Output(File3, Rec1);
            CopyRest(File1, File3);
            EXIT;
          END; (* IF *)
        END; (* IF *)
        (* NOT File1.eof AND NOT File2.eof *)
      END; (* LOOP *)
    END; (* IF *)
  END ; (* IF *)
END MergeFiles;

(********** Test program for MergeFiles procedure **********)

VAR InFile1, InFile2, OutFile: File;
    Rec: Item;
    Index: CARDINAL;

BEGIN (* MergeFilesTest *)
  Lookup(InFile1, "File1.dat", FALSE);
  IF InFile1.res # done THEN
    WriteString("Cannot open first input file");
    WriteLn;
```

```
    ELSE
      Lookup(InFile2, "File2.dat", FALSE);
      IF InFile2.res # done THEN
        WriteString("Cannot open second input file");
        WriteLn;
      ELSE
        Lookup(OutFile, "File3.dat", TRUE);
        IF OutFile.res # done THEN
          WriteString("Cannot open output file");
          WriteLn;
        ELSE
          MergeFiles( InFile1, InFile2, OutFile, ReadRecord, WriteRecord, Smaller );
          Close(OutFile);
          Lookup(OutFile, "File3.dat", FALSE);
          IF OutFile.res # done THEN
            WriteString("Unable to reopen output file");
            WriteLn;
          ELSE
            LOOP
              ReadRecord(OutFile, Rec);
              IF OutFile.eof THEN
                EXIT;
              END; (* IF *)
              FOR Index := 1 TO KeyLength DO
                Write(Rec.Key[Index]);
              END; (* FOR *)
              WriteLn;
            END; (* LOOP *)
            WriteLn;
            Close(OutFile);
          END; (* IF *)
        END; (* IF *)
        Close(InFile2);
      END; (* IF *)
      Close(InFile1);
    END; (* IF *)
END MergeFilesTest.
```

We have added a main program to test our MergeFiles procedure. It opens files, producing an error message if the files cannot be opened properly. Once the files are opened, it merges them by calling the MergeFiles procedure. Then it closes the output file and reopens it in order to read and print its contents.

Procedure ReadRecord reads a key followed by an information field; if it encounters an end of file, it returns to the caller. Procedure WriteRecord writes a record to the output file, first writing the record key and then writing the information field of the record. Our ReadRecord and WriteRecord procedures can be adapted to other record structures based on the elements of the actual files. Procedure Smaller compares two keys one character at a time; as soon as two characters differ, it returns the correspond-

> ### User's Manual for MergeFiles
>
> MergeFiles is a procedure to merge two sorted files of records of user-defined type Item. It uses procedure ReadRecord to read each record from input files and procedure WriteRecord to output each record. It also uses a Boolean function Smaller, returning the comparison result of two record keys. These three procedures must be defined by the user and passed as parameters to procedure MergeFiles.
>
> Procedure MergeFiles takes six parameters. The first three are file parameters: two input files, and an output file. The last three are procedure parameters—read, write, and comparison—having the following types:
>
> ```
> TYPE ReadProc = PROCEDURE (VAR File, VAR Item);
>      WriteProc = PROCEDURE (VAR File, Item);
>      CompareProc = PROCEDURE (Item, Item): BOOLEAN;
> ```
>
> MergeFiles must be called once the three files have been opened. It does not close any of the files. Call example:
>
> ```
> MergeFiles( InputFile1, InputFile2, OutputFile,
>             Read, Write, Compare );
> ```

ing result. The function returns false if the two keys have the same length and all characters are equal.

Procedure MergeFiles comprises local procedure CopyRest. CopyRest reads one by one the remaining items in the input file given as the first parameter and writes them to the output file. It stops when it encounters the end of the input file.

Procedure MergeFiles implements the pseudocode solution we developed earlier. Note, however, that the Merge Both Files algorithm has not been implemented as a separate procedure but rather as an internal loop of procedure MergeFiles. We decided to do so because the length of procedure MergeFiles, including the loop, is less than a page. The program follows exactly the pseudocode.

The program was run using the test cases defined in our testing strategy and gave the expected results.

Complete the Documentation The MergeFiles procedure could be used as a general utility procedure in a library module. Therefore, a short user's manual as shown above is required for the procedure.

Summary

Data types are a combination of the type values and the operations that can be applied to these values. We have reviewed the available standard data types of Modula-2:

scalar or simple types, as well as structured types. Values for simple types cannot be decomposed any further and are said to be atomic. Values for structured types can be decomposed.

Modula-2 simple types are CARDINAL, INTEGER, BOOLEAN, REAL, CHAR, subranges, and enumeration. The pointer type, which will be reviewed in Chapter 5, is also a simple type. Modula-2 structured types are ARRAY, RECORD, and SET. Procedure types allow variables to be assigned procedure values and make it possible to pass procedures as parameters. The TYPE declaration allows the user to define new types by combining the existing standard types.

Files represent a particular data structure. They are not standard Modula-2 types, but are found in all implementations. Their format and the available operations might differ slightly from one implementation to the other, but are usually very similar.

■ *Exercises*

1. Which operation or operations are supported for all built-in Modula-2 data types?

2. The following declarations are given:

   ```
   TYPE Range = [0..100];
        String = ARRAY [0..79] OF CHAR;
        Square = (black, white, empty);
        CheckerBoard = ARRAY [1..8],[1..8] OF Square;
   VAR  Game: CheckerBoard;
        Grade: Range;
        Exams: ARRAY [1..3] OF Range;
        History: ARRAY [1..50] OF CheckerBoard;
        Card: CARDINAL;
        Int: INTEGER;
        S1, S2: String;
        S3: ARRAY [0..79] OF CHAR;
   ```

   If all variables have been assigned values, which of the following are valid assignments?

   ```
   Int := Grade;
   Exams[1] := Int;
   Exams[3] := Card;
   S3[1] := "string processing";
   S1 := S2;
   S2 := S3;
   S2[1] := 'A';
   S1[79] := S3[4];
   History[1, 1, 2] := black;
   History[50] := white;
   Game[3, 8] := Grade;
   History[7] := Game;
   ```

   How many Square elements are there in History?

3. A cattle ranch has a number of buildings, a number of horses, a number of cattle of various breeds, an inventory of tools, and also some personnel. Give all the declarations needed to define new data types to be used in an application dealing with the inventory and the management of the ranch. Try to think of different possible organizations for all the data involved.

■ *Programming Problems*

4. Modify the MergeFiles procedure and test program, so that it runs on your Modula-2 implementation.

5. Revise the MergeFiles procedure so that input files are validated, i.e., their values are checked for order. Test the modified procedure.

6. Transform the MergeFiles procedure into a more general library procedure that will ask the user for the input and output file names, open those files, and close them once the merge is done. Test your new procedure.

7. Write a program to read a file and check that it is sorted in either ascending or descending order on a given key field. Try to make your program general enough so that it can accommodate files of elements of various types with a minimum of changes to the program.

8. Design and implement a program with interactive input, which will read in the x- and y-coordinates of two points and then determine the slope of the line connecting the points and the quadrants in which the points lie. To resolve ambiguities in determining the quadrants, assume that the first quadrant contains the positive x- and y-axes, the second contains the negative x-axis, the third contains the negative y-axis, and the fourth contains no points on the axes.

9. Design and implement a program with interactive input to repeatedly read in the coefficients of a quadratic equation and then compute and display all the roots of the equation.

*10. In chess a queen can take any piece on the same row, same column, or either diagonal. Since there are eight rows and eight columns on a chess board, it is an interesting problem to find if it is possible to place eight queens on a chess board such that no queen can take any other queen. An appropriate data structure for this problem is suggested in Appendix A. Write and test a procedure to solve the Eight Queens problem.

Note: Problems marked with an asterisk (*) have a higher level of difficulty.

Arrays

INTRODUCTION

The array structure is among the oldest data structures used in computer science. *Arrays* can be found in the first high-level programming languages like FORTRAN, COBOL, and ALGOL 60. Even programming languages offering few explicit data types, such as BASIC, have the necessary mechanisms for using arrays because of their importance in numerical analysis, in applied mathematics, or in engineering. The array type is used for implementing many other types, as we will see in the coming chapters. Some computers have been designed with built-in array operations implemented in the hardware.

Central memory in a computer is a linear array (vector) of words of the same size, identified by cardinal numbers (addresses). Because of this, vectors play an important role in the implementation of various data structures. Although arrays are common, their implementations can be varied depending on their use. In many programming languages, memory must be allocated to arrays before starting execution of programs, while in other programming languages, memory for arrays is allocated dynamically during program execution according to need.

Chapter 2 Arrays

2.1 Definition

> **Array** A finite, ordered set of homogeneous elements of the same type. The number of elements is specifically defined; the order of the elements is such that we can identify a first element, a second element, and so on; and the elements are all of the same type.

A simple array type always includes a component type and an index type. The component type is the type of the elements in the array, while the index type is the type of values used to select individual elements. The component type can be any type, while the index type must be a scalar type.

The main operations on an array are the following: storing a value in a specified element, extracting a value from a specified element, or assigning one array to another array of the same type. In Modula-2 an array is defined by a component type and a scalar index type. For example, in the following declaration:

```
VAR A,B: ARRAY [1955..2000] OF INTEGER;
```

INTEGER is the component type and [1955..2000], a subrange of CARDINAL, is the scalar index type.

The three operations that are discussed above are illustrated in the following Modula-2 statements:

```
A[Index] := Elt;        (* Store *)
Elt := A[Index];        (* Extract *)
A := B;                 (* Assign *)
```

Other programming languages offer similar operations.

The component type of an array may also be an array; the resulting structure is a multidimensional array. In Modula-2 we could have:

```
TYPE Vector = ARRAY [0..5] OF CARDINAL;
     Table = ARRAY [1..Max] OF Vector;
VAR A: Table;
```

Access to the elements of A could be indicated in two ways:

A[I][J]   access to element J of array A[I]

or

A[I, J]   using a common mathematics notation

Let's give a few definitions here. A vector is a one dimensional array with an index bounded by a first element index (F) and a last element index (L). The number of elements in a vector is:

$$ORD(L) - ORD(F) + 1$$

An array with n dimensions is an ordered collection of homogeneous components identified by an ordered set of indices $\{i_1, i_2, i_3, \ldots, i_n\}$ where each of i_j is such that:

$$F_j \leq i_j \leq L_j$$

The rank of an array is the number of indices: a vector has rank 1, a matrix has rank 2, and so forth. Using notation similar to Modula-2, an n-dimensional array, T, can be declared by:

```
T: ARRAY [F₁..L₁, F₂..L₂, ..., Fₙ..Lₙ] OF ElementType;
```

and an individual element is specified by:

$$T[i_1, i_2, \ldots, i_n] \quad \text{where } F_k \leq i_k \leq L_k$$

Of course, for an actual Modula-2 declaration, the missing items indicated by the ellipsis (. . .) must be completely specified. The number of elements in this array is:

$$\prod_{j=1}^{n} (ORD(L_j) - ORD(F_j) + 1)$$

Suppose we have the following declarations:

```
TYPE CorpType      = (Marine, Signal, Engineer);
     DivisionType  = [1..5];
     RegimentType  = [100..108];
     BattalionType = [10..16];
     EnlistedMen   = RECORD
                       .
                       .
                       .
                     END;
VAR Army: ARRAY CorpsType, DivisionType, RegimentType,
                BattalionType OF EnlistedMen;
```

For the array Army, we can compute the number of elements by using the above formula:

$$\prod_{j=1}^{4} (ORD(L_j) - ORD(F_j) + 1)$$

$$= (ORD(Engineer) - ORD(Marine) + 1)(5 - 1 + 1)(108 - 100 + 1)(16 - 10 + 1)$$
$$= 3 \times 5 \times 9 \times 7 = 945.$$

2.2 Applications

Applications of arrays are so numerous that it won't be possible to cover them all, or even to give a representative sample. We will use two short examples to illustrate the syntactic notation for arrays in Modula-2.

Transpose of a Square Matrix

A square matrix has the same number of rows and columns. The transpose of a square matrix M is defined by:

$$M^t_{i,j} = M_{j,i} \quad \text{for all i, j}$$

For example,

```
1  5   9  13                      1   2   3   4
2  6  10  14   is the transpose of 5   6   7   8
3  7  11  15                      9  10  11  12
4  8  12  16                     13  14  15  16
```

Given the declaration

```
TYPE Matrix = ARRAY [1..N], [1..N] OF INTEGER;
```

the following procedure would transpose a matrix:

```
PROCEDURE TransposeMatrix (VAR  A: Matrix);
VAR  Row, Col: CARDINAL;
     Temp: INTEGER;
BEGIN
   FOR Row := 1 TO N - 1 DO
      FOR Col := Row + 1 TO N DO (* swap elements *)
         Temp := A[Row,Col];
         A[Row, Col] := A[Col, Row];
         A[Col, Row] := Temp;
      END; (* FOR *)
   END; (* FOR *)
END TransposeMatrix;
```

When we develop an algorithm, we should analyze its efficiency. One crude way of analyzing an algorithm is to count the number of statements executed upon completion. This gives us a basis for comparing two algorithms. Executing procedure TransposeMatrix will execute the three swapping statements (N − 1) times with Row = 1, (N − 2) times with Row = 2, (N − 3) times with Row = 3, etc. Thus, the total number of executed statement is: 3[(N − 1) + (N − 2) + (N − 3) + ··· + 1] or 3N(N − 1)/2, and we can say that the execution time of the TransposeMatrix procedure is proportional to N^2. We will look at the analysis of algorithms in a more complete way in the next chapter.

Matrix Multiplication

In mathematics, matrix multiplication is defined for a matrix A of size m × n (i.e., with m rows and n columns) and a matrix B of size n × p as producing matrix C of size m × p whose elements are:

$$c_{ik} = \sum_{j=1}^{n} a_{ij}b_{jk} \quad \begin{array}{l} \text{for } 1 \leq i \leq m \\ \text{and } 1 \leq k \leq p \end{array}$$

To implement this operation we can write the following Modula-2 procedure:

```
TYPE Matrix1 = ARRAY [1..M], [1..N] OF INTEGER;
     Matrix2 = ARRAY [1..N], [1..P] OF INTEGER;
     Matrix3 = ARRAY [1..M], [1..P] OF INTEGER;
PROCEDURE MatrixMult(VAR C: Matrix3; A: Matrix1; B: Matrix2);
VAR I, J, K: CARDINAL;
BEGIN
  FOR I := 1 TO M DO
    FOR K := 1 TO P DO
      C[I, K] := 0;
      FOR J := 1 TO N DO
        C[I, K] := C[I, K] + A[I, J] * B[J, K];
      END; (* FOR *)
    END; (* FOR *)
  END; (* FOR *)
END MatrixMult;
```

This execution of procedure MatrixMult will execute the "C[I, K] := 0" statement M × P times, and the inner assignment statement M × P × N times. If we have square matrices, then M = N = P, and the number of statements executed is $N^2 + N^3$. Therefore, we can say that the execution time of the MatrixMult procedure is proportional to N^3; this execution time is greater than that of the transposition algorithm.

2.3 Implementation of General Arrays

For each implementation of an array, we will have to develop a mapping function, which, when applied to a set of indices, will compute the memory address of the place where an array element will be stored. If we consider a vector (one-dimensional array) whose elements use one word of memory, it is easy to see that:

$$\text{address of } V[I] = \text{address of } V[F] + ORD(I) - ORD(F)$$

where F is the lower bound of the indices, and the address of V[F] is the address of the vector's first element. The address of the vector's last element is

$$\text{address of } V[L] = \text{address of } V[F] + L - F.$$

Figure 2-1
Sequential
Allocation

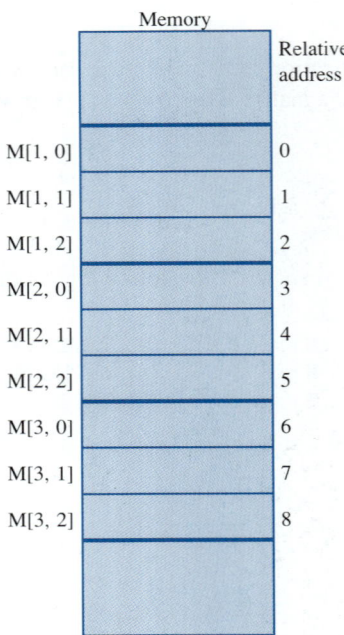

Lexicographic Allocation

When memory is allocated for the elements of an array, it is necessary to choose the order of the array elements in memory. In the case of a vector, there is no problem, as the mapping is direct and simple. In the case of a matrix (two-dimensional array), space is usually allocated to the elements row by row (row-major order). For matrix M: ARRAY[1..3], [0..2] OF INTEGER, space is allocated as shown on Figure 2-1. Notice that the index of the elements increases with the lexicographic order. (If we concatenate the two indices, we obtain numbers in increasing order.) For example:

$$\text{address of } M[1, 2] < \text{address of } M[2, 1] \text{ because } (1\ 2) < (2\ 1)$$

By examining Figure 2-1 we can find an allocation function to compute the relative address from the values of the indices.

$$\text{relative address of } M[i, j] = 3(i - 1) + j$$

This computation can be interpreted in the following way: to find the jth element of the ith row, skip the preceding $i - 1$ rows, where each row contains three elements, and skip another j elements before reaching the relative address you are interested in.

In some cases memory space is allocated to the matrix elements column by column (column-major order). The formula to compute the elements relative address is then slightly different (see problem 2 in the Exercises section).

We do need a formula to compute the relative address of an element for a general array like $A[F_1..L_1, F_2..L_2, \ldots, F_n..L_n]$. We can use lexicographic ordering so that

Figure 2-2 Decomposition of a Four-Dimensional Array

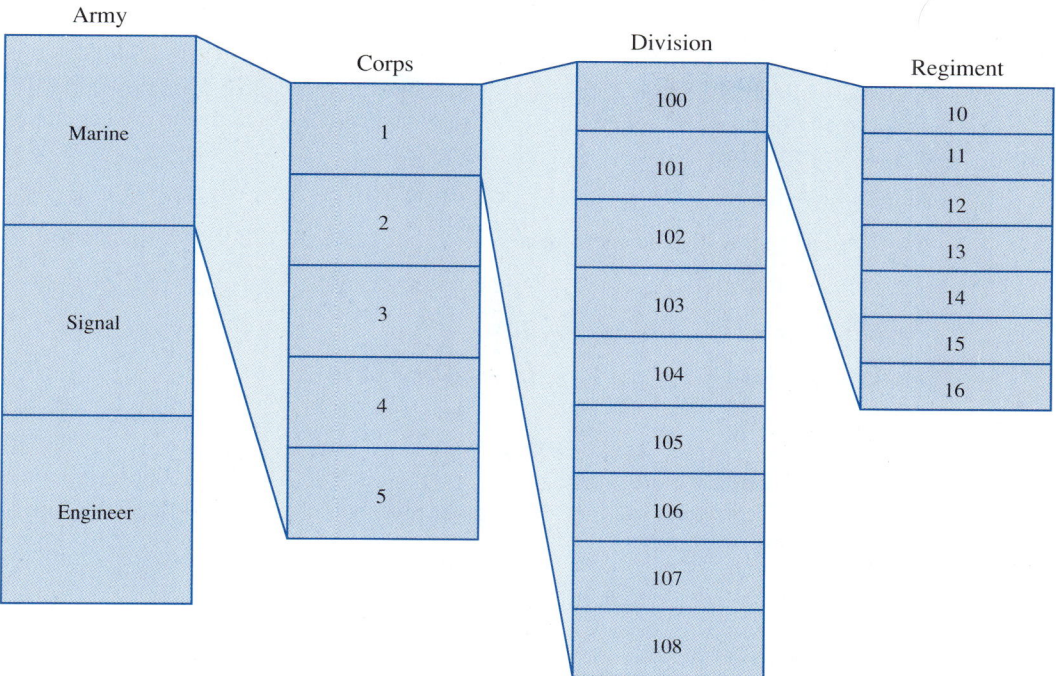

$$\text{address of } A[a_1, a_2, \ldots, a_n] < \text{address of } A[b_1, b_2, \ldots, b_n]$$
$$\text{if } (a_1 \; a_2 \; \ldots \; a_n) < (b_1 \; b_2 \; \ldots \; b_n)$$

If we consider the following two elements of array A: $A[F_1, F_2, \ldots, F_n]$ and $A[F_1 + 1, F_2, \ldots, F_n]$, storing the elements in lexicographic order guarantees us that all elements having their first index equal to F_1 and valid values for the other indices are stored between these two elements. So, between elements $A[F_1, F_2, \ldots, F_n]$ and $A[F_1 + 1, F_2, \ldots, F_n]$, we must have enough space to store a subarray comprising all elements having F_1 as first index, and whose other indices vary within the limits of their definition. Figure 2-2 illustrates this using the Army array seen earlier. Between element Army[Marine, 1, 100, 10] and Army[Signal, 1, 100, 10] there must be space for $5 \times 9 \times 7$ elements.

In a similar manner, we must have the same amount of storage for the subarray that includes all elements between $A[F_1 + 1, F_2, \ldots, F_n]$ and $A[F_1 + 2, F_2, \ldots, F_n]$. In fact, we will need $(L_1 - F_1 + 1)$ such spaces to store the same number of subarrays whose size is given by:

$$(L_2 - F_2 + 1)(L_3 - F_3 + 1) \cdots (L_n - F_n + 1).$$

We can use the same reasoning about the space needed to store the elements between $A[F_1, F_2, \ldots, F_n]$ and $A[F_1, F_2 + 1, \ldots, F_n]$. The size of the needed space will be: $(L_3 - F_3 + 1)(L_4 - F_4 + 1) \cdots (L_n - F_n + 1)$ for a subarray where elements have fixed first and second indices. Using the example in Figure 2-2, we see that between elements Army[Marine, 1, 100, 10] and Army[Marine, 2, 100, 10] we must have 9×7 elements.

Continuing in this fashion, index by index, we reach the case where all indices are fixed but the last one. Space allocation is then limited to a vector of size $(L_n - F_n + 1)$. This can be illustrated by computing the address of an element relative to the beginning of the corresponding subarray. For instance:

address of $A[I_1, I_2, \ldots, I_{n-1}, I_n]$ = address of $A[I_1, I_2, \ldots, I_{n-1}, F_n] + I_n - F_n$

since this is only a displacement in a vector. In Figure 2-2, this corresponds to:

address of $Army[I_1, I_2, I_3, I_4]$ = address of $Army[I_1, I_2, I_3, 10] + I_4 - 10$.

With the preceding subarray, we have:

address of $A[I_1, I_2, \ldots, I_{n-1}, I_n]$ = address of $A[I_1, I_2, \ldots, F_{n-1}, F_n]$ +
$(L_n - F_n + 1)(I_{n-1} - F_{n-1}) + (I_n - F_n)$

where we must "skip" $(I_{n-1} - F_{n-1})$ vectors, each of size $(L_n - F_n + 1)$, before reaching the vector we are interested in. In Figure 2-2, we would skip $(I_3 - 100)$ vectors of size 7. We can back up still another level and consider the preceding subarray. In that case we have:

address of $A[I_1, I_2, \ldots, I_{n-2}, I_{n-1}, I_n]$
= address of $A[I_1, I_2, I_3, \ldots, F_{n-2}, F_{n-1}, F_n]$
+ $(L_{n-1} - F_{n-1} + 1)(L_n - F_n + 1)(I_{n-2} - F_{n-2})$
+ $(L_n - F_n + 1)(I_{n-1} - F_{n-1}) + (I_n - F_n)$

since we must skip $(I_{n-2} - F_{n-2})$ matrices, each of size $(L_{n-1} - F_{n-1} + 1)(L_n - F_n + 1)$, and $(I_{n-1} - F_{n-1})$ vectors, each of size $(L_n - F_n + 1)$, before reaching the vector we are interested in. We can back up this way, up to the first index, and we obtain a general formula for computing the address of an array element relative to the first array element (the element identified by the minimum values of every index).

address of $A[I_1, I_2, \ldots, I_n]$ = address of $A[F_1, F_2, \ldots, F_n]$

$$+ \sum_{k=1}^{n} \left[\prod_{j=k+1}^{n} (L_j - F_j + 1) \right] (I_k - F_k)$$

This formula assumes a single memory word is used for each element. You can easily modify the formula to accommodate elements of size k.

We can apply this formula to the Army array we defined earlier and compute the address of element Army[Marine, 2, 102, 13].

address of Army[Marine, 2, 102, 13]
= address of Army[Marine, 1, 100, 10] +
$(5 - 1 + 1)(108 - 100 + 1)(16 - 10 + 1)(ORD(Marine) - ORD(Marine))$ +
$(108 - 100 + 1)(16 - 10 + 1)(2 - 1)$ +
$(16 - 10 + 1)(102 - 100)$ +
$(13 - 10)$
= address of Army[Marine,1,100,10]+80

Lexicographic allocation for arrays is efficient for the following reasons.

- Moving in an array along one of the indices is very simple (addition of a constant).
- Allocation is done in a contiguous manner, which leads to a good use of memory space.
- Access to arbitrary elements is easily calculated; we will present an iterative version of this calculation in the next section.

This implementation of arrays can be used whether the arrays are static (existing from the beginning to the end of a block execution), or dynamic (created during program execution by explicit calls to a memory allocation procedure and explicitly freed when not needed anymore).

Auxiliary Vectors

Some languages, like Modula-2, allow indices of various types that are not necessarily integer values. Since each of the indices of an array can be of a different type, arrays are treated as vectors whose elements are themselves vectors, each vector having its own index. A type declaration like:

```
TYPE Alphabet = ['A'..'Z'];
     Index = [1..20];
     Table = ARRAY Index, BOOLEAN, Alphabet OF REAL;
```

will be interpreted as:

```
TYPE Table = ARRAY Index OF
               ARRAY BOOLEAN OF
                 ARRAY Alphabet OF REAL;
```

With such an interpretation one can use descriptive vectors. These vectors allow us to check array accesses at compilation time in order to elaborate run time checks. If an array A is declared as being of type Table, its representation will correspond to Figure 2-3.

This representation uses three types of vectors because type Table is a combination of three types. Such a representation makes index checking very simple at execution time, since the lower and upper bounds of the indices are kept. Address computation for an array element will be done iteratively by using sizes of the various elements of the vectors, indices for the elements, and lower bounds of each index.

Given a general array, $A[F_1..L_1, F_2..L_2, \ldots, F_n..L_n]$, address computation for element $A[I_1, I_2, \ldots, I_n]$ can be performed by the following pseudocode:

```
Address ← Start Adress; (* beginning address *)
For J ← 1 to N
   Address ← Address + Size_J * (I_J − F_J);
End For
```

Chapter 2   Arrays

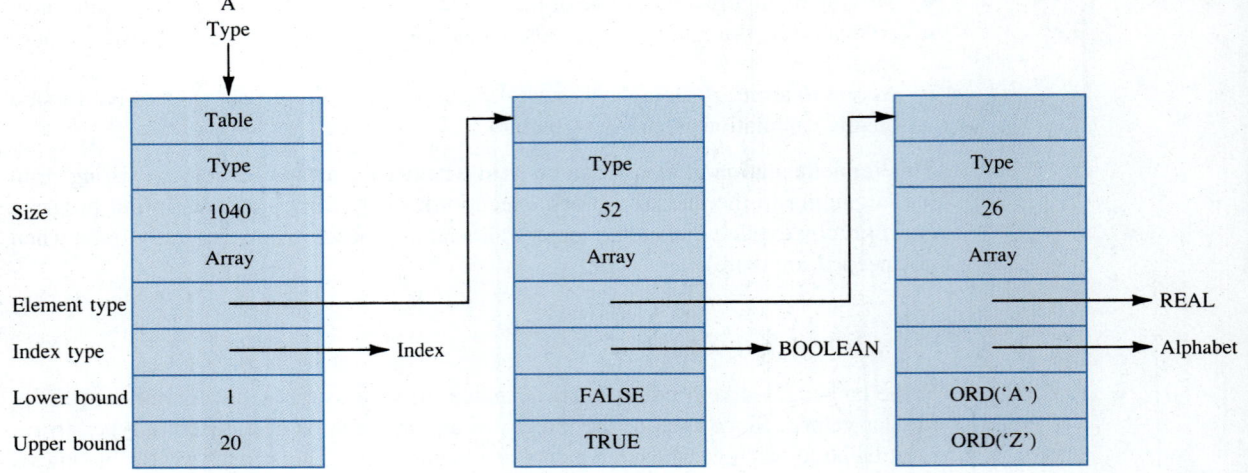

Figure 2-3   Representation of Array A of Type Table

The value of Start Adress is usually obtained from the table associated with the variables.

With the example of Figure 2-3, we would have N = 3 and:

```
F₁ = 1
F₂ = FALSE (or zero)
F₃ = ORD('A')
Size₁ = 52
Size₂ = 26
Size₃ = 1
```

Address of element A[5, TRUE, 'G'] will be computed from those values and $I_1 = 5$, $I_2 = $ TRUE (or one), $I_3 = $ ORD('G').

```
Address = Adr + 4 * 52 + 1 * 26 + 1 * 6 = Adr + 240.
```

2.4 Implementation of Specialized Arrays

In many applications, arrays may have many elements with zero values. For example, in *diagonal matrices*, all elements are zero except those on the diagonal. In a *tridiagonal matrix*, the only nonzero elements are those on the diagonal and two lines of elements parallel to this diagonal. *Triangular matrices* have all zero elements on one side of the diagonal. Other matrices, which we will call *sparse matrices*, have only a few nonzero elements placed randomly in the array. All these cases correspond to given applications. These applications can use the general representation seen previously, but its use leads to inefficient space utilization. It is often possible to represent partially filled arrays by vectors of nonzero values, thus saving space; however, address computation for accessing an element is usually more complicated and takes more time.

Diagonal Matrices

Suppose that you wanted to multiply the n columns of an m × n matrix M by constant values, $c_1, c_2, \ldots, c_n$, respectively. This could be accomplished by multiplying M on the right by the n × n matrix

$$\begin{matrix} c_1 & 0 & 0 & \ldots & 0 \\ 0 & c_2 & 0 & \ldots & 0 \\ 0 & 0 & c_3 & \ldots & 0 \\ \vdots & \vdots & \vdots & & \vdots \\ 0 & 0 & 0 & \ldots & c_n \end{matrix}$$

Let's call this diagonal matrix C. Clearly it would be very space inefficient to store this matrix with n × n entries. C can be represented by a vector V where V[I] corresponds to C[I, I]. The space has been reduced from n × n to n, and the access time is faster than the two-dimensional representation.

Tridiagonal Matrices

In a tridiagonal matrix, the only nonzero elements are those on the main diagonal and two lines of elements parallel to this diagonal, as shown in the following example.

$$\begin{matrix} c_1 & c_2 & 0 & 0 & 0 & \ldots & 0 \\ c_3 & c_4 & c_5 & 0 & 0 & \ldots & 0 \\ 0 & c_6 & c_7 & c_8 & 0 & \ldots & 0 \\ 0 & 0 & c_9 & c_{10} & c_{11} & \ldots & 0 \\ 0 & 0 & 0 & c_{12} & c_{13} & \ldots & 0 \\ 0 & 0 & 0 & 0 & c_{15} & \ldots & 0 \\ \vdots & \vdots & \vdots & \vdots & \vdots & & \vdots \\ 0 & 0 & 0 & 0 & 0 & \ldots & c_n \end{matrix}$$

A tridiagonal matrix can be represented by three vectors, each corresponding to elements M[i − 1, i], M[i, i], M[i, i + 1]. It can also be represented by a single vector with a simple address computation formula:

$$\text{address of M}[i, j] = \text{address of M}[1, 1] + 2(i - 1) + (j - 1)$$

For example, if the above conditions are respected, then the vector contains the following sequential elements: M[1, 1], M[1, 2], M[2, 1], M[2, 2], M[2, 3], M[3, 2], M[3, 3], M[3, 4], M[4, 3], etc. Notice that these elements are in increasing lexicographic order.

Triangular Arrays

For many tables of data, the table entry at the *i*th row and *j*th column is always the same as the entry at the *j*th row and the *i*th column. One such example can be seen in a table for distances between two cities. In this case it is necessary to store the distance between each pair of cities only once. When a map contains such a table, that table often appears in triangular form. In fact, any table that is symmetric about the diagonal is a candidate for triangularization. We can make a distinction between a lower-triangular matrix like:

$$
\begin{array}{cccccc}
c_1 & 0 & 0 & 0 & 0 & \cdots 0 \\
c_2 & c_3 & 0 & 0 & 0 & \cdots 0 \\
c_4 & c_5 & c_6 & 0 & 0 & \cdots 0 \\
c_7 & c_8 & c_9 & c_{10} & 0 & \cdots 0 \\
c_{11} & c_{12} & c_{13} & c_{14} & c_{15} & \cdots 0 \\
c_{16} & c_{17} & c_{18} & c_{19} & c_{20} & \cdots 0 \\
\vdots & \vdots & \vdots & \vdots & \vdots & \vdots \\
c_{n-k-4} & c_{n-k-3} & c_{n-k-2} & c_{n-k-1} & c_{n-k} & \cdots c_n
\end{array}
$$

and an upper-triangular matrix like:

$$
\begin{array}{cccccc}
c_1 & c_2 & c_3 & c_4 & c_5 & \cdots c_k \\
0 & c_{k+1} & c_{k+2} & c_{k+3} & c_{k+4} & \cdots c_{2k-1} \\
0 & 0 & c_{2k} & c_{2k+1} & c_{2k+2} & \cdots c_{3k-3} \\
0 & 0 & 0 & c_{3k-2} & c_{3k-1} & \cdots c_{4k-6} \\
0 & 0 & 0 & 0 & c_{4k-5} & \cdots c_{5k-10} \\
0 & 0 & 0 & 0 & 0 & \cdots c_{6k-15} \\
\vdots & \vdots & \vdots & \vdots & \vdots & \vdots \\
0 & 0 & 0 & 0 & 0 & \cdots c_n
\end{array}
$$

A triangular matrix can also be stored in a vector with a simple address computation function. Notice that a given row of a lower-triangular matrix contains one more element than the previous row. Thus, space reserved for row i begins after the area reserved for the first $(i-1)$ rows. These take $1 + 2 + 3 + \cdots + (i-1)$ memory cells, which you may recall, is equal to $i(i-1)/2$ cells. Therefore:

$$\text{address of } M[i, j] = \text{address of } M[1, 1] + i(i-1)/2 + (j-1)$$

The vector used to represent the lower-triangular matrix contains the following sequential elements: M[1, 1], M[2, 1], M[2, 2], M[3, 1], M[3, 2], M[3, 3], M[4, 1], etc.

If by chance, we have two triangular matrices of the same size, we can store them in a rectangular matrix as shown below:

$$
\begin{array}{llllllll}
A_{11} & B_{nn} & B_{nn-1} & \cdots & & & & B_{n1} \\
A_{21} & A_{22} & B_{n-1n-1} & \cdots & & & & B_{n-11} \\
A_{31} & A_{32} & A_{33} & B_{n-2n-2} & \cdots & & & B_{n-21} \\
& & & \cdots & & & & \\
A_{n1} & A_{n2} & A_{n3} & \cdots & & & A_{nn} & B_{11}
\end{array}
$$

Mapping formulas for $1 \leq i \leq n$ and $1 \leq j \leq n + 1$ are:

```
A[i, j] = C[i, j]
B[i, j] = C[n - i + 1, n - j + 2]
```

Combined matrix C will be represented by a vector and addresses of its elements will be computed in the following manner:

address of A[i, j] = address of C[1, 1] + $(n + 1)(i - 1) + (j - 1)$
address of B[i, j] = address of C[1, 1] + $(n + 1)n - 1 - ((n + 1)(i - 1) + (j - 1))$

Notice that in the case of the elements of B, we proceed in the same way as for the elements of A, but backing up from the last element of the combined matrix.

The case of triangular matrices can be generalized to one more dimension. We have then tetrahedral arrays, which correspond graphically to the cut corner of a cube. It is possible to define a formula for computing the addresses of elements by using the fact that $1^2 + 2^2 + 3^2 + 4^2 + \cdots + n^2 = n(n + 1)(2n + 1)/6$:

address of M[i, j, k] = address of M[1, 1, 1] + $i(i - 1)(i + 1)/6 + j(j - 1)/2 + (k - 1)$

This formula can be generalized to the case of n-dimensional arrays using binomial coefficients.

Sparse Matrices

A diagonal matrix has at most n nonzero elements, a tridiagonal matrix has at most $(3n - 2)$ nonzero elements, and a triangular matrix has at most $n(n + 1)/2$ nonzero elements. The occupation ratios of diagonal and tridiagonal matrices are $1/n$ and $3/n - 2/n^2$. These values are proportional to $1/n$ and become very small when n increases. As we have seen, in these cases there are much more efficient storage schemes that avoid storing the zero values. However, there are many other applications where matrices are sparse, in the sense of having a low occupancy ratio, yet the nonzero elements may be more randomly placed. We will now explore methods for representing sparse matrices with randomly placed nonzero elements.

First let's consider an actual application for sparse matrices. Suppose that you are employed by a cattle ranch that owns several thousand cows and several hundred bulls. Mating is carefully controlled, and it is your job to keep track of the number of calves produced by every possible pair of cattle. You might choose a matrix to represent this data, with the first index representing the bull, the second index representing the cow, and the matrix entry representing the number of calves produced by this pair. Obviously, most pairs will never produce offspring at all, thus most entries in the matrix would be zero. Suppose that there were 1000 cows, 100 bulls, and during one breeding season there were 250 births (each from a different cow). This means that only 250 entries out of a potential 100,000 entries would be nonzero, so the occupancy ratio is 0.00250. It is obvious that we would not want to use a general matrix to represent these data.

Storing Indices with Element Values

The simplest and most obvious method is to keep only the nonzero elements with their indices. We will illustrate this using a much smaller (and much less sparse) matrix than the cattle-breeding data discussed above. Consider, the following matrix:

```
4 0 0 6
9 7 0 0
0 0 0 0
0 0 2 0
```

We could store this data as a sequence of triplets, where each triplet represents an element identified by its row, its column, and its value.

(1, 1, 4),   (1, 4, 6),   (2, 1, 9),   (2, 2, 7),   (4, 3, 2)

We need 3N memory cells if there are N nonzero elements in the matrix. Accessing an element will require a sequential search whose execution time is proportional to N.

It is also possible to use a pseudo-address instead of row and column indices. The pseudo-address is the relative address the element would have in a complete matrix, assuming lexicographic ordering across the rows. For the data above we would have:

(0, 4),   (3, 6),   (4, 9),   (5, 7),   (14, 2)

The necessary memory space is 2N. Since elements are ordered by their pseudo-address, it is possible to use a binary search (see Chapter 3), and the search time is proportional to log N. This improvement is possible at the cost of the pseudo-address computation, which only involves simple arithmetic. In the example above, the pseudo-address for a nonzero element in the ith row and jth column is $4(i - 1) + j - 1$. (Given a pseudo-address, p, the row number is (p DIV 4) + 1 and the column number would be (p MOD 4) + 1.)

Storing Elements Row by Row

Another method is to keep matrix elements row by row, with elements of the same row kept in a contiguous space. For the small, sparse matrix

```
4 0 0 6
9 7 0 0
0 0 0 0
0 0 2 0
```

this would mean storing:

Row Number	Column Value . . .	Column Value . . .
1	1 4	4 6
2	1 9	2 7
3		
4	3 2	

2.4 Implementation of Specialized Arrays

The required memory space is 2N + r, where r is the number of rows. Each row can have a different size: this makes it impossible to use a binary search. However, it is possible to create a row directory with starting index for each row. In our example the directory would be:

1 1
2 1
3 0
4 3

This directory will require r memory cells and can be searched using a binary search whose execution time is proportional to log r. Once a row is found, a binary search over its elements will be done in a time proportional to log L, if L is the number of nonzero elements in the row.

Using a Bit Map

Yet another method is to use a bit map of the matrix elements. For instance, the bit map for our sample matrix is shown below.

Matrix   **Bit Map**
4 0 0 6   1 0 0 1
9 7 0 0   1 1 0 0
0 0 0 0   0 0 0 0
0 0 2 0   0 0 1 0

The bit map shows the positions of the nonzero elements, and only these elements (4, 6, 9, 7, 2 in our example) are kept in a vector. The bit map itself must also be kept, but it is made of values that are either 0 or 1. These values can be represented by bits, and the bit map can be compressed by a factor equal to the word size of the computer. With the vector of nonzero elements and the bit map, we must also have an efficient access method to the matrix elements. As we have done earlier, we can use a row directory giving the address of the first element of each row, and use masking and indexing techniques to find a given element.

Vector	Bit Map	Row	Directory
4	1 0 0 1	1	1
6	1 1 0 0	2	3
9	0 0 0 0	3	0
7	0 0 1 0	4	5
2			

For example, to find element M[2, 2], the row directory gives 3 as the starting address in the vector for row 2. Masking bit map 1100 shows that the element in column 2 exists, that there is one element in front of it, and results in the computation of address 4.

Using an Augmented Bit Map

The bit map can be extended to hold for each row a continuous sequence of 1-bits, from the first to the last nonzero element of a row. The augmented bit map for our last example is:

Matrix	Augmented Bit Map
4 0 0 6	1 1 1 1
9 7 0 0	1 1 0 0
0 0 0 0	0 0 0 0
0 0 2 0	0 0 1 0

In that case we must keep all the elements corresponding to 1 bits in the augmented bit map: 4, 0, 0, 6, 9, 7, 2. Obviously, this forces us to keep elements with value zero. We compute the first column used in each row (C), the number of elements found in the preceding rows (N), and the difference of those two values (D), as shown below.

Matrix	Bit Map	i	C	N	$D = N - C$
4 0 0 6	1 1 1 1	1	1	0	−1
9 7 0 0	1 1 0 0	2	1	4	3
0 0 0 0	0 0 0 0	3	0	6	6
0 0 2 0	0 0 1 0	4	3	6	3

Address computation is given by:

$$\text{address of } M[i, j] = \text{address of first} + D[i] + j$$

where "address of first" is the address of the first nonzero element of the matrix. Using this formula, we find the address of M[4, 3] = address of first + D[4] + 3 = 1 + 3 + 3 = 7.

Linked Representation

A linked (or dynamic) representation is generally used in cases where arrays must grow in arbitrary directions, but is rarely used for complete arrays. Linked representation is also used for sparse matrices where the nonzero elements are randomly placed. These representations are usually based on linked lists and are not as efficient as static representations. However, they offer a flexibility important in certain applications. They will be introduced in Chapter 5 as applications of linear lists.

Summary

Arrays are ordered sets of homogeneous elements; they exist in most high-level programming languages. Their implementations vary greatly depending on the system being used.

Lexicographic allocation is the method most often used, as it allows efficient use of computer memory as well as easy access to array elements. Other storage techniques have been developed for specialized matrices, such as diagonal matrices, tridiagonal matrices, triangular matrices, and other very sparse matrices.

■ *Exercises*

1. An array A is declared in each of the following parts; each element uses a memory word. What is the address of the indicated element if the first element of A is at memory address 200?
   (a) VAR A: ARRAY [1..150] OF EltType; address of A[20]?
   (b) VAR A: ARRAY [-10..10],[10..20] OF EltType; address of A[1, 15]?
   (c) VAR A: ARRAY [0..10],[0..20] OF EltType; address of A[10, 20]?
   (d) VAR A: ARRAY [0..10],[0..20] OF EltType; address of A[6, 0]?
   (e) VAR A: ARRAY [0..10],[0..20] OF EltType; address of A[0, 20]?

2. In FORTRAN, arrays have at most three dimensions, indices vary from 1 up, arrays are stored **column by column,** that is, with the first index varying first.
   (a) For array T declared by DIMENSION T(L, M, N), where L, M, N are constants corresponding to the upper bounds of the indices, give the formula to compute the address of element T(I, J, K), assuming one element occupies one word.
   (b) With declaration DOUBLE PRECISION T(10, 20, 30), where array elements use two words each, compute the address of element T(5, 10, 20), assuming that T's first element is at address 100. What element is at address 1100?

3. Define a mapping function that will store array

   A[0..4],[1..3],[-2..0]

   in addresses 200 to 244 so that

   address of A[0, 1, -2] = 200 and address of A[4, 3, 0] = 244.

4. Modify the general formula for lexicographic space allocation so that it takes into account the size of array elements.

5. A triangular 10 × 10 matrix is represented by a vector as shown in Figure 2-1. Its first element is placed at address 100 (one word per element). Give the address of M[9, 8]. What element is at address 150?

6. Establish the formula to compute the address of element M[i, j] of an upper-triangular matrix represented by a vector.

*7. For a tetrahedral array such that for all elements T[i, j, k] we have $1 \leq k \leq j \leq i \leq 4$, define an address computation function for element T[i, j, k].

Note: Problems marked with an asterisk (*) have a higher level of difficulty.

8. With the following declarations:

   ```
   TYPE Employee = RECORD
                      Name: ARRAY [1..N] OF CHAR;
                      Address: ARRAY [1..L] OF CHAR;
                   END;
   VAR Employees: ARRAY [1..Max] OF Employee;
   ```

   if memory addressing is by bytes and a character occupies one byte, and if the first element of Employees is stored starting at address A:
   (a) draw the representation of memory allocation to the array elements.
   (b) define a formula to compute the address of Employees[I].Address.

9. To represent a sparse matrix, one can use a bit matrix and a vector of nonzero values. The bit matrix indicates the position of nonzero elements in the matrix. For instance:

0	0	0	1	0	will be represented by	0	0	0	1	0	and	1
0	2	0	3	0		0	1	0	1	0		2
4	0	0	0	0		1	0	0	0	0		3
0	0	0	0	0		0	0	0	0	0		4
0	5	0	0	6		0	1	0	0	1		5
												6

   If each element occupies one word of memory and if each word contains b bits, what memory size should be used to represent an m × n matrix with p nonzero elements?

10. In a representation for sparse matrices, each element is represented by a triplet (row, column, value) stored in an array. The first triplet gives the number of rows, the number of columns, and the number of nonzero elements of the matrix. Give an algorithm that produces the transposed matrix using the same representation. Recall that the transposed A^t of a matrix A is such that $A^t[i, j] = A[j, i]$.

■ Programming Problems

11. Write a procedure ComputeAddress that computes the address of an array element relative to the array first element. The procedure will have three parameters, Lower, Upper, and Index, each a vector. Vectors Lower and Upper contain the lower and upper bounds of each dimension. Vector Index contains the indices of the element whose address we want to compute. For example, if Lower = (2, 1, 0, −4), Upper = (5, 10, 3, 0) and Index = (3, 8, 0, −1), we will compute the address of T[3, 8, 0, −1] of array T[2..5],[1..10],[0..3],[−4..0].

12. A 200 × 200 sparse matrix is represented by three vectors: R (row), C (column), and V (values). Write two procedures, Get and Put, to get the value of element M[i, j], and to assign a value to it.

13. Write the necessary procedures to implement the augmented bit map representation method by computing vectors C, N, D, and the address of M[i, j].

14. A saddle point in an m × n matrix exists if M[i, j] is the smallest value of its row and the largest value of its column. Write a procedure to determine if a saddle point exists in a given matrix.

15. Write a program to keep a register of students' grades and to print the grade sheet. For each student the program will read: name, number, address (street, city, state, zip code), grades (for each course: course number and grade). The program will read the grades for each course and update the students' records. The data are pairs of integers for student number and grade. You may assume that student numbers are integers (1..N) and can be used as indices in the students table. A student cannot take more than six courses. The program will print a grade sheet, which will show the name and address of student and, for each course taken, the final grade as well as the semester average.

*16. Write a program to solve the problem of the Knight's Tour on a chessboard. Given a knight at a specific position on the chessboard, move the knight so that it moves according to chess rules and visits each of the 64 squares once and only once. A simple way of doing this is to place numbers 1, 2, 3, . . . , 64 in each square to indicate in which order they have been visited. The Knight's Tour does not have to end where it started. From one position on the chessboard B[i, j], the knight has eight possible moves.

```
    -   3   -   2   -
    4   -   -   -   1
    -   -   K   -   -
    5   -   -   -   8
    -   6   -   7   -
```

Each move is identified by a pair of integers. These are the values to add to (i, j) to reach the new position: move 1 = (2, 1), move 2 = (1, 2), move 3 = (−1, 2), move 4 = (−2, 1), move 5 = (−2, −1), move 6 = (−2, −2), move 7 = (1, −2), move 8 = (2, −1). We can keep those pairs in two parallel vectors, Row and Column, and use them to compute a new position.

```
NewI := OldI + Row[k];    NewJ := OldJ + Column[k];
```

Your algorithm can follow the general pattern:

```
Try next move
   Repeat
      Choose next move from remaining possible moves
      If move is valid
         Store move
         If chessboard not full
            Try next move
            If failure
               Erase stored move
            End if
         End if
      End if
   Until a move is accepted or no more move possible
End Try next move
```

Searching, Sorting, and the Analysis of Algorithms

INTRODUCTION

In Chapter 2, we presented an informal analysis of a matrix transpose algorithm and a matrix multiplication algorithm. That discussion provided just a glimpse into a very important area of computer science called *analysis of algorithms*. It is not enough to know that we have an algorithm to solve a problem; we must also know that the algorithm can be executed in some reasonable amount of time. For instance, the algorithm that determines if the game of chess is a forced victory for the white pieces is impractical because it would require eons to execute, even on our fastest computers. We must be able to analyze algorithms to determine if they are practical; this chapter is devoted to that topic.

We start off by introducing the Big-O notation as the mathematical basis for analyzing an algorithm to determine its time complexity. We use the word "complexity" here to refer to the efficiency of an algorithm, rather than its subtlety or intricacy. You may wish to think of the complexity of an algorithm as an estimate of its execution time, but the estimate should be independent of any particular computer or programming language.

We introduce two simple searching algorithms and analyze their complexity. Next we introduce several simple sorting algorithms, and analyze their complexity. Then, we introduce another well-known sorting procedure, which is significantly faster than the simple sorting algorithms. The chapter concludes with a case study involving yet another sorting algorithm, whose efficiency is better than the simple sorts.

3.1 Analysis of Algorithms

In Chapter 2, we said that one way of analyzing an algorithm was to count the number of statements it will have executed on its completion. In fact, this gives us a basis for comparing two algorithms: a measure of the time necessary for their execution.

The Big-O Notation

To determine the *time complexity* of an algorithm, we first find an expression that gives us an estimate of the execution time of the algorithm, and then we analyze that expression. The expression for execution time is usually a function of a variable (or variables) that is a measure of the size of the particular task that the algorithm is being asked to perform. For example, the size of a search would be the length, say n, of the sequence to be searched. So, when we say that the run time for a searching algorithm is proportional to n, we are expressing a functional relationship between the size of the searching job and the amount of work required to complete the job. The mathematical notation used to express such relationships is called the Big-O notation. To determine the Big-O value for a given expression, we must find the dominant term or terms in the expression.

We can formally define Big-O notation as follows:

Big-O Notation We say that g(n) is O(f(n)) if there exist two constants C and k such that $|g(n)| \leq C\,|f(n)|$ for all $n > k$.

EXAMPLE 1

For some algorithm, let's assume that we have $g(n) = n^2/2 + 5n/2 - 3$. In order to show that g(n) is $O(n^2)$ according to our definition, we take $f(n) = n^2$. Now, we must find values of C and k that cause the inequality $|g(n)| \leq C\,|f(n)|$ for all $n > k$, to be satisfied. Table 3-1 gives the values (truncated to integers) of the three terms in g(n), for small values of n.

Notice that, for very small n, the second term is larger than the first, because the second is multiplied by $\frac{5}{2}$ while the first is divided by 2. However, this does not last long. By the time n is equal to 5, the terms are equal, and when n is 10, the first is double the second. Thus the first term dominates the other two, and so we say that g(n) is $O(n^2)$.

To prove that this is true, using our definition and Table 3-1 we note that $g(6) = 30$, and since $6^2 = 36$, we take $C = \frac{5}{6}$, and $k = 5$. Actually, we can take C to be any value greater than or equal to $\frac{5}{6}$, and k to be any value greater than or equal to 5, but it is common to give the least possible values if they are not too difficult to find.

Two things should be noted:

1. A proportionality constant, such as $\frac{1}{2}$ in the example above, does not affect the complexity of an algorithm.

Table 3-1
Growth of Terms of $g(n)$

n	$n^2/2$	$5n/2$	-3
2	2	5	-3
3	4	7	-3
4	8	10	-3
5	12	12	-3
6	18	15	-3
7	24	17	-3
8	32	20	-3
9	40	22	-3
10	50	25	-3
50	1250	125	-3
100	5000	250	-3

2. The domination need only be true from a particular value of n, such as 5 in the example above, and beyond.

EXAMPLE 2

Suppose we want to find the complexity of an algorithm whose execution time can be estimated by the expression $1^2 + 2^2 + 3^2 + \cdots + n^2$. To do our analysis, we first need to find a closed form (eliminating the $\cdots$ notation) for this summation. By using induction, it can be shown that:

$$1^2 + 2^2 + 3^2 + \cdots + n^2 = n(n + 1)(2n + 1)/6$$

If we choose C to be 1 and k to be 1, then

$$|n(n + 1)(2n + 1)/6| \leq |n^3| \text{ for all } n \geq 1$$

so we say the complexity is $O(n^3)$. Of course, our original sum of squares is also bounded by n^4 or n^5, etc., so the Big-O notation only provides an upper bound.

There is another notation, called Big-omega, that is used to specify a lower bound. We say that g(n) is $\Omega(f(n))$ if there exists a constant c such that $|g(n)| \geq |c\, f(n)|$ for an infinite number of values of n. A third notation, called theta, is defined in terms of these other two notations: we say g(n) is $\Theta(f(n))$ if g(n) is both $O(f(n))$ and $\Omega(f(n))$. It is beyond the scope of this text to use these alternative notations; rather, we will use the Big-O notation in a "common sense" way. We will not give the complexity of an algorithm as $O(n^4)$ if we could also show it is $O(n^3)$.

Common Complexity Classes

The complexity of an algorithm can be expressed by many Big-O classifications. However, there are some commonly occurring classifications, which we will examine in this section. Table 3-2 gives a list of common complexity classes.

We refer to the first six complexity classes as polynomial classes, and, of course, there are many other polynomial classes, such as $O(n^4)$.

Table 3-2 Common Complexity Classes

constant	$O(1)$
logarithmic	$O(\log n)$
linear	$O(n)$
n log n	$O(n \log n)$
quadratic	$O(n^2)$
cubic	$O(n^3)$
exponential	$O(2^n)$, $O(10^n)$, $O(C^n)$ for any constant $C > 1$

A constant complexity means that the run time is independent of the size of the problem, clearly an uncommon situation for an entire algorithm, but more common for a component of an algorithm.

Some of the other complexities involve the logarithmic function. Since converting logarithms from one base to another only involves multiplying by a constant, the choice of the logarithm base does not affect the algorithm complexity. We have:

$$\log_b x = \frac{\log_a x}{\log_a b} = \log_a x \log_b a$$

We will write log to indicate base two logarithms.

An exponential complexity involves raising a constant (greater than 1) to the nth power.

In order to appreciate how fast each of these functions grow, we will make a table for small values of n. We choose powers of two so that the logarithms result in integer values. The data is given in tabular form in Table 3-3; a graphical presentation is given in Figure 3-1.

It is evident from the rates of growth that the complexity of an algorithm can make a big difference in run time, especially for larger values of n. In particular, notice how the exponential 2^n surges past the polynomials at about n = 10. For this reason, algorithms of exponential complexity are called "intractable," since they would not be practical computing methods for larger problems.

For algorithms with polynomial complexity, we obviously prefer those with complexity of low order, such as n and n log n, since they will be more efficient for large problems. We will now introduce two simple searching methods with time complexities $O(n)$ and $O(\log n)$; then we will introduce several simple sorting methods, each

Table 3-3 Values for Various Functions

	log n	n	n log n	n^2	n^3	2^n
n = 1	0	1	0	1	1	2
n = 2	1	2	2	4	8	4
n = 4	2	4	8	16	64	16
n = 16	4	16	64	256	4096	65536
n = 256	8	256	2048	65536	16777216	1.16×10^{77}
n = 1024	10	1024	10240	1048576	1.07×10^9	1.80×10^{308}

Figure 3-1
A Graphical Comparison of Complexities

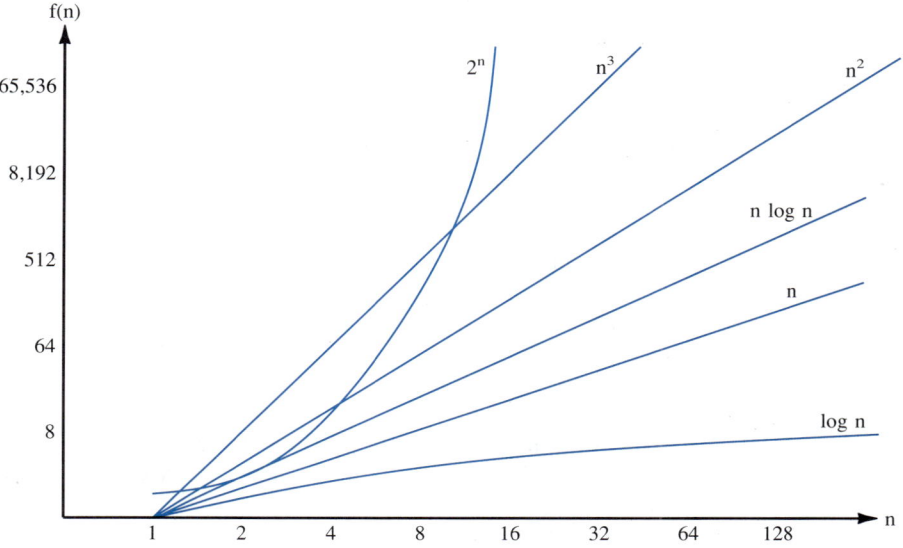

with a complexity of $O(n^2)$. Later, we will show other sorting techniques with lower complexity, like $O(n \log n)$. We would expect a substantial difference in run time for these two classes of sorting algorithms for problems with large n.

Another aspect of the complexity of an algorithm is what is often called its *space complexity*. The space complexity of an algorithm is a measure of the memory space needed to execute the algorithm. Some algorithms with a good time complexity might have a large space complexity, rendering their use on small computers somewhat problematic.

3.2 Simple Searching Algorithms

Although searching for information may appear simple, the speed with which it can be done will determine whether a method is practical or not. The searching of a collection of records will be done using a specific field of the records as a "key." Searching a collection of records normally involves comparing record keys to a given search key with the intent of finding a record with the search key, or determining that no such record is present in the collection. For example, we could search an array of employee records on the name field, in order to find a record with a given name.

Sequential Search

The simplest form of a search is the sequential search, as shown below for an array of records. Elements are examined one after the other until either a record that has the same key is found, or the end of the array is reached.

```
PROCEDURE SequentialSearch(Table: ArrayType; K: KeyType): IndexType;
VAR Index: IndexType;
BEGIN
  Index := 1;
  WHILE Index <= TableSize DO
    (* K is not a key of elements Table[1]..Table[Index-1] *)
    IF K = Table[Index].Key THEN(* found *)
      RETURN Index;
    ELSE
      INC(Index);            (* continue *)
    END; (* IF *)
  END; (* WHILE *)
  RETURN 0;                  (* not found *)
END SequentialSearch;
```

The SequentialSearch function returns the index of the element if key K is in Table, or returns a zero value otherwise. We have assumed that elements of Table have a field Key that is used for the search.

There are several variations of this algorithm, the best-known one involves the storing of the searched key K in an extra element of the table as a sentinel (either at position 0 or at position TableSize +1). This device simplifies the loop:

```
WHILE K # Table[Index].Key DO INC(Index) END
```

but requires checking the index at the end of that loop to find out if the sentinel was reached.

The time complexity of a search is based on the number of comparisons C_n between the key and the elements during the execution of the algorithm. In order to count the number of statements executed by SequentialSearch, we note that the WHILE loop is repeated at most n times, if n is the number of elements in the array. For each repetition of that loop, three statements are executed: the comparison for the end of array; the keys comparison, which can stop the repetition; and the increment of the index. The number of statements executed is therefore equal to $3C_n$.

The expected number of comparisons required to locate an element with key K, using a sequential search, is given by:

$$C_n = 1 \ p_1 + 2 \ p_2 + \cdots + n \ p_n$$

where p_i is the probability that the ith element searched contains the search key, and where $p_1 + p_2 + p_3 + \cdots + p_n = 1$. If each element is equally likely to be accessed during a search, then $p_i = 1/n$ and $C_n = (n + 1)/2$. This result means that about half the elements are inspected on the average, each time a search is performed.

In that case, the number of statements executed is: $g(n) = 3(n + 1)/2$. Using our definition for the Big-O notation, we can choose $f(n) = n$ because $g(n) < C f(n)$ if we choose C to be 2 and $n > 3$. (For $n = 3$, we have $g(n) = 6$ and $2f(n) = 6$.) Thus the complexity of SequentialSearch is O(n).

Using what is called Zipf distributions (the nth most frequent word in a natural language text occurs with a frequency proportional to 1/n), and the 80/20 rule observed in data processing applications (80% of the transactions deal with the most active 20% of the elements of a file), Knuth has found that $C_n = 0.122n$. Therefore, whatever the distribution, sequential search algorithms will always be O(n), although the performance can be much improved if the most frequently used keys are placed at the front of the table.

The space complexity of SequentialSearch is equal to the size needed to store the array, as the searching is done directly in the original array, and does not require extra storage beyond the temporary variable (Index) used by the algorithm.

Binary Search

If the names in a telephone book were not kept in alphabetical order, looking for somebody's telephone number would be a horrendous task. We could use the sequential search algorithm we have just seen, but that would not be particularly efficient. In fact, the efficiency of searching the telephone book is dependent on the fact that its elements are kept in order.

The reason why a search in an ordered table is more efficient than a search in an unordered table is easy to see: a single comparison in a sequential search can eliminate only the key under consideration, while such a comparison in an ordered table can eliminate either all the elements preceding or all the elements following the key.

The simplest and most efficient method of searching an ordered sequential table is the binary search. The search key is compared to the middle element of the table: if the keys match then the search is over, otherwise the same method is applied either to the first half or to the second half of the table. This recursive description indicates that a recursive algorithm should be easy to define.

```
BinarySearch (Data, First, Last, Name)
   Set Middle to (First + Last) div 2
   If First < Last then
      If Name precedes entry at Middle position then
         { Name not in second half }
         BinarySearch(Data, First, Middle − 1, Name)
      Elsif Name comes after entry at Middle position then
         { Name not in first half }
         BinarySearch(Data, Middle + 1, Last, Name)
      End if
   End if
End BinarySearch
```

However, since recursion introduces overhead (see Chapter 6), such a recursive solution might be impractical when efficiency is a prime consideration. The following is a nonrecursive version of the binary search algorithm.

```
PROCEDURE BinarySearch(Table: ArrayType; K: KeyType): INTEGER;
VAR Low, High, Middle: INTEGER;
BEGIN
  Low := 1;
  High := ArraySize;                    (* table limits *)
  WHILE Low <= High DO
    Middle := (Low + High) DIV 2;       (* middle index *)
    IF K = Table[Middle].Key THEN       (* found *)
      RETURN Middle;
    ELSIF K < Table[Middle].Key THEN    (* search in first half *)
      High := Middle - 1;
    ELSE                                (* search in second half *)
      Low := Middle + 1;
    END; (* IF *)
  END; (* WHILE *)
  RETURN 0;                             (* not found *)
END BinarySearch;
```

In this method each comparison reduces the number of possible candidates by a factor of 2. Considering the worst-case behavior when an item isn't present, the approximate number of items remaining after each comparison is as follows:

Comparison	1	2	3	...	p
Remaining items	n/2	n/4	n/8	...	$n/2^p$

We can stop searching when only one item remains, thus when $n/2^p = 1$ or simply $n = 2^p$. It follows that the maximum number of key comparisons, p, is approximately $\log_2 n$. The WHILE loop is repeated log n times. Each repetition, except the last one, executes two comparisons (IF and ELSIF) and two assignment statements. The number of statements executed is therefore approximately equal to 4 log n, thus the BinarySearch procedure complexity is O(log n).

The space complexity of BinarySearch is equal to the size needed to store the array, as the searching is done directly in the original array, and does not require extra storage beyond the temporary variables (Low, High, Middle) used by the algorithm.

3.3 Simple Sorts

In this section, we will develop three simple sorting algorithms and analyze their complexity. The algorithms will sort an array of records into ascending order. The sorting will be done using a specific field of the record as a "key," so that the records order is based on that key field. For example we could sort an array of employee records on the name field, so that the records are ordered alphabetically by name.

In thinking about how to sort an array, your first reaction may be to use another array of equal size to hold the result. Unfortunately, this is not practical if the array is very large—the memory of your computer may not be able to hold both arrays, along with the program and the run time system. Since this is a common situation, we will avoid using another array and try to do the sorting using only the original array. We say that such a sort is *in situ* (or "in place").

Selection Sort

This method can be described by the following steps:

Find the smallest element of the array.
Swap this element with the first element of the array.
Repeat this algorithm on the subarray of remaining elements.

We can illustrate it with a twelve-element array as shown in Figure 3-2. This figure shows the contents of the array elements (represented by a numerical key value) after each pass of the algorithm.

Original array	74	66	20	96	14	57	61	83	55	71	94	3
Pass 1	3	66	20	96	14	57	61	83	55	71	94	74
Pass 2	3	14	20	96	66	57	61	83	55	71	94	74
Pass 3	3	14	20	96	66	57	61	83	55	71	94	74
Pass 4	3	14	20	55	66	57	61	83	96	71	94	74
Pass 5	3	14	20	55	57	66	61	83	96	71	94	74
Pass 6	3	14	20	55	57	61	66	83	96	71	94	74
Pass 7	3	14	20	55	57	61	66	83	96	71	94	74
Pass 8	3	14	20	55	57	61	66	71	96	83	94	74
Pass 9	3	14	20	55	57	61	66	71	74	83	94	96
Pass 10	3	14	20	55	57	61	66	71	74	83	94	96
Pass 11	3	14	20	55	57	61	66	71	74	83	94	96

Figure 3-2 Selection Sort

The algorithm can be formulated by the following pseudocode, assuming an array with indices going from 0 to n, and a sort in ascending order.

> SelectionSort
>   For i from 0 to n − 1 do
>   Find the index of the smallest element of Table[i] through
>   Table[n], call it small
>   Swap Table[i] and Table[small]
>   { Elements Table[0] through Table[i] are in proper positions }
>   End for
>   { Elements Table[0] through Table[n] are in their proper positions }
> End SelectionSort

Notice that if Table has one element, n − 1 = −1, so no iterations are performed. If Table has more than one element, after the first iteration of the loop the smallest element will be in its proper place, after the second iteration the two smallest elements will be in their proper places, and, in general, after the *i*th iteration, the i smallest elements will be in their proper places. This observation is documented by the assertion at the bottom of the loop. After n iterations, the elements Table[0] through Table[n − 1] are in their proper places, and so Table[n] must also be in its proper place. Thus, all elements are in order, as documented by the assertion at the end of the algorithm.

The algorithm is called SelectionSort, because in each pass we "select" the smallest remaining element to place in its proper position, working from the lowest index to the highest index. Using the example of Figure 3-2, the first iteration, or "pass" as it is often called in sorting, looks for the index of the smallest element in the entire array; the index is 11 in this case. We then swap Table[11], which has value 3, with Table[0], which has value 74. The second pass looks for the index of the smallest element in the subarray Table[1] through Table[11]; that index is 4. We then swap the value 14 at Table[4] with the value 66 at Table[1]. The algorithm continues by leaving the value 20 in its position, exchanging the values 55 and 96, and so on. The following procedure implements this algorithm in a more general way, as it allows the caller to specify the sorting order and uses a comparison procedure provided by the user to compare the records on a given field. It uses the following types:

```
TYPE SomeRecord = RECORD
                    Key: KeyType;
                    Info: . . . .;
                    . . . . . . . .
                  END;
     Order = (Ascending, Descending);
     CompareProc = PROCEDURE(SomeRecord, SomeRecord, Order): BOOLEAN;
```

```
PROCEDURE SelectionSort(VAR Table: ARRAY OF SomeRecord;
                       Number: CARDINAL; SortingOrder: Order;
                       Ordered: CompareProc);
(* Sort Number elements of open array Table into given order
   on key field defined by comparison procedure *)
VAR Index, SearchIndex, LastIndex, Extreme: CARDINAL;
BEGIN
  LastIndex := Number - 1;    (* indices go from 0 to Number-1 *)
  FOR Index := 0 TO LastIndex-1 DO
    Extreme := Index;
    FOR SearchIndex := Index+1 TO LastIndex DO
        (* Find Extreme, index of the element of
           Table[Index] .. Table[LastIndex] with the largest
           (or smallest) key *)
      IF Ordered(Table[SearchIndex], Table[Extreme], SortingOrder) THEN
          Extreme := SearchIndex;
      END; (* IF *)
        (* Table[Extreme] is >= (or <=) Table[Index]..Table[SearchIndex] *)
    END; (* FOR *)
    (* Table[Extreme] is >= (or <=) Table[Index]..Table[LastIndex] *)

    Swap(Table[Extreme], Table[Index]);
    (* Table[0]..Table[Index] are in their proper positions. *)
  END; (* FOR *)

  (* Table[0]..Table[LastIndex] are in their proper positions. *)
END SelectionSort;
```

Note that, because array Table is an open array, its indices will vary from 0 to Number − 1, which must be less than HIGH(Table). Some additional assertions have been included as documentation for the inner FOR loop, which finds the index of the largest (or smallest) element of A[Index] through A[N]. Procedure Swap is used to exchange the values of two record variables:

```
PROCEDURE Swap(VAR X, Y: SomeRecord);
VAR Copy: SomeRecord;
BEGIN
  Copy := X;
  X := Y;
  Y := Copy;
END Swap;
```

If the procedure is to sort the first 156 elements of an array A and the sort is to be in ascending order then we would use the call:

```
SelectionSort(A, 156, Ascending, Comparison);
```

If we want to sort the same array in descending order, we only have to modify our call to:

```
SelectionSort(A, 156, Descending, Comparison);
```

Procedure Comparison returns true if the two elements are in sorting order, false otherwise. It can be built simply, as in the following example, assuming the key field type is some basic Modula-2 type.

```
PROCEDURE Comparison(Rec1, Rec2: SomeRecord; Sort: Order): BOOLEAN;
BEGIN
   IF Sort = Ascending THEN
     RETURN Rec1.Key < Rec2.Key;
   ELSE
     RETURN Rec1.Key > Rec2.Key;
   END;
END Comparison;
```

It should be pointed out that several variations of these approaches are possible. There might be separate procedures for a less-than comparison and a greater-than comparison, thus dispensing with the need of a parameter of type Order. The caller would simply supply the correct procedure parameter to produce the desired sort. Also, we have written a general procedure to sort an initial subarray of a size specified by the parameter Number. If this flexibility is not required, then the sorting procedure can be simplified slightly by dispensing with this parameter and using the function HIGH to recover the size of the entire array. Finally, it should be noted that there is nothing sacred about processing the array from left to right and searching for the index of the smallest remaining element. A selection sort algorithm that processes the array from right to left and searches for the index of the largest remaining element is also possible.

An analysis of the efficiency of a sorting algorithm must take into consideration the number of times elements are moved, as well as the number of comparisons.

Let us first find the expected number of comparisons:

On the first pass, there are N comparisons, N + 1 being the length of the array.
On the second pass, there are N − 1 comparisons.
On the third pass, there are N − 2 comparisons.

.
.
.

On the last pass, there is 1 comparison.

Thus there are:

$$1 + 2 + \cdots + (N - 1) + N = \frac{N(N + 1)}{2} \quad \text{comparisons.}$$

Since the number of elements in the array is n = N + 1, the number of comparisons expressed as a function of the number of elements is $n(n - 1)/2$.

There is at most one exchange, comprising three moves (or assignments), for each pass; so the number of moves is equal to 3N, because there are N passes. As a function of the number of elements in the array, the number of moves is 3(n − 1).

Thus, assuming that a comparison and an assignment have equal weight, an expression giving an estimate for execution time of the algorithm is:

$$g(n) = n(n - 1)/2 + 3(n - 1)$$

or

$$g(n) = n^2/2 + 5n/2 - 3$$

As we have seen in Example 1 in Section 3.1, we say that g(n) is $O(n^2)$, or, less formally, we say that the selection sort is order n^2. Note that the time complexity is independent of the initial order of the data.

The space complexity of SelectionSort is equal to the size needed to store the array, as the sorting is done directly in the original array, and does not require extra storage beyond the temporary variables (Index, SearchIndex, LastIndex, Extreme) used by the algorithm.

Linear Insertion Sort

This method is often used by card players to put their cards in order. We can illustrate it with a 12-element array as shown on Figure 3-3, where only the numerical key values appear.

At each step, an element of the original sequence is transferred into the resulting sequence. At the beginning, the resulting sequence includes only the last element of the original sequence: 3 in the example of Figure 3-3. Then, the next element in the original sequence, 94, is inserted into the expanded resulting sequence, 3　94, which is then expanded to 3　71　94, and so on. At each iteration, the element that immediately precedes the resultant sequence is inserted into its proper position. This leads to the following pseudocode solution.

```
InsertionSort
    For i from n − 1 down to 0 do
        Insert Table[i] in its proper place in Table[i+1]..Table[n]
        { Table[i] through Table[n] are in order }
    End for
    { Table[0] through Table[n] are in order }
End InsertionSort
```

Naturally, the insertion will involve finding the proper place as well as doing the insertion itself. We can use a sequential search to find the proper position. Also, the insertion will involve moving some elements to make room for the insertion. Using these ideas, we obtain the following procedure:

Figure 3-3 Insertion Sort

Original array	74	66	20	96	14	57	61	83	55	71	94	3
Pass 1	74	66	20	96	14	57	61	83	55	71	3	94
Pass 2	74	66	20	96	14	57	61	83	55	3	71	94
Pass 3	74	66	20	96	14	57	61	83	3	55	71	94
Pass 4	74	66	20	96	14	57	61	3	55	71	83	94
Pass 5	74	66	20	96	14	55	3	55	61	71	83	94
Pass 6	74	66	20	96	14	3	55	57	61	71	83	94
Pass 7	74	66	20	96	3	14	55	57	61	71	83	94
Pass 8	74	66	20	3	14	55	57	61	71	83	94	96
Pass 9	74	66	3	14	20	55	57	61	71	83	94	96
Pass 10	74	3	14	20	55	57	61	66	71	83	94	96
Pass 11	3	14	20	55	57	61	66	71	74	83	94	96

Figure 3-3 Insertion Sort

```
PROCEDURE InsertionSort(VAR Table: ARRAY OF SomeRecord;
                       Number: CARDINAL; SortingOrder: Order;
                       Ordered: CompareProc);
(* Sort open array Table into given order. *)
VAR Index, Position, LastIndex, MoveIndex: CARDINAL;
    Copy: SomeRecord;
BEGIN
  LastIndex := Number - 1;   (* indices go from 0 to Number-1 *)
  FOR Index := LastIndex-1 TO 0 BY -1 DO
    (* Set Position to proper position within
       Table[Index+1]..Table[LastIndex] to put Table[Index] *)
    Position := Index+1;
```

```
    WHILE (Position <= LastIndex)
        AND Ordered(Table[Position], Table[Index], SortingOrder) DO
      INC(Position);
    END; (* WHILE *)
    DEC(Position);

    (* Move Table[Index+1]..Table[Position] to make room for Table[Index] *)
    Copy := Table[Index];
    FOR MoveIndex := Index+1 TO Position DO
      Table[MoveIndex-1] := Table[MoveIndex];
    END; (* FOR *)

    Table[Position] := Copy;
    (* Table[Index]..Table[LastIndex] are in order *)
  END (* FOR *)
  (* Table[0]..Table[LastIndex] are in order *)
END InsertionSort;
```

The sequential search for the position at which to insert element Table[Index] is done simply with a WHILE loop, which advances in the sorted part of the array until an element is found that is already in the proper sorting order relative to Table[Index]. Once this is found, the insertion must be made at the preceding position. Notice that moving elements to make room for the insertion is done by processing elements to be moved from the lowest index to the highest index. Think about why it would not work if we started with the highest element.

There are several variations of an insertion sort. We could, for instance, process the array in the opposite direction. It would also be possible to combine the loop structure that searches for the proper place to insert the element with the loop that moves the elements. In this single loop, we would see if we had reached the proper position yet, and, if not, we would move the element we just looked at and continue searching. We have not presented this version of the algorithm, since there are advantages, that we will see shortly, in keeping the search process separate from the movement of data.

As with the selection sort, the average number of comparisons for the simple insertion sort is proportional to n^2. To see this, note that the comparisons are done in the WHILE statement by calling function procedure Ordered. The first pass through the external FOR loop, we have at most one comparison. The second pass will make at most two comparisons (it could make only one, depending on the data). The third pass will make at most three comparisons. The last pass will make at most n comparisons. The total of comparisons made is thus at most equal to $1 + 2 + 3 + \cdots + (n - 1) = n(n - 1)/2$. The average number of comparisons will usually be less than this worst-case behavior but still proportional to n^2.

The number of moves will also vary, depending on the data in the array, and on the average the number of moves will also be proportional to n^2. To see this, observe that for n − 1 elements, we must find the place to insert the element and then do the insertion. On the average, we will have to search through half of the elements to find the position for the insertion and then those elements must be moved to make room for the insertion. So, on the average, the number of moves will be one half of $1 + 2 + \cdots + (n - 1)$, which is proportional to n^2, as claimed.

The space complexity of this algorithm is the same as for selection sort. The reason that the space complexities are the same is that the only additional storage space needed for this insertion sort is for local variables, since the sort is done in place.

In an insertion sort we have to search the sorted part of the array in order to find the proper position to insert the next value. In the above procedure, we search sequentially. However, since the data being searched is ordered, we could use a binary search whose complexity is $O(\log n)$, as compared to $O(n)$ for a sequential search. Although this would reduce the number of comparisons needed, it would not reduce the number of data movements, and the algorithm complexity would remain $O(n^2)$. This binary insertion sort will be left as an exercise (see problem 12 in the Exercise section).

Bubble Sort

As with the previous sorts, this method makes several passes over the array elements to put them in order. In each pass, pairs of adjacent elements are compared, and, if the two elements comprising the pair are not in order, they are exchanged. The first pass considers all the elements in this pairwise fashion. When the pass is completed, the largest element will have "bubbled" to its correct position as the last element of the array. Also, some localized reordering will have taken place. The second pass considers all the elements but the last one, and, when completed, the second largest value will have bubbled to the next to last position of the array. This process continues until there is only one element left to be considered, and that element is already in its final position.

Figure 3-4 illustrates the first pass of this process applied to a 12-element array, while Figure 3-5 shows the resulting array after each pass.

The corresponding algorithm can be expressed in pseudocode in the following manner.

```
Bubble Sort
    For all elements in array do
        For all remaining elements in array do
            If neighbor elements are not in order
                Exchange them
            End if
        End for
    End for
End Bubble Sort
```

The Modula-2 procedure follows directly.

3.3 Simple Sorts

Original array	74	66	20	96	14	57	61	83	55	71	94	3
Comparison 1	66	74	20	96	14	57	61	83	55	71	94	3
Comparison 2	66	20	74	96	14	57	61	83	55	71	94	3
Comparison 3	66	20	74	96	14	57	61	83	55	71	94	3
Comparison 4	66	20	74	14	96	57	61	83	55	71	94	3
Comparison 5	66	20	74	14	57	96	61	83	55	71	94	3
Comparison 6	66	20	74	14	57	61	96	83	55	71	94	3
Comparison 7	66	20	74	14	57	61	83	96	55	71	94	3
Comparison 8	66	20	74	14	57	61	83	55	96	71	94	3
Comparison 9	66	20	74	14	57	61	83	55	71	96	94	3
Comparison 10	66	20	74	14	57	61	83	55	71	94	96	3
Comparison 11	66	20	74	14	57	61	83	55	71	94	3	96

Figure 3-4 First Pass of Bubble Sort

```
PROCEDURE BubbleSort(VAR Table: ARRAY OF SomeRecord;
                     Number: CARDINAL; SortingOrder: Order;
                     Ordered: CompareProc);
(* Sort open array Table in given order *)
VAR Limit, Index: CARDINAL;
    Copy: SomeRecord;
BEGIN
    FOR Limit := Number-1 TO 1 BY -1 DO  (* indices go from 0 to Number-1 *)
       FOR Index := 1 TO Limit DO
         IF NOT Ordered(Table[Index-1], Table[Index], SortingOrder) THEN
            Swap(Table[Index], Table[Index-1]);
         END; (* IF *)
       END; (* FOR *)
     END; (* FOR *)
END BubbleSort;
```

Original array	74	66	20	96	14	57	61	83	55	71	94	3
Pass 1	66	20	74	14	57	61	83	55	71	94	3	96
Pass 2	20	66	14	57	61	74	55	71	83	3	94	96
Pass 3	20	14	57	61	66	55	71	74	3	83	94	96
Pass 4	14	20	57	61	55	66	71	3	74	83	94	96
Pass 5	14	20	57	55	61	66	3	71	74	83	94	96
Pass 6	14	20	55	57	61	3	66	71	74	83	94	96
Pass 7	14	20	55	57	3	61	66	71	74	83	94	96
Pass 8	14	20	55	3	57	61	66	71	74	83	94	96
Pass 9	14	20	3	55	57	61	66	71	74	83	94	96
Pass 10	14	3	20	55	57	61	66	71	74	83	94	96
Pass 11	3	14	20	55	57	61	66	71	74	83	94	96

Figure 3-5 Passes of Bubble Sort

The outer FOR loop controls the number of passes, with values of Limit going from the last index to 1 (open array Table indices start at zero). So, Limit always indicates the final position for a given pass. The inner FOR loop starts comparing the first two elements in the array and goes up to position Limit, the final position of the pass. If two adjacent values are found not to be in order, they are swapped.

In analyzing BubbleSort, we notice that each pass involves a diminishing number of comparisons, from $n - 1$ on the first pass, to one on the last pass, where n is the number of elements of the array. Thus, the total number of comparisons is $n(n - 1)/2$.

The number of moves will vary depending on the data in the array. The worst possible case for BubbleSort is when it sorts an array that is in reverse order. It then takes $n - 1$ exchanges for the first pass, $n - 2$ exchanges for the second pass, down to 1 for the last pass. An exchange requires three assignments, and the total number of assignments is $3n(n - 1)/2$ in the worst case. The best case, an array already sorted, will involve no moves, so for the average case we will have half the moves of the worst case, or 3n(n − 1)/4 moves. However, without having to go into more details, we can note that the number of comparisons and the number of moves are both proportional to n^2, so the complexity of BubbleSort is $O(n^2)$.

The space complexity of this algorithm is the same as for the previously illustrated selection sort and insertion sort. The only additional storage space needed for this bubble sort is for local variables, since the sort is done in place.

There are small variations to this bubble sort that enable us to sort the data into descending order or to process the array in the opposite direction. Another variation, which can improve efficiency where the data is already partially sorted, is a *bubble sort with flag*. In this sort, for each pass a BOOLEAN flag is used to indicate if any exchanges have been made during the pass. Once we have a pass with no exchanges, then the array must be sorted and the procedure can be exited. This improvement will be left as an exercise (see problem 8 in the Exercise section). Another small improvement, called a *shaker sort*, is to process the data in alternate directions for consecutive passes. This is left as an exercise (see problem 10 in the Exercise section).

3.4 A More Efficient Sort: Quicksort

The three simple sorts we have seen above all have a complexity of $O(n^2)$. We have noted possible improvements, but these alone will not change the complexity. We will now consider a sorting method that is a bit more challenging to code, but has a smaller complexity.

A sorting algorithm developed in 1961 by C. A. R. Hoare was promptly named Quicksort because of its excellent performance. Apparently Hoare had the idea for this algorithm several years earlier but was unable to implement it. He subsequently read about recursion in the ALGOL 60 Report and, a short time later, while attending a tutorial session on the "new" programming language ALGOL 60, he again attempted an implementation. This time he used recursion and was successful. The resulting program delighted the instructors of the tutorial, and has subsequently delighted generations of computer scientists because of its elegance and efficiency.

Quicksort is a "divide and conquer" sorting method: it partitions the array of elements to be sorted into two smaller parts, and then recursively sorts each smaller part. More specifically, an element, call it P, is chosen arbitrarily and the array is partitioned in such a way that:

all of the elements in the left partition are less than or equal to P
all of the elements in the right partition are greater than or equal to P

The element P is usually called a *pivot*. The result of the partition is illustrated in Figure 3-6.

Figure 3-6 Result of Partitioning

Left partition	Right partition
≤ P	≥ P

The result of the partitioning step is illustrated repeatedly on the complete sorting example in Figure 3-7. The element at the middle position in the original array, 57, was initially chosen as the pivot. The first partitioning was achieved by exchanging several values as indicated. In this figure, we have used brackets ([and]) to delimit the partitions remaining to be sorted.

After the first partition is done, the sorting method is applied recursively to the left and right partitions. The base case for the recursion is a partition with one element or no element, since this partition is already sorted. For clarity, in Figure 3-7 we have shown the subarray about to be partitioned in bold print. Notice that subarray selection

Original array		74	66	20	96	14	57	61	83	55	71	94	3
Partition 1 Pivot value 57 Exchange 74 3 Exchange 66 55 Exchange 96 57		[3	55	20	57	14]	[96	61	83	66	71	94	74]
Partition 2 Pivot value 20 Exchange 55 14		[3	14]	20	[57	55]	[96	61	83	66	71	94	74]
Partition 3 Pivot value 3		3	14	20	[57	55]	[96	61	83	66	71	94	74]
Partition 4 Pivot value 57 Exchange 57 55		3	14	20	55	57	[96	61	83	66	71	94	74]
Partition 5 Pivot value 66 Exchange 96 66		3	14	20	55	57	[66	61]	[83	96	71	94	74]
Partition 6 Pivot value 66 Exchange 66 61		3	14	20	55	57	61	66	[83	96	71	94	74]
Partition 7 Pivot value 71 Exchange 83 71		3	14	20	55	57	61	66	71	[96	83	94	74]
Partition 8 Pivot value 83 Exchange 96 74		3	14	20	55	57	61	66	71	74	83	[94	96]
Partition 9 Pivot value 94		3	14	20	55	57	61	66	71	74	83	94	96

Figure 3-7   Example of Quicksort

proceeds from left to right. Since it is not necessary to partition subarrays of size 1, we have not shown the partition boundaries for subarrays of size 1.

Our pseudocode algorithm is:

> Quicksort
>   If there is more than one element in the subarray
>   Choose pivot value
>   Partition array based on pivot value
>   Quicksort left partition
>   Quicksort right partition
>   End if
> End Quicksort

We need to refine the algorithm by giving more detail for the partitioning step. To do the partitioning, we scan the array from its left end until we find an element greater than or equal to the pivot. We then scan the array from its right end until we find an element less than or equal to the pivot. These two elements are not in the correct partitions, so they are exchanged. We continue this process of scanning and exchanging until the scans meet. When they meet, we can be sure that all elements greater than or equal to the pivot were swapped to the right partition, and all elements less than or equal to the pivot were swapped to the left partition, as illustrated in Figures 3-6 and 3-7.

Using this description of the partitioning process and our pseudocode, we implement Quicksort as a procedure to sort an array of records on some key field specified by a comparison function.

```
PROCEDURE QuickSort(Left, Right: INTEGER; VAR Table: ARRAY OF SomeRecord;
                    SortingOrder: Order; Ordered: CompareProc);
(* Application of C.A.R. Hoare's Quicksort method to the sorting of
   an array of records Table on the Key field. A pivot (middle element)
   is chosen and the vector is partitioned in such a way that all
   the elements with a key less than or equal to the pivot are in
   the left partition and all the elements with a key greater than
   or equal to the pivot are in the right partition. The process
   is then applied to each partition. *)

VAR Lindex, Rindex: INTEGER;
    Pivot: SomeRecord;

BEGIN
  IF Left < Right THEN (* more than one element, sort *)
    Lindex := Left;
    Rindex := Right;
    Pivot := Table[(Lindex + Rindex) DIV 2];
    REPEAT
      WHILE (Lindex < Right)   (* Scan left *)
          AND Ordered(Table[Lindex], Pivot, SortingOrder) DO
        INC(Lindex);
      END; (* WHILE *)
```

```
        WHILE (Rindex > Left)           (* Scan right *)
           AND Ordered(Pivot, Table[Rindex], SortingOrder) DO
          DEC(Rindex);
        END; (* WHILE *)
        IF Lindex <= Rindex THEN        (* Exchange records *)
          Swap(Table[Lindex], Table[Rindex]);
          INC(Lindex);
          DEC(Rindex);
        END; (* IF *)
      UNTIL Lindex > Rindex;            (* Partition done *)
      (* Table[Left]..Table[Rindex] <= Pivot
         AND  Pivot <= Table[Lindex]..Table[Right] *)
      QuickSort(Left, Rindex, Table, SortingOrder, Ordered);
      QuickSort(Lindex, Right, Table, SortingOrder, Ordered);
    END; (* IF *)
END QuickSort;
```

Procedure Quicksort has five parameters, the array to be sorted, Table, the limits of the partition to sort, Left and Right, the sorting order, and a comparison procedure. Provided there is more than one element in the array, the partitioning process is applied. The pivot value chosen is the value of the middle element. The REPEAT loop partitions the array by applying the method we presented earlier. The array is scanned from the left and from the right until values are found that must be exchanged or until the scans meet. Once the partition of the array is done, Quicksort is called recursively on each of the partitions.

We split the analysis of the Quicksort algorithm into finding the complexity of forming the partition and finding the number of passes that need to be made.

Let n be the number of elements to be partitioned. Since every element is examined, exactly n comparisons are made. The number of exchanges depends on the ordering of the data.

- The best case would be an array with the pivot value at the center and all elements less than the pivot to the left and all elements greater than the pivot to the right. No exchanges would be necessary for this array.
- The worst case is just the opposite (namely, the pivot at the center, larger elements to the left and smaller elements to the right). This case would require n/2 exchanges.
- Using statistical methods, it can be shown that the average case will require approximately n/6 exchanges. Thus, the average case is n comparisons plus n/6 exchanges and so the complexity of the partitioning step is O(n).

The number of passes required depends on the pivot value selected.

- The best case for selection of the pivot is when the pivot value is the median value (that is, the value such that half of the items are less than this value and half of the items are greater than this value). The data are partitioned into two equal halves, so if this process continues, the partition sizes will reach one element in $\log_2 n$ passes.
- The worst selection for the pivot is when it is either the smallest or the largest value in the array. In this case, given an original array of n elements, the partition sizes

are 1 and n − 1 elements. If this unlucky choice is made again for the remaining n − 1 elements, the resulting partitions will be 1 and n − 2 elements. If this continues, then n passes will be required.
- Surprisingly, for the average case where we assume the initial data is in random order and thus the pivot value is random, the number of passes can be shown to be 1.39 log n, only slightly worse than the best case.

The overall complexity of the algorithm will be the product of the complexity for the partitioning times the number of passes. So we can summarize our results from above:

Best case: n log n   which is O(n log n)
Average case: 1.39 n log n   which is O(n log n)
Worst case: n × n   which is $O(n^2)$

A few words need to be said about the selection of the pivot. Two obvious choices are the first element of the partition or the last element of the partition. If the data is in totally random order, these choices are as good as any other. However, if the data is already partially sorted, these would be poor choices because they would tend to be extreme values. Therefore the algorithm given in this section selects the pivot at the center of the array. (Note that this does not imply the value will be the median value, that is, the middle element of the ordered values.) Another alternative is to find the median of three values—the first, the last, and the central element—and use that as the pivot. In this way we are more likely to be close to the median for all of the data (see problem 13 in the Exercise section).

The space complexity of this algorithm seems to be the same as for the simple sorts, as the only additional storage space needed for the algorithm is for local variables. However, being a recursive algorithm, QuickSort also uses a built-in, run time stack. As we will see in Chapter 6, this requires extra storage. The number of elements (each element includes space for all parameters and local variables of the procedure) needed on the stack is equal to the number of passes, which is normally log n, and at worst n.

A slight improvement in the algorithm would be to sort the smallest partition first so as to minimize the size of the recursion stack (see problem 16 in the Exercise section). Since recursion involves substantial overhead at run time, when partitions become small enough, it is possible to use some other sorting method on the smaller subarrays in order to improve efficiency even further. It is also possible to implement Quicksort using iteration rather than recursion (see Chapter 6).

The approach used in Quicksort can be adapted to give a useful technique for finding the median for unsorted arrays of data without having to sort the entire array first. The general strategy is to select a pivot and partition the data. Rather than recursively sorting both partitions, we only select the partition that will contain the median element (the (n + 1) DIV 2 position). For example, in Figure 3-7 the array has 12 elements, so we would expect the median to end up in the sixth position if the array was sorted. After the first partition, we see that the sixth position is in the right partition, so we only have to sort the right partition. We continue selecting the correct partition each time until we reach a partition with one element at the position of the median (see problem 14 in the Exercise section). That element is the median. It can be shown that this algorithm has complexity of O(n). A similar approach can be used to find the kth element in the sorted array without having to sort the entire array (see problem 15 in the Exercise section).

3.5 Case Study: Developing a Merge Sort Algorithm

In the case study of Chapter 1, we developed an algorithm to merge two sorted files. The merging process is simple and can be used to sort a sequence of elements.

Design

Define the Problem Our objective is to develop a general sorting procedure, using sorting methods based on merging sequences of sorted elements. As the sorting procedures we have seen in this chapter, we want to develop a flexible procedure that can sort in ascending or descending order, and is also able to sort arrays of records on some predefined field.

Design of a Solution We start with an unordered array of data. In order to be able to merge two sequences of data, we consider that the array comprises a series of ordered *runs*. Given a sequence $x_1, x_2, \ldots, x_n$, we say a subsequence $x_i, x_{i+1}, \ldots, x_k$ is a run if $x_m \leq x_{m+1}$ for $i \leq m < k$.

The original array can be considered to be a series of runs of length 1. During the first pass, it is easy to scan the elements from the original array, to create runs of length 2, and to store the result in a temporary array. The second pass of merge sort will combine pairs of runs of length 2 from that temporary array, and create runs of length 4, which will be stored in the original array. These two arrays will then be used in the next pass which will build runs of length 8, and store them in the temporary array. The process will be repeated until we obtain a final run containing all elements in sorted order. This merge sort process is illustrated by Figure 3-8, where square brackets are used to delimit runs.

In Figure 3-8, we start with 12 elements in the original array, which is considered to be a sequence of runs of length 1. In the first pass, the original array is scanned, and runs of length 2 are formed and stored in a second array. The second pass of merge sort combines the runs of length 2 from the second array into runs of length 4, which are then stored in the original array. Pass 3 combines runs of length 4 into runs of length 8 stored again in the second array; note that a run of length 4 remains, as there is no matching run with which to merge it. Pass 4 is the last pass, and combines the two remaining runs into a single run of length 12 in the original array.

The structure chart for our solution is shown in Figure 3-9. It is very simple: Merge Sort will call repeatedly procedure Merge Runs in order to merge runs of length 1, then runs of length 2, then runs of length 4, etc.

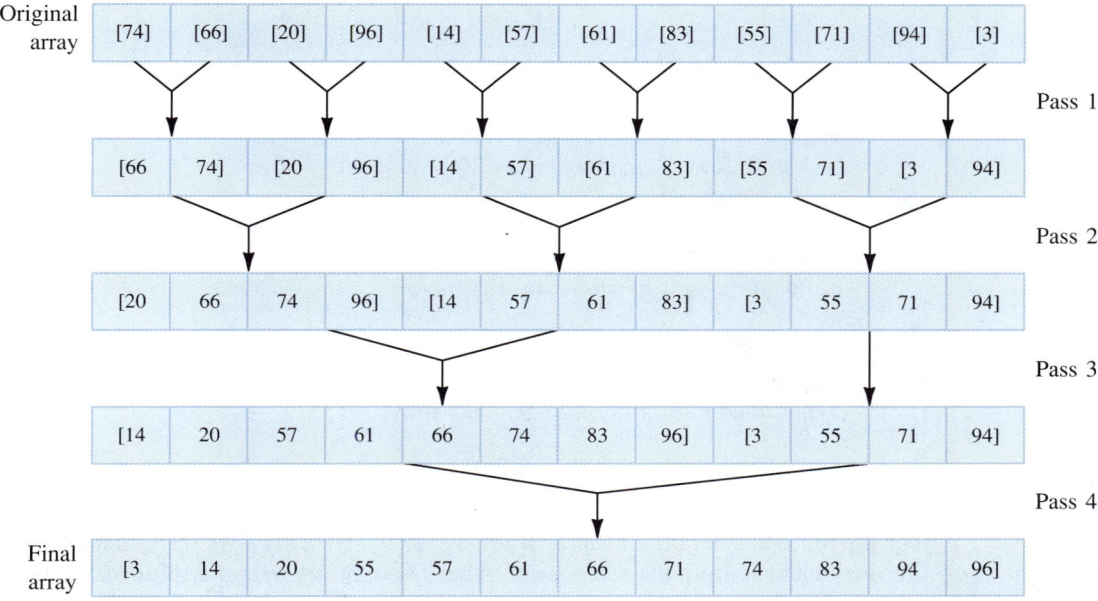

Figure 3-8 Example of Merge Sort

Refine the Solution Based on the preceding example, we are now ready to define a pseudocode solution. We choose to call Merge Runs repeatedly, and actually to call it twice for each iteration. This way, at the end of an iteration the result will always be in the original array. This process will require us to check that we have a minimum number of elements in the array before calling Merge Runs twice. Looking back on the example of Figure 3-8, we see that, if we have more than two elements in the original array, we will need at least two calls to Merge Runs. When the run length, which is doubled constantly, becomes greater than half the array size, it is not possible to call Merge Runs twice, and the loop is exited. If necessary, one last call to Merge Runs is done, with a compulsory copy of the resulting array into the original array, which is used to return the sorted result.

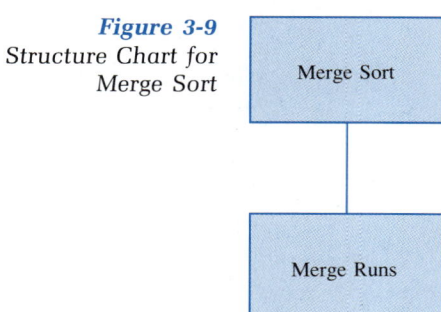

Figure 3-9
Structure Chart for Merge Sort

> Merge Sort
>   Set run length to 1
>   If there are more than 2 elements in the array
>   Repeat
>   Merge Runs from original array to temporary array
>   Double run length
>   Merge Runs from temporary array to original array
>   Double run length
>   Until run length greater than half the array
>   End if
>   If run length less than array size
>   Merge Runs from original array to temporary array
>   Copy temporary array into original array
>   End if
> End Merge Sort

The pseudocode solution for Merge Runs is easy to define once we understand that we are merging runs from the same array. After two runs are identified, we merge them before advancing to the next pair of runs in the array. When merging two runs, we will generally exhaust one of the runs before the other, so we will need to copy the remaining elements to the resulting array, before advancing to the next pair of runs. This process is similar to our merge files routine in Chapter 1.

> Merge Runs
>   Identify first and second runs
>   While first run still inside original array do
>   Repeat
>   If first key is in proper order compared with second key
>   Copy first key to resulting array
>   Else
>   Copy second key to resulting array
>   End if
>   Until the end of one of the runs is reached
>   If elements remain in first run
>   Copy them to resulting array
>   Else
>   Copy remaining elements from second run to resulting array
>   End if
>   Advance to next runs
>   End while
> End Merge Runs

Develop a Testing Strategy In testing sorting procedures it is important to consider extreme cases: empty array, full array, data without duplicate values, data with duplicate values, array already sorted, array already sorted in reverse order, random array. For our Merge Sort procedure, we will assume that the original array has at least one element, and our test cases will include the following:

1. An array of one element
2. A full array
3. An array where all elements have the same value
4. An array of random data with no duplicates
5. An array of random data with some duplicates
6. An array where the data is already sorted
7. An array where the data is initially sorted in reverse order
8. An array whose number of elements is a power of 2
9. An array whose number of elements is not a power of two

Cases 1 and 3 are easy to cover. We can combine case 2 with one of the next cases. Cases 8 and 9 can be combined with other cases. To illustrate case 4, we can use a testing program which will generate random entries in the array before calling the MergeSort procedure. The following code fragment could be part of our testing program.

```
CONST MaxLength = 30;
      Maxi = 1000;
TYPE KeyType = INTEGER;
     SomeRecord = RECORD
                     Key: KeyType;
                     Info: ARRAY [1..MaxLength] OF CHAR;
                  END;
     Order = (Ascending, Descending);
     CompareProc = PROCEDURE(SomeRecord, SomeRecord, Order): BOOLEAN;
VAR T: ARRAY [1..Maxi] OF SomeRecord;
       .
       .
       .
  FOR k := 1 TO 930 DO
    T[k].Key := Random(25000);
  END;
  WriteString("Merge Sort: random data"); WriteLn;
  Display(T, 930); WriteLn;
  MergeSort(T, 930, Ascending, Comparison);
  Display(T, 930); WriteLn;
       .
       .
       .
```

Once the results from that sort have been checked, they can be used as data for case 6. Then the call:

```
MergeSort(T, 930, Descending, Comparison);
```

will generate data for test case 7.

Implementation

Code and Test the Program We will only show here the code for procedures MergeSort and MergeRuns. The code for procedure MergeSort follows the pseudocode given earlier, albeit with more details. Besides the original array to be sorted, we have added a number of parameters: the number of elements to sort as the array to be sorted is seldom full, the sorting order (ascending or descending), and a comparison procedure.

```
PROCEDURE MergeSort(VAR SortArray: ARRAY OF SomeRecord;
                    NumberOfElements: CARDINAL;
                    SortingOrder: Order; Compare: CompareProc);
(* Sort array SortArray in SortingOrder on field defined
   in procedure Compare, using merge sort method *)
VAR TempArray: ARRAY [0..Maxi] OF SomeRecord;
    Index, RunLength, Limit: CARDINAL;
BEGIN
  RunLength := 1;
  Limit := NumberOfElements DIV 2;
  WHILE RunLength < Limit DO
    (* merge runs until at most one last merge is needed *)
    MergeRuns(SortArray, TempArray, RunLength,
              NumberOfElements, SortingOrder, Compare);
    RunLength := 2 * RunLength;
    MergeRuns(TempArray, SortArray, RunLength,
              NumberOfElements, SortingOrder, Compare);
    RunLength := 2 * RunLength;
  END; (* WHILE *)
  IF RunLength < NumberOfElements THEN          (* final merge *)
    MergeRuns(SortArray, TempArray, RunLength,
              NumberOfElements, SortingOrder, Compare);
    FOR Index := 0 TO NumberOfElements-1 DO     (* copy result *)
      SortArray[Index] := TempArray[Index];
    END; (* FOR *)
  END; (* IF *)
END MergeSort;
```

Note that we have replaced a combination of an If statement and a Repeat loop from the pseudocode by a While loop that calls MergeRuns twice, with a different value for RunLength. Thus, at the end of each iteration, the resulting runs are stored in the original array (which is used to return the sorted result). This loop stops when there remains at most one last merge to do. The final merge is done only if necessary, and its results, which are stored in the temporary array, must then be copied into the original array.

The code for procedure MergeRuns follows the pseudocode given earlier, except for the replacement of a Repeat loop by a While loop, and expanding an If statement into two While loops, one for each alternative. It uses indices Run1 and Run2 to mark the positions of the two runs being merged, and makes sure these indices do not go beyond the number of elements being sorted. It also uses OutIndex as an index into the resulting array. The main While loop is repeated as long as the position of the first run to merge remains in the array. Indices EndRun1 and EndRun2 mark the ends of the two runs to merge. The internal While loop does the actual merge of the two runs, and stops when one of the runs is exhausted. The two following While loops copy the remaining elements from one of the runs to the resulting array (note that only one of these loops will be executed). Following this, the run indices are moved to the next pair of runs for the next iteration.

```
PROCEDURE MergeRuns(VAR SortArray,OutArray:ARRAY OF SomeRecord;
                    RunLength, NumberOfElements: CARDINAL;
                    SortingOrder: Order; Compare: CompareProc);

(* Array SortArray contains initially sorted runs of length RunLength.
   This procedure places in array OutArray runs of length 2*RunLength *)
VAR OutIndex,Run1,Run2,EndRun1,EndRun2: CARDINAL;
BEGIN
  Run1 := 0;                          (* index of first run *)
  Run2 := RunLength;                  (* index of second run *)
  OutIndex := 0;                      (* index of resulting array *)
  WHILE Run1 < NumberOfElements DO
    EndRun1 := Run1 + RunLength;          (* end of first run *)
    IF EndRun1 > NumberOfElements THEN
      EndRun1 := NumberOfElements;
    ELSE
      EndRun2 := Run2 + RunLength;  (* end of second run *)
      IF EndRun2 > NumberOfElements THEN
        EndRun2 := NumberOfElements;
      END; (* IF *)
      WHILE (Run1 # EndRun1) AND (Run2 # EndRun2) DO
        (* merge runs until one of them is exhausted *)
        IF Compare(SortArray[Run1], SortArray[Run2], SortingOrder) THEN
          OutArray[OutIndex] := SortArray[Run1];
          INC(Run1);
        ELSE
          OutArray[OutIndex] := SortArray[Run2];
          INC(Run2);
        END; (* IF *)
        INC(OutIndex);
      END; (* WHILE *)
    END; (* IF *)
    WHILE Run1 < EndRun1 DO  (* add remaining elements from longest run *)
      OutArray[OutIndex] := SortArray[Run1];
      INC(OutIndex); INC(Run1);
    END; (* WHILE *)
```

```
    WHILE Run2 < EndRun2 DO  (* add remaining elements from longest run *)
      OutArray[OutIndex] := SortArray[Run2];
      INC(OutIndex); INC(Run2);
    END; (* WHILE *)
    Run1 := Run2;                  (* advance to next runs *)
    Run2 := Run2 + RunLength;
  END; (* WHILE *)
END MergeRuns;
```

The Compare procedure returns true if the two elements are in sorted order, false otherwise. It checks some specific field of type SomeRecord. An example of such a procedure has been seen in the previous section entitled SelectionSort.

Now that we have the final code for procedure MergeSort, we must try and establish its time and space complexities. Procedure MergeSort calls procedure MergeRuns with run lengths of 1, 2, 4, . . . , max, where max is less than or equal to the number of elements. From this, we see that there are $\log_2 n$ calls to MergeRuns. A call to MergeRuns corresponds to a pass on the entire array.

Procedure MergeRuns moves all the elements of the entire array each time it is called. The number of comparisons done by MergeRuns depends on the order of the data: if runs of length 1 are being merged, then there will be n/2 comparisons. If runs of length n/2 are being merged, there will be as few as n/2 and as many as n − 1 comparisons.

The total number of moves of MergeSort is thus n log n, and the total number of comparisons is between n/2 log n and n log n. The time complexity of our MergeSort procedure is therefore O(n log n).

To establish the space complexity of MergeSort, note that the procedure requires two arrays—SortArray, which initially holds the original data to be sorted, and TempArray, an array of the same type. The merge process uses the two arrays during each pass. MergeSort requires space for 2n elements, twice as much as the simple sorting methods we have seen in this chapter, and probably more than QuickSort for larger values of n.

Complete the Documentation Since we have only developed two procedures, it is not deemed necessary to provide a user's manual. However, it is always recommended to document some of the design decisions, (such as the use of pairs of calls to MergeRuns in the general case, so as to avoid unnecessary copies of the sorted array). The test data and results should also be included in the documentation.

Summary

This chapter started by defining what is meant by the complexity of an algorithm. The Big-O notation was introduced as a way to mathematically classify algorithms according to complexity. Some commonly occurring classifications are logarithmic, linear, n log n, quadratic, cubic, and exponential. Algorithms of exponential complexity are considered intractable because they are not practical for large problems.

Two simple searching algorithms for arrays of records were introduced and illustrated. Their time complexity was shown to be O(n) for the sequential search, and O(log n) for the binary search. A sequential search can be applied to any data while a binary search requires sorted data.

Sorting algorithms for arrays were also introduced and illustrated. It was shown that they are typically O(n log n), like the Quicksort algorithm, or $O(n^2)$, like the selection sort, insertion sort, and bubble sort algorithms. The case study developed another type of sorting algorithm based on merging, and whose complexity is also O(n log n). Procedure parameters were used to make sorting algorithms more general.

■ *Exercises*

1. Find the complexity classification for the following expressions:
   (a) 3000n + 45000000
   (b) $(x^3 - 1)/(x - 1)$
   (c) $y^5 - 3y^3 + 2^y$

2. Prove that function f(n) is O(log n):
   f(1) = 1
   f(n) = f(n − 1) + 1/n for n > 1

3. The following is a version of the binary search that assumes that indices for Table go from 1 to TableSize. Prove as formally as possible that the algorithm is correct. What are the advantages and disadvantages of this method over the one presented in the text?

```
PROCEDURE Search(Table: TableType; Key: KeyType): INTEGER;
VAR Finish: BOOLEAN;
    Length, Middle: INTEGER;
BEGIN
  Middle := (TableSize+1) DIV 2;
  Length := TableSize DIV 2;
  Finish := FALSE;
  WHILE (Key # Table[Middle].key) AND NOT Finish DO
    IF Key < Table[Middle].key THEN
      Middle := Middle - (Length + 1) DIV 2;
    ELSE
      Middle := Middle + (Length + 1) DIV 2;
    END; (* IF *)
    IF Length = 1 THEN
      Finish := TRUE;
    ELSE
      Length := Length DIV 2;
    END; (* IF *)
  END; (* WHILE *)
  IF Key = Table[Middle].key THEN
    RETURN Middle;
  ELSE
    RETURN -1;
  END; (* IF *)
END Search;
```

4. Given the following 20 integers: 472, 623, 161, 322, 767, 278, 624, 310, 139, 757, 456, 268, 790, 66, 365, 222, 754, 116, 193, 970, sort them showing each pass using:
   (a) InsertionSort
   (b) SelectionSort
   (c) BubbleSort
   (d) Quicksort
   (e) MergeSort

5. Any sorting algorithm that moves elements only one position at a time has a complexity $O(n^2)$. True or false? Explain your answer.

6. Some sorting algorithms keep the original order of keys having the same value: they are said to be *stable*. Explain why and when this is useful. Which of the sorting algorithms we have seen in the text are stable?

7. Given a sorted array of strings $S_1, S_2, S_3, \ldots, S_n$, write a procedure to determine whether a given string S is a member of the sorted array. Find the complexity of your procedure as a function of n and the length of S.

8. The bubble sort can be improved somewhat by stopping the sort after any pass in which no exchanges are made. Implement this improved bubble sort.

9. What is the complexity of the improved bubble sort described in problem 8? Explain.

10. Implement a version of the bubble sort, called *shaker sort*, in which consecutive passes are done in alternate directions.

11. What is the complexity of the shaker sort described in problem 10? Explain.

12. Modify procedure InsertionSort so that it searches the sorted part of the array using a binary search.

13. Modify the Quicksort program to use the median of the first entry, the last entry, and the central entry as the pivot value.

14. Modify the Quicksort program to find the median of an unsorted array without sorting all elements.

15. Given an unsorted array, modify the Quicksort program to find the kth element of the sorted array without sorting all the elements.

16. Modify the Quicksort program so that the smallest partition is always sorted first. This method will ensure that the number of recursive calls at any one time never exceeds log n.

■ Programming Problems

17. Write and test a recursive version of the binary search procedure.

18. Time the binary search algorithm and the sequential search algorithm as implemented on your computer. Find N, the number of elements beyond which the binary search is the fastest.

19. Implement all five internal sorting algorithms as described in the text. Exercise these procedures on sets of data containing 5000 random numbers (using your system's number generator to generate the data sets), and produce a comparison table indicating the procedure length, the necessary memory space, and the execution time.

20. Modify the simple sort procedures so that they compute the number of moves and the number of comparisons done. Generate sequences of random numbers, store them in arrays, sort these and plot the number of moves and of comparisons as a function of n. Draw your own conclusions.

21. Repeat problem 20 for Quicksort and MergeSort.

22. Modify the simple sort procedures to record the distance and frequency, each time an element is moved. The distance of a move is simply the difference between the indices of the two elements being exchanged. The frequency is simply the number of moves. For each of the algorithms, draw a table giving the frequency of moves and the average distance moved.

23. Modify the Quicksort procedure to use partitioning into three parts: elements less than the pivot, elements equal to the pivot, and elements greater than the pivot. Test your new procedure.

24. Define, program, and test a sorting procedure to sort an array in three parts. The elements stored in the array can only have one of three values: red, white, and blue. The sorting algorithm must be O(n), and the array must be sorted in place.

25. Write and test a sort procedure such that on odd numbered passes, it compares Arr[i] and Arr[i + 1] for all odd i, and exchanges the elements if Arr[i] > Arr[i + 1]. On even numbered passes, it compares Arr[i] and Arr[i + 1] for all even i, and exchanges the elements if Arr[i] > Arr[i + 1]. The process is continued until the array is sorted. What is its complexity?

Abstract Data Types

INTRODUCTION

In this chapter we will introduce the most important concept related to data structures, that of an abstract data type (ADT). This concept will be used throughout the rest of the book. Abstraction is very important in mathematics and computer science; we will see how it can help us develop reusable software components. The ADT is first presented informally, along with Modula-2 features supporting ADT implementation. The definition module defines an ADT in sufficient detail for proper use; the implementation module deals with details of data representation and implementation of the ADT operations.

Chapter 4 Abstract Data Types

4.1 Definitions and Formal Specifications

An abstract data type (ADT) helps us specify the logical properties of a data type. It is a mathematical model that includes a collection of values and a set of operations on those values. When defining an abstract data type we are not concerned with how it will be implemented on the computer, but only with the operations that can be performed on values of the type. As indicated by its name, an ADT is first an abstraction that makes it possible for us to define new types that can themselves be used in various algorithms. When the time comes to implement those algorithms on a computer, we will have to implement the ADT as well; the abstraction will become an actual realization. In fact, an ADT is the generalization of the idea of data type we saw in Chapter 1.

Abstract data types should be implemented in accordance with the *information hiding principle,* which states that software should be designed such that:

- users have all the information needed to use the software correctly and nothing more.
- implementors have all the information needed to implement the software and nothing more.

To illustrate the concept of ADT, let's show an application in which we are using a deck of cards that will be distributed to four players. We will use an ADT with three types (Card, Hand, and DeckOfCards) and several operations (Shuffle, InitHand, PickCard, Place a card, and Display a hand). The following program segment illustrates the dealing of the cards to the players and the display of the four hands.

```
TYPE Position = (East, South, West, North);
VAR Players: ARRAY Position OF Hand;
    Deck: DeckOfCards;
    C: Card;
    I, Pos: Position;
    J: CARDINAL;
       .
       .
       .
    Shuffle( Deck );              (* shuffle 52 cards in deck *)
    FOR Pos := East TO North DO
      InitHand(Player[Pos]);
    END;   (* FOR *)
    I := east;
    FOR J := 52 TO 1 BY -1 DO
      C := PickCard( Deck );      (* select a card *)
      Place( C, Players [I] );    (* give to a player *)
```

```
      IF (I = North) THEN
         I := East;
      ELSE
         INC(I);
      END; (* IF *)
   END; (* FOR *)
   FOR Pos := East TO North DO
      Display( Players [Pos] );
   END; (* FOR *)
```

.
.
.

It is relatively easy to follow what the program does, if we already know about cards and how to play card games. In a way, the program is self-explanatory: we can deduce that Hand will hold 13 cards, DeckOfCards will hold 52 cards, and that Card represents a playing card (suit and value). Procedure Shuffle will randomly mix up the cards, InitHand will initialize the various players and their hands, PickCard will randomly pick a card from the remaining cards in the deck, Place will put a card in a player's hand, and Display will show a hand. Even though the program does not give any detail as to how those operations are done or how the data are represented, we can use the types and operations to perform the desired task. These types and their operations can be defined in a way that is independent of any application, and, even more important, so that their representation can change without affecting the applications using them.

In a more formal way we will specify our abstract data types with two parts: a value definition part and an operation definition part. The value definition part will define the collection of values for the ADT (domain) as well as the type of the components for a structured type; it might also include some conditions on the values. For instance, if we are defining an abstract data type Fraction, we will indicate that a fraction is a pair of values—two integers, with the condition that the second must be positive and nonzero.

The operation definition part specifies what operations are available to manipulate the values defined. Each operation is defined by a heading in the first part giving the operation name and its parameters, some optional pre-conditions and some post-conditions. A pre-condition is an assertion that must be true in order for the operation to execute correctly; some operations will have no pre-conditions. A post-condition is the assertion that is true after completion of the operation.

There are two important rules about the operations of an ADT:

- An ADT must include enough operations to be able to generate all possible values of the type.
- An ADT must include enough testing operations so that the user can verify all the pre-conditions.

The following example illustrates the application of these concepts to the operation of creating a fraction:

```
CreateFraction(A, B: INTEGER; VAR F: Fraction)
```
    pre-condition: B > 0
    post-condition: numerator(F) = A
                          denominator(F) = B

We will develop a Fractions ADT in the case study at the end of this chapter.

4.2 Definition Module

Modula-2 is a modern programming language that offers all the necessary tools to define and implement abstract data types. We will use the definition module to formally specify our abstract data types. The syntax of a definition module is:

```
DEFINITION MODULE identifier;
{[FROM identifier]   IMPORT list-of-identifiers ';'}
{definition}
END identifier.
```

As usual, braces indicate a number of occurrences of their contents (zero or more), and square brackets indicate zero or one occurrences (either zero or one) of their contents. The complete syntax description of Modula-2 can be found in Appendix B. A definition module can have import lists, and the definition part will include constant, type, and variable declarations as well as procedure headings.

The value definition part of the ADT will usually be defined by means of type declarations, whose syntax is:

> TYPE { identifier ['=' type representation]';' }

If the type representation is included, the type is said to be transparent, whereas if it is not included, the type is called opaque. As we are defining abstract data types, the type representation should *not* be included; it is related to implementation, and not to the abstraction.

The operation definition part of the ADT is defined by the procedure headings which indicate what operations are available. Those headings must include comments explaining what the operations do in terms of their parameters. Those comments should also include pre-conditions and post-conditions, when appropriate.

Definition modules are compiled separately and must be compiled before their corresponding implementation module, or any modules importing from them. This early compilation helps check the various operation interfaces for consistency.

We will illustrate the concept of ADT with two applications of sequences. A sequence is an ordered set of elements usually written as:

$S = \{s_0, s_1, s_2, s_3, \ldots, s_n\}$.

4.2 Definition Module

A sequence has a length (number of elements), a first element, and a last element. It can also be empty.

EXAMPLE 1

Strings Our first example will define the ADT String, in which we define a string as a sequence of characters with some maximum length, Max, as well as a number of operations. The following definition module completely defines the ADT Strings. In the documentation, we use the prime notation to indicate the value of a parameter after an operation is applied: Dest' = Source indicates that the value of parameter Dest after the operation is the value that parameter Source had before the operation. We also used the vertical bar character, '|', in the comments to indicate string concatenation.

```
DEFINITION MODULE Strings;

TYPE String;   (* a string is a sequence of characters, where
                  characters are numbered starting with index 0 *)

PROCEDURE InitString(VAR S: String);
(* Initialize a string; this operation is absolutely
   necessary before using string S.
   Pre-condition: none
   Post-condition: S' is an empty string *)

PROCEDURE Length(S: String): CARDINAL;
(* Give length of a string.
   Pre-condition: S is an initialized string
   Post-condition: return the number of characters in S *)

PROCEDURE Assign(VAR Dest: String; Source: String);
(* String assignment.
   Pre-condition: Dest and Source are initialized strings
   Post-condition: Dest' = Source *)

PROCEDURE AssignConst(VAR Dest: String; Source: ARRAY OF CHAR);
(* Assignment of a Modula-2 string constant to a variable of type
   String.
   Pre-condition: Dest is an initialized string and Source is a
                  string constant
   Post-condition: Dest' = Source *)

PROCEDURE Copy(Source: String; Index, Count: CARDINAL;
               VAR Dest: String);
(* Copy part of a string into another string.
   Pre-condition: Index+Count-1 < Length(Source) and Index >= 0
   Post-condition: Dest' = Source [Index..Index+Count-1] *)

PROCEDURE Delete(VAR Source: String; Index, Count: CARDINAL);
(* Delete part of a string.
   Pre-condition: Index+Count-1 < Length(Source) and Index >= 0
   Post-condition: Source' = Source [0..Index-1]
                   | Source [Index+Count-1 .. Length(Source)-1] *)
```

```
PROCEDURE Insert(Source: String; VAR Dest: String;
                 Index: CARDINAL);
(* Insert a string into another string.
   Pre-condition: 0 <= Index <= Length(Dest)
                  Length(Dest) + Length(Source) <= Max
   Post-condition: If Index = Length(Dest) then Source is
                      concatenated to Dest
                   else Dest' = Dest [0..Index-1] | Source |
                          Dest[Index .. Length(Dest) - 1] *)

PROCEDURE Concat(Str1, Str2: String; VAR Dest: String);
(* Concatenate Str1 and Str2 and store result in Dest.
   Pre-condition: Length(Str1) + Length(Str2) <= Max
   Post-condition: Dest' = Str1 | Str2 *)

PROCEDURE StringGreater(Str1, Str2: String): BOOLEAN;
(* String comparison in lexical order according to character set.
   Pre-condition: Str1 and Str2 are initialized strings
   Post-condition: if Str1 > Str2 return TRUE
                   otherwise return FALSE *)

PROCEDURE StringEqual(Str1, Str2: String): BOOLEAN;
(* String comparison in lexical order according to character set.
   Pre-condition: Str1 and Str2 are initialized strings
   Post-condition: if Str1 = Str2 return TRUE
                   otherwise return FALSE *)

PROCEDURE FetchChar(Source: String; Index: CARDINAL): CHAR;
(* Extract a character from a string.
   Pre-condition: 0 <= Index < Length(Dest)
   Post-condition: return Source[Index] *)

PROCEDURE AssignChar(Ch: CHAR; VAR Dest: String; Index: CARDINAL);
(* Store a character into a string.
   Pre-condition: 0 <= Index < Length(Dest)
   Post-condition: Dest[Index]' = Ch *)

PROCEDURE Pos(Sub, Source: String): CARDINAL;
(* Search string Source for substring Sub.
   Pre-condition: Sub and Source are initialized strings
   Post-condition: if there is no match Pos = Length(Source)
                   otherwise 0 <= Pos < Length(Source) and
                       Source[Pos..Pos+Length(Sub)-1] = Sub
                       and there is no match before Pos *)

PROCEDURE DisposeString(VAR S: String);
(* Delete string S.
   Pre-condition: S is an initialized string
   Post-condition: S' does not exist anymore *)

PROCEDURE ToString(Ch: CHAR; VAR Str: String);
(* Conversion between type CHAR and type String.
   Pre-condition: Str is an initialized string
   Post-condition: Str' = Ch *)
```

```
PROCEDURE InputString(VAR Str: String);
(* Input string Str from standard input, string will be terminated
   by a blank, a return or any other control character.
   Pre-condition: Str is an initialized string
   Post-condition: Str' = string value read from standard input *)
PROCEDURE OutputString(Str: String);
(* Output string Str on standard output.
   Pre-condition: Str is an initialized string
   Post-condition: Str is output to standard output *)
PROCEDURE ReadLine(VAR Str: String);
(* Input a string which may contain spaces, terminated by an end of
   line.
   Pre-condition: Str is an initialized string
   Post-condition: Str' = sequence of characters from current input
                   device, input terminated by an end of line *)
END Strings.
```

This module defines entirely the ADT Strings: the user can create and dispose of strings, assign them, compare them, search for, delete or insert substrings, concatenate two strings, access individual characters of strings, input strings, and output strings. The user is not given any information as to the actual representation chosen for strings or the algorithms used for implementing the operations, as no information is needed to use the String data type. We end up with two assignment operations, because we want to be able to assign one string to another and we also want to be able to assign a Modula-2 string constant ("like this string constant") to a string.

EXAMPLE 2

Files Our second example will illustrate files: sequences of elements stored in secondary (permanent) memory. The elements of a file can be of any type, but are often bytes or words, component units of computer memory. Usually a byte is a collection of eight bits, and the smallest memory component that can be accessed; words are normally made of several bytes. Files can also have different organizations, but we are only interested here in the simplest kind of files—sequential files where an item cannot be accessed before all items preceding it have been accessed. The following definition module specifies our ADT Files. This module varies slightly from the one given in Chapter 1, but this is to be expected in Modula-2 since the Files module is non-standard. The Files module on your system probably provides similar operations but in a slightly varied form.

```
DEFINITION MODULE Files;
FROM SYSTEM IMPORT WORD;

TYPE File;
     Direction = (input, output);
```

```
PROCEDURE Open(VAR F: File; Name: ARRAY OF CHAR;
               Dir: Direction; Replace: BOOLEAN;
               VAR Code: INTEGER);
(* Open file Name for input or output
   Post-condition: Code' = 0 normal result, file opened,
                           file created if it did not exist
                           if Dir = output, Replace is true and file
                           already exists, the old file is destroyed
                   Code' = -1 if Dir = output, Replace is false
                           and file exists
                   Code' = -2 if directory full
                   Code' = -3 if device cannot handle direction *)

PROCEDURE Close(VAR F: File);
(* Close file F
   Pre-condition: F is an open file
   Post-condition: F is closed *)

PROCEDURE Reset(VAR F: File);
(* Reset file F to its beginning
   Pre-condition: F is an open file
   Post-condition: the next item read will be the first item in
                   the file *)

PROCEDURE Rename(VAR F: File; Name: ARRAY OF CHAR;
                 VAR Code: INTEGER);
(* Give a new name to file F
   Post-condition: Name is the new name of file F
                   File F is closed, Code' = 0
                   If a file Name existed previous to the
                   operation, the operation is cancelled and
                   Code' = -1 *)

PROCEDURE Delete(VAR F: File; Name: ARRAY OF CHAR): INTEGER;
(* Delete file Name
   Post-condition: if F is deleted then return 0
                   if no such file as Name then return -1 *)

PROCEDURE ReadByte(VAR F: File; VAR Ch: CHAR);
(* Read a byte (character) from file F
   Pre-condition: F open for input
   Post-condition: Ch' = next byte from F *)

PROCEDURE ReadWord(VAR F: File; VAR W: WORD);
(* Read a word from file F
   Pre-condition: F open for input
   Post-condition: W' = next word from F *)

PROCEDURE WriteByte(VAR F: File; Ch: CHAR);
(* Write a byte (character) to file F
   Pre-condition: F open for output
   Post-condition: byte Ch written to F at the end of the file *)
```

```
PROCEDURE WriteWord(VAR F: File; W: WORD);
(* Write a word to file F
   Pre-condition: F open for output
   Post-condition: word W written to F at the end of the file *)
PROCEDURE EOF(VAR F: File): BOOLEAN;
(* Check end of file F. An end of file can only be detected after
   a Read operation.
   Pre-condition: F open for input
   Post-condition: if at end of file return TRUE
                   otherwise return FALSE *)
END Files.
```

This definition module specifies our File ADT.

4.3 Applications

Now that ADT Strings and ADT Files are defined, we can use them to develop application programs.

Let us develop a short program to count the words in a paragraph, assuming that words are delimited by single blanks, and that the line starts and ends with a word. We can decompose this simple problem by defining a procedure to count the words in a line and calling it repeatedly. The simple structure chart in Figure 4-1 shows our solution.

The structure of CountWords is clear. We repeatedly read a line and call ProcessLine until the end of the paragraph indicated by a blank line. Procedure ProcessLine deletes the first word delimited by a blank or the end of the line, counts it, and repeats this process until the line is empty.

```
MODULE CountWords;
(* This program counts the words in a paragraph that is entered
   interactively. The entry of an empty line indicates the end
   of the paragraph, at which time the word count is printed. *)
FROM InOut IMPORT WriteString, WriteCard, WriteLn;
FROM Strings IMPORT String, Pos, ToString, Length, Delete,
                   InitString, ReadLine;

VAR WordCount: CARDINAL;
    Line: String;

PROCEDURE ProcessLine (Line: String; VAR Count: CARDINAL);
VAR BlankPosition: CARDINAL;
    Blank: String;
BEGIN
  InitString(Blank);
  ToString(' ', Blank);
```

```
        WHILE Length(Line) > 0 DO              (* count words *)
          Count := Count + 1;
          BlankPosition := Pos(Blank, Line);   (* next blank *)
          IF BlankPosition = Length(Line) THEN (* finished *)
            Delete(Line, 0, Length(Line));
          ELSE                                 (* delete word *)
            Delete (Line, 0, BlankPosition+1);
          END; (* IF *)
        END; (* WHILE *)
      END  ProcessLine;
      BEGIN   (* CountWords *)
        InitString(Line);
        WordCount: = 0;
        LOOP
          ReadLine(Line);
          IF Length(Line) = 0 THEN             (* end of paragraph *)
            EXIT
          END;   (* IF *)
          ProcessLine(Line, WordCount);
        END; (* LOOP *)
        WriteString("The word count is ");
        WriteCard(WordCount, 3); WriteLn;
      END CountWords.
```

Using ADT Strings, we had no difficulty implementing our algorithm. We were able to concentrate on the problem to solve without getting involved in string representation details.

Similarly we can use ADT Files to develop a procedure to copy a file into another one while displaying a dot every 100 characters to show that the operation is active. Here again the solution is relatively easy. We open the two files and check that the operations are successful. We then call a procedure to actually copy the first file into the second file character by character, counting the characters and displaying a dot after processing each 100 characters. Once this is done the two files are closed.

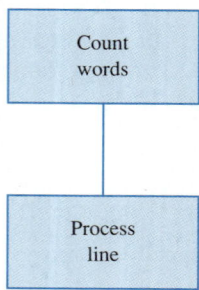

Figure 4-1
Structure Chart for Counting Words

```
FROM Files IMPORT File, Open, Close, WriteByte, ReadByte, EOF,
                  Direction;
FROM InOut IMPORT WriteString, WriteLn, Write, Read;
    .
    .
    .
PROCEDURE FileCopy(File1, File2: ARRAY OF CHAR);
CONST MaxChar = 100;
VAR F1, F2: File;
    Reply: INTEGER;

PROCEDURE Copy(F1, F2: File);
VAR Counter: CARDINAL;
    Ch: CHAR;
BEGIN
  Counter := 0;
  LOOP
    ReadByte(F1, Ch);
    IF EOF(F1) THEN EXIT END;   (* end of input file *)
    WriteByte(F2, Ch);
    INC(Counter);
    IF Counter = MaxChar THEN   (* write a dot *)
      Write('.');
      Counter := 0;             (* reset counter *)
    END; (* IF *)
  END; (* LOOP *)
END Copy;

BEGIN
  Open(F1, File1, input, FALSE, Reply);
  IF Reply # 0 THEN
    WriteString("Cannot open input file"); WriteLn;
    RETURN;
  END;
  Open(F2, File2, output, FALSE, Reply);
  IF Reply # 0 THEN
    WriteString("Cannot open output file"); WriteLn;
    Close(F1);
    RETURN;
  END;
  Copy(F1, F2);
  Close(F2);
  Close(F1);
END FileCopy;
```

Here again we have had no difficulty defining our algorithms, using the ADT Files and its available operations.

4.4 Implementation Module

As we have just seen, we can use the ADTs we have defined to write programs and we can compile these programs provided the definition modules for the ADTs used are compiled. However, we won't be able to execute the programs until we have compiled the implementation modules for these ADTs. To fully implement an ADT, we have to choose a representation for the abstract data type and we have to choose algorithms to implement its operations. Those implementation details are not needed by the user of the ADT and are therefore encapsulated in an implementation module. The Modula-2 syntax of an implementation module resembles the syntax of a main module.

```
IMPLEMENTATION MODULE identifier;
{[FROM identifier]  IMPORT list-of-identifiers ';'}
{declaration}
[BEGIN
   {statement}]
END identifier.
```

The word IMPLEMENTATION indicates that there exists a corresponding DEFINITION module, which must be compiled before compiling that implementation module. The BEGIN and the statements that follow it are optional. If they are present, the statements are executed exactly once when the module is imported. They are often used for initialization operations. An implementation module does not have to import from its own definition module; this is done automatically.

Since only the information in the definition module can be accessed, the user is not allowed to access and manipulate the data hidden in the implementation module.

To illustrate implementation modules, we will look again at our previous examples. However, because of the size of the modules and also because of system dependencies, we will not show complete implementation modules here.

Our Strings ADT will be implemented in the following way.

```
IMPLEMENTATION MODULE Strings;
FROM Storage IMPORT ALLOCATE, DEALLOCATE;
FROM InOut IMPORT Read, Write, Done, EOL;

CONST Max = 80;
      EndOfString = 0C;

TYPE String = POINTER TO CharSequence;
             (* opaque types must be pointers *)
     CharSequence = ARRAY [0..Max] OF CHAR;

(* This type of string is provided for applications where a maximum
   of Max characters is appropriate.  The string is always
   terminated by a null character (0C). *)
```

```
PROCEDURE InitString(VAR S: String);
(* Initialize S to empty string *)
VAR I: CARDINAL;
BEGIN
  S := NIL;
END InitString;

PROCEDURE Length(S: String): CARDINAL;
(* Return the current length of S *)
VAR Count: CARDINAL;
BEGIN
  Count := 0;
  IF S # NIL THEN
    WHILE S^[Count] # EndOfString DO
      INC(Count);
    END; (* WHILE *)
  END; (* IF *)
  RETURN Count;
END Length;

PROCEDURE Assign(VAR Dest: String; Source: String);
(* Assignment of Source to Dest *)
BEGIN
  IF Source = NIL THEN
    IF Dest # NIL THEN       (* empty string *)
      DEALLOCATE(Dest, SIZE(CharSequence));
      Dest := NIL;
    END; (* IF *)
  ELSE
    IF Dest = NIL THEN       (* allocate space *)
      ALLOCATE(Dest, SIZE(CharSequence));
    END; (* IF *)
    Dest^ := Source^;        (* copy character array *)
  END; (* IF *)
END Assign;

PROCEDURE Delete(VAR Source: String; Index, Count: CARDINAL);
(* Delete a substring of Source *)
VAR J, K, L: CARDINAL;
BEGIN
  L := Length(Source);
  IF (Index+Count-1 < L) AND (Count > 0) AND (Index >= 0) THEN
    K := Index;
    FOR J := Index+Count TO L DO
      Source^[K] := Source^[J];
      INC(K);
    END; (* FOR *)
    FOR J := K TO Max DO
      Source^[J] := EndOfString;
    END; (* FOR *)
  END; (* IF *)
END Delete;
```

```
PROCEDURE DisposeString(VAR S: String);
(* Delete string S *)
BEGIN
  IF S # NIL THEN
    DEALLOCATE(S, SIZE(CharSequence));
    S := NIL;
  END; (* IF *)
END DisposeString;

PROCEDURE Copy(Source: String; Index, Count: CARDINAL;
               VAR Dest: String);
(* Copy Count characters from Source starting at position Index
   into Dest *)
VAR Intermediate: String;
BEGIN
  InitString( Intermediate );  (* The use of pointers as value
     parameters does not protect the source string, so we must make
     a working copy of it *)
  Assign(Intermediate, Source );
  IF (Index+Count-1 < Length(Intermediate)) (* valid substring *)
     AND (Count <= Max) THEN                (* fits into Dest *)
       (* delete characters preceding and following substring *)
    Delete(Intermediate, 0, Index);
    Delete(Intermediate, Count, Length(Intermediate)-Count);
    Assign(Dest, Intermediate); (* keep substring *)
  ELSE
    DisposeString(Dest);   (* no extraction possible *)
  END; (* IF *)
  DisposeString( Intermediate );
END Copy;
    .
    .
    .
END Strings.
```

These declarations illustrate part of the implementation of the ADT Strings; the remaining procedures are straightforward. Many use some other operations (as Copy does) and are left as an exercise (see problem 8 in the Exercise section). The use of opaque types forces us to use pointers, because Modula-2 systems implement opaque types through pointers.

Had we declared type String in the definition module as:

```
TYPE String = ARRAY [0..Max] OF CHAR;
```

we would have avoided the use of pointers, but we would have made String a transparent type accessible to the user, violating the information hiding principle.

With an opaque type, even if you know about the choice of an array for implementing type String, you cannot access directly individual characters in a string. The compiler will prevent the use of constructs like S^[3] (which is allowed only in the implementation module), and therefore will force you to use operations FetchChar and AssignChar. One disadvantage of defining String as an opaque type is the fact that it is not directly compatible with Modula-2 string constants. However, we have already defined a special operation AssignConst to permit assignment of a string constant to one of our strings. Similarly, we cannot use ReadString and WriteString from module InOut with our strings, but we have defined our own input/output operations, InputString and OutputString. Another disadvantage of opaque types is that it puts the burden of memory management on programmers: once a string is no longer in use, it is the responsibility of the programmer to dispose of it. Despite these drawbacks, the use of opaque types and information hiding is highly encouraged, because an implementation module using one representation can be replaced with an entirely different module with a different representation and not affect any user programs.

A Review of Pointers

Before going any further, let's review the Modula-2 POINTER type. Pointers are used to reference dynamic data structures that do not exist at compile time and are created during program execution. A pointer variable (like a variable of type String in the above example) is a static variable that contains the memory address of the dynamic data structure it references. Dynamic data structures are created at execution time by explicit calls to the procedure ALLOCATE imported from module Storage, which allocates the memory space necessary for the structures. An example of this is the call:

```
ALLOCATE(S, SIZE(CharSequence))
```

in procedure InitString; in some systems, you can replace this call by standard procedure call NEW(S). This call allocates enough space to store a value of type CharSequence (Max+1 characters) and stores the address of that space in pointer variable S. Note that standard function SIZE returns the amount of memory space needed by its parameter, which may either be a type or a variable. The newly created object is called a dynamic variable that has no name and can only be accessed through its associated pointer, using a dereference sign (^): S^ is called the referent of S and represents the dynamic variable of type CharSequence. Since this is an array of characters we can index an individual character as S^[i].

In short, direct reference to a pointer variable, like S, refers to the memory address stored in that pointer variable. On the other hand, a dereferenced pointer variable, like S^, specifies the object pointed to, an array of characters in this case, and has meaning only after a call to ALLOCATE (or to NEW) has been executed. In a similar manner, when a dynamic variable is no longer needed, the space it occupies may be released explicitly by a call to procedure DEALLOCATE, as we have in procedure DisposeString:

```
DEALLOCATE(S, SIZE(CharSequence)).
```

In some systems you can replace that call by standard procedure call DISPOSE(S). In procedure DisposeString also note the use of NIL, a special pointer value that can be assigned to any pointer variable and that indicates that the pointer points nowhere.

This implementation for strings is not the only possible one; in fact, it is possible to define many different String data structures (see Chapter 13) and implement each one of them in an implementation module. You do not have to know the implementation in order to use an ADT: you only need to know the definition module. Once an ADT has been defined and programmed, it is possible to change its implementation part without forcing the user to modify her application program. Such changes should not affect the results of the application program, but they may affect the performance.

An implementation module for ADT Files is written in a manner similar to the Strings implementation module. However, it is extremely machine dependent and therefore we will not show it here.

4.5 Case Study: An Abstract Data Type for Fractions

The focus of this case study will be the development of an ADT for fractions. Since an ADT should be thoroughly tested before release, we will also develop a short test program.

Design

Definition of the Problem Our Fraction ADT should perform the following operations:

- create a fraction and dispose of a fraction
- perform the operations of addition, subtraction, multiplication, and division
- provide conversions from and to a string and a conversion to a real number

The fraction representation should be hidden from the user. Fractions can be either positive or negative; they should always be maintained in reduced form. Division by zero should print an error message and halt the program. The conversion from a string to a fraction should indicate the success or failure of the conversion. The allowed string inputs should be mixed numbers, such as 2 1/2, improper fractions, such as 5/2, and whole numbers, such as 2. The conversion from a fraction to a string should allow choice of format—either as a mixed number or in improper form.

Design of a Solution We decompose our task into three types of operations: creation/removal, arithmetic operations, and conversions. We note that the arithmetic operations will use the creation operation to formulate the resultant fraction. We will also need a reduction procedure to insure that the numerator and denominator of frac-

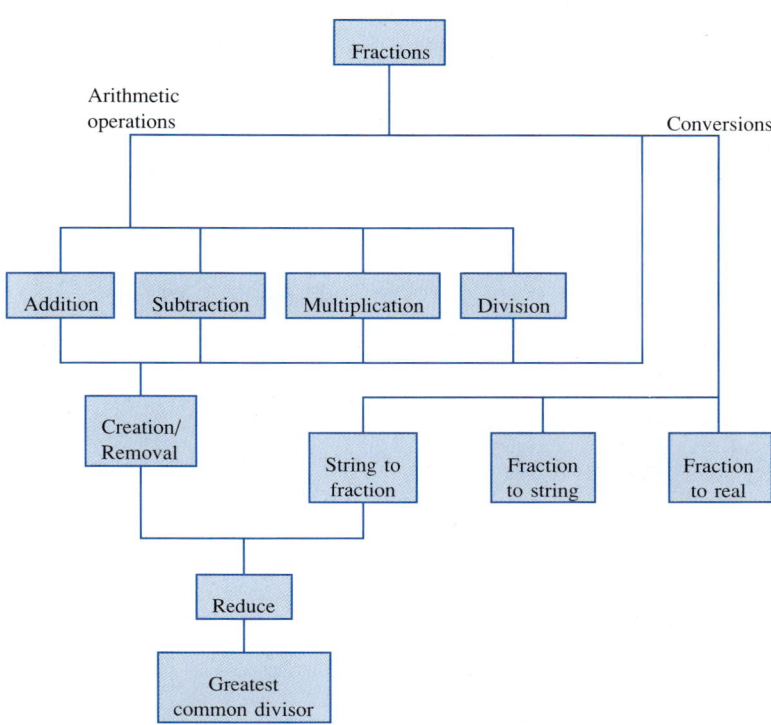

Figure 4-2
Structure Chart for Fraction Operations

tions contain no common factors; so fraction reduction needs a function to compute the greatest common divisor. The string-to-fraction conversion will also use the reduction procedure to ensure the fraction is stored in reduced form. This organization is reflected in the structure chart of Figure 4-2 above.

Refine the Solution The first step of refining our solution will be to decide which operations will be accessible to the user. Since fractions will always be kept in reduced form, the reduce and greatest common divisor operations will be private to the implementation module. The other operations are public; they are specified in the following definition module.

```
DEFINITION MODULE Fractions;
(* Provides operations to create, dispose, add, subtract, multiply,
   and divide fractions. There are three conversion routines: string
   to fraction, fraction to string, and fraction to real. Fraction is
   an opaque type. Fractions are always stored and processed in
   reduced form. *)
TYPE Fraction;     (* a fraction has a numerator and a denominator *)
```

```
PROCEDURE CreateFraction(Numerator, Denominator: INTEGER;
                        VAR F: Fraction);
(* Create a fraction with the specified components.  Only the
   numerator may be negative and the denominator must be greater
   than zero. Fractions will automatically be reduced.
   Pre-condition: Denominator > 0
   Post-condition: F' is the desired fraction or undefined if
                   pre-condition not met *)

PROCEDURE DisposeFraction(VAR F: Fraction);
(* Dispose of the fraction F, which becomes undefined
   Pre-condition: F is defined
   Post-condition: F' is undefined *)

PROCEDURE AddFractions( F1, F2: Fraction; VAR Result: Fraction);
(* Add fractions F1 and F2 to produce Result.
   Pre-condition: F1 and F2 are defined
   Post-condition: Result' = F1 + F2 *)

PROCEDURE SubtractFractions( F1, F2: Fraction; VAR Result: Fraction);
(* Subtract fraction F2 from fraction F1 to produce Result.
   Pre-condition: F1 and F2 are defined
   Post-condition: Result' = F1 - F2 *)

PROCEDURE MultiplyFractions( F1, F2: Fraction; VAR Result: Fraction);
(* Multiply fractions F1 and F2 to produce Result.
   Pre-condition: F1 and F2 are defined
   Post-condition: Result' = F1 * F2 *)

PROCEDURE DivideFractions( F1, F2: Fraction; VAR Result: Fraction);
(* Divide fraction F1 by F2 to produce Result. If F2 is initially
   equal to zero, then the program HALTS after printing an error
   message.
   Pre-condition: F1 and F2 are defined and F2 # 0
   Post-condition: Result' = F1 / F2 or program HALT if F2 = 0 *)

PROCEDURE StringToFraction(S: ARRAY OF CHAR; VAR F: Fraction;
                           VAR Success: BOOLEAN);
(* Attempt to convert the string input to a fraction.  The string
   input may either be in mixed form, such as -2 1/3, or improper
   form, such as 17/3.  Whole numbers are accepted and set to fraction
   form, such as 5/1.
   Pre-condition: S is a well-formed string
   Post-condition: Success = TRUE and F' is the desired fraction
                   or Success = FALSE and F' is undefined *)

PROCEDURE FractionToString(F: Fraction; ProperFraction: BOOLEAN;
                           VAR S: ARRAY OF CHAR);
(* Convert the fraction F to string format either as a mixed
   number, such as 2 1/5, or as an improper fraction, such as 11/5,
   depending on the BOOLEAN parameter ProperFraction.
   Pre-condition: F is defined
   Post-condition: S' is the character representation of the desired
                   fraction or empty if the pre-condition is not met *)
```

```
PROCEDURE FractionToReal(F: Fraction): REAL;
(* Convert fraction F to the corresponding REAL number.
   Pre-condition: F is defined
   Post-condition: return real value corresponding to value of F *)
END Fractions.
```

We do not need to decide on the exact representation of a fraction before we develop pseudocode for our operations in the refinement step, but we do need some more information. Since all operations will be easier if we store fractions in improper form with a numerator and denominator, we will store fractions like $12\frac{3}{4}$ as $\frac{51}{4}$. To show the sign of a fraction, we will associate the sign with the numerator only. Thus fractions will be represented with two parts: a numerator part and a denominator part.

The operations for creation and disposal will simply allocate memory and deallocate memory for the fraction representation. Since fractions will be kept in reduced form, the creation operation will also use the reduction operation. The arithmetic operations follow directly from the mathematical definitions, so we will only illustrate the pseudocode for the addition operation.

> Add Fractions
>   Set Numerator to numerator of first fraction * denominator of second fraction
>   + numerator of second fraction * denominator of first fraction
>   Set Denominator to
>   denominator of first fraction * denominator of second fraction
>   Create resulting fraction with Numerator and Denominator
> End Add Fractions

The conversion of a fraction to a real value is straightforward; however, converting fractions to and from strings needs to be discussed in some detail. Given a string input, there may be one number present, as in 3 for the fraction $\frac{3}{1}$, there may be two numbers present, separated by a divide symbol, as in 2/3, or there may be three numbers present, the first one followed by a space and the second two separated by a divide symbol, as in 4 7/8. When there are so many possibilities for a correct formulation of a fraction and so many possibilities for ill-formed fractions, the underlying logic can be better described by a decision tree as in Figure 4-3.

We will also have to allow for an optional sign (+ or −) at the start of the string. Using our decision tree we can develop the following pseudocode:

> String To Fraction
>   If first nonblank character is '+'
>   Set positive flag
>   Advance to next character
>   Elsif first nonblank character is '−' then
>   Set negative flag
>   Advance to next character
>   End if

102 Chapter 4 Abstract Data Types

Figure 4-3
Decision Tree for Conversion

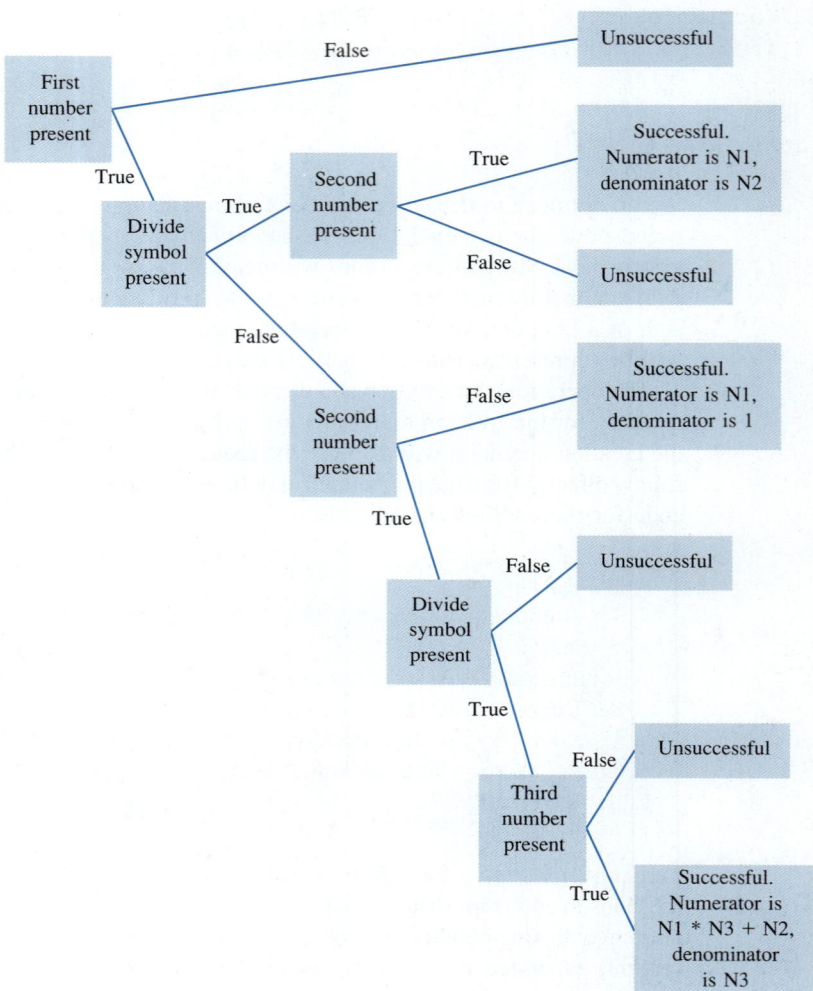

```
Skip blank characters
If current character is a digit
    Get first number
    Skip blank characters
    If current character is a digit
        Get second number
        Skip blank characters
        If current character is '/'
            Advance current character and skip blank characters
```

```
            If current character is a digit
               Get third number
               Set the numerator to the second number +
                  the first number * the third number using proper sign
               Set the denominator to the third number
               Reduce fraction
            Else
               Set failure flag { third number missing after / }
            End if
         Else
            Set failure flag
            { two numbers present and / symbol missing }
         End if
      Elsif current character is '/'
         Advance current character and skip blank characters
         If current character is a digit
            Get second number
            Set the numerator to the first number using proper sign
            Set the denominator to the second number
            Reduce fraction
         Else
            Set failure flag { second number missing after / }
         End if
      Elsif current character is not '+' or '−'
         { fraction must be a whole number }
         Set the numerator to the first number
         Set the denominator to 1
      Else
         Set failure flag { extraneous sign }
      End if
   Else { no number present }
      Set failure flag
   End if
End String To Fraction
```

We will need a Skip Blanks procedure that is straightforward and will not be presented in pseudocode. We will also need a procedure Get Number to convert a sequence of numerical characters into the corresponding number.

```
Get Number
    Set number to 0
    While current character is a digit
        Set number to number * 10 + value of digit
        Advance current character
    End while
End Get Number
```

The utility operation to reduce fractions will be easy, provided that we have a greatest common divisor function.

```
Reduce
    Set common divisor to the greatest common divisor of
        numerator and denominator
    If common divisor > 1
        Divide both the numerator and denominator by the common
            divisor
    End if
End Reduce
```

The greatest common divisor operation will accept two positive numbers and return their greatest common divisor (GCD), which must be greater than or equal to 1. Although the simplest form of the greatest common divisor algorithm is recursive (see Chapter 6), for the sake of efficiency we will develop here an iterative version. Using Euclid's algorithm, one of the oldest mathematical algorithms, we repeatedly subtract the smaller number from the larger number until the two numbers are equal, to obtain the GCD.

```
GCD
    While N1 # N2
        If N1 > N2
            Set N1 to N1 - N2
        Else
            Set N2 to N2 - N1
        End if
    End while
    Return N1 {same as N2}
End GCD
```

This algorithm works, but, like its recursive version, it is inefficient. Suppose that N1 is 10000 and N2 is 3, then the algorithm will do 3333 subtractions before N1 becomes less than N2. Repeated subtraction like this can be avoided if we note that it is equivalent to division, and use instead the remainder from division, called the modulus, which is always less than the divisor. We will repeatedly compute the modulus of the

4.5 Case Study: An Abstract Data Type for Fractions

larger number divided by the smaller one and stop when it becomes zero; then the greatest common divisor is the last divisor. Here is the new version of our algorithm based on division.

```
GCD
    While N1 # 0 and N2 # 0
        If N1 > N2
            Set N1 to N1 mod N2
        Else
            Set N2 to N2 mod N1
        End if
    End while
    If N1 = 0
        Return N2
    Else
        Return N1
    End if
End GCD
```

Finally, converting a fraction to a string should have a Boolean parameter to indicate if the string is supposed to be in mixed-number or improper form. We will assume that procedure ConvertNumber converts a number parameter to a sequence of numerical characters that are added to a string.

```
Fraction To String
    Set Numerator to numerator of fraction
    If Numerator < 0
        Set Numerator to absolute value of Numerator
        Add '−' to Str
    End if
    If mixed number form and Numerator >= denominator of fraction
        Set whole number to Numerator divided by denominator of fraction
        Set Numerator to Numerator modulus denominator of fraction
        Convert whole number to string and add to Str
        Add space to Str
    End if
    If Numerator > 0
        Convert Numerator to string and add to Str
        Add '/' to Str
        Convert denominator of fraction to string and add to Str
    Elsif Str is empty { fraction is 0 }
        Add '0' to Str
    End if
    Add null character to end of string
End Fraction To String
```

Developing the pseudocode for converting a number to a string requires careful thought, since using modulus 10 on the number will produce the least significant digit, which must be added to the string at the rightmost position, and we are building the string from left to right. Recursion is a useful way to save postponed obligations. In this case, we will save the least significant digit to be added at the end of the string, once the recursive process has already added the numerical characters to the string for the more significant digits. The recursion stops when the number to be processed is zero.

```
Convert
    If Number > 0
        Set Digit to Number mod 10
        Convert Number div 10
        Assign character value of Digit to next character in string
    End if
End Convert
```

Develop a Testing Strategy A definition and an implementation module form a library unit that cannot be run as a stand-alone program. Therefore, we will need to develop a test program for our fractions ADT. The test program will be menu driven and have the following options: add fractions, subtract fractions, multiply fractions, divide fractions, toggle print mode (mixed number or improper fraction), print equivalent real number, and exit. The string conversion routines will be used to solicit input from the user and to print results of computations.

When testing our Fractions ADT we should include limiting cases and abnormal cases, such as division by zero. Here is a set of test cases:

Add, subtract, multiply, and divide two positive fractions
Add, subtract, multiply, and divide a negative fraction by a positive fraction
Add, subtract, multiply, and divide a positive fraction by a negative fraction
Add, subtract, multiply, and divide two negative fractions
Add, subtract, multiply, and divide zero by a nonzero fraction
Add, subtract, and multiply a nonzero fraction by zero
Add, subtract, and multiply two zero fractions
Perform operations where the result needs to be reduced (e.g., 2/3 * 3/2)
Divide any fraction by zero (error condition, program should halt)

The Modula-2 code for our test program is quite straightforward and easy to write as shown below.

```
MODULE TestFractions;
FROM InOut IMPORT ReadCard, ReadString, WriteString, WriteLn, WriteReal;
FROM Fractions IMPORT Fraction, AddFractions, SubtractFractions,
                MultiplyFractions, DivideFractions, CreateFraction,
                DisposeFraction, StringToFraction, FractionToString,
                FractionToReal;
FROM Strings IMPORT ReadLine;
```

```
PROCEDURE GetChoice (): CARDINAL;
(* Display options menu and insure a valid option is input *)
VAR Choice: CARDINAL;
BEGIN
  WriteString("1. Add two fractions"); WriteLn;
  WriteString("2. Subtract two fractions"); WriteLn;
  WriteString("3. Multiply two fractions"); WriteLn;
  WriteString("4. Divide two fractions"); WriteLn;
  WriteString("5. Toggle print mode (proper or improper)"); WriteLn;
  WriteString("6. Print equivalent real number to fraction"); WriteLn;
  WriteString("7. Exit program"); WriteLn;
  LOOP
    WriteString("Please enter your selection and press return > ");
    ReadCard(Choice);
    IF Choice IN {1..7} THEN
      RETURN Choice;
    ELSE
      WriteString("Your selection must be between 1 and 7."); WriteLn;
    END;  (* IF *)
  END; (* LOOP *)
END GetChoice;

PROCEDURE GetFraction(VAR F: Fraction);
(* Prompt user for a fraction and input as a string. If the
   conversion to a fraction is not successful, the process is
   repeated. *)
VAR Success: BOOLEAN;
    StrFraction: ARRAY[0..79] OF CHAR;
BEGIN
  REPEAT
    WriteString("enter fraction > "); ReadLine(StrFraction);
    StringToFraction(StrFraction, F, Success);
    IF NOT Success THEN
      WriteString("Conversion unsuccessful, try again"); WriteLn;
    END; (* IF *)
  UNTIL Success;
END GetFraction;

VAR F1, F2, Result: Fraction;
    InOutProperFractions: BOOLEAN;
    StrFraction: ARRAY[0..79] OF CHAR;

BEGIN  (* TestFractions *)
  InOutProperFractions := TRUE;
  LOOP
    CASE GetChoice() OF
    | 1 : GetFraction(F1); GetFraction(F2);
          AddFractions(F1, F2, Result);
          FractionToString(Result, InOutProperFractions, StrFraction);
          WriteString('result> '); WriteString(StrFraction); WriteLn;
```

```
    | 2 : GetFraction(F1); GetFraction(F2);
          SubtractFractions(F1, F2, Result);
          FractionToString(Result, InOutProperFractions, StrFraction);
          WriteString('result> '); WriteString(StrFraction); WriteLn;
    | 3 : GetFraction(F1); GetFraction(F2);
          MultiplyFractions(F1, F2, Result);
          FractionToString(Result, InOutProperFractions, StrFraction);
          WriteString('result> '); WriteString(StrFraction); WriteLn;
    | 4 : GetFraction(F1); GetFraction(F2);
          DivideFractions(F1, F2, Result);
          FractionToString(Result, InOutProperFractions, StrFraction);
          WriteString('result> '); WriteString(StrFraction); WriteLn;
    | 5 : InOutProperFractions := NOT InOutProperFractions;
    | 6 : GetFraction(F1);
          WriteString('real value> ');
          WriteReal(FractionToReal(F1), 15, 6); WriteLn;
    | 7 : EXIT;
    END; (* CASE *)
    DisposeFraction(F1); DisposeFraction(F2); DisposeFraction(Result);
  END; (* LOOP *)
END TestFractions.
```

Remember that this "test" program is simple, and that using it will test our ADT only if we feed it fraction examples covering the various test cases we have identified above. Our test program is interactive, but it could easily be converted to accept input from a file and write output to a file. It also could be automated to generate "random" fractions, perform all operations, and verify that the results are correct. Verification could be done by converting the fractions to real numbers, performing the same operation on the real numbers, then comparing, within a small tolerance for round-off error, the real result with the fraction result converted to a real number (see problem 12 in the Exercise section).

Implementation

We have already given code for the definition module and the test program, so this section develops the code for the implementation module Fractions.

Code and Test the Program Our code follows directly from the pseudocode developed earlier.

```
IMPLEMENTATION MODULE Fractions;
(* Provide operations to create, dispose, add, subtract, multiply, and
   divide fractions. Also provide three conversion routines: string
   to fraction, fraction to string, and fraction to real. Type
   fraction is an opaque type. Fractions are always stored and
   processed in reduced form. *)
FROM Storage IMPORT ALLOCATE, DEALLOCATE;
FROM InOut IMPORT WriteString, WriteLn; (* for fatal error messages *)
```

4.5 Case Study: An Abstract Data Type for Fractions

```
TYPE FractionType = RECORD
                      Numerator, Denominator: INTEGER;
                    END;
     Fraction = POINTER TO FractionType;
PROCEDURE GCD(N1, N2: CARDINAL):CARDINAL;
(* Return the greatest common divisor of two numbers >= 1 *)
BEGIN
  WHILE (N1 # 0) AND (N2 # 0) DO
    IF N1 > N2 THEN
      N1 := N1 MOD N2;
    ELSE
      N2 := N2 MOD N1;
    END; (* IF *)
  END;  (* WHILE *)
  IF N1 = 0 THEN
    RETURN N2;
  ELSE
    RETURN N1;
  END;   (* IF *)
END GCD;

PROCEDURE Reduce(VAR F: Fraction);
(* Reduce Fraction F so that numerator and denominator have no
   common factors. *)
VAR CommonFactor: INTEGER;
BEGIN
  CommonFactor := GCD(ABS(F^.Numerator), F^.Denominator);
  IF CommonFactor > 1 THEN
    F^.Numerator := F^.Numerator DIV CommonFactor;
    F^.Denominator := F^.Denominator DIV CommonFactor;
  END;  (* IF *)
END Reduce;

PROCEDURE CreateFraction(Numerator, Denominator: INTEGER;
                         VAR F: Fraction);
(* Create a fraction with the specified components. Only the
   numerator may be negative and the denominator must be greater than
   zero. Values greater than one are specified in improper form, such
   as 5/2 for 2 1/2. Fractions will automatically be reduced. *)
BEGIN
  IF Denominator > 0 THEN
    ALLOCATE(F, SIZE(FractionType));
    F^.Numerator := Numerator;
    F^.Denominator := Denominator;
    Reduce(F);
  ELSE
    WriteString("Fraction cannot have negative or zero denominator");
    WriteLn; HALT;
  END; (* IF *)
END CreateFraction;
```

```
PROCEDURE DisposeFraction(VAR F: Fraction);
(* Dispose of the fraction F, which becomes undefined *)
BEGIN
  DEALLOCATE(F, SIZE(FractionType));
  F := NIL;
END DisposeFraction;

PROCEDURE AddFractions( F1, F2: Fraction; VAR Result: Fraction);
(* Add fractions F1 and F2 to produce Result. *)
VAR Numerator, Denominator: INTEGER;
BEGIN
  Numerator := F1^.Numerator * F2^.Denominator +
               F2^.Numerator * F1^.Denominator;
  Denominator := F1^.Denominator * F2^.Denominator;
  CreateFraction(Numerator, Denominator, Result);
END AddFractions;

PROCEDURE SubtractFractions( F1, F2: Fraction; VAR Result: Fraction);
(* Subtract fraction F2 from fraction F1 to produce Result. *)
VAR Numerator, Denominator: INTEGER;
BEGIN
  Numerator := F1^.Numerator * F2^.Denominator -
               F2^.Numerator * F1^.Denominator;
  Denominator := F1^.Denominator * F2^.Denominator;
  CreateFraction(Numerator, Denominator, Result);
END SubtractFractions;

PROCEDURE MultiplyFractions( F1, F2: Fraction; VAR Result: Fraction);
(* Multiply fractions F1 and F2 to produce Result. *)
VAR Numerator, Denominator: INTEGER;
BEGIN
  Numerator := F1^.Numerator * F2^.Numerator;
  Denominator := F1^.Denominator * F2^.Denominator;
  CreateFraction(Numerator, Denominator, Result);
END MultiplyFractions;

PROCEDURE DivideFractions( F1, F2: Fraction; VAR Result: Fraction);
(* Divide fraction F1 by F2 to produce Result. If F2 is initially
   equal to zero, then the program HALTS after printing an error
   message. *)
VAR Numerator, Denominator: INTEGER;
BEGIN
  Numerator := F1^.Numerator * F2^.Denominator;
  Denominator := F1^.Denominator * F2^.Numerator;
  IF Denominator > 0 THEN
    CreateFraction(Numerator, Denominator, Result);
  ELSE (* CreateFraction will HALT if zero denominator *)
    CreateFraction(- Numerator, - Denominator, Result);
  END; (* IF *)
END DivideFractions;
```

4.5 Case Study: An Abstract Data Type for Fractions

```
PROCEDURE StringToFraction(S: ARRAY OF CHAR; VAR F: Fraction;
                           VAR Success: BOOLEAN);
(* Attempt to convert the string input to a fraction. The string
   input may either be in proper form, such as -2 1/3, or improper
   form, such as 17/3. Whole numbers are accepted and set to fraction
   form, such as 5/1.
   If successful, then F is set to the fraction and Success is TRUE;
   otherwise Success is FALSE and F is undefined. *)

PROCEDURE IsDigit(Ch: CHAR): BOOLEAN;
(* Return TRUE is Ch is a digit, FALSE otherwise *)
BEGIN
  RETURN ('0' <= Ch) AND (Ch <= '9');
END IsDigit;

PROCEDURE SkipBlanks(S: ARRAY OF CHAR; VAR Index: CARDINAL);
(* Advance Index to the position of a nonblank character *)
VAR LastIndex: CARDINAL;
BEGIN
  LastIndex := HIGH(S);
  WHILE (Index <= LastIndex) AND (S[Index] = ' ') DO
    INC(Index);
  END; (* WHILE *)
END SkipBlanks;

PROCEDURE GetNumber(S: ARRAY OF CHAR; VAR Index, Number: CARDINAL);
(* Assuming Index points to a digit character in S, GetNumber scans
   all contiguous digits forming the corresponding number. Index
   ends up on the first nondigit character. *)
VAR LastIndex: CARDINAL;
BEGIN
  LastIndex := HIGH(S);
  Number := 0;
  WHILE (Index <= LastIndex) AND IsDigit(S[Index]) DO
    Number := Number * 10 + ORD(S[Index]) - ORD('0');
    INC(Index);
  END; (* WHILE *)
END GetNumber;

PROCEDURE AssignFraction(Negative: BOOLEAN;
                         Whole, Num, Denom: CARDINAL;
                         VAR F: Fraction; VAR Success: BOOLEAN);
(* Using the negative flag and numbers for the whole number part,
   numerator and denominator, this procedure forms the corresponding
   reduced fraction, provided that the denominator is nonzero. *)
BEGIN
  IF Denom = 0 THEN
    Success := FALSE;
  ELSE
    ALLOCATE(F, SIZE(FractionType));
    F^.Numerator := Num + Whole * Denom;
```

```
        IF Negative THEN
           F^.Numerator := - F^.Numerator;
        END;
        F^.Denominator := Denom;
        Reduce(F);
        Success := TRUE;
    END; (* IF *)
END AssignFraction;

VAR Index, LastIndex, FirstNum, SecondNum, ThirdNum: CARDINAL;
    Negative: BOOLEAN;
BEGIN   (* StringToFraction *)
  Negative := FALSE;
  LastIndex := HIGH(S);
  Index := 0;
  SkipBlanks(S, Index);

  (* look for leading sign *)
  IF (Index <= LastIndex) AND (S[Index] = '+') THEN
    INC(Index);
  ELSIF (Index <= LastIndex) AND (S[Index] = '-') THEN
    Negative := TRUE;
    INC(Index);
  END; (* IF *)

  SkipBlanks(S, Index);

  IF (Index <= LastIndex) AND IsDigit(S[Index]) THEN
    GetNumber(S, Index, FirstNum);   (* get first number *)
    SkipBlanks(S, Index);
    IF (Index <= LastIndex) AND IsDigit(S[Index]) THEN
      GetNumber(S, Index, SecondNum);
      SkipBlanks(S, Index);
      IF (Index <= LastIndex) AND (S[Index] = '/') THEN
        INC(Index);   (* move past / *)
        SkipBlanks(S, Index);
        IF (Index <= LastIndex) AND IsDigit(S[Index]) THEN
          GetNumber(S, Index, ThirdNum);
          AssignFraction(Negative, FirstNum, SecondNum, ThirdNum,
                         F, Success);
        ELSE (* failure, no third number after / *)
          Success := FALSE;
        END; (* IF *)
      ELSE (* failure, more than one number and / not found *)
        Success := FALSE;
      END; (* IF *)
    ELSIF (Index <= LastIndex) AND (S[Index] = '/') THEN
      INC(Index);   (* move past / *)
      SkipBlanks(S, Index);
```

```
        IF (Index <= LastIndex) AND IsDigit(S[Index]) THEN
          GetNumber(S, Index, SecondNum);
          AssignFraction(Negative, 0, FirstNum, SecondNum, F, Success);
        ELSE (* failure, no second number after / *)
          Success := FALSE;
        END; (* IF *)
      ELSIF (S[Index] # '-') AND (S[Index] # '+') THEN
        (* string only contains one number *)
        AssignFraction(Negative, 0, FirstNum, 1, F, Success);
      ELSE
        Success := FALSE;  (* extraneous sign *)
      END; (* IF *)
  ELSE (* failure, no first number *)
    Success := FALSE;
  END;  (* IF *)
END StringToFraction;

PROCEDURE FractionToString(F: Fraction; ProperFraction: BOOLEAN;
                           VAR S: ARRAY OF CHAR);
(* Convert the fraction F to string format either as a mixed
   number, such as 2 1/5, or as an improper fraction, such as 11/5,
   depending on the BOOLEAN parameter ProperFraction. *)

  PROCEDURE ConvertNumber(Num: CARDINAL; VAR S: ARRAY OF CHAR;
                          VAR Index: CARDINAL);
  (* Convert Num into a sequence of digit characters that are assigned
     to the string S starting at position Index. *)
  VAR Digit: CARDINAL;
  BEGIN
    IF Num > 0 THEN
      Digit := Num MOD 10;
      ConvertNumber(Num DIV 10, S, Index);
      S[Index] := CHR(ORD('0') + Digit);
      INC(Index);
    END; (* IF *)
  END ConvertNumber;

VAR Index: CARDINAL;
    WholeNumber, Numerator: INTEGER;
BEGIN  (* FractionToString *)
  Index := 0;
  Numerator := F^.Numerator;
  IF Numerator < 0 THEN
    Numerator := ABS(Numerator);
    S[Index] := '-';
    INC(Index);
  END;  (* IF *)
```

```
  IF ProperFraction AND (Numerator >= F^.Denominator) THEN
    WholeNumber := Numerator DIV F^.Denominator;
    Numerator := Numerator MOD F^.Denominator;
    ConvertNumber(WholeNumber, S, Index);
    S[Index] := ' '; INC(Index);
  END; (* IF *)
  IF Numerator > 0 THEN
    ConvertNumber(Numerator, S, Index);
    S[Index] := '/'; INC(Index);
    ConvertNumber(F^.Denominator, S, Index);
  ELSIF Index = 0 THEN    (* special case, fraction is 0 *)
    S[Index] := '0'; INC(Index);
  END; (* IF *)
  S[Index] := CHR(0);     (* end string with a null character *)
END FractionToString;

PROCEDURE FractionToReal(F: Fraction): REAL;
(* Convert fraction F to the corresponding REAL number. *)
BEGIN
  RETURN  FLOAT(F^.Numerator)/FLOAT(F^.Denominator);
END FractionToReal;

END Fractions.
```

The Modula-2 code for function procedure GCD and procedure Reduce is similar to the pseudocode. If the pre-condition that the denominator is positive is respected, CreateFraction allocates the space needed for a fraction and assigns values to numerator and denominator; if the pre-condition is not met, the program halts after displaying a message. Procedure DisposeFraction simply deallocates the space allocated to the fraction parameter.

The arithmetic operation procedures AddFractions, SubtractFractions, MultiplyFractions, and DivideFractions are straightforward and apply the computation rules we know for doing arithmetic on fractions.

Procedure StringToFraction is the longest procedure of the Fractions module, but we have seen why in the design discussion. It closely follows the pseudocode and uses four local procedures. Function procedure IsDigit just checks whether or not a character is numerical. Procedure SkipBlanks reads characters one at a time and stops when the character read is not a blank. Procedure GetNumber reads numerical characters one at a time, and converts them to a numerical value; it stops when reading a nonnumerical character. Procedure AssignFraction checks to see if the fraction is acceptable; if it is, it allocates the space for a fraction and assigns numerator and denominator values. (Note that the numerator value becomes negative if the negative flag is set.) Once the fraction has a value, it is reduced by procedure Reduce. AssignFraction returns flag Success to indicate whether or not the operation was successful. Note how closely the code for StringToFraction follows the pseudocode developed earlier.

Procedure FractionToString uses local procedure ConvertNumber, whose code follows the pseudocode. The code for FractionToString follows closely the pseudocode solution. Procedure FractionToReal is very simple, as it performs the division of numerator by denominator to find the real value corresponding to the fraction value.

Since the denominator of a fraction is defined to be always greater than zero, we could have declared it to be of type CARDINAL, while the numerator had to be of type INTEGER. With an integer numerator and a cardinal denominator, appropriate conversions would have to be performed so that the arithmetic operations are performed on operands of the same type. Special care would have had to be taken with division, since the result denominator is formed by multiplying the denominator of the first fraction by the numerator of the second fraction, possibly producing a negative result. We opted instead to avoid these complications, by declaring both numerator and denominator to be of type INTEGER, and by making sure that denominators were always greater than zero. We tested our ADT Fractions with the given test program and data corresponding to the identified test cases, and it performed correctly. Here is a sample of the test data used:

```
 2/3  +   4/3        2/34  -   1/17        3/4  *   4/3        3/4  /   3/4
-2/3  +   4/3       -2/34  -   1/17       -3/4  *   4/3       -3/4  /   3/4
 2/3  +  -4/3        2/34  -  -1/17        3/4  *  -4/3        3/4  /  -3/4
-2/3  +  -4/3       -2/34  -  -1/17       -3/4  *  -4/3       -3/4  /  -3/4
   0  +   4/3           0  -   1/17          0  *   4/3          0  /   3/4
 2/3  +    0         2/34  -    0           3/4  *    0
   0  +    0            0  -    0             0  *    0
 2 5/6 + 47/12        4/3  /   0
```

We have used open arrays of characters as parameters rather than the String type developed in the ADT in Sections 4.2 and 4.3. Therefore, although the Fractions module is independent of any other user defined ADTs, it lacks the security of dealing with a string as an opaque type.

Complete the Documentation Since we have developed a library module to be used by other programmers, it is not necessary to prepare a user's manual. The internal documentation in the definition module is sufficient for proper use of the ADT, while the internal documentation in the implementation module is sufficient to aid the programmer making small modifications to the module. It is wise to document some of the design decisions, such as the representation of fractions as a pair of integers, halting the program on a division by zero error, and the use of an iterative algorithm based on division to find the GCD. The code for converting from a string to a fraction is quite complex, so the decision tree should be retained to supplement the program code. The test data and results could also be included in the documentation.

Summary

Abstract data types offer us a way of formulating data types based on modularity and information hiding. The process of abstraction that we use results in simplified solutions. With abstraction, our specifications are clearer, as they are not overloaded with representation and implementation details.

An ADT consists of three components: specification, representation and implementation. Once the specifications of an ADT are done, we have to consider representation, implementation, and performance issues. We implement ADTs using Modula-2 modules, which make it possible to separate the specification from implementation. This approach helps protect the integrity of the data structures used in the representation because the user is given only limited and controlled access to these structures. We illustrated the partial development of two ADTs: Strings and Files. The case study developed a complete ADT and test program for fractions.

External modules not only provide information hiding, as illustrated by the development of an abstract data type, but they are also very useful in the development of large programs. When a definition module that is part of a large program is changed, most of the other parts of the program must be recompiled. But when only an implementation module is changed in a system, the only part of the system that has to be recompiled is this implementation module. The entire program can then be executed after relinking it with the newly compiled implementation module. Thus, an implementation module may be changed without requiring any change in the importing programs, as long as the corresponding definition module is not changed.

■ *Exercises*

1. The user is supposed to check the pre-condition before using an operation. However, since users do make mistakes, to what extent does the implementation have to check its pre-conditions?

*2. Add operations to the String data type:
   - conversion procedures: IntToStr, CardToStr, RealToStr, StrToInt, StrToCard, StrToReal
   - Caps (convert string to upper case)
   - Match (matches a wildcard pattern, where ? matches any single character, and * matches any sequence of characters, including one with no characters)
   - NextPos (identical to Pos but start search at given position in string)

3. Study the file system of your Modula-2 implementation and note the differences with the Files definition module presented in Section 4.2.

4. Define a complex number ADT. A complex number contains a real and an imaginary part (both REAL).

5. Define a real number ADT, where each real number is made of two parts: the part in front of the decimal point, which is an integer, and the part after the decimal point, which is a cardinal.

6. Define a sequence ADT based on the mathematical notion of a sequence: a sequence is a numbered set of elements; a sequence has a length (the number of its elements) and can be empty; a sequence's first and last elements can be accessed, added, deleted.

Note: Problems marked with an asterisk (*) have a higher level of difficulty.

Programming Problems

7. Implement all the procedures of the text Strings module.

8. Expand the Strings module implemented in problem 7 by implementing the added procedures of problem 2.

9. Rewrite and test procedure CountWords so that it works on your system.

10. Rewrite and test procedure FileCopy so that it works on your system.

11. Implement the complex number ADT that was defined in problem 4. Define a testing strategy and write a test program for it.

12. Complete the Fractions ADT test program so that it generates a sequence of test data using a random number generator, and so that it automatically checks its results by doing computations in parallel on REALs equivalent to the tested fraction values.

13. Implement the real number ADT defined in problem 5. Define a testing strategy and write an automatic testing program for this ADT, which uses a random number generator to generate test data, and parallel operations on REALs to verify ADT operations results.

14. Implement the sequence ADT as defined in problem 6. After defining a testing strategy, write a test program for the sequence ADT.

Fundamental Data Structures

PART TWO

CHAPTER

5 Linear Lists
6 Stacks and Recursion
7 Queues
8 Trees
9 Binary Search Trees

The topics covered in Part Two are fundamental to any study of data structures. Each chapter introduces an abstract data type (ADT) as a definition module, uses this ADT in several applications, develops alternative implementations, and concludes with a case study that either investigates another application or implementation. The linear structures, linear lists, stacks, and queues are presented in Chapters 5, 6, and 7. Tree structures, in the form of general trees, binary trees, and binary search trees, are covered in Chapters 8 and 9. These five chapters form the basis for more advanced studies of data structures and algorithms that follow in Part Three of this text.

Linear Lists

INTRODUCTION

In computer science, lists are extremely important. Informally, the word "list" is used to cover a large number of data types. Formally, a *list* is an ordered set of elements, where each element may contain one or more fields or may itself be a list. This general definition makes it possible to design complex structures based on lists. We will see this in Chapter 14 when we cover *generalized lists*.

In this chapter, we will limit ourselves to *linear lists,* where each element is made of two parts: the information related to the element, which may be subdivided into a number of fields, and a component that will define the order of elements in an implicit or explicit manner. Neither part may be a list itself. Simple linear lists are also called *sequences*.

5.1 Abstraction: The Linear List

A linear list is a sequence of n elements (n ≥ 0) of a given type. A list will be denoted by:

$(e_1, e_2, e_3, \ldots, e_n)$ $n \geq 0$

where

e_i denotes an arbitrary element,
e_1 is the first element, and
e_n is the last element.

The length of the list is denoted by n; when n is zero, the list is empty and denoted by ( ).

The linear list ADT will include a type List based on this definition. One of the principal characteristics of lists is their flexibility. The number of elements in a list is not fixed and may vary dynamically as a program executes. Elements in a list are all of the same type, and may be examined, inserted, or deleted at any place in the list. Usual operations applied to linear lists are:

insert an element
delete an element
search for an element
combine two lists into one list (concatenate)
copy a list
count the elements in a list
display a list
make a list empty

Because of their flexibility and of their dynamic nature, lists are used to build more complex data structures. They are used in a large number of applications, like simulation, where they match, in a natural way, the data structures needed to sequence events.

Given the dynamic nature of linear lists, our ADT List will be defined in the following manner.

```
DEFINITION MODULE ListADT;
FROM ListElements IMPORT ListElement, ListIndex;

TYPE List;      (* A linear list is a sequence of elements *)

VAR ListError: BOOLEAN;   (* Result of list operation *)

PROCEDURE CreateList(VAR L: List);
(* Create list L. Any program using objects of type List must
   first call this procedure.
   Pre-condition: L does not exist
   Post-condition: L' exists and is empty; ListError' = FALSE *)
```

```
PROCEDURE Insert(VAR L: List; i: ListIndex; Item: ListElement);
(* Insert Item immediately after the ith element in L
   Pre-condition: L exists, 0 ≤ i ≤ length of L
   Post-condition: if pre-condition satisfied then
                     L' = (e1, e2, ..., ei, Item, ei+1, ..., en)
                     length' = length + 1; ListError' = FALSE
                   otherwise ListError' = TRUE *)
PROCEDURE Delete(VAR L: List; i: ListIndex; VAR Item: ListElement);
(* Delete the ith element in L, and assign it to Item
   Pre-condition: L exists, 0 ≤ i ≤ length of L
   Post-condition: if pre-condition satisfied then
                     L' = (e1, e2, ..., ei-1, ei+1, ..., en)
                     length' = length - 1;
                     ListError' = FALSE and Item' = ei
                   otherwise ListError' = TRUE *)
PROCEDURE SearchList(L: List; VAR i: ListIndex; Item: ListElement);
(* Search L for Item and return index i or zero if not found
   Pre-condition: L exists
   Post-condition: if length > 0 & ei = Item then
                     i' = Item index in list
                   otherwise i' = 0 *)
PROCEDURE MakeListEmpty(VAR L: List);
(* Make list L empty
   Pre-condition: L exists
   Post-condition: L' = () *)
PROCEDURE ListLength(L: List): CARDINAL;
(* Return length of list L
   Pre-condition: L exists
   Post-condition: return current number of elements in list *)
PROCEDURE Get(L: List; i: ListIndex; VAR Item: ListElement);
(* Return value of ei in L
   Pre-condition: L exists, 0 < i ≤ length of L
   Post-condition: if pre-condition satisfied then
                     Item' = ei; ListError' = FALSE
                   otherwise ListError' = TRUE *)
PROCEDURE Put(VAR L: List; i: ListIndex; Item: ListElement);
(* Update value of ei in L
   Pre-condition: L exists, 0 < i ≤ length of L
   Post-condition: if pre-condition satisfied then
                     L' = (e1, e2, ..., ei-1, Item, ei+1, ..., en);
                     ListError' = FALSE
                   otherwise ListError' = TRUE *)
END ListADT.
```

Note that we have imported types ListElement and ListIndex from a user-defined module called ListElements, where procedures to compare two elements and to display an element should also be defined. This ListElements module might be defined as:

```
DEFINITION MODULE ListElements;

TYPE ListIndex   = ........      (* type of list index *)
     ListElement = ........      (* type of list elements *)

PROCEDURE EqualElements(E1, E2: ListElement): BOOLEAN;
(* Return TRUE if elements E1 and E2 are equal *)

PROCEDURE WriteElement(E: ListElement);
(* Write element E's value to standard output *)

END ListElements.
```

Variable ListError is a global variable for module ListADT, which will return the result of the latest operation invoked. We have used a prime (') to indicate the value of a constant or a parameter *after* applying an operation. In other words, after executing successfully the CreateList procedure, variable ListError has value FALSE and parameter L is the empty list.

This definition module does not include a procedure to display a list, to copy a list, or to combine two lists into one. Note that with the given ADT operations it is possible to implement DisplayList, CopyList, and ConcatLists in a user's module. When defining an ADT, our objective will always be to include only primitive operations, and to avoid redundancy.

5.2 Applications

Because lists are part of our everyday life (for example, the familiar lists of things to do, lists of students, lists of members, price lists, and so on), they are used in a large number of applications. For instance, simulation systems are always based on lists. As we will see in the rest of this text, lists constitute a basic data type that is used to implement many other data types.

We will show here applications involving arithmetic operations on elements of two very different kinds.

High-Precision Arithmetic

We want to be able to perform arithmetic operations on integer values of large magnitude, in cases when using types INTEGER or CARDINAL or even LONGINT or LONGCARD would be too limiting. By using linear lists to represent integer values, we can do computations with values of extremely large numbers. We could represent our positive integers in base-ten form, one digit per element. However, this would not be an efficient use of storage, since numerical types may hold larger integers. Instead, we will view each "digit" as if it was in base 10000 (therefore with four decimal digits). A high-precision integer is thus sliced into four-digit pieces, each piece being an element of a list. The first element in the list should be the least significant "digit," as we need to handle the carry operation in an efficient manner. The representation of the integer 1236789234590l2 is the list:

(9012, 2345, 6789, 0123)

Module ListElements defines the element type in the following manner.

```
DEFINITION MODULE ListElements;
TYPE ListElement = INTEGER;
     ListIndex = [0..Max];
     ..........
END ListElements.
```

The addition operation can then be defined by the following procedure.

```
PROCEDURE AddIntegers(X, Y: List; VAR Sum: List);
(* Add long integers X and Y and put result in Sum *)
CONST MaxSlice = 10000;
VAR Carry, XSlice, YSlice, PartialSum: ListElement;
    Index, LengthX, LengthY: ListIndex;
BEGIN
  Carry := 0;
  MakeListEmpty(Sum);           (* resulting list *)
  LengthX := ListLength(X);
  LengthY := ListLength(Y);
  Index := 1;
  WHILE (Index <= LengthX) OR (Index <= LengthY) DO
  (* add corresponding number slices *)
    IF Index > LengthX THEN     (* end of list *)
      XSlice := 0;
    ELSE                        (* get integer slice *)
      Get(X, Index, XSlice);
    END; (* IF *)
    IF Index > LengthY THEN     (* end of list *)
      YSlice := 0;
    ELSE                        (* get integer slice *)
      Get(Y, Index, YSlice);
    END; (* IF *)
    PartialSum := XSlice + YSlice + Carry;    (* add slices *)
    IF PartialSum > MaxSlice-1 THEN      (* too big *)
      Insert(Sum, Index-1, PartialSum-MaxSlice);
      Carry := 1;
    ELSE                                      (* keep it *)
      Insert(Sum, Index-1, PartialSum);
      Carry := 0;
    END; (* IF *)
    INC(Index);
  END; (* WHILE *)
```

```
        IF Carry = 1 THEN    (* add extra element *)
          Insert(Sum, Index-1, 1);
        END; (* IF *)
      END AddIntegers;
```

The resulting list, Sum, is built by adding each new element as its last element. The AddIntegers procedure takes into account that the two integers may be of different lengths, and the WHILE loop is repeated as long as the *two* lists are not empty. If one list is exhausted before the other, a zero value is supplied for the missing element. The carry starts at zero, and is either zero or one depending on the actual addition operation. We have not forgotten the possibility for the resulting list to be longer than either of the original lists because of a last carry.

The procedure was called with the following parameters:

(9012, 5678, 1234)
(4321, 8765, 9012, 9999)

and produced the following result: (3333, 4444, 0247, 0000, 0001), which corresponds to the following addition:

$$123456789012 + 9999901287654321 = 10000024744443333$$

Polynomial Arithmetic

In some applications, the objects manipulated are not numbers but polynomials, and it is useful to be able to add or multiply polynomials. For instance:

$$(x^4 + 2x^3y + 3x^2y^2 + 4xy^3 + 5y^4) * (x^2 - 2xy + y^2) = (x^6 - 6xy^5 + 5y^6)$$

We can represent polynomials with three variables using our ADT List with the following type.

```
TYPE ListElement = RECORD
            Coefficient, XPower, YPower, ZPower: INTEGER;
         END;
```

We will assume that the polynomial's terms are ordered lexicographically on the combined powers of x, y, and z. For instance, x^3yz^2 (312) comes before x^2z^3 (203). With such a representation, polynomial $x^6 - 6xy^5 + 5y^6$ would be represented by:

([1, 6, 0, 0], [−6, 1, 5, 0], [5, 0, 6, 0])

The following procedures implement the addition of two polynomials.

```
PROCEDURE ComparePowers(Monomial1, Monomial2: ListElement): INTEGER;
(* Compare lexicographically the powers of two polynomial terms
   if power of Monomial1 > power of Monomial2 return  1
   if power of Monomial1 = power of Monomial2 return  0
   if power of Monomial1 < power of Monomial2 return -1 *)
```

5.2 Applications

```
BEGIN
  IF Monomial1.XPower > Monomial2.XPower THEN
    RETURN 1
  ELSIF Monomial1.XPower < Monomial2.XPower THEN
    RETURN -1
  ELSIF Monomial1.YPower > Monomial2.YPower THEN
    RETURN 1
  ELSIF Monomial1.YPower < Monomial2.YPower THEN
    RETURN -1
  ELSIF Monomial1.ZPower > Monomial2.ZPower THEN
    RETURN 1
  ELSIF Monomial1.ZPower < Monomial2.ZPower THEN
    RETURN -1
  ELSE
    RETURN 0;
  END;
END ComparePowers;

PROCEDURE AddPolynomials(Polynomial1, Polynomial2: List; VAR Polynomial3: List);
(* Add Polynomial1 and Polynomial2 and store results in Polynomial3 *)
VAR Index1, Index2, Index3, Length1, Length2: ListIndex;
    Monomial1, Monomial2: ListElement;
BEGIN
  Index1 := 1;   (* term index in Polynomial1 *)
  Index2 := 1;   (* term index in Polynomial2 *)
  Length1 := ListLength(Polynomial1);
  Length2 := ListLength(Polynomial2);
  Index3 := 0;   (* index in Polynomial3 *)
  MakeListEmpty(Polynomial3);
  Get(Polynomial1, Index1, Monomial1);
  IF ListError THEN Monomial1 := Null END;
  Get(Polynomial2, Index2, Monomial2);
  IF ListError THEN Monomial2 := Null END;
  WHILE (Index1 <= Length1) OR (Index2 <= Length2) DO
    IF ComparePowers(Monomial1, Monomial2) = -1 THEN      (* copy Monomial2 *)
      Insert(Polynomial3, Index3, Monomial2);
      INC(Index3);
      INC(Index2); Get(Polynomial2, Index2, Monomial2);
      IF ListError THEN Monomial2 := Null END;
    ELSIF ComparePowers(Monomial1, Monomial2) = 1 THEN    (* copy Monomial1 *)
      Insert(Polynomial3, Index3, Monomial1);
      INC(Index3);
      INC(Index1); Get(Polynomial1, Index1, Monomial1);
      IF ListError THEN Monomial1 := Null END;
    ELSE                                                  (* add two terms *)
      Monomial2.Coefficient := Monomial2.Coefficient + Monomial1.Coefficient;
      IF Monomial2.Coefficient # 0 THEN      (* keep only if nonzero *)
        Insert(Polynomial3, Index3, Monomial2);
        INC(Index3);
      END; (* IF *)
```

```
      INC(Index1); Get(Polynomial1, Index1, Monomial1);
      IF ListError THEN    (* no more terms in Polynomial1 *)
        Monomial1 := Null;
      END; (* IF *)
      INC(Index2); Get(Polynomial2, Index2, Monomial2);
      IF ListError THEN    (* no more terms in Polynomial2 *)
        Monomial2 := Null;
      END; (* IF *)
    END; (* IF *)
  END; (* WHILE *)
END AddPolynomials;
```

We use procedure Get to obtain the polynomial terms (monomials). If we reach the end of a polynomial, Get will return with ListError set to TRUE, and, in that case, we assign the value Null (a list element with four zero values) to the element.

With

Polynomial1 = ([12, 3, 1, 0], [4, 2, 2, 0], [−3, 1, 0, 1], [−2, 0, 3, 2])
Polynomial2 = ([3, 4, 0, 1], [−4, 2, 2, 0], [9, 1, 0, 1], [−4, 0, 3, 2], [2, 0, 1, 1])

the procedure produces:

Polynomial3 = ([3, 4, 0, 1], [12, 3, 1, 0], [6, 1, 0, 1], [−6, 0, 3, 2], [2, 0, 1, 1])

This corresponds to

$$\text{Polynomial1} = 12x^3y + 4x^2y^2 - 3xz - 2y^3z^2$$
$$\text{Polynomial2} = 3x^4z - 4x^2y^2 + 9xz - 4y^3z^2 + 2yz$$

whose sum is:

$$\text{Polynomial3} = 3x^4z + 12x^3y + 6xz - 6y^3z^2 + 2yz$$

We could develop a complete ADT for polynomial operations. We will leave polynomial multiplication as problem 6 in the Exercises section.

5.3 Implementation

Several representations are possible for linear lists, and each offers advantages as well as some disadvantages. The application and its context will help determine what representation to choose.

Static Implementation

With static implementation, the list elements are kept in a contiguous array, as shown in Figure 5-1. An index is kept with the array to show the last element's position, which is the number of elements in the list.

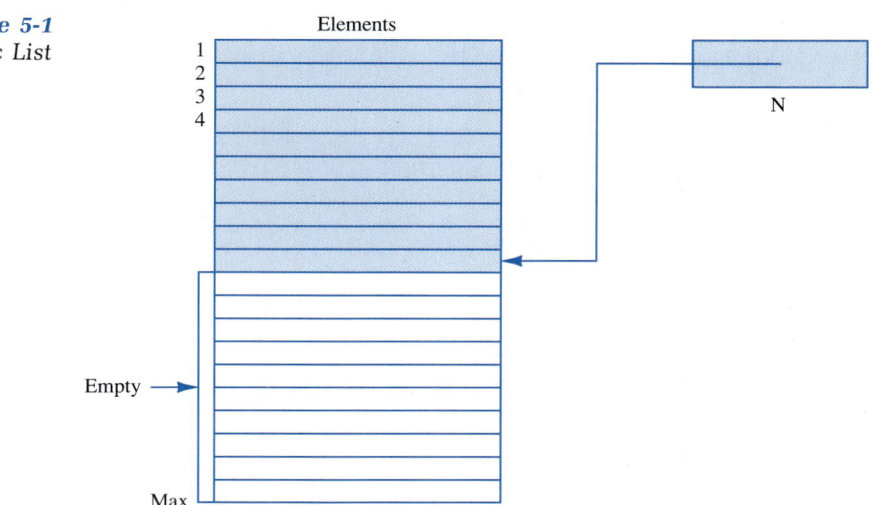

Figure 5-1
Static List

The following implementation module defines the various operations based on this representation, using the previously defined ListElements module.

```
IMPLEMENTATION MODULE ListADT;
(* A static contiguous implementation of linear lists *)
FROM ListElements IMPORT ListElement, ListIndex, EqualElements;
FROM InOut IMPORT WriteString, WriteLn, WriteInt;
FROM Storage IMPORT ALLOCATE;

CONST Max = 500;

TYPE List = POINTER TO Node;    (* opaque type *)
     Node = RECORD
              N: [0..Max];
              Elements: ARRAY [1..Max] OF ListElement;
            END;

PROCEDURE CreateList(VAR L: List);
(* Create list L *)
BEGIN
  ALLOCATE(L, SIZE(Node));
  IF L # NIL THEN
    L^.N := 0;
    ListError := FALSE;
  ELSE
    ListError := TRUE;
  END; (* IF *)
END CreateList;
```

```
PROCEDURE Insert(VAR L: List; i: ListIndex; Item: ListElement);
(* Insert element Item immediately after the ith element in L *)
VAR Index: ListIndex;
BEGIN
  WITH L^ DO
    IF (i >= 0) & (i <= N) & (N < Max) THEN
      (* 0 <= i <= N <= Max *)
      (* shift positions e[i+1]..e[N] forward one position to e[i+2]..e[N+1] *)
      Index := N;
      INC(N);
      WHILE Index >= i+1 DO
        (* i < Index <= N &
           L=(e[1]..e[i],e[i+1]..e[Index-1],e[Index+1]..e[N]) *)
        Elements[Index+1] := Elements[Index];
        DEC(Index);
      END; (* WHILE *)
      ListError := FALSE;
      Elements[i+1] := Item;   (* insert new entry *)
    ELSE
      ListError := TRUE;
    END; (* IF *)
    (* N' = N + 1 & L' = (e[1]..e[i], Item, e[i+1]..e[N']) *)
  END; (* WITH *)
END Insert;

PROCEDURE Delete(VAR L: List; i: ListIndex; VAR Item: ListElement);
(* Delete the ith element in L, and assign it to Item *)
VAR Index: ListIndex;
BEGIN
  WITH L^ DO
    IF (i >= 0) & (i <= N) THEN
      (* shift positions e[i+1]..e[N] backward one position to
         e[i]..e[N-1] since e[i] is deleted *)
      DEC(N);
      Item := Elements[i];
      FOR Index := i TO N DO
        Elements[Index] := Elements[Index+1];
      END; (* FOR *)
      ListError := FALSE;
    ELSE
      ListError := TRUE;
    END; (* IF *)
  END; (* WITH *)
END Delete;
```

```
PROCEDURE SearchList(L: List; VAR i: ListIndex; Item: ListElement);
(* Search L for Item and return index i or zero if not found *)
BEGIN
  WITH L^ DO
    (* examine the list serially from the beginning until either a
       matching element is found or the list is exhausted *)
    i := 1;
    WHILE (i <= N) & NOT EqualElements(Item, Elements[i]) DO
      (* sequential search *)
      INC(i);
    END; (* WHILE *)
    IF i > N THEN      (* list exhausted without a match *)
      i := 0;
    END; (* IF *)
  END; (* WITH *)
END SearchList;

PROCEDURE MakeListEmpty(VAR L: List);
(* Make list L empty *)
BEGIN
  L^.N := 0;
END MakeListEmpty;

PROCEDURE ListLength(L: List): CARDINAL;
(* Return length of list L *)
BEGIN
  RETURN L^.N;
END ListLength;

PROCEDURE Get(L: List; i: ListIndex; VAR Item: ListElement);
(* Return value of ith element of L *)
BEGIN
  WITH L^ DO
    IF (i > 0) & (i <= N) THEN
      Item := Elements[i];
      ListError := FALSE;
    ELSE
      ListError := TRUE;
    END; (* IF *)
  END; (* WITH *)
END Get;

PROCEDURE Put(VAR L: List; i: ListIndex; Item: ListElement);
(* Update value of ith element of L *)
BEGIN
  IF (i > 0) & (i <= L^.N) THEN
    L^.Elements[i] := Item;
    ListError := FALSE;
  ELSE
    ListError := TRUE;
  END;
END Put;
```

```
BEGIN
  ListError := FALSE;
END ListADT.
```

We should note here that there are cases where the list elements must be ordered with respect to a particular field; for instance, a list of names might have to be kept in alphabetical order. In such cases, the insertion operation must be defined differently, so that an element is always inserted in its proper position in the ordered list. For instance, the insertion of "Murray" in the following ordered list of names (Abernathy, Beaudoin, Black, Dorchester, Hanigan, O'Flaherty, Smith), will produce the list (Abernathy, Beaudoin, Black, Dorchester, Hanigan, Murray, O'Flaherty, Smith). However, this type of list is used only in specific instances; we have therefore implemented a simpler and more general insertion operation.

In our list implementation, the complexity of operations CreateList, ListLength, MakeListEmpty, Get, and Put is O(1): each procedure will be executed in a fixed number of steps, as it contains no loop. Operations Delete, Insert, SearchList all have a complexity of O(n), since the corresponding procedures contain a loop whose number of repetitions depends on the size of the list. Table 5-1 shows the complexity of all the procedures.

The space complexity of all the operations is simple, as they all use one list which is represented as a record. The fixed size of this record includes the space for Max elements and a counter.

This static contiguous implementation of linear lists is straightforward. Notice, however, that the representation we have chosen is somewhat wasteful of memory space, especially when Max is large and the actual number of elements is much smaller than Max. Also, the implementation of operations Insert and Delete is inefficient, since we have to shift a whole block of elements each time either operation is carried out.

Dynamic Implementation

With a dynamic implementation, the memory space necessary for a list is not allocated in one block at the start of the program. Instead, memory is allocated as needed, a list

Table 5-1 Operations Complexity

Procedure	Complexity
CreateList	O(1)
Insert	O(n)
Delete	O(n)
SearchList	O(n)
MakeListEmpty	O(1)
ListLength	O(1)
Get	O(1)
Put	O(1)

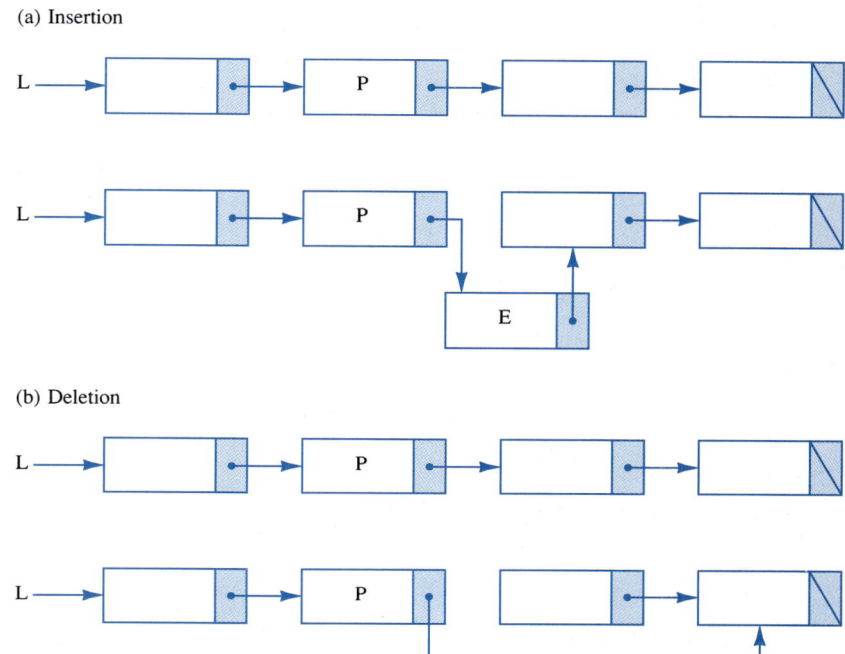

Figure 5-2
Insertion and Deletion in a Linked List

(a) Insertion

(b) Deletion

element is represented by a *node*, and a list is made of nodes linked together. Figure 5-2 above illustrates the processes of insertion and deletion.

In this dynamic implementation, a node is made of two parts: the actual list element and a pointer to the next node. The corresponding implementation module follows.

```
IMPLEMENTATION MODULE ListADT;
(* Dynamic implementation of linear lists *)
FROM ListElements IMPORT ListElement, ListIndex, EqualElements, WriteElement;
FROM Storage IMPORT ALLOCATE, DEALLOCATE;

TYPE List = POINTER TO Node;
     Node = RECORD
                Info: ListElement;
                Next: List;
            END;

PROCEDURE CreateList(VAR L: List);
(* Create list L *)
BEGIN
  L := NIL;
  ListError := FALSE;
END CreateList;
```

```
PROCEDURE FindNode(L: List; i: ListIndex): List;
(* Find pointer to node i. Return NIL if index out of range *)
VAR Index: ListIndex;
    Link: List;
BEGIN
  IF i <= 0 THEN
    RETURN NIL;
  ELSE
    Index := 1;
    Link := L;
    WHILE Index # i DO
      INC(Index);
      Link := Link^.Next;
    END; (* WHILE *)
    RETURN Link;
  END; (* IF *)
END FindNode;

PROCEDURE Insert(VAR L: List; i: ListIndex; Item: ListElement);
(* Insert element Item immediately after the ith element in L *)
VAR Link1, Link2: List;
BEGIN
  Link1 := FindNode(L, i);
  IF ((i > 0) & (Link1 # NIL)) OR (i = 0) THEN
    (* 0 <= i <= N *)
    ALLOCATE(Link2, SIZE(Node));
    Link2^.Info := Item;
    ListError := FALSE;
    IF i = 0 THEN     (* Insert at head of list *)
      (* i = 0 & L = (Item, e1, ..., eN) *)
      Link2^.Next := L;
      L := Link2;
    ELSE
      (* i > 0 & L = (e1, ..., ei, Item, ei+1, ..., eN) *)
      Link2^.Next := Link1^.Next;
      Link1^.Next := Link2;
    END; (* IF *)
  ELSE
    ListError := TRUE;
  END; (* IF *)
END Insert;

PROCEDURE Delete(VAR L: List; i: ListIndex; VAR Item: ListElement);
(* Delete the ith element in L, and assign it to Item *)
VAR Link1, Link2: List;
BEGIN
  Link1 := FindNode(L, i);
  IF Link1 # NIL THEN
    ListError := FALSE;
    Item := Link1^.Info;
```

```
        IF i = 1 THEN     (* first element *)
          Link2 := L;
          L := L^.Next;
          DEALLOCATE(Link2, SIZE(Node));
        ELSE
          Link2 := FindNode(L, i-1);
          Link2^.Next := Link1^.Next;
          DEALLOCATE(Link1, SIZE(Node));
        END; (* IF *)
      ELSE
        ListError := TRUE;
      END;
END Delete;

PROCEDURE SearchList(L: List; VAR i: ListIndex; Item: ListElement);
(* Search L for Item and return index i or zero if not found *)
VAR Link: List;
BEGIN
   Link := L;
   i := 1;
   WHILE (Link # NIL) & NOT EqualElements(Item, Link^.Info) DO
      (* Check sequentially *)
      Link := Link^.Next;
      INC(i);
   END;
   IF Link = NIL THEN
      i := 0;
   END;
END SearchList;

PROCEDURE MakeListEmpty(VAR L: List);
(* Make list L empty *)
VAR Link: List;
BEGIN
   WHILE L # NIL DO    (* delete element *)
      Link := L;
      L := L^.Next;
      DEALLOCATE(Link, SIZE(Node));
   END;
END MakeListEmpty;

PROCEDURE ListLength(L: List): CARDINAL;
(* Return length of list L *)
VAR Link: List;
    Count: CARDINAL;
BEGIN
   Link := L;
   Count := 0;
```

```
  WHILE Link # NIL DO        (* count elements *)
    INC(Count);
    Link := Link^.Next;
  END;
  RETURN Count;
END ListLength;

PROCEDURE Get(L: List; i: ListIndex; VAR Item: ListElement);
(* Return value of ei in L *)
VAR Link: List;
BEGIN
  Link := FindNode(L, i);
  IF Link # NIL THEN
    Item := Link^.Info;
    ListError := FALSE;
  ELSE
    ListError := TRUE;
  END;
END Get;

PROCEDURE Put(VAR L: List; i: ListIndex; Item: ListElement);
(* Update value of ei in L *)
VAR Link: List;
BEGIN
  Link := FindNode(L, i);
  IF Link # NIL THEN
    Link^.Info := Item;
    ListError := FALSE;
  ELSE
    ListError := TRUE;
  END;
END Put;

BEGIN
  ListError := FALSE;
END ListADT.
```

With this dynamic implementation of linear lists, all operations, except CreateList, which is O(1), are O(n), because they all contain a loop based on the list length or a call to FindNode (which contains a similar loop). Table 5-2 sums up the complexities of all operations in the dynamic implementation.

With this representation, the space complexity is exactly the space needed for storing the elements of the list, each element being associated with a pointer.

Although static and dynamic implementations have insertion and deletion algorithms of the same complexity, we can see that, compared to the static contiguous implementation, the dynamic implementation uses memory more efficiently at the cost of slightly slower operations.

The static implementation is best suited to applications where the size of the list is stable and the number of insertions and deletions is small, while the dynamic implementation should be chosen for applications with more insertions and deletions, or

Table 5-2
Operations Complexity

Procedure	Complexity
CreateList	O(1)
Insert	O(n)
Delete	O(n)
SearchList	O(n)
MakeListEmpty	O(n)
ListLength	O(n)
Get	O(n)
Put	O(n)

where the size of the list is unknown. With the dynamic implementation, the link part of each node is a pointer. With the static contiguous implementation we've seen earlier, this pointer is not needed. The neighbor is implied by its location; the next element in the list is the next element in the array. We can define another static implementation based on an array in which each element indicates its successor in the list. The type declarations then become:

```
TYPE List = POINTER TO Table;
     Index = [1..Max];
     Node = RECORD
               Item: ListElement;
               Next: Index;
            END;
     Table = RECORD
                Free: [0..Max];
                Elements: ARRAY Index OF Node;
             END;
```

Such an organization, illustrated by the example of Figure 5-3, is very similar to our dynamic implementation, but pointers are replaced by indices (pseudo-pointers).

Since procedures ALLOCATE and DEALLOCATE can be used only with pointers, we will have to manage the allocation and the liberation of free space for nodes. In particular, we will need to initialize the array so that each node of the array points to its successor:

```
FOR i := 1 TO Max-1 DO
   L^.Elements[i].Next := i+1;
END;
L^.Elements[Max].Next := 0;
L^.Free := 1;
```

We can then define procedures Allocate and Deallocate in the following manner.

Figure 5-3
Static Implementation with Pseudo-Pointers

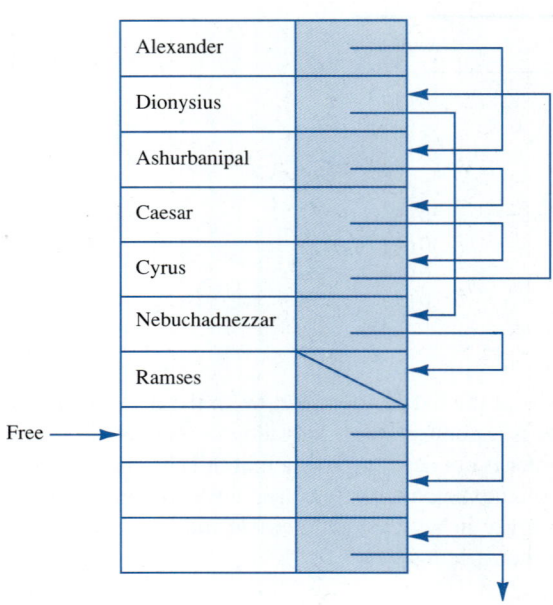

```
PROCEDURE Allocate(VAR L: List; VAR Link: Index);
BEGIN
   IF L^.Free = 0 THEN
      ListError := TRUE;
   ELSE
      ListError := FALSE;
      Link := L^.Free;
      L^.Free := L^.Elements[L^.Free].Next;
   END;
END Allocate;

PROCEDURE Deallocate(VAR L: List; Link: Index);
BEGIN
   L^.Elements[Link].Next := L^.Free;
   L^.Free := Link;
END Deallocate;
```

With these two procedures we can easily adapt the dynamic implementation we have just defined. Procedures like FindNode or Insert remain very much as they are, once calls to ALLOCATE and DEALLOCATE have been replaced by calls to Allocate and Deallocate.

With pointers, we have considerably more flexibility because the system will allocate storage dynamically as we need it and as long as there is free memory space left. With arrays, we have a static implementation and we must therefore decide in advance how many elements there will be in all the lists of a user program. It is possible with the static implementation that several lists can share the same data structure. However, there is less difference than it might seem between the two implementations because in

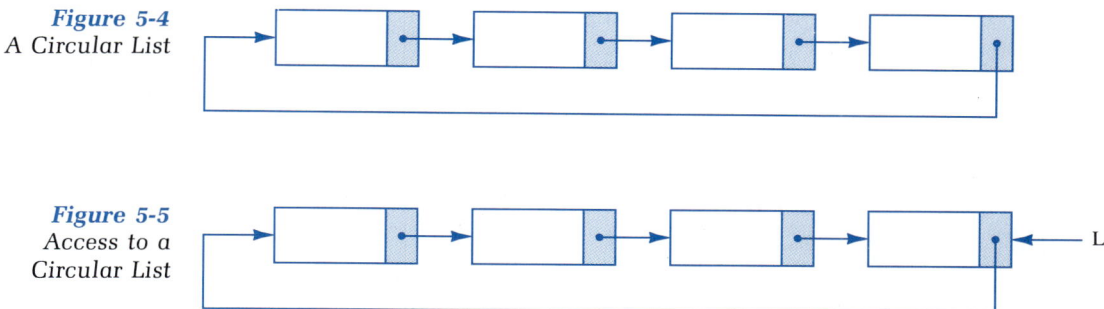

Figure 5-4
A Circular List

Figure 5-5
Access to a Circular List

any actual case the memory space is always limited. If you have a good implementation of Modula-2, there should be no need to use arrays similar to what we have just shown, as these only simulate a dynamic implementation.

Circular Lists

Linear lists do have some disadvantages. For instance, from a given element in the list other than the first one, it is impossible to access all previous elements, as it is impossible to go backwards in the list. By having the last element's pointer (whose value is normally NIL) pointing to the first element, we obtain a *circular list*, as illustrated in Figure 5-4.

From any circular list element, it is possible to access all the other elements in the list. We should note that access to elements in a circular list is usually through the first or the last element of that list. However, the choice is arbitrary, and any element could be used. If the list is accessed through its last element, as shown in Figure 5-5, then we can access the head of the list by following a single pointer.

We can implement our ADT List with circular lists. However, we should note that, even though it is possible to define circular lists with a static implementation, these lists are more interesting with a dynamic implementation. For such a dynamic implementation many operations remain like those we have shown earlier, with noncircular linear lists. Some operations like insertion will be almost identical as before, while others, like FindNode, might have to be modified a little more, as the following two examples show.

```
PROCEDURE FindNode(L: List; i: ListIndex): List;
(* Find pointer to node i. Return NIL if index out of range *)
VAR j: ListIndex;
    Link: List;
BEGIN
  IF i <= 0 THEN
    RETURN NIL;
  ELSE
    j := 1;
    Link : = L^.Next;
```

```
        WHILE (j < i) AND (Link # L) DO
          INC(j);
          Link := Link^.Next;
        END; (* WHILE *)
        IF j = i THEN
          RETURN Link;
        ELSE
          RETURN NIL;
        END; (* IF *)
      END; (* IF *)
    END FindNode;

    PROCEDURE Insert(VAR L: List; i: ListIndex; item: ListElement);
    (* Insert element item immediately after the ith element in L *)
    VAR Link1, Link2: List;
    BEGIN
      Link1 := FindNode(L, i);
      IF ((i > 0) AND (Link1 # NIL)) OR (i=0) THEN
        (* 0 <= i <= N *)
        ALLOCATE(Link2, SIZE(Node));
        Link2^.Info := item;
        ListError := FALSE;
        IF i = 0 THEN      (* Insert at head of list *)
          (* i=0, L=(item, e[1], ..., e[N]) *)
          Link2^.Next : = L^.Next;
          L^.Next := Link2;
        ELSE
          (* i>0, L=(e[1], ..., e[i], item, e[i+1], ..., e[N]) *)
          Link2^.Next := Link1^.Next;
          Link1^.Next := Link2;
        END; (* IF *)
      ELSE
        ListError := TRUE;
      END; (* IF *)
    END Insert;
```

This implementation might be used if some operations of our ADT were to be modified. For instance, the search operation could start at any element of the list instead of the beginning of the list.

Symmetric Lists

Even though it is possible to access any element of a circular list from a given element in the list, it is possible to move from one element to another in only one direction. With a static contiguous implementation, successor elements are contiguous to their predecessors, and this problem does not exist. But with a dynamic implementation, most operations will require the use of an extra pointer to the preceding element. For instance, to delete an element it is necessary to know its predecessor. If we must scan the list from the beginning to find this predecessor, the operation can become ineffi-

Figure 5-6
A Symmetric List

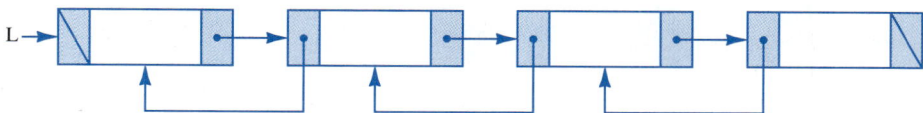

cient. In order to be able to move in the list in both directions, each element of a *symmetric list* or *doubly linked list* will have two fields to connect it to the element preceding it and to the element following it, as shown in Figure 5-6.

In the previous high-precision arithmetic application, we had to keep the number slices in reverse order in the list because of the way the carry propagates. The display of a number was thus rendered awkward, and a symmetric list would improve that particular situation. Of course, there is a price to pay for that extra flexibility. We need space for these extra links, and we will have more links to manipulate in the operations implementation.

In a symmetric list implemented with pointers, we have the following identity:

```
P^.Predecessor^.Successor = P^.Successor^.Predecessor = P
```

This identity holds true except for the first and the last elements of the list.

In general, deletion of an element is simply done by:

```
P^.Predecessor^.Successor = P^.Successor;
P^.Successor^.Predecessor = P^.Predecessor;
DEALLOCATE(P, SIZE(Node));
```

Nevertheless, in procedure Delete it will still be necessary to check for the empty list, the deletion of the only element in the list, or the deletion of the first or last elements. A symmetric list may also be circular, a situation that might simplify some of the operations.

List Headers

It is sometimes useful to keep a special element at the head of the list. This element is not a member of the list and is called a *list header*. This header might carry information on the number of elements in the list, the list name, the position of the last element, and so on. Figure 5-7 shows a list with its header.

Operations on this type of list are the same as we have seen before. Some modifications in their implementation will be necessary. An empty list will have only one element, its header.

List headers can also be used with circular lists and symmetric lists. Checking to see if a list is empty is easier when list headers are used. The various empty lists are shown in Figure 5-8.

Figure 5-7
List with a List Header

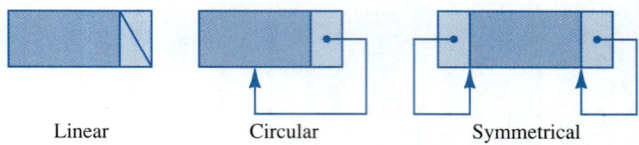

Figure 5-8
Header Nodes for Various Empty Lists

Linear Circular Symmetrical

5.4 Multilinked Lists

In a symmetric or doubly linked list, both series of links represent an ordering and each ordering is the logical inverse of the other. The second set of pointers could, in fact, be used to indicate a completely different ordering. This introduces the concept of *multilinked lists*.

Large amounts of data are usually organized in what is called a *database*. For instance, we could have a database containing information on each student in a university. A *database management system* (DBMS) includes all the facilities to manipulate information in the database. Let's assume that we have a rudimentary database including all the students in the university. Each student is characterized by an information record with a number of fields like student number, name, address, department, year of study, as shown in Figure 5-9.

In that database, we might want to search for all records with a specific value in a given field, such as all second-year students or all computer science students. If such queries are often used, it is best to keep auxiliary lists of the records that have the same value in a particular field. These auxiliary lists are usually called *inverted lists*. For instance, we can establish an inverted list for the department field with value CS:

Buckle, Gorki, Patna, Tremblay, Wagner

Instead of keeping this auxiliary list independently, we can use the record fields to keep pointers and to establish external list headers with the field value. In Figure 5-10, pointers will be represented by numbers for the sake of clarity.

This organization improves the efficiency of the query operations. However, if we want to know where a student lives, the information is not in the student's record any

Figure 5-9
Students Database

Number	Name	Address	Department	Year
BUC122156	Buckle	Boston	CS	1
DAR031460	Darwin	Hartford	Economy	2
FLA111062	Flanagan	Boston	Management	2
GOR011561	Gorki	Montreal	CS	1
JON111259	Jones	New York	History	3
LOI032462	Loiselle	Boston	Management	4
MIN101360	Minor	Albany	Management	2
PAT052063	Patna	New York	CS	4
RIC031964	Ricotta	Hartford	Economy	3
SMI022358	Smith	Boston	Management	1
TRE121859	Tremblay	Montreal	CS	3
WAG111251	Wagner	New York	CS	2

Figure 5-10
Students Database

Number	Name	Address	Department	Year
BUC122156	Buckle	3	4	4
DAR031460	Darwin	9	9	3
FLA111062	Flanagan	6	6	7
GOR011561	Gorki	11	8	10
JON111259	Jones	8	0	9
LOI032462	Loiselle	10	7	8
MIN101360	Minor	0	10	12
PAT052063	Patna	12	11	0
RIC031964	Ricotta	0	0	11
SMI022358	Smith	0	0	0
TRE121859	Tremblay	0	12	0
WAG111251	Wagner	0	0	0

Address		Department		Year	
Boston	1	CS	1	1	1
Hartford	2	Economy	2	2	2
Montreal	4	Management	3	3	5
New York	5	History	5	4	6
Albany	7				

more, and it is impossible to obtain it from that record. For instance, if we want to find out where Flanagan lives, starting with his record number 3 and following the Address field provides us with the information that he lives in the same city as Loiselle and Smith, but does not give us the city. The NIL (or zero in Figure 5-10) pointers may be replaced by pointers to the various list headers. To find a field value for a given student is then possible, but requires us to traverse the entire field list. In our previous example, Smith's record Address field might point to Boston and thus give us Flanagan's address. To extract all information on a given student would be time-consuming if we had a database with tens of thousands of students.

5.5 Linked Implementations of Arrays*

In Chapter 2 we mentioned that arrays are sometimes implemented using what we called *linked implementations,* based on linear list concepts. We will present here some of the methods and structures used in linked implementations of arrays. These linked implementations are used for partially filled arrays or sparse arrays (arrays where most elements have value zero).

The Iliffe vectors method is a well-known method that has been used to represent complete arrays. It requires a little more memory space, but allows for quicker access to array elements than the regular method described in Chapter 2. To each array dimen-

*Section may be skipped without loss of continuity.

sion is associated a number of vectors. Figure 5-11 gives a representation for array A defined by:

```
VAR A: ARRAY [3..5], [1..4], [1..2] OF INTEGER;
```

In this example, the address computation for an element is done by using pointers kept in various vectors:

$$\text{address of } A[i, j, k] = V1[i][j] + (k - 1)$$

because $V1[i]$ points to a vector, where we use the pointer indexed by j, which brings us to the values vector. The address computation is very simple and involves only additions. Here, accessing an element is quicker than with the regular address computation for arrays seen in Chapter 2. In Figure 5-11, the pointers point to elements with index 1. In practice those pointers point to elements with index 0 (which simplifies slightly the computation) even if these elements do not exist. A part of a vector is then considered to consist of virtual elements, as shown in Figure 5-12. In the figure, pointer P points to element of index 0, while actual index values are restricted to 3 to 5.

Index validity is supposed to be checked. (Upper and lower bounds can be kept with the array main vector.) With this method, it is sufficient to add the index to P to obtain the next level pointer. The virtual area, to which P points, is used for other things, and index-validity checks make sure indices are not used in an erroneous way.

Access to those values is fast but at the expense of using more memory. In Figure 5-11 we use 15 elements more than the 24 needed to store the actual elements. This method is more economical if the index ranges are in increasing order; that is, if the last index has the largest range. In our example, the representation would be more efficient if we had declared the array as:

```
VAR A: ARRAY [1..2], [3..5], [1..4] OF INTEGER;
```

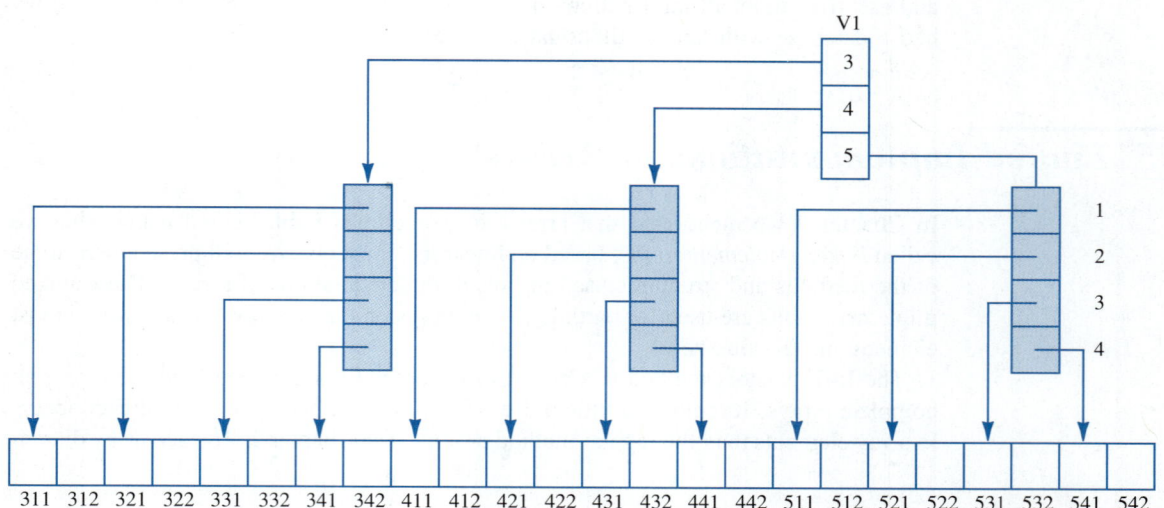

Figure 5-11   Iliffe Vectors Representation

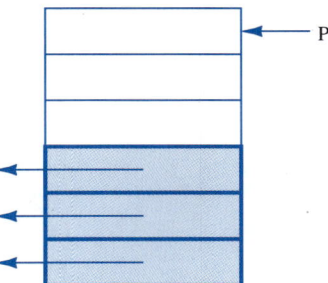

Figure 5-12
Virtual Elements

This declaration would have required only 8 extra elements for the vectors: a first vector of two elements, and two other vectors of three elements each. If the first index has the largest range, the method yields the least efficient use of memory. If we had declared the array as:

```
VAR A: ARRAY [1..4], [3..5], [1..2] OF INTEGER;
```

it would have required 16 extra elements: a first vector of 4 elements and four other vectors with 3 elements each.

Linked representations are also used for sparse matrices in which all the elements of a row are linked together and all the elements of a column are also linked together. This linkage makes it possible to process all elements in a row or in a column. With each element, we keep the value, the row index, and the column index. Each element will have five fields: two integers for index values and two pointers for a column list and a row list, and the element value.

```
TYPE Pointer = POINTER TO Element;
     Element = RECORD
                 Row, Column, Value: INTEGER;
                 RowPoint, ColPoint: Pointer;
               END;
```

Figure 5-13 shows the representation of the following matrix.

```
1 0 0 0 2
0 3 0 0 0
0 0 0 0 0
4 5 0 0 6
```

Memory space necessary for this representation will be 5N for the N nonzero elements, plus $2(r + c)$ for rows and columns headers. Access time for an element will be of the order p, where p is the maximum number of elements in a row or in a column. (This access is achieved by direct access of the row or column directory, followed by sequential search of the list). Note that access to all elements of a list (row or column) will be of the same order of magnitude as access to a single element. Complete processing of the matrix will not be much longer than with the static representations we

Figure 5-13
Sparse Matrix

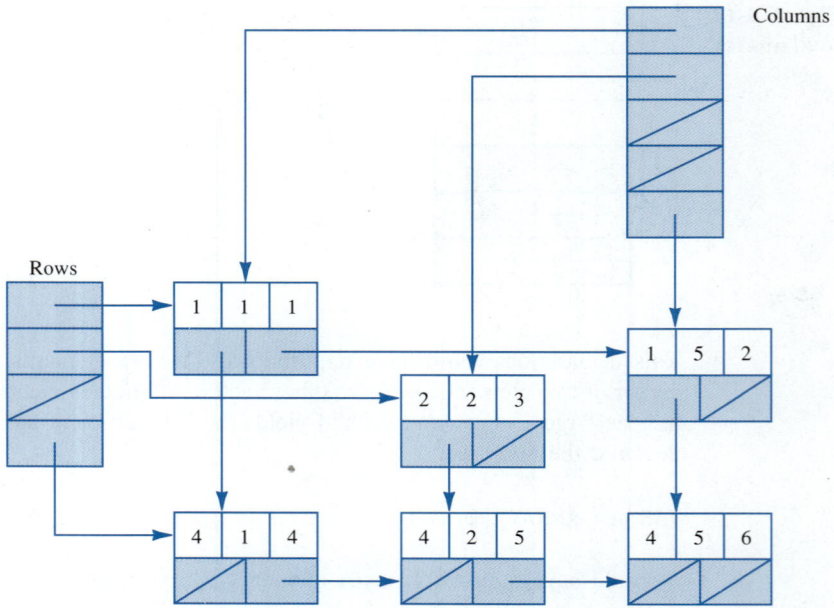

have seen earlier. With this representation, we benefit from the flexibility of inserting and deleting elements in linear lists.

Row and column directories can be represented, as in Figure 5-13, by vectors in which elements have a NIL value if the corresponding row or column is absent. However, if we have a 1,000 × 1,000 matrix where only 12 elements are nonzero, space used will not be efficient if we keep two 1,000 element vectors for list headers. To increase efficiency, row and column directories can be organized somewhat differently, by keeping the row or the column number with each pointer, by ordering the directory on the row or the column number, and by not keeping NIL pointers. Memory utilization is then much better and access time for an element will be of the order (log m) + p. Here m is the number of rows or columns (depending on whether elements are accessed by rows or by columns) and p is the maximum number of elements in a row or in a column (binary search of row or column directory, followed by sequential search of the list). It is also possible to use circular or symmetric linear lists for the row and column lists. We will explore in depth a particular representation for sparse matrices in the case study in Section 5.7.

It is also possible to adapt some of the static methods we have seen earlier to a linked representation. For instance, the matrix:

```
4 0 0 6
9 7 0 0
0 0 0 0
0 0 2 0
```

can be represented by Figure 5-14.

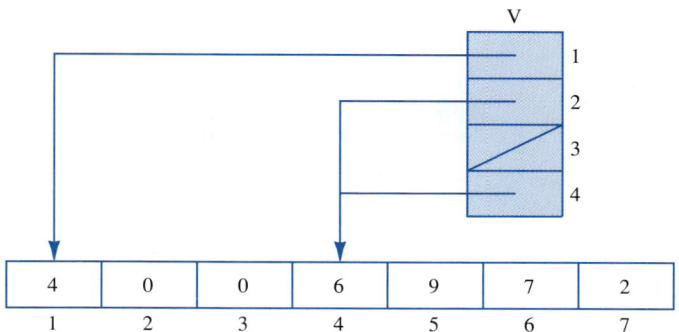

Figure 5-14 Associated Vector

With a vector of the values, we keep a vector giving the position of the elements preceding the first element of a row. Address computation is simple:

$$\text{Address of } M[i, j] = V[i] + j$$

For instance, the address of M[1, 4] will be (0 + 4), which corresponds to value 6, and the address of M[4, 3] will be (4 + 3), which corresponds to value 2. Note that V[4] points to the predecessor of the pseudo-first element of row 4 (rows 2, 3, and 4 have been collapsed).

This method can be generalized to arrays having more dimensions. Consider an array declared as:

```
VAR A: ARRAY [3..6], [1..3], [1..5] OF ElementType;
```

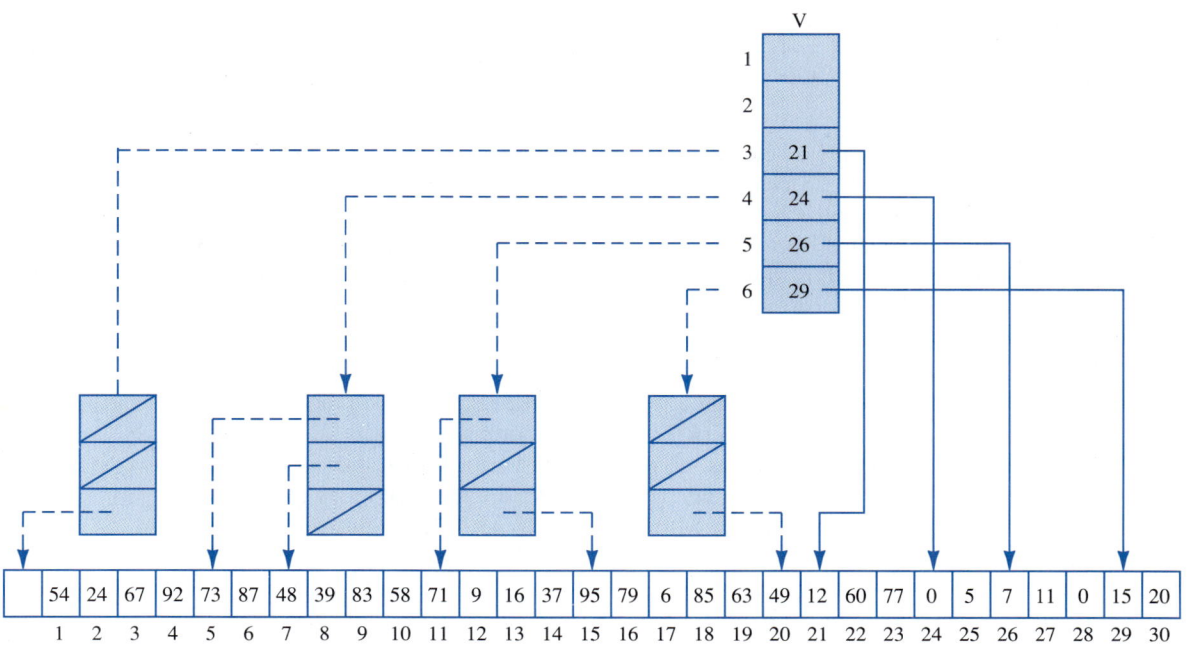

Figure 5-15 Associated Vectors for a Three-Dimensional Array

Table 5-3
Address Calculation for a Three-dimensional Array Using Associated Vectors

Index i,j,k	Value	V[i]	V[i] + j	B[V[i] + j]	B[V[i] + j] + k	
3,3,1	54	21	24	0	1	so B[1] is 54
3,3,2	24	21	24	0	2	so B[2] is 24
3,3,3	67	21	24	0	3	so B[3] is 67
3,3,4	92	21	24	0	4	so B[4] is 92
3,3,5	73	21	24	0	5	so B[5] is 73
4,1,1	87	24	25	5	6	so B[6] is 87
4,1,2	48	24	25	5	7	so B[7] is 48
4,2,1	39	24	26	7	8	so B[8] is 39
4,2,2	83	24	26	7	9	so B[9] is 83
4,2,3	58	24	26	7	10	so B[10] is 58
4,2,4	71	24	26	7	11	so B[11] is 71
5,1,1	9	26	27	11	12	so B[12] is 9
5,1,2	16	26	27	11	13	so B[13] is 16
5,1,3	37	26	27	11	14	so B[14] is 37
5,1,4	95	26	27	11	15	so B[15] is 95
5,3,1	79	26	29	15	16	so B[16] is 79
5,3,2	6	26	29	15	17	so B[17] is 6
5,3,3	85	26	29	15	18	so B[18] is 85
5,3,4	63	26	29	15	19	so B[19] is 63
5,3,5	49	26	29	15	20	so B[20] is 49
6,1,1	12	29	30	20	21	so B[21] is 12
6,1,2	60	29	30	20	22	so B[22] is 60
6,1,3	77	29	30	20	23	so B[23] is 77

where only 23 elements are present of the 60 possible elements. The indices and values for these 23 elements are shown in the left two columns of Table 5-3.

We will assume the other possible array elements are never accessed. We will use associated vectors to store this information, as shown in Figure 15-15. The second-level vectors shown with dotted lines to the left of the figure are virtual; the actual values are stored at the end of the array B, as shown by the solid lines to the right.

Unused indices are not stored. For instance, if the first index is 3, then the values 1 and 2 for the second index are not used and no provision is made to store these values. To access the element at position M[3,3,4], we obtain the value V[3] because 3 is the first index, and we add 3, the second index, to obtain 21 + 3 = 24. Then we access B[24] to find the starting index of the vector for the third dimension. So we add 4, the third index, to the value at B[24] to obtain the final index in B, 0 + 4 = 4, in order to retrieve the value for M[3,3,4], which is 92. The right-hand side of Table 15-3 shows the access paths for the other elements in M.

This technique usually produces faster access to elements of a multidimensional array than the formula in Section 2.3, since only additive operations are involved. In this case, we also saved some space because we required 23 elements for the values used and 11 elements for the associated vectors, compared with 60 elements for the complete array. However, to make a fair comparison, we should allow for all 60 elements to be accessed. In this case, the space using associated vectors is $60 + 3 * 6 + 4 = 82$ elements. In general, storage using associated vectors will be greater than the corresponding storage for conventional methods, but access to elements will be faster.

5.6 Memory Management*

The memory space required for the data structures of a program can be allocated at the time the block declaring the variables is entered. Memory allocation happens in this way with static structures, such as arrays and records. As we have seen, with the static implementation of linked lists, the amount of memory allocated must be the maximum amount needed, or greater. If one wants to use only the minimum necessary memory space, it is best to use a dynamic implementation, where memory space is allocated only as needed during program execution. "Only as needed" implies that mechanisms exist to obtain memory space when it is wanted and also to release memory space when it is no longer needed.

Free memory space must also be organized in such a way that the allocation and liberation operations are easy and efficient. This organization must allow allocation of blocks of different sizes because data structures are often composed of elements of various sizes. For practical reasons, it might be desirable to allocate only blocks of a given size. In most cases this size will be too large, and some parts of the allocated memory will not be used; this is called *internal fragmentation*. In other cases, only what is strictly necessary is allocated, perhaps leading to a splitting of the free space in small size blocks—*external fragmentation*. To avoid this situation, one must have a recovery process that can either merge adjacent free blocks or compact the existing structures.

Allocation

The free space list is assumed to be a linear list of memory blocks, as shown in Figure 5-16.

There are several allocation strategies. The first one is the *first fit* method, in which the free list is searched until a block whose size is greater than or equal to the desired size is found. The block is then split, and the remainder is left in the free space list. The following pseudocode illustrates this method.

---

*Section may be skipped without loss of continuity.

Figure 5-16
Free Memory Space List

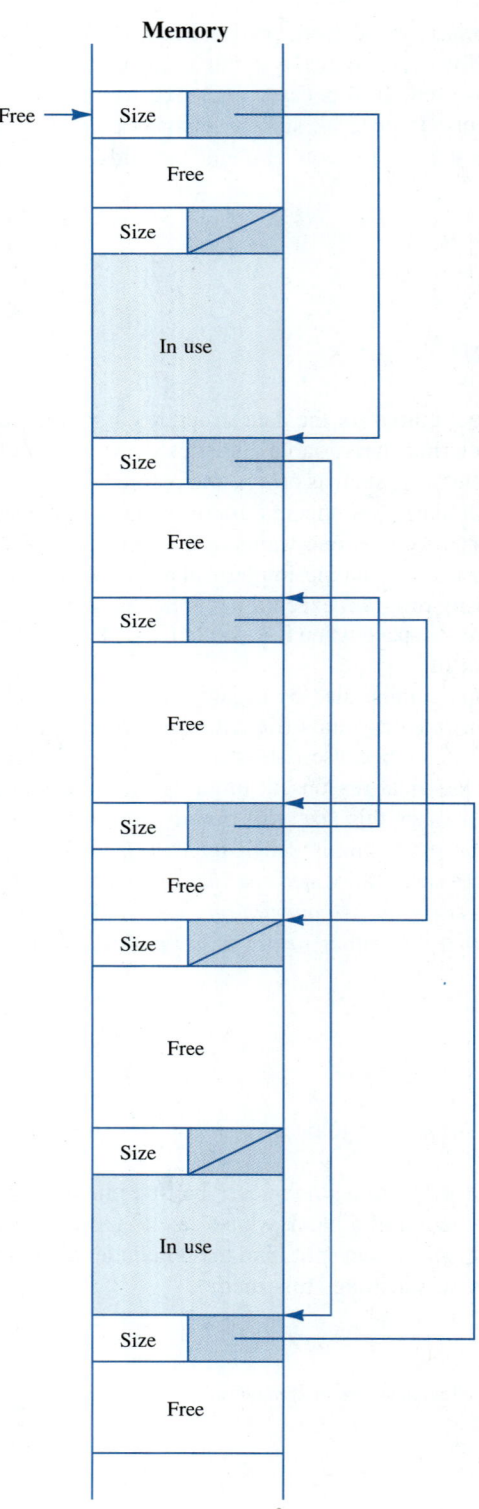

> First fit
>   Set current block to first block of free space
>   While size of current block < N do
>   Get next block
>   End while
>   If current block size > N + epsilon then
>   Split current block
>   End if
>   Allocate current block
> End First fit

The value epsilon is the smallest memory fragment that will be allowed. This method is efficient if the liberation process merges adjacent blocks.

A second method, the *best fit* method, searches the free list for the block with a size closest to the desired size. In order to avoid having to traverse the entire list, the list can be kept in ascending order of block sizes. The main disadvantage of this method is that the number of small blocks in the free list keeps increasing, as the unused part of a "best fit" block is necessarily small. Also the return of a block to the free list is less efficient, since every block must be inserted in ascending order, an O(n) operation for a linked structure.

A third method, the *next fit* method, is only a modified version of the "first fit" method, since the free list is searched not from its beginning, but rather from the point reached by the last search. The free list can be implemented as a circular list; thus it is only necessary to make sure the whole list has been searched in cases where no block can satisfy the request. The advantage of "next fit" over "first fit" is that the small blocks resulting from splitting are evenly distributed over the entire free list rather than accumulated at the start of the list.

A fourth method is the *worst fit* method, where the largest block is used to satisfy a request. The free list is ordered according to block sizes in a descending order. If a request can be satisfied, it is dealt with immediately, and the unused portion, which is probably a large block, is inserted back in the free list. Since the list is sorted, this will be an O(n) operation for a linked list.

The *fixed size* method allocates memory blocks without splitting them. This way, more memory is allocated than necessary most of the time. However, the management of the free list is much simpler.

Finally the *buddy system* always splits blocks in half. Initially, free memory is only made of one block that will be split for the first request. There will be as many block splits as necessary to obtain a satisfactory block size. Free memory is represented by several lists, each comprising blocks of a given size. For instance, if there are only blocks of size 64 and there is a request for a block of size 16, a block will be split into two blocks of size 32. One of these will be put in the list for size 32, and the other one will be split into two blocks of size 16. One of these will then be placed in the corresponding free list for size 16, while the other will be returned to the caller. The original buddy method used blocks whose size was a power of two, but later similar methods used blocks whose size was based on other sequences, such as the Fibonacci numbers.

Liberation

In order for dynamic memory management to be complete, it is necessary to have efficient means to free memory blocks that are no longer used. Fixed-size blocks only have to be linked to the free list, while variable size blocks must be merged with their neighbors, if at all possible.

If the free list is a symmetric list in increasing order of addresses, the following pseudocode defines an algorithm for freeing a block and merging it with its neighbors.

```
Free block
    Set current block to first block
    While current block address < freed block address do
        Set current block to next block
    End while
    Set previous block to block preceding current block
    If end of previous block adjacent to freed block then
        Combine previous block and freed block
    Else
        Link previous block and freed block
    End if
    If end of freed block adjacent to beginning of current
            block then
        Combine freed block and current block
    Else
        Link freed block and current block
    End if
End free block
```

This method may be improved by keeping at the head and at the end of each block a flag indicating whether the block belongs to the free list or not, and the block size. Once a block is freed, it is sufficient to examine the memory word preceding or following the block to know immediately whether or not a merge is possible.

In the buddy system, a simple computation gives the address of a block's buddy. If it is free, then a merge is possible that can generate other merges. Each merge implies in turn an update of the size lists.

5.7 Case Study: Sparse Matrices

Design

Definition of the Problem We are to design and implement an ADT for matrices that are very, very sparse, that is, for matrices in which the density of nonzero elements is less than 0.0001. The user must be able to specify the number of rows and columns, up to a maximum of 10,000. Both row and column indices will be zero-

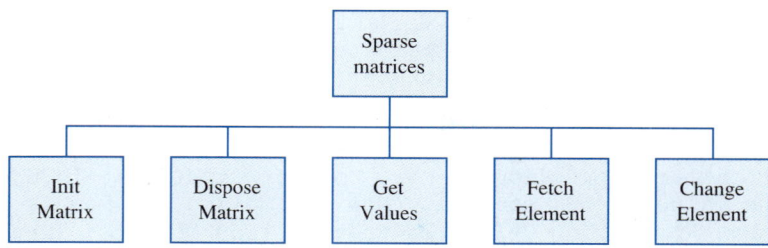

Figure 5-17
Sparse Matrices Operations

based. Although there will be no arbitrary restrictions on the number of nonzero elements beyond system memory limitations, it is assumed the matrices have usually less than 10,000 nonzero elements.

We will assume that the type of the data is integer, but this should be easily changeable to any data type. The ADT should make it possible to initialize a matrix, to dispose of a matrix, to fetch the value of an element, and to change the value of an element. Even though the matrix type is not visible, the user should be able to find out the number of rows, the number of columns, and the number of nonzero elements in a given matrix. The ADT should be tested by writing user-defined operations to display a matrix, to copy matrix values to a file, and to multiply two matrices.

Design of a Solution Since we are designing an ADT, we need only to define a data type and the corresponding operations. Because we want to apply the information hiding principle, we will define an opaque type for sparse matrices. The operations are as described in the previous step and can be integrated in the structure chart of Figure 5-17.

These operations can be completely specified by the following definition module.

```
DEFINITION MODULE SparseMatrix;
(* This module implements an abstract data type for sparse matrices
   with up to 10,000 rows and 10,000 columns. The type is Matrix
   and the operations are:
   InitMatrix and DisposeMatrix for creation and removal;
   GetMatrixValues returns the number of rows, the number of columns
      and the number of nonzero elements;
   FetchElement and ChangeElement get and change element values *)
TYPE Matrix;
PROCEDURE InitMatrix(VAR M: Matrix; NbrRows, NbrCols: CARDINAL);
(* Initialize sparse matrix M with at most NbrRows rows and NbrCols
   columns. All entries are initially zero. *)
PROCEDURE DisposeMatrix(VAR M: Matrix);
(* Dispose of all data associated with matrix M, which is considered
   undefined after this operation. *)
```

```
PROCEDURE GetMatrixValues(M: Matrix; VAR NbrRows, NbrCols,
                         NonzeroElements: CARDINAL);
(* Return the number of rows, the number of columns, and the number
   of nonzero elements for matrix M. If M is not defined, then all
   three values are set to zero. *)
PROCEDURE FetchElement(M: Matrix; Row, Column: CARDINAL): INTEGER;
(* Return the value at the specified Row and Column. If Row is
   greater than NbrRows or Column is greater than NbrCols, then
   MAX(INTEGER) is returned. *)
PROCEDURE ChangeElement(VAR M: Matrix; Row, Column: CARDINAL;
                       Value: INTEGER);
(* Add an element in matrix M at Row and Column with value specified
   by Value. If an element already exists at this position, change
   its value to Value. If Row is greater than NbrRows or Column is
   greater than NbrCols, this procedure does nothing to matrix M. *)
END SparseMatrix.
```

Refine the Solution Before we start thinking about the various algorithms we need for the operations, let's take some time to discuss the data structures we will use. The design of the data structure for the sparse matrix should provide reasonably fast access to data and efficient use of memory space. The rows and columns of the matrix will be linked lists, as suggested by Figure 5-13. Each element will contain its row number, its column number, an integer value, a link to the next nonzero row element, and a link to the next nonzero column element. Since we are assuming an individual row or column will have very few nonzero elements, traversing a linked list to find an element will be acceptable. The header node for the sparse matrix will contain the number of rows, the number of columns, the number of nonzero elements, and access to the row and column pointers.

This access mechanism will involve choices between space efficiency and time efficiency. An array of row pointers and an array of column pointers, as suggested by Figure 5-13, will provide the fastest access to columns and rows. It also means that we will have to set aside memory for the worst-case number of rows and columns, even if the matrix rarely becomes that large. To illustrate, let's assume that our array has actually only 1,500 rows and 2,500 columns, and that there is a total of 3,000 nonzero entries. If, as specified, we allow a maximum of 10,000 rows and 10,000 columns, then each matrix header will require space for the actual header (3 words), space for the 10,000 row pointers, and space for the 10,000 column pointers, thus $2 \times 10,000 + 3 = 20,003$ words. If there were 3,000 nonzero entries, where each entry is an integer value and takes up 5 words (row, column, value, two pointers), then the data would require $5 \times 3,000 = 15,000$ words. The matrix header actually takes more memory space than the data itself! However, the total required space, 35,003 words, would still be less than one percent of the $1500 \times 2500 = 3,750,000$ words required for an ordinary array.

One technique to reduce the space needed for the row and column pointers would be using a linked list of pointers instead of an array of pointers, and only allocate the pointers needed for the array being stored. Each column or row header would now take two words instead of one, one for the pointer to the first nonzero item and one for the next header item. The number of rows and columns would have to be less than half the maximum in order to save space. Assuming a 1,500 by 2,500 array, as above, the matrix header would now require $1500 \times 2 + 2500 \times 2 + 3 = 8003$ words. Although this is a substantial space improvement over the 20,003 words required by the worst-case model above, the loss of direct access to a column or row header is too steep a price to pay in efficiency. Unlike the rows or columns themselves, the header lists will be very long, and to traverse them sequentially every time we need to access an array element will be unacceptably lengthy.

The technique we will use combines space efficiency and time efficiency. We will use a two-tiered array of pointers. Figure 5-18 illustrates this organization for 16 elements. At the first level is an array with four pointers to the second-level arrays. At the second level are four arrays of four pointers to the actual data (note that some of these pointers might be NIL). There are 16 elements, and if we want to access the element having index 13, we compute 13 DIV 4 to find the first level pointer, then 13 MOD 4 to find the second-level pointer (this is shown with bold arrows in Figure 5-18).

Based on this representation, in our ADT the matrix header will contain an array of 100 pointers for rows and 100 pointers for columns. Each of these pointers, if used, will point to another array of 100 pointers, which will be the column or row pointers. This second tier will only be allocated on an as-needed basis. In general, there may be some unused pointers in the first tier, and the number of second-tier arrays could be much less than the maximum possible as illustrated by Figure 5-19. There will also be a nonnegligible number of NIL pointers in the second-tier arrays.

For the 1,500 by 2,500 array discussed previously, the second tier of row pointers would have a maximum of 15 arrays of 100 pointers each, and the second tier of column pointers would have at most 25 arrays of 100 pointers each. If the size of the matrix is not divisible by 100, then there may also be some unused pointers in the last 100 pointers of the second tier. This technique has reduced the space for the matrix header and secondary tiers to a maximum of $3 + 2 \times 100 + 15 \times 100 + 25 \times 100 = 4203$ words. But what is most important is that because both tiers use array indexing, we have retained constant access time to a row or column pointer. If we want to access

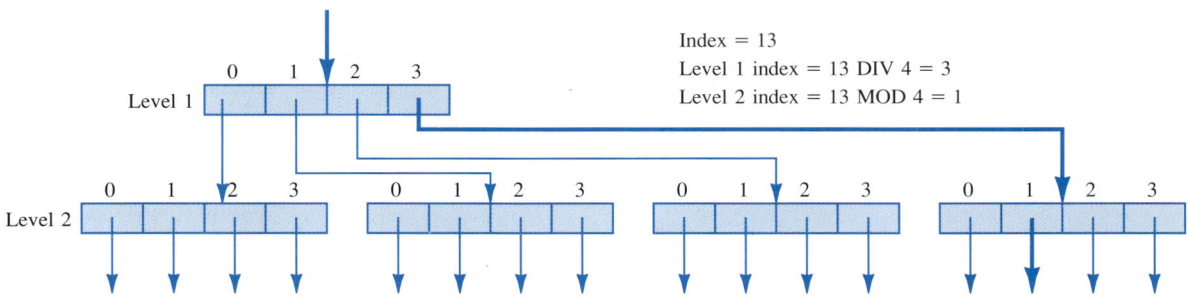

Figure 5-18 Two-Tiered Array of Pointers

Figure 5-19
Two-Tiered Array
of Pointers with
Missing Elements

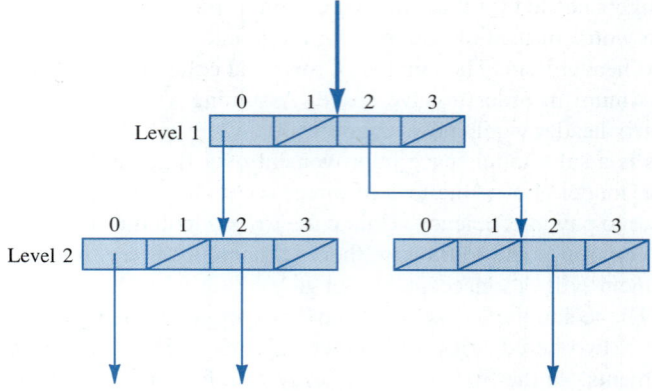

row 1251, then we go to the pointer indexed by 12 (1251 DIV 100) of the first row tier to find the pointer with index 51 (1251 MOD 100) of the second row tier. Figure 5-20 illustrates this approach on a much smaller scale; each tier has only four pointers.

Even though the matrix of Figure 5-20 is fairly small and not very sparse, our sparse matrix data structure still occupies less space than the $12 \times 15 = 180$ word structure for an ordinary array. The total space used is:

$$3 + 2 \times 4 + 3 \times 4 + 4 \times 4 + 5 \times 11 = 94 \text{ words}$$

With a large and very sparse matrix the savings would be even more substantial.

Now that we have decided what data structures to use, we can specify them using Modula-2 syntax and then define our algorithms.

```
CONST ArrayMax = 99;
      ArrayMaxPlusOne = ArrayMax + 1;

TYPE Matrix = POINTER TO MatrixHeader;
     ElementPtr = POINTER TO MatrixElement;
     ArrayIndex = [0..ArrayMax];
     MinorHeaderArray = ARRAY ArrayIndex OF ElementPtr;
     MinorHeaderArrayPtr = POINTER TO MinorHeaderArray;
     MajorHeaderArray = ARRAY ArrayIndex OF MinorHeaderArrayPtr;
     MatrixHeader =
       RECORD
         NbrRows, NbrCols, NonzeroElements: CARDINAL;
         RowHeader, ColumnHeader: MajorHeaderArray;
       END;
     MatrixElement =
       RECORD
         Row, Column: CARDINAL;
         Value: INTEGER;
         NextRowEntry, NextColEntry: ElementPtr;
       END;
```

5.7 Case Study: Sparse Matrices 157

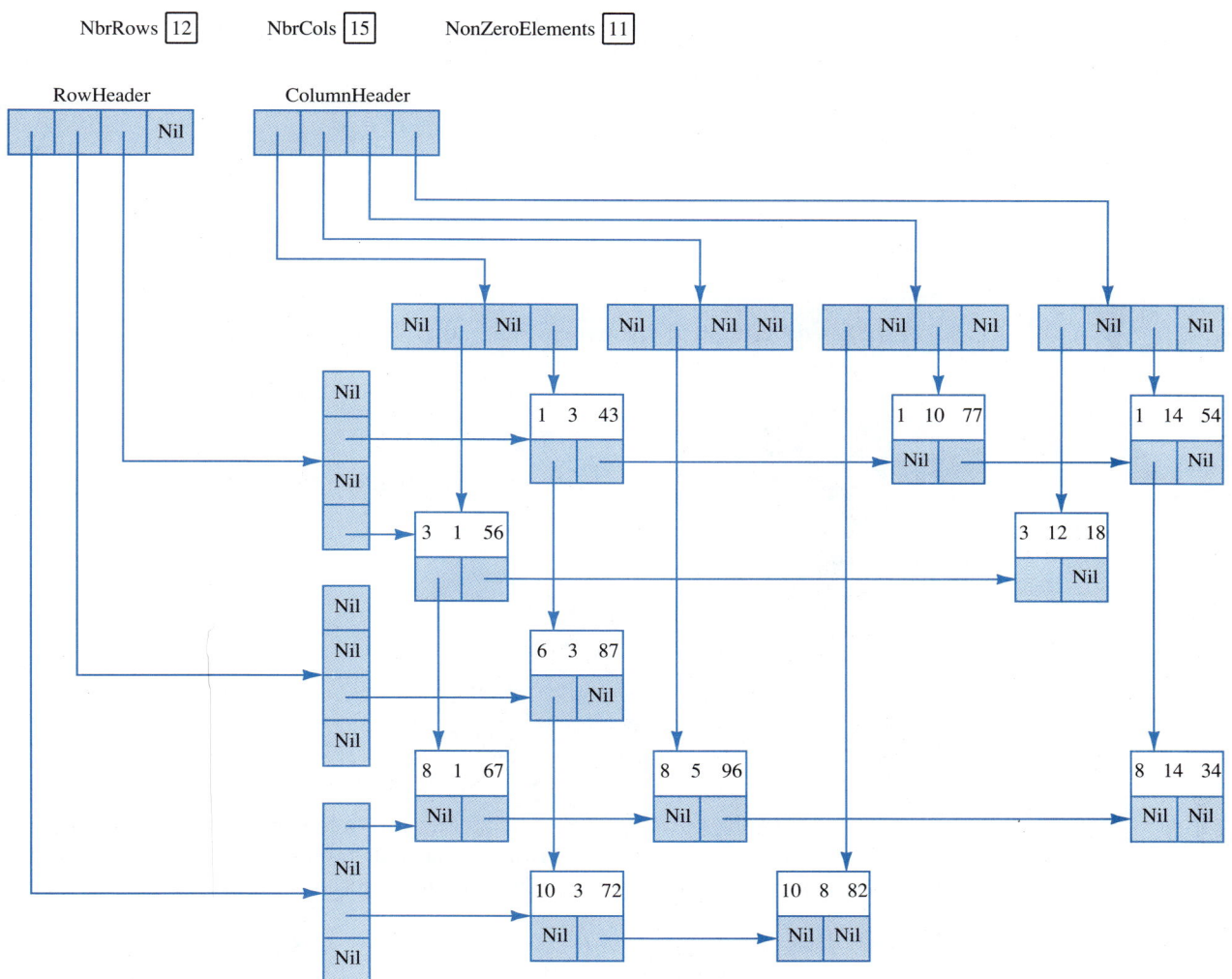

Figure 5-20 Sparse Matrix Data Structure and Data Using Two Tiers of Four Pointers

Matrix initialization is simple: we have to allocate space for the matrix header and to initialize the first tier pointers to NIL.

> Initialize Matrix
>   Allocate matrix header node
>   Assign values for the number of rows, columns, and nonzero elements

>   Set Major Header row pointers to NIL
>   Set Major Header column pointers to NIL
> End Initialize Matrix

To dispose of a matrix, we have to remove all matrix elements first, then remove the minor header arrays, and finally remove the matrix header.

> Dispose Matrix
>   For each major index of rows
>   If minor row header array exists
>   For each minor index of rows
>   Set Scan to first nonzero column element
>   While Scan is not NIL
>   Set Trail to Scan
>   Advance Scan to next nonzero column element
>   Dispose of element at Trail
>   End while
>   End for
>   Dispose of minor row header array
>   End if
>   End for
>   Dispose of all minor column header arrays
>   Dispose of matrix header
> End Dispose Matrix

To fetch a matrix value, we can either search for it across a row or down a column. The pseudocode below searches across a row. An invalid row or column value will be indicated by returning the value of the maximum integer.

> Fetch Element
>   If Row and Column indices are valid
>   If row header not NIL { row exists }
>   Set RowScan to first nonzero element in row
>   While RowScan is not NIL and RowScan column is less than Column
>   Advance RowScan to next nonzero entry in Row
>   End while
>   If RowScan is NIL then
>   Set Value to 0
>   Elsif element exists at Row and Column
>   Set Value to element value
>   Else
>   Set Value to 0
>   End if

```
        Else
            Set Value to 0
    Else
        Set value to maximum integer value
    End if
End Fetch Element
```

Changing a matrix element uses a search pattern similar to that used in fetching an element. If the element exists and the new value is nonzero, then we simply change the existing value. If the new value is zero, then we have to delete the existing node. This process is illustrated in Figure 5-21, which is a portion of the matrix of Figure 5-20 where the value of the element at row 8 and column 5 is changed from 96 to 0.

We find the node to be deleted and assign it to Element. We then find the previous row element, RowScan, which in this example is the entry at row 8 and column 1. We find the prior column entry, but since there is none, our ColumnScan pointer ends up at Element itself. Since RowScan is a prior element, we assign to RowScan's next row entry pointer the value of Element's next row entry pointer. Since ColumnScan is Element itself, there is no prior column entry, so we set the column header pointer to the next column entry of Element. Finally, we delete the node at Element.

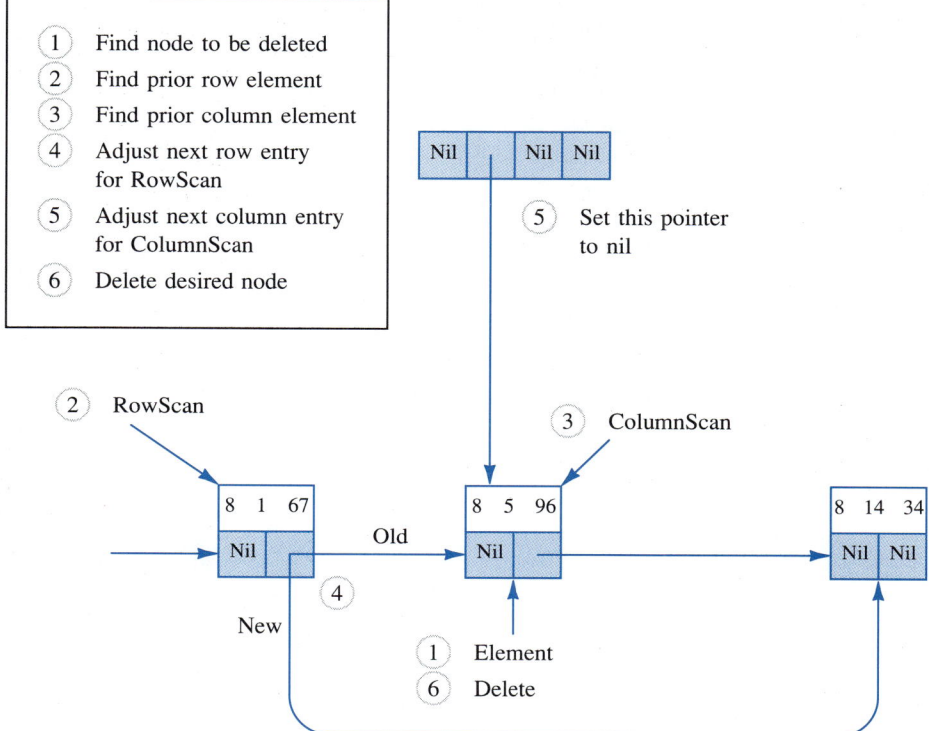

Figure 5-21
Deleting an Element from a Sparse Matrix

The most common case occurs when the element to be changed is not found in the original search. We illustrate this case in Figure 5-22 by changing the value of the node at row 8 and column 4 from 0 to 57, in the sparse matrix of Figure 5-20.

Once it is determined that the node is not present, we position RowScan to the prior row element, which in this case is the node at row 8 and column 1. We position ColumnScan to the prior column element, which in this case is NIL, since there is no prior element in column 4. We create the new node, called Element, and fill in the appropriate values for Row, Column, and Value. If RowScan is not NIL, as in this case, then we assign the value from RowScan's next row entry pointer to Element's next row entry pointer. If ColumnScan is NIL, as in Figure 5-22, or if ColumnScan is an entry with a row value greater than Element, then Element will be the first entry in the column. In this case we assign the value of the column header to the next column entry field of Element. Finally, we must connect Element in the appropriate row and column. For the row, we set RowScan's next row entry field to Element. For the column, we set the column header pointer to Element. This completes the insertion of Element.

The pseudocode on page 161 reflects all of the alternatives discussed above. To minimize the necessary conditional tests, we have organized the code to scan a row and change pointers before scanning a column and changing pointers.

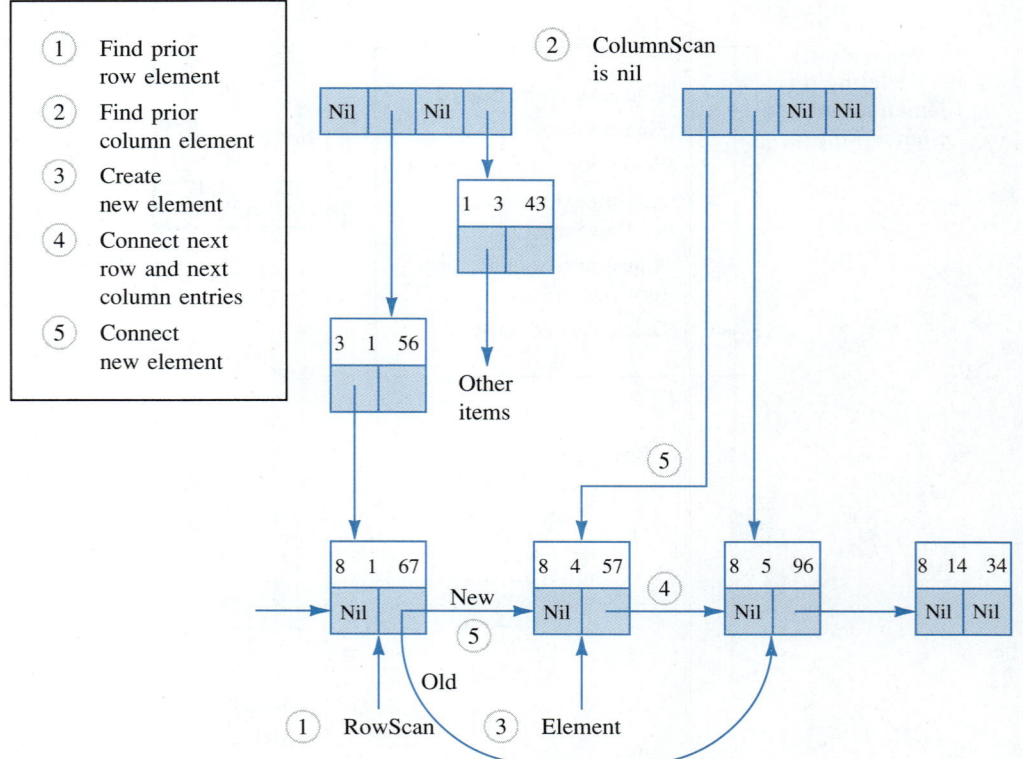

Figure 5-22 *Inserting an Element in a Sparse Matrix*

```
Change Element
    If Row and Column values are within the valid range
        If row and column headers are not NIL
            Set RowScan to first nonzero Row element
            Set ColumnScan to first nonzero Column element
            While RowScan is not NIL and there are more nonzero entries
                    and RowScan column is less than Column
                Advance RowScan to next nonzero entry in Row
            End while
            If the element currently exists
                If new value is not zero
                    Set element value to new value
                Else { element node must be removed }
                    Delete Element
                End if
            Elsif Value not zero { adding a new nonzero element }
                Insert Element
        Elsif Value not zero
            If row header is NIL
                Allocate minor row header array
            Else
                Set RowScan to first nonzero Row element
            End if
            If column header is NIL
                Allocate minor column header array
            Else
                Set ColumnScan to first element
            End if
            Insert Element
        End if
    End if
End Change Element
```

Change Element calls on two procedures to delete an element from a couple of lists, and to insert an element into a couple of lists. Delete Element deletes the element from the row list and then from the column list. When this is done, it removes the element and updates the number of elements in the matrix.

```
Delete Element
    If Element first in row
        Connect header to next element in row
    Else
        Set RowScan to prior nonzero row element
        Connect RowScan element to successor of Element in row
    End if
```

>   If Element first in column
>   Connect header to next element
>   Else
>   Set ColumnScan to prior nonzero column element
>   Connect ColumnScan element to successor of Element in column
>   End if
>   Remove Element
>   Decrement number of nonzero values
> End Delete Element

Insert Element inserts the element into the column list, and then into the row list. To insert an element, it is necessary to know if the element inserted is the only one in the list, if it is inserted as the first element in the list, or if it is inserted in any other position in the list.

> Insert Element
>   Set ColumnScan to prior nonzero column element
>   Allocate a new element and assign Row, Column, Value
>   Increment number of nonzero values
>   If ColumnScan is NIL { new element is first column entry }
>   or Row is smaller than first element row value
>   Set next column entry in new element to column header
>   Attach new element to column header node
>   Else
>   Attach next column entry to new element
>   Attach new element to ColumnScan element
>   End if
>   If RowScan is NIL { new element is first row entry }
>   or Column is smaller than first element column value
>   Set next row entry in new element to row header
>   Attach new element to row header node
>   Else
>   Attach next row entry to new element
>   Attach new element to RowScan
>   End if
> End Insert Element

Develop a Testing Strategy We will write procedures external to the ADT to read data from a file and build the corresponding sparse matrix, to display a matrix in the usual manner (including zero values), to save a sparse matrix in a file (excluding zero values), and to multiply two matrices. We will test the read, display and write matrix procedures with:

a sparse matrix with approximately 1% nonzero elements
a sparse matrix with approximately 0.1% nonzero elements
a matrix with all zero entries
a matrix with all nonzero entries
a matrix with all zero entries, except for the last column and the last row

Since the matrix multiplication procedure will use a variety of ADT operations, we will test it for a variety of matrices. Let matrices labeled A be sparse matrices with 1% nonzero elements, let B matrices have all zero elements, and let C matrices have all nonzero elements. We will test the matrix multiply routine, and thus our ADT, for the following pairs:

two matrices that cannot be multiplied
two matrices of the "same" type
an A matrix times a B matrix and a B matrix times an A matrix
an A matrix times a C matrix and a C matrix times an A matrix
a B matrix times a C matrix and a C matrix times a B matrix

As part of this testing we will read matrices from files, store them in files, and display the matrix values. The procedures to read and write matrix values use the same format (row and column numbers start at zero):

Number of rows	Number of columns	Number of nonzero values
Row	Column	Value
:	:	:
:	:	:
Row	Column	Value

Input and output redirection will be used to read from a file and to write to a file. The following pseudocode defines the read and write matrix operations.

```
Read Matrix
    Open input
    Read number of rows, number of columns, nonzero elements
    Initialize matrix
    For each nonzero element
        Read row, column, value
        Change corresponding element
    End for
    Close input
End Read Matrix

Write Matrix
    Open output
    Write number of rows, number of columns, nonzero elements
```

> For all the rows
>   For all the columns
>   Fetch Element at row, column
>   If Element value is not zero
>   Write row, column, value
>   End if
>   End for
>   End for
>   Close output
> End Write Matrix

We have included an interactive test program here as an example to allow for simple testing.

```
MODULE TestSpMatrix;
FROM SparseMatrix IMPORT Matrix, GetMatrixValues, FetchElement,
                         DisposeMatrix, ChangeElement, InitMatrix;
FROM InOut IMPORT ReadCard, WriteString, WriteInt, WriteLn, WriteCard,
                 ReadInt, OpenInput, CloseInput, OpenOutput, CloseOutput;

PROCEDURE GetChoice() : CARDINAL;
(* Display menu of choices; return valid choice or reprompt user for
   input. *)
VAR Choice: CARDINAL;
BEGIN
  WriteString("1. Find A × B"); WriteLn;
  WriteString("2. Find (A × B) × C"); WriteLn;
  WriteString("3. Find B × C"); WriteLn;
  WriteString("4. Find A × (B × C)"); WriteLn;
  WriteString("5. Quit"); WriteLn;

  LOOP
    WriteString("Enter your choice> ");
    ReadCard(Choice); WriteLn;
    CASE Choice OF
      1..5: RETURN Choice;
      ELSE
      WriteString("Valid choices are 1 through 5"); WriteLn;
    END; (* CASE *)
  END; (* LOOP *)
END GetChoice;
```

```
PROCEDURE ReadMatrix (VAR M: Matrix;
                     VAR NbrRows, NbrCols, NonzeroElements: CARDINAL);
(* Read matrix data from the specified file. It is assumed the first
   three entries in the file are NbrRows, NbrCols, and NonzeroElements.
   The remaining entries are triplets of the form: Row, Col, Value.
   The process terminates when the end of file is reached. If the data
   is read successfully, then NbrRows, NbrCols, and NonzeroElements are
   set to the appropriate values. If, for any reason, the data was not
   read successfully, these values are set to zero and matrix M is
   undefined. *)
VAR ElementCount, Row, Column: CARDINAL;
    Value: INTEGER;
BEGIN
  OpenInput('dat');
  ReadCard(NbrRows); ReadCard(NbrCols); ReadCard(NonzeroElements);
  InitMatrix(M, NbrRows, NbrCols);
  FOR ElementCount := 1 TO NonzeroElements DO
    ReadCard(Row); ReadCard(Column); ReadInt(Value);
    ChangeElement(M, Row, Column, Value);
  END; (* FOR *)
  CloseInput;
END ReadMatrix;

PROCEDURE DisplayMatrix (VAR M: Matrix);
(* Display matrix M in the usual manner *)
VAR Row, Column, NbrRows, NbrCols, Temp: CARDINAL;
BEGIN
  GetMatrixValues(M, NbrRows, NbrCols, Temp);
  FOR Row := 0 TO NbrRows - 1 DO
    FOR Column := 0 TO NbrCols - 1 DO
      WriteInt(FetchElement(M, Row, Column), 8);
    END; (* FOR *)
    WriteLn;
  END; (* FOR *)
END DisplayMatrix;

PROCEDURE WriteMatrix (VAR M: Matrix);
(* Write matrix M using output redirection, so the user can specify a file
   or the terminal. The nonzero values are printed as triplets,
   Row-Column-Value, with a linefeed between each triplet. *)
VAR Row, Column, NbrRows, NbrCols, NonZeroElements: CARDINAL;
    Value: INTEGER;
BEGIN
  OpenOutput('dat');
  GetMatrixValues(M, NbrRows, NbrCols, NonZeroElements);
  WriteCard(NbrRows, 8); WriteCard(NbrCols, 8);
  WriteCard(NonZeroElements, 8); WriteLn;
  FOR Row := 0 TO NbrRows-1 DO
    FOR Column := 0 TO NbrCols-1 DO
      Value := FetchElement(M, Row, Column);
```

```
        IF Value # 0 THEN
          WriteCard(Row, 8); WriteCard(Column, 8);
          WriteInt(Value, 8); WriteLn;
        END;
      END; (* FOR *)
    END; (* FOR *)
    CloseOutput;
  END WriteMatrix;

  PROCEDURE MatrixMult (VAR Left, Right, Result: Matrix);
  (* Multiplies matrix Left times matrix Right to produce the Result matrix.
     Result is initialized and the appropriate entries made if matrix
     multiplication is possible (the number of columns of Left equals the
     number of rows of Right). If multiplication is not possible, Result
     is left undefined. *)
  VAR LeftRows, LeftCols, RightRows, RightCols, Temp, I, J, K: CARDINAL;
      Sum: INTEGER;
  BEGIN
    GetMatrixValues(Left, LeftRows, LeftCols, Temp);
    GetMatrixValues(Right, RightRows, RightCols, Temp);
    IF LeftCols = RightRows THEN    (* multiplication possible *)
      InitMatrix(Result, LeftRows, RightCols);
      FOR I := 0 TO LeftRows - 1 DO
        FOR K := 0 TO RightCols - 1 DO
          Sum := 0;
          FOR J := 0 TO LeftCols - 1 DO
            Sum := Sum + FetchElement(Left, I, J)
                         * FetchElement(Right, J, K);
          END; (* FOR *)
          ChangeElement(Result, I, K, Sum);
        END; (* FOR *)
      END; (* FOR *)
    END; (* IF *)
  END MatrixMult;

VAR A, B, C, Result1, Result2: Matrix;
    NbrRows, NbrCols, NonzeroElements: CARDINAL;
BEGIN
  WriteString("data file for matrix A"); WriteLn;
  ReadMatrix(A, NbrRows, NbrCols, NonzeroElements);
  WriteString("data file for matrix B"); WriteLn;
  ReadMatrix(B, NbrRows, NbrCols, NonzeroElements);
  WriteString("data file for matrix C"); WriteLn;
  ReadMatrix(C, NbrRows, NbrCols, NonzeroElements);
  DisplayMatrix(A); WriteLn;
  DisplayMatrix(B); WriteLn;
  DisplayMatrix(C); WriteLn; WriteLn;
```

```
  LOOP
    CASE GetChoice() OF
      1: MatrixMult(A,B,Result1); DisplayMatrix(Result1);
         WriteMatrix(Result1);
    | 2: MatrixMult(A,B,Result1); MatrixMult(Result1,C,Result2);
         DisplayMatrix(Result2); WriteMatrix(Result2);
    | 3: MatrixMult(B,C,Result1); DisplayMatrix(Result1);
    | 4: MatrixMult(B,C,Result1); MatrixMult(A,Result1,Result2);
         DisplayMatrix(Result2);
    | 5: EXIT;
    END; (* CASE *)
  END; (* LOOP *)
  DisposeMatrix(A); DisposeMatrix(B); DisposeMatrix(C);
END TestSpMatrix.
```

It would also be possible to write a more extensive program that would generate random matrices (let's call them MA, MB, and MC) and verify in all cases that (MA × MB) × MC equals MA × (MB × MC). A procedure would be needed to generate a random sparse matrix with the desired characteristics, such as a specified percentage of nonzero values, along with a procedure to test the equality of matrices. We leave these tasks as exercises (see problems 26, 27, and 28 in the Exercise section).

Implementation

Code and Test the Program The implementation module for our ADT follows directly from the pseudocode developed during the design phase.

```
IMPLEMENTATION MODULE SparseMatrix;
(* Implementation of the abstract data type for sparse matrices.
   Maximum 10,000 rows and 10,000 columns. *)
FROM Storage IMPORT ALLOCATE, DEALLOCATE;

CONST ArrayMax = 99;
      ArrayMaxPlusOne = ArrayMax + 1;

TYPE Matrix = POINTER TO MatrixHeader;
     ElementPtr = POINTER TO MatrixElement;
     ArrayIndex = [0..ArrayMax];
     MinorHeaderArray = ARRAY ArrayIndex OF ElementPtr;
     MinorHeaderArrayPtr = POINTER TO MinorHeaderArray;
     MajorHeaderArray = ARRAY ArrayIndex OF MinorHeaderArrayPtr;
     MatrixHeader =
       RECORD
         NbrRows, NbrCols, NonzeroElements: CARDINAL;
         RowHeader, ColumnHeader: MajorHeaderArray;
       END;
```

```
    MatrixElement =
      RECORD
        Row, Column: CARDINAL;
        Value: INTEGER;
        NextRowEntry, NextColEntry: ElementPtr;
      END;
PROCEDURE InitMatrix(VAR M: Matrix; NbrRows, NbrCols: CARDINAL);
(* Initialize sparse matrix M with at most NbrRows rows and NbrCols
   columns. Set all entries to zero. *)

  PROCEDURE AssignMajorHeader(VAR MajorHeader: MajorHeaderArray);
  VAR Index: ArrayIndex;
  BEGIN
    FOR Index := 0 TO ArrayMax DO
      MajorHeader[Index] := NIL;
    END; (* FOR *)
  END AssignMajorHeader;

BEGIN
  ALLOCATE(M, SIZE(MatrixHeader));
  M^.NbrRows := NbrRows;
  M^.NbrCols := NbrCols;
  M^.NonzeroElements := 0;
  AssignMajorHeader(M^.RowHeader);        (* rows *)
  AssignMajorHeader(M^.ColumnHeader);     (* columns *)
END InitMatrix;

PROCEDURE DisposeMatrix(VAR M: Matrix);
(* Dispose of all data associated with matrix M, which is considered
   undefined after this operation. *)
VAR MajorIndex, MinorIndex: ArrayIndex;
    Scan, Trail: ElementPtr;
BEGIN
  FOR MajorIndex := 0 TO M^.NbrRows DIV ArrayMaxPlusOne DO
    IF M^.RowHeader[MajorIndex] # NIL THEN
      FOR MinorIndex := 0 TO ArrayMax DO
        Scan := M^.RowHeader[MajorIndex]^[MinorIndex];
        WHILE Scan # NIL DO     (* dispose of column list *)
          Trail := Scan;
          Scan := Scan^.NextColEntry;
          DEALLOCATE(Trail, SIZE(MatrixElement));
        END; (* WHILE *)
      END; (* FOR *)
      DEALLOCATE(M^.RowHeader[MajorIndex], SIZE(MinorHeaderArray));
    END; (* IF *)
  END; (* FOR *)

  FOR MajorIndex := 0 TO M^.NbrCols DIV ArrayMaxPlusOne DO
    DEALLOCATE(M^.ColumnHeader[MajorIndex], SIZE(MinorHeaderArray));
  END; (* FOR *)
  DEALLOCATE(M, SIZE(MatrixHeader));
END DisposeMatrix;
```

```
PROCEDURE GetMatrixValues(M: Matrix; VAR NbrRows, NbrCols,
                         NonzeroElements: CARDINAL);
(* Return the number of rows, the number of columns, and the number
   of nonzero elements for the matrix M. If M is not defined, then
   all three values are set to zero. *)
BEGIN
  NbrRows := M^.NbrRows;
  NbrCols := M^.NbrCols;
  NonzeroElements := M^.NonzeroElements;
END GetMatrixValues;

PROCEDURE FetchElement(M: Matrix; Row, Column: CARDINAL): INTEGER;
(* Return the value of M[Row, Column]. If Row is greater than NbrRows
   or Column is greater than NbrCols, then MAX(INTEGER) is returned. *)
VAR RowScan: ElementPtr;
    Header: MinorHeaderArrayPtr;
BEGIN
  IF (Row < M^.NbrRows) AND (Column < M^.NbrCols) THEN
    Header := M^.RowHeader[Row DIV ArrayMaxPlusOne];
    IF Header # NIL THEN   (* find element *)
      RowScan := Header^[Row MOD ArrayMaxPlusOne];
      WHILE (RowScan # NIL) AND (RowScan^.Column < Column) DO
        RowScan := RowScan^.NextColEntry;
      END; (* WHILE *)
      IF RowScan = NIL THEN    (* no element *)
        RETURN 0;
      ELSIF (RowScan^.Row = Row) AND (RowScan^.Column = Column) THEN
        (* element exists *)
        RETURN RowScan^.Value;
      ELSE  (* element doesn't match, so value is zero *)
        RETURN 0;
      END; (* IF *)
    ELSE   (* no element *)
      RETURN 0;
    END; (* IF *)
  ELSE
    RETURN MAX(INTEGER);   (* bad column or row number *)
  END; (* IF *)
END FetchElement;

PROCEDURE ChangeElement(VAR M: Matrix; Row, Column: CARDINAL;
                        Value: INTEGER);
(* Perform M[Row, Column] := Value. If element does not exist,
   create it; if an element already exists at this position,
   change its value to Value. If Row > NbrRows or
   Column > NbrCols do nothing. *)
```

```
PROCEDURE Delete(Element: ElementPtr; ColumnScan: ElementPtr;
                 VAR M: Matrix; Row, Column: CARDINAL);
VAR RowScan: ElementPtr;
BEGIN
  (* position RowScan to prior column *)
  RowScan := M^.RowHeader[Row DIV ArrayMaxPlusOne]^
              [Row MOD ArrayMaxPlusOne];
  IF RowScan = Element THEN    (* first element in row *)
    M^.RowHeader[Row DIV ArrayMaxPlusOne]^
              [Row MOD ArrayMaxPlusOne] := Element^.NextColEntry;
  ELSE
    WHILE RowScan^.NextColEntry # Element DO
      RowScan := RowScan^.NextColEntry;
    END; (* WHILE *)
    (* adjust pointer *)
    RowScan^.NextColEntry := Element^.NextColEntry;
  END;
  (* position ColumnScan to prior row *)
  IF ColumnScan = Element THEN    (* first element in column *)
    M^.ColumnHeader[Column DIV ArrayMaxPlusOne]^
              [Column MOD ArrayMaxPlusOne] := Element^.NextRowEntry;
  ELSE
    WHILE ColumnScan^.NextRowEntry # Element DO
      ColumnScan := ColumnScan^.NextRowEntry;
    END; (* WHILE *)
    (* adjust pointer *)
    ColumnScan^.NextRowEntry := Element^.NextRowEntry;
  END;
  DEALLOCATE(Element, SIZE(MatrixElement));
  DEC(M^.NonzeroElements);
END Delete;

PROCEDURE Insert(Value: INTEGER; RowScan, ColumnScan: ElementPtr;
                 VAR M: Matrix; Row, Column: CARDINAL);
VAR Element: ElementPtr;
BEGIN
  WHILE (ColumnScan # NIL) AND (ColumnScan^.NextRowEntry # NIL)
        AND (ColumnScan^.NextRowEntry^.Row <= Row) DO
    ColumnScan := ColumnScan^.NextRowEntry;
  END; (* WHILE *)
  ALLOCATE(Element, SIZE(MatrixElement));
  Element^.Row := Row;
  Element^.Column := Column;
  Element^.Value := Value;
  INC(M^.NonzeroElements);
  IF(ColumnScan = NIL) OR (Row < ColumnScan^.Row) THEN (* first element *)
    M^.ColumnHeader[Column DIV ArrayMaxPlusOne]^
        [Column MOD ArrayMaxPlusOne] := Element;
    Element^.NextRowEntry := ColumnScan;
```

```
      ELSE   (* insert in column list *)
        Element^.NextRowEntry := ColumnScan^.NextRowEntry;
        ColumnScan^.NextRowEntry := Element;
      END; (* IF *)
      Element^.NextColEntry := ColumnScan;
      IF (RowScan = NIL) OR (Column < RowScan^.Column) THEN  (* first element *)
        M^.RowHeader[Row DIV ArrayMaxPlusOne]^
            [Row MOD ArrayMaxPlusOne] := Element;
        Element^.NextColEntry := RowScan;
      ELSE   (* insert in row list *)
        Element^.NextColEntry := RowScan^.NextColEntry;
        RowScan^.NextColEntry := Element;
      END; (* IF *)
    END Insert;

    PROCEDURE AllocateMinorHeader(VAR MinorHeader: MinorHeaderArrayPtr);
    VAR Index: ArrayIndex;
    BEGIN
      ALLOCATE(MinorHeader, SIZE(MinorHeaderArray));
      FOR Index := 0 TO ArrayMax DO
        MinorHeader^[Index] := NIL;
      END; (* FOR *)
    END AllocateMinorHeader;

VAR RowScan, ColumnScan, Element: ElementPtr;
    RowHead, ColumnHead: MinorHeaderArrayPtr;
BEGIN
  IF (Row < M^.NbrRows) AND (Column < M^.NbrCols) THEN
    RowHead := M^.RowHeader[Row DIV ArrayMaxPlusOne];
    ColumnHead := M^.ColumnHeader[Column DIV ArrayMaxPlusOne];
    IF (RowHead # NIL) AND (ColumnHead # NIL) THEN
      RowScan := RowHead^[Row MOD ArrayMaxPlusOne];
      ColumnScan := ColumnHead^[Column MOD ArrayMaxPlusOne];
      WHILE (RowScan # NIL) AND (RowScan^.NextColEntry # NIL)
            AND (RowScan^.NextColEntry^.Column <= Column) DO
        RowScan := RowScan^.NextColEntry;
      END; (* WHILE *)
      IF (RowScan^.Row = Row) AND (RowScan^.Column = Column) THEN
        (* element exists *)
        RowScan^.Value := Value;
        IF Value = 0 THEN    (* value zero so element must be deleted *)
          Delete(RowScan, ColumnScan, M, Row, Column);
        END; (* IF *)
      ELSIF Value # 0 THEN     (* insert element *)
        Insert(Value, RowScan, ColumnScan, M, Row, Column);
      END; (* IF *)
```

```
      ELSIF Value # 0 THEN   (* insert new element *)
        IF RowHead = NIL THEN
          AllocateMinorHeader(M^.RowHeader[Row DIV ArrayMaxPlusOne]);
          RowScan := NIL;
        ELSE
          RowScan := RowHead^[Row MOD ArrayMaxPlusOne];
          WHILE (RowScan # NIL) AND (RowScan^.NextColEntry # NIL)
                AND (RowScan^.NextColEntry^.Column <= Column) DO
            RowScan := RowScan^.NextColEntry;
          END; (* WHILE *)
        END; (* IF *)
        IF ColumnHead = NIL THEN
          AllocateMinorHeader(M^.ColumnHeader[Column DIV ArrayMaxPlusOne]);
          ColumnScan := NIL;
        ELSE
          ColumnScan := ColumnHead^[Column MOD ArrayMaxPlusOne];
        END;
        Insert(Value, RowScan, ColumnScan, M, Row, Column);
      END; (* IF *)
    END; (* IF *)
  END ChangeElement;

END SparseMatrix.
```

We tested our ADT using the test program given previously and with a variety of data. The program performed as expected. Here is a simple output example.

```
              1         0         0         0         2
              0         3         0         0         0
              0         0         0         0         0
              4         5         0         0         6

              1         0         0         4
              0         3         0         5
              0         0         0         0
              0         0         0         0
              2         0         0         6

              1         0         0         1
              0         1         0         0
              0         0         1         0
              1         0         0         1

      1. Find A × B
      2. Find (A × B) × C
      3. Find B × C
      4. Find A × (B × C)
      5. Quit
      Enter your choice> 1
              5         0         0        16
              0         9         0        15
              0         0         0         0
             16        15         0        77
```

```
1. Find A × B
2. Find (A × B) × C
3. Find B × C
4. Find A × (B × C)
5. Quit
Enter your choice> 2
        21              0               0              21
        15              9               0              15
         0              0               0               0
        93             15               0              93
1. Find A × B
2. Find (A × B) × C
3. Find B × C
4. Find A × (B × C)
5. Quit
Enter your choice> 3
         5              0               0               5
         5              3               0               5
         0              0               0               0
         0              0               0               0
         8              0               0               8
1. Find A × B
2. Find (A × B) × C
3. Find B × C
4. Find A × (B × C)
5. Quit
Enter your choice> 4
        21              0               0              21
        15              9               0              15
         0              0               0               0
        93             15               0              93
1. Find A × B
2. Find (A × B) × C
3. Find B × C
4. Find A × (B × C)
5. Quit
Enter your choice> 5
```

Complete the Documentation The documentation internal to the code should be supplemented by a discussion of the design decisions made before the coding. The design decisions for the sparse matrix representation should be discussed in detail. The test program, including the ReadMatrix, DisplayMatrix, PrintMatrix, and MatrixMult procedures, should be included. The complete testing results should also be provided.

Maintenance If one needs to multiply matrices frequently, the external matrix multiply procedure given in the test program would be very inefficient. Every time an element is required, including each of the nonzero elements, a search is initiated starting from the matrix header node. If one designed a matrix multiply from inside the ADT, then the scan across the row of the left matrix and the scan down the column of the right matrix would proceed directly from the row and column header nodes and only nonzero nodes would be considered. The pseudocode for an internal matrix multiply is:

> MultMatrix
>   If matrix multiplication is possible
>   Initialize the result matrix
>   For each row of the left matrix
>   For each column of the right matrix
>   Set Sum to 0
>   Set LeftScan to first nonzero element of row in left matrix
>   Set RightScan to first nonzero element of column in right matrix
>   While LeftScan and RightScan are not nil
>   If LeftScan column number = RightScan row number
>   Set Sum to Sum plus product of LeftScan and RightScan entries
>   Advance both LeftScan and RightScan
>   Elsif LeftScan column number < RightScan row number
>   Advance LeftScan
>   Else
>   Advance RightScan
>   End if
>   End while
>   If Sum is not zero
>   Change element in the result matrix
>   End if
>   End for
>   End for
>   Else
>   Set result matrix to nil
>   End if
> End MultMatrix

The program code for an internal matrix multiplication follows directly from the pseudocode. We can add it to the SparseMatrix implementation module after adding the procedure header to the SparseMatrix definition module.

```
PROCEDURE MultMatrix (VAR Left, Right, Result: Matrix);
(* Multiply matrix Left times matrix Right to produce the Result
   matrix. Result is initialized and the appropriate entries made if
   matrix multiplication is possible (the number of columns of Left
   equals the number of rows of Right). If multiplication is not
   possible, Result is left undefined. *)
```

```
VAR Row, Column: CARDINAL;
    Sum: INTEGER;
    LeftScan, RightScan: ElementPtr;
BEGIN
  IF Left^.NbrCols = Right^.NbrRows THEN (* multiplication possible *)
    InitMatrix(Result, Left^.NbrRows, Right^.NbrCols);
    FOR Row := 0 TO Left^.NbrRows - 1 DO
      FOR Column := 0 TO Right^.NbrCols - 1 DO
        Sum := 0;
        LeftScan :=
            Left^.RowHeader[Row DIV ArrayMaxPlusOne]^
                    [Row MOD ArrayMaxPlusOne];
        RightScan :=
            Right^.ColumnHeader[Column DIV ArrayMaxPlusOne]^
                    [Column MOD ArrayMaxPlusOne];
        WHILE (LeftScan # NIL) AND (RightScan # NIL) DO
          IF (LeftScan^.Column = RightScan^.Row) THEN
            Sum := Sum + LeftScan^.Value * RightScan^.Value;
            LeftScan := LeftScan^.NextColEntry;
            RightScan := RightScan^.NextRowEntry;
          ELSIF LeftScan^.Column < RightScan^.Row THEN
            LeftScan := LeftScan^.NextColEntry;
          ELSE
            RightScan := RightScan^.NextRowEntry;
          END; (* IF *)
        END; (* WHILE *)
        IF Sum # 0 THEN
          ChangeElement(Result, Row, Column, Sum);
        END; (* IF *)
      END; (* FOR *)
    END; (* FOR *)
  ELSE
    Result := NIL;
  END; (* IF *)
END MultMatrix;
```

Similarly, in order to improve efficiency, we can include in the SparseMatrix module procedures for DisplayMatrix, and WriteMatrix.

Summary

Linear lists are one of the basic data structures in computer science. They are used in a variety of applications, and in implementing other ADTs. Basic operations on linear lists include list creation, inserting, deleting, searching, and counting the list elements.

Linear lists can be implemented statically using arrays and indices, or dynamically using dynamic structures and pointers. Linked lists can take several forms, such as circular lists, symmetric, or doubly linked lists; each implementation offers various advantages or disadvantages. Linear lists can also be used to implement various forms of arrays, including sparse arrays.

When using a dynamic implementation, it is necessary to obtain memory space as it is needed. This process, in turn, implies a method to allocate and free blocks of memory. The best-known memory allocation methods include first fit, best fit, next fit, worst fit, fixed size, and the buddy system.

■ *Exercises*

1. Write a procedure to reverse an entire linear list represented by a dynamic linked list, so that the first element becomes the last element, the second element becomes the next to last element, and so on.

2. Write a procedure to attach a linked list L2 to the end of another linked list L1.

3. Write a procedure that splits a linked list into two lists starting at a given element, which becomes the first element of the second list.

4. Modify the dynamic implementation of linear lists so that every list has a list header.

5. Write a multiplication procedure for the high-precision arithmetic application given in Section 5.2.

6. Write a multiplication procedure for the polynomial arithmetic application given in Section 5.2.

7. Given two linked lists $A = (a_1, a_2, \ldots, a_n)$ and $B = (b_1, b_2, \ldots, b_m)$, write a procedure to combine these two lists into a third list $C = (a_1, b_1, a_2, b_2, \ldots, a_m, b_m, \ldots, a_n)$ if $m \leq n$ or $C = (a_1, b_1, a_2, b_2, \ldots, a_n, b_n, \ldots, b_m)$ if $n \leq m$. This merge should be done using only the existing elements (no copy; change only the links).

8. Write a procedure to insert an element E *before* element P in the list, where only these pointers P and E are known. (Hint: A swap is needed.)

9. Write a procedure to free a circular list represented with a list header.

10. Write a procedure to divide a circular linked list into two circular lists from a given element E, which then becomes the first element of the new circular list.

11. Write a procedure to reverse a circular linked list, the first element becoming the last element, and so on.

12. For the multilinked lists seen in Section 5.4, define the necessary operations to display all records corresponding to:
    (a) Management and Boston
    (b) Management or Boston

13. For the representation of Iliffe shown in the text, establish a general formula giving the required total space as a function of the array rank, each dimension (D_i for $1 \leq i \leq n$), and the space necessary to store an element.

14. Instead of using Iliffe vectors, one can use the multiplication table method, where two vectors T and V represent an m × n matrix as shown in Figure 5-23. Compare this representation with the total space required and the access time to an element for Iliffe vectors. Is this representation acceptable? What are its principal characteristics?

15. A 300 × 300 matrix has at most five nonzero elements per row. Assume that one uses five words per node, except for the list headers that take up only one word. How much space is needed to represent this matrix using a linked representation?

16. Write a procedure that outputs the values of a sparse matrix represented with linked lists as in Figure 5-13.

17. Write procedures ALLOCATE and DEALLOCATE for cases in which memory blocks are all the same size.

18. If memory blocks have a header with the following fields:

    ```
    FreeBlock: BOOLEAN;
    Size: CARDINAL;
    Forward, Backward: POINTER TO Block;
    ```

    and if we use the following liberation algorithm:

    ```
    Q := FreeList^.Forward;
    P^.Forward := Q;
    P^.Backward := FreeList;
    Q^.Backward := P;
    FreeList^.Forward := P;
    P^.FreeBlock := TRUE;
    ```

    adjacent free blocks are not merged. Define an allocation algorithm that merges adjacent free blocks during the free list search. The free list header is a block of size 2. Its Forward pointer shows the first free block, while its Backward pointer indicates the last free block.

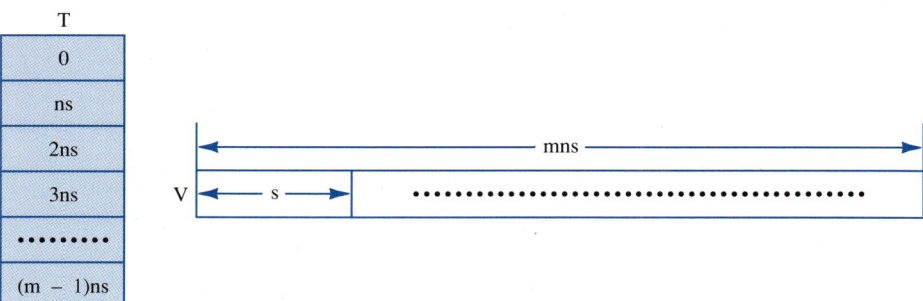

Figure 5-23
Multiplication Table Method

Programming Problems

19. Define and implement an ADT, based on linear lists, with the following operations:

    union of two lists
    intersection of two lists
    sum of two integer elements of lists
    advance a list element one position
    copy a list
    swap the mth and the nth elements of a list
    order a list so that its elements are in increasing order

*20. A character string is represented as a list of single characters. Write and test the following procedures to manipulate such strings.

    Convert(S, L)   convert the Modula-2 string S into the corresponding list L
    ConvertList(S, L)   convert the character list L into the Modula-2 string S
    Compare(L1, L2)   compare two character lists and return -1, 0, 1
                           if L1 is $<$, $=$, or $>$ than L2
    Substring(L, B, E)   create a list representing a substring of list L between
                           positions B and E
    Substitute(L1, B, N, L2)   replace n elements of L1 starting at B by the
                           elements of L2, which is not changed

21. Modify the high-precision arithmetic representation seen in the text to use symmetric lists with list headers. Write and test a procedure AddSameSign, which adds two long integers having the same sign.

22. Define a representation for polynomials with three variables, based on circular lists. Each element will represent a term. Write and test procedures for addition and multiplication of two polynomials.

*23. A survey done on a large number of persons has produced the following information.

    Sex: (1) male, (2) female
    Income: (1) less than $10,000 (2) $10,001–$25,000 (3) $25,001–$40,000
            (4) $40,001–$50,000 (5) more than $50,000
    Political party: (1) Democratic (2) Republican (3) other
    Age: (1) less than 20 (2) 20–29 (3) 30–39 (4) 40–49 (5) 50–59
         (6) 60 or more
    Smoking habits: (1) never (2) cigars only (3) pipe only
         (4) less than 1 pack a day (5) 1–2 packs a day
         (6) more than 2 packs a day

    Write a program to read in these data (each piece of data consisting of an identification followed by a five-digit number). Create an information structure in which each element has an identification and belongs to five lists, each list grouping people with the same answer to a given question.

Note: Problems marked with an asterisk (*) have a higher level of difficulty.

24. Write a procedure to manipulate the structure of problem 23. This procedure accepts a five-digit code representing answers to the survey's five questions, but where zero indicates that answers to that question are not considered. For instance, code 13041 represents non-smoking males in their forties with earnings of $25,001 to $40,000. The procedure will display the identification of all persons corresponding to the given code.

25. Implement and test the static implementation simulating pointers with indices in an array as introduced on page 137, at the end of the section Dynamic Implementation.

26. Add a procedure to the sparse matrix ADT that will generate a random sparse matrix with integer entries. The procedure parameters should include the number of rows, the number of columns, the decimal percentage of nonzero elements, the maximum entry value, and the minimum entry value.

27. Add a Boolean function to the sparse matrix ADT that will test the equality of two sparse matrices.

28. Use the procedures from problems 26 and 27 to generate an automated test program for the matrix multiply procedure that generates random matrices A, B, and C such that multiplication is possible and verifies that (MA × MB) × MC = MA × (MB × MC).

Stacks and Recursion

INTRODUCTION

Stacks are among the most useful tools of computer science. In this chapter we examine this simple, yet powerful, data structure, and show why it is so important in computer science. Many computer systems have machine instructions to manipulate hardware stacks. In programming language run time systems, stacks are used to implement procedure and function calls and to evaluate arithmetic expressions. After defining the stack by using abstraction, we will illustrate its use in some applications. Then two implementations of the stack ADT will be presented: a static implementation based on the record and array types, and a dynamic implementation based on pointers. Further applications of the stack ADT will be covered in a discussion of recursion and in a case study.

6.1 Abstraction: The Stack

A stack is a structured data type best defined by the rules governing the insertion and deletion of its elements. A stack is an ordered collection of elements; the only element that can be removed is the one that was inserted most recently. Such a structure is said to have a last-in/first-out (LIFO) behavior. More formally, a stack is a sequence of items into which new items may be inserted, and from which items may be removed, at an end called the top of the stack.

As an informal example of a stack, consider the stack of empty trays kept in a spring-loaded chamber in a cafeteria. Only the top tray is accessible; it can be seen, and can be removed. The second tray from the top is not accessible or visible. The only way to add a tray to the stack is by putting it on top of the stack. If there are no trays, then the stack is empty. Figure 6-1 illustrates a stack of names: Wilkinson is the only item that can be removed, in which case the top will move down one position. On the other hand, if we want to add element Muldoon to the stack of Figure 6-1, it will be added above Wilkinson and the top of the stack will move up one position. Such a stack of names could be used, for instance, as a re-hire list for employees temporarily laid off, where the rules call for re-hiring the employee most recently laid off.

The operation of adding an element to the stack is usually called Push, while the operation of removing one element from the stack is usually called Pop. Because of the first operation, stacks are sometimes called pushdown lists. Conceptually, there is no upper limit on the number of elements that can be stored on a stack, as our definition did not include any such limitation. We can therefore assume that elements can be pushed onto the stack as needed. However, in practice there will always exist a limit on implemented stacks, as computer memory is only finite. On the other hand a Pop operation applied to a stack containing one element results in an empty stack. Another Pop operation on that stack would be impossible, since there is no element to remove.

A stack is essentially a dynamic structure, continually changing as a result of insertions and removals. Figure 6-2 illustrates the dynamic changes in a stack of characters.

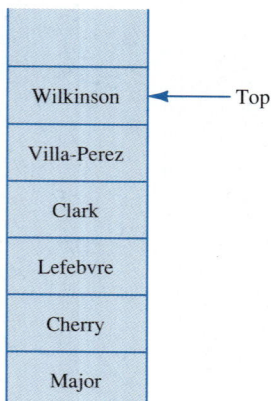

Figure 6-1
A Stack of Names

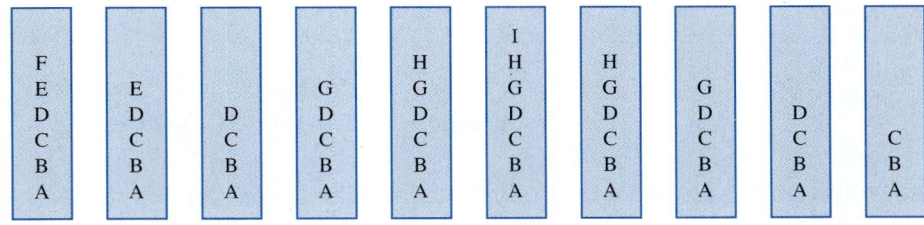

Figure 6-2
Dynamic Behavior
of Stack

The leftmost view of the stack was reached after a series of six Push operations:

Push(A); Push(B); Push(C); Push(D); Push(E); Push(F);

Then the stack is shown after each of the following operations:

Pop; Pop; Push(G); Push(H); Push(I); Pop; Pop; Pop; Pop;

All the elements of a stack should be of the same type (stack of dishes, stack of bricks, stack of books) as it is usually impossible to stack objects of different sizes and shapes. In fact, a stack is not really a single data type: we should define different stack types for different element types. Using a strongly typed language such as Modula-2 means that the elements must be of the same type. However, by using variant records, it is possible to have items of the same type, the variant record type, that contain different information. In this chapter we will concentrate on stacks of a fixed type and will define the stack ADT independently of the type of elements. This independence will be accomplished in our definition module by the import of type StackElementType from module StackElements, a technique we have already used in our List ADT.

```
DEFINITION MODULE StackElements;
TYPE StackElementType = ...   (* type of stack element *)
      .
      .
      .
END StackElements.
```

Note that such a definition module will require us to define the corresponding implementation module, even when it is empty, as in this case.

The following definition module defines our ADT Stack.

```
DEFINITION MODULE Stacks;
FROM StackElements IMPORT StackElementType;

TYPE Stack;

VAR StackError: BOOLEAN;   (* Status of last operation *)

PROCEDURE CreateStack( VAR S: Stack);
(* Create a stack
   post-condition: S' exists and is empty *)
```

```
PROCEDURE Push( VAR S: Stack; Elt: StackElementType);
(* Add element to stack
   pre-condition: S exists and is not full
   post-condition: if S is full then StackError' is TRUE,
                   else S' includes Elt as top element,
                   StackError' is FALSE *)

PROCEDURE Pop( VAR S: Stack; VAR Elt:StackElementType);
(* Retrieve top element from stack
   pre-condition: S exists and is not empty
   post-condition: if S is empty then StackError' is TRUE,
                   else Elt' = last stored element of S,
                   Elt is removed from S, and StackError' is FALSE *)

PROCEDURE Empty( S: Stack): BOOLEAN;
(* Check if stack is empty
   pre-condition: S exists
   post-condition: Empty is true if S has no element in it
                   Empty is false if S has elements in it *)

PROCEDURE StackTop( S: Stack; VAR Elt: StackElementType);
(* Return top of stack without changing stack
   pre-condition: S exists and is not empty
   post-condition: if S is empty then StackError' is TRUE
                   else Elt' = top of stack S, and StackError'
                   is FALSE *)

PROCEDURE DisposeStack( VAR S: Stack);
(* Dispose of the stack
   pre-condition: S exists
   post-condition: S' does not exist any more *)
END Stacks.
```

Besides the two basic operations Push and Pop, we need an operation to create a stack, an operation to check if a stack is empty, and an operation to dispose of a stack. An operation to examine the top element of the stack, StackTop, has been added, but it should be noted that it could be replaced by the two calls:

```
Pop(S, E);
Push(S, E);
```

An assignment operation has been omitted because the need to copy a whole stack seldom arises.

6.2 Applications

Infix to Postfix Conversion

Our first application will be a simple program to convert an arithmetic expression from infix notation to postfix notation. To simplify matters, variables will be represented by single uppercase letters and operations will be limited to $+, -, *, /$. The input expression will not contain any parentheses and will be terminated by a ';' sign. Since we want to be able to interpret infix expression A+B*C as A+(B*C) and translate it to the postfix expression ABC*+, we will give different precedences to operators. As you can see in this example, in a postfix expression an operator immediately follows its operands. Here are some examples of infix expressions and the postfix equivalent of each:

```
A+B              AB+
A+B*C            ABC*+
A+B-C/D*E+F      AB+CD/E*-F+
A+B+C+D+E        AB+C+D+E+
A+B*C/D-E        ABC*D/+E-
```

The overall translation algorithm is presented below. We have added to it a simple verification that the input expression is well formed: a counter, call it Rank, is incremented by 1 each time a variable is encountered in the input, and decremented by 1 each time an operator is found. Rank helps us check if the infix expression is well formed as a sequence of the form: operand {operator operand}.

```
Conversion
    Initialize precedence array
    Push $ on stack
    Read next character
    While next character not a semicolon
        While Precedence(next character) ≤ Precedence(top of stack)
            Pop and output character
        End while
        If Rank is 0 or 1
            Push next character
            Read next character
            Update Rank
        Else
            Set Valid to false
            Skip input to next semicolon
        End if
    End while
```

> While top of stack not $ and Valid
>   Pop and output character
> End while
>   Output postfix expression with validity message
> End Conversion

In order for the variables not to be kept on the stack, they are given the highest precedence. Then come * and /, followed by + and − with still lower precedence, and finally by $ with the lowest precedence. We use $ as a marker for the last element on the stack because it simplifies our testing of the stack top precedence; otherwise it would suffice to use ADT operation Empty.

Given the input expression:

A+B*C;

where ";" marks the expression end, our algorithm will produce the following stack and output:

```
Stack      Output
$
$A
$+         A
$+B        A
$+*        AB
$+*C       AB
$          ABC*+
```

One of the reasons why postfix notation is so widely used, is that it produces completely unambiguous expressions. Furthermore, a postfix expression can be evaluated very simply with the use of a stack. While scanning the expression from left to right, push all operands onto the stack and apply all operators to the two operands on top of the stack pushing the result back onto the stack. This is left as problem 10 in the Exercises section at the end of this chapter.

Another approach is used by compilers that have to generate the machine code to evaluate the arithmetic expression. Here again, the use of a stack makes it possible to obtain a simple solution. We will assume here that we have a very simple set of instructions: LOAD to load a value into a register, STORE to store a value from a register, and the four arithmetic operations ADD, SUB, MUL, DIV. For instance, with these instructions, the statement

A := B + C;

would be translated as:

```
LOAD   R0,B
ADD    R0,C
STORE  R0,A
```

Notice that we have used R0 (register zero) as an accumulator. In some instruction sets a built-in accumulator is assumed, and the instructions would be: LOAD B, ADD C, STORE A. We will also have to use intermediate variables to store intermediate results, and we will call them T1, T2, T3, and so forth. We will reuse temporary variables not in use anymore. Otherwise we would quickly run out of temporary variables. For a multiple register instruction set with available registers R1 through Rn, we could use registers instead of temporary memory locations provided that n registers are sufficient, but here we will keep to a simple and somewhat crude code generation solution. The overall simple code generation algorithm is the following.

> Generation
>   For all characters of postfix expression
>   If character is operand
>   Push it
>   Else
>   Pop right operand, if temporary variable decrement n
>   Pop left operand, if temporary variable decrement n
>   Print "LOAD R0," left operand
>   Case character of
>   +: Print "ADD R0," right operand
>   −: Print "SUB R0," right operand
>   *: Print "MUL R0," right operand
>   /: Print "DIV R0," right operand
>   End case
>   Increment n
>   Print "STORE R0,T" n
>   Push Tn
>   End if
>   End for
> End Generation

Applied to the postfix expression ABC*+ produced earlier by our conversion algorithm, this generation algorithm produces the following code that will evaluate the expression:

```
LOAD   R0,B
MUL    R0,C
STORE  R0,T1
LOAD   R0,A
ADD    R0,T1
STORE  R0,T1
```

It is a simple task to adapt the algorithm to the generation of instructions with a different syntax.

The following program (which reads a sequence of infix expressions, converts each to a postfix expression, and then generates the assembly code) illustrates the two algorithms. It imports the Stack type and stack operations CreateStack, Pop, Push and StackTop. In this example, StackElementType has been defined as being equal to CHAR. Procedure Conversion follows closely the pseudocode algorithm given above, with some additional input data validation provided by procedure Get. Procedure Generation reflects the pseudocode algorithm, but has been organized in a slightly different manner. Since we are dealing with a stack of characters, note the double popping needed for intermediate variables whose names take up two characters. Don't forget that popping the stack returns the elements in the reverse order they were pushed on it.

```
MODULE InfixToCode;
(* Conversion of an arithmetic expression from infix notation to
   postfix notation and generation of corresponding assembly code *)
FROM Stacks IMPORT Stack, Push, Pop, StackTop, CreateStack;
FROM InOut IMPORT Write, WriteString, WriteLn, Read, OpenOutput,
                  CloseOutput, OpenInput, CloseInput;
CONST Max = 100;
TYPE Index = [1..Max];
     Vector = ARRAY Index OF CHAR;
PROCEDURE Conversion(VAR Postfix: Vector; VAR N: CARDINAL; VAR Valid: BOOLEAN);
(* Conversion of an infix expression which is read in and terminated
   by a semicolon, into a postfix string. Valid is true if the
   expression is valid, false otherwise *)
VAR S: Stack;
    Ch, Next: CHAR;
    Out: CARDINAL;
    Rank: INTEGER;
    Precedence, Ranks: ARRAY [' '..'Z'] OF INTEGER;

  PROCEDURE Get(VAR C: CHAR);
  BEGIN      (* Skip spaces and read a valid character *)
    Read(C); Write(C);
    WHILE C = ' ' DO
      Read(C); Write(C);
    END;
    IF (C = '*') OR (C = '/') OR (C = '+') OR (C = '-')
        OR (C = ';') OR (C >= 'A') AND (C <= 'Z') THEN
      RETURN;
    ELSE     (* invalid character, skip to ; *)
      Valid := FALSE;
      WHILE C # ';' DO
        Read(C); Write(C);
      END;
    END;
  END Get;
```

```
BEGIN
  (* Initialize precedence and ranks table *)
  Precedence['*'] := 2; Ranks['*'] := -1;
  Precedence['/'] := 2; Ranks['/'] := -1;
  Precedence['+'] := 1; Ranks['+'] := -1;
  Precedence['-'] := 1; Ranks['-'] := -1;
  Precedence['$'] := 0; Ranks['$'] := 0;
  FOR Ch := 'A' TO 'Z' DO
    Precedence[Ch] := 3;
    Ranks[Ch] := 1;
  END; (* FOR *)
  CreateStack(S);
  Push(S, '$');      (* Marker to facilitate precedence comparisons *)
  Rank := 0;
  Out := 0;
  Valid := TRUE;
  WriteString("Give an expression ended by ;"); WriteLn;
  Get(Next);
  WHILE Next # ';' DO      (* Read and process input *)
    LOOP
      StackTop(S, Ch);
      IF Precedence[Next] > Precedence[Ch] THEN EXIT END; (* IF *)
      INC(Out);
      Pop(S, Ch);          (* Pop and output *)
      Postfix[Out] := Ch;
    END; (* LOOP *)
    IF (Rank = 0) OR (Rank = 1) THEN
      Push(S, Next);
      INC(Rank, Ranks[Next]);
      Get(Next);
    ELSE
      Valid := FALSE;
      WHILE Next # ';' DO
        Get(Next);
      END; (* WHILE *)
    END; (* IF *)
  END; (* WHILE *)
  LOOP
    StackTop(S, Ch);
    IF (Ch = '$') OR NOT Valid THEN EXIT END; (* IF *)
    (* Empty stack *)
    INC(Out);
    Pop(S, Ch);
    Postfix[Out] := Ch;
  END; (* LOOP *)
  N := Out;
  WriteString(" the expression: ");
  FOR Out := 1 TO N DO
    Write(Postfix[Out]);
  END; (* FOR *)
```

```
      IF Valid THEN
        WriteString(" is valid");
      ELSE
        WriteString(" is invalid");
      END; (* IF *)
      WriteLn;
    END Conversion;

    PROCEDURE Generation(Postfix: Vector; N: CARDINAL);
    (* Assembler code generation for evaluation of postfix expression *)
    VAR S: Stack;
        Index: CARDINAL;
        TempVar: INTEGER;    (* Because ORD returns an integer *)
        Next: CHAR;

        PROCEDURE PrintCode(VAR S: Stack; OpCode: ARRAY OF CHAR;
                            VAR VarNum: INTEGER);
        (* Actual code generation *)
        VAR Ch, CharLeft, CharRight, Left, Right: CHAR;
        BEGIN
          CharRight := ' ';
          CharLeft := ' ';
          Pop(S, Right);
          IF Right = 'T' THEN
            Pop(S, CharRight);
            DEC(VarNum);            (* Recuperate temporary variable *)
          END; (* IF *)
          Pop(S, Left);
          IF Left = 'T' THEN
            Pop(S, CharLeft);
            DEC(VarNum);            (* Recuperate temporary variable *)
          END; (* IF *)
          WriteString("LOAD R0,"); Write(Left); Write(CharLeft); WriteLn;
          WriteString(OpCode); Write(Right); Write(CharRight); WriteLn;
          INC(VarNum);
          Ch := CHR(ORD('0') + VarNum);
          WriteString("STORE R0,T"); Write(Ch); WriteLn;
          Push(S, Ch);
          Push(S, 'T');
        END PrintCode;

    BEGIN  (* Generation *)
      CreateStack(S);
      TempVar := 0;
      FOR Index := 1 TO N DO
        Next := Postfix[Index];
```

```
      CASE Next OF
        '+' : PrintCode(S, "ADD R0,", TempVar); |
        '-' : PrintCode(S, "SUB R0,", TempVar); |
        '*' : PrintCode(S, "MUL R0,", TempVar); |
        '/' : PrintCode(S, "DIV R0,", TempVar);
        ELSE Push(S, Next);
      END; (* CASE *)
    END; (* FOR *)
END Generation;

VAR Postfix: Vector;
    N: CARDINAL;
    Stop: CHAR;
    Good: BOOLEAN;

BEGIN    (* InfixToCode *)
  OpenOutput("out"); OpenInput("dat");
  REPEAT
    Conversion(Postfix, N, Good);
    IF Good THEN
      Generation(Postfix, N);
    END; (* IF *)
    Read(Stop); Write(Stop);
  UNTIL Stop = '%';
  CloseOutput; CloseInput;
END InfixToCode.
```

The program was run with the following test data set:

```
A+B*C;
A+B-C/D*E+F;
A+B+C+D+E;
A+B*C/D-E;
A;
ABC++;
A+-C;
A+B-f*H;
A+B^C;%
```

and produced the following output.

```
Give an expression ended by ;
A+B*C; the expression: ABC*+ is valid
LOAD   R0,B
MUL    R0,C
STORE  R0,T1
LOAD   R0,A
ADD    R0,T1
STORE  R0,T1
```

Chapter 6   Stacks and Recursion

```
Give an expression ended by ;
A+B-C/D*E+F; the expression: AB+CD/E*-F+ is valid
LOAD    R0,A
ADD     R0,B
STORE   R0,T1
LOAD    R0,C
DIV     R0,D
STORE   R0,T2
LOAD    R0,T2
MUL     R0,E
STORE   R0,T2
LOAD    R0,T1
SUB     R0,T2
STORE   R0,T1
LOAD    R0,T1
ADD     R0,F
STORE   R0,T1

Give an expression ended by ;
A+B+C+D+E; the expression: AB+C+D+E+ is valid
LOAD    R0,A
ADD     R0,B
STORE   R0,T1
LOAD    R0,T1
ADD     R0,C
STORE   R0,T1
LOAD    R0,T1
ADD     R0,D
STORE   R0,T1
LOAD    R0,T1
ADD     R0,E
STORE   R0,T1

Give an expression ended by ;
A+B*C/D-E; the expression: ABC*D/+E- is valid
LOAD    R0,B
MUL     R0,C
STORE   R0,T1
LOAD    R0,T1
DIV     R0,D
STORE   R0,T1
LOAD    R0,A
ADD     R0,T1
STORE   R0,T1
LOAD    R0,T1
SUB     R0,E
STORE   R0,T1

Give an expression ended by ;
A; the expression: A is valid
```

```
Give an expression ended by ;
ABC++; the expression: AB is invalid

Give an expression ended by ;
A+-C; the expression: A+ is invalid

Give an expression ended by ;
A+B-f*H; the expression: AB+ is invalid

Give an expression ended by ;
A+B^C; the expression: A is invalid
%
```

Solving a Maze

An old puzzle that has fascinated—and still fascinates—children and adults is how to find a path through a maze. A maze constructed for people can be made of carefully trimmed hedges or mirror walls, but if it is for rats in a psychology experiment, it might be made of small wooden panels. Here we consider only an abstract maze. We will develop a simple program for finding a path in a maze, with no claim to producing the shortest or most efficient path. We represent our maze in Figure 6-3.

Once we are in a given position, a move can be made in four directions: north, east, south, or west. Our strategy will be to try successively all directions to make a move. If we try a direction and the move is possible, we make the move. We also save the current position and the direction the move was made. We save this information in

Figure 6-3
A Maze

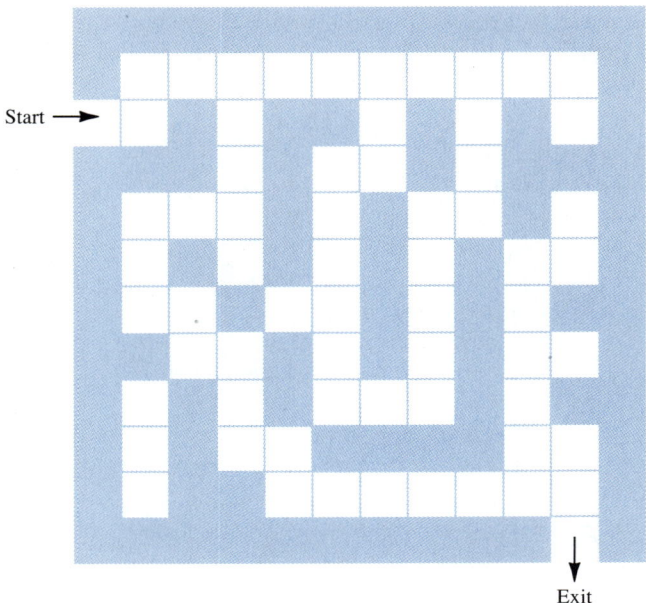

order to be able to come back to our starting point and try another direction, in case we follow a dead-end branch. This strategy of saving and restoring positions is a last-in/first-out strategy, so we will use a stack to save and restore positions.

This plan will not be sufficient, however, to prevent us from going down the same path twice, which would result in running around in circles. In order to avoid trying a path that was already tried, we will mark the paths we try so that we will not try them again, by changing a "white" square to a "visited" square. We will use our stack ADT as we did for the preceding application. However this time our StackElements definition module will look like this.

```
DEFINITION MODULE StackElements;

TYPE Direction = (North, East, South, West, None);
     StackElementType = RECORD
                          X, Y: CARDINAL;
                          dir: Direction;
                        END;
END StackElements.
```

StackElementType defines a position in the maze identified by its row coordinate and column coordinate and by the direction in which to make the next move. Note that we have to define the type Direction here as we use it in the declaration of StackElementType. Also we have added an extra direction, None, to indicate that all directions have been tried.

We will define a maze as a record with three fields: a starting position, an end position, and a matrix of "colors" (black, white, visited, and path). If we reach the end square, then the squares whose values have been saved on the stack will be marked as "path" squares so that the maze can be printed with the solution path clearly marked. The following pseudocode describes our path-searching algorithm.

> Solve maze
>   Initialize maze and stack
>   Push starting position on stack
>   While stack not empty
>   Pop current position from stack
>   While more moves are possible
>   Try a move to new position
>   If new position is end position
>   Push current position on stack
>   Push end position on stack
>   Record path from stack
>   Print maze and path
>   Halt

Figure 6-4
Input File for Maze

```
11  11
1 1 1 1 1 1 1 1 1 1 1 1
1 0 0 0 0 0 0 0 0 0 0 1
1 0 1 0 1 1 0 1 0 1 0 1
1 1 1 0 1 0 0 1 0 1 1 1
1 0 0 0 1 0 1 0 0 1 0 1
1 0 1 0 1 0 1 0 1 0 0 1
1 0 0 1 0 0 1 0 1 0 1 1
1 1 0 0 1 0 1 0 1 0 0 1
1 0 1 0 1 0 0 0 1 0 1 1
1 0 1 0 0 1 1 1 1 0 0 1
1 0 1 1 0 0 0 0 0 0 0 1
1 1 1 1 1 1 1 1 1 1 1 1
2 1 10 10
```

```
            Else
               Mark new position as visited
               Push current position on stack
               Set current position to new position
            End if
         End while
      End while
      Print ''impossible to find a path''
   End Solve maze
```

Our complete solution will include a procedure to initialize the maze: reading input from a file for maze dimensions, followed by the maze definition as a sequence of zeros (white) and ones (black), followed by the start and end positions (two pairs of coordinates), as shown in Figure 6-4.

It will also include a procedure to print the maze in its final form (showing walls as asterisks and the path as dots), a procedure to make a move from a given position going in a specified direction, and a procedure to copy the information in the stack into the maze matrix. This leads to the following program.

```
MODULE SolveMaze;
(* Program to read in a maze, find a path which goes from start
   position to end position, and print the path
                          P. Gabrini   August 1991 *)
FROM StackElements IMPORT StackElementType, Direction;
FROM Stacks IMPORT Stack, CreateStack, Empty, Pop, Push;
FROM InOut IMPORT OpenInput, CloseInput, ReadCard, WriteString, WriteLn;

CONST XMax = 15;
      YMax = 15;
```

```
TYPE PositionType = StackElementType;
     Color = (White, Black, Path, Visited);
     MazeType = RECORD
                   NumRows, NumCols: CARDINAL;
                   Board: ARRAY [0..XMax], [0..YMax] OF Color;
                   Start, End: PositionType;
                END;
VAR PathStack: Stack;
    Maze: MazeType;
    CurrentPosition, NewPosition: PositionType;
    Success: BOOLEAN;
PROCEDURE InitMaze(VAR M: MazeType);
(* Initialization of maze M by reading data from a file *)
VAR Row, Column, Box: CARDINAL;
BEGIN
  OpenInput("dat");
  WITH M DO
    ReadCard(NumRows);
    ReadCard(NumCols);
    FOR Row := 0 TO NumRows DO
      FOR Column := 0 TO NumCols DO
        ReadCard(Box);
        IF Box = 0 THEN
          Board[Row, Column] := White;
        ELSE
          Board[Row, Column] := Black;
        END; (* IF *)
      END; (* FOR *)
    END; (* FOR *)
    ReadCard(Start.x); ReadCard(Start.y);
    ReadCard(End.x); ReadCard(End.y);
    Start.dir := North;
    End.dir := North;
  END; (* WITH *)
END InitMaze;

PROCEDURE PrintMaze(M: MazeType);
VAR Row, Column: CARDINAL;
BEGIN
  WITH M DO
    FOR Row := 0 TO NumRows DO
      FOR Column := 0 TO NumCols DO
        IF Board[Row, Column] = Black THEN WriteString('*');
        ELSIF (Board[Row, Column] = White) OR (Board[Row, Column] = Visited) THEN
          WriteString(' ');
        ELSIF Board[Row, Column] = Path THEN WriteString('.');
        END; (* IF *)
      END; (* FOR *)
```

```
      WriteLn;
    END; (* FOR *)
  END; (* WITH *)
END PrintMaze;

PROCEDURE RecordPath(VAR path: Stack; VAR M: MazeType);
(* Transcribes the stacked path to the maze board *)
VAR Position: PositionType;
BEGIN
  WHILE NOT Empty(path) DO
    Pop(path, Position);
    M.Board[Position.x, Position.y] := Path;
  END; (* WHILE *)
END RecordPath;

PROCEDURE TryMove(VAR CurrentPosition, NewPosition: PositionType);
(* Make a move from current position *)
VAR X, Y: CARDINAL;
BEGIN
  X := CurrentPosition.x;
  Y := CurrentPosition.y;
  CASE CurrentPosition.dir OF
    North: NewPosition.x := X - 1;
           NewPosition.y := Y;
  | East:  NewPosition.x := X;
           NewPosition.y := Y + 1;
  | South: NewPosition.x := X + 1;
           NewPosition.y := Y;
  | West:  NewPosition.x := X;
           NewPosition.y := Y - 1;
  END; (* CASE *)
  NewPosition.dir := North;
  INC(CurrentPosition.dir);
END TryMove;

BEGIN
  Success := FALSE;
  CreateStack(PathStack);
  InitMaze(Maze);
  Push(PathStack, Maze.Start);
  WHILE NOT Empty(PathStack) DO
    Pop(PathStack, CurrentPosition);
    WHILE CurrentPosition.dir # None DO
      TryMove(CurrentPosition, NewPosition);
      IF (NewPosition.x = Maze.End.x) AND (NewPosition.y = Maze.End.y) THEN
        Push(PathStack, CurrentPosition);
        Push(PathStack, NewPosition);
        RecordPath(PathStack, Maze);
        PrintMaze(Maze);
        Success := TRUE;
```

```
        ELSIF Maze.Board[NewPosition.x, NewPosition.y] = White THEN
          Maze.Board[NewPosition.x, NewPosition.y] := Visited;
          Push(PathStack, CurrentPosition);
          CurrentPosition := NewPosition;
        END; (* IF *)
      END; (* WHILE *)
  END; (* WHILE *)
  IF NOT Success THEN
    WriteString("Impossible to get out of maze"); WriteLn;
  END; (* IF *)
END SolveMaze.
```

To compile the program we must compile first:

the StackElements definition module
the Stacks definition module

The compilations must take place in that order, since module Stacks imports from module StackElements. Before we can run the SolveMaze program we also must compile the StackElements implementation module. (It is an empty module, but the loader will be looking for it.) Then we must compile the Stacks implementation module. Execution of the SolveMaze program with the input of Figure 6-4 produces the result shown in Figure 6-5.

Note that the path found is not the shortest possible path, as the last three moves can be replaced by a single move. However, our strategy always tries North first. If we tried East first we would end up with a result that would be shorter for this particular maze.

Figure 6-5
Solved Maze

```
* * * * * * * * * * *
*  .  .  .           *
* . * . * *    *   *   *
* * * . *      *   * * *
* .  .  . *  *      *   *
* . *    *  *   *     *
* .  . *    *   *  * *
* *  .  . *  *  *     *
*   *  . *      *   * *
*   * .  . * * *  .  .  *
*   * *  .  .  .  .  .  .  *
* * * * * * * * * * *
```

6.3 Implementation

Before we can execute our application programs, we must define our implementation for stacks. We will consider two implementations here: a static implementation using arrays and a dynamic implementation using linear lists.

Static Implementation

Our first implementation will use a record containing a scalar value for the stack top index and an array of elements. The representation must define a maximum size for the stack, which will be imported from module Elements, as it is best defined by the user. This, in turn, requires us to check if the stack is full before pushing an element on it. To do that, we have defined a function procedure local to the implementation module, Full. The following implementation represents our solution.

```
IMPLEMENTATION MODULE Stacks;
FROM StackElements IMPORT Max, StackElementType;
FROM Storage IMPORT ALLOCATE, DEALLOCATE;

TYPE Stack = POINTER TO StackType; (* opaque types must be pointers *)
     StackType = RECORD
                   Top: [0..Max];
                   Data: ARRAY [1..Max] OF StackElementType;
                 END;

PROCEDURE CreateStack( VAR S: Stack);
(* Create a stack *)
BEGIN
  ALLOCATE(S, SIZE(StackType));
  S^.Top := 0;
END CreateStack;

PROCEDURE Full( S: Stack): BOOLEAN;
(* Internal procedure to check if stack is full *)
BEGIN
  RETURN S^.Top = Max;
END Full;

PROCEDURE Push( VAR S: Stack; Elt:StackElementType);
(* Add element to stack *)
BEGIN
  IF Full(S) THEN
    StackError := TRUE;
  ELSE
    INC(S^.Top);
    S^.Data[S^.Top] := Elt;
    StackError := FALSE;
  END; (* IF *)
END Push;
```

```
PROCEDURE Empty( S: Stack): BOOLEAN;
(* Check if stack is empty *)
BEGIN
  RETURN S^.Top = 0;
END Empty;

PROCEDURE Pop( VAR S: Stack; VAR Elt:StackElementType);
(* Retrieve top element from stack *)
BEGIN
  IF Empty(S) THEN
    StackError := TRUE;
  ELSE
    Elt := S^.Data[S^.Top];
    DEC(S^.Top);
    StackError := FALSE;
  END; (* IF *)
END Pop;

PROCEDURE StackTop( S: Stack; VAR Elt: StackElementType);
(* Return top of stack without changing stack *)
BEGIN
  IF Empty(S) THEN
    StackError := TRUE;
  ELSE
    Elt := S^.Data[S^.Top];
    StackError := FALSE;
  END; (* IF *)
END StackTop;

PROCEDURE DisposeStack( VAR S: Stack);
BEGIN
  DEALLOCATE(S, SIZE(StackType));
END DisposeStack;

END Stacks.
```

The use of an opaque type forces us to use a pointer and consequently a call to ALLOCATE for the creation of a stack, and a call to DEALLOCATE to dispose of the stack. This is the price we have to pay for enforcing the information hiding principle. Both our application programs execute correctly with this implementation.

Procedure CreateStack allocates space for our representation and sets the top index to zero, indicating an empty stack. Function procedure Full just checks if the top index has reached the array limit. Procedure Push checks to see if the stack is full, in which case the error flag is set. Otherwise the top index is incremented and the value is copied into the new stack top. Function procedure Empty checks to see if the top index is zero. Procedure Pop checks to see if the stack is empty. If it is, the error flag is set; otherwise the stack top element is copied, and the top index is decremented. Procedure StackTop is very similar to procedure Pop, except that the top index is not changed. Procedure DisposeStack just deallocates the memory space previously allocated for the stack representation.

The time complexity of all these operations is O(1), as they all execute in constant time. In other words, the number of statements executed is fixed, whatever the number of elements in the stack. The space complexity of the algorithms is bound to the memory size necessary to represent a stack: there will be space for Max elements and the top index.

Dynamic Implementation

Our second implementation will be based on a linear list. We define a stack node as a record comprising an element and a pointer to the next node. All the operations are defined accordingly. Push and Pop dynamically modify the stack structure by adding or deleting elements through the use of procedures ALLOCATE and DEALLOCATE imported from module Storage. Note that in this implementation we do not need a Full function, as memory space is allocated as needed and each call to ALLOCATE will detect whether or not the allocation is successful. The following implementation module illustrates our solution.

```
IMPLEMENTATION MODULE Stacks;
(* Dynamic implementation of stacks *)
FROM StackElements IMPORT StackElementType;
FROM Storage IMPORT ALLOCATE, DEALLOCATE;

TYPE Stack = POINTER TO StackNode;
     StackPtr = Stack;
     StackNode = RECORD
                     element: StackElementType;
                     next: StackPtr;
                 END;

PROCEDURE CreateStack(VAR S: Stack);
(* Create a stack *)
BEGIN
  S := NIL;
END CreateStack;

PROCEDURE Empty(S: Stack): BOOLEAN;
(* Check if stack is empty *)
BEGIN
  RETURN S = NIL;
END Empty;

PROCEDURE Push(VAR S: Stack; Elt: StackElementType);
(* Add element to stack *)
VAR P: StackPtr;
BEGIN
  ALLOCATE(P, SIZE(StackNode));    (* create new element *)
  IF P # NIL THEN
    P^.next := S;
    P^.element := Elt;
    S := P;
    StackError := FALSE;
```

```
    ELSE      (* memory full *)
      StackError := TRUE;
    END; (* IF *)
  END Push;

  PROCEDURE Pop(VAR S: Stack; VAR Elt: StackElementType);
  (* Retrieve top element from stack *)
  VAR P: StackPtr;
  BEGIN
    IF Empty(S) THEN    (* nothing to pop *)
      StackError := TRUE;
    ELSE
      P := S;
      Elt := S^.element;
      S := S^.next;
      DEALLOCATE(P, SIZE(StackNode));  (* dispose of old element *)
      StackError := FALSE;
    END; (* IF *)
  END Pop;

  PROCEDURE StackTop(S: Stack; VAR Elt: StackElementType);
  (* Return top of stack without changing stack *)
  BEGIN
    IF Empty(S) THEN    (* nothing *)
      StackError := TRUE;
    ELSE
      Elt := S^.element;
      StackError := FALSE;
    END; (* IF *)
  END StackTop;

  PROCEDURE DisposeStack(VAR S: Stack);
  (* Dispose of the stack *)
  VAR P: StackPtr;
  BEGIN
    WHILE S # NIL DO
      P := S;
      S := S^.next;
      DEALLOCATE(P, SIZE(StackNode));
    END; (* WHILE *)
  END DisposeStack;

END Stacks.
```

Our two application programs executed correctly after we substituted this dynamic implementation for the static implementation given previously. The only compilation needed was that of the Stacks implementation module and then the application program needed to be re-linked. This is the beauty of the modular approach: one component of a large program can be changed without starting a ripple of changes throughout the rest of the program.

Procedure CreateStack just sets the stack pointer to NIL to indicate an empty stack. Procedure Empty checks to see whether or not the stack pointer is NIL. Procedure Push first allocates space for a new element; if this allocation is not successful, the memory is full and the error flag is set. Otherwise the element value is copied into the new element, the element is linked to the top element pointed to by the stack pointer, and the stack pointer is made to point to the new element. Procedure Pop checks to see if the stack is empty. If it is, the error flag is set; otherwise the top stack element is copied and deallocated, and the stack pointer is set to point to the next element. Procedure StackTop is similar to the Pop procedure except for the removal of the top element. Procedure DisposeStack traverses the list of the stack elements and deallocates them as it encounters them.

The time complexity of all ADT operations except DisposeStack is $O(1)$, as the number of statements executed for each operation is fixed. The complexity of DisposeStack is $O(n)$, as it is necessary to repeat the deallocation for each element in the stack. The space complexity is variable and depends on the number of elements in the stack. Clearly we need space for all the nodes in the stack list, that is, n records of type StackNode, whose size is based on the element type size.

6.4 Generic ADTs

When we developed our ADTs for lists and stacks, we have had to bind the ADT element type to the ADT because of the strong type checking of Modula-2. In the applications we have seen in Chapter 5 and in this chapter, we dealt with lists of integers, lists of polynomial elements, stacks of characters, and stacks of records, and each time we had to use a different ADT, specifically designed for the element type.

The ADT element type can be declared directly in the ADT definition module. When this is the case, this definition module must be modified whenever the element type is changed. However, in our presentation of ADTs, you might have noted that element types were declared in a user-defined module (ListElements for ListADT, and StackElements for Stacks), and you might have wondered about these modules. By putting the element type declaration in an external module, changing the type does not require us to modify the ADT definition and implementation modules, but only to recompile them with the newly recompiled Elements module.

If we want stacks of characters we must first define StackElementType as equal to CHAR, then compile the StackElements definition module, the StackElements implementation module, the Stacks definition module, and the Stacks implementation module. Now, if we want stacks of records we must first define StackElementType as equal to the desired record type, then compile the StackElements definition module, the StackElements implementation module, the Stacks definition module, and the Stacks implementation module. This has a "ripple effect" of requiring recompilation of every module that imports from Stacks. This does not seem to be an ideal solution, but Modula-2 strong type checking makes it imperative to have the ADT bound to a specific type of element.

Another alternative would be using an opaque type for the data item imported from StackElements. This would have the advantage of localizing changes to the StackElements implementation module when the type is changed. However, since the type is now dynamic, there would have to be operations to create and dispose of a stack item that would be used by the stack operations Push, Pop, and Dispose.

The ideal solution would be for us to be able to define a Stack ADT that can push and pop any type of element. This is what is called a *generic ADT*, or an ADT that can operate on any type of element. In order to define such a generic ADT, we must circumvent Modula-2 strong type checking. This is possible in Modula-2 using either variant records or the so-called low level facilities, but it will be **at the expense of making the programs less portable** and **particularly vulnerable to programming errors.** We will illustrate here a simple technique for defining generic ADTs.

We can use Modula-2's low-level facilities to implement generic ADTs. In Modula-2, the pseudo-module SYSTEM provides several types and procedures dealing with machine-specific characteristics. Main memory is taken to be an array of bytes or words, depending on the addressing scheme of the processor used. Types BYTE and WORD may be imported from SYSTEM, and in Modula-2, arrays of BYTE (or WORD in some cases) are compatible with any type. We can define our element type as an array of BYTE and use open array type parameters for our stacks procedures: this will make our ADT able to deal with all kinds of types.

```
DEFINITION MODULE GenericStacks;
FROM SYSTEM IMPORT BYTE;

CONST Max = 32;           (* Size of stack elements *)

VAR StackError: BOOLEAN;

TYPE Stack;

PROCEDURE CreateStack( VAR S: Stack);
(* Create a stack *)

PROCEDURE Push( VAR S: Stack; Elt: ARRAY OF BYTE);
(* Add element to stack *)

PROCEDURE Pop( VAR S: Stack; VAR Elt: ARRAY OF BYTE);
(* Retrieve top element from stack *)

PROCEDURE Empty( S: Stack): BOOLEAN;
(* Check if stack is empty *)

PROCEDURE StackTop( S: Stack; VAR Elt: ARRAY OF BYTE);
(* Return top of stack without changing stack *)

PROCEDURE DisposeStack( VAR S: Stack);
(* Dispose of the stack *)

END GenericStacks.
```

The GenericStacks definition module is not very different from our earlier Stacks definition module. Note the definition of the maximum size, Max, of the elements to be stacked, the import of type BYTE, and the use of parameter type ARRAY OF

BYTE for the Push, Pop, and StackTop procedures. The GenericStacks implementation module is not very different from our earlier solutions.

```
IMPLEMENTATION MODULE GenericStacks;
FROM Storage IMPORT ALLOCATE, DEALLOCATE;
FROM SYSTEM IMPORT BYTE;

CONST Last = 50;           (* Size of stack *)

TYPE Stack = POINTER TO StackType; (* opaque types must be pointers *)
     StackElementType = ARRAY [1..Max] OF BYTE;
     StackType = RECORD
                   Top: [0..Last];
                   Data: ARRAY [1..Last] OF StackElementType;
                 END;
     .
     .
     .

PROCEDURE Push( VAR S: Stack; Elt: ARRAY OF BYTE);
VAR i: CARDINAL;
BEGIN
  IF Full(S) OR (HIGH(Elt) >= Max) THEN
    StackError := TRUE;
  ELSE
    INC(S^.Top);
    FOR i := 0 TO HIGH(Elt) DO     (* copy element onto stack *)
      S^.Data[S^.Top][i+1] := Elt[i];
    END; (* FOR *)
    StackError := FALSE;
  END; (* IF *)
END Push;
     .
     .
     .

PROCEDURE Pop( VAR S: Stack; VAR Elt: ARRAY OF BYTE);
VAR i: CARDINAL;
BEGIN
  IF Empty(S) OR (HIGH(Elt) >= Max) THEN
    StackError := TRUE;
  ELSE
    FOR i := 0 TO HIGH(Elt) DO     (* copy stack top into element *)
      Elt[i] := S^.Data[S^.Top][i+1];
    END; (* FOR *)
    DEC(S^.Top);
    StackError := FALSE;
  END; (* IF *)
END Pop;
```

```
PROCEDURE StackTop( S: Stack; VAR Elt: ARRAY OF BYTE);
VAR i: CARDINAL;
BEGIN
  IF Empty(S) OR (HIGH(Elt) >= Max) THEN
    StackError := TRUE;
  ELSE
    FOR i := 0 TO HIGH(Elt) DO        (* copy stack top into element *)
      Elt[i] := S^.Data[S^.Top][i+1];
    END; (* FOR *)
    StackError := FALSE;
  END; (* IF *)
END StackTop;



END GenericStacks.
```

Besides the use of an array of bytes for the element type, the only differences appear in procedures Push, Pop, and StackTop, which must now copy the entire array of bytes. With this implementation, it is possible to use the stack for elements of any type whose size is not larger than Max bytes. Without changing anything in our implementation or even having to recompile any part of it, we can use GenericStacks with elements of the following types:

```
ARRAY [1..Max] OF CHAR
LONGCARD
LONGINT
CARDINAL
INTEGER
REAL
LONGREAL
CHAR
RECORD
    Name: ARRAY[1..10] OF CHAR;
    Salary: LONGCARD;
    AverageHours: REAL;
END
```

If you use GenericStacks for values of a single type, the implementation will work very well, even though you will lose some protection because of the lack of checking you have introduced. You need to remember that if you make a mistake and use an element of a different type, the compiler will not tell you, as everything is compatible with ARRAY OF BYTE. The problem with such an implementation of generic stacks is that it makes it possible to stack objects of different types: this is a practice to **avoid absolutely,** but **the system will not prevent you from doing it!**

In practice, the careful programmer must define a complete package for handling generic types in a safe way. This safe approach can be achieved by designing all the tools needed to handle a full data type: declaration of a specific type that is able to

6.4 Generic ADTs

represent all generic types, and a number of procedures to handle objects of the various generic types. For instance,* two opaque types GenericType and Object could be defined along with the following procedures:

```
PROCEDURE AllocateGeneric(VAR Type: GenericType; TypeName: ARRAY OF CHAR;
                         Allocate: AllocateProc; Free:    FreeProc;
                         Equal: EqualProc; Compare: CompareProc; Copy: CopyProc);
(* Define a new generic type *)

PROCEDURE FreeGeneric(VAR Type: GenericType);
(* Dispose of a generic type *)

PROCEDURE Allocate(VAR X: Object; Type: GenericType);
(* Allocate an object of a generic type *)

PROCEDURE Free(VAR X: Object; Type: GenericType);
(* Free an object of a generic type *)

PROCEDURE EqualObjects(X, Y: Object; Type: GenericType): BOOLEAN;
(* Compare two objects of a generic type for equality *)

PROCEDURE CompareObjects(X, Y: Object; Type: GenericType): Relation;
(* Compare two objects of a generic type *)

PROCEDURE AssignObject(VAR X: Object; Y: Object; Type: GenericType);
(* Perform assignment X := Y for two objects of a generic type *)

PROCEDURE GetValue(X: Object; VAR Y: ARRAY OF BYTE; Type: GenericType);
(* Copy value of generic X into ordinary variable Y *)

PROCEDURE PutValue(Y: ARRAY OF BYTE; VAR X: Object; Type: GenericType);
(* Copy value of ordinary variable Y into generic X *)
```

A generic type could be defined as:

```
GenericType = POINTER TO RECORD
                  Name:     ARRAY [0..MaxLength] OF CHAR;
                  Size:     SizeType;
                  Valid:    ValidationMark;
                  Rep:      RepresentationType;
                  Alloc:    AllocateProc;
                  Free:     FreeProc;
                  Equal:    EqualProc;
                  Compare:  CompareProc;
                  Copy:     CopyProc;
              END;
```

where AllocateProc, FreeProc, EqualProc, CompareProc, and CopyProc are procedure types using type ADDRESS imported from module SYSTEM. This small example,

---

*Private communication from Luc Lavoie.

which has been greatly reduced in size and does not show local procedures to check type compatibility and other handling tools, shows nevertheless that the development of a true generic type facility in Modula-2 may involve a lot of work.

6.5 Recursion

The divide-and-conquer problem-solving technique is applicable if the original problem can be subdivided into smaller subproblems. This technique is used in the structural design step of the problem-solving method we use in the case studies (see Appendix A). A special case of the divide-and-conquer technique occurs when the subproblems are just smaller versions of the original problem. In that case, the problem can be solved using a method known as recursion.

Recursion is based on solving the original problem by solving smaller versions of the same problem. However, for recursion to be successful, we must eventually reach a smallest version, called the base case, that can be solved directly. Pseudocode for a recursive solution will have the following aspect:

> If the problem is a base case then
>   Solve the base case directly
> Else
>   Solve the general case using solutions of simpler cases
> End if

Let's take a few examples to illustrate this.

A mathematical definition of the factorial function of a nonnegative integer is:

```
0! = 1                      (base case)
n! = n(n - 1)!  for n > 0   (general case)
```

A Modula-2 function procedure to compute factorials follows directly from the definition:

```
PROCEDURE Factorial( K: CARDINAL ): CARDINAL;
(* Recursive computation of K! *)
BEGIN
  IF K = 0 THEN
    RETURN 1;
  ELSE
    RETURN K * Factorial( K - 1 );
  END; (* IF *)
END Factorial;
```

Function Factorial calls itself: it is a recursive function procedure. The base case is for K = 0.

For our second example, suppose that we have to develop a procedure to print an integer using only procedure Write (which outputs one character). We know that we can isolate the last digit of the integer by using MOD and eliminate it by using DIV. However this gives the digits in the wrong order to print them. We can use recursion to overcome this difficulty, as we have already done in the ConvertNumber procedure in the fraction case study of Chapter 4.

```
PROCEDURE PrintNum( N: INTEGER);
(* Print an integer using Write *)

  PROCEDURE DigitChar( Digit: INTEGER ): CHAR;
  BEGIN
    RETURN CHR(Digit + ORD('0'));
  END DigitChar;

BEGIN
  IF N < 10 THEN                  (* Base case *)
    Write(DigitChar(N));
  ELSE
    PrintNum(N DIV 10);           (* most significant digits *)
    Write(DigitChar(N MOD 10));(* least significant digit *)
  END; (* IF *)
END PrintNum;
```

The procedure will repeatedly call itself without printing anything until it reaches the base case. Unlike the case of an iterative control structure, where execution of the loop body must be completed before starting the next one, in a recursive control structure, a new recursive cycle may begin before completion of the preceding cycle. You should trace the procedure with a value like 1234 to check that 1234 is actually printed.

We could have also solved the problem of the reversed digits by pushing them onto a stack, and then popping them off in the correct order. As we will see shortly, recursion is implemented using a stack and our recursive solution takes advantage of this "built-in" stack.

Our third example will look at one of the oldest algorithms, Euclid's algorithm, for finding the greatest common divisor of two integers A and B. We have already seen an iterative version of this algorithm in the case study of Chapter 4. This algorithm is based on the fact that the GCD of A and B is the same as the GCD of B and R, where R is the remainder of the division of A by B. The following function implements Euclid's algorithm.

```
PROCEDURE GCD(X, Y: CARDINAL): CARDINAL;
(* Compute greatest common divisor of X and Y *)
VAR Remainder, Z: CARDINAL;
BEGIN
  IF X < Y THEN     (* Exchange X and Y *)
    Z := X;
    X := Y;
    Y := Z;
  END; (* IF *)
```

```
            Remainder := X MOD Y;
            IF Remainder = 0 THEN
              RETURN Y;
            ELSE
              RETURN GCD(Y, Remainder);
            END; (* IF *)
          END GCD;
```

Our algorithm assumes that the first parameter X is greater than the second parameter Y, and we have made sure of this by adding statements to exchange the values of X and Y if X is less than Y.

To complete our presentation of recursion we will include the solution of the Towers of Hanoi puzzle. This puzzle has three towers (or pegs) and a set of disks of increasing size that can be slid onto the pegs. The initial puzzle position for four disks is shown in Figure 6-6.

The goal of the game is to move all the disks from the peg labeled A (start) to the peg labeled C (destination) while respecting the two following rules:

- Only one disk can be moved at a time.
- It is forbidden to place a larger disk on top of a smaller disk.

We can easily find a recursive solution for n disks by assuming we know how to solve the puzzle for (n − 1) disks:

Move (n − 1) disks from start to intermediate.
Move the largest disk from start to destination.
Move (n − 1) disks from intermediate to destination.

The base case will be when we are left with one disk, which we move directly from the start to the destination. The following procedure solves the Towers of Hanoi puzzle.

```
PROCEDURE Hanoi(N: CARDINAL; Start,Intermediate,Destination: CHAR);
(* Solve Towers of Hanoi puzzle recursively for N disks *)
  PROCEDURE PrintMove(Disk: CARDINAL; From, To: CHAR);
  BEGIN
    WriteString("Move disk"); WriteCard(Disk, 2);
    WriteString(" from peg ");
    Write(From); WriteString(" to peg "); Write(To); WriteLn;
  END PrintMove;

BEGIN
  IF N = 1 THEN
    PrintMove(1, Start, Destination);
  ELSE
    Hanoi(N-1, Start, Destination, Intermediate);
    PrintMove(N, Start, Destination);
    Hanoi(N-1, Intermediate, Start, Destination);
  END; (* IF *)
END Hanoi;
```

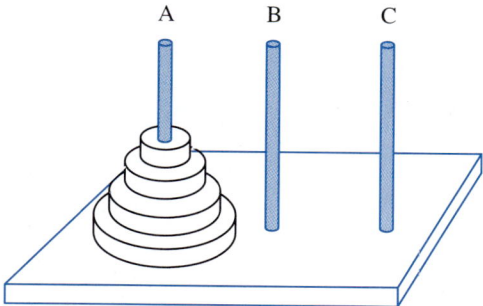

Figure 6-6
Towers of Hanoi Puzzle

The call Hanoi(4, 'A', 'B', 'C') generates the following.

```
Move disk   1 from peg A to peg B
Move disk   2 from peg A to peg C
Move disk   1 from peg B to peg C
Move disk   3 from peg A to peg B
Move disk   1 from peg C to peg A
Move disk   2 from peg C to peg B
Move disk   1 from peg A to peg B
Move disk   4 from peg A to peg C
Move disk   1 from peg B to peg C
Move disk   2 from peg B to peg A
Move disk   1 from peg C to peg A
Move disk   3 from peg B to peg C
Move disk   1 from peg A to peg B
Move disk   2 from peg A to peg C
Move disk   1 from peg B to peg C
```

Implementing Recursion

Each time a procedure is invoked, a separate procedure activation record is created that contains the procedure's local environment (local variables and parameters) as well as the instruction currently being executed. When a procedure is invoked recursively, several activation records are created, each describing a distinct invocation. Within each activation record, the identifier names are exactly the same. However, only the last activation record is accessible and, therefore, there is no ambiguity.

Procedure calls are accomplished by using a stack to keep the successive activation records, and this stack is maintained by the Modula-2 system in a manner invisible to the user. Each time a recursive call is made, a new activation record is created and pushed on the stack. When the procedure returns to its caller, the stack is popped; the previous activation record then becomes the current stack top used for referencing variables.

Figure 6-7 illustrates the stack states during execution of the call Factorial(4). For reasons of space, the figure shows only the top two activation records in the stack.

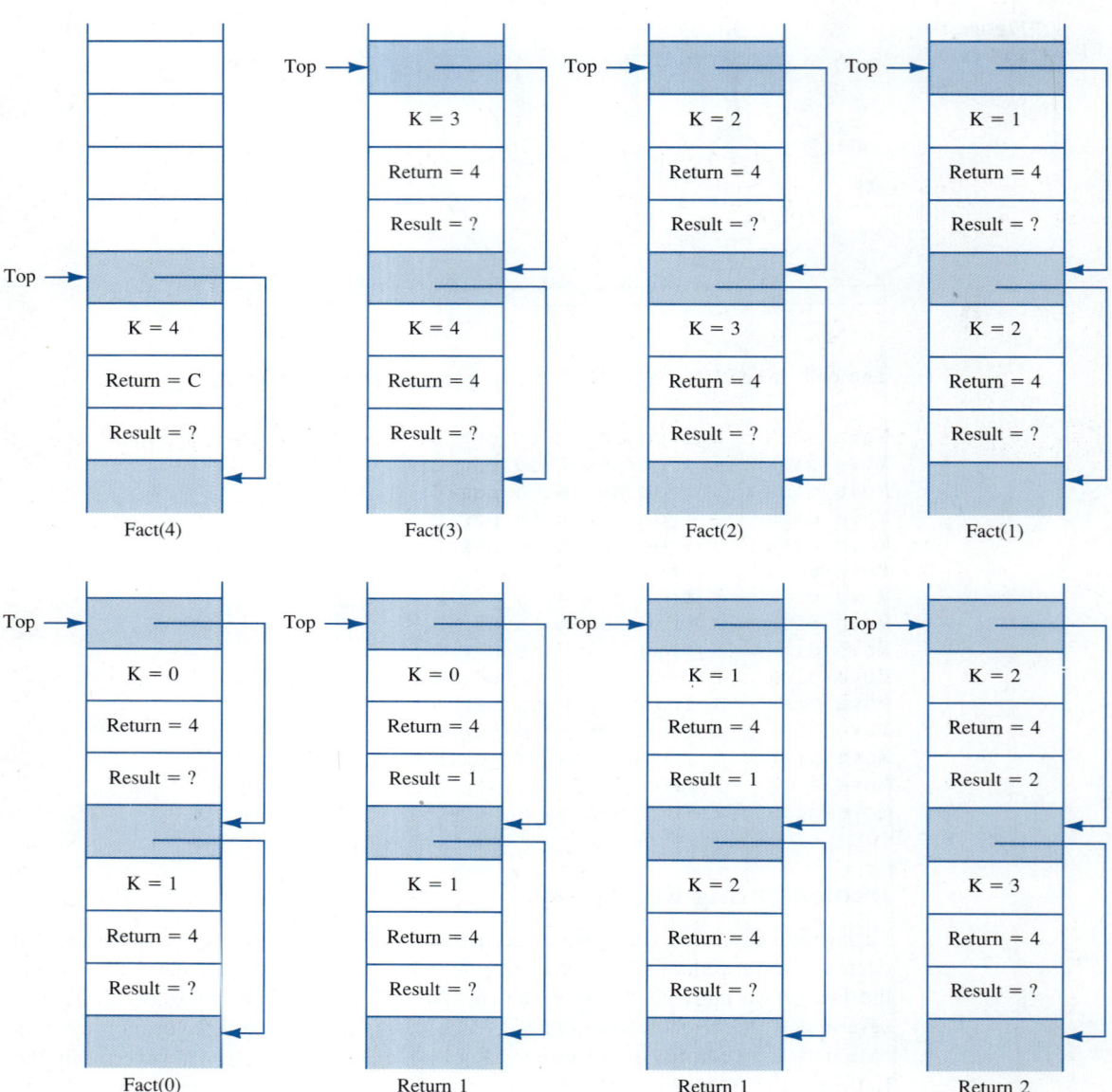

Figure 6-7 Stack During Execution of Factorial(4)

In Figure 6-7 we have represented an activation record with four elements: a pointer to the previous stack frame (needed for popping the stack, as stack frames do not necessarily have the same size), the value of the parameter K, the return address (using statement numbers from the definition of Factorial), and the value of the returned results. A question mark indicates an undefined value. Return address C represents the address following the original call. If our procedure had had more parameters and some local variables, the stack frame would have included them.

Figure 6-7
Continued

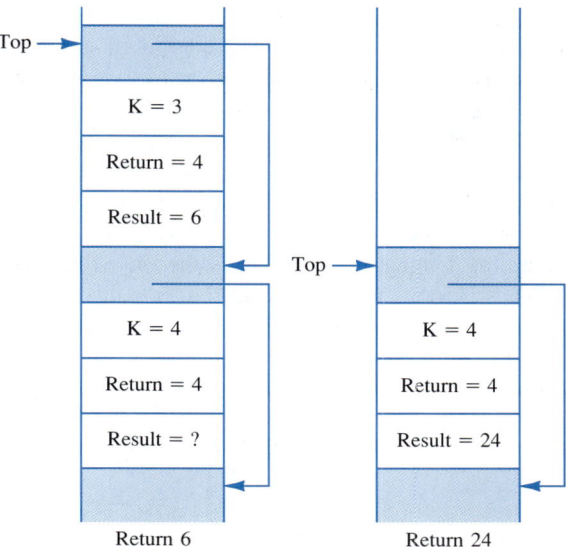

The actual stack model for activation records is slightly more complex than we have shown here. Since we are dealing with recursion, the environment of the call and the environment of declaration are the same, so we have only shown a single link back to the caller. It is possible for the environment of the call and the environment of declaration to be different, as in the case when a nested procedure calls a more global procedure. To handle this situation we need two links: a static link to the environment of declaration and a dynamic link to the environment of the call. The chain of static links is followed when searching for the most local declaration of a variable. The dynamic link is used when an activation record is popped off the stack.

The use of a stack is the most common approach to implement recursion. (By comparison, programming language systems that do not use a stack, like FORTRAN or COBOL, do not allow recursion.) The simplicity of the stack makes it possible to solve the recursion problem in an elegant manner. However, there is a price to pay, and recursive solutions might turn out to be slower than iterative solutions. It should be noted that a stack is not sufficient to allow functions to *first-class citizens*. For a function to be a first-class citizen, we must have both an instruction pointer (ip) and an environment pointer (ep). This ip/ep pair must be retained even after the procedure is exited, therefore a stack cannot be used. We would need a *heap* structure to implement functions as first class citizens.

Recursion and Iteration

In general, a recursive version of a program will execute less efficiently with respect to time and memory space than will a nonrecursive version. The explanation for this difference can be found in the overhead involved in a recursive call—in stacking a number of variables and values, and in unstacking them on a return. This is not to say that recursion should be dropped entirely for reasons of efficiency because some recursive solutions are the most natural and logical way of solving a problem. The example of the Towers of Hanoi would be difficult to solve were it not for recursion. When we talk about efficiency, we have to remember that we have a conflict between machine efficiency and programmer efficiency. If a recursive solution is the simplest and most straightforward way of solving a given problem, it is usually not worth the effort to find a nonrecursive solution that is more "efficient."

In a limited way, recursion can be viewed as a special case of iteration. In fact, in some programming languages recursion is the only repetitive control structure. For example, a WHILE loop can be replaced by an equivalent recursive procedure:

```
WHILE condition DO           PROCEDURE While;
   BodyOfLoop;               BEGIN
END; (* WHILE *)                IF condition THEN
                                   BodyOfLoop;
                                   While;
                                END; (* IF *)
                             END While;
```

A call to While will have the same effect as executing the WHILE loop. That is, each call to While when the condition is true will execute BodyOfLoop once before invoking While recursively. When the condition becomes false, the current activation of the procedure as well as the previous activations will return because the recursive call is at the very end of the procedure.

Thus every loop can be replaced by recursion, but the reverse is not true: not all recursion can be replaced by a loop.

The additional storage and execution time required to allocate and release activation records for recursive calls can sometimes be saved if recursion can be simply replaced by iteration. Our earlier Factorial example had only a sequence of multiplications expressed as:

$$n! = n * (n - 1) * (n - 2) * \cdots * 2 * 1 \qquad \text{for } n > 0$$

It can be rewritten using only iteration:

```
PROCEDURE IterFactorial(N: CARDINAL): CARDINAL;
VAR i, Fact: CARDINAL;
BEGIN
  Fact := 1;
  FOR i := 1 TO N DO
    Fact := Fact * i;
  END; (* FOR *)
  RETURN Fact;
END IterFactorial;
```

The recursive solution is very much like the mathematical recursive definition of factorial; however, the iterative solution is more efficient, even though it requires the use of two local variables. The Factorial example might not be a very convincing example for efficiency, though. The solution uses CARDINALs and most systems will not be able to compute more than 8! (40320) or 12! even on larger computers. In that case, it is probably more efficient to keep factorial values in a table.

Our point here is that whenever it is possible, it is more "machine efficient" to have an iterative version of a solution than a recursive version, but, as we will see, it sometimes takes a considerable effort to transform a fully recursive solution like the Towers of Hanoi solution into a nonrecursive solution. Before looking into those transformations from recursive to iterative, let's take another example illustrating recursion vs. iteration. Consider the Fibonacci sequence of integers:

0, 1, 1, 2, 3, 5, 8, 13, 21, 34, 55, 89, . . .

where each number is the sum of the two preceding numbers. Fibonacci numbers of order 2 are formally defined by:

$$F(n) = n \quad \text{if } n = 0 \text{ or } n = 1$$
$$F(n) = F(n-2) + F(n-1) \quad \text{if } n \geq 2$$

From this definition it is easy to write a recursive procedure to compute Fibonacci numbers.

```
PROCEDURE Fibonacci(N : CARDINAL): CARDINAL;
(* Compute Nth Fibonacci number *)
BEGIN
  IF N <= 1 THEN
    RETURN N;
  ELSE
    RETURN Fibonacci(N-2) + Fibonacci(N-1);
  END; (* IF *)
END Fibonacci;
```

In order to get a better idea of the way the procedure works, consider what it does if called by Fibonacci(5). Figure 6-8 illustrates the series of recursive calls generated.

Even though this computation is simple, we notice that Fibonacci(3) was computed twice, Fibonacci(2) was computed three times, Fibonacci(1) was computed five times, and Fibonacci(0) was computed three times. Clearly, this is inefficient, especially when N becomes large. For instance, the call Fibonacci(25) will generate 242,784 recursive calls! It can be shown that the number of additions to compute Fibonacci(N) is equal to Fibonacci(N + 1) − 1. From this we can establish that the complexity of this algorithm is $O(c^N)$ where c is a constant greater than 1. Obviously the complexity of this algorithm is exponential! Since the rule used to compute the Fibonacci numbers is so simple (a number is the sum of its two predecessors), we can easily write an equivalent iterative solution.

Figure 6-8
Recursive Calls

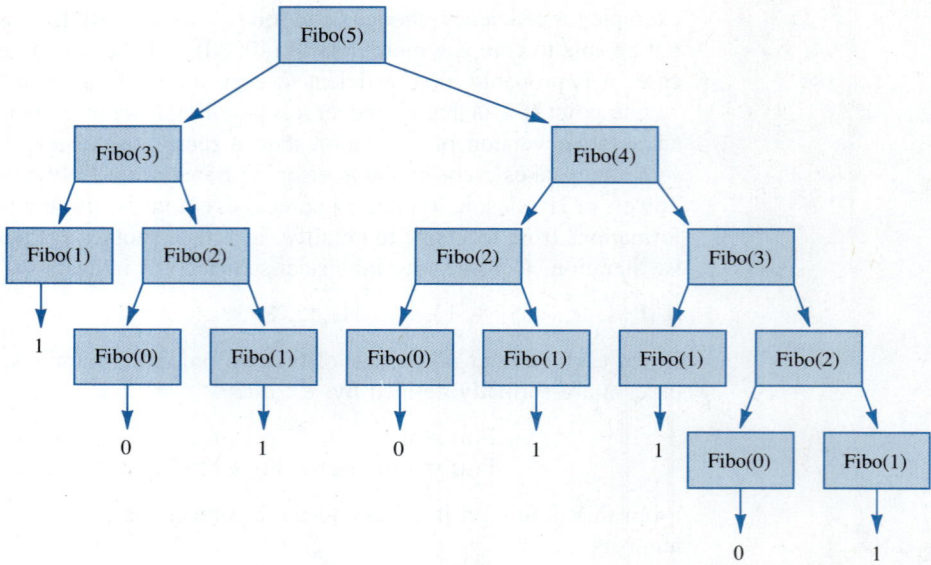

```
PROCEDURE IterFibonacci(N: CARDINAL): CARDINAL;
VAR Previous, Current, New, I: CARDINAL;
BEGIN
  IF N = 0 THEN
    RETURN 0;
  ELSIF N = 1 THEN
    RETURN 1;
  ELSE
    Previous := 0;
    Current := 1;
    FOR I := 2 TO N DO
      New := Previous + Current;
      Previous := Current;
      Current := New;
    END; (* FOR *)
    RETURN New;
  END; (* IF *)
END IterFibonacci;
```

We now have an algorithm with one single loop whose complexity is O(N), a much better result. For instance, the call IterFibonacci(25) will loop 24 times, which should be contrasted with the 242,784 recursive calls generated by the call Fibonacci(25). But this iterative procedure is larger than the previous one, requires local variables, and its correspondence to the mathematical definition is not immediately clear.

In our recursive Fibonacci calculation, recursion is not the culprit, but rather the way recursion was applied, as the recurrence relation

$$F(N) = F(N-2) + F(N-1)$$

is only intended to define the mathematical property of a sequence and is not necessarily an appropriate computational method. Consider the following functions:

```
PROCEDURE Fibo(Previous, Current, Count, N: CARDINAL): CARDINAL;
BEGIN
  IF Count = N THEN
    RETURN Current;
  ELSE
    RETURN Fibo(Current, Previous + Current, Count + 1, N);
  END; (* IF *)
END Fibo;
PROCEDURE FastFibo(N: CARDINAL): CARDINAL;
BEGIN
  IF N = 0 THEN
    RETURN 0;
  ELSE
    RETURN Fibo(1,1,1, N);
  END; (* IF *)
END FastFibo;
```

The function FastFibo handles the special case of $N = 0$ and provides the parameters necessary to activate the recursive function Fibo. Since Count is incremented for each recursive call and recursion stops when Count reaches N, there will be N recursive calls for this recursive version of the Fibonacci function.

Converting Tail Recursion to Iteration

It is sometimes easy to convert a recursive solution to an equivalent nonrecursive solution. There is a special case of recursion called tail recursion, where the last executed statement in a recursive procedure is the recursive call. This special case is easy to convert to an iterative equivalent. We can observe that once the recursive call is done, the procedure does nothing but return. The recursive call is therefore like a repetition of the procedure body with different values for parameters and local variables. The recursive call can therefore be replaced by assignment statements and iteration.

Among our previous examples, While is tail recursive, and we have already seen that it can be transformed into an iterative statement. PrintNum is not tail recursive, as the recursive call is not the last statement of the procedure. GCD is tail recursive, whereas Hanoi, with two recursive calls, is certainly not tail recursive. At first it may appear that Factorial is tail recursive, but actually it is not, since we do the multiplication operation on the way out of recursion. The difference is that the recursive call is part of a more complex expression and not the last statement or an expression that only involves the recursive call.

Let's convert GCD to an iterative equivalent. We know that it is tail recursive and that we can replace the recursive call by iteration.

```
PROCEDURE GCD(X, Y: CARDINAL): CARDINAL;
(* Compute greatest common divisor of X and Y *)
VAR Remainder, Z: CARDINAL;
BEGIN
  IF X < Y THEN     (* Exchange X and Y *)
    Z := X;
    X := Y;
    Y := Z;
  END; (* IF *)
  Remainder := X MOD Y;
  IF Remainder = 0 THEN
    RETURN Y;
  ELSE
    RETURN GCD(Y, Remainder);
  END; (* IF *)
END GCD;
```

The tail recursive call wants to reapply the same algorithm not to X and Y, but now to Y and Remainder. Therefore, before looping we just have to modify X and Y so that they have those values.

```
PROCEDURE IterGCD(X, Y: INTEGER): INTEGER;
VAR Remainder, Z: INTEGER;
BEGIN
  IF X < Y THEN
    Z := X;
    X := Y;
    Y := Z;
  END; (* IF *)
  LOOP
    Remainder := X MOD Y;
    IF Remainder = 0 THEN
      RETURN Y;
    ELSE
      X := Y;
      Y := Remainder;
    END; (* IF *)
  END; (* LOOP *)
END IterGCD;
```

Note that we have moved the start of the LOOP statement below the first statement of the procedure. We move the beginning of the LOOP because we know the new values are in order, and we can now avoid testing the order of X and Y once we start looping. Whenever we end up with a tail recursive solution, we should transform it to an iterative solution using similar methods. As you can see, such a transformation does not involve too much effort.

Converting General Recursion to Iteration

To construct a nonrecursive solution to a problem that is most naturally solved recursively will require a substantial effort. If a program is run very frequently, then an increase in execution efficiency will justify the cost involved in the transformation of the program to a nonrecursive version. In such cases, the best way to do the transformation is not by attempting to create a nonrecursive solution from the problem specifications, but rather by first simulating recursion using a stack, and then through various refinements, eliminating all stacks and variables that are not needed.

We should keep in mind that when we introduce modifications to a program, we also run the risk of introducing unexpected errors. Also, if the final nonrecursive version still requires a stack, it is very probable that the original, recursive version is as fast as the nonrecursive one, particularly when we use a stack ADT rather than a "built-in" stack structure. Sometimes, we have no choice if we have to use a language like FORTRAN or COBOL or use an assembler that does not support recursion.

In order to deduce what should be done to simulate a recursive call, let's take a look at what happens when such a call is made, and also when the called procedure returns to the caller. When a procedure is called, the following sequence occurs:

1. Arguments are evaluated and passed.
2. Local variables are allocated and may be initialized.
3. The return address is saved and control is transferred to the called procedure.

When a called procedure returns to its caller, the following events occur:

1. The procedure's data area (local variables and copies of arguments) is freed.
2. A branch is executed to the return address.

The same actions occur whether or not the procedure call is recursive, since each recursive call is treated as a normal procedure call and creates an activation record for the procedure. On returning to the caller, the act of freeing the data area also restores the caller's data area.

In order to simulate recursive calls, we can establish the following replacement rules.

Replace a recursive call with the following steps:

1. Save the return address, local variables, and parameters.
2. Set the local variables and parameters to their new values.
3. Transfer to the beginning of the procedure.

At each return point, add the following:

1. Restore the return address, local variables, and parameters.
2. Return to the proper position in the recursive procedure.

We can apply these conversion steps to produce an iterative solution for the Towers of Hanoi problem. Recall our recursive solution in pseudocode:

```
Hanoi(N, Start, Intermediate, Destination)
   If N = 1
      Move disk 1 from Start to Destination
   Else
      Hanoi(N−1, Start, Destination, Intermediate) { Call #1 }
      Move disk N from Start to Destination
      Hanoi(N−1, Intermediate, Start, Destination) { Call #2 }
   End if
End Hanoi
```

We will replace Call #1 and Call #2 by applying our first rule, namely, replacing the recursive call with saving the return location and parameters (we have no local variables), setting the parameters to their new values, and transferring control to the beginning of the procedure. Each time there is a return we have to check if there are any saved values; if so, we restore the saved values and transfer control to the proper location in the procedure. This leads us to the following pseudocode solution.

```
IterHanoi(N, Start, Intermediate, Destination) { version #1 }
   Call: If N = 1
            Print move disk 1 from Start to Destination
         Else
            { actions to replace Call #1 }
            Save return to after Call #1, N, Start, Intermediate, Destination
            Set parameters to N−1, Start, Destination, Intermediate
            Go to Call
         End if
   Return: If there are saved values on the stack
              Restore return location, N, Start, Intermediate, Destination
              If return is after Call #1
                 Print move disk N from Start to Destination
                 { actions to replace Call #2 }
                 Save return to after Call #2, Start, Intermediate, Destination
                 Set parameters to N−1, Intermediate, Start, Destination
                 Go to Call
              Else { return after Call #2 }
                 Go to Return
              End if
           End if
End IterHanoi { version #1 }
```

To facilitate the transfer of control, we have introduced a Go to statement and labels into our pseudocode. However, programming with Go to's, which are supported in languages like FORTRAN and BASIC, is not recommended and this facility is not even available in Modula-2. To eliminate our uses of Go to, we must try to simplify and restructure this iterative solution. First we can do some simplification, since there is no code, other than a return, after Call #2. Studying this last solution brings to light the fact that for our Call #2 we save the return to after Call #2 along with the values of the parameters. When this call is completed, these values will be restored and then a Go to Return will be executed. If the stack is empty, that completes the procedure; otherwise other values will be restored, destroying those just restored without using them. Saving them can be eliminated, and then only one return address will be used, return to after Call #1. This simplifies our next version.

```
IterHanoi(N, Start, Intermediate, Destination) { version #2 }
   Call : If N = 1
            Print move disk 1 from Start to Destination
         Else
            Save N, Start, Intermediate, Destination
            Set parameters to N−1, Start, Destination, Intermediate
            Go to Call { Call #1 }
         End if
         If there are saved values on the stack
            Restore N, Start, Intermediate, Destination
            Print move disk N from Start to Destination
            Set parameters to N−1, Intermediate, Start, Destination
            Go to Call { Call #2 }
         End if
End IterHanoi   { version #2 }
```

This version still has two Go to statements that branch to the start of the procedure. The first If with its Go to can be replaced by a WHILE statement. The second Go to can be replaced by an outer WHILE statement controlled by a local Boolean variable set to true when the stack is empty. We obtain our final pseudocode version.

```
IterHanoi(N, Start, Intermediate, Destination) { version #3 }
   Set Finished to False
   While not Finished
      While N > 1
         Save N, Start, Intermediate, Destination
         Set parameters to N−1, Start, Destination, Intermediate
      End while
      Print move disk 1 from Start to Destination
      If there are saved values on the stack
         Restore N, Start, Intermediate, Destination
         Print move disk N from Start to Destination
         Set parameters to N−1, Intermediate, Start, Destination
```

> Else
>   Set Finished to True
> End if
> End while
> End IterHanoi { version #3 }

Our implementation in Modula-2 follows from this last pseudocode version. We must define StackElementType in the StackElements module as an activation record (a cardinal and three characters) and we must recompile the ADT for Stacks.

```
TYPE StackElementType = RECORD
                          Card: CARDINAL;
                          Char1, Char2, Char3: CHAR;
                        END;
PROCEDURE Save(S: Stack; N: CARDINAL; T1, T2, T3: CHAR);
VAR ActRec: StackElementType;
BEGIN
  WITH ActRec DO
    Card := N;
    Char1 := T1;
    Char2 := T2;
    Char3 := T3;
  END; (* WITH *)
  Push(S, ActRec);
END Save;

PROCEDURE Restore(S: Stack; VAR N: CARDINAL; VAR T1, T2, T3: CHAR);
VAR ActRec: StackElementType;
BEGIN
  Pop(S, ActRec);
  WITH ActRec DO
    N := Card;
    T1 := Char1;
    T2 := Char2;
    T3 := Char3;
  END; (* WITH *)
END Restore;

PROCEDURE IterHanoi(N: CARDINAL; Start, Intermediate,
                    Destination: CHAR);
(* Iterative version of towers of Hanoi puzzle solution *)
VAR S: Stack;
    Finished: BOOLEAN;

PROCEDURE PrintMove(Disk: CARDINAL; From, To: CHAR);
BEGIN
  WriteString("Move disk"); WriteCard(Disk, 2);
  WriteString(" from peg ");
  Write(From); WriteString(" to peg "); Write(To); WriteLn;
END PrintMove;
```

```
PROCEDURE SetPar(M: CARDINAL; A, B, C: CHAR);
BEGIN
  N := M;
  Start := A;
  Intermediate := B;
  Destination := C;
END SetPar;

BEGIN
  CreateStack(S);
  Finished := FALSE;
  WHILE NOT Finished DO
    WHILE N > 1 DO
      Save(S, N, Start, Intermediate, Destination);
      SetPar(N-1, Start, Destination, Intermediate);
    END; (* WHILE *)
    PrintMove(1, Start, Destination);
    IF NOT Empty(S) THEN
      Restore(S, N, Start, Intermediate, Destination);
      PrintMove(N, Start, Destination);
      SetPar(N-1, Intermediate, Start, Destination);
    ELSE
      Finished := TRUE;
    END; (* IF *)
  END; (* WHILE *)
END IterHanoi;
```

This iterative version of the program is very probably more efficient than the recursive version. However, the amount of work involved in the transformation from recursive to iterative was substantial and always has the risk of introducing new errors in the code. This version of our program is well designed, nicely modularized into procedures, and easy to understand. However, the modularization into procedures is not as efficient as we might wish, since we still have the overhead of procedure calls, the same sort of overhead that makes the simpler, recursive version inefficient. If we eliminate the procedure calls and simply duplicate the procedure body directly in the IterHanoi procedure, then our solution will be time efficient but not very space efficient because of the duplicated code.

There is no absolute rule to help us choose between a recursive and a nonrecursive algorithm. Many recursive procedures are more concise and easier to read and maintain than the corresponding nonrecursive procedures. The trade-off is between the concise legibility of recursion versus the machine efficiency of iteration. If both recursive and nonrecursive solutions have similar code complexity, as we saw with the factorial and Fibonacci problems, then the nonrecursive algorithm would be preferred because of its better efficiency. If, on the other hand, the nonrecursive version leads to a more complex algorithm or data structures, then recursion should be preferred.

6.6 Case Study: A Nonrecursive Version of Quicksort

The Quicksort algorithm we presented in Chapter 3 is a recursive algorithm. In order to make it more efficient or to implement it in a language that does not support recursion, we will design an iterative version of that same algorithm. The original Quicksort algorithm is recursive, which, in general, means it is easy for the programmer to implement, but hard on the machine during execution.

Design

Definition of the Problem Write a procedure to perform a Quicksort on an array of records without using recursion. Our nonrecursive procedure should be functionally equivalent to the recursive version given in Section 3.4. We will still sort an open array of records and use parameters to indicate the sorting order and the comparison procedure for array elements.

Design of a Solution Figure 6-9 shows a structure chart for our original algorithm.

Instead of blindly applying the conversion method we have just seen, we will instead try to reason our way out of the recursive solution. This will show that a good understanding of a recursive algorithm is sometimes sufficient to convert it. In Quicksort, recursion is used to sort the left and right partitions, provided that they have more than one element. Recursion helps us remember postponed obligations: when the program is sorting the left partition, it has postponed the obligation to sort the right partition. In particular, to sort the right partition, the program must know the values of the boundary of the partition, given by variables Lindex and Right in our recursive algorithm. When the program is recursively sorting the left partition, the values of parameter Right and local variable Lindex may change according to local conditions, but when the sort of the left partition is completed, the values of Lindex and Right are restored and the sort of the right partition can proceed. We depend on recursion and the scoping rules to retain these original values so that processing can pick up where it left off. If we don't use recursion, then it becomes the programmer's responsibility to retain the necessary values for postponed obligations. In the case of Quicksort, the necessary values are the partition boundaries for all partitions waiting to be sorted.

In the discussion of the Quicksort algorithm it was noted that we would have fewer recursive calls if we postponed sorting the larger partition and immediately started processing the smaller partition. The number of recursive calls is reduced because it is easier to remember the boundaries of a few large partitions than to remember the boundaries of many more smaller partitions. Since it will be the programmer's obligation to remember the boundaries of postponed partitions in our nonrecursive (or iterative) Quicksort, we will adopt this strategy to minimize the number of things to be remembered. Figure 6-10 gives our structure chart for the iterative Quicksort.

Figure 6-9
Structure Chart for Recursive Quicksort

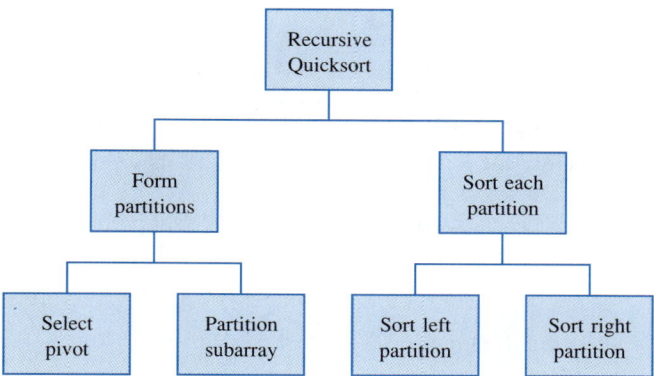

Refine the Solution Initially, the entire array is considered a partition, so we save its bounds as a partition to be sorted. Repeatedly, we get the partition boundaries for the last postponed partition and process it. To do that, we form partitions of this subarray just as in the recursive version. We save the boundaries of the larger partition and process the smaller partition. Eventually the smaller partition will be empty or contain just a single element, in which case it will require no further processing. Then we get the partition boundaries for the last postponed partition and process it. This sequence continues until there are no more postponed obligations and the sort is completed.

We now form a high-level pseudocode solution that we will refine after discussing the choice of data structures.

Figure 6-10
Structure Chart for Iterative Quicksort

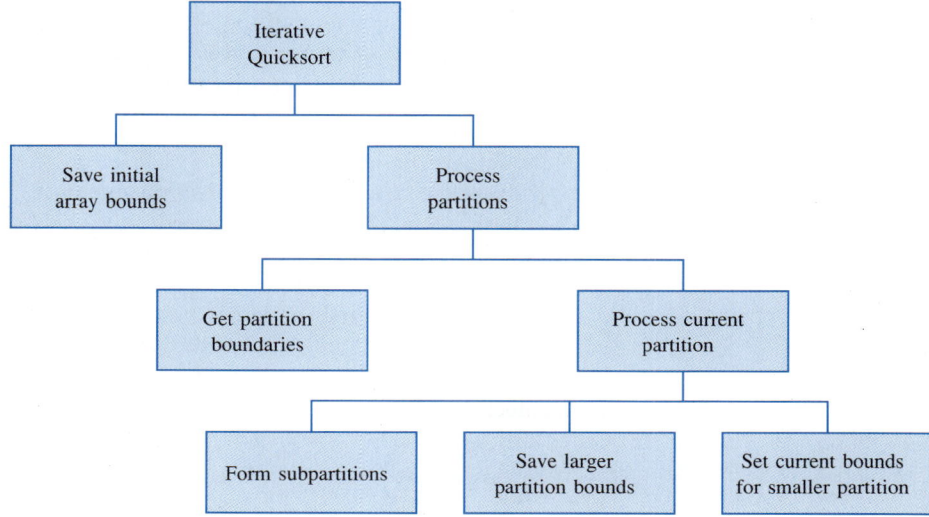

> Iterative Quicksort
>   Save the array bounds
>   While there are partitions to be processed
>   Get the current partition boundaries
>   While the current partition has more than one element
>   Form the subpartitions
>   Save the boundaries of the larger subpartition
>   Set the current partition to the smaller subpartition
>   End while
>   End while
> End Iterative Quicksort

We must now decide on a data structure for saving and getting the boundaries of a partition waiting to be sorted. For each partition, we must save a lower bound and an upper bound, so a record structure is appropriate. Since we must save the boundaries for many partitions waiting to be sorted and retrieve them in the reverse order of their saving, we will use a stack of record structures. This selection comes as no surprise because we already know from Section 6.5 that a stack is needed for converting from recursion to iteration, even though we have not followed the method that was shown in that section.

Using the language of stack processing, we refine the pseudocode of procedure Quicksort to operate on an open array with bounds Left and Right.

> Iterative Quicksort
>   Create stack
>   Push Left and Right on stack
>   While the stack is not empty
>   Pop the current values for Left and Right off the stack
>   While Left < Right { the partition has more than one element }
>   Form the left partition from Left to Rindex and
>   the right partition from Lindex to Right
>
>   If the left partition is larger
>   If the left partition has more than one element
>   Push bounds Left and Rindex onto the stack
>   End if
>   Set Left to Lindex { prepare to process the right partition }
>   Else { the right partition is larger }
>   If the right partition has more than one element
>   Push bounds Lindex and Right onto the stack
>   End if
>   Set Right to Rindex { prepare to process the left partition }
>   End if
>   End while
>   End while
> End Iterative Quicksort

We have not expanded the pseudocode for forming the left and right partitions, since that part of the algorithm is identical to what can be found in the recursive Quicksort algorithm already developed. These details of the partitioning will determine the order of sorting; we will assume the sorting order is given as a parameter.

Develop a Testing Strategy In testing sorting algorithms it is important to consider extreme cases for the allowed size of the array, different types of data (both with and without duplicate values), and different initial orderings of the data. For our iterative Quicksort we will assume the initial array has at least one element. Our test cases will include:

- an array of random data with no duplicates
- an array of random data with some duplicates
- an array in which all elements are duplicates of a single value
- an array of one element
- an array in which the data are already in ascending order
- an array in which the data are already in descending order

We will test all cases with both sorting orders, and the expected outcome in all cases is the data sorted into ascending order or descending order. In order not to clutter the text, we won't give actual examples of test data, but these are easy to build.

Implementation

We will only present here the code for the iterative Quicksort procedure itself. We have assumed the same data structure, an open array of records, that was used in the recursive Quicksort program.

Code and Test the Program The program code given below follows directly from the pseudocode and from the partitioning process from the recursive Quicksort.

```
PROCEDURE IterQuickSort(Left, Right: INTEGER;
                  VAR Table: ARRAY OF SomeRecord;
                  SortingOrder: Order; Ordered: CompareProc);
(* Application of C.A.R. Hoare's Quicksort method to the sorting of
   an array of records Table on the Key field. A pivot (middle element)
   is chosen and the vector is partitioned in such a way that all
   the elements with a key less than or equal to the pivot are in
   the left partition and all the elements with a key greater than
   or equal to the pivot are in the right partition. The process
   is then applied iteratively to each partition. *)

VAR Lindex, Rindex: INTEGER;
    Pivot: SomeRecord;
    Item: StackElementType;
    S: Stack;
```

```
BEGIN
  CreateStack(S);
  Right := Right - Left;   (* adjust to zero based for open array *)
  Left := 0;
  Item.LowerBound := Left;
  Item.UpperBound := Right;
  Push(S, Item);
  REPEAT   (* until stack is empty *)
    Pop(S, Item);
    Left := Item.LowerBound;
    Right := Item.UpperBound;
    REPEAT
      Lindex := Left;
      Rindex := Right;
      Pivot := Table[(Lindex + Rindex) DIV 2];
      REPEAT       (* until partition is formed *)
        WHILE (Lindex < Right)
            AND Ordered(Table[Lindex], Pivot, SortingOrder) DO
          INC(Lindex);   (* Scan left *)
        END; (* WHILE *)
        WHILE (Rindex > Left)
            AND Ordered(Pivot, Table[Rindex], SortingOrder) DO
          DEC(Rindex);    (* Scan right *)
        END; (* WHILE *)
        IF Lindex <= Rindex THEN            (* Exchange records *)
          Swap(Table[Lindex], Table[Rindex]);
          INC(Lindex);
          DEC(Rindex);
        END; (* IF *)
      UNTIL Lindex > Rindex;      (* Partition done *)
      (* Table[Left]..Table[Rindex] <= Pivot
         AND Pivot <= Table[Lindex]..Table[Right] *)
      IF (Rindex - Left) > (Right - Lindex) THEN (* left partition is larger *)
        IF Left < Rindex THEN   (* more than 1 element in partition *)
          Item.LowerBound := Left;
          Item.UpperBound := Rindex;
          Push(S, Item);
        END;
        Left := Lindex;    (* prepare for sorting right partition *)
      ELSE
        IF Lindex < Right THEN      (* more than 1 element in partition *)
          Item.LowerBound := Lindex;
          Item.UpperBound := Right;
          Push(S, Item);
        END;
        Right := Rindex;   (* prepare for sorting left partition *)
      END; (* IF *)
    UNTIL Left >= Right;
  UNTIL Empty(S);
END IterQuickSort;
```

We tested this procedure with the data described in our testing strategy and the data were always sorted into ascending or descending order, as desired. Notice that the outer While loops of the pseudocode have been programmed as REPEAT loops; otherwise, the program code follows directly from the pseudocode. Also note at the beginning of the procedure that the two statements:

```
Right := Right - Left;

Left := 0;
```

are necessary because the values for Left and Right must be zero-based, as Table is an open array parameter. The caller to IterQuickSort will use the actual indices to the array, and these two statements will adjust correctly the values of Left and Right. For instance, if the actual indices go from 1 to 50, then the first action done in the procedure is to decrement Left and Right by one.

Procedure IterQuickSort uses types SomeRecord, Order, CompareProc, as well as procedures Swap and Comparison. Some examples of their possible declarations follow.

```
TYPE SomeRecord = RECORD
                    Key: KeyType;
                    Info: ARRAY [1..Max] OF CHAR;
                  END;
     Order = (Ascending, Descending);
     CompareProc = PROCEDURE(SomeRecord, SomeRecord, Order): BOOLEAN;
PROCEDURE Swap(VAR X, Y: SomeRecord);
VAR Copy: SomeRecord;
BEGIN
     Copy := X;
     X := Y;
     Y := Copy;
END Swap;

PROCEDURE Comparison(Rec1, Rec2: SomeRecord; Sort: Order): BOOLEAN;
(* Comparison of keys if key type is a basic Modula-2 type *)
BEGIN
  IF Sort = Ascending THEN
    RETURN Rec1.Key < Rec2.Key;
  ELSE
    RETURN Rec1.Key > Rec2.Key;
  END;
END Comparison;
```

The Stacks module will use a StackElementType, imported from module StackElements, defined as:

```
TYPE StackElementType = RECORD
                          LowerBound, UpperBound: INTEGER;
                        END;
```

Since we are studying the stack ADT in this chapter, we have used an external stack ADT with procedure calls to Push and Pop. Since we have developed a nonrecursive algorithm to eliminate the recursive procedure calls, using calls to Push and Pop may not provide much improvement. If efficiency is critically important, the external stack ADT could be replaced by a local array containing partition bounds.

We should choose a stack size that is as small as possible yet is sufficiently large to hold all partition boundaries waiting to be sorted. If there are n items to be sorted, a stack of size $\log_2 n$ is sufficient. This is based on the assumption that the largest partition is always stacked and the smallest partition is processed. The smallest partition after the first iteration could contain at most n/2 items. After the second iteration, the smallest partition could have at most n/4 items. The process of stacking could continue until the smallest partition has one element. But the sequence n/2, n/4, . . . , 2, 1 has at most $\log_2 n$ values, so the stack will never have more than $\log_2 n$ values at any one time. Therefore, if we sort an array of 1000 records, a stack size of 10 is sufficient.

Complete the Documentation Since we have only developed a single procedure for this case study, it is not necessary to prepare a user's manual. However, it is good to document some of the design decisions. Some of the important design decisions we have discussed are: the stacking of the bounds of the largest partition, determining the size of the stack needed for a given size array, the choice of the pivot value, and using an appropriate comparison in the partitioning process to produce the desired sort into ascending or descending order.

Summary

The Stack ADT is one of the most useful data types in computer science. It is a simple type which has a last-in/first-out behavior and two major operations, Push and Pop. Applications of stacks are numerous and most often involve backtracking, as when looking for a path through a maze. Stacks can be implemented in a static way (where the maximum size of the stack is fixed in advance) or in a dynamic way (where the stack size is increased each time a Push operation is done, and is decreased with each Pop operation).

Stacks are used to implement recursion, a technique to solve a problem by solving smaller versions of the same problem. Recursion is a way of thinking that offers many advantages, but it also has some disadvantages, as it adds some overhead to the algorithm execution time. A recursive solution must have a base case to stop the chain of recursive calls; otherwise the sequence of recursive calls becomes infinite, and the computer soon runs out of memory as each recursive call saves the current environment (activation record) on a stack. Examples of recursive algorithms are numerous. However, it is often possible to find a more machine-efficient iterative method that is equivalent. A special case of recursion, tail recursion, makes it possible to replace a recursive algorithm by a nonrecursive one with little effort. It is also possible to simulate recursion using a stack, but many recursive algorithms require too much effort to convert to nonrecursive versions.

Exercises

1. What conditions are required for a sequence of Push and Pop operations on a stack to leave the stack empty without trying to Pop from an empty stack? What conditions are required for such a sequence to leave the stack unchanged?

2. Given a sequence of Push and Pop operations on a stack (such as Push, Push, Push, Pop, Pop, Push, Pop, Pop) and the stack size, design an algorithm that determines whether or not the operations will go beyond the stack limits, i.e., pop from an empty stack or push on a full stack.

3. If integers 1, 2, 3 are input in order for a sequence of operations Push and Pop, what outputs are possible? For instance Push, Push, Pop, Push, Pop, Pop would produce 2, 3, 1. Of the six distinct combinations of 1, 2, 3, one cannot be produced by the preceding method: which one and why?

4. Why is it all right to implement a stack as a linear list in which the first element is the top of the stack, but not recommended to implement a stack as a linear list for which the top of the stack is the last element of the list?

5. Design the algorithms to keep two stacks growing toward each other from each end of a single vector. Write the procedures to manipulate the two stacks: Push1, Push2, Pop1, Pop2. Neither stack will run out of space until all the array is full. Give the advantages and disadvantages of the method.

6. Write a procedure CheckBalance that checks whether an arithmetic expression is balanced with respect to parentheses. The procedure will use a stack.

7. Modify CheckBalance from problem 6 so that it prints the arithmetic expressions back with numbered parentheses, as in:

    (a + (b − c * (d − e) + f) / g)
    1   2   3   3   2   1

8. Write an algorithm to determine if a string of characters is a palindrome. (A palindrome reads the same way from left to right as from right to left.) For example, "MADAM IM ADAM," and "ABLE WAS I ERE I SAW ELBA," and "EIN NEGER MIT GAZELLE ZAGT IM REGEN NIE" are palindromes. Choose either a recursive algorithm or one that uses a stack.

9. Transform the following infix expressions into postfix expressions.

    A + B / C − D
    (A + B) * (C − D) + (E * F) / (G − H)
    (A − B) * C / (D + E) * (F + G)

10. Write an algorithm to evaluate a postfix expression.

11. Using induction, prove that the number of additions to compute recursively Fibonacci(N) is equal to Fibonacci(N + 1) − 1.

12. What is the number of moves our Hanoi algorithm uses? Why does the recursive solution to the Towers of Hanoi problem use the minimum number of moves? What can you say of the complexity of recursive procedure Hanoi and of procedure IterHanoi?

13. The following algorithm is a nonrecursive solution to the Towers of Hanoi puzzle.

    - Assume the pegs are arranged in a triangle.
    - On odd numbered moves, move the smallest disk one peg clockwise.
    - On even moves, make the only legal move not involving the smallest disk.

    Convince yourself that this algorithm solves the puzzle correctly. Is the recursive version or this nonrecursive one easier to understand?

14. Convert the following procedure into an iterative version without using a stack.

    ```
    PROCEDURE Recurse(N: INTEGER);
    BEGIN
      IF NOT End(N) THEN
        WriteString("Recurse"); WriteCard(N, 5); WriteLn;
        Recurse(Trans(N));
      END; (* IF *)
    END Recurse;
    ```

15. If Table is an array of cardinals, give recursive algorithms to compute:
    (a) the maximum element of Table
    (b) the minimum element of Table
    (c) the sum of the elements of Table

16. Ackermann's function is defined recursively for nonnegative integers.

    $A(M, N) = N + 1$ if $M = 0$
    $A(M, N) = A(M-1, 1)$ if $M \neq 0, N = 0$
    $A(M, N) = A(M-1, A(M, N-1))$ if $M \neq 0, N \neq 0$

    (a) Using this definition, show that $A(3, 2) = 29$.
    (b) Can you find an iterative method for computing $A(M, N)$?

    Warning: This function is highly recursive. If you program it, be sure to use very small values for M and N when running your program!

17. Find what the following recursive procedure computes.

    ```
    PROCEDURE F(N: CARDINAL): CARDINAL;
    BEGIN
      IF N = 0 THEN
        RETURN 0;
      ELSE
        RETURN N + F(N-1);
      END; (* IF *)
    END F;
    ```

    Write an iterative version of that procedure.

18. Given the following program:

    ```
    PROCEDURE SeriesPrint(N: CARDINAL);
    BEGIN
      IF N # 0 THEN
        SeriesPrint(N DIV 2);
        WriteCard(N, 2); Write(',');
        SeriesPrint(N DIV 2);
      END; (* IF *)
    END SeriesPrint;
    ```

    Show what SeriesPrint(11) prints.

Programming Problems

19. Implement and test the Stacks of problem 5.

20. Implement and test the algorithms of problem 15.

21. Implement and test Ackermann's function, and time its execution.
    Warning: This function is highly recursive. Be sure to use very small values for M and N when running your program!

22. Add a Retrieve operation for the stack that returns the value of the nth most recently arrived element without modifying the stack (the top element is of depth 1). Add a depth operation for the stack that returns the current number of elements in the stack. Is this operation useful? Implement both those operations with the static representation of stacks.

23. Implement both Retrieve and Depth for the stacks of problem 22 with the dynamic representation of stacks.

24. Implement and test the iterative solution of the Towers of Hanoi given in problem 13.

25. Modify the final version of IterHanoi to use a local stack structure. Notice that you need not have an opaque type nor any operations beyond that required by the program.

26. Write a test program for IterHanoi that compares its results with a recursive version of the algorithm.

27. If timing functions are available on your system, time the execution of both versions of Hanoi to see if iteration is more efficient than recursion. You might need to eliminate all input/output activities so that the measured time reflects execution time and not input/output wait time.

28. Write a test program for IterQuickSort that compares its results with a recursive version of the algorithm.

29. If timing functions are available on your system, time the execution of both versions of Quicksort to see if iteration is more efficient than recursion.

30. Rewrite the SolveMaze program so that the explicit use of a stack is replaced by recursion.

31. Modify the IterQuickSort procedure in the case study to use a local "stack" built into the procedure.

Queues

INTRODUCTION

Queues occur all too often in everyday life: we find waiting lines at the bank, at the supermarket, at the post office, and in many other places. For this reason, queues are an intuitively obvious data structure. People waiting to be served by a cashier normally form a line in which their position is an indication of their arrival time. The person closest to the cashier is at the head of the queue and was the first to arrive, while the person farthest from the cashier is the last in line and was the last to arrive. People arriving go to the end of the line, people being served are taken from the head of the line. There are also other systems of queues where physical positioning in a line is not necessary, as in some stores or government offices where arriving persons take a number, and numbers are distributed in increasing order. When a clerk is ready to serve a customer, she calls the next number, and the person holding that number comes forward to be served.

These two real-life examples illustrate the concept of queue. A queue is a data type with a first-in/first-out (or, in short, FIFO) behavior. Elements can be added one at a time to a queue in any order, but only the element that was added the least recently may be removed. Some real-life queues do not have this behavior; for instance, the queue in a hospital emergency room does not respect the first-in/first-out rule, but rather uses a priority scheme to determine the first patient out of the queue, based on the seriousness of the injury or illness of all the patients in the queue. This type of queue is called a priority queue.

In this chapter, we will concentrate on first-in/first-out queues, their applications, and implementations. We will study priority queues in Chapter 10.

7.1 Abstraction: The Queue

A queue is essentially a linear list in which insertions can be made only at the tail end, and deletions can be made only at the head. We will denote a queue by $Q = (e_1, e_2, e_3, \ldots, e_n)$. A deletion in that queue would give $Q' = (e_2, e_3, \ldots, e_n)$, while an insertion after this deletion would give $Q'' = (e_2, e_3, \ldots, e_n, e_{n+1})$. For instance, if we have a queue of customers:

(Finley, Kieran, Anderson, McGibbon, Davidson, Shorrock)

the first customer to be served will be Finley. When Finley is taken off the queue, it becomes:

(Kieran, Anderson, McGibbon, Davidson, Shorrock)

New customer Galanos will be added at the end of the queue, which would become:

(Kieran, Anderson, McGibbon, Davidson, Shorrock, Galanos)

The operations associated with queues are creation, deletion, insertion of an element, deletion of an element, counting the number of elements in a queue, and examining the first element in a queue. The following definition module gives a precise definition of each operation.

```
DEFINITION MODULE QueueADT;
FROM QueueElements IMPORT QElementType;
TYPE Queue;

VAR QueueError: BOOLEAN;
(* Result of operation: QueueError is always false unless the
   operation failed *)

PROCEDURE CreateQueue(VAR Q: Queue);
(* Create an empty queue Q
   Precondition: Q does not exist
   Postcondition: Q' exists and is empty and QueueError' is FALSE
                  otherwise QueueError' is TRUE *)

PROCEDURE DisposeQueue(VAR Q: Queue);
(* Dispose of queue Q
   Precondition: Q exists
   Postcondition: Q' does not exist anymore *)

PROCEDURE Enqueue(VAR Q: Queue; Item: QElementType);
(* Insert element Item at the end of queue Q
   Precondition: Q exists
   Postcondition: Item is the last element of Q' and QueueError'
                  is FALSE otherwise QueueError' is TRUE *)
```

```
PROCEDURE Dequeue(VAR Q: Queue; VAR Item: QElementType);
(* Delete first element of queue Q and return it in Item
   Precondition: Q is not empty
   Postcondition: Item is a copy of the first element of Q and
                  Q' no longer contains Item and QueueError' is FALSE
                  otherwise QueueError' is TRUE *)
PROCEDURE CountQueue(Q: Queue): CARDINAL;
(* Return the current number of elements in queue Q
   Precondition: Q exists
   Postcondition: number of elements in queue is returned *)
PROCEDURE QueueHead(Q: Queue; VAR Item: QElementType);
(* Return value of first element of queue Q in Item
   Precondition: Q exists
   Postcondition: Q' = Q and Item' = first queue element and
                  QueueError' is FALSE otherwise QueueError' is TRUE *)
END QueueADT.
```

Note that type Queue is an opaque type and that we have imported the queue's element type from user module QueueElements. Variable QueueError is a global variable from module QueueADT, whose value will indicate whether or not the result of the latest operation invoked is valid. Here again, we have used a prime (') to indicate the value of a parameter or a variable *after* applying an operation. There is no operation to display a queue and its contents, but it is possible to define such an operation based on the other ones.

7.2 Applications

Since queues occur frequently in everyday life, it should not be surprising to encounter them in a large number of computer science applications. As a matter of fact, *queuing theory* can be considered a field of computer science. We will discuss some common applications; the first is a *simulation* example involving queues. Operating systems, whose main role is to control the sharing of computer resources between users, also need to use queues, and we will discuss operating system applications as well. The case study in Section 7.4 involves the simulation of a simple computer system.

Simulation of Central Station Wickets

A simulation program models a real situation: each object and each operation of the real situation are represented in the simulation. The results of the simulation can be used to understand the real phenomenon, without having to observe it. Simulation imitates how an actual situation would develop, while accelerating the times involved.

Let's consider the ticket windows—wickets—in Central Station. Assume first that there are five wickets. When you (a traveler) arrive, a wicket might be free and you could buy your ticket directly without any wait. In general, if all wickets are busy you can choose the shortest waiting line and wait for your turn. In such cases, you must spend a total time equal to the transaction time plus the waiting time. In order to improve service and determine the optimal number of wickets, we will simulate the wickets operation. A simulation program will make it possible for us to compute the average time spent by a traveler in buying a ticket as a function of various conditions such as the time interval between traveler arrivals, the number of wickets, and the number of queues (if there is not one queue per wicket).

Such a simulation program is more useful than observations of the actual wicket operation, as it allows us to modify conditions very easily and collect new data quickly. Obviously, the validity of the results will depend completely on how well the model matches the actual situation.

In our program to simulate the wicket situation of Central Station, travelers will be characterized by two pieces of data: arrival time and duration of the transaction at the wicket. We will make the simplifying assumption that everyone acts independently. We will have five wickets represented by five different queues. Each element in a queue will be a traveler waiting to be served. The first element of each queue will represent a traveler currently being served. Each newly arriving traveler is added to the shortest queue. After being served, a traveler leaves the queue. We will have six possible actions:

traveler arrival
traveler departure from queue 1
traveler departure from queue 2
traveler departure from queue 3
traveler departure from queue 4
traveler departure from queue 5

These actions constitute simulation *events*.

The simulation program will use an event list. This list will consist of at most one element for each event type; that is, six elements in our case: one element for the next arrival, and five elements corresponding to the serving of the queue heads. If all queues are not busy, the event list will consist of less than six elements. Our model can be illustrated by Figure 7-1.

The event list is ordered on the event time. This way, the first event to process is the first element in the list, the list elements carry information as to the kind of event they represent, and the event list makes it possible to know what the next event will be. The elements of the queues carry two pieces of information: the arrival time and the time needed for service. In Figure 7-1, the times of departure events in the event list are departure times, whereas the times indicated in the queues are arrival times. For example, the customer shown at the head of Queue 2 arrived at 9:41 and is currently in the process of service for seven minutes. She will depart at 9:54, resulting in a waiting time of 6 minutes since her total time is 13 minutes.

The general simulation algorithm is given by the following pseudocode.

7.2 Applications 239

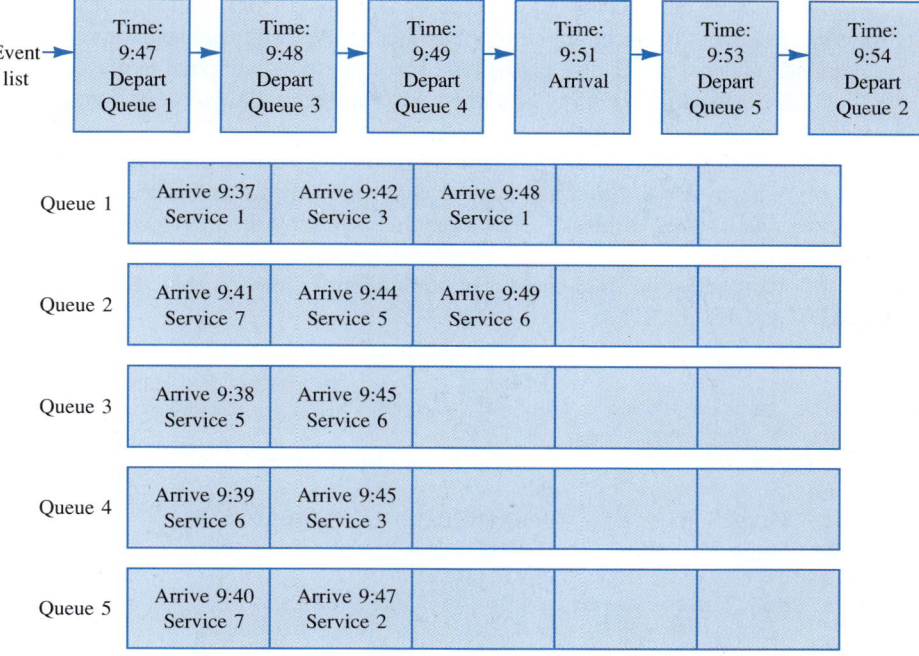

Figure 7-1 Simulation Model

```
Simulation
    Initialize
    Repeat
        Find next event
        Case event of
        Arrival:    register arrival
                    generate next arrival
        Departure:  register departure and time spent
                    generate next departure
        End case
    Until end of simulation
    Compute and display results
End simulation
```

Adapting this general simulation algorithm to our specific simulation gives the following.

Initialize: When the simulation starts, the first event must necessarily be the arrival of the first traveler. It is therefore necessary to generate this traveler arrival by placing a corresponding element in the event list.

Find next event: The next event is copied and deleted from the event list.

Arrival: The event is placed in the shortest queue, and, if this queue comprises only one element, its departure is also generated. The corresponding event is placed in the event list. Then, the next arrival is generated, so that there will always be an arrival in the event list until the end of the simulation.

Departure: The corresponding element is taken off its queue and the total time is computed. A departure is generated for the next element in that queue.

Compute and display results: The average time spent by the travelers is computed and displayed.

The following program implements the simulation. It imports tools from modules QueueADT and ListADT.

```
MODULE CentralStation;
(* Simulation of travelers served at a number of wickets
            Ph. Gabrini    November 1991 *)
FROM QueueADT IMPORT Queue, CreateQueue, Enqueue, Dequeue, QueueHead,
                  CountQueue;
FROM ListADT IMPORT List, Insert, Delete, CreateList, ListEmpty;
FROM InOut IMPORT WriteString, WriteLn, WriteCard,
                  OpenOutput, CloseOutput, WriteReal;
FROM QueueElements IMPORT NbWickets, Kind, QElementType, QRange;

TYPE QType = ARRAY QRange OF Queue;

MODULE PseudoRandom;
  EXPORT Random;

  VAR Seed: REAL;

  PROCEDURE Random(): REAL;
  (* Return pseudo-random value from zero up to
     but not including 1 *)
  BEGIN
    Seed := 27.182313 * Seed + 31.415917;
    Seed := Seed - FLOAT(TRUNC(Seed));
    RETURN Seed;
  END Random;

BEGIN (* PseudoRandom *)
  Seed := 1.23456789;
END PseudoRandom;

PROCEDURE AddTime(Time, Duration: CARDINAL): CARDINAL;
(* Add Duration to a given Time *)
VAR Hours, Minutes: CARDINAL;
BEGIN
  Hours := Time DIV 100;
  Minutes := Time MOD 100 + Duration;
```

```
    IF Minutes > 59 THEN
      Minutes := Minutes - 60;
      INC(Hours);
    END; (* IF *)
    RETURN Hours * 100 + Minutes;
  END AddTime;

  PROCEDURE TimeDiff(Time1, Time2: CARDINAL): CARDINAL;
  (* Compute time difference Time1 - Time2. Time values, as created by
     Generate are correct and represented by integers.
     For example 1136 stands for 11 hours 36 minutes. *)
  VAR Min1, Min2, Hour1, Hour2, DiffMin: CARDINAL;
  BEGIN
    IF Time1 > Time2 THEN      (* compute difference *)
      Min1 := Time1 MOD 100;
      Min2 := Time2 MOD 100;
      Hour1 := Time1 DIV 100;
      Hour2 := Time2 DIV 100;
      IF Min1 > Min2 THEN      (* straight difference *)
        DiffMin := Min1 - Min2;
      ELSE  (* add 60 minutes to Min1 *)
        DiffMin := Min1 + 60 - Min2;
        DEC(Hour1);
      END; (* IF *)
      RETURN (Hour1 - Hour2) * 100 + DiffMin;
    ELSE     (* no difference possible *)
      RETURN 0;
    END; (* IF *)
  END TimeDiff;

  PROCEDURE Generate(VAR Clock: CARDINAL; VAR EventList: List);
  (* Generate next random arrival and advance clock. Times are represented
     by integers on the 2400 scale. *)
  VAR Hour, Minute: CARDINAL;
      Item: QElementType;
  BEGIN
    Minute := TRUNC(Random()*3.0);     (* 0-3 minutes to next arrival *)
    Minute := (Clock MOD 100) + Minute;(* new minutes *)
    IF Minute >= 60 THEN               (* convert to hour-minute *)
      Minute := 100 + Minute - 60;
    END; (* IF *)
    Hour := (Clock DIV 100)*100;       (* old hour *)
    Clock := Hour + Minute;            (* advance clock *)
    IF Clock < 1100 THEN               (* no more arrivals after 1100 *)
      (* 0-10 minutes of service time *)
      Item.Event := Arrival;
      Item.Hour := Clock;
      Item.Duration := TRUNC(10.0*Random());
      Item.QueueNumber := 0;
      Insert(EventList, Item);
    END; (* IF *)
  END Generate;
```

```
PROCEDURE Arrive(VAR EventList: List; ArrTime, ServTime: CARDINAL;
                VAR Clock: CARDINAL; VAR Queues: QType);
(* Register and process new arrival *)
VAR Small, i, QNumber, Number: CARDINAL;
    Item: QElementType;
BEGIN
  QNumber := 1;
  Small := CountQueue(Queues[1]);
  FOR i := 2 TO NbWickets DO        (* find shortest queue *)
    Number := CountQueue(Queues[i]);
    IF Number < Small THEN
      Small := Number;
      QNumber := i;
    END; (* IF *)
  END; (* FOR *)
  WriteString("Arrival: ");WriteCard(ArrTime, 5); WriteString("service:");
  WriteCard(ServTime, 5); WriteLn;
  Item.Event := Departure;
  Item.QueueNumber := QNumber;
  Item.Hour := ArrTime;
  Item.Duration := ServTime;
  (* insert in queue *)
  Enqueue(Queues[QNumber], Item);
  (* if only one element in queue put departure in event list *)
  IF CountQueue(Queues[QNumber]) = 1 THEN
    Item.Hour := AddTime(ArrTime, ServTime);
    Insert(EventList, Item);
  END; (* IF *)
  Generate(Clock, EventList);
END Arrive;

PROCEDURE Quit(QNumber, DepTime: CARDINAL; VAR Q: QType;
               VAR EvList: List; VAR TotTime, Count: CARDINAL);
(* Process a departure *)
VAR Item: QElementType;
BEGIN
  Dequeue(Q[QNumber], Item);                          (* take off queue *)
  Item.Duration := TimeDiff(DepTime, Item.Hour);      (* update counters *)
  TotTime := TotTime + Item.Duration;
  INC(Count);
  WriteString("Departure:"); WriteCard(DepTime, 5);
  WriteString(" waited :"); WriteCard(Item.Duration, 5); WriteLn;
  (* If more customers in queue, prepare next departure *)
  IF CountQueue(Q[QNumber]) > 0 THEN
    QueueHead(Q[QNumber], Item);
    Item.Hour := AddTime(DepTime, Item.Duration);
    Insert(EvList, Item);
  END; (* IF *)
END Quit;
```

```
  VAR Queues: QType;
      EventList: List;
      TotTime, Count, Clock, QueueNumber: CARDINAL;
      Item: QElementType;
BEGIN (* CentralStation *)
  OpenOutput("dat");
  CreateList(EventList);
  Count := 0;
  TotTime := 0;
  FOR QueueNumber := 1 TO NbWickets DO
     CreateQueue(Queues[QueueNumber]);
  END; (* FOR *)
  Clock := 900;                          (* simulation starts at 9 o'clock *)
  Generate(Clock, EventList);            (* first customer *)
  WHILE NOT ListEmpty(EventList) DO (* repeat as long as there are events *)
     Delete(EventList, Item);
     IF Item.Event = Arrival THEN       (* arrival *)
        Arrive(EventList, Item.Hour, Item.Duration, Clock, Queues);
     ELSE                               (* departure *)
        Quit(Item.QueueNumber, Item.Hour, Queues, EventList, TotTime, Count);
     END; (* IF *)
  END; (* WHILE *)
  WriteLn; WriteString("Average time spent: ");
  WriteReal(FLOAT(TotTime)/FLOAT(Count), 6, 2); WriteLn;
  CloseOutput;
END CentralStation.
```

Figure 7-2 shows the end of the output generated by executing the CentralStation program.

Figure 7-2
Simulation Results

Departure:	1055	waited :	3
Arrival:	1056	service:	6
Departure:	1056	waited :	11
Departure:	1057	waited :	7
Arrival:	1057	service:	6
Arrival:	1059	service:	3
Departure:	1100	waited :	9
Departure:	1101	waited :	8
Departure:	1101	waited :	7
Departure:	1102	waited :	9
Departure:	1102	waited :	17
Departure:	1103	waited :	6
Departure:	1104	waited :	12
Departure:	1106	waited :	7
Departure:	1106	waited :	11
Departure:	1108	waited :	12

Average time spent: 6.4

The CentralStation program uses type Queue imported from module QueueADT, as well as type List imported from module ListADT, where list elements are ordered by arrival time (see Chapter 5). Both data types Queue and List use type QElementType, defined in module QueueElements.

```
DEFINITION MODULE QueueElements;
CONST NbWickets = 5;
TYPE Kind = (Arrival, Departure);
     QRange = [1..NbWickets];
     QElementType = RECORD
                      Hour, Duration: CARDINAL;
                      Event: Kind;
                      QueueNumber: QRange;
                    END;
END QueueElements.
```

where

field Hour indicates the arrival time
field Duration indicates the time needed for service
field Event is used to distinguish between arrivals and departures
field QueueNumber is zero in the case of arrivals, or indicates the queue number for departures

The five queues are part of a queue array. Local module PseudoRandom provides a crude pseudorandom number generator through function Random. Its global variable, Seed, used by Random, exists during all the execution of program CentralStation but is not accessible from the other parts of the program, as it is not exported. Procedures AddTime and TimeDiff are utility procedures to add or subtract the times given, which are represented as integers less than 2400. Procedure Generate randomly generates an arrival with a 3-minute maximum interval between arrivals, updates the clock, and adds the corresponding element to the event list. Arrival generation starts at 900 hours and stops at 1100 hours.

Procedure Arrive processes an arrival by first finding the shortest queue and inserting the new element in it. If this queue has only one element (the newly inserted one), a departure is generated and the corresponding element inserted in the event list. Finally, the next arrival is generated. Procedure Quit processes a departure by taking the element off its queue, computing and updating the total time and the number of customers served. If there are other elements in this queue, a departure is generated.

The main program initializes the event list, the five queues, and the clock. It generates the first arrival and loops on event processing. That is, the first event is taken off the event list and is processed according to its kind. Once the simulation is over, results are computed and displayed.

Changing the maximum interval between arrivals to 2 minutes and running the simulation again gives quite different results. Figure 7-3 shows the end of the output generated. Arrivals still stop at 1100 hours, but the system is now quite clogged, and it

Figure 7-3
Results for Second Simulation

```
Departure: 1234 spent :  146
Departure: 1238 spent :  150
Departure: 1239 spent :  140
Departure: 1240 spent :  150
Departure: 1240 spent :  147
Departure: 1240 spent :  144
Departure: 1241 spent :  150
Departure: 1244 spent :  148
Departure: 1245 spent :  146
Departure: 1246 spent :  148
Departure: 1246 spent :  149
Departure: 1246 spent :  147
Departure: 1249 spent :  150
Departure: 1249 spent :  150
Departure: 1250 spent :  151

Average time spent:     71
```

takes until 1250 hours to serve the last customer. This person will have waited 151 minutes to get a ticket, while the average waiting time is 71 minutes! Undoubtedly, in real life many customers would have left before being served! Our results indicate that for such an arrival rate the number of wickets is insufficient. A next simulation run might increase the number of wickets to 8 to see what improvement results.

Queues in Operating Systems

Without an operating system, a modern computer would be useless, as the operating system acts as an interface between the user and the computer hardware. Microcomputer operating systems are usually simple because they have to deal with a single user and to control an environment including memory, one application program, a couple of disk drives, a keyboard, a screen, and a printer. By contrast, larger computers have more complex operating systems, as they usually allow a number of simultaneous users. The operating system is then seen as a resource manager for system resources that are shared between active users. The programs of an operating system allocate memory, perform input-output operations, control the execution of each application program, schedule input-output requests on the various devices, and manage the queues associated with the various computer resources.

Figure 7-4 represents the states of executing programs in a computer system. An executing program is often called a *process*. With a single processor computer, only one process can be in the Running state at a given time, while several processes might be in states Ready and Blocked. A Running process becomes Blocked whenever it requests a resource, and later passes from Blocked to Ready whenever the requested resource is allocated to it. Provided it has not been blocked, a Running process becomes Ready whenever it has used up the processor time it was allocated.

Since there can be a number of processes in the computer system at a given time, it is necessary to keep them in queues. Thus, we will have a queue of all processes in the Ready state, as well as a queue of all processes in the Blocked state. In fact Blocked

Figure 7-4
Process States in a
Computer System

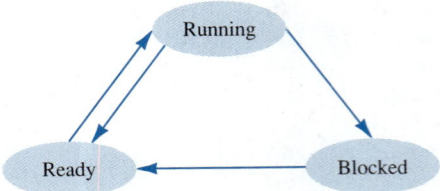

processes are usually distributed in a number of queues as they await allocation of a particular resource: access to a disk file, access to a printer, etc. In order to serve the processes, it is necessary to be able to manage queues. For instance, if a print request is issued by the running process, this process is enqueued in the printer queue. Assuming the printing operation itself does not require central processing unit (CPU) intervention, when the printer completes a task, it notifies the control program, which then takes the corresponding process on the printer queue and transfers it back to the Ready queue.

In operating systems on large computers, it is usual to deal with hundreds of simultaneous users. In such cases, it is typical to have several classes of processes and to give higher priorities to processes in one class over those in another. If all ready processes are kept in one queue, the first-in/first-out property of the queue will have to be replaced by some selection scheme based on the priorities of its elements. This need has led to the development of priority queues, which will be discussed in Chapter 10.

With regular first-in/first-out queues, it is still possible to deal with processes with priorities. If we had four levels of priority, the Ready queue could be replaced by four queues, one for each priority level. Then, when it comes time to select a process for Running, the highest priority queue is used first. If it is empty, the second highest priority queue is then used, and so on. We will use such a scheme in our case study.

7.3 Implementation

As with linear lists, we can implement queues with static arrays or with dynamic nodes.

Static Implementation

With this implementation, the queue elements are kept in an array as shown in Figure 7-5. Two indices are kept with the array to show the head and the tail of the queue. The array is used cyclically; that is, when the tail reaches the last array position, the next element is inserted in the first position. In an empty queue, the head index value will be MaxQueue and the tail index will be zero. In a full queue, the head and tail indices will be equal.

The following implementation module defines the various operations based on this representation.

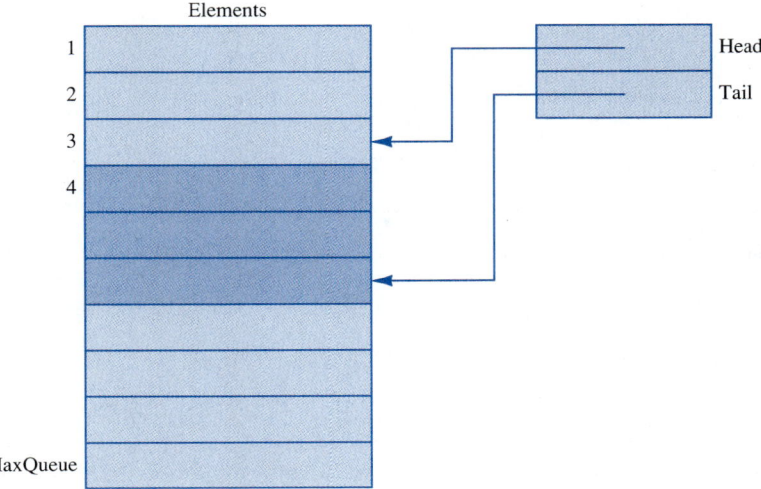

Figure 7-5
Static Queue

```
IMPLEMENTATION MODULE QueueADT;
FROM QueueElements IMPORT QElementType;
FROM Storage IMPORT ALLOCATE, DEALLOCATE;

CONST MaxQueue = 50;

TYPE Queue = POINTER TO QueueRec;
     QueueRec = RECORD
                  Head, Tail, Number: [0..MaxQueue];
                  Data: ARRAY [1..MaxQueue] OF QElementType;
                END;
(* Empty queue: Tail = 0, Head = MaxQueue, Number = 0
   Full queue:  Tail = Head, Number = MaxQueue
   Other queue: Tail indicates actual last element
                Head indicates previous first element *)

PROCEDURE CreateQueue(VAR Q: Queue);
(* Create queue Q *)
BEGIN
  ALLOCATE(Q, SIZE(QueueRec));
  IF Q # NIL THEN
    Q^.Tail := 0;
    Q^.Number := 0;
    Q^.Head := MaxQueue;
    QueueError := FALSE;
  ELSE
    QueueError := TRUE;        (* no allocation possible *)
  END; (* IF *)
END CreateQueue;
```

```
PROCEDURE DisposeQueue(VAR Q: Queue);
(* Dispose of queue Q *)
BEGIN
  DEALLOCATE(Q, SIZE(QueueRec));
END DisposeQueue;

PROCEDURE Enqueue(VAR Q: Queue; E: QElementType);
(* Insert element E in queue Q *)
BEGIN
  IF Q^.Number < MaxQueue THEN
    WITH Q^ DO
      Tail := (Tail MOD MaxQueue) + 1;
      Data[Tail] := E;
      INC(Number);
    END;
    QueueError := FALSE;
  ELSE
    QueueError := TRUE;        (* full queue *)
  END;
END Enqueue;

PROCEDURE Dequeue(VAR Q: Queue; VAR E: QElementType);
(* Retrieve in E and delete head of queue Q *)
BEGIN
  IF Q^.Number # 0 THEN
    WITH Q^ DO
      Head := (Head MOD MaxQueue) + 1;
      E := Data[Head];
      DEC(Number);
      IF Number = 0 THEN       (* queue is now empty *)
        Tail := 0;
        Head := MaxQueue;
      END;
    END;
    QueueError := FALSE;
  ELSE
    QueueError := TRUE;        (* no element to retrieve *)
  END;
END Dequeue;

PROCEDURE CountQueue(Q: Queue): CARDINAL;
(* Return number of elements in Q *)
BEGIN
  RETURN Q^.Number;
END CountQueue;

PROCEDURE QueueHead(Q: Queue; VAR Item: QElementType);
(* Return value of first element of queue Q in Item *)
BEGIN
  IF (Q # NIL) AND (Q^.Number # 0) THEN
    Item := Q^.Data[Q^.Head MOD MaxQueue + 1];
    QueueError := FALSE;
```

```
    ELSE
      QueueError := TRUE;     (* no queue *)
    END; (* IF *)
END QueueHead;

END QueueADT.
```

Note that an empty queue is indicated by the tail index and the number of elements equal to zero (the head index is then set to MaxQueue). If indices Head and Tail are equal, or if the number of elements is equal to MaxQueue, then the queue is full.

The time complexity of all the operations CreateQueue, CountQueue, DisposeQueue, QueueHead, Enqueue, Dequeue is $O(1)$: each procedure will be executed in a fixed number of steps. The space complexity is the space necessary to store MaxQueue elements and three integers.

Dynamic Implementation

With this implementation, the queue is a linked list made of nodes allocated as needed. Each queue element is made of two parts: the element proper and a pointer to the next queue element. Type Queue is a record with three fields: two pointers to head and tail elements and a number indicating how many elements are in the queue. The implementation module follows.

```
IMPLEMENTATION MODULE QueueADT;
FROM QueueElements IMPORT QElementType;
FROM Storage IMPORT ALLOCATE, DEALLOCATE;

TYPE PointerToElement = POINTER TO Element;
     Queue = POINTER TO QueueType;
     QueueType = RECORD
                     Head, Tail: PointerToElement;
                     Number: CARDINAL;
                 END;
     Element = RECORD
                   Data: QElementType;
                   Next: PointerToElement;
               END;

PROCEDURE CreateQueue(VAR Q: Queue);
(* Initialize queue *)
BEGIN
  ALLOCATE(Q, SIZE(QueueType));
  IF Q # NIL THEN
    Q^.Number := 0;
    Q^.Head := NIL;
    Q^.Tail := NIL;
    QueueError := FALSE;
  ELSE
    QueueError := TRUE;     (* no allocation possible *)
  END; (* IF *)
END CreateQueue;
```

```
PROCEDURE DisposeQueue(VAR Q: Queue);
(* Dispose of queue Q *)
VAR node: PointerToElement;
BEGIN
  IF Q # NIL THEN
    node := Q^.Head;
    WHILE node # NIL DO
      Q^.Head := node^.Next;
      DEALLOCATE(node, SIZE(Element));
      node := Q^.Head;
    END; (* WHILE *)
    DEALLOCATE(Q, SIZE(QueueType));
  END; (* IF *)
END DisposeQueue;

PROCEDURE Dequeue(VAR Q: Queue; VAR Item: QElementType);
(* Take off element from head of queue *)
VAR Point: PointerToElement;
BEGIN
  IF (Q = NIL) OR (Q^.Number = 0) THEN
    QueueError := TRUE;            (* no element to dequeue *)
  ELSE
    Point := Q^.Head;
    Item := Point^.Data;
    DEC(Q^.Number);                (* update counter *)
    Q^.Head := Point^.Next;
    IF Q^.Head = NIL THEN          (* last element was deleted *)
      Q^.Tail := NIL;
    END; (* IF *)
    DEALLOCATE(Point, SIZE(Element));
    QueueError := FALSE;
  END; (* IF *)
END Dequeue;

PROCEDURE Enqueue(VAR Q: Queue; Item: QElementType);
(* Put element at end of queue *)
VAR New: PointerToElement;
BEGIN
  IF Q # NIL THEN
    ALLOCATE(New,SIZE(Element));    (* new element *)
    IF New # NIL THEN
      QueueError := FALSE;
      New^.Data := Item;
      New^.Next := NIL;
      IF Q^.Tail = NIL THEN         (* only element *)
        Q^.Head := New;
      ELSE                          (* last element *)
        Q^.Tail^.Next := New;
      END; (* IF *)
      Q^.Tail := New;
      INC(Q^.Number);               (* update counter *)
```

```
      ELSE
        QueueError := TRUE;          (* no allocation possible *)
      END;
    ELSE
      QueueError := TRUE;            (* no queue *)
    END; (* IF *)
  END Enqueue;

  PROCEDURE QueueHead(Q: Queue; VAR Item: QElementType);
  (* Get information of head of queue *)
  BEGIN
    IF (Q = NIL) OR (Q^.Number = 0) THEN
      QueueError := TRUE;        (* no element *)
    ELSE
      Item := Q^.Head^.Data;
      QueueError := FALSE;
    END; (* IF *)
  END QueueHead;

  PROCEDURE CountQueue(Q: Queue): CARDINAL;
  (* Get number of elements in queue *)
  BEGIN
    RETURN Q^.Number;
  END CountQueue;

END QueueADT.
```

The time complexity of operations CreateQueue, QueueHead, CountQueue, Enqueue, and Dequeue is $O(1)$, as each procedure requires only a fixed number of steps (no loop). Operation DisposeQueue has a complexity of $O(n)$, since the linked list must be traversed in order to free all elements. The space complexity of all operations is the space necessary to store the number of elements needed.

7.4 Case Study: A Computer Simulation

Queues are used in operating systems to hold tasks ready to execute. A simple operating system would have at least one queue to hold tasks ready for the central processing unit, a queue for each disk drive for tasks needing to read or write to the disk, a queue for printing, and so forth. In this case study, we will simulate the behavior of a simple computer system that can comprise a user-specified number of CPUs, disks, and printers.

Design

It is beyond the scope of this example to study the design of real operating systems. Rather, we will simulate a system where a user-defined workload can be tested using various numbers of devices. For a given workload, the simulation should be able to help the user determine the minimum number of devices of each type needed to produce acceptable job throughput without having devices sitting idle most of the time.

Definition of the Problem In our simulation, jobs will be of four types: system jobs, timeshare jobs, batch jobs, and background jobs, in order of highest priority to lowest priority access to the CPUs. In other words, all system jobs will be executed or begin executing before any timeshare jobs can start executing. Batch jobs will only execute when a CPU has no system or timeshare jobs ready for execution. Background jobs have the lowest priority and will only run when there are no other jobs of higher priority waiting for execution.

For reading and writing to a disk, each job will be associated with a particular disk drive. There will be no priority for disk access; jobs will be handled on a round-robin basis. A job can have a specified amount of printing that will be assigned to the first available printer. It is assumed all printers are of the same type and in the same location, so a user can accept output on any printer.

The simulation will depend on a system clock with discrete units of time that start counting at zero. Jobs will be put into an input queue and will enter the system when the clock reaches the job start time. Each job will be specified by a job number, the job type (system, timeshare, batch, or background), a job start time, the number of units of CPU time required, a disk number, the number of units of disk time required, and the number of units of printer time required.

We will assume that all CPU activity will be completed before disk activity, and that all disk activity will be completed before printing. Relaxing these simplifying assumptions will be left as program extensions. The number of devices (CPUs, disks, and printers) must be specified for a particular simulation. A job can run on any CPU and execution can be interrupted between clock cycles. In other words, a job need not run to completion once it has started. A higher priority job may enter the system and pre-empt the execution of a lower priority job. Disk activity will also be interruptible, but all jobs in the queue will have equal priority. So, if there are three jobs in a queue, they will each have one unit of disk access time before the first job gets a second unit of access. Printing jobs cannot be interrupted and must complete once they reach a printer. All printers share a single queue, which works on a first-come, first-served basis (there is no priority). The diagram in Figure 7-6 illustrates a system that has two CPUs, four disks, and three printers.

The simulation program should read the job data using input redirection. Each input line will contain seven integers: job number, job type, start time, CPU time, disk number, disk time, print time, as in the following:

```
1 1 0 3 3 1 2
```

This input indicates job number 1 of type timeshare, starting at time zero, needing a CPU time of 3 units, using disk #3 for 1 unit, and printing for 2 units. A job number equal to zero will indicate the input end. The user will have the choice to display the input data if desired, using a format we will discuss later. There will be two modes of output display the user can select: show all active jobs after each clock cycle or show only final results. The results for each job will be the job number and job type, the start

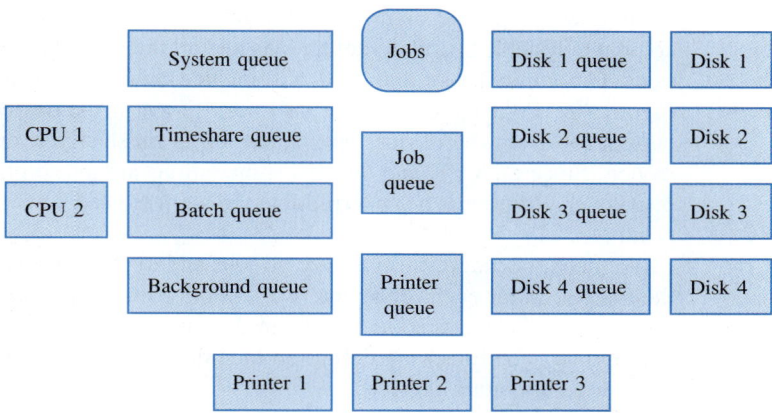

Figure 7-6
A Computer Simulation with Two CPUs, Four Disks, and Three Printers

and finish times, the wait and execution times for each device, and the total wait and total execution times.

Design of a Solution The structure of our simulation is straightforward. At each clock cycle we have to enter the new jobs, schedule the CPUs, schedule the disks, and schedule the printers. When a job is completed, the job statistics are output automatically, but we want the option to output the machine state at each clock cycle. This organization is reflected in the structure chart in Figure 7-7.

Each device can process one job at a time. Since we have several CPUs, several disk units, and several printers, we will need an array associated with each class of device to store the job currently assigned to each device. When not being processed, a job will be waiting in a queue. The input job queue holds jobs waiting to start. There are four CPU queues corresponding to the four priority levels: system, timeshare, batch, and background. Each disk will have its own queue. All of the printers will share a single queue. All queues will hold elements of the same type, that is jobs. Each job will be characterized by the job number; the job type; the start time; the entry time to a queue; the associated disk drive; the required time for CPU, disk, and printer; the wait time for each device; and the execution time completed for each device.

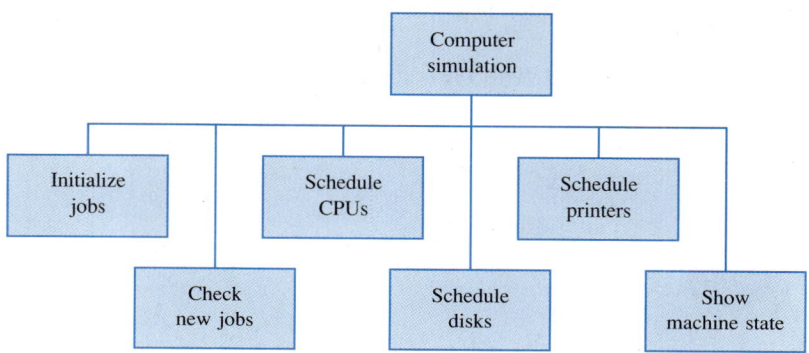

Figure 7-7
Structure Chart for the Computer Simulation

In order to keep the simulation program simple, we will use an ADT to represent the computer system, that is, to define jobs and all the related types, variables, and operations. Our computer system ADT will include, in particular, all the elements found in Figure 7-6. For each device, we will need to test if the device is active, retrieve the current job from the device, test if that job is finished yet, and start a new job on a device. Since the CPU and disk drive operations are interruptible, we will need a job dispatcher. Printing is not interruptible, so we will need a way to tell a job to continue printing.

We need procedures to initialize all jobs and to check if there are any active jobs in the system. After each time slice, we will have to check if new jobs have entered the system. Finally, we need to be able to display the machine state and job statistics, as appropriate. The following definition module gives the complete specification for our computer simulation ADT.

```
DEFINITION MODULE ComputerSystem;
(* Provide operations on the abstract type Job to simulate a simple
   computer system. The global variables MaxCPU, MaxDisk, and
   MaxPrinter are set interactively during module initialization. *)

VAR MaxCPU, MaxDisk, MaxPrinter: CARDINAL;

TYPE Job;

PROCEDURE InitJobs(ShowInput: BOOLEAN);
(* Read data from a file via redirection and place all jobs in the
   input job queue. It is assumed the jobs in the data file are
   already sorted from earliest to latest entry time. The input data
   is displayed as it is read if ShowInput is true. *)

PROCEDURE CheckNewJobs(Time: CARDINAL);
(* Check entry time for job at head of the job entry queue and
   activate job if the current time matches the entry time. More than
   one job can be activated for a given entry time. *)

PROCEDURE CPUActive(CPUNumber: CARDINAL): BOOLEAN;
(* Return TRUE if the specified CPU is active,
   otherwise return FALSE. *)

PROCEDURE GetCPUJob(VAR J: Job; CPUNumber: CARDINAL);
(* Get currently active job J from the specified CPU and set the CPU
   to idle. *)

PROCEDURE StartNewCPUJob(CPUNumber: CARDINAL; Time: CARDINAL);
(* Start highest priority ready job on the inactive CPU specified. *)

PROCEDURE DiskActive(DiskNumber: CARDINAL): BOOLEAN;
(* Return TRUE if the specified Disk is active,
   otherwise return FALSE. *)
```

```
PROCEDURE GetDiskJob(VAR J: Job; DiskNumber: CARDINAL);
(* Get currently active job J from the specified disk and set the disk
   to idle. *)
PROCEDURE StartNewDiskJob(DiskNumber: CARDINAL; Time: CARDINAL);
(* Start the job at the head of the specified disk queue on the
   inactive Disk specified. *)
PROCEDURE PrinterActive(PrinterNumber: CARDINAL): BOOLEAN;
(* Return TRUE if the specified Printer is active,
   otherwise return FALSE. *)
PROCEDURE GetPrinterJob(VAR J: Job; PrinterNumber: CARDINAL);
(* Get currently active job J from the specified printer and set the
   printer to idle. *)
PROCEDURE PrinterFinished(PrinterNumber: CARDINAL): BOOLEAN;
(* Return TRUE if job J has completed on PrinterNumber,
   otherwise return FALSE. *)
PROCEDURE ContinuePrinting(PrinterNumber: CARDINAL);
(* Continue current print job for one more clock cycle *)
PROCEDURE StartNewPrinterJob(PrinterNumber: CARDINAL; Time: CARDINAL);
(* Start the job at the head of the printer queue on the inactive
   Printer specified. *)
PROCEDURE DispatchJob(VAR J: Job; Time: CARDINAL; ShowTrace: BOOLEAN);
(* A job completes all CPU activity first, then all disk activity, and
   finally all printing. Dispatch puts the job in the appropriate
   device queue. If the job is complete, the job statistics are
   printed in the appropriate format for summary or trace. *)
PROCEDURE JobsActive(): BOOLEAN;
(* Return TRUE if there are any active jobs in the system,
   FALSE otherwise. *)
PROCEDURE ShowMachineState(Time: CARDINAL);
(* Display active CPU, Disk and Printer jobs *)
END ComputerSystem.
```

As can be expected, Job is an opaque type. Also note that variables MaxCPU, MaxDisk, and MaxPrinter are used to parameterize the simulated computer system; their values will be defined by the user for each simulation.

Refine the Solution We will first refine the computer simulation program whose structure is displayed in Figure 7-7. The procedures to schedule the various devices are all very similar; here is the pseudocode for the CPU scheduler.

```
Schedule CPUs
    For each CPU
        If the CPU is active
            Get the current CPU job
            Dispatch the current job
        End if
        Start a new CPU job
    End for
End Schedule CPUs
```

Notice that we do not need to check directly if the job is finished, because that will be handled by the dispatcher. Every CPU job is rescheduled at each clock cycle, whether or not there are any other pending jobs. If the job is not finished, then the dispatcher will put it in the appropriate CPU queue. If there are no other jobs in that queue, then the original job will be restarted as a new job. The pseudocode for the disk scheduler is similar to the CPU scheduler, as disk units are also interruptible. The printer scheduler pseudocode is slightly different, since print jobs must run to completion.

```
Schedule Printers
    For each printer
        If the printer is active
            If the current job is finished
                Get the current printer job
                Dispatch the current job
                Start a new printer job
            Else
                Continue printing
            End if
        Else
            Start a new printer job
        End if
    End for
End Schedule Printers
```

The main simulation program will use our computer system ADT, keep track of the system clock, and schedule the devices after each clock cycle. The user will have the option to specify if the input is to be displayed and if a complete trace of active jobs is to be shown or not.

7.4 Case Study: A Computer Simulation

```
Computer Simulation
    Set device limits
    Get input display option
    Get trace option
    Initialize jobs
    Set clock to zero
    If trace is on then show machine state
    Repeat
        Increment clock
        Check for entry of new jobs
        Schedule CPUs
        Schedule disks
        Schedule printers
        If trace is on then show machine state
    Until there are no active jobs
End Computer Simulation
```

The pseudocode developed so far will appear in the main computer simulation program.

We now focus on the development of pseudocode for several of the operations inside the computer system ADT. Many of the procedures are "one liners" that don't require pseudocode development. For example, the Printer Finished procedure is:

```
Printer Finished
    Return true if time required is equal to time completed,
        false otherwise
End Printer Finished
```

We will leave these very short procedures until coding time; rather we will concentrate on the more complex operations. We will use input redirection to read job data; a job number of zero will terminate input.

```
Initialize Jobs
    Open input
    If ShowInput then print heading
    Loop
        Read job number
        Exit if job number = 0
        Read job data
        If ShowInput then print job data
        Set wait times and completed times to 0
    End loop
```

```
        Close input
        Check for jobs entering at clock 0
        For each CPU
            Start a new job
        End for
End Initialize Jobs
```

At each clock cycle, we will have to check for new jobs entering the system. We will assume that the input data read via redirection were in order, from the earliest starting time to the latest starting time. We will use queue operations for enqueuing, dequeuing, checking the front of the queue and checking for an empty queue from our queue ADT.

```
Check New Jobs
    Loop
        Exit if the job queue is empty
        Get the job at the front of the job queue
        Exit if the entry time is later than the current time
        Dequeue the job at the front of the queue
        Set the entry time to the current time
        Enqueue the job into the appropriate CPU queue
    End loop
End Check New Jobs
```

Starting a CPU job will involve fetching the highest priority job waiting for execution and sending it to the appropriate CPU.

```
Start New CPU Job
    Check CPU Job Queues
    If there is a Job
        Set CPU to active
        Increment CPU completed time for Job
        Assign Job to CPU
    End if
End Start New CPU Job

Check CPU Job Queues
    If system queue is not empty
        Dequeue Job
    Elsif timeshare queue is not empty
        Dequeue Job
    Elsif batch queue is not empty
        Dequeue Job
```

```
    Elsif background queue is not empty
        Dequeue Job
    Else
        No Job
    End if
End Check CPU Job Queues
```

The procedures for disks and printers are similar to the procedures for CPUs and will not be presented in pseudocode. The procedures to show the machine state or print job statistics are sequences of write statements and will not be developed in pseudocode. The dispatch procedure reflects the completion of CPU activities first, then disk activities, and finally print activities.

```
Dispatch Job
    If CPU required time > CPU completed time
        Enqueue in appropriate CPU queue
    Elsif Disk required time > Disk completed time
        Enqueue in appropriate disk queue
    Elsif Printer required time > Printer completed time
        Enqueue in printer queue
    Else { job finished }
        Print job statistics
    End if
End Dispatch Job
```

The simulation ends when there are no active jobs on any device. We will associate to each device type an array of Boolean flags indicating whether or not the device is active.

```
Jobs Active
    Set Active to false
    For each CPU Number
        Set Active to Active OR CPU Active[CPU Number]
    End for
    For each DiskNumber
        Set Active to Active OR Disk Active[Disk Number]
    End for
    For each PrinterNumber
        Set Active to Active OR Printer Active[Printer Number]
    End for
    Return Active
End Jobs Active
```

When the computer simulation begins, the computer system ADT solicits the number of CPUs, disks, and printers, and then initializes the appropriate queues and sets all devices to idle. This code will appear in the body of the ADT implementation module so that it executes once when the module is imported:

> Computer System
>   Print program explanation
>   Get number of CPUs, disks and printers
>   Define the four CPU queues (system, timeshare, batch and background)
>   Set each CPU to idle
>   For each disk drive
>   Define a disk queue
>   Set the disk to idle
>   End for
>   Define a printer queue
>   Set each printer to idle
> End Computer System

Develop a Testing Strategy Before we outline a variety of test conditions, we should first carefully trace an example so that we understand how the computer simulation progresses. Figure 7-8 shows the input data for a four job simulation, as we wish it to be displayed by the program upon user request.

To describe the operation of the simulation we will make a chart of where each job is located at each clock cycle, and a short discussion will follow. The triplet of values for each job is the *remaining* required time for the CPU, disk, and printer. These values correspond to the start of the clock cycle, so that at time 0 the values match the original data. When the triplet reaches (0,0,0), then the job is finished. For this simulation, we have assumed there are two CPUs, four disks (but disk 4 is never requested), and three printers. Figure 7-9 shows the corresponding chart.

At time 0, Job 1 has been placed in the timeshare queue and then on CPU 1 while other jobs are waiting for their entry time.

At time 1, Job 1 is dispatched to the timeshare queue and Job 2 is in the system queue. System jobs have highest priority so Job 2 is assigned CPU 1 while Job 1 is assigned CPU 2. Jobs 3 and 4 are still waiting in the job entry queue.

At time 2, jobs enter the system first, so Job 3 is put in the batch queue and Job 4 is put in the system queue. Neither of the current CPU jobs is finished yet, so Job 1

Job #	Job Type	Entry Time	CPU Time	Disk #	Disk Time	Printer Time
1	timshr	0	3	3	1	2
2	system	1	2	3	2	1
3	batch	2	1	1	1	1
4	system	2	2	2	1	3

Figure 7-8 Display of Job Input Data

7.4 Case Study: A Computer Simulation

Clock	Job 1		Job 2		Job 3		Job 4	
0	(3,1,2)	CPU 1	(2,2,1)	Job Entry	(1,1,1)	Job Entry	(2,1,3)	Job Entry
1	(2,1,2)	CPU 2	(2,2,1)	CPU 1	(1,1,1)	Job Entry	(2,1,3)	Job Entry
2	(1,1,2)	Timeshare	(1,2,1)	CPU 2	(1,1,1)	Batch	(2,1,3)	CPU 1
3	(1,1,2)	CPU 2	(0,2,1)	Disk 3	(1,1,1)	Batch	(1,1,3)	CPU 1
4	(0,1,2)	Disk 3	(0,1,1)	Disk 3 Q	(1,1,1)	CPU 1	(0,1,3)	Disk 2
5	(0,0,2)	Printer 2	(0,1,1)	Disk 3	(0,1,1)	Disk 1	(0,0,3)	Printer 1
6	(0,0,1)	Printer 2	(0,0,1)	Printer Q	(0,0,1)	Printer 3	(0,0,2)	Printer 1
7	(0,0,0)	finished	(0,0,1)	Printer 2	(0,0,0)	finished	(0,0,1)	Printer 1
8	(0,0,0)	finished	(0,0,0)	finished	(0,0,0)	finished	(0,0,0)	finished

Figure 7-9 Simulation Chart Following Clock Cycle

goes to the timeshare queue and Job 2 goes to the system queue. Only two CPUs are available and they are used by the system jobs: Job 4 is assigned to CPU 1 and Job 2 is assigned to CPU 2. Jobs 1 and 3 are waiting in the timeshare and batch queues, respectively.

At time 3, Job 2 has finished its CPU execution and moves to the disk 3 queue and then to disk 3. Job 4 is dispatched to the system queue. CPU 1 is assigned to the highest priority job, Job 4, and CPU 2 is assigned the next highest priority job, Job 1. Job 3 remains in the batch queue.

At time 4, Jobs 4 and 1 have finished their CPU execution. Job 4 goes to disk 2 queue, Job 1 goes to disk 3 queue, and Job 3 leaves the batch queue and is assigned to CPU 1. Job 2 is dispatched back to the disk 3 queue, putting it behind Job 1. The disks are assigned the jobs at the heads of their queues: Job 4 is on disk 2 and Job 1 is on disk 3.

At time 5, Job 3 has finished CPU execution and is dispatched to disk 1 queue. Job 4 on disk 2 is dispatched to the printer queue, then Job 1 on disk 3 is dispatched to the printer queue. The disks are assigned, Job 3 going to disk 1 and Job 2 going to disk 3. The printers are assigned, Job 4 going to printer 1 and Job 1 going to printer 2.

At time 6, all disk activity is completed, so Job 3 goes to the printer queue followed by Job 2. Job 4 continues printing on printer 1, Job 1 continues printing on printer 2, and Job 3 is assigned to printer 3. Job 2 remains in the printer queue since no more printers are available.

At time 7, Job 1 on printer 2 and Job 3 on printer 3 are finished. Job 4 continues on printer 1 and Job 2 is removed from the printer queue and assigned to printer 2.

At time 8, Jobs 4 and 2 are finished printing, so there are no active jobs in the system and the simulation ends. Figure 7-10 shows the final job statistics in the "nontrace" form.

If the user had selected the trace output, the information displayed would have been as shown in Figure 7-11. The trace includes all jobs active on devices at the start of each clock cycle. It does not include the contents of the various queues, because we have not assumed a print queue operation in our queue ADT. Adding this feature to the trace printout is left as an exercise (see problem 20).

Job Num	Job Type	Start Time	Stop Time	CPU Wait	CPU Exec	Disk Num	Disk Wait	Disk Exec	Printer Wait	Printer Exec	Total Wait	Total Exec
1	timshr	0	7	1	3	3	0	1	0	2	1	6
3	batch	2	7	2	1	1	0	1	0	1	2	3
4	system	2	8	0	2	2	0	1	0	3	0	6
2	system	1	8	0	2	3	1	2	1	1	2	5

Figure 7-10 Final Job Statistics

Now that we understand better how the simulation program works, we can define our testing strategy. The program should be tested with a variety of configurations and a variety of data. The configurations should include:

one device of each type
the maximum allowable number of devices of each type
a mixture of device counts, including "bottleneck" situations

The job data should include:

jobs requiring only one device
jobs requiring two devices but not a third
jobs requiring all three devices
jobs with all the same entry time
jobs with a variety of entry times
jobs with all the same CPU priority
jobs with a variety of CPU priorities
jobs all using the same disk drive (a bottleneck situation)
jobs using a variety of disk drives

The various configurations should be tested with the different job data. For instance, the input data of Figure 7-12 represents a mixture of device counts, jobs requiring all three devices, jobs with a variety of entry times, jobs with a variety of CPU priorities, and jobs using a variety of disk drives. As stated earlier, each line comprises seven integers: job number, job type, start time, CPU time, disk number, disk time, print time.

Implementation

The program presented next only gives the computer system ADT implementation module and the computer simulation main module. The QueueADT module is identical to the module presented in the text except for the line:

FROM QueueElements IMPORT ElementType;

which has been replaced by

FROM SYSTEM IMPORT ADDRESS;
TYPE ElementType = ADDRESS;

```
_____ clock       0 _____
CPUs (cpu#, job#) > (1, 1) (2, none)
Disks (disk#, job#) > (1, none) (2, none) (3, none) (4, none)
Printers (printer#, job#) > (1, none) (2, none) (3, none)
_____ clock       1 _____
CPUs (cpu#, job#) > (1, 2) (2, 1)
Disks (disk#, job#) > (1, none) (2, none) (3, none) (4, none)
Printers (printer#, job#) > (1, none) (2, none) (3, none)
_____ clock       2 _____
CPUs (cpu#, job#) > (1, 4) (2, 2)
Disks (disk#, job#) > (1, none) (2, none) (3, none) (4, none)
Printers (printer#, job#) > (1, none) (2, none) (3, none)
_____ clock       3 _____
CPUs (cpu#, job#) > (1, 4) (2, 1)
Disks (disk#, job#) > (1, none) (2, none) (3, 2) (4, none)
Printers (printer#, job#) > (1, none) (2, none) (3, none)
_____ clock       4 _____
CPUs (cpu#, job#) > (1, 3) (2, none)
Disks (disk#, job#) > (1, none) (2, 4) (3, 1) (4, none)
Printers (printer#, job#) > (1, none) (2, none) (3, none)
_____ clock       5 _____
CPUs (cpu#, job#) > (1, none) (2, none)
Disks (disk#, job#) > (1, 3) (2, none) (3, 2) (4, none)
Printers (printer#, job#) > (1, 4) (2, 1) (3, none)
_____ clock       6 _____
CPUs (cpu#, job#) > (1, none) (2, none)
Disks (disk#, job#) > (1, none) (2, none) (3, none) (4, none)
Printers (printer#, job#) > (1, 4) (2, 1) (3, 3)
Job #1 timshr   start/finish 0/7 CPU wait/exec 1/3
 Disk num/wait/exec 3/0/1 Print wait/exec 0/2 Total wait/exec 1/6
Job #3 batch    start/finish 2/7 CPU wait/exec 2/1
 Disk num/wait/exec 1/0/1 Print wait/exec 0/1 Total wait/exec 2/3
_____ clock       7 _____
CPUs (cpu#, job#) > (1, none) (2, none)
Disks (disk#, job#) > (1, none) (2, none) (3, none) (4, none)
Printers (printer#, job#) > (1, 4) (2, 2) (3, none)
Job #4 system   start/finish 2/8 CPU wait/exec 0/2
 Disk num/wait/exec 2/0/1 Print wait/exec 0/3 Total wait/exec 0/6
Job #2 system   start/finish 1/8 CPU wait/exec 0/2
 Disk num/wait/exec 3/1/2 Print wait/exec 1/1 Total wait/exec 2/5
_____ clock       8 _____
CPUs (cpu#, job#) > (1, none) (2, none)
Disks (disk#, job#) > (1, none) (2, none) (3, none) (4, none)
Printers (printer#, job#) > (1, none) (2, none) (3, none)
```

Figure 7-11 Simulation Trace

Figure 7-12
Sample Input Data

```
1 1 0 3 3 1 2
2 0 1 2 3 2 1
3 2 2 1 1 1 1
4 0 2 2 2 1 3
0
```

In Modula-2, type ADDRESS is compatible with all pointer types. This modification makes our queue ADT more generic, as it now can deal with all elements defined as pointer types; in particular, all opaque types like type Job.

Code and Test the Program The code presented here follows directly from the pseudocode developed during the design phase. It completes the computer system ADT.

```
IMPLEMENTATION MODULE ComputerSystem;
(* Provides operations on the abstract type Job to simulate a simple
   computer system. The global variables MaxCPU, MaxDisk, and
   MaxPrinter are set interactively during module initialization. *)
FROM Storage IMPORT ALLOCATE, DEALLOCATE;
FROM QueueADT IMPORT Queue, CreateQueue, Enqueue, Dequeue, CountQueue, QueueHead;
FROM InOut IMPORT OpenInput, CloseInput, ReadCard, WriteCard,
                  WriteString, WriteLn;

CONST DeviceMax = 10;

TYPE
  JType = (system, timeshare, batch, background);
  Job = POINTER TO JobRec;
  JobRec =
    RECORD
      JobNumber: CARDINAL;
      JobType: JType;
      StartTime, EntryTime: CARDINAL;
      CPURequired, CPUWait, CPUCompleted: CARDINAL;
      DiskNumber, DiskRequired, DiskWait, DiskCompleted: CARDINAL;
      PrintRequired, PrintWait, PrintCompleted: CARDINAL;
    END; (* Job *)

VAR ActiveCPUs : ARRAY [1..DeviceMax] OF BOOLEAN;
    ActiveDisks : ARRAY [1..DeviceMax] OF BOOLEAN;
    ActivePrinters : ARRAY [1..DeviceMax] OF BOOLEAN;
    CPUJobs : ARRAY [1..DeviceMax] OF Job;
    DiskJobs : ARRAY [1..DeviceMax] OF Job;
    PrinterJobs : ARRAY [1..DeviceMax] OF Job;
    CPUQueues : ARRAY [system..background] OF Queue;
    DiskQueues : ARRAY [1..DeviceMax] OF Queue;
    JobQueue, PrinterQueue : Queue;
```

```
PROCEDURE InitJobs(ShowInput: BOOLEAN);
(* Read data from a file via redirection and place all jobs in the
   input job queue. It is assumed the jobs in the data file are sorted
   from earliest to latest entry time. *)
VAR J: Job;
    ORDJobType, JobNumber, CPUNumber: CARDINAL;
BEGIN (* InitJobs *)
  OpenInput("dat");
  IF ShowInput THEN
    WriteString(
       "Job #  Job Type  Entry Time  CPU Time  Disk #  Disk Time Printer Time");
    WriteLn;
  END; (* IF *)
  LOOP
    ReadCard(JobNumber);
    IF JobNumber = 0 THEN
      EXIT
    ELSE
      ALLOCATE(J, SIZE(JobRec));
      J^.JobNumber := JobNumber;
    END;
    WITH J^ DO
      ReadCard(ORDJobType);
      JobType := VAL(JType, ORDJobType);
      ReadCard(StartTime);
      ReadCard(CPURequired); CPUWait := 0; CPUCompleted := 0;
      ReadCard(DiskNumber); ReadCard(DiskRequired);
      DiskWait := 0; DiskCompleted := 0;
      ReadCard(PrintRequired); PrintWait := 0; PrintCompleted := 0;
      IF ShowInput THEN
        WriteCard(JobNumber, 4);
        CASE JobType OF
          system : WriteString("   system ");
        | timeshare : WriteString("   timshr ");
        | batch : WriteString("   batch ");
        | background : WriteString("   bckgnd ");
        END; (* CASE *)
        WriteCard(StartTime, 10);
        WriteCard(CPURequired, 10);
        WriteCard(DiskNumber, 10);
        WriteCard(DiskRequired, 10);
        WriteCard(PrintRequired, 10); WriteLn;
      END; (* IF *)
    END; (* WITH *)
    Enqueue(JobQueue, J);
  END; (* LOOP *)
  CloseInput;
```

```
    CheckNewJobs(0);
    FOR CPUNumber := 1 TO MaxCPU DO
      StartNewCPUJob(CPUNumber,0);
    END; (* FOR *)
END InitJobs;

PROCEDURE CheckNewJobs(Time: CARDINAL);
(* Check entry time for job at head of the job entry queue and
   activates job if the current time matches the entry time. More
   than one job can be activated for a given entry time. *)

VAR J: Job;
BEGIN
  LOOP
    IF CountQueue(JobQueue) = 0 THEN EXIT END;
    QueueHead(JobQueue, J);
    IF J^.StartTime > Time THEN EXIT END;
    Dequeue(JobQueue, J);
    J^.EntryTime := Time;
    Enqueue(CPUQueues[J^.JobType], J);
  END; (* LOOP *)
END CheckNewJobs;

PROCEDURE CPUActive(CPUNumber: CARDINAL) : BOOLEAN;
(* Return TRUE if the specified CPU is active,
   otherwise return FALSE. *)
BEGIN (* CPUActive *)
  RETURN ActiveCPUs[CPUNumber];
END CPUActive;

PROCEDURE GetCPUJob(VAR J: Job; CPUNumber: CARDINAL);
(* Get currently active job J from the specified CPU and set the CPU
   to idle. *)
BEGIN (* GetCPUJob *)
  J := CPUJobs[CPUNumber];
  ActiveCPUs[CPUNumber] := FALSE;
END GetCPUJob;

PROCEDURE CPUFinished(CPUNumber: CARDINAL) : BOOLEAN;
(* Return TRUE if job J has completed on the specified CPU,
   otherwise FALSE *)
BEGIN (* CPUFinished *)
  RETURN CPUJobs[CPUNumber]^.CPURequired =
              CPUJobs[CPUNumber]^.CPUCompleted;
END CPUFinished;

PROCEDURE JobToCPU(VAR J: Job; CPUNumber: CARDINAL);
(* Place job J at the specified CPU and set that CPU to active. *)
BEGIN (* JobToCPU *)
  ActiveCPUs[CPUNumber] := TRUE;
  INC(J^.CPUCompleted);
  CPUJobs[CPUNumber] := J;
END JobToCPU;
```

```
PROCEDURE CheckCPUJobQueues(VAR J: Job; Time: CARDINAL);
(* Check for higher priority job in ready queues to see which job to
   execute for the next time slice. *)
BEGIN (* CheckCPUJobQueues *)
  IF CountQueue(CPUQueues[system]) # 0 THEN
    Dequeue(CPUQueues[system], J);
  ELSIF CountQueue(CPUQueues[timeshare]) # 0 THEN
    Dequeue(CPUQueues[timeshare], J);
  ELSIF CountQueue(CPUQueues[batch]) # 0 THEN
    Dequeue(CPUQueues[batch], J);
  ELSIF CountQueue(CPUQueues[background]) # 0 THEN
    Dequeue(CPUQueues[background], J);
  ELSE
    J := NIL;
  END; (* IF *)
  IF J # NIL THEN
    J^.CPUWait := J^.CPUWait + Time - J^.EntryTime;
  END; (* IF *)
END CheckCPUJobQueues;

PROCEDURE StartNewCPUJob(CPUNumber: CARDINAL; Time: CARDINAL);
(* Start any ready job on the inactive CPU specified. *)
VAR J: Job;
BEGIN (* StartNewCPUJob *)
  CheckCPUJobQueues(J, Time);
  IF J # NIL THEN
    JobToCPU(J, CPUNumber);
  END; (* IF *)
END StartNewCPUJob;

PROCEDURE DiskActive(DiskNumber: CARDINAL) : BOOLEAN;
(* Return TRUE if the specified Disk is active,
   otherwise return FALSE. *)
BEGIN (* DiskActive *)
  RETURN ActiveDisks[DiskNumber];
END DiskActive;

PROCEDURE GetDiskJob(VAR J: Job; DiskNumber: CARDINAL);
(* Get currently active job J from the specified disk and set the
   disk to idle. *)
BEGIN (* GetDiskJob *)
  J := DiskJobs[DiskNumber];
  ActiveDisks[DiskNumber] := FALSE;
END GetDiskJob;

PROCEDURE DiskFinished(DiskNumber: CARDINAL) : BOOLEAN;
(* Return TRUE if job J has completed on the specified Disk,
   otherwise FALSE. *)
BEGIN (* DiskFinished *)
  RETURN DiskJobs[DiskNumber]^.DiskRequired =
              DiskJobs[DiskNumber]^.DiskCompleted;
END DiskFinished;
```

```
PROCEDURE JobToDisk(VAR J: Job; DiskNumber: CARDINAL);
(* Send job J to the specified disk and set that disk to active. *)
BEGIN (* JobToDisk *)
  ActiveDisks[DiskNumber] := TRUE;
  INC(J^.DiskCompleted);
  DiskJobs[DiskNumber] := J;
END JobToDisk;

PROCEDURE StartNewDiskJob(DiskNumber: CARDINAL; Time: CARDINAL);
(* Start any ready job on the inactive Disk specified. *)
VAR J: Job;
BEGIN (* StartNewDiskJob *)
  IF CountQueue(DiskQueues[DiskNumber]) # 0 THEN
    Dequeue(DiskQueues[DiskNumber], J);
    J^.DiskWait := J^.DiskWait + Time - J^.EntryTime;
    JobToDisk(J, DiskNumber);
  END; (* IF *)
END StartNewDiskJob;

PROCEDURE PrinterActive(PrinterNumber: CARDINAL) : BOOLEAN;
(* Return TRUE if the specified Printer is active,
   otherwise return FALSE *)
BEGIN (* PrinterActive *)
  RETURN ActivePrinters[PrinterNumber];
END PrinterActive;

PROCEDURE GetPrinterJob(VAR J: Job; PrinterNumber: CARDINAL);
(* Get currently active job J from the specified printer and set the
   printer to idle. *)
BEGIN (* GetPrinterJob *)
  J := PrinterJobs[PrinterNumber];
  ActivePrinters[PrinterNumber] := FALSE;
END GetPrinterJob;

PROCEDURE PrinterFinished(PrinterNumber: CARDINAL) : BOOLEAN;
(* Return TRUE if job J has completed on PrinterNumber,
   otherwise FALSE *)
BEGIN (* PrinterFinished *)
  RETURN PrinterJobs[PrinterNumber]^.PrintRequired =
                    PrinterJobs[PrinterNumber]^.PrintCompleted;
END PrinterFinished;

PROCEDURE ContinuePrinting(PrinterNumber: CARDINAL);
(* Continue current print job for one more time slice *)
BEGIN
  INC(PrinterJobs[PrinterNumber]^.PrintCompleted);
END ContinuePrinting;
```

```
PROCEDURE JobToPrinter(VAR J: Job; PrinterNumber: CARDINAL);
(* Send job J to the specified printer and set that printer to
   active. *)
BEGIN (* JobToPrinter *)
  ActivePrinters[PrinterNumber] := TRUE;
  INC(J^.PrintCompleted);
  PrinterJobs[PrinterNumber] := J;
END JobToPrinter;

PROCEDURE StartNewPrinterJob(PrinterNumber: CARDINAL; Time: CARDINAL);
(* Start any ready job on the inactive Printer specified. *)
VAR J: Job;
BEGIN (* StartNewPrinterJob *)
  IF CountQueue(PrinterQueue) # 0 THEN
    Dequeue(PrinterQueue, J);
    J^.PrintWait := J^.PrintWait + Time - J^.EntryTime;
    JobToPrinter(J, PrinterNumber);
  END; (* IF *)
END StartNewPrinterJob;

PROCEDURE PrintJobStats(J: Job; CurrentTime: CARDINAL;
                        ShowTrace: BOOLEAN);
(* Print job number, total cpu wait time, total cpu execution time,
   total disk wait time, total disk execution time, total print wait
   time, total print execution time, percent execution time of total
   time. *)
VAR TotalExecutionTime, TotalWaitTime: CARDINAL;
BEGIN (* PrintJobStats *)
  WITH J^ DO
    TotalExecutionTime := CPUCompleted + DiskCompleted +
                          PrintCompleted;
    TotalWaitTime := CurrentTime - StartTime - TotalExecutionTime;
    IF ShowTrace THEN
      WriteString("Job #"); WriteCard(JobNumber, 1);
      CASE JobType OF
        system : WriteString(" system ");
      | timeshare : WriteString(" timshr ");
      | batch : WriteString(" batch ");
      | background : WriteString(" bckgnd ");
      END; (* CASE *)
      WriteString(" start/finish "); WriteCard(StartTime,1);
      WriteString("/"); WriteCard(CurrentTime, 1);
      WriteString(" CPU wait/exec "); WriteCard(CPUWait,1);
      WriteString("/"); WriteCard(CPUCompleted, 1); WriteLn;
      WriteString(" Disk num/wait/exec "); WriteCard(DiskNumber, 1);
      WriteString("/"); WriteCard(DiskWait,1);
      WriteString("/"); WriteCard(DiskCompleted, 1);
      WriteString(" Print wait/exec "); WriteCard(PrintWait, 1);
      WriteString("/"); WriteCard(PrintCompleted, 1);
      WriteString(" Total wait/exec "); WriteCard(TotalWaitTime, 1);
      WriteString("/"); WriteCard(TotalExecutionTime, 1);
```

```
      ELSE
        WriteCard(JobNumber, 3);
        CASE JobType OF
          system : WriteString(" system ");
        | timeshare : WriteString(" timshr ");
        | batch : WriteString(" batch ");
        | background : WriteString(" bckgnd ");
        END; (* CASE *)
        WriteCard(StartTime, 6);
        WriteCard(CurrentTime, 6);
        WriteCard(CPUWait, 6);
        WriteCard(CPUCompleted, 6);
        WriteCard(DiskNumber, 6);
        WriteCard(DiskWait, 6);
        WriteCard(DiskCompleted, 6);
        WriteCard(PrintWait, 6);
        WriteCard(PrintCompleted, 6);
        WriteCard(TotalWaitTime, 6);
        WriteCard(TotalExecutionTime, 6);
      END; (* IF *)
      WriteLn;
    END; (* WITH *)
    DEALLOCATE(J, SIZE(JobRec));
END PrintJobStats;

PROCEDURE DispatchJob(VAR J: Job; Time: CARDINAL; ShowTrace: BOOLEAN);
(* A job completes all CPU activity first, then all disk activity, and
   finally all printing. Dispatch puts the job in the appropriate
   device queue. If the job is complete, the job statistics are
   printed in the appropriate format for summary or trace. *)

BEGIN (* DispatchJob *)
  J^.EntryTime := Time;
  IF J^.CPURequired > J^.CPUCompleted THEN
    Enqueue(CPUQueues[J^.JobType], J);
  ELSIF J^.DiskRequired > J^.DiskCompleted THEN
    Enqueue(DiskQueues[J^.DiskNumber], J);
  ELSIF J^.PrintRequired > J^.PrintCompleted THEN
    Enqueue(PrinterQueue, J);
  ELSE (* job is finished *)
    PrintJobStats(J, Time, ShowTrace);
  END; (* IF *)
END DispatchJob;
```

```
PROCEDURE JobsActive() : BOOLEAN;
(* Return TRUE if there are any active jobs in the system,
   FALSE otherwise *)
VAR Active: BOOLEAN;
    Count: CARDINAL;
BEGIN (* JobsActive *)
  Active := FALSE;
  FOR Count := 1 TO MaxCPU DO
    Active := Active OR ActiveCPUs[Count];
  END; (* FOR *)
  FOR Count := 1 TO MaxDisk DO
    Active := Active OR ActiveDisks[Count];
  END; (* FOR *)
  FOR Count := 1 TO MaxPrinter DO
    Active := Active OR ActivePrinters[Count];
  END; (* FOR *)
  RETURN Active;
END JobsActive;

PROCEDURE ShowMachineState(Time: CARDINAL);
(* Display active jobs for CPUs, Disks and Printers *)
VAR Index: CARDINAL;
BEGIN
  WriteString('___ clock '); WriteCard(Time, 6);
  WriteString(' ___'); WriteLn;
  (* show active CPU jobs *)
  WriteString('CPUs (cpu#, job#) > ');
  FOR Index := 1 TO MaxCPU DO
    WriteString(" ("); WriteCard(Index,1); WriteString(", ");
    IF CPUActive(Index) THEN
      WriteCard(CPUJobs[Index]^.JobNumber, 1);
      WriteString(')');
    ELSE
      WriteString('none)');
    END; (* IF *);
  END; (* FOR *)
  WriteLn;
  (* show active disk jobs *)
  WriteString('Disks (disk#, job#) > ');
  FOR Index := 1 TO MaxDisk DO
    WriteString(" ("); WriteCard(Index,1); WriteString(", ");
    IF DiskActive(Index) THEN
      WriteCard(DiskJobs[Index]^.JobNumber, 1);
      WriteString(')');
    ELSE
      WriteString('none)');
    END; (* IF *);
  END; (* FOR *)
  WriteLn;
```

```
  (* show active printer jobs *)
  WriteString('Printers (printer#, job#) > ');
  FOR Index := 1 TO MaxPrinter DO
    WriteString(" ("); WriteCard(Index,1); WriteString(", ");
    IF PrinterActive(Index) THEN
      WriteCard(PrinterJobs[Index]^.JobNumber, 1);
      WriteString(')');
    ELSE
      WriteString('none)');
    END; (* IF *)
  END; (* FOR *)
  WriteLn;
END ShowMachineState;

PROCEDURE PrintExplanation;
BEGIN
  WriteLn; WriteString(
 "This program simulates the behavior of a simple computer system.");
  WriteLn; WriteString(
 "You will be asked to specify the number of CPUs, disks, and printers.");
  WriteLn; WriteString(
 "CPU work is completed first and access is based on the job type: ");
  WriteLn; WriteString(
 "system, timeshare, batch and background from highest to lowest priority.");
  WriteLn; WriteString(
 "Each disk has a separate queue of jobs handled on a round robin basis.");
  WriteLn; WriteString(
 "Printer jobs execute until completion on a first come, first served basis.");
  WriteLn; WriteString(
 "Data input for each job is: job number, job type, start time, cpu time,");
  WriteLn; WriteString(
 "disk number, disk time, and printer time. Input is via redirection.");
  WriteLn; WriteString(
 "You may choose either a trace showing all active jobs at each clock cycle");
  WriteLn; WriteString(
 "or the final output summary. For each job, the summary contains the job");
  WriteLn; WriteString(
 "number, start and finish times, wait and execution times for each device,");
  WriteLn; WriteString(
    "total wait time, and total execution time.");
  WriteLn; WriteLn;
END PrintExplanation;
```

```
PROCEDURE GetDeviceNumbers(VAR MaxCPU, MaxDisk, MaxPrinter: CARDINAL);
  PROCEDURE GetValidDeviceCount(Msg: ARRAY OF CHAR): CARDINAL;
  VAR Choice: CARDINAL;
  BEGIN
    WriteString(Msg);
    LOOP
      WriteString("(1..");
      WriteCard(DeviceMax,1); WriteString(") > ");
      ReadCard(Choice); WriteLn;
      IF (1 <= Choice) AND (Choice <= DeviceMax) THEN EXIT END;
      WriteString("Please enter a valid choice ");
    END; (* LOOP *)
    RETURN Choice;
  END GetValidDeviceCount;
BEGIN
  MaxCPU := GetValidDeviceCount("Enter number of CPUs ");
  MaxDisk := GetValidDeviceCount("Enter number of disks ");
  MaxPrinter := GetValidDeviceCount("Enter number of printers ");
END GetDeviceNumbers;

VAR CPUIndex: JType;
    DeviceCount: CARDINAL;
BEGIN (* ComputerSystem initialization *)
  PrintExplanation;
  GetDeviceNumbers(MaxCPU, MaxDisk, MaxPrinter);
  FOR DeviceCount := 1 TO MaxDisk DO
    CreateQueue(DiskQueues[DeviceCount]);
    ActiveDisks[DeviceCount] := FALSE;
  END; (* FOR *)
  CreateQueue(JobQueue);
  CreateQueue(PrinterQueue);
  FOR CPUIndex := system TO background DO
    CreateQueue(CPUQueues[CPUIndex]);
  END; (* FOR *)
  FOR DeviceCount := 1 TO MaxCPU DO
    ActiveCPUs[DeviceCount] := FALSE;
  END; (* FOR *)
  FOR DeviceCount := 1 TO MaxPrinter DO
    ActivePrinters[DeviceCount] := FALSE;
  END; (* FOR *)
END ComputerSystem.
```

The computer simulation program is our main program and uses the computer system ADT. The Modula-2 program is very similar to the pseudocode.

```
MODULE ComputerSimulation;
(* This module simulates the runtime behavior of a simple computer
   system with a user defined number of CPUs, disks and printers.
   Data is read from an input file and output can be redirected to the
   console or to a file. The user can choose to have a trace of
   active jobs for each clock cycle or a summary of job activity.
   "Job" is an opaque type described in the module CPUSim.
                  Barry Kurtz          October 1991 *)
FROM InOut IMPORT OpenOutput, CloseOutput, WriteString, WriteLn, Read;
FROM ComputerSystem IMPORT Job, InitJobs, DispatchJob, JobsActive, GetCPUJob,
     CPUActive, StartNewCPUJob, GetDiskJob, DiskActive, StartNewDiskJob,
     GetPrinterJob, PrinterActive, PrinterFinished, StartNewPrinterJob,
     ContinuePrinting, MaxCPU, MaxDisk, MaxPrinter, ShowMachineState,
     CheckNewJobs;

PROCEDURE GetBooleanResponse(Msg: ARRAY OF CHAR;
                             VAR Response: BOOLEAN);
(* Print Msg and solicit a yes/no answer. Response is set to TRUE
   if answer is yes and to FALSE if answer is no. Reprompt user
   until either a Y for yes or N for no is entered. *)
VAR Choice: CHAR;
BEGIN
  WriteString(Msg); WriteLn;
  WriteString('Do you want this option? (Y/N) ');
  LOOP
    Read(Choice); WriteLn;
    Choice := CAP(Choice);
    IF (Choice = 'Y') OR (Choice = 'N') THEN EXIT END;
    WriteString('Please enter Y or N if you want this option. ');
  END; (* LOOP *)
  Response := Choice = 'Y';
END GetBooleanResponse;

PROCEDURE ScheduleCPUs(Time: CARDINAL; Trace: BOOLEAN);
(* For each CPU that is active, the current job is retrieved and
   dispatched. A new job is started on the CPU (if any jobs are
   ready). *)
VAR CPUNumber: CARDINAL;
    CurrentJob: Job;
BEGIN (* ScheduleCPUs *)
  FOR CPUNumber := 1 TO MaxCPU DO
    IF CPUActive(CPUNumber) THEN
      GetCPUJob(CurrentJob, CPUNumber);
      DispatchJob(CurrentJob, Time, Trace);
    END; (* IF *)
    StartNewCPUJob(CPUNumber, Time);
  END; (* FOR *)
END ScheduleCPUs;
```

```
PROCEDURE ScheduleDisks(Time: CARDINAL; Trace: BOOLEAN);
(* For each disk that is active, the current job is retrieved and
   dispatched. A new job is started on the disk (if any jobs are
   ready). *)
VAR DiskNumber: CARDINAL;
    CurrentJob: Job;
BEGIN (* ScheduleDisks *)
  FOR DiskNumber := 1 TO MaxDisk DO
    IF DiskActive(DiskNumber) THEN
      GetDiskJob(CurrentJob, DiskNumber);
      DispatchJob(CurrentJob, Time, Trace);
    END; (* IF *)
    StartNewDiskJob(DiskNumber, Time);
  END; (* FOR *)
END ScheduleDisks;

PROCEDURE SchedulePrinters(Time: CARDINAL; Trace: BOOLEAN);
(* For each printer, if the printer is active and the job is finished,
   then the job is retrieved, dispatched, and a new job is started.
   If the printer is active and the job is not finished, the job
   continues printing. If the printer is not active, then a new job
   is started if any print jobs are waiting. *)
VAR PrinterNumber: CARDINAL;
    CurrentJob: Job;
BEGIN (* SchedulePrinters *)
  FOR PrinterNumber := 1 TO MaxPrinter DO
    IF PrinterActive(PrinterNumber) THEN
      IF PrinterFinished(PrinterNumber) THEN
        GetPrinterJob(CurrentJob, PrinterNumber);
        DispatchJob(CurrentJob, Time, Trace);
        StartNewPrinterJob(PrinterNumber, Time);
      ELSE
        ContinuePrinting(PrinterNumber);
      END; (* IF *)
    ELSE
      StartNewPrinterJob(PrinterNumber, Time);
    END; (* IF *)
  END; (* FOR *)
END SchedulePrinters;

VAR Time: CARDINAL;
    ShowInput, ShowTrace: BOOLEAN;

BEGIN (* ComputerSimulation *)
  GetBooleanResponse("You have the option to display the input data.",
                    ShowInput);
  GetBooleanResponse("You have the option to trace execution.",
                    ShowTrace);
  InitJobs(ShowInput);   (* enters job data via redirection *)
  OpenOutput("out");
  Time := 0;
```

```
    IF NOT ShowTrace THEN    (* print summary heading *)
      WriteString(
" Job Job     Start   Stop         CPU             Disk            Printer         Total");
      WriteLn;
      WriteString(
" Num Type    Time    Time   Wait  Exec  Num   Wait  Exec   Wait  Exec   Wait  Exec");
      WriteLn;
    ELSE
      ShowMachineState(Time);
    END; (* IF *)
    REPEAT
      INC(Time);
      CheckNewJobs(Time);
      ScheduleCPUs(Time, ShowTrace);
      ScheduleDisks(Time, ShowTrace);
      SchedulePrinters(Time, ShowTrace);
      IF ShowTrace THEN
        ShowMachineState(Time);
      END; (* IF *)
    UNTIL NOT JobsActive();
    CloseOutput;
END ComputerSimulation.
```

We tested the ComputerSimulation program with two CPUs, four disk units, three printers, and the input data of Figure 7-12. When we asked for the input data display, we obtained Figure 7-8. When running the program in trace mode, we obtained the results of Figure 7-11. When not in trace mode, the final results were those of Figure 7-10. We tested further with a variety of system configurations and data; the simulation program performed as expected.

Complete the Documentation The documentation internal to the code should be supplemented by discussing the design decisions made before the coding. The operation of the simulation should be discussed in detail and several traces, similar to the trace in Figure 7-11, should be provided. The complete testing results should also be provided.

Summary

Queues are data structures in which the storage and retrieval of elements are limited to a single element at a time: the user has access only to the least recently added element. Queues are used in a variety of applications, especially in simulation and within computer operating systems.

Implementations of queues must keep track of the first and last elements of the queue in order to have efficient storage and retrieval operations. Static and dynamic implementations of queues generally have the same overall performance characteristics. All operations have constant complexity, with the exception of the operation disposing of a linked queue.

■ *Exercises*

1. Write a procedure to display the elements of a queue from head to tail,
   (a) using only the operations for the queue ADT.
   (b) working directly with the static representation.
   (c) working directly with the dynamic representation.

2. Write a procedure to display the elements of a queue from tail to head.
   (a) using only the operations for the queue ADT.
   (b) working directly with the static representation.
   (c) working directly with the dynamic representation.

3. Assuming a queue of integers, write a program that uses only ADT operations to increment the value of each item in the queue.

4. Using only the ADT operations for a queue, write a procedure to reverse a queue,
   (a) using recursion.
   (b) using the Stack ADT.

5. Using only ADT operations, write a procedure to split a queue into a queue of "even" elements and a queue of "odd" elements.

6. Using only ADT operations, write a procedure to merge two queues, Q1 and Q2, into a single queue with an element from Q1, then an element from Q2, etc.

7. In the CentralStation simulation program, modify procedure Generate so that it generates bursts of arrivals at one-minute maximum intervals during the first five minutes of each hour.

8. Define another operation for the ADT Queue, Cancel(Key), which will cancel the element with the given Key in the queue.

9. Define a new Boolean operation InQueue(Key) for the ADT Queue. This operation returns TRUE if an element with a key equal to the procedure parameter Key is indeed in the queue.

10. A *dequeue* is a double ended queue, where insertions and deletions are done at either end. Define completely the ADT Dequeue.

11. An input-restricted deque allows insertions at one end only. Modify your ADT Deque to specify an input-restricted deque.

12. An output-restricted deque allows deletions at one end only. Modify your ADT Deque to specify an output-restricted deque.

Programming Problems

13. Implement and test your ADT Deque defined in problem 10.

14. Modify the static implementation of queues so that the first element of the queue is *always* the first element of the array.

15. Modify the CentralStation simulation program so that, instead of five queues, there is only one queue for the five wickets. Run the modified program and compare the results with those of the original program.

16. Modify the queue implementation of your choice so that it becomes a priority queue implementation: operation Enqueue will keep the queue in order of its elements' priority.

17. Modify the queue implementation of your choice so that it becomes a priority queue implementation: operation Dequeue will search the queue for the element with the higher priority, and if there are several to choose from, the least recently inserted will be taken.

18. Modify the computer simulation so that CPU activity and Disk activity alternate. If a job has four units of CPU time and five units of disk time, there will be one unit of CPU, one unit of disk, another unit of CPU, etc., until execution is completed.

19. A more elaborate variation of problem 18 is to have CPU bursts and disks bursts that are satisfied alternately. The job data should include the total CPU time, the minimum burst time, the maximum burst time, and similar data for the disk. For example, if there are 32 units of total CPU time with bursts ranging from 3 units to 7 units, then a burst time within this range would be selected and the CPU would execute for that length of time before swapping to the disk. This disk burst would be determined in a similar manner; then, if required CPU time remains, the job switches back to the CPU. For either the CPU or disk, it is permissible for the final burst time to be less than the minimum.

20. Add a print queue routine to the computer simulation so that the contents of each queue is displayed if the trace option is selected. This routine should be external to the ADT. You may rely on the fact that job numbers are unique as you print the elements in the queue by a sequence of dequeues and enqueues.

Trees

INTRODUCTION

The abstract data types we have seen so far have all been linear or one-dimensional. Even though they offer advantages of flexibility, they are basically sequential, so that moving through the corresponding structures is done one position at a time. Linear representations are often inadequate for conceptualizing problems or for use in many computer applications. A tree is a nonlinear data structure that is particularly important in computer science, as it is extremely useful in a wide variety of computer applications. Trees provide the basis for numerous methods of quick information retrieval. Trees may be used in sorting and searching applications; they are used to implement priority queues; and they are also used in game playing applications, in theorem proving, and in knowledge representations.

This chapter introduces the tree abstraction as well as a number of varied applications and some implementations. A specific type of tree, the binary search tree, will be introduced in Chapter 9. More advanced topics on trees will be covered in Chapter 10.

Chapter 8 Trees

8.1 Definitions

A *tree* is a collection of elements called *nodes* as illustrated in Figure 8-1. The first node of a tree is called the *root* of the tree.

More formally a tree is either:

empty

or

a node (the tree root), with a finite number of associated trees called its *subtrees*

A *leaf* is a node that has no subtree. A *branch* is a connection between a node and one of its subtrees. The root of a given node's subtree is a direct *descendant* of that node. A node is also called the *parent* of its subtrees. For example, in Figure 8-1, J, F, C, K, L, H, and I are leaves. Nodes B, C, and D are direct descendants of root A, and D is the parent of G, H, and I.

If $n_1, n_2, n_3, \ldots, n_m$ is a sequence of nodes in a given tree such that n_{i+1} is a direct descendant of n_i for $1 \leq i \leq m$, then this sequence is called a *path* from tree node n_1 to tree node n_m. The length of a path is one less than the number of nodes in the path. For instance, in Figure 8-1 there is a path of length 3 between nodes A and L. The *height* of a node in a tree is the length of the longest path from that node to a leaf. In Figure 8-1, the height of node B is 2. The height of a tree is the height of its root. The *depth* of a node is the length of the path from the root to that node. The *degree* of a node is the number of its direct descendants, while the degree of a tree is the maximum degree of all its nodes. The *level* of a node is such that the level of the root is 1, and each node has a level that is one greater than the level of its parent. An *ordered tree* is a tree in which the order of each node's subtrees is fixed. The descendants of a node are usually ordered from left to right. Figure 8-2 shows two different ordered trees. Finally, a *forest* is a collection of zero or more trees.

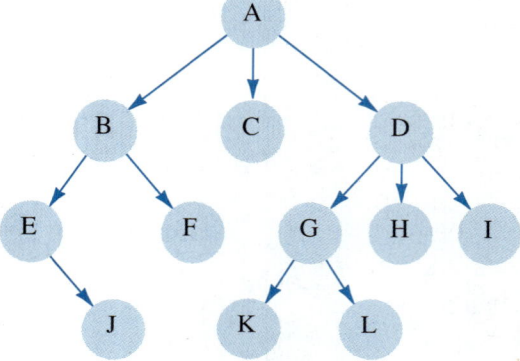

Figure 8-1
A Tree

Figure 8-2
Ordered Trees

There are several ways to denote trees. As seen in figures 8-1 and 8-2, the representation most often used is that with the root on top and the leaves at the bottom. As trees represent hierarchies, we can also use the Modula-2 RECORD structure to represent a tree. The following represents the tree of Figure 8-1:

```
A: RECORD
      B: RECORD
            E: RECORD
                  J;
               END;
            F;
         END;
      C;
      D: RECORD
            G: RECORD
                  K;
                  L;
               END;
            H;
            I;
         END;
   END;
```

As a matter of fact, the table of contents of this book also represents a tree. Here is a chapter example representing a hierarchy: node 5 has nine descendants, node 5.3 has five descendants, etc.

5. Linear Lists
    5.1 Abstraction: The Linear List
    5.2 Applications
        High-Precision Arithmetic
        Polynomial Arithmetic
    5.3 Implementation
        Static Implementation
        Dynamic Implementation
        Circular Lists
        Symmetric Lists
        List Headers
    5.4 Multilinked Lists
    5.5 Linked Implementations of Arrays

5.6 Memory Management
    Allocation
    Liberation
5.7 Case Study: Sparse Matrices
    Design
    Implementation
5.8 Summary
5.9 Exercises

It is also possible to use other notations. The tree of Figure 8-1 can be represented by Figure 8-3 or by the following parenthesized form, where the first element of each list (following the left parenthesis) is the root and the other elements are the root's subtrees:

(A (B (E J) F) C (D (G K L) H I))

Some representations might only be good for unordered trees, however, since it is not always possible to deduce the order of the subtrees from the representation alone.

Many computer science applications are based on a subset of trees called *binary trees*. A binary tree is a tree in which nodes have at most two descendants. The empty tree is also a binary tree. Each subtree of a node is identified either as the left descendant (or *child*) or as the right descendant (or child) of that node. Children of the same parent are called *siblings*.

It is interesting to note that a forest of trees of any degree can be represented by binary trees if, for each node

    the first descendant becomes the left subtree root
    the next sibling becomes the right subtree root

Figure 8-4 shows the binary tree representing the tree of Figure 8-1.

Binary trees are sometimes used to store information for searching. Binary trees can be organized into *binary search trees* so that searching operations can be more efficient. Binary search trees will be presented in Chapter 9.

8.2 Abstraction

An abstract data type Tree will define types Tree and Node and offer a number of operations including:

CreateTree(root)	Create a new tree
LeftmostChild(node, tree)	Return leftmost child of node in tree
RightSibling(node, tree)	Return right sibling of node in tree
Graft(subtree, tree, node)	Add subtree as rightmost descendant of node in tree
Parent(node, tree)	Return parent of node in tree
Traverse(tree, process)	Visit every node in the tree and apply process to each of them

Figure 8-3
A Tree
Representation

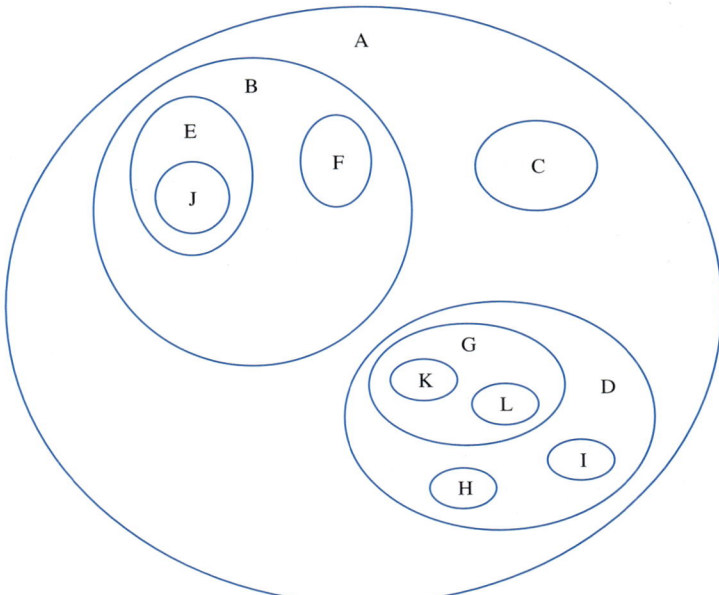

The Traverse operation is of special interest, as it implies visiting every node in a tree exactly once and applying some processing operation to every node element. Linear lists were traversed in an intuitively obvious way from beginning to end, but trees may be traversed in a number of different ways.

For instance, we could start at the root and proceed to the root of the leftmost subtree, and then to the root of its leftmost subtree until a leaf is found. This leaf is the first node to be visited. After that, we backtrack along the path we have taken until finding a node with no more subtrees, which we proceed to visit. Or we backtrack until

Figure 8-4
Binary Tree
Representing a Tree

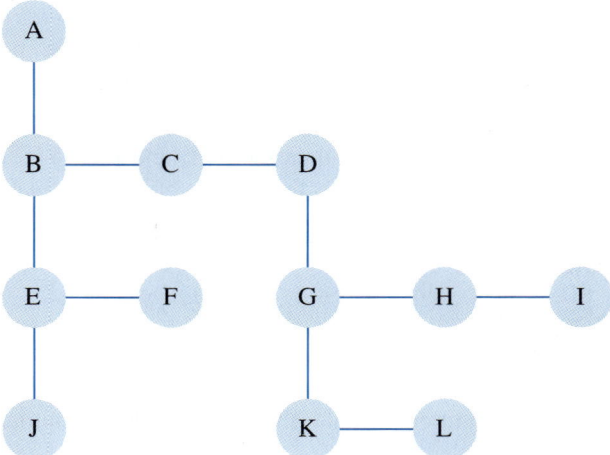

we find a node with other subtrees, and the leftmost node of these subtrees is followed in the same manner until a leaf is found and visited. The backtracking process continues until there are no more nodes left to visit. This traversal method is called *depth-first traversal,* as we always go as deep as we can to visit the next node. Traversal of the tree in Figure 8-1 using depth-first traversal would visit the nodes in the following order: J E F B C K L G H I D A.

Another traversal method is called *breadth-first traversal*. Here we proceed level by level, visiting the whole breadth of a level before going down to the next level. We start at the root and visit it first, and then we visit the roots of all its subtrees (or descendants) in left-to-right order, and then each of the first descendant's descendants, and so forth. Breadth-first traversal of the tree in Figure 8-1 would visit the nodes in the following order: A B C D E F G H I J K L.

Besides traversals, there are a great variety of other operations that can be performed on trees; many of them will be specific to given applications.

Since it is always possible to represent a tree as a binary tree, and since most applications are based on this kind of tree, in this chapter we will concentrate on binary trees. As a consequence, we will not complete the development of the ADT Tree here, but rather define completely the ADT Binary Tree.

Binary Tree

To define an ADT Binary Tree we will need nodes containing some kind of "standard" element. As we have done before, we will define a type TreeElementType as specified by the user and import it into our BinaryTreeADT module. From a given tree node it is possible to go two ways, left or right, and we must take that into account when defining our operations. Thus, we will include in our ADT a type Position, which will be used to indicate the position of the next node as the root of the tree, the left descendant, or the right descendant.

A global variable TreeError will be used to signal the success or failure of the operations. When we have a binary tree, it is very useful to keep track of the most recently visited node, called the *current node*. Most operations will affect the current node or alter it.

Although traversal methods for trees can be numerous, in the case of binary trees only three traversal strategies are commonly used, all of them depth-first methods:

Preorder: Visit the root, then its left subtree, and finally its right subtree.
Inorder: Visit the left subtree, then the root, and finally its right subtree.
Postorder: Visit the left subtree, the right subtree, and finally the root.

To illustrate these strategies, traversals of the tree in Figure 8-4 will visit the nodes in the following orders:

Preorder: A B E J F C D G K L H I
Inorder: J E F B C K L G H I D A
Postorder: J F E L K H I G D C B A

The following definition module gives a complete definition of ADT Binary Tree.

```
DEFINITION MODULE BinaryTreeADT;
FROM BinTreeElements IMPORT TreeElementType;

TYPE BinaryTree;      (* opaque type *)
     TreePointer;     (* opaque type *)
     TraverseProc = PROCEDURE(TreeElementType);
     Position = (ToRoot, ToLeft, ToRight);

VAR TreeError: BOOLEAN; (* result of operation *)

PROCEDURE CreateTree(VAR Tree: BinaryTree);
(* The first procedure to call, which allocates and initializes a tree.
   Pre-condition: Tree does not exist
   Post-Condition: empty Tree exists, TreeError' is false *)

PROCEDURE DeleteTree(VAR Tree: BinaryTree);
(* All informations about the Tree and the data records it contains are
   deleted.
   Pre-condition: Tree exists
   Post-Condition: Tree does not exist, TreeError' is false *)

PROCEDURE InsertNode(VAR Tree: BinaryTree; VAR Element: TreeElementType;
                     Where: Position);
(* Insert Element into the tree. The key is in the element.
   Pre-condition: Tree and Element exist. Where=ToRoot and Tree is empty,
                  Where=ToLeft & no left child,
                  Where=ToRight & no right child
   Post-Condition: node is inserted in Tree and TreeError' is false
                   otherwise TreeError' is true *)

PROCEDURE DeleteNode(VAR Tree: BinaryTree);
(* Delete current node from the Tree.
   This procedure should not be called during a TraverseTree.
   Pre-condition: Tree and current node exist
   Post-Condition: current node is deleted, and TreeError' is false
                   otherwise TreeError' is true *)

PROCEDURE TraverseTree(Tree: BinaryTree; TravProc: TraverseProc);
(* Call "TravProc" for each node using an Inorder traversal.
   Pre-condition: Tree exists
   Post-Condition: all nodes have been visited and TravProc applied to them *)

PROCEDURE SearchTree(Tree: BinaryTree; Element: TreeElementType);
(* Search for Element in the Tree.
   Pre-condition: Tree and Element exist
   Post-Condition: if element occurs in Tree then the current node is
                   set to the first occurrence found in order otherwise
                   TreeError' is true and current node is not changed *)
```

```
PROCEDURE NextNode(VAR Tree: BinaryTree; Where: Position);
(* Advance current node in given direction.
   Pre-condition: Tree and current node exist
   Post-Condition: Where = ToRoot then current node is Tree root
                   Where = ToLeft then current node is left child
                   Where = ToRight then current node is right child
                   otherwise there is no change and TreeError' is false *)
PROCEDURE StoreNode(VAR Tree: BinaryTree; Element: TreeElementType);
(* Store Element as the new value of the current node.
   Pre-condition: Tree, current node and Element exist
   Post-Condition: current node value' = Element and TreeError' is false
                   otherwise TreeError' is true *)
PROCEDURE RetrieveNode(Tree: BinaryTree; VAR Element: TreeElementType);
(* Assign value of current node to element.
   Pre-condition: Tree and current node exist
   Post-Condition: Element' = current node value and TreeError' is false
                   otherwise TreeError' is true *)
PROCEDURE TreeSize(Tree: BinaryTree): CARDINAL;
(* Return number of nodes in tree.
   Pre-condition: Tree exists
   Post-Condition: number of nodes in Tree is returned *)
PROCEDURE DisplayTree(Tree: BinaryTree; PrintElement: TraverseProc);
(* Print tree with indentations to show structure.
   Pre-condition: Tree exists
   Post-Condition: Tree is displayed vertically on screen with elements
                   indented *)
PROCEDURE GetCurrentNode(Tree: BinaryTree; VAR Node: TreePointer);
(* Return pointer to Tree current node.
   Pre-condition: Tree exists
   Post-Condition: Node' points to current node *)
PROCEDURE SetCurrentNode(Tree: BinaryTree; Node: TreePointer);
(* Reset Tree current node to Node.
   Pre-condition: Tree exists, Node exists in tree
   Post-Condition: current node is set to Node *)
PROCEDURE ExistNode(Tree: BinaryTree; Where: Position): BOOLEAN;
(* Return TRUE if a node exists at position indicated.
   Pre-condition: Tree exists
   Post-Condition: return true if node exists Where
                   otherwise return false *)
END BinaryTreeADT.
```

Note that a procedure type was introduced that is needed for the parameters of operations TraverseTree and DisplayTree. In the case of TraverseTree, a procedure parameter is used to define the processing to apply to every node in the tree. In the case of DisplayTree, a procedure parameter is necessary to display the node values, which are of imported type TreeElementType. The procedures used in TraverseTree and in DisplayTree are intended to be different but have the same parameter type, and are of the same procedure type.

8.3 Applications

In computer science, trees are considered one of the most fundamental subjects because they and their variations have many applications. Trees are also useful as a data structure used to implement other abstract data types. Tree applications are so rich and varied that it is impossible to cover them all. We will show here a few applications of the tree abstract data type and of the tree data structure as well.

Searching

Most tree applications will use the tree searching operation of our ADT Binary Tree. The searching algorithm used will be described in detail with the implementations in Section 8.4.

Searching is an operation that can be applied to all sorts of trees and is not confined to binary trees. Basically, searching a tree is very similar to traversing it. It is thus not surprising to find two ways of doing searches that are similar to those used in tree traversals: depth-first search and breadth-first search.

In depth-first search, we start at the root and, following a sequence of left pointers, we go to the root of the leftmost and deepest subtree. Then we examine this root by comparing it (or its key) to the desired element. If the comparison is negative, we backtrack along the path we followed and, using recursion, we examine the next successor of the node reached while backtracking. Using the example of the general tree of Figure 8-5 and searching for Q, we start at the root A and follow left pointers to B, F, and N. N is examined, as it has no successor. We backtrack to F and try its next successor O, which leads us to T, which is examined. We backtrack again to O and examine U, then O and F. We then examine G, P, H, and B. We backtrack to A and apply the same method to its other successors: we examine C, I, Q, and stop there as we have found a node corresponding to our goal.

We assume a tree whose structure is defined by:

```
TYPE NodePointer = POINTER TO Node;
     Node = RECORD
              Info: CHAR;
              Successors: ARRAY [1..Max] OF NodePointer;
            END;
```

This representation assumes there will be at most Max children for any node. This representation is adequate when the number of children is relatively uniform. (In the case study of Section 8.5, we will use a left-child, right-sibling representation that is

Figure 8-5
A General Tree

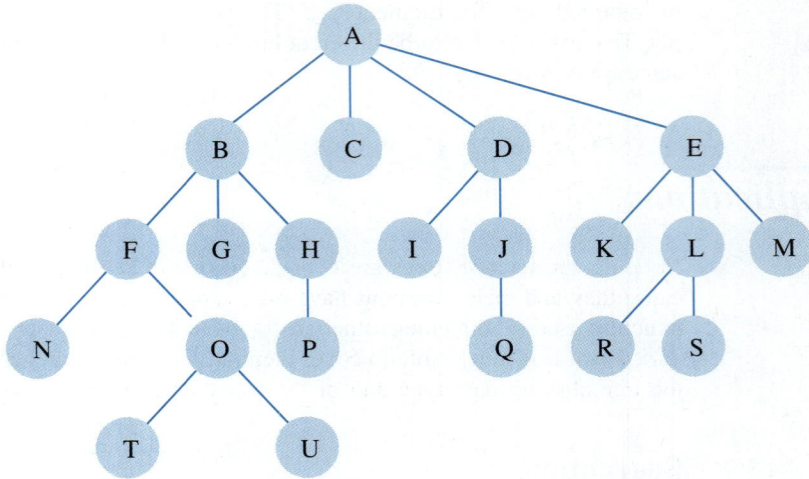

more appropriate when the number of children is not as uniform as in this example.) The following procedure implements our depth-first search algorithm.

```
PROCEDURE DepthFirstSearch(Tree: NodePointer; Element: CHAR;
                           VAR Node: NodePointer; VAR Found: BOOLEAN);
VAR Index: CARDINAL;
BEGIN
  IF (Tree # NIL) AND NOT Found THEN
    Index := 1;
    WHILE (Index <= Max) AND (Tree^.Successors[Index] # NIL) DO
      (* search all successors *)
      DepthFirstSearch(Tree^.Successors[Index], Element, Node, Found);
      INC(Index)
    END; (* WHILE *)
    IF Tree^.Info = Element THEN   (* stop search *)
      Found := TRUE;
      Node := Tree;
    END; (* IF *)
  END; (* IF *)
END DepthFirstSearch;
```

The procedure is recursive, as we apply the same process to various subtrees. It assumes that the Successors array comprises a NIL pointer to mark the end of a node's descendants. The procedure considers a given node and calls itself recursively for each of the node's successors. Once this is done, the node is examined and the search stops as soon as the element is found.

In a breadth-first search, we start at the root and examine it first. If it is not the element we are looking for, we examine all its successors from left to right. Then, if we are still searching, we examine the first descendant's children from left to right, then the second descendant's children, and so forth, until we find what we are looking for or we have examined all the tree nodes. Using the general tree of Figure 8-5 we will examine A, then B, C, D, and E, then F, G, H, I, J, K, L, and M, then N, O, P, and Q.

In order to use this method, we will need a queue to keep a list of all the descendants of a node that we must examine later. If we use the same tree structure as before, our algorithm is described by procedure BreadthFirstSearch.

```
PROCEDURE BreadthFirstSearch(Tree: NodePointer; Element: CHAR;
                 VAR Point: NodePointer; VAR Found: BOOLEAN);
VAR Index: CARDINAL;
    Node: NodePointer;
    Q: Queue;
BEGIN
  CreateQueue(Q);
  Enqueue(Q, Tree);
  WHILE (CountQueue(Q) # 0) AND NOT Found DO  (* examine queue *)
    Dequeue(Q, Node);
    IF Node^.Info = Element THEN              (* stop search *)
      Point := Node;
      Found := TRUE;
      RETURN;
    END; (* IF *)
    Index := 1;
    WHILE (Index <= Max) AND (Node^.Successors[Index] # NIL) DO
      Enqueue(Q, Node^.Successors[Index]);
      INC(Index);
    END; (* WHILE *)
  END; (* WHILE *)
END BreadthFirstSearch;
```

The first node is examined and then its successors are enqueued. The next node to examine is the first in the queue; this process is repeated as long as we have not found what we are looking for and there are elements in the queue.

Expression Trees

As we have seen, the three ways of traversing a binary tree are called preorder, inorder, and postorder. The choice of these names was not accidental, but rather related to a specialized kind of tree, the expression tree. An expression tree is used to represent algebraic expressions. It is a binary tree made of simple operands and operators, with the simple operands as tree leaves and the operators as interior nodes. Figure 8-6 gives the expression tree corresponding to the expression a+b/c.

The tree traversal methods applied to the expression tree in Figure 8-6 give the following node order:

Preorder: +a/bc
Inorder: a+b/c
Postorder: abc/+

Figure 8-6
Expression Tree for
$a+b/c$

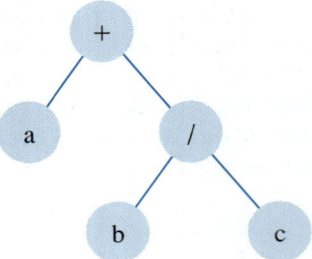

It is easy to note that the traversals correspond to the prefix, infix, and postfix forms of the algebraic expression. When an expression comprises a unary operator, one of the subtrees of the unary operator will be empty. Figure 8-7 gives an example of a more complete expression tree, which we use to represent a whole statement.

Once an expression tree has been built, it is easy to obtain either the prefix or the postfix form of the expression. We have already seen one conversion method from infix to postfix in Section 6.2. An expression tree may also be used to evaluate the expression.

To build an expression tree we must parse an algebraic expression. One easy way of doing this is to use the method of recursive descent. The structure used in this method is similar to the one used to define an expression following EBNF (Extended Backus Naur Form—used to define the syntax of languages like Modula-2):

Expression = SimpleExpression [Relation SimpleExpression]
SimpleExpression = [''+'' | ''−''] Term {AddOperator Term}
Term = Factor [MulOperator Factor]
Factor = Number | Identifier | ''('' Expression '')'' | NOT Factor
Relation = ''='' | ''#'' | ''<'' | ''>'' | ''<='' | ''>=''
AddOperator = ''+'' | ''−'' | OR
MulOperator = '' * '' | ''/'' | DIV | MOD | AND

Figure 8-7
Expression Tree for
$c := (-x + y/n) < (z * k)$

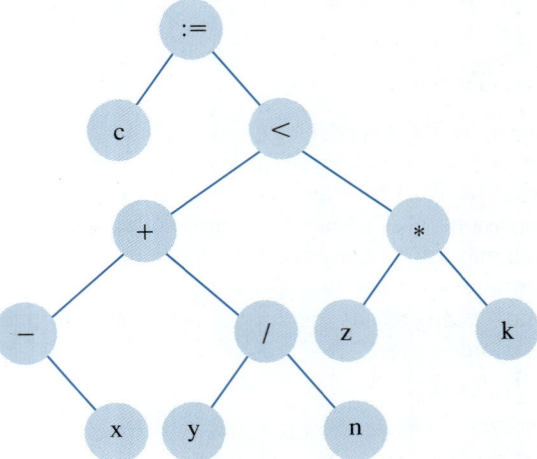

We can design our recursive descent parser on this model, with procedures Expression, SimpleExpression, Term, and Factor. Relation, AddOperator, and MulOperator can be represented by sets of enumeration types. For instance, procedure Term would simply be:

```
PROCEDURE Term(VAR ExpressionTree: Tree);
BEGIN
  Factor(ExpressionTree);
  WHILE Symbol IN MulOperator DO
    AddNode(ExpressionTree, Symbol);
    GetNextSymbol(Symbol);
    Factor(ExpressionTree^.Right);
  END;
END Term;
```

Completion of such a parser is left as problem 26.

Expression trees may be used as means to evaluate expressions in language interpreters. They may also be used in the optimization phase of a compiler: an expression tree is scanned to detect identical subexpressions. Identical subexpressions will be represented by subtrees having the same structure and the same node contents. Once two identical subexpressions have been detected, the global expression must be rewritten so that the subexpression is evaluated only once and the evaluation result is used several times. The rewriting is not always simple. We will leave a simple application of this method to problems 27 and 28, while noting that there are other expression optimization techniques that do not necessarily use expression trees.

Huffman Codes

In computers, character codes are usually based on a fixed number of bits: seven bits for the ASCII code (see Appendix C) and eight bits for the EBCDIC code. When sending messages through telecommunication lines it is always better to try to have the shortest messages possible, for efficiency. With fixed-length character codes, message lengths are always fixed. However, for smaller sets of characters it is possible to define special character codes that will reduce the message lengths.

If we have five characters and a three-bit character code, as in the following:

    A   000
    B   001
    C   010
    D   011
    E   100

then the message ''BADCABDEAD'' will be coded

001000011010000010111000000011

which has a length of 30 bits. To minimize the length of messages to send we can define a Huffman code. In our message, letters A and D occurred three times, while letters C and E occurred only once. Consequently, if we choose a short code for letters A and D and a longer code for letters C and E, our message length will be decreased. We could choose the following codes:

A   10
B   01
C   000
D   11
E   001

which gives a 22-bit message: 0110110001001110011011. For this message, the savings are not that spectacular, but for longer messages, savings can be substantial. Note that a code cannot be the prefix of another code. This requirement is needed in order to read the message from left to right. In our message, 01 is encountered first (B), then 10 (A), then 11 (D), then 000(C), etc. There are no ambiguities. Since character codes have different lengths, the message cannot be divided into equal slices; rather, it must be examined bit by bit.

To get a particular code, we must use the probability of occurrence of each symbol in the message. In fact, what is used is the frequency of occurrence of the symbols in a group of messages to send, and, if the messages are written in a given language, the frequency of the symbols in the language.

Huffman's algorithm makes it possible to obtain such character codes. It works in the following way: the two symbols with the lowest frequency, x and y, are first chosen and then they are replaced by a pseudo-symbol z with a frequency equal to the sum of the two frequencies. This process is applied repeatedly until all symbols have been replaced. The optimal code for the original symbols is the code of the pseudo-symbol that replaced them, with an extra zero in the case of x, and an extra 1 in the case of y.

The codes may be seen as the paths in a binary tree: the path from a node to its left descendant adds a zero to the code, while the path from a node to its right descendant adds a 1 to the code. Figure 8-8 shows the binary tree corresponding to the previous example, where leaves represent the original symbols. This guarantees that no internal node corresponds to a character code.

Figure 8-8
Huffman Code Binary Tree

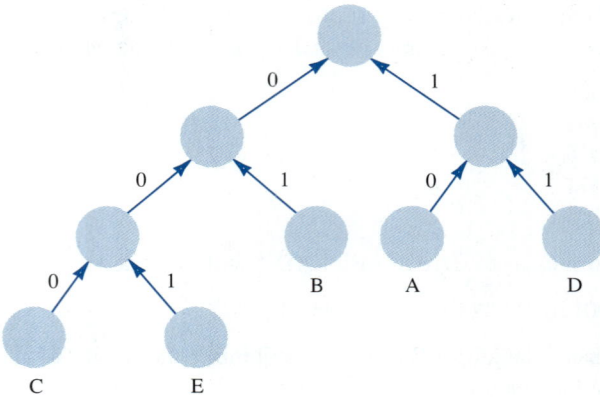

It is possible to build such a tree from the original symbols. Once the tree is built, we have only to start at a leaf and go up the tree to the root to get the corresponding code. This is done for each leaf: each time we climb a left branch, a zero is added in front of the code, while each time we climb a right branch a 1 is added in front of the code. From Figure 8-8 we can see that the code for A is 10, the code for B is 01, the code for C is 000, etc.

Note that with this method it is only necessary to keep a link between a node and its parent, and that links from a parent to its children are not used. We will not be able to use our ADT Binary Tree, as our needs are specific to our particular application. Instead, we will design our own tree structure in anticipation of the next section on implementation.

Each node will include three fields: the frequency of occurrence (of the symbol for leaves or the sum of the descendants' frequencies for internal nodes), a pointer to its parent (in order to be able to climb up the tree from the leaves), and a flag to indicate whether the node is a left or a right descendant (for code creation). Using this structure, the tree of Figure 8-8 can be represented as shown in Figure 8-9. The symbols could be included in the leaves, but can also be kept in a separate array of characters. We will define a node type with three fields: Frequency, Parent, Descendant, and use an array of nodes to represent our tree. The array shown in Figure 8-10 is another representation of the tree of Figure 8-8.

The program to build such a tree from a given set of data, and to produce the corresponding Huffman codes is the following.

Figure 8-9
Huffman Code
Binary Tree

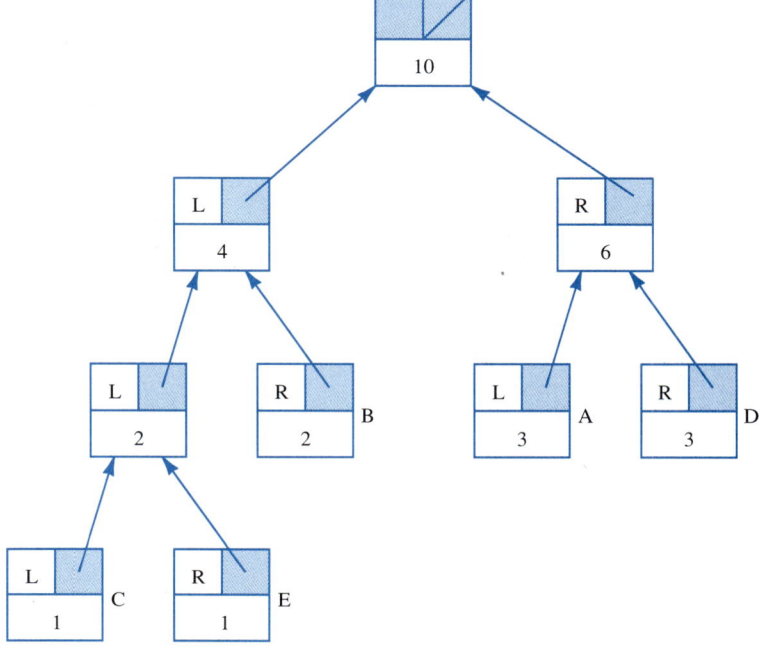

Figure 8-10
Huffman Code Binary Tree in Array

	Nodes		
1	3	8	L
2	2	7	R
3	1	6	L
4	3	8	R
5	1	6	R
6	2	7	L
7	4	9	L
8	6	9	R
9	10	0	*

Alphabet
A
B
C
D
E

```
MODULE HuffmanCodes;
FROM InOut IMPORT WriteString, WriteLn, Read, ReadCard, Write,
                  WriteCard, OpenInput, CloseInput;

CONST MaxBits = 20;                         (* maximum number of bits in code *)
      MaxPos = MaxBits + 1;
      MaxSymbols = 26;                      (* maximum number of different codes *)
      MaxNodes = MaxSymbols * 2 - 1;        (* maximum number of tree nodes *)

TYPE DescendantType = (Left, Right);
     IndexType = [0..MaxNodes];
     Bit = ['0'..'1'];
     CodeType = RECORD
                  Bits: ARRAY [1..MaxBits] OF Bit;  (* symbol code *)
                  Start: [1..MaxPos];               (* index of first code bit *)
                END;
     NodeType = RECORD                              (* tree element *)
                  Frequency: CARDINAL;
                  Parent: IndexType;
                  Descendant: DescendantType;
                END;

VAR Alphabet: ARRAY [1..MaxSymbols] OF CHAR;   (* symbols *)
    Codes: ARRAY [1..MaxSymbols] OF CodeType;  (* codes *)
    Nodes: ARRAY [1..MaxNodes] OF NodeType;    (* tree nodes *)
    Index, N: [0..MaxSymbols];                 (* symbol indices *)
    Node, Free, Index1, Index2: IndexType;     (* tree indices *)
    Code: CodeType;
    BitIndex: [1..MaxBits];                    (* code index *)
    Symbol: CHAR;
    Small1, Small2: CARDINAL;                  (* smallest frequencies *)
```

```
BEGIN
  (* Initialization *)
  FOR Node := 1 TO MaxNodes DO        (* empty tree *)
    Nodes[Node].Frequency := 0;
    Nodes[Node].Parent := 0;
  END; (* FOR *)
  FOR Index := 1 TO MaxSymbols DO   (* empty alphabet *)
    Alphabet[Index] := ' ';
  END; (* FOR *)

  (* read alphabet and frequencies *)
  OpenInput("dat");
  ReadCard(N);
  FOR Index := 1 TO N DO
    ReadCard(Nodes[Index].Frequency); Read(Alphabet[Index]);
  END; (* FOR *)
  CloseInput;

  (* build the tree *)
  FOR Free := N+1 TO 2*N-1 DO (* Free indicates the next free node *)
    (* look for two unused symbols with smallest frequencies *)
    Index1 := 0; Index2 := 0;
    Small1 := MAX(CARDINAL);
    Small2 := MAX(CARDINAL);
    FOR Node := 1 TO Free-1 DO
      IF Nodes[Node].Parent = 0 THEN            (* Node not used yet *)
        IF Nodes[Node].Frequency < Small1 THEN  (* new smallest *)
          Small2 := Small1;
          Small1 := Nodes[Node].Frequency;
          Index2 := Index1;
          Index1 := Node;
        ELSIF Nodes[Node].Frequency < Small2 THEN (* second smallest *)
          Small2 := Nodes[Node].Frequency;
          Index2 := Node;
        END; (* IF *)
      END; (* IF *)
    END; (* FOR *)
    (* new node Free has Index1 as Left descendant and Index2 as
       Right descendant *)
    Nodes[Index1].Parent := Free;
    Nodes[Index1].Descendant := Left;
    Nodes[Index2].Parent := Free;
    Nodes[Index2].Descendant := Right;
    Nodes[Free].Frequency:= Nodes[Index1].Frequency + Nodes[Index2].Frequency;
  END; (* FOR *)
```

```
    (* extract codes from tree *)
    FOR Index := 1 TO N DO
      Code.Start := MaxPos;
      Node := Index;
      WHILE Nodes[Node].Parent # 0 DO                    (* go up in tree *)
        IF Nodes[Node].Descendant = Left THEN            (* Left descendant: 0 *)
          DEC(Code.Start);
          Code.Bits[Code.Start] := '0';
        ELSE                                             (* Right descendant: 1 *)
          DEC(Code.Start);
          Code.Bits[Code.Start] := '1';
        END; (* IF *)
        Node := Nodes[Node].Parent;
      END; (* WHILE *)
      Codes[Index] := Code;                              (* keep new code *)
    END; (* FOR *)

    (* display results *)
    FOR Index := 1 TO N DO
      Write(Alphabet[Index]); Write(' ');
      WriteCard(Nodes[Index].Frequency, 3); Write(' ');
      FOR BitIndex := Codes[Index].Start TO MaxBits DO   (* display code *)
        Write(Codes[Index].Bits[BitIndex]);
      END; (* FOR *)
      WriteLn;
    END; (* FOR *)
END HuffmanCodes.
```

For brevity in presentation, we have not modularized the code into procedures; however, the logical divisions of the code are clearly presented and the program could be easily modularized. Program HuffmanCodes starts by initializing the Nodes array to empty, then reads in the number of symbols followed by each symbol and its frequency. The symbol is kept in array Alphabet and its frequency is kept in array Nodes. After all the data have been read in, the first N elements in Nodes represent the leaves of the Huffman tree, which has yet to be built. Internal nodes will be located in elements N + 1 and beyond, in array Nodes.

Using the fact that in a *full binary tree* (a tree where each node is either a leaf or has two descendants) the number of leaves exceeds the number of internal nodes by one (see problem 13 of the Exercises section), we know the tree we are building will have 2N − 1 nodes. We repeatedly find the nodes with the two lowest frequencies (Small1 and Small2) and create their parent node Free. Once the tree is built, for each leaf we climb the tree up to the root and construct the code as we go by adding a 0 (left) or a 1 (right) in front of the code. After this is done, we only have to print the various codes. The complexity of Huffman's algorithm is $O(n^2)$, as the tree building operation is based on two nested loops.

With the following input:

9, 16A, 8B, 24C, 6D, 12E, 4F, 16G, 2H, 6I

program HuffmanCodes produces the following codes:

A	111	D	1010	G	00		
B	1101	E	100	H	11000		
C	01	F	11001	I	1011		

8.4 Implementation

As with most ADTs, we can use two kinds of implementation.

Dynamic Implementation

Since trees are nonlinear dynamic structures, it is more natural to use an implementation based on pointers. The BinaryTreeADT implementation module will define the following structures and procedures.

```
TYPE BinaryTree = POINTER TO TreeHeader;
     TreePointer = POINTER TO TreeNode;
     TreeHeader = RECORD
                     Root: TreePointer;
                     Current: TreePointer;
                     Size: CARDINAL;
                  END;
     TreeNode = RECORD
                   Element: TreeElementType;
                   Left, Right: TreePointer;
                END;
```

As expected, BinaryTree is a pointer to a tree header where information is kept in three fields: Root is a pointer to the root node, Current is a pointer to the current node (that is, the node to which most operations will apply), Size indicates the number of nodes in the tree. A tree node has three fields: the element comprising all the information associated with the node, and two pointers to the node's descendants.

```
PROCEDURE CreateTree(VAR Tree: BinaryTree);
(* The first procedure to call, which allocates and initializes a Tree *)
BEGIN
  ALLOCATE(Tree, SIZE(TreeHeader));
  Tree^.Root := NIL;
  Tree^.Current := NIL;
  Tree^.Size := 0;
END CreateTree;
```

```
PROCEDURE DeleteTree(VAR Tree: BinaryTree);
(* All information about the Tree and the data records it contains are
   deleted *)

  PROCEDURE DeleteNodes(VAR Node: TreePointer);
  BEGIN
    IF Node # NIL THEN
      DeleteNodes(Node^.Left);
      DeleteNodes(Node^.Right);
      DEALLOCATE(Node, SIZE(TreeNode));
    END; (* IF *)
  END DeleteNodes;

BEGIN
  DeleteNodes(Tree^.Root);
  DEALLOCATE(Tree, SIZE(TreeHeader));
  Tree := NIL;
END DeleteTree;
```

Procedures CreateTree and DeleteTree are self-explanatory. DeleteTree calls on a local recursive procedure DeleteNodes, which, starting with the root node, uses a postorder traversal to deallocate all the tree nodes.

```
PROCEDURE InsertNode(VAR Tree: BinaryTree; VAR Element: TreeElementType;
                     Where: Position);
(* Insert Element into the Tree. The key is in the Element. *)

  PROCEDURE NewNode(VAR Node: TreePointer; Element: TreeElementType);
  (* Create a new Node *)
  BEGIN
    ALLOCATE(Node, SIZE(TreeNode));
    Node^.Element := Element;
    Node^.Left := NIL;
    Node^.Right := NIL;
  END NewNode;

VAR Node: TreePointer;

BEGIN
  TreeError := FALSE;
  WITH Tree^ DO
    CASE Where OF
      ToRoot: IF Size = 0 THEN
                NewNode(Node, Element);
                Root := Node;
                Current := Node;
                Size := 1;
              ELSE
                TreeError := TRUE;
              END; (* IF *)
```

```
| ToLeft:  IF (Current # NIL) AND (Current^.Left = NIL) THEN
            NewNode(Node, Element);
            Current^.Left := Node;
            Current := Node;
            INC(Size);
          ELSE
            TreeError := TRUE;
          END;
| ToRight: IF (Current # NIL) AND (Current^.Right = NIL) THEN
            NewNode(Node, Element);
            Current^.Right := Node;
            Current := Node;
            INC(Size);
          ELSE
            TreeError := TRUE;
          END;
    END; (* CASE *)
  END; (* WITH *)
END InsertNode;
```

Procedure InsertNode uses internal procedure NewNode, which creates a new node and assigns a value to its associated element. Insertion can only take place at the root if there is no root. Insertion takes place at the left (or right) of the current node if there is a current node with no left (or right) descendant. Figure 8-11 illustrates the insertion of a new node N into tree T. Tree T has four nodes, its root node is node A, and its current node is B and has no children. The insertion is done at the left of the current node. Note that, once the insertion is done, the current node becomes the new node.

Figure 8-11
Insertion at Left of Current Node

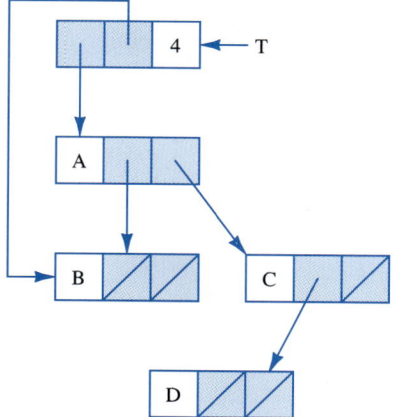
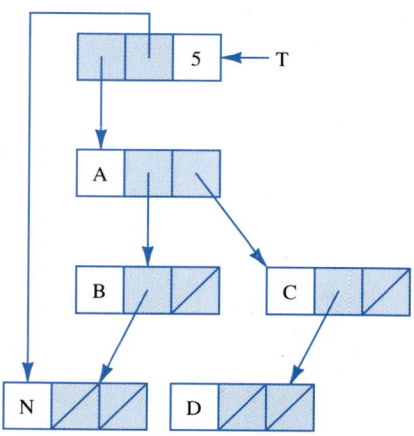

```
PROCEDURE DeleteNode(VAR Tree: BinaryTree);
(* Delete current Node *)

  PROCEDURE FindPredecessor(Node: TreePointer; VAR Found: BOOLEAN;
                            VAR Predecessor: TreePointer);
  (* Find Node which points to Current *)
  BEGIN
    IF NOT Found AND (Node # NIL) THEN
      IF NOT ((Node^.Right = Tree^.Current)
           OR (Node^.Left = Tree^.Current)) THEN
        FindPredecessor(Node^.Left, Found, Predecessor);
        FindPredecessor(Node^.Right, Found, Predecessor);
      ELSE
        Found := TRUE;
        Predecessor := Node;
      END; (* IF *)
    END; (* IF *)
  END FindPredecessor;

VAR Parent, Node: TreePointer;
    Found: BOOLEAN;

BEGIN
  TreeError := FALSE;
  WITH Tree^ DO
    IF Current # NIL THEN
      Found := FALSE;
      FindPredecessor(Tree^.Root, Found, Parent);
      IF Current^.Left = NIL THEN (* empty Left branch *)
        IF Parent^.Left = Current THEN
          Parent^.Left := Current^.Right;
        ELSE
          Parent^.Right := Current^.Right;
        END; (* IF *)
      ELSIF Current^.Right = NIL THEN (* empty Right branch *)
        IF Parent^.Left = Current THEN
          Parent^.Left := Current^.Left;
        ELSE
          Parent^.Right := Current^.Left;
        END; (* IF *)
      ELSE (* no branch empty *)
        Node := Current^.Left;
        WHILE Node^.Right # NIL DO
          Node :^ Node^.Right;
        END; (* WHILE *)
        IF Parent^.Left = Current THEN
          Parent^.Left := Current^.Left;
        ELSE
          Parent^.Right := Current^.Left;
        END; (* IF *)
        Node^.Right := Current^.Right;
      END; (* IF *)
```

```
      DEALLOCATE(Current, SIZE(TreeNode));
      Current := NIL;
      DEC(Size);
    END; (* IF *)
  END; (* WITH *)
END DeleteNode;
```

Procedure DeleteNode operates on the current node and, after checking that it exists, calls internal procedure FindPredecessor to find the parent of that current node. FindPredecessor examines all the tree nodes starting from the root until it finds one that has the current node as a descendant. (We could have improved efficiency and made this search unnecessary by keeping an extra pointer Parent in each node.) Once the predecessor is found, DeleteNode checks to see if one of the current node's descendants is missing, in which case the current node's parent is linked to the only descendant. In the case in which the current node has two descendants, we first find the rightmost node of the current node's left subtree. The current node's parent is then linked to the current node's left subtree, and the rightmost node is linked to the current node's right subtree. This process is illustrated in Figure 8-12, where we delete current node C from tree T. Tree T has eight elements, node A is its root node, and the current node is node C (we might have reached that node as a result of a search, for instance). Node C has two descendants, and its parent node is node A. Parent node A is made to point to the current node's left descendant, D, and the rightmost element of the current node's left subtree, F, is made to point to the current node's right descendant, E. The current node is then deleted and the tree is left with an undefined current node.

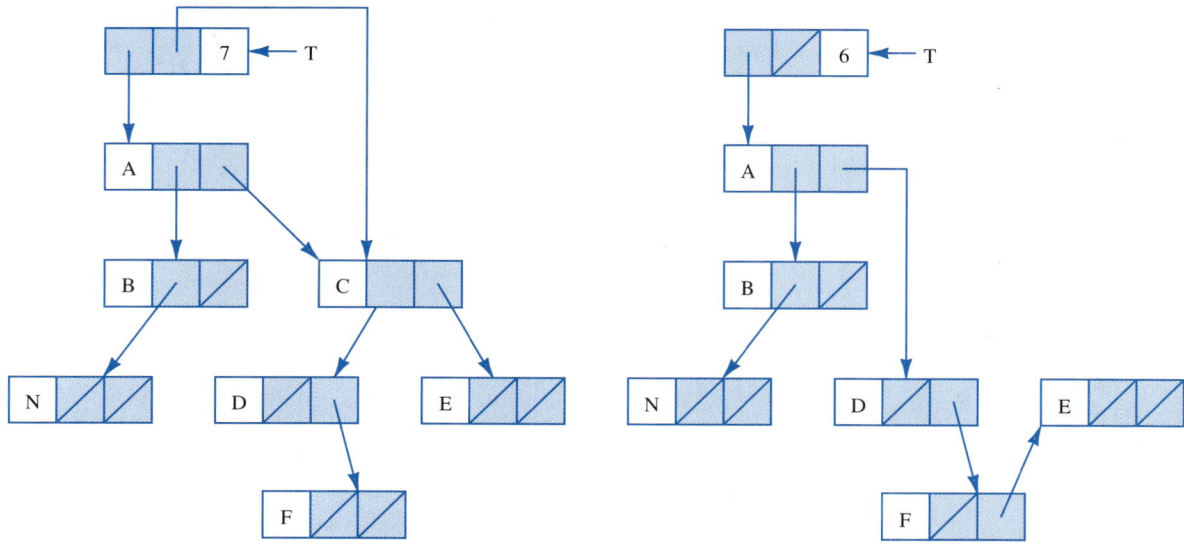

Figure 8-12   Deletion of Current Node C

```
PROCEDURE TraverseTree(Tree: BinaryTree; TravProc: TraverseProc);
(* Call "TravProc" for each Node in order. Don't call any procedures
   that modify links while in mid traversal, like InsertNode,
   DeleteNode, DeleteTree. *)
PROCEDURE Traverse(Node: TreePointer; TravProc: TraverseProc);
BEGIN
  IF Node # NIL THEN
    Traverse(Node^.Left, TravProc);
    TravProc(Node^.Element);
    Traverse(Node^.Right, TravProc);
  END; (* IF *)
END Traverse;

BEGIN
  Traverse(Tree^.Root, TravProc);
END TraverseTree;

PROCEDURE SearchTree(Tree: BinaryTree; Element: TreeElementType);
(* Search for Element in the Tree. If Found then Element will contain
   the node information, otherwise TreeError is true *)
VAR Node: TreePointer;
    Found: BOOLEAN;

  PROCEDURE InOrderSearch(Node: TreePointer);
  BEGIN
    IF (Node # NIL) AND NOT Found THEN
      InOrderSearch(Node^.Left);
      IF Equal(Node^.Element, Element) THEN
        Tree^.Current := Node;
        Found := TRUE;
        RETURN;
      ELSE
        InOrderSearch(Node^.Right);
      END; (* IF *)
    END; (* IF *)
  END InOrderSearch;

BEGIN
  TreeError := FALSE;
  Found := FALSE;
  Node := Tree^.Root;
  InOrderSearch(Node);
  IF NOT Found THEN
    Tree^.Current := NIL;
    TreeError := TRUE;
  END; (* IF *)
END SearchTree;
```

Procedure TraverseTree is a simple inorder traversal. Procedure SearchTree examines all nodes in the tree using an inorder search and stops as soon as a node with the desired element is found. It uses function procedure EqualKeys, imported from TreeElements, which, given two elements, compares their keys for equality.

```
PROCEDURE NextNode(VAR Tree: BinaryTree; Where: Position);
(* Advance current Node in given direction *)
BEGIN
  WITH Tree^ DO
    TreeError := FALSE;
    IF Where = ToRoot THEN
      Current := Root;
    ELSIF Current= NIL THEN
      TreeError := TRUE;
    ELSIF Where= ToLeft THEN
      Current := Current^.Left;
    ELSE
      Current := Current^.Right;
    END; (* IF *)
  END; (* WITH *)
END NextNode;

PROCEDURE DisplayTree(Tree: BinaryTree; PrintElement: TraverseProc);
(* Print Tree with indentations to show structure *)
  PROCEDURE PrintNodes(Node: TreePointer; indent: CARDINAL;
                      PrintElement: TraverseProc);
  VAR i: CARDINAL;
  BEGIN
    IF Node # NIL THEN
      PrintNodes(Node^.Right, indent+1, PrintElement);
      FOR i := 1 TO indent DO WriteString("   "); END; (* FOR *)
      PrintElement(Node^.Element);
      WriteLn;
      PrintNodes(Node^.Left, indent+1, PrintElement);
    END; (* IF *)
  END PrintNodes;
BEGIN
  PrintNodes(Tree^.Root, 0, PrintElement);
END DisplayTree;

PROCEDURE ExistNode(Tree: BinaryTree; Where: Position): BOOLEAN;
(* Return TRUE if a Node exists at position indicated *)
BEGIN
  TreeError := FALSE;
  WITH Tree^ DO
    IF Where = ToRoot THEN
      RETURN Root # NIL;
    ELSIF Current = NIL THEN
      TreeError := TRUE;
      RETURN FALSE;
```

```
    ELSIF Where = ToLeft THEN
      RETURN Current^.Left # NIL;
    ELSE
      RETURN Current^.Right # NIL;
    END; (* IF *)
  END; (* WITH *)
END ExistNode;
```

Procedures NextNode and ExistNode are self-explanatory. Procedure DisplayTree displays the tree nodes in order vertically on the output device, using indentation to convey the tree structure. The displayed tree is tilted 90 degrees. For instance, the original tree of Figure 8-12 will be displayed as shown on the left of Figure 8-13. If lines are drawn in for branches, as is done on the right of Figure 8-13, this sideways tree becomes very legible. Procedures StoreNode, RetrieveNode, TreeSize, SetCurrentNode, and GetCurrentNode are very simple and left as part of problem 31.

From an efficiency point of view, procedures CreateTree, InsertNode, NextNode, StoreNode, RetrieveNode, TreeSize, GetCurrentNode, SetCurrentNode, and ExistNode are all O(1), in large part because of the use of a tree header with a current node and a size field. On the other hand, procedures DeleteTree, TraverseTree, SearchTree, and DisplayTree, which must examine all the tree nodes, are all O(n), as is procedure DeleteNode (because of FindPredecessor). The space complexity of all operations requires memory space for n nodes (an element and two pointers each), a header (two pointers and an integer), and occasional variables.

Static Implementation

In a static implementation, the various nodes will be elements of an array, and the pointers will be replaced by indices in that array. We have already seen such a static implementation in the Huffman codes application of the preceding section. Figure 8-10 illustrated this sequential organization of a binary tree. We can redefine the implementation of our binary tree ADT using the following types.

```
TYPE BinaryTree = POINTER TO TreeStructure;
     TreeIndex = [0..Max];
     TreeNode = RECORD
                  Element: TreeElementType;
                  Left, Right: TreeIndex;
                END;
     TreeStructure = RECORD
                       Root, Current: TreeIndex;
                       Size: CARDINAL;
                       Nodes: ARRAY [1..Max] OF TreeNode;
                     END;
```

The CreateTree procedure will have to initialize all pseudo-pointers Left and Right to zero. However, a static implementation uses a fixed array, and in a dynamic application where nodes are inserted and deleted often, it becomes necessary to organize the

Figure 8-13
Display of a Tree

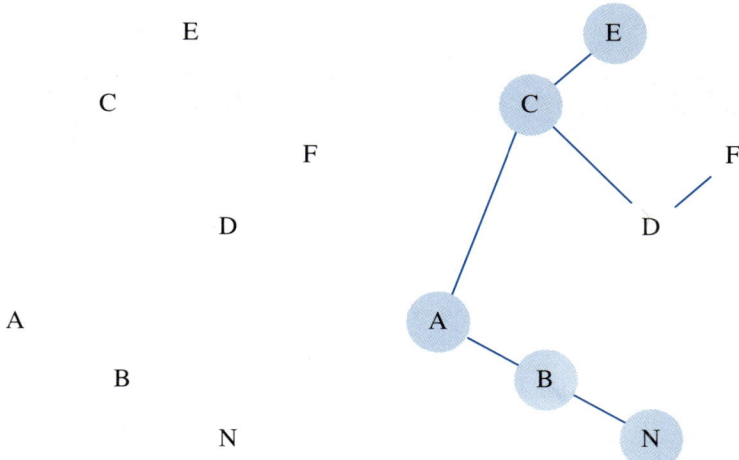

array in order to be able to reuse the deleted nodes. This organization is achieved by adding a field to the TreeStructure record:

```
FreeSpace: TreeIndex;
```

FreeSpace will always indicate where to find the first free tree node in the Nodes array. Moreover, free elements will be linked together as a linear list through their Left field.

Figure 8-14 illustrates such an organization: at left is the static implementation of the tree shown in the usual manner at right. With this organization, we will define two procedures Allocate and Deallocate, which will allow us to use the dynamic implementation programs by simply replacing calls to ALLOCATE and DEALLOCATE by calls to Allocate and Deallocate.

```
PROCEDURE Allocate(VAR Node: TreeIndex; Tree: BinaryTree);
BEGIN
   WITH Tree^ DO
     IF (Tree # NIL) AND (FreeSpace # 0) THEN
       Node := FreeSpace;
       FreeSpace := Nodes[FreeSpace].Left;
       TreeError := FALSE;
     ELSE
       TreeError := TRUE;
       Node := 0;
     END; (* IF *)
   END; (* WITH *)
END Allocate;
```

306 Chapter 8 Trees

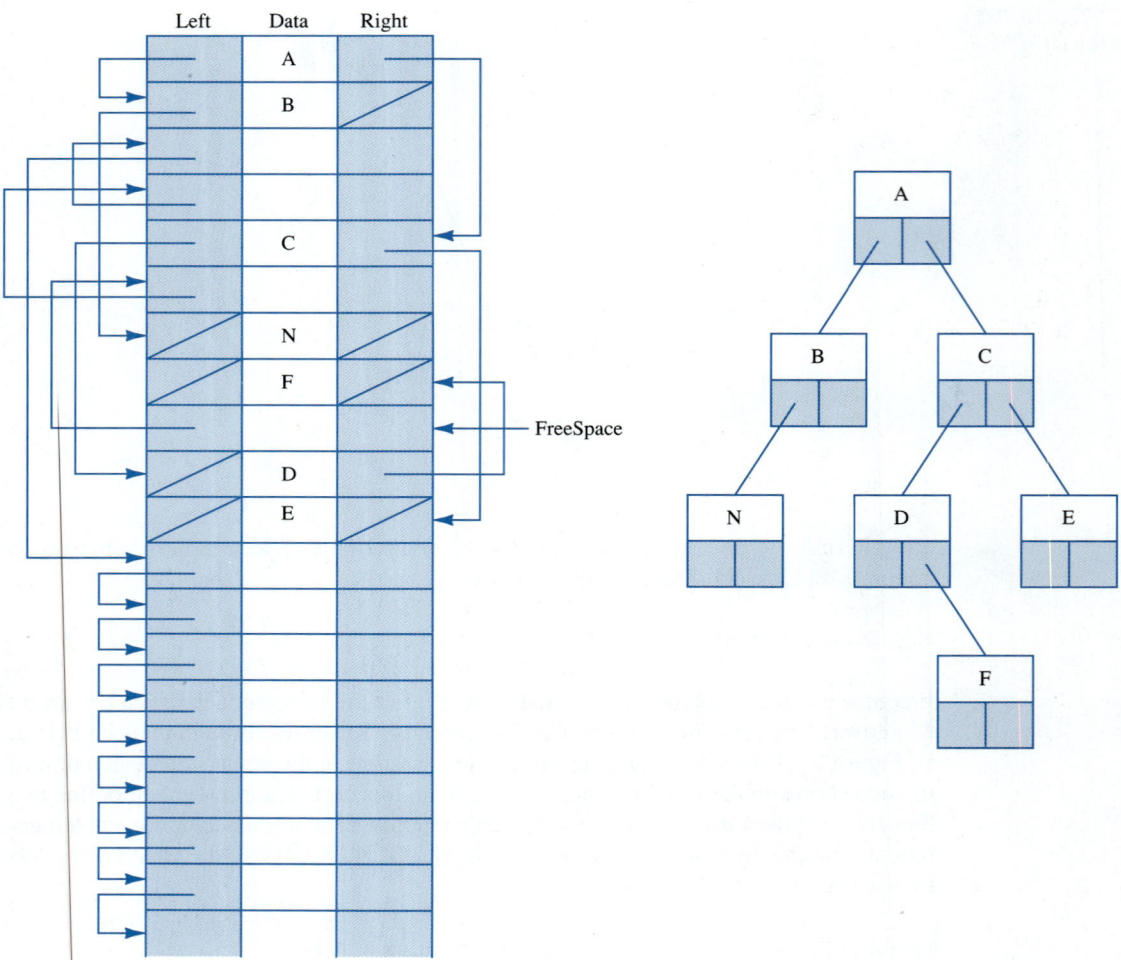

Figure 8-14 Static Implementation of Trees

```
PROCEDURE Deallocate(Node: TreeIndex; VAR Tree: BinaryTree);
BEGIN
  WITH Tree^ DO
    Nodes[Node].Left := FreeSpace;
    FreeSpace := Node;
    Node := 0;
  END; (* WITH *)
END Deallocate;
```

8.5 Case Study: A Tic-Tac-Toe Playing Program

A well-known application of trees is found in computer games where the various states of a game are represented using trees. We will design and implement a simple game playing program as an illustration.

Design

We will develop a program that plays the game of Tic-Tac-Toe. This game is very simple but will allow us to illustrate some of the techniques used in game playing programs.

Definition of the Problem The game of Tic-Tac-Toe is played on a square divided into nine boxes by two players. The first player puts a mark (usually a cross) in one of the nine boxes. The next player puts a mark (usually a small circle) in one of the remaining free boxes. The players take turns placing their marks. The aim is to fill a row, a column, or a diagonal with three crosses or circles. If this happens, the game is over and the player with the combination of three has won. Figure 8-15 shows the square initially and after a win.

We are to implement a program that plays the game of Tic-Tac-Toe. The program will play the part of one player; the user will be the other player. The game will be played interactively, and the user will be able to choose who starts playing. Each time the computer plays, the Tic-Tac-Toe square will be displayed and the user will be prompted for a move. The moves of the user will be validated: it is forbidden to play outside the square, or to play in a box where someone has already played. The program will detect a win and stop the game with an appropriate congratulation or commiseration message. The program will also recognize a tie.

Design of a Solution From the problem definition it follows that the program will execute in an interactive manner, be able to accept a move from the user, be able to make its own move, be able to detect if a game state is a win or a tie, and be able to display the Tic-Tac-Toe square. Figure 8-16 presents the structure chart corresponding to this situation.

In computer game playing, trees are used to represent the various possible states of the game based on all possible moves from a given state. The tree root corresponds to the current game state. Its direct descendants represent all game states that can be

Figure 8-15
Tic-Tac-Toe States

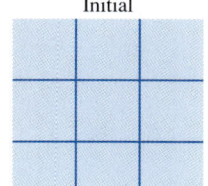

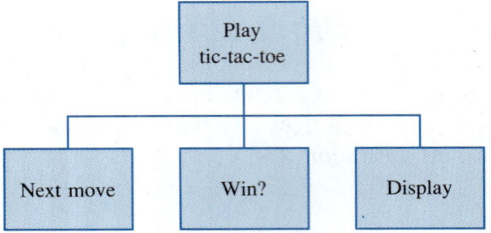

Figure 8-16
Structure Chart for Tic-Tac-Toe

reached by making one move. The next level of the tree represents all the game states that can be reached after playing two moves, and so forth. Figure 8-17 shows such a tree built from a game state where player O just played. If the game is complex, like chess, the tree quickly becomes too large, and it becomes necessary to find heuristics in order to reduce its size. For games that are simpler, like Tic-Tac-Toe, it is possible to use the complete tree.

From this figure we can see that, to decide what the next move is, we must build the game tree. In order to do that, we must be able to generate all the game states that can be reached with a single move, and for each of these, to expand them in the same manner. Once this is done, we have to choose the best solution, and select the corresponding move. In order to evaluate the expanded game tree, we need to be able to evaluate a specific game state: this can be done by computing some values for a game

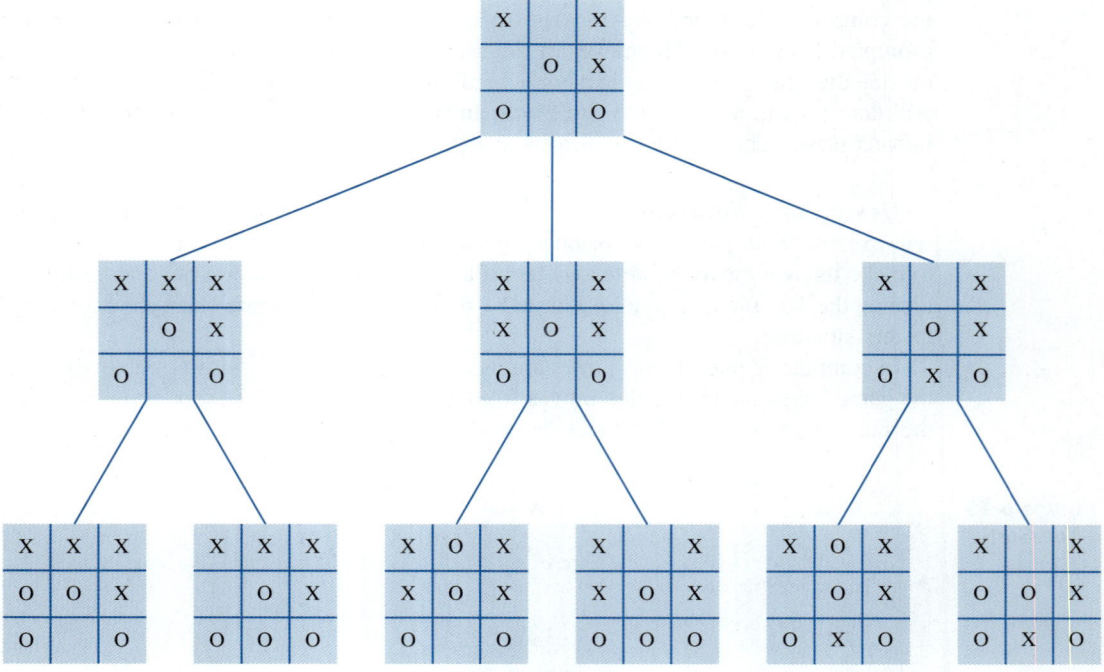

Figure 8-17 A Tic-Tac-Toe Game Playing Tree

8.5 Case Study: A Tic-Tac-Toe Playing Program

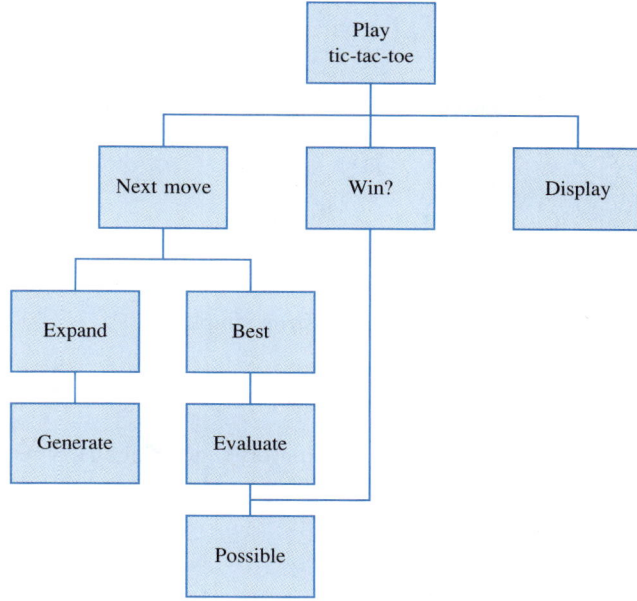

Figure 8-18
Complete Structure Chart for Tic-Tac-Toe

state and evaluating the results of this computation. We can expand the structure chart of Figure 8-16 into the structure chart in Figure 8-18, noting that to decide if a situation is a win we will have to use the previously computed values of the game state.

Refine the Solution We can define directly the algorithms needed at the higher level of our structure chart. Here is the pseudocode for the main program.

```
Tic Tac Toe
    Initialize square to empty
    If user plays first
        Place first move of X on square
    Else
        Place computer move O in center of square
    End if
    Repeat
        If last move was not computer's move
            Next move for O
        End if
        Display square
        If O does not win and square is not full
            Ask player for move on square
        End if
    Until X wins or O wins or square full
```

```
        If X wins
            Display Bravo!
        Elsif O wins
            Display I win!!
        Else
            Display This is a tie!
        End if
End Tic Tac Toe
```

The pseudocode for procedure Win is simple.

```
Win
    Possible position for Player
    If 3 in a row or 3 in a column or 3 in a diagonal
        Return true
    Else
        Return false
    End if
End Win
```

The pseudocode for Display is simple and will not be shown here.

In order to define the algorithms needed for the other components of the structure chart of Figure 8-18, we must study the tree expansion and evaluation process in more detail. In the tree of Figure 8-17, we will compute for each node a value that will be used to evaluate the corresponding game state. Such an evaluation function could be defined in a number of ways; we will choose a simple function. Since we are looking in that figure for the best move for X, the computed game state value will be the number of rows plus the number of columns plus the number of diagonals that can still be filled by Xs, less the number of rows, columns, and diagonals that O can fill. In cases where X wins, we use the value of 9, while in cases where O wins we use value −9. All children of a winning state will have the same winning value. This computed value is static; it corresponds to one game state only and does not indicate other game states that might be reached. Figure 8-19 shows the same game tree as Figure 8-17, with added computed values for the lowest level. These values will be carried to the upper levels using a method called minimax.

The tree of Figure 8-19 is used to evaluate a game state as a function of the possible moves, and it shows projections for two moves. To evaluate X's best move, the lowest game states are evaluated for X. Then we go up in the tree, taking with us alternatively the maximum and the minimum of the values associated with the nodes (a high value indicates a better chance to win, while a low value is an indication of a good chance to lose). Nodes are labeled alternatively "+" and "−", where "+" indicates the player whose turn it is to play at the root and "−" indicates the opponent.

When all the descendant game states of a + node have been evaluated, a + player must choose the game state yielding the maximum value. Also, the opponent will choose the game state yielding the minimum value for the + player. This method is called minimax because both functions are used alternatively as we go up in the tree. In

8.5 Case Study: A Tic-Tac-Toe Playing Program

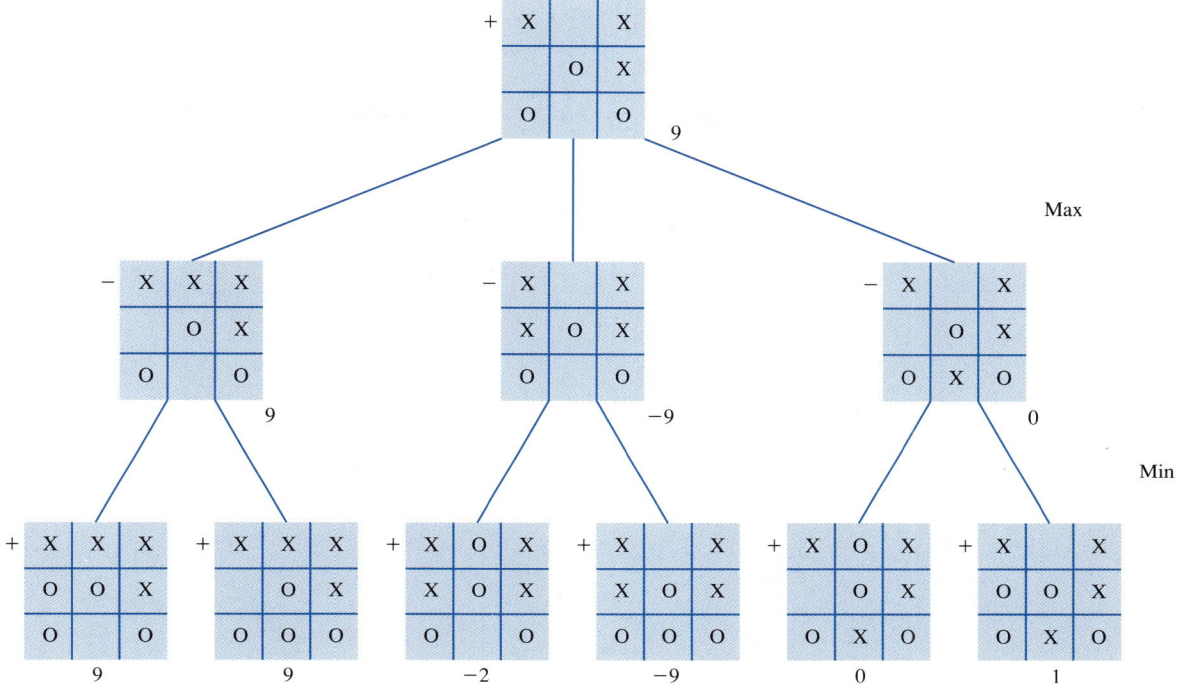

Figure 8-19 Tic-Tac-Toe Tree with Computed Values

Figure 8-19, the − nodes get the minimum of their descendants' values, while the + nodes get the maximum of their descendants' values—a winning game state in that particular case.

To find the best move for a given player from a given game state, the tree is built up to a given level, then the game states of the leaves are evaluated. These values are passed up the tree and give values to the upper nodes by choosing maximum and minimum values for nodes + and −, respectively.

The tree in Figure 8-19 is a generalized tree with multiple children (up to nine for the first move). If we use a left-child, right-sibling representation, as shown in Figure 8-20, we will be able to use our binary ADT, where our data will be the square plus a flag indicating whether the node is a + or − node.

We can now develop the pseudocode for the remaining procedures. NextMove is easy to understand: after creating a tree and expanding it to the desired level, a best move is selected and returned.

```
Next Move
    Create a tree with Square at the root
    Expand Tree to given level for Player
    Best Move for Player
    Delete tree
End Next Move
```

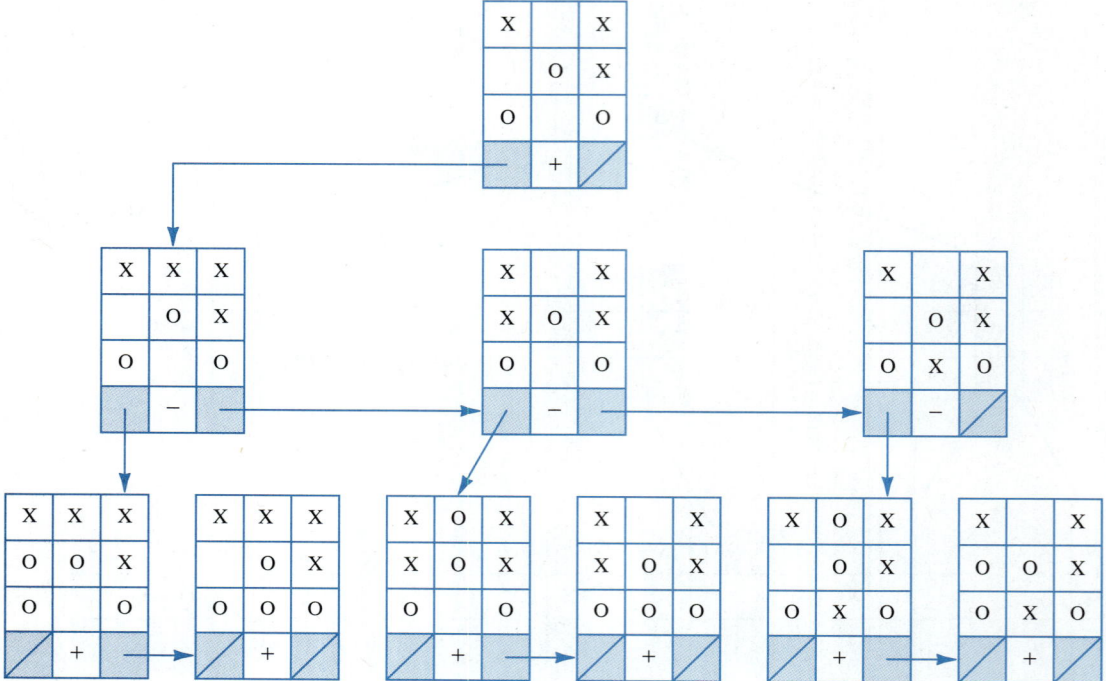

Figure 8-20 Representation of Tic-Tac-Toe Tree

Procedure Expand Tree calls Generate Squares to generate all the squares possible for a move from a given position. It then expands the generated squares and repeats the process until the desired expansion level is reached.

```
Expand Tree
    If depth not reached
        Generate Squares
        If there are descendants
            Move to first descendant
            While descendant exists
                Set status (+ or −) opposite to parent's status
                Expand Tree for next player
                Move to next right descendant
            End while
        End if
    End if
End Expand Tree
```

8.5 Case Study: A Tic-Tac-Toe Playing Program

Procedure Generate Squares generates one square for each unfilled position on a given square. All the generated squares are inserted as descendants of the initial position in the game tree.

```
Generate Squares
    For all positions on square
        If empty
            Set player in empty position
            If first element
                Insert element to the left using left child pointer
            Else
                Insert element to the right following right sibling pointer
            End if
        End if
    End for
End Generate Squares
```

Procedure Best Move is applied to all the squares that are descendants of the original game state. It applies the minimax method and returns the minimum or maximum value along with the corresponding move.

```
Best Move
    If no more descendants
        Set Value to Evaluate Square
        Return Element
    Else
        Best Move for first successor
        Set Value to minimum or maximum
        While there are nodes at the same level
            Move right to next node
            Best Move for node
            If Element −
                Set Value to minimum
            Else
                Set Value to maximum
            End if
        End while
    End if
End Best Move
```

Procedure Possible fills two vectors with values indicating what positions in a square can be filled by a player: horizontals, verticals, or diagonals.

> Possible
>   Set Horizontal and Vertical to zero
>   For each square position
>   Update Horizontal count
>   Update Vertical count
>   Update first diagonal count
>   Update second diagonal count
>   End for
> End Possible

Procedure Evaluate Square returns a single measure for a given square.

> Evaluate Square
>   Set Count1 to number of rows, columns and diagonals open to Player
>   Set Count2 to number of rows, columns and diagonals open to opponent
>   Return Count1 − Count2
> End Evaluate Square

Develop a Testing Strategy The testing of the program is simple, since it involves playing games. We will systematically try the various possible moves in the following cases:

- The computer plays first.
- The user plays first.

We will also try the program with different levels of expansion:

- Expansion to one level
- Expansion to two levels
- Expansion to three levels

To check the validation of the moves entered by the user, we will also try entering moves outside the square, and moves to a position already occupied.

Implementation

Code and Test the Program Our game playing program will use our Binary Tree ADT, and the following BinTreeElements module.

```
DEFINITION MODULE BinTreeElements;

CONST MaxSize = 3;

TYPE PlayType = (X, O, Empty);
    LevelType = (Plus, Minus);
    SquareType = ARRAY [1..MaxSize], [1..MaxSize] OF PlayType;
    TreeElementType = RECORD
                        Square: SquareType;
                        Turn: LevelType;
                      END;
END BinTreeElements.

MODULE TicTacToe;
(* A program for playing Tic Tac Toe in an interactive manner *)
FROM InOut IMPORT ReadCard, Write, WriteString, WriteLn, Read,
                  WriteCard;
FROM BinTreeElements IMPORT TreeElementType, PlayType, LevelType,
                            SquareType, MaxSize;
FROM BinaryTreeADT IMPORT BinaryTree, TreePointer, Position, CreateTree,
                          InsertNode, SetCurrentNode, GetCurrentNode,
                          RetrieveNode, StoreNode, TreeError, NextNode,
                          DeleteTree, ExistNode;

TYPE PlayerType = [X..O];
    Vector = ARRAY [1..4] OF CARDINAL;

PROCEDURE Possible(Square: SquareType; VAR Horizontal, Vertical: Vector;
                   Player: PlayerType);
(* Generate vectors representing the positions of Player on Square *)
VAR Row, Column, Value: CARDINAL;
BEGIN
  FOR Row := 1 TO 4 DO                              (* initialize to zero *)
    Horizontal[Row] := 0;
    Vertical[Row] := 0;
  END; (* FOR *)
  FOR Row := 1 TO MaxSize DO
    FOR Column := 1 TO MaxSize DO
      IF Square[Row, Column] = Player THEN          (* player *)
        Value := 1;
      ELSIF Square[Row, Column] = Empty THEN
        Value := 0;
      ELSE                                          (* opponent *)
        Value := 4;
      END; (* IF *)
      Horizontal[Row] := Horizontal[Row] + Value;   (* Horizontal *)
      Vertical[Column] := Vertical[Column] + Value; (* Vertical *)
      IF Row = Column THEN
        Vertical[4] := Vertical[4] + Value;         (* First diagonal *)
      END; (* IF *)
```

```
      IF ((Row = 1) AND (Column = MaxSize))
        OR ((Row = 2) AND (Column = 2))
        OR ((Row = MaxSize) AND (Column = 1)) THEN (* Second diagonal *)
        Horizontal[4] := Horizontal[4] + Value;
      END; (* IF *)
    END; (* FOR *)
  END; (* FOR *)
END Possible;
```

Procedure Possible fills two vectors with values indicating the number of possible positions that can be occupied by a player. The first vector describes the horizontal groups and its last value is associated to the second diagonal. The second vector describes the vertical groups and its last value represents the first diagonal.

```
PROCEDURE GenerateSquares(Tree: BinaryTree; Player: PlayerType);
(* Generate squares obtained from Square where Player will play *)
VAR Row, Column: CARDINAL;
    FirstTime: BOOLEAN;
    Element: TreeElementType;
    Square: SquareType;
BEGIN
  FirstTime := TRUE;
  RetrieveNode(Tree, Element);       (* get square *)
  Square := Element.Square;
  FOR Row := 1 TO MaxSize DO
    FOR Column := 1 TO MaxSize DO
      IF Square[Row, Column] = Empty THEN
        (* create list of possible moves starting at left *)
        Element.Square := Square;
        Element.Square[Row, Column] := Player;
        IF FirstTime THEN              (* first descendant left *)
          InsertNode(Tree, Element, ToLeft);
          FirstTime := FALSE;
        ELSE                           (* other descendants right *)
          InsertNode(Tree, Element, ToRight);
        END; (* IF *)
      END; (* IF *)
    END; (* FOR *)
  END; (* FOR *)
END GenerateSquares;
```

Procedure GenerateSquares creates a list of the nodes comprising the various squares that can be obtained from a given square. This list will include as many nodes as there are possibilities of playing one move. This list is the list of descendants of the given node.

```
PROCEDURE DisplaySquare(Square: SquareType);
(* Display a square on screen *)
VAR Row, Column: CARDINAL;
BEGIN
   WriteString("-------------"); WriteLn;
   FOR Row := 1 TO MaxSize DO
     FOR Column := 1 TO MaxSize DO
       IF Square[Row, Column] = X THEN
          WriteString("| X ");
       ELSIF Square[Row, Column] = O THEN
          WriteString("| O ");
       ELSE
          WriteString("|   ");
       END; (* IF *)
     END; (* FOR *)
     Write('|'); WriteLn;
   END; (* FOR *)
   WriteString("-------------"); WriteLn;
END DisplaySquare;
```

Procedure DisplaySquare just displays a square on the screen.

```
PROCEDURE EvaluateSquare(Square: SquareType;
                         Player: PlayerType): INTEGER;
(* Evaluate strength of a square for Player *)
VAR Horizon, Vertical: Vector;
    CountPlayer, CountOpponent: INTEGER;
    Row: CARDINAL;
BEGIN
   Possible(Square, Horizon, Vertical, Player);
   (* Number of rows, columns, diagonals open to player *)
   CountPlayer := 0;
   (* Number of rows, columns, diagonals open to opponent *)
   CountOpponent := 0;
   FOR Row := 1 TO 4 DO
     IF Horizon[Row] < 3 THEN    (* 0, 1, 2: open to player *)
        INC(CountPlayer);
     END; (* IF *)
     IF (Horizon[Row] = 0) OR (Horizon[Row] = 4) OR (Horizon[Row] = 8) THEN
        INC(CountOpponent); (* 0, 4, 8: open to opponent *)
     END; (* IF *)
     IF (Horizon[Row] = 3) OR (Vertical[Row] = 3) THEN
        INC(CountPlayer, 10);    (* Player's winning position *)
     END; (* IF *)
     IF (Horizon[Row] = 12) OR (Vertical[Row] = 12) THEN
        INC(CountOpponent, 10);  (* Opponent wins *)
     END; (* IF *)
```

```
        IF Vertical[Row] < 3 THEN    (* 0, 1, 2: player *)
          INC(CountPlayer);
        END; (* IF *)
        IF (Vertical[Row] = 0) OR (Vertical[Row] = 4) OR (Vertical[Row] = 8) THEN
          INC(CountOpponent);        (* 0, 4, 8: opponent *)
        END; (* IF *)
      END; (* FOR *)
      IF CountPlayer >= 10 THEN
        RETURN 9;
      ELSIF CountOpponent >= 10 THEN
        RETURN -9;
      ELSE
        RETURN CountPlayer - CountOpponent;
      END; (* IF *)
    END EvaluateSquare;
```

Procedure EvaluateSquare returns a value corresponding to a given square. The value returned is the number of rows, columns, and diagonals that can be filled by the player minus the number that can be filled by the opponent, or 9 if the player wins, or −9 if the opponent wins.

```
PROCEDURE ExpandTree(Tree: BinaryTree; Level, Depth: CARDINAL;
                     Player: PlayerType);
(* Expansion of Tree from a square: generation of all possible squares
   then repeat for each of them until desired Depth *)
VAR Parent: TreePointer;
    Player2: PlayerType;
    Element: TreeElementType;
    ParentTurn: LevelType;
BEGIN
  IF Level < Depth THEN
    RetrieveNode(Tree, Element);
    ParentTurn := Element.Turn;
    GetCurrentNode(Tree, Parent);
    GenerateSquares(Tree, Player);      (* list of possible moves *)
    SetCurrentNode(Tree, Parent);
    IF ExistNode(Tree, ToLeft) THEN
      NextNode(Tree, ToLeft);
      WHILE NOT TreeError DO     (* traverse list of ToRight nodes *)
        RetrieveNode(Tree, Element);
        IF ParentTurn = Plus THEN
          Element.Turn := Minus;
        ELSE
          Element.Turn := Plus;
        END; (* IF *)
        StoreNode(Tree, Element);
```

```
          IF Player = X THEN                 (* other player's turn *)
             Player2 := O;
          ELSE
             Player2 := X;
          END; (* IF *)
          GetCurrentNode(Tree, Parent);
          ExpandTree(Tree, Level+1, Depth, Player2);    (* expand other levels *)
          SetCurrentNode(Tree, Parent);
          NextNode(Tree, ToRight);
        END; (* WHILE *)
    END; (* IF *)
  END; (* IF *)
END ExpandTree;
```

Procedure ExpandTree realizes the expansion of the game tree from the square in the tree root. The procedure calls GenerateSquares for the generation of a list of the squares obtained after one move. It then uses recursive calls to generate the moves of the other levels. The Turn indicator is alternated with each level.

```
PROCEDURE BestMove(Tree: BinaryTree; Player: PlayerType;
                   VAR Better: TreeElementType; VAR Value: INTEGER);
(* Find best move from the expanded Tree *)
VAR Val: INTEGER;
    Element, Maybe: TreeElementType;
    Node: TreePointer;
BEGIN
  RetrieveNode(Tree, Element);
  IF NOT ExistNode(Tree, ToLeft) THEN        (* no more expansion *)
     Value := EvaluateSquare(Element.Square, Player);
     Better := Element;
  ELSE       (* normal Node, traverse list of sons *)
     NextNode(Tree, ToLeft);
     GetCurrentNode(Tree, Node);
     BestMove(Tree, Player, Better, Value);  (* evaluate head of list *)
     SetCurrentNode(Tree, Node);
     RetrieveNode(Tree, Better);
     IF Element.Turn = Minus THEN            (* take minimum *)
        Value := -Value;
     END; (* IF *)
     WHILE ExistNode(Tree, ToRight) DO
        NextNode(Tree, ToRight);
        GetCurrentNode(Tree, Node);
        BestMove(Tree, Player, Maybe, Val);  (* evaluate rest of list *)
        SetCurrentNode(Tree, Node);
        IF Element.Turn = Minus THEN         (* minimum *)
           Val := -Val;
        END; (* IF *)
```

```
          IF Val > Value THEN
            Value := Val;
            RetrieveNode(Tree, Better);
          END; (* IF *)
      END; (* WHILE *)
      IF Element.Turn = Minus THEN          (* minimum *)
        Value := -Value;                    (* min(a, b) = -max(-a, -b) *)
      END; (* IF *)
    END; (* IF *)
END BestMove;
```

Procedure BestMove is the most important of all, as it chooses the tree node that will lead to the best solution for a given player. It goes down to the leaves, evaluates the corresponding squares, and returns these values in the upper nodes using the minimax method. If a node has a $+$ flag, then the maximum is taken; if it has a $-$ flag, then the minimum is taken. The minimum is obtained by taking the maximum of the negated values, and by negating it, since:

$$\text{Min}(a, b) = -\text{Max}(-a, -b)$$

```
PROCEDURE NextMove(VAR Square: SquareType; Level: CARDINAL;
                   Player: PlayerType);
(* Look for best move of Player at a projection level *)
VAR Tree: BinaryTree;
    BetterElement: TreeElementType;
    Value: INTEGER;
BEGIN
  CreateTree(Tree);                         (* create Tree root and initialize *)
  BetterElement.Square := Square;
  BetterElement.Turn := Plus;               (* root is plus by definition *)
  InsertNode(Tree, BetterElement, ToRoot);
  ExpandTree(Tree, 0, Level, Player);       (* add possible moves to Tree *)
  NextNode(Tree, ToRoot);
  BestMove(Tree, Player, BetterElement, Value);
  Square := BetterElement.Square;
  DeleteTree(Tree);
END NextMove;
```

Procedure NextMove is called by the main program to generate the computer's next move. It creates a tree and then calls procedure ExpandTree to expand it to a given level. It calls on procedure BestMove to return the square corresponding to the player's best move.

```
PROCEDURE Win(Square: SquareType; Player: PlayerType): BOOLEAN;
(* Look if Player wins *)
VAR Index: CARDINAL;
    Horizontal, Vertical: Vector;
    Finished: BOOLEAN;
```

```
BEGIN
  Finished := FALSE;
  Possible(Square, Horizontal, Vertical, Player);
  Index := 1;
  REPEAT
    IF Horizontal[Index]= 3 THEN
      Finished := TRUE;
    ELSIF Vertical[Index] = 3 THEN
      Finished := TRUE
    END; (* IF *)
    INC(Index);
  UNTIL Finished OR (Index = 5);
  RETURN Finished;
END Win;
```

Procedure Win returns a Boolean indicating whether or not a player has won the game. It calls on Possible to measure the game state and checks to see if a row, a column, or a diagonal is filled by the player.

```
VAR Game: SquareType;
    Row, Column, Moves: CARDINAL;
    Answer, Ch: CHAR;
    ComputerFirst: BOOLEAN;

BEGIN (* Game between a player X and the computer O *)
  FOR Row := 1 TO MaxSize DO
    FOR Column := 1 TO MaxSize DO
      Game[Row, Column] := Empty;    (* Initialize square *)
    END; (* FOR *)
  END; (* FOR *)
  WriteString("Do you want to play first? (Y/N)"); WriteLn;
  Read(Answer); Read(Ch); WriteLn;
  IF CAP(Answer) = 'Y' THEN
    REPEAT
      WriteString("Where do you play? (m n)"); WriteLn;
      ReadCard(Row); ReadCard(Column);
    UNTIL (Column>0) AND (Column<4) AND (Row>0) AND (Row<4);
    Game[Row, Column] := X;     (* Register first player move *)
    ComputerFirst := FALSE;
  ELSE
    Game[2, 2] := O;      (* Otherwise computer plays at center *)
    ComputerFirst := TRUE;
  END; (* IF *)
  Moves := 0;
  REPEAT
    IF ComputerFirst THEN
      (* computer played first, skip to user's move *)
      ComputerFirst := FALSE;
    ELSE
      NextMove(Game, 2, O); (* computer move *)
    END; (* IF *)
```

```
      INC(Moves);
      DisplaySquare(Game);
      IF NOT Win(Game, 0) AND (Moves < 5) THEN   (* player move *)
        REPEAT
          REPEAT
            WriteString("Where do you play? (m  n)"); WriteLn;
            ReadCard(Row); ReadCard(Column);
          UNTIL (Column > 0) AND (Column < 4) AND (Row > 0) AND (Row < 4);
        UNTIL Game[Row, Column] = Empty;
        Game[Row, Column] := X;
      END; (* IF *)
    UNTIL Win(Game, X) OR Win(Game, O) OR (Moves = 5);
    IF Win(Game, X) THEN
      WriteString("Bravo!"); WriteLn;
    ELSIF Win(Game, O) THEN
      WriteString("I won!"); WriteLn;
    ELSE
      WriteString("This is a tie!"); WriteLn;
    END; (* IF *)
END TicTacToe.
```

When the program was tested according to our testing strategy, it performed quite well: it was impossible to beat it with expansion levels 1, 2, and 3. The only way to beat the program was by choosing an expansion level of zero, which prevented the computer from playing! Here is an example of a short game.

```
Do you want to play first? (Y/N)
Y
Where do you play? (m  n)
2  1
-----------
|   |   |   |
| X | O |   |
|   |   |   |
-----------
Where do you play? (m  n)
1  1
-----------
| X |   |   |
| X | O |   |
| O |   |   |
-----------
Where do you play? (m  n)
3  1
-----------
| X |   | O |
| X | O |   |
| O |   | X |
-----------
I won!
```

Complete the Documentation At this point, all the discussion about the minimax method used should be added to the structure chart. The documentation should include the problem specifications, the structure chart, the program, the strategy of verification, and the various tests done, along with their results. For reasons of space, the program was sparsely documented. At this stage, however, it would be a good idea to improve on this aspect of the documentation by inserting more complete comments in the program statements as well as at the beginning of each procedure.

Summary

In this chapter you have been introduced to a data structure that is very common in computer applications, the tree. We have defined the binary tree ADT. Since all trees can be represented by binary trees, the use of the ADT Binary Tree should make it possible to solve most problems. However, it it difficult to define an ADT general enough for all applications because applications of trees are numerous and may require some particular operations. Trees are also data structures that can be used to implement other ADTs, as we will see in later chapters.

Implementations of trees or binary trees can be static or dynamic; however the dynamic nature of trees usually makes dynamic implementations more interesting.

■ Exercises

1. Given the tree that follows,
    (a) give a list of the tree leaves
    (b) indicate what node is the tree root

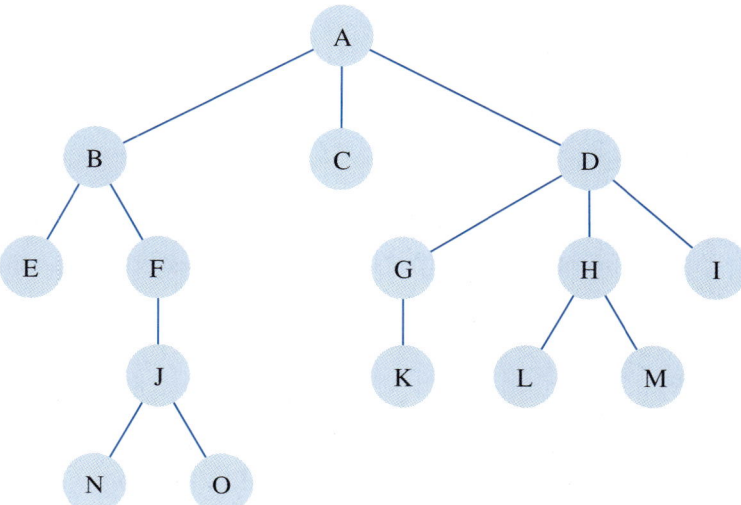

(c) indicate what node is the parent of node H
(d) indicate what nodes are the descendants of node D
(e) indicate what nodes are the siblings of node H
(f) give the tree height
(g) give the depth of node F
(h) indicate all the paths of length 3

2. List the nodes of Figure 8-7 in preorder, inorder, and postorder sequence.

3. Draw the tree representation of the expressions:
   a. $5(x + yz)$
   b. $x - y + 2/z$

4. Find the Huffman tree and codes for the following characters and their frequencies u(25), v(17), w(15), x(11), y(8), z(5).

5. Draw all the binary trees with four nodes. (Hint: There are 14.)

6. Show that a binary tree is uniquely defined by the preorder and inorder lists of its nodes.

7. Do the inorder and postorder lists of a binary tree's nodes define uniquely that binary tree? Explain.

8. Do the preorder and postorder lists of a binary tree's nodes define uniquely that binary tree? Explain.

9. Find all binary trees whose nodes appear exactly in the same order in both:
   - Preorder and inorder
   - Preorder and postorder
   - Inorder and postorder

10. Is it true that c is a descendant of d if and only if c precedes d in preorder, and d precedes c in postorder?

11. Is it true that leaf nodes of a binary tree appear in the same relative order in preorder, inorder, and postorder?

12. If we define two new traversal methods as:
    - Right subtree, root, left subtree
    - Root, right subtree, left subtree

    are there any simple relations between the order of the nodes produced by these two methods and the three "classical" methods of preorder, inorder, and postorder?

13. Prove that in a full binary tree the number of leaves is equal to the number of internal nodes plus 1.

14. Use induction to show that the maximum number of nodes in a binary tree of height h is $2^{h+1} - 1$.

15. Using one of the tree implementations from the text, write a procedure to compute the height of a tree.

16. Give an algorithm to build a full binary tree (a binary tree whose nodes have either zero or two descendants) from the preorder enumeration of its nodes, where each node is marked either as internal or as leaf.

17. Define a postorder traversal algorithm for a binary tree that uses a stack instead of recursion.

18. Write two procedures, one that will count the nodes and another one that will count the leaves of a binary tree.

19. Write an algorithm that will build a binary tree from the preorder and inorder enumerations of its nodes. Write another algorithm that will build a binary tree from the postorder and inorder enumerations of its nodes.

■ Programming Problems

20. Write and test a recursive procedure that will make a copy of a binary tree.

21. Write and test an iterative procedure that will make a copy of a binary tree.

22. Write and test a procedure which, given an expression tree, produces the fully parenthesized corresponding expression.

23. Write and test a procedure which, given an expression tree, produces the correct and minimally parenthesized corresponding expression.

24. Write and test a TreeSelectionSort procedure that sorts m distinct values by the following algorithm (also called tournament sort).

> Store the values to be sorted in the leaves of a binary tree
> While root value # $-\infty$ do
>   Going up the tree and starting from the leaves place largest
>   elements in parent nodes
>   Write out the root value and replace it in its leaf by $-\infty$

25. Implement the six operations for the tree ADT given on page 282, at the beginning of Section 8.2.

26. Complete the expression parser described on page 291 in Section 8.3, using the EBNF definition of an expression. The parser will produce an expression tree.

27. Write and test a Boolean procedure SameTree that returns TRUE if its two tree parameters are identical, and returns FALSE otherwise. Two trees are considered to be identical if they have the same structure and the same values in the corresponding nodes.

28. Write and test a procedure Optimize that detects identical subtrees in an expression tree and modifies the tree structure to replace them by 2*Subtree, or by 0 or 1 if the operator separating the two subexpressions is +, −, or /.

29. Write and test a Predecessor procedure that, given a tree node, returns its inorder predecessor.

30. A Fibonacci tree is defined as follows:
    - The empty tree is a Fibonacci tree of order 0.
    - A single node is a Fibonacci tree of order 1.
    - A Fibonacci tree of order n consists of a root with the Fibonacci tree of order n − 1 as left subtree, and the Fibonacci tree of order n − 2 as right subtree.

    Write and test a procedure to build a Fibonacci tree of order n.

31. Complete and test the BinaryTreeADT implementation module by writing procedures StoreNode, RetrieveNode, TreeSize, SetCurrentNode, and GetCurrentNode.

32. Complete and test the static implementation of binary trees introduced in the text by writing the BinaryTreeADT implementation module.

33. Modify the Tic-Tac-Toe program so that it uses 12 x 12 squares, and the winner has largest number of 3-sequences.

34. The game of Nim starts with N piles of sticks. Two players alternate in removing one or more sticks from a given pile. The player removing the last stick loses.

    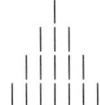

    Write and test a procedure to determine the best move in Nim. Write and test a complete program making it possible to play Nim with the computer.

35. A family tree is a figure representing a group of persons and their relationships to each other. There are two kinds of relationships: a relationship of marriage and a relationship between descendants.
    (a) Define a structure making it possible to represent a family tree. (Assume there is only one marriage per person and there are no incestuous marriages.)
    (b) Modify the structure to allow for multiple marriages. Exceptional cases such as marriages between first cousins must be allowed.
    (c) Write and test a procedure to build a family tree from data such as "John Doe married to Helen Fortin" or any other understandable form.

Binary Search Trees

INTRODUCTION

As we have seen in the preceding chapter, trees are the basis for numerous methods of quick information retrieval. Binary trees are often used in searching applications, and for that reason, a special kind of binary tree has been defined: the binary search tree. This chapter introduces the binary search tree concept and abstraction, as well as a number of applications and some implementations.

9.1 Abstraction: The Binary Search Tree

A binary search tree is a binary tree in which all the elements in the left subtree of a given node have key values less than or equal to that node's key value, and all the elements in the right subtree of the given node have key values greater than or equal to that node's key value. Figure 9-1 shows a binary search tree in which node values are single characters.

In a binary search tree, each node's location in the tree is determined by the value of the node's element. Either the whole element or only one of its parts, the "key," is used to determine the position. The organization of binary search trees makes searches efficient because a unique path can be followed from the tree root to the target node.

Our ADT Binary Search Tree is somewhat similar to the Binary Tree ADT seen in Chapter 8, albeit simpler. Here, however, we do not need a current node and the number of operations is reduced. We use type CompProc to pass a comparison procedure for keys or elements to operations insertion, deletion, and searching. The following definition module defines our Binary Search Tree ADT.

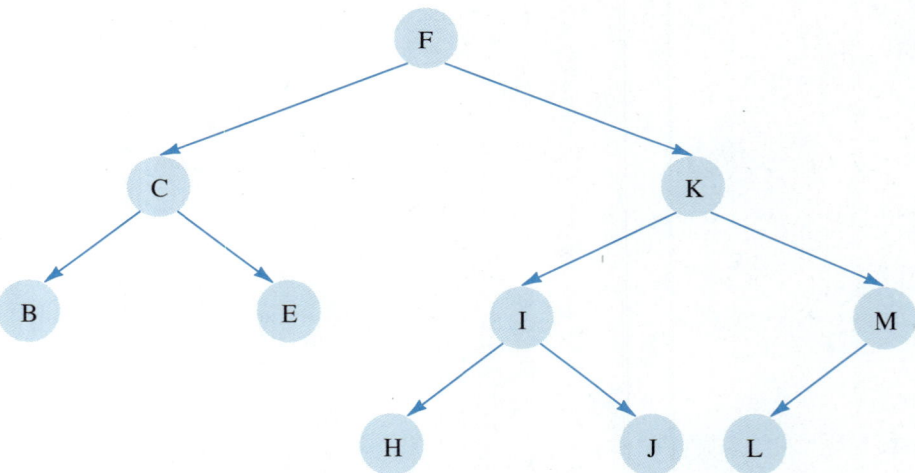

Figure 9-1
A Binary Search Tree

```
DEFINITION MODULE BSTreeADT;
FROM BSTreeElements IMPORT ElementType, KeyType;

TYPE BinarySearchTree;      (* opaque type *)
     TraverseProc = PROCEDURE(ElementType);
     CompProc     = PROCEDURE(KeyType,KeyType): INTEGER;
     PrintKeyProc = PROCEDURE(KeyType);

PROCEDURE CreateTree(VAR Tree: BinarySearchTree);
(* This procedure must be called first, it allocates and
   initializes a Tree.
   Pre-condition: Tree does not exist
   Post-condition: Tree' exists and is empty *)
```

```
PROCEDURE DeleteTree(VAR Tree: BinarySearchTree);
(* All information about the Tree and the data records it
   contains are deleted.
   Pre-condition: Tree exists
   Post-condition: Tree' does not exist *)
PROCEDURE InsertNode(VAR Tree: BinarySearchTree;
                     Element: ElementType; Comp: CompProc);
(* Insert Element at proper position into the Tree according to the
   Element's key. Use Comp for key comparisons. If a node
   already existed with same key, it is updated with value Element.
   Pre-condition: Tree and Element exist
   Post-condition: Tree' contains node with value Element *)
PROCEDURE DeleteNode(VAR Tree: BinarySearchTree; Key: KeyType;
                     Comp: CompProc);
(* Find the element with this Key and delete it from the tree.
   Use Comp for key comparisons. If no node has this Key,
   Tree is unchanged.
   Pre-condition: Tree exists
   Post-condition: Tree' does not contain node with Key anymore *)
PROCEDURE TraverseTree(VAR Tree: BinarySearchTree;
                       TravProc: TraverseProc);
(* Apply TravProc to each node of Tree using an Inorder traversal.
   Pre-condition: Tree exists
   Post-condition: all nodes of Tree have been visited in order and
                   TravProc has been applied to them *)
PROCEDURE SearchKey(Tree: BinarySearchTree; Key: KeyType;
                    VAR Element: ElementType; Comp: CompProc): BOOLEAN;
(* Search for an Element identified by Key in the Tree. Use Comp
   for key comparisons.
   Pre-condition: Tree and Element exist
   Post-condition: if Key occurs in Tree return True and set Element
                   to node value otherwise return False *)
PROCEDURE DisplayTree(Tree: BinarySearchTree; PrintKey: PrintKeyProc);
(* Display Tree keys with indentations to show Tree structure
   Pre-condition: Tree exists
   Post-condition: Tree is displayed vertically on screen with
                   elements indented to the right *)
END BSTreeADT.
```

Note that, here again, we have used procedure types in order to create more general operations for traversing a tree and printing a tree. In the case of TraverseTree, we apply a procedure provided by the user to each and every element in the tree. In the case of DisplayTree, we use a procedure parameter to be able to print values of a specific key type.

9.2 Application

Creation of an Index for a Text

Let's design a program that will read in a text, collect all significant words of this text together with the numbers of the pages in which every word occurs, and that will display an index of the collected words in alphabetical order with the ordered page references of their occurrences. We will define a word to be a sequence of letters and digits starting with a letter. A word will be deemed to be significant if it does not appear in a dictionary of trivial words. For our purpose, the end of a page will be indicated by the character "@" (this could be easily changed to any other character including the form feed character).

We will use two binary search trees, one for the dictionary of trivial words and one to store the text words. Nodes of the text word binary search tree will contain two parts: the word and a list of associated page numbers. Words from the text vary greatly in length. In order for the program to use memory space efficiently, the significant words from the text, each terminated by an end-of-string character, will be kept in a linear buffer (array of characters), and the tree nodes will only contain the index of the word's first character in the buffer. Since page numbers must be printed in ascending order, they will be kept in the nodes as a queue with no duplicates. Figure 9-2 illustrates this organization.

Program MakeIndex is listed below. It uses modules BSTreeADT and QueueADT. The queue element type is CARDINAL for page numbers, while the tree element type is a record comprising the key (word index), the last page number, and the page queue.

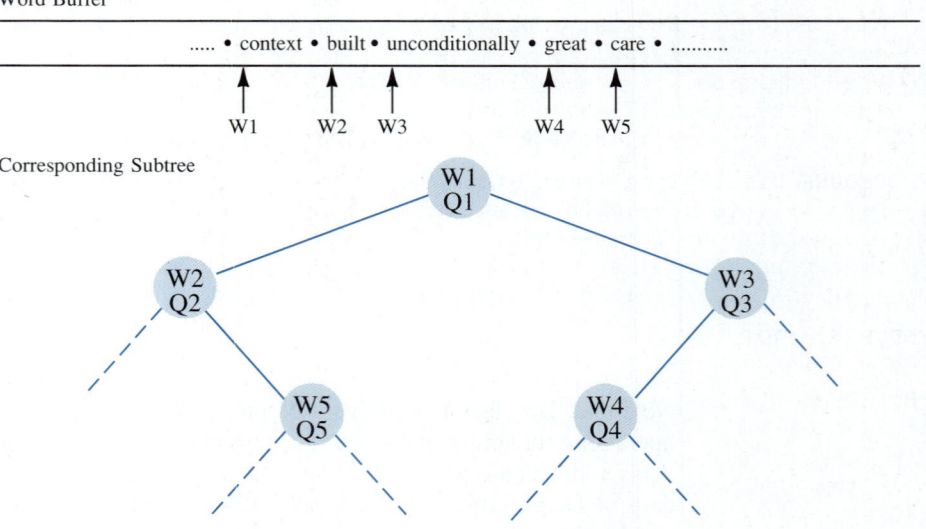

Figure 9-2 Organization of Tree and Word Buffer

```
              TYPE KeyType     = CARDINAL;
                   ElementType = RECORD
                                   Key: KeyType;
                                   LastPage: QElementType;
                                   Pages: Queue;
                                 END;
```

The program has three main steps: reading the list of trivial words and construction of the binary search tree Dictionary, reading the text and building the binary search tree Words, and, finally, listing the elements of Words by traversing the binary search tree.

```
MODULE MakeIndex;
FROM InOut IMPORT OpenInput, OpenOutput, CloseInput, CloseOutput,
                  Read, Done, EOL, Write, WriteCard, WriteLn, WriteString;
FROM BSTreeElements IMPORT KeyType, ElementType;
FROM BSTreeADT IMPORT BinarySearchTree, CreateTree, InsertNode,
                  TraverseTree, SearchKey;
FROM QueueElements IMPORT QElementType;
FROM QueueADT IMPORT Queue, Enqueue, Dequeue, CountQueue, CreateQueue;

CONST BufferLength = 10000;
      WordLength = 16;
      EndOfString = 0C;
      EndOfPage = '@';
      Space = ' ';
      ItemsPerLine = 8;

VAR Buffer: ARRAY [1..BufferLength] OF CHAR;  (* Global word buffer *)

PROCEDURE DisplayWord(Index: CARDINAL);
(* Display a word from global buffer in WordLength width *)
VAR Limit: CARDINAL;
BEGIN
  Limit := Index + WordLength;
  WHILE Buffer[Index] > EndOfString DO    (* output word *)
    Write(Buffer[Index]);
    INC(Index);
  END; (* WHILE *)
  WHILE Index < Limit DO    (* pad with blanks *)
    Write(Space);
    INC(Index);
  END; (* WHILE *)
END DisplayWord;

PROCEDURE DisplayElement(element: ElementType);
(* Display an index element: word and page references *)
VAR Index, NumbersDisplayed: CARDINAL;
    Item: QElementType;
BEGIN
  DisplayWord(element.Key);
  NumbersDisplayed := 0;
```

```
  WHILE CountQueue(element.Pages) # 0 DO
    IF NumbersDisplayed = ItemsPerLine THEN        (* line is full *)
      WriteLn;
      NumbersDisplayed := 0;
      FOR Index := 1 TO WordLength DO      (* skip space under word *)
        Write(Space);
      END; (* FOR *)
    END; (* IF *)
    Dequeue(element.Pages, Item);
    WriteCard(Item, 6);             (* output page number *)
    INC(NumbersDisplayed);
  END; (* WHILE *)
  WriteLn;
END DisplayElement;

PROCEDURE Difference(i, j: KeyType): INTEGER;
(* Compute difference between two words in global buffer *)
BEGIN
  LOOP
    IF Buffer[i] # Buffer[j] THEN      (* not identical *)
      RETURN INTEGER(ORD(Buffer[i])-ORD(Buffer[j]));
    ELSIF Buffer[i] = EndOfString THEN      (* identical *)
      RETURN 0;
    END; (* IF *)
    INC(i); INC(j);
  END; (* LOOP *)
END Difference;

PROCEDURE GetWord(VAR Ch: CHAR; VAR New, Old: CARDINAL);
(* Read a word and store it into global buffer *)
BEGIN
  New := Old;
  REPEAT (* for all letters including accented *)
    Write(Ch);
    Buffer[New] := Ch;
    INC(New);
    Read(Ch);
  UNTIL (Ch < '0') OR (Ch > '9') AND (Ch < 'A')
     OR (Ch > 'Z') AND (Ch < 'a')
     OR (Ch > 'z') AND (Ch < 200C) OR (Ch > 237C)
     OR NOT Done;
  Buffer[New] := EndOfString;
  INC(New);
END GetWord;

PROCEDURE InsertWord(VAR Root: BinarySearchTree; Page: CARDINAL;
                    VAR New, Old: CARDINAL);
(* Insert a word in index tree if not already there. Add new reference
   to its page number queue *)
VAR Word: ElementType;
    AlreadyIn: BOOLEAN;
    Last: QElementType;
```

```
BEGIN
  AlreadyIn := SearchKey(Root, Old, Word, Difference);
  IF AlreadyIn THEN
    IF Word.LastPage # Page THEN           (* add only new page references *)
      Enqueue(Word.Pages, Page);
      Word.LastPage := Page;
      InsertNode(Root, Word, Difference);       (* update existing node *)
    END; (* IF *)
  ELSE                   (* new word *)
    Word.Key := Old;
    CreateQueue(Word.Pages);
    IF Page # 0 THEN              (* page is zero for dictionary *)
      Enqueue(Word.Pages, Page);
      Word.LastPage := Page;
    END; (* IF *)
    InsertNode(Root, Word, Difference);
    Old := New;                 (* keep word in global buffer *)
  END; (* IF *)
END InsertWord;

VAR Words, Dictionary: BinarySearchTree;
    OldIndex, NewIndex, PageNumber, LineNumber: CARDINAL;
    Char: CHAR;
    Word: ElementType;
BEGIN
  CreateTree(Words);
  CreateTree(Dictionary);
  OldIndex := 1;
  PageNumber := 1;
  LineNumber := 1;
  WriteString("Give name of dictionary file: ");OpenInput("text");
  Read(Char);
  WHILE Done DO
    CASE Char OF
      'A'..'Z','a'..'z':
            GetWord(Char, NewIndex, OldIndex);
            InsertWord(Dictionary, 0, NewIndex, OldIndex);
    ELSE Read(Char);
    END; (* CASE *)
  END; (* WHILE *)
  CloseInput; WriteLn;
  WriteString("Give name of text file: "); OpenInput("text");
  WriteString("Give name of output file: "); OpenOutput("xref");
  WriteCard(LineNumber, 6);
  Write(Space);
  Read(Char);
```

```
  WHILE Done DO
    CASE Char OF
      EOL: WriteLn; Read(Char); INC(LineNumber);
           WriteCard(LineNumber, 6); Write(Space);
    | 'A'..'Z','a'..'z':
           GetWord(Char, NewIndex, OldIndex);
           IF NOT SearchKey(Dictionary, OldIndex, Word, Difference) THEN
             InsertWord(Words, PageNumber, NewIndex, OldIndex);
           END; (* IF *)
    | EndOfPage: INC(PageNumber); Write(Char); Read(Char);
    ELSE Write(Char); Read(Char);
    END; (* CASE *)
  END; (* WHILE *)
  WriteLn; WriteLn; CloseInput;
  TraverseTree(Words, DisplayElement);
  CloseOutput;
  WriteString("Index complete"); WriteLn;
END MakeIndex.
```

Procedure DisplayWord displays a word from the word buffer left-justified in 16 columns.

Procedure DisplayElement displays a word and all the page numbers in its associated queue, but with no more than eight page numbers per line.

Procedure Difference examines two words from the word buffer and compares them character by character, returning the difference of the first two characters that do not match.

Procedure GetWord reads a word from the input text and stores it temporarily in the word buffer, ending it with an end-of-string character. There are two indices associated with the word buffer: OldIndex and NewIndex. When a word is first read, the value of OldIndex is not changed: it refers to the new word. The value of NewIndex is updated to refer to the next word space in the word buffer. If the word is kept, OldIndex is advanced to NewIndex; otherwise, the next call to GetWord will read the new word in the word buffer over the word that was not kept.

Procedure InsertWord is called after it has been decided that the input word is significant. The procedure starts by checking to see if the word is already stored in binary search tree Words. If it is, and if the current page number has not already been stored, it adds the new page number to the associated queue, and updates the corresponding node in the Words tree. The word just read will not be kept in the buffer, since it is already there. If the word is not in the Words tree, a new node is inserted in Words, and the word is kept in the word buffer. Note that procedure InsertWord is also used to create the dictionary of trivial words, but in creating the dictionary, the page number is zero and is not enqueued.

The main program creates the two binary search trees and initializes the counters and indices. It asks for the name of the file for the dictionary of trivial words, opens that file, reads its contents, and builds the Dictionary tree. The program then asks the user for the name of the text file and opens it. The text file is read: an end-of-line character will increment the line counter, an end-of-page character will increment the page number. Words begin with a letter. The program reads the words and checks if each one appears in the dictionary. If it does, the word is ignored; if it does not, it is inserted in the Words tree. Punctuation characters and numbers are ignored. Once the file is read, the index is output by simply traversing binary search tree Words and applying DisplayElement to each node.

The dictionary file might contain the following words. You might note that the words are not in order, as we want to obtain a reasonably balanced binary search tree. (We will say more on this subject in Chapter 10.)

like   much   me   mine   my   My   Much
and   a   as   at   an   are   am   all   An   At   As   A   All   Am
no   not   nor   No   but   by   be   By   But
etc   did   do   Did   Do   or   of   on   off   our   ours   On   Our
for   from   For   From   she   so   She   So
her   him   hers   his   he   has   have   had   He   His   Has   Had   Have
the   to   this   that   these   those   there   them   their   they   The   To   This   That
in   its   if   I   is   it   It   Its   If   In   us   up
who   whom   whose   was   we   will   with   when   We   Will   With
your   you   yours   You   Your

The following is a sample of program output for the latter part of the alphabet.

```
through            6     9    12
thus               9
time               1     2     4     5     8     9    11    13
                  16    19
too                2     3
took               6     9    10
true               4
two                3     4     7     8    13
understanding      5
very               2     4     5     9
week               6    10
weeks              3
well               3     7     8
went               2     7
were               2     3     4     6     7    15    18
what               2     6     8
whatever           9
where              9    17
```

9.3 Implementation

The implementation of a binary search tree is simpler than that of a binary tree, because the number of operations is less. We do not need to have a tree header. The implementation module includes the following:

```
TYPE BinarySearchTree = POINTER TO TreeNode;
     TreeNode = RECORD
                  Element: ElementType;
                  Left, Right: BinarySearchTree;
                END;
PROCEDURE CreateTree(VAR Tree: BinarySearchTree);
(* The first procedure to call, which allocates and initializes a tree *)
BEGIN
  Tree := NIL;
END CreateTree;

PROCEDURE DeleteTree(VAR Tree: BinarySearchTree);
(* All information about the tree and the data records it contains are
   deleted *)
BEGIN
  IF Tree # NIL THEN
    DeleteTree(Tree^.Left);
    DeleteTree(Tree^.Right);
    DEALLOCATE(Tree, SIZE(TreeNode));
  END; (* IF *)
END DeleteTree;

PROCEDURE InsertNode(VAR Tree: BinarySearchTree;
                     Element: ElementType; Comp: CompProc);
(* Insert Element into the Tree. The key is in the Element. *)
VAR Diff: INTEGER;
BEGIN
  IF Tree = NIL THEN
    ALLOCATE(Tree, SIZE(TreeNode));
    Tree^.Element := Element;
    Tree^.Left := NIL;
    Tree^.Right := NIL;
  ELSE
    Diff := Comp(Element.Key, Tree^.Element.Key);
    IF Diff < 0 THEN
      InsertNode(Tree^.Left, Element, Comp);
    ELSIF Diff > 0 THEN
      InsertNode(Tree^.Right, Element, Comp);
    ELSE (* already in Tree update node *)
      Tree^.Element := Element;
    END; (* IF *)
  END; (* IF *)
END InsertNode;
```

Procedure CreateTree is self-explanatory. Procedure DeleteTree is recursive: it deletes the left subtree, then deletes the right subtree, and finally deallocates the root. The recursive procedure InsertNode is also relatively simple. The element to insert is compared to the root; if its key is less than the root, the element is inserted into the left subtree. If its key is greater than the root, the element is inserted into the right subtree.

If the keys are equal, an element with the same key already exists in the tree, and that tree node is simply updated with the element's value.

```
PROCEDURE DeleteNode(VAR Tree: BinarySearchTree; Key: KeyType;
                    Comp: CompProc);
(* Find the Element with this Key and delete it from the Tree *)
  PROCEDURE FindPredecessor(Tree: BinarySearchTree;
                            VAR Node: BinarySearchTree);
  (* Find rightmost node in left subtree *)
  BEGIN
    Node := Tree^.Left;
    WHILE Node^.Right # NIL DO
      Node := Node^.Right;
    END; (* WHILE *)
  END FindPredecessor;
VAR Diff: INTEGER;
    Node: BinarySearchTree;
BEGIN
  IF Tree # NIL THEN
    Diff := Comp(Tree^.Element.Key, Key);
    IF Diff = 0 THEN
      IF Tree^.Left = NIL THEN (* empty left branch *)
        Node := Tree;
        Tree := Tree^.Right;
        DEALLOCATE(Node, SIZE(TreeNode));
      ELSIF Tree^.Right = NIL THEN (* empty right branch *)
        Node := Tree;
        Tree := Tree^.Left;
        DEALLOCATE(Node, SIZE(TreeNode));
      ELSE (* no branch empty, find inorder predecessor *)
        FindPredecessor(Tree, Node);
        Tree^.Element := Node^.Element;
        DeleteNode(Tree^.Left, Tree^.Element.Key, Comp);
      END; (* IF *)
    ELSIF Diff < 0 THEN
      DeleteNode(Tree^.Left, Key, Comp);
    ELSE
      DeleteNode(Tree^.Right, Key, Comp);
    END; (* IF *)
  END; (* IF *)
END DeleteNode;
```

Procedure DeleteNode is similar to the binary tree delete operation. The node to be deleted is searched for recursively. After the node has been found, if it has only one descendant, its parent is linked with that descendant. If the node to be deleted has two descendants, the rightmost node of its left subtree is copied into it, and that element, which has at most one descendant, is deleted. Notice the use of recursion and the VAR parameter Tree to change the value of the pointer in the parent of the node to be deleted.

```
PROCEDURE TraverseTree(VAR Tree: BinarySearchTree;
                      TravProc: TraverseProc);
(* Call TravProc for each node in order. Don't call any procedures
   that modify links while in mid traversal, like InsertNode,
   DeleteNode, DeleteTree. *)
BEGIN
  IF Tree # NIL THEN
    TraverseTree(Tree^.Left, TravProc);
    TravProc(Tree^.Element);
    TraverseTree(Tree^.Right, TravProc);
  END; (* IF *)
END TraverseTree;

PROCEDURE SearchKey(Tree: BinarySearchTree; Key: KeyType;
                    VAR Element: ElementType; Comp: CompProc): BOOLEAN;
(* Search for "Key" in the Tree. If found then return true and
   Element will contain the node information, otherwise return
   false. *)
VAR Diff: INTEGER;
BEGIN
  IF Tree = NIL THEN
    RETURN FALSE;
  ELSE
    Diff := Comp(Key, Tree^.Element.Key);
    IF Diff = 0 THEN
      Element := Tree^.Element;
      RETURN TRUE;
    ELSIF Diff < 0 THEN
      RETURN SearchKey(Tree^.Left, Key, Element, Comp);
    ELSE
      RETURN SearchKey(Tree^.Right, Key, Element, Comp);
    END; (* IF *)
  END; (* IF *)
END SearchKey;
```

Procedure TraverseTree is a self-explanatory recursive procedure. Procedure SearchKey is also very simple: if the tree is empty, the search obviously fails; otherwise, either the element is found or the search is continued in the appropriate subtree.

```
PROCEDURE PrintTree(Tree: BinarySearchTree; Indentation: CARDINAL;
                    PrintKey: PrintKeyProc);
(* Print Tree with indentations to show structure *)
VAR Indent: CARDINAL;
BEGIN
  IF Tree # NIL THEN
    PrintTree(Tree^.Right, Indentation+1, PrintKey);
```

```
      FOR Indent := 1 TO Indentation DO
         WriteString("    ");
      END; (* FOR *)
      PrintKey(Tree^.Element.Key);
      WriteLn;
      PrintTree(Tree^.Left, Indentation+1, PrintKey);
   END; (* IF *)
END PrintTree;

PROCEDURE DisplayTree(Tree: BinarySearchTree; PrintKey: PrintKeyProc);
(* Calls Print Tree with indentation set to 0 *)
VAR Indent: CARDINAL;
BEGIN
   PrintTree(Tree, 0, PrintKey);
END DisplayTree;
```

Procedure DisplayTree is similar to the binary tree operation DisplayTree.

From an efficiency point of view, only procedure CreateTree is O(1), while procedures DeleteTree, TraverseTree, and DisplayTree (which must examine all the tree nodes) are all O(n). The complexity of procedures InsertNode, DeleteNode, and SearchKey is not as easy to establish. It will depend on the shape of the tree: in the worst case, the tree is a *degenerate binary tree*, i.e., a tree in which every internal node has exactly one child. In that case, the tree is similar to a linear list, and therefore the complexity of the procedures will be O(n), as it would be for a linear list. In the best case, the tree is a completely balanced full binary tree, i.e., a full binary tree in which all the leaves occur at the same level, as illustrated by Figure 9-3.

Applying procedures InsertNode, DeleteNode, or SearchKey to such a tree, we see that each comparison of a node element eliminates half of the remaining tree. In fact,

Figure 9-3
A Completely Balanced, Full Binary Tree and a Search Path

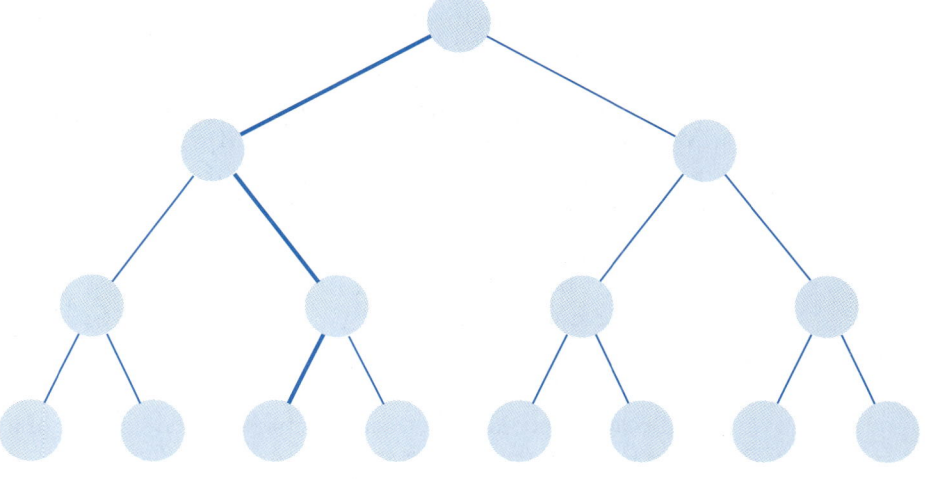

the longest search path length is equal to the tree height. A completely balanced, full binary tree with n nodes has a height h such that:

$$n = 2^h - 1$$

which gives:

$$h = \log_2(n + 1)$$

Thus, in the best case, the complexity of procedures InsertNode, DeleteNode, and SearchKey is O(log n). The average case would be based on random binary search trees. It has been shown (not here) that the search length is 1.38 log n, which is only 40% worse than the best case, and still O(log n).

The space complexity of all operations is the space needed to store n nodes, where each node includes an element of a given size as well as two pointers, and some occasional local variables.

9.4 Case Study: Threaded Binary Search Trees

In a binary search tree, nodes are ordered according to a key value such that an inorder traversal of the tree will visit the nodes in sorted order. The traversal algorithm for such a tree was very simple to program using recursion. However, as we have seen with other recursive problems, such as the Towers of Hanoi or Quicksort in Chapter 6, an iterative solution will usually be more time and space efficient than the corresponding recursive solution. In this case study, we will explore one technique for developing a nonrecursive algorithm for a tree traversal.

Design

We know that any recursive algorithm can be replaced by a corresponding iterative algorithm, provided we use a stack to remember postponed obligations. In our iterative Quicksort, the stack stored the partition bounds for unsorted partitions. Since traversal algorithms visit the left subtree before visiting the right subtree, we could use a stack to save all the nodes when we are in the left subtree of the node and the right subtree remains to be explored. This is the most straightforward iterative traversal technique, but it has several drawbacks:

It requires an auxiliary data structure, the stack, for each traversal process.
It could not be implemented incrementally, allowing the traversal to be started anywhere in the tree.
If both forward and reverse traversals were to be performed at the same time, two stacks would be required.

Because other iterative techniques based on the structure of a binary tree are possible, we will not develop the stack traversal algorithm in this case study.

Definition of the Problem You may have noticed that binary tree nodes in a dynamic implementation often contain nil pointers: a leaf node will have two nil pointers and a node with only one child will have one nil pointer. Two questions naturally come to mind:

How many nil pointers are there in a binary tree?
Can the nil pointers be used for another purpose?

To answer the first question, we observe that a binary tree with n nodes will have exactly 2n pointers (two pointers per node). Notice that we have not counted the pointer to the root node, since the pointer is not part of the tree structure itself. There must be exactly n − 1 nonnil pointers in the tree because every node except the root is pointed to by some pointer in the tree. This means that every binary tree with n nodes has n + 1 nil pointers.

To answer the question of how to use these nil pointers to our advantage, we note that the recursive traversal algorithm returns to a prior procedure call when the nil pointer is encountered. This means that we move back up the tree closer to the root when we encounter the nil. Since a nil pointer takes as much space as a "real" pointer, it is possible to replace these nil pointers with other pointers, which we will call *threads*, that will help us move back up the tree. For an inorder traversal of a binary search tree, we would replace a right nil pointer with the inorder successor of the node we are currently visiting, and we would replace a left nil pointer with the node's inorder predecessor. Figure 9-4 shows a diagram of a fully threaded tree. The only nil pointers would be the left thread for B, since it has no predecessor, and the right thread for Z, which has no successor.

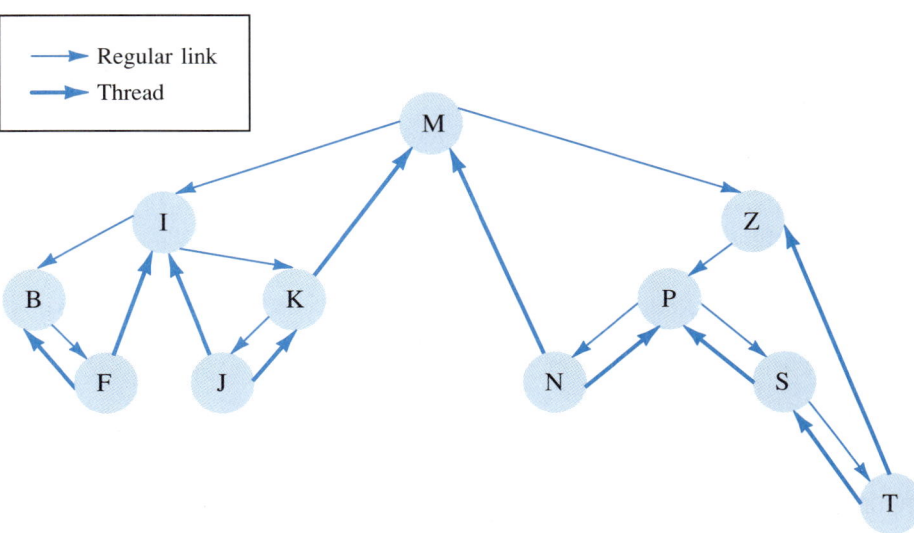

Figure 9-4
A Fully Threaded Tree

We want to construct an abstract data type for our threaded binary search tree that includes the following operations: creation of a tree, deletion of a tree, insertion and deletion of a node, search for a successor and a predecessor, forward and backward traversals, and display of a node element and of the entire tree. The tree type should be opaque, so that an alternative search tree structure could be implemented without affecting the definition of the operations. In addition to being potentially more efficient than the recursive algorithm, the traversal should be incremental, in the sense that the traversal can start at any node in the tree and move a specified number of nodes either in the forward or backward direction.

Design of a Solution We first present the definition module for our abstract data type.

```
DEFINITION MODULE ThreadedBSTrees;
(* This module implements a binary search tree using a doubly threaded
   tree. The use of threads makes it not only possible to traverse the
   tree iteratively in either direction, it also makes incremental
   traversals possible. *)
FROM ThreadElements IMPORT ElementType;
TYPE ThreadedBSTree;
PROCEDURE CreateTree(VAR Tree: ThreadedBSTree);
(* Create an empty Tree *)

PROCEDURE EmptyTree(Tree: ThreadedBSTree) : BOOLEAN;
(* Return TRUE if the Tree is empty, otherwise return FALSE *)

PROCEDURE DisposeTree(VAR Tree: ThreadedBSTree);
(* Dispose of the entire Tree structure *)

PROCEDURE FindPredecessor(Tree: ThreadedBSTree): ThreadedBSTree;
(* Return the predecessor of a given Tree node *)

PROCEDURE FindSuccessor(Tree: ThreadedBSTree): ThreadedBSTree;
(* Return the successor of a given Tree node *)

PROCEDURE FindNode(Tree: ThreadedBSTree; Key: ElementType): ThreadedBSTree;
(* Return a pointer to the node that has the given Key; if Key is not
   present in the Tree, NIL is returned *)

PROCEDURE InsertNode(VAR Tree: ThreadedBSTree; Element: ElementType);
(* Insert Element into Tree; if Element already exists in the Tree, then
   the Tree is not altered *)

PROCEDURE DeleteNode(VAR Tree: ThreadedBSTree; Element: ElementType);
(* Delete the node with same key as Element from Tree; if there is no
   node with same key as Element, then the Tree is not altered *)

PROCEDURE ForwardTraversal(Tree: ThreadedBSTree);
(* Perform an inorder traversal of the search Tree and displays elements in
   ascending key values; use the display procedure from ThreadElements and
   separate values by a space *)
```

```
PROCEDURE BackwardTraversal(Tree: ThreadedBSTree);
(* Perform a reverse inorder traversal of the search Tree and displays
   elements in descending Key values; use the display procedure from
   ThreadElements and separate values by a space *)
PROCEDURE DisplayNode(Tree: ThreadedBSTree);
(* Print value of element at node Tree *)
PROCEDURE DisplayTree(Tree: ThreadedBSTree);
(* Display entire Tree from left to right with root at left *)
END ThreadedBSTrees.
```

For simplicity, we have not used procedure parameters for comparisons, processes to be applied during traversal, and display routines. This generalization to the threaded binary search tree ADT is left as problem 13 in the Exercise section.

Refine the Solution Before refining our solution we need to define the data structure we will use. To distinguish between a thread and a regular link, we need a tag field for each pointer. The threads shown in Figure 9-4 allow us to perform a nonrecursive inorder traversal, the most common traversal for a binary search tree. Other traversals could be performed recursively, provided a thread is treated just like a nil pointer. A fully threaded tree, like the one in Figure 9-4, allows one to perform an entire traversal either forwards or backwards; it even makes it possible to search through a sorted list either forwards or backwards over a specified number of items. If only forward movement through the data is needed, then one can construct a right-threaded tree where a thread replaces all nil right links, but where nil left links are not replaced by threads.

The opaque data structure can be defined by the following type declarations:

```
TYPE ThreadedBSTree = POINTER TO Node;
     Node = RECORD
              Element: ElementType;
              Left, Right: ThreadedBSTree;
              LeftThread, RightThread: BOOLEAN;
            END;
```

The new fields LeftThread and RightThread will be TRUE if the corresponding Left and Right fields are threads; otherwise, they will be FALSE. We could have used a tagged variant record structure to distinguish threads from real links. However, such a structure offers no advantage, and since good programming style encourages the avoidance of variant records and their dangers, we prefer the normal record structure. It should be noted that we have paid a price for our threaded tree: each node in the tree will require space to store two extra Boolean values that are not present in a regular binary search tree. The code for inserting and deleting nodes will also be more complex, as we will see below.

The tree creation operation is so simple it will not be developed in pseudocode. The traversal operations will be based on the primitive operations of FindSuccessor and FindPredecessor, so we will develop the pseudocode for these operations first. To find a given node's successor, we inspect its right link: if it is a thread, then it points directly to the node's successor, or it will be nil if the node has no successor. On the other hand, if the node's right link is a regular link, then we must go to the right child and then move down regular left links as far as possible. We will end up on the successor node.

> Find Successor
>   Set successor to the right link of current node
>   If right link of current node is a regular link
>   While left link of successor is a regular link
>   Set successor to the left link of successor
>   End while
>   End if
> End Find Successor

The code for Find Predecessor is similar: either the left link is a thread that points directly to the predecessor or it is a regular link to the left child, from which we traverse along right regular links as far as we can.

> Find Predecessor
>   Set predecessor to the left link of current node
>   If left link of current node is a regular link
>   While right link of predecessor is a regular link
>   Set predecessor to the right link of predecessor
>   End while
>   End if
> End Find Predecessor

If a node has no successor because it is the last node of the traversal, or if a node has no predecessor because it is the first node of a traversal, then the appropriate procedure will return NIL. We will use this fact to halt the traversal process. Algorithms for forward and reverse traversals of threaded trees are very similar. We give the corresponding pseudocode now, first for a forward traversal, then for a reverse traversal.

> Forward Traversal
>   Set Current to given tree node
>   While left link of Current is a regular link
>   Set Current to left link of Current
>   End while
>   While Current ≠ nil
>   Apply process to Current
>   Set Current to the successor of Current
>   End while
> End Forward Traversal

> Reverse Traversal
>   Set Current to given tree node
>   While right link of Current is a regular link
>   Set Current to right link of Current
>   End while
>   While Current # nil
>   Apply process to Current
>   Set Current to the predecessor of Current
>   End while
> End Reverse Traversal

Finding a node with a particular key value is similar to the search of a regular binary search tree, except that we must end descending into the tree when we encounter a thread.

> Find Node
>   If Node is nil or key of Node equals Element
>   Return Node
>   Elsif key of Node is less than Element
>   If right link of Node is a thread
>   Return nil
>   Else
>   Return result of Find Node applied to right link of Node
>   End if
>   Else
>   If left link of Node is a thread
>   Return nil
>   Else
>   Return result of Find Node applied to left link of Node
>   End if
>   End if
> End Find Node

Inserting a new node into our threaded tree will be relatively easy, since a new node in a binary search tree is always a leaf node. Thus the parent of our new node will have a thread in the place where the new node must be attached. Figure 9-5 illustrates such a case. Here we have assumed the new node will be inserted as the parent's right child. Since the new node will be a leaf, it will contain two threads: the left thread will point to the parent node, the right thread will inherit the parent's right thread, and the right subtree of the parent will be a regular link pointing to the new node.

Inserting a new node as the left child of the parent will be similar; in this case the parent will become the successor of the new node, and the new node will inherit the parent's left thread as its left thread. In our pseudocode for the insertion we have assumed that a utility procedure Create Node creates a new node with the element key

Figure 9-5
Insertion of a Right Child

Inserting a new node in place of a right thread

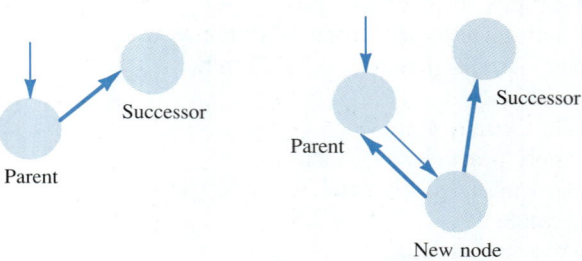

value, attaches it to the current node, and sets its successor and predecessor. All links of a new node are threads.

```
Insert Node
    If tree = nil
        Create Node tree with no successor or predecessor
    Else
        While node with key element has not been found
            If element < key at tree
                If left link of tree is a thread
                    Set link to a regular link
                    Create Node, set left link to tree's left link
                                    and tree as a successor
                    Exit while loop
                Else
                    Set tree to its left link
                End if
            Elsif element = key at tree
                Exit while loop
            Else    { element must be greater than key at tree }
                If right link of tree is a thread
                    Set link to a regular link
                    Create Node, set right link to tree's successor
                                    and tree as a predecessor
                    Exit while loop
                Else
                    Set tree to its right link
                End if
            End if
        End while
    End if
End Insert Node
```

Deletion of a node is more complex than insertion, because the node to be deleted may be a leaf, have one child, or have two children. Recall that in the unthreaded binary search tree, we dealt with the case of two children by finding the predecessor of the node to be deleted. We swapped the values in these two nodes, and then deleted the predecessor, which was either a leaf or had at most one child. We will use a similar strategy here. The easiest case is when the node to be deleted is a leaf.

Figure 9-6 shows the case of a leaf node that is the right child of its parent, so the parent is the predecessor of the node to be deleted. The successor of the node to be deleted is found by following its right thread. After the deletion is completed, the parent's right link becomes this thread.

The deletion of a left child that is a leaf is analogous: the parent will inherit the left thread of the child.

The deletion of a node with a single child is a bit more complex. We will first consider the case when the node to be deleted, call it D, is the right child of its parent and has a real right child. This means that the parent is the predecessor of D. This situation is shown at the left of Figure 9-7. We find the successor of D by going right one node and then left as far as possible along regular links. The successor will have a left thread that points back to D; this will have to be changed to point to the parent (and predecessor) of D. The parent's right link, which pointed to D, will have to point to the right child of D. Then D can be deleted, as shown at the right side of Figure 9-7.

The other case that occurs in deleting the right child of a parent is when the left child of the node to be deleted, D, is a regular link. This case is pictured at the left of Figure 9-8. We must find the predecessor of D, since it will have a thread pointing to D. Since the right thread of D points to its successor, the predecessor node will inherit this thread. The right pointer of the parent will be changed to point to the left child of D. Then D can be deleted, as shown at the right side of Figure 9-8.

There will be two symmetric cases when the node to be deleted is the left child of its parent. The pseudocode for the deletion of a right child is given below.

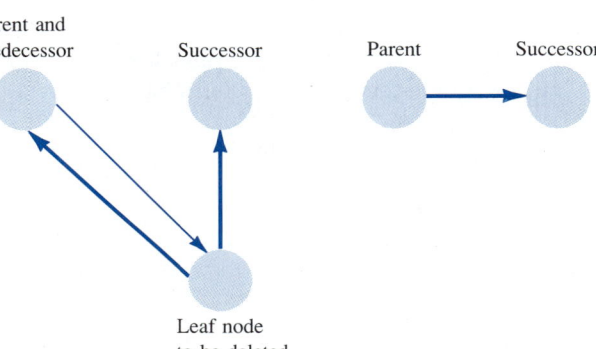

Figure 9-6
Deletion of a Right Child That is a Leaf

Figure 9-7
Deletion of a Right Child with a Left Thread and a Right Child

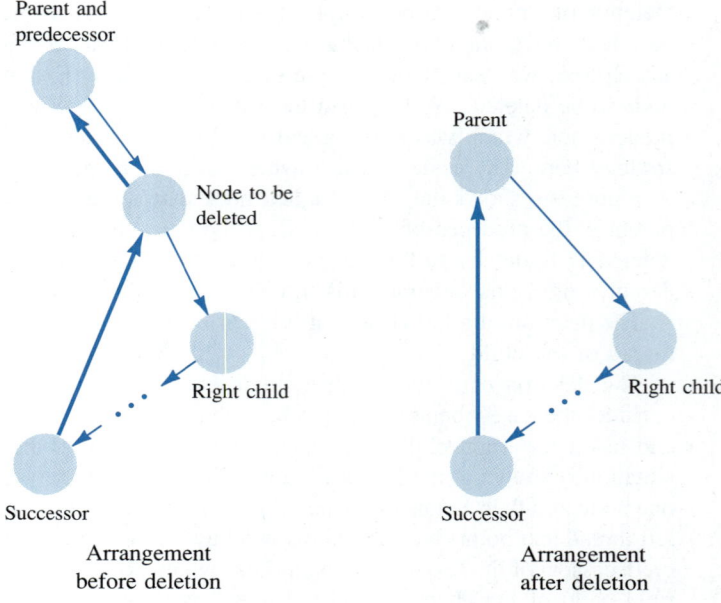

```
Delete Right Child
    Set D to right child of parent
    If D is a leaf
        Set parent's right link to a thread and D's right link
        Deallocate D
    Elsif D has one child to the right
        Set current to D's successor
        Set current's left link to D's left link
        Set parent's right link to D's right link
        Deallocate D
    Elsif D has one child to the left
        Set current to D's predecessor
        Set current's right link to D's right link
        Set parent's right link to D's left link
    Else { D has two children }
        Set current to D's predecessor
        Swap data for D and current
        Delete the node current
    End if
End Delete Right Child
```

There will be an analogous procedure for deleting a node's left child. Since the root of the tree has no parent, we handle it with a separate algorithm.

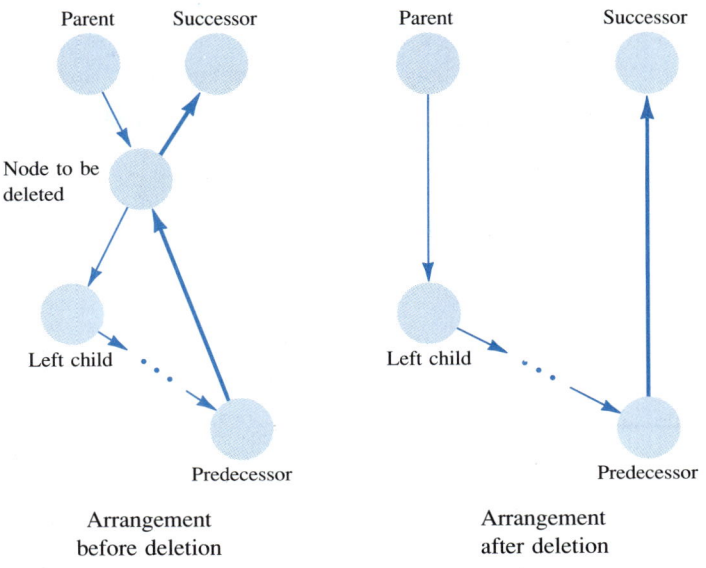

Figure 9-8
Deletion of a Right Child with a Right Thread and a Left Child

Arrangement before deletion

Arrangement after deletion

```
Delete Root
    If root has no children then
        Deallocate root
        Set root to nil
    Elsif root has one child to the left
        Set D to root
        Set root to its left link
        Deallocate D
    Elsif root has one child to the right
        Set D to root
        Set root to its right link
        Deallocate D
    Else { root has two children }
        Set current to root's predecessor
        Swap data for root and current
        Delete node current
    End if
End Delete Root
```

We now have the algorithms necessary to complete the Delete Node algorithm.

```
Delete Node
    If tree is not empty and key at tree equals element
        Delete Root
    Else
        Set parent to the parent of element
        If parent is not nil and element is the left child
            Delete Left Child
        Elsif parent is not nil and element is the right child
            Delete Right Child
        End if
    End if
End Delete Node
```

The remaining algorithms, Dispose Tree and Display Tree, are not presented here in pseudocode; they are very similar to the same algorithms for a binary search tree with the threads acting as nil links.

Develop a Testing Strategy Since our threaded trees are search trees, we can insert nodes in a particular order to obtain a tree with a desired shape. Some of the trees we should use to test our algorithm are:

- several *random* trees in which the nodes are inserted in random order
- a linear right tree in which the nodes are inserted in ascending order
- a linear left tree in which the nodes are inserted in descending order
- an empty tree
- a tree with one node
- the two possible trees with two nodes
- deletion of a node with two children
- deletion of a node with one child
- deletion of a leaf node
- deletion of a node with no predecessor
- deletion of a node with no successor
- deletion of the root node
- deletion of the root node when it is the only node in the tree

We have designed a menu-driven test program in order to check out all of these cases. The code for the test program appears below.

```
MODULE TestThreadedBST;
(* This driver program provides a menu of choices that allows the
   user to test all of the procedures available from the threaded
   tree abstract data type. Test cases are developed through user
   interaction. *)
FROM ThreadedBSTrees IMPORT ThreadedBSTree, CreateTree, DisposeTree,
                            InsertNode, DeleteNode, FindNode,
                            FindPredecessor, FindSuccessor,
                            ForwardTraversal, BackwardTraversal,
                            DisplayNode, DisplayTree, EmptyTree;
FROM ThreadElements IMPORT ElementType, InputElement,
                           DisplayElement;
FROM InOut IMPORT ReadCard, WriteString, WriteLn;

PROCEDURE DisplayMenu;
(* Print list of available options *)
BEGIN
  WriteLn;
  WriteString('1. Create tree'); WriteLn;
  WriteString('2. Delete tree'); WriteLn;
  WriteString('3. Insert node'); WriteLn;
  WriteString('4. Delete node'); WriteLn;
  WriteString('5. Find node'); WriteLn;
  WriteString('6. Move to predecessor node'); WriteLn;
  WriteString('7. Move to successor node'); WriteLn;
  WriteString('8. Forward traversal of tree'); WriteLn;
  WriteString('9. Reverse traversal of tree'); WriteLn;
  WriteString('10. Display value at current node'); WriteLn;
  WriteString('11. Display entire tree'); WriteLn;
  WriteString('12. Quit program'); WriteLn; WriteLn;
  WriteString('Please enter your choice (1..12) : ');
END DisplayMenu;

PROCEDURE GetChoice() : CARDINAL;
(* Solicits user input in the range of 1..12, the valid choices. If
   the user inputs any other number, a prompt for proper input is
   printed and another input read in. This function only returns a
   valid value. *)
VAR Choice: CARDINAL;
BEGIN
  DisplayMenu;
  LOOP
    ReadCard(Choice); WriteLn;
    IF (1 <= Choice) AND (Choice <= 12) THEN
      RETURN Choice
    ELSE
      WriteString('Please enter a choice between 1 and 12 > ');
    END; (* IF *)
  END;   (* LOOP *)
END GetChoice;
```

```
VAR Tree, Current : ThreadedBSTree;
    Element: ElementType;
BEGIN
  LOOP
    CASE GetChoice() OF
      1: CreateTree(Tree); Current := Tree;
    | 2: DisposeTree(Tree);
    | 3: WriteString('enter node value to be inserted > ');
         InputElement(Element); DisplayElement(Element);
         InsertNode(Tree, Element);
    | 4: WriteString('enter node value to be deleted > ');
         InputElement(Element); DisplayElement(Element);
         DeleteNode(Tree, Element);
    | 5: WriteString('enter node value to be found > ');
         InputElement(Element); DisplayElement(Element);
         Current := FindNode(Tree, Element);
         IF EmptyTree(Current) THEN
           WriteString('node not found, Current node set to root'); WriteLn;
           Current := Tree;
         END; (* IF *)
    | 6: Current := FindPredecessor(Current);
         IF EmptyTree(Current) THEN
           WriteString('node has no predecessor, Current node set to root');
           Current := Tree;
         ELSE
           WriteString('Current node is ');
           DisplayNode(Current);
         END; (* IF *) WriteLn;
    | 7: Current := FindSuccessor(Current);
         IF EmptyTree(Current) THEN
           WriteString('node has no successor, Current node set to root');
           Current := Tree;
         ELSE
           WriteString('Current node is ');
           DisplayNode(Current);
         END; (* IF *) WriteLn;
    | 8: ForwardTraversal(Current);
    | 9: BackwardTraversal(Current);
    |10: WriteString('Current node is ');
         DisplayNode(Current); WriteLn;
    |11: DisplayTree(Tree);
    |12: EXIT
    END; (* CASE *)
  END; (* LOOP *)
END TestThreadedBST.
```

9.4 Case Study: Threaded Binary Search Trees

When running this program, the user will have to provide data to test the various cases we have identified earlier.

Implementation

We assume the existence of a module ThreadElements that will supply the type for ElementType and operations for input, display, and comparison of elements. If the element type cannot use assignment to transfer values, then we would have to add an assign operation to this module.

Code and Test the Program The following implementation module was developed directly from the pseudocode.

```
IMPLEMENTATION MODULE ThreadedBSTrees;
(* This module implements a binary search Tree using a doubly threaded
   Tree. The use of threads makes it not only possible to traverse the
   Tree iteratively in either direction, it also makes incremental
   traversals, a node at a time, possible. *)
FROM InOut IMPORT WriteString, WriteLn, Write;
FROM ThreadElements IMPORT ElementType, DisplayElement, LessThanElement,
                           EqualElement;
FROM Storage IMPORT ALLOCATE, DEALLOCATE;
TYPE ThreadedBSTree = POINTER TO TreeNode;

     TreeNode = RECORD
                     Element: ElementType;
                     Left, Right: ThreadedBSTree;
                     LeftThread, RightThread: BOOLEAN;
                END;

PROCEDURE CreateTree(VAR Tree: ThreadedBSTree);
BEGIN
  Tree := NIL;
END CreateTree;

PROCEDURE EmptyTree(Tree: ThreadedBSTree) : BOOLEAN;
(* Return TRUE if the Tree is empty, otherwise return FALSE *)
BEGIN
  RETURN Tree = NIL
END EmptyTree;
```

```
PROCEDURE DisposeTree(VAR Tree: ThreadedBSTree);
(* Dispose of the entire Tree structure *)
BEGIN
  IF Tree # NIL THEN
    IF NOT Tree^.LeftThread THEN
      DisposeTree(Tree^.Left)
    END; (* IF *)
    IF NOT Tree^.RightThread THEN
      DisposeTree(Tree^.Right)
    END; (* IF *)
    DEALLOCATE(Tree, SIZE(TreeNode));
  END; (* IF *)
END DisposeTree;
```

Procedures CreateTree and EmptyTree are quite straightforward. Procedure DisposeTree is very similar to procedure DeleteTree in the binary search tree ADT. However, here left and right links must be checked, and recursive calls are made only if the links are regular links and not threads.

```
PROCEDURE FindPredecessor(Tree: ThreadedBSTree): ThreadedBSTree;
(* Return the predecessor of a given Tree node *)
VAR Node: ThreadedBSTree;
BEGIN
  IF Tree = NIL THEN
    RETURN NIL
  ELSE
    Node := Tree^.Left;
    IF NOT Tree^.LeftThread THEN
      WHILE NOT Node^.RightThread DO
        Node := Node^.Right;
      END; (* WHILE *)
    END; (* IF *)
    RETURN Node;
  END; (* IF *)
END FindPredecessor;
```

Procedure FindPredecessor is simple: if the tree is empty, it returns NIL. If the left pointer is a thread, it points to the predecessor, which is returned. If the left pointer is not a thread, we follow a chain of regular right pointers from the left descendant to get the desired predecessor.

```
PROCEDURE FindSuccessor(Tree: ThreadedBSTree): ThreadedBSTree;
(* Return the successor of a given Tree node *)
VAR Node: ThreadedBSTree;
BEGIN
  IF Tree = NIL THEN
    RETURN NIL
```

```
    ELSE
      Node := Tree^.Right;
      IF NOT Tree^.RightThread THEN
        WHILE NOT Node^.LeftThread DO
          Node := Node^.Left;
        END; (* WHILE *)
      END; (* IF *)
      RETURN Node;
    END;  (* IF *)
END FindSuccessor;
```

Procedure FindSuccessor is also simple: if the tree is empty, it returns NIL. If the right pointer is a thread, it points to the successor, which is returned. If the right pointer is not a thread, we follow a chain of regular left pointers from the right descendant to get the desired successor.

```
PROCEDURE FindNode(Tree: ThreadedBSTree; Key: ElementType): ThreadedBSTree;
(* Return a pointer to the node that has the given Key; if Key is not
   present in the Tree, NIL is returned *)
VAR Where: ThreadedBSTree;
BEGIN
  Where := Tree;
  IF (Where = NIL) OR (EqualElement(Where^.Element, Key)) THEN
    RETURN Where
  ELSIF LessThanElement(Where^.Element, Key) THEN
    IF Where^.RightThread THEN
      RETURN NIL;
    ELSE
      RETURN FindNode(Where^.Right, Key);
    END; (* IF *)
  ELSE
    IF Where^.LeftThread THEN
      RETURN NIL;
    ELSE
      RETURN FindNode(Where^.Left, Key);
    END; (* IF *)
  END; (* IF *)
END FindNode;
```

Procedure FindNode returns NIL if the tree is empty. If the desired node was the starting node, it is returned. Depending on the Key value, the search is done recursively left or right. Before calling FindNode recursively, we check to see if we have reached a thread. If this is the case, the key will not be found and NIL is returned.

```
PROCEDURE InsertNode(VAR Tree: ThreadedBSTree; Element: ElementType);
(* Insert Element into Tree; if Element already exists in the Tree,
   then the Tree is not altered *)
VAR Parent: ThreadedBSTree;
    Found: BOOLEAN;
```

```
    PROCEDURE CreateNode(VAR Tree:ThreadedBSTree; Elt:ElementType;
                        Left, Right:ThreadedBSTree);
  (* Allocate the specified node with both threads set to TRUE *)
  BEGIN
    ALLOCATE(Tree, SIZE(TreeNode));
    Tree^.Element := Elt;
    Tree^.Left := Left;
    Tree^.Right := Right;
    Tree^.LeftThread := TRUE;
    Tree^.RightThread := TRUE;
  END CreateNode;
BEGIN
  IF Tree = NIL THEN
    CreateNode(Tree, Element, NIL, NIL);
  ELSE
    Found := FALSE;
    Parent := Tree;
    WHILE NOT Found DO
      IF LessThanElement(Element, Parent^.Element) THEN (* look Left *)
        IF Parent^.LeftThread  THEN
          (* insert as Left child of Parent *)
          Parent^.LeftThread := FALSE;
          CreateNode(Parent^.Left, Element, Parent^.Left, Parent);
          Found := TRUE;
        ELSE (* keep looking *)
          Parent := Parent^.Left;
        END; (* IF *)
      ELSIF EqualElement(Element, Parent^.Element) THEN (* already in Tree *)
        Found := TRUE;
      ELSE       (* look Right *)
        IF Parent^.RightThread THEN
          (* insert as Right child of Parent *)
          Parent^.RightThread := FALSE;
          CreateNode(Parent^.Right, Element, Parent, Parent^.Right);
          Found := TRUE
        ELSE
          Parent := Parent^.Right;
        END; (* IF *)
      END; (* IF *)
    END; (* WHILE *)
  END; (* IF *)
END InsertNode;
```

Procedure InsertNode is a little more complicated because it does not use recursion. If it finds a leaf, it inserts a new node and connects it to that leaf by calling CreateNode. Depending on the value of the element to insert, it follows left or right pointers. If it finds it has to go left and the left pointer is a thread, it inserts the element as the left child of that node. If it finds it has to go right and the right pointer is a thread, it inserts the element as the right child of that node.

```
PROCEDURE DeleteNode(VAR Tree: ThreadedBSTree; Element: ElementType);
(* Delete the Node with same key as Element from Tree; if there is no
   node with same key as Element, then the Tree is not altered *)
BEGIN
  (* this complex procedure has been discussed in detail in the
     design section. Actual implementation is left as programming
     problem number 12. *)
END DeleteNode;

PROCEDURE ForwardTraversal(Tree: ThreadedBSTree);
(* Perform an inorder traversal of the search Tree and display
   elements in ascending key values; use the display procedure
   from ThreadElements and separate values by a space *)
VAR Current: ThreadedBSTree;
BEGIN
  IF Tree # NIL THEN
    Current := Tree;
    WHILE NOT Current^.LeftThread DO
      (* find first Element of traversal *)
      Current := Current^.Left;
    END; (* WHILE *)
    WHILE Current # NIL DO
      (* finds remaining elements using FindSuccessor *)
      DisplayElement(Current^.Element); Write(' ');
      Current := FindSuccessor(Current);
    END; (* WHILE *)
  ELSE
    WriteString("empty tree"); WriteLn;
  END; (* IF *)
END ForwardTraversal;
```

Procedure ForwardTraversal starts at a given node, and if it is not empty, follows regular left pointers to find the first element of the traversal. From that element, it follows a chain of successors using calls to FindSuccessor, and displays the value of each element.

```
PROCEDURE BackwardTraversal(Tree: ThreadedBSTree);
(* Perform a reverse inorder traversal of the search Tree and
   display elements in descending key values; use the display
   procedure from ThreadElements and separate values by a space *)
VAR Current: ThreadedBSTree;
BEGIN
  IF Tree # NIL THEN
    Current := Tree;
    WHILE NOT Current^.RightThread DO
      Current := Current^.Right;
    END; (* WHILE *)
    WHILE Current # NIL DO
      DisplayElement(Current^.Element); Write(' ');
      Current := FindPredecessor(Current);
    END; (* WHILE *)
  ELSE
    WriteString("empty tree"); WriteLn;
  END; (* IF *)
END BackwardTraversal;
```

> Procedure BackwardTraversal is similar to ForwardTraversal: it starts at a given node, and if it is not empty, follows regular right pointers to find the first element of the traversal. From that element, BackwardTraversal follows a chain of predecessors by using calls to FindPredecessor, and displays the value of each element.

```
PROCEDURE DisplayNode(Tree: ThreadedBSTree);
(* Print value of element at node Tree *)
BEGIN
  DisplayElement(Tree^.Element);
END DisplayNode;

PROCEDURE PrintTree(Tree: ThreadedBSTree; Indentation: CARDINAL);
(* Utility procedure that actually prints the Tree *)
VAR Indent: CARDINAL;
BEGIN
  IF Tree # NIL THEN
    IF NOT Tree^.RightThread THEN
      PrintTree(Tree^.Right, Indentation+1);
    END;
    FOR Indent := 1 TO Indentation DO
      WriteString("    ");
    END; (* FOR *)
    DisplayElement(Tree^.Element); WriteLn;
    IF NOT Tree^.LeftThread THEN
      PrintTree(Tree^.Left, Indentation+1);
    END;
  END; (* IF *)
END PrintTree;
```

Procedure PrintTree is similar to the PrintTree procedure of the binary search tree ADT. It is recursive, but before each recursive call it checks to make sure the left or right pointer, as the case may be, is not a thread. If the pointer is a thread, it must be treated as a nil pointer. Procedure DisplayTree given below is "syntactic sugar" for this PrintTree procedure.

```
PROCEDURE DisplayTree(Tree: ThreadedBSTree);
(* Display entire Tree from left to right with the root at the left;
   Procedure supplying Indentation to PrintTree *)
BEGIN
  PrintTree(Tree, 0);
END DisplayTree;

END ThreadedBSTrees.
```

We tested our program with ElementType = CHAR, but a more complex type, such as a record with a key field, could be used. We used the testing program developed earlier, with data that we created corresponding to the various cases that were identified in the testing strategy development.

Complete the Documentation The documentation internal to the code should be supplemented by a discussion of the design decisions made before the coding. The design decisions for the threaded tree structure are fairly straightforward; however, materials on the design of the insertion and the deletion algorithms should be saved. The test program, test data, and test results should be included as part of the documentation.

Summary

This chapter has been an extension of the preceding one. Here we have introduced the binary search tree, a kind of binary tree especially designed for improved performance of the search operation.

The applications that require binary search trees usually need a limited number of operations. Threaded binary trees take advantage of the fact that, in a binary tree, half the pointers are nil, and thus they can be used to accelerate traversal operations in the tree, provide incremental traversals, and allow traversals in either direction.

As was the case with binary trees, implementations of binary search trees are usually dynamic because of the dynamic nature of the tree.

■ Exercises

1. Explain why, in the binary search tree ADT, we do not need a current node.

2. Explain why we need fewer operations in the binary search tree ADT than in the binary tree ADT.

3. Since we can use the TraverseTree operation in conjunction with a display element procedure to display the tree elements' values, what is the use of ADT operation PrintTree?

4. In the MakeIndex application, suggest another way of keeping the page number associated with a word. Modify the application and test it.

5. Can the static implementation suggested in Chapter 8 for binary trees be used for binary search trees?

6. In the text we have described the inorder successor of a node depending on whether the node is a left or a right descendant. Is it possible to describe in a similar manner the location of:

   - a node's preorder successor
   - a node's postorder successor

7. Write an inorder traversal algorithm for a binary search tree that uses a stack instead of recursion.

Programming Problems

8. Write and test a Boolean procedure that examines a binary tree to determine if it is a binary search tree.

9. Write and test a procedure to convert a binary tree into a binary search tree with the same elements.

10. Define, implement, and test two new operations for the threaded binary search trees, Advance and GoBack, which, given a tree node, traverse the tree for a number of nodes in either direction.

11. Modify the threaded binary search tree ADT so that it becomes a right-threaded binary search tree ADT.

12. Complete the implementation of the DeleteNode procedure in the threaded binary search tree implementation given in the case study of Section 9.4.

13. Add procedure parameters for comparisons, processes to be applied during traversal, and display routines to the threaded binary search tree ADT.

14. If the text read by MakeIndex is scanned from beginning to end, then the page references will be sorted. However, if sections of the text are read in an unknown order, then the queue structure for storing page numbers should be replaced by a binary search tree. Make this change and test your program by reading pages in "random" order to see if the results are the same as reading pages from beginning to end. The page number will have to be part of the data read. Note that this change means we have a binary search tree structure inside of another binary search tree! This may be surprising, but it is a natural structure for this problem.

15. Write and test a TreeInsertionSort procedure that sorts m distinct values by first inserting them into a binary search tree, and then listing the tree in inorder. Analyze the running time of your procedure.

Advanced Data Structures

PART THREE

CHAPTER

10 Special Purpose Trees
11 Internal and External Sorting
12 Tables
13 Character Strings
14 Generalized Lists
15 Graphs
16 Sets

Although this part of the text is titled "advanced," the data structures it introduces are no less nor inherently more difficult than those studied earlier. Some structures are more specialized, such as Special Purpose Trees (Chapter 10) or Character Strings (Chapter 13), while others are more general, such as Generalized Lists (Chapter 14), Graphs (Chapter 15), and Sets (Chapter 16). Additional algorithms for internal and external sorting are studied in Chapter 11. Searching for data in Table structures, with particular emphasis on hash functions, is studied in Chapter 12. The topics covered in Part Three are relatively independent of each other and can be selected for study based on interest and need.

Special Purpose Trees

INTRODUCTION

In the preceding two chapters we introduced the tree data structure and several abstract data types. We covered binary trees and a few applications, but a complete and exhaustive presentation of trees would undoubtedly require a separate book. Our focus in this chapter is to introduce a few new concepts related to trees. This third chapter on trees will introduce height-balanced or AVL trees, multiway trees implemented as B-trees, as well as optimal search tree concepts and a tree implementation of priority queues.

10.1 Height-Balanced Trees

When we discussed the complexity of operation SearchKey for binary search trees, we pointed out that in the worst case the binary search tree was a degenerate binary tree similar to a linear list. If we build a binary search tree by repeatedly calling InsertNode, and if the input elements are already ordered, we will indeed end up with a degenerate binary tree and will have lost all the benefits of the binary search tree: the search operation will be O(n)!

A *perfectly balanced tree* is a tree in which, for each node, the number of nodes in its left and right subtrees differ by at most 1. Although it is possible to build a perfectly balanced tree from a given set of data, it is fairly difficult to restore a perfect balance after an insertion or a deletion in such a tree. The implementation of perfectly balanced trees is impractical, and so we must find a definition of balance that is less strict and leads to practical implementations, while retaining most of the qualities of perfectly balanced trees.

The definition of balance we will use was given by Adelson-Velskii and Landis: a tree will be said to be balanced if and only if, for every node, the difference in height of its two subtrees is at most 1. The trees that satisfy this condition are usually called AVL trees, and Figure 10-1 gives an example of such a tree. AVL trees may be used as binary trees or binary search trees. We will assume in this section that we are working with binary search trees.

Binary trees and binary search trees can actually be implemented by AVL trees. In fact, the representation of AVL trees is similar to the representation of binary trees, and the operations are identical except for insertion and deletion, which are more complex for AVL trees. To help implement these operations in a simple way, we associate with each node a *balance factor* indicating whether the node is perfectly balanced (same height for left and right subtrees), or whether the left or the right subtree is higher. The balance factor will represent $h_R - h_L$ for a given node (height of right subtree minus height of left subtree).

Assuming a node N with a left subtree L and a right subtree R, if we want to insert a new node in L, which increases its height by 1, then there are three possible cases:

(a) $h_L = h_R$ The balance of the node is changed but will remain acceptable.
(b) $h_L < h_R$ The balance is improved as the two subtrees become of equal height.
(c) $h_L > h_R$ The balance is changed. The tree must be restructured, since the left subtree is now two levels deeper than the right subtree.

To remedy the imbalance in this last case, we will need to adjust the tree structure. A detailed study of the various possibilities shows that there are only two general cases to consider: single rotation and double rotation.

A single rotation is illustrated in Figure 10-2, where a subtree with root Y becomes unbalanced as a result of an insertion, and is restructured in a subtree with root X. In Figure 10-2, subtrees are shown as rectangles that may contain any number of elements, the added element is represented by a crossed rectangle, and the digits represent the balance factor of the corresponding node. After the insertion, X's balance factor is changed from 0 to 1. Then it is discovered that Y's balance factor was already 1, which

Figure 10-1
An AVL Tree

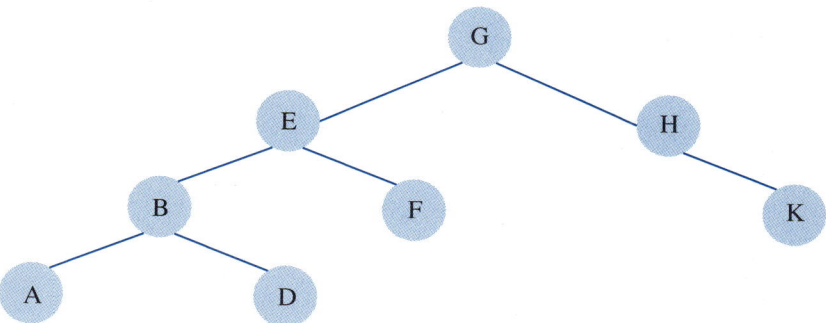

indicates that its right side was already higher than its left and that the subtree requires restructuring. The left subtree of X comprises values that are greater than Y and less than X: it can become the right subtree of Y without changing the order of the elements in the subtree. Similarly, since X is the right child of Y, the value of Y is less than the value of X, and Y can become X's left child without disturbing the order in the subtree.

The remainder of the tree, which is not shown in Figure 10-2, is not affected by this restructuring, as the height of the subtree has not changed. This restructuring is called a single left rotation. The mirror image of Figure 10-2 would illustrate a single right rotation.

A double rotation is slightly more complex; it is illustrated in Figure 10-3. The new node has been added to the left of node X, but could have been added to its right without changing the resulting structure. After the insertion, X's balance factor is changed from 0 to -1. Then Y's balance factor is changed from 0 to -1. Then it is discovered that Z's balance factor is already 1, which indicates that the subtree was already higher on its right and requires restructuring. In Figure 10-3, the value of X is greater than the value of Z and less than the value of Y: X can therefore become the parent of left child Z and right child Y. Similarly X's left subtree comprises values that

Figure 10-2
Single Left Rotation

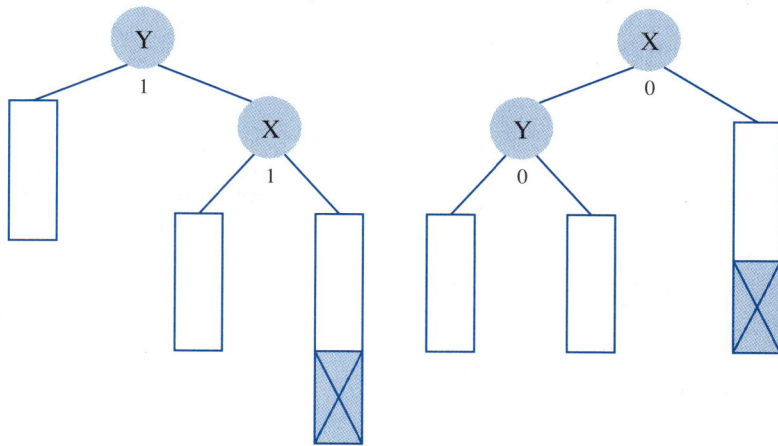

Figure 10-3
Double Right-Left Rotation

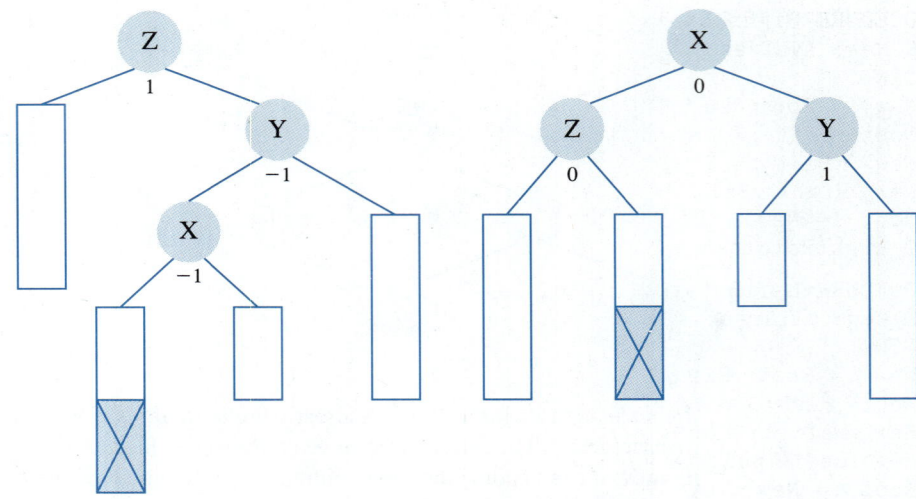

are greater than Z's value, and less than X's value and Y's value: it can become the right child of Z. The right subtree of X contains values that are greater than Z's value and X's value, and less than Y's value: it can become the left child of Y. The balance factors are then adjusted. It should be noted that the double-left rotation is the composition of two single rotations: a single right rotation about Y followed by a single left rotation about Z.

As with the single rotation, the remainder of the tree is not affected by the double rotation restructuring, as the height of the subtree is not changed. The mirror image of Figure 10-3 would illustrate a double right rotation.

Our implementation will use the following definitions.

```
TYPE AVLTree = POINTER TO NodeType;
     NodeType = RECORD     (* An internal node of a tree *)
                    Element: ElementType;
                    Left, Right: AVLTree;
                    Bal: INTEGER;
                END;
```

The balance factor, Bal, will represent $h_R - h_L$ for a given node, i.e., the difference of the height of its right and left subtrees. The single and double rotations will be realized by the following procedures, which implement the transformations we have just described. You should trace LeftRotate with the tree of Figure 10-2, and RightLeftRotate with Figure 10-3.

```
PROCEDURE RightRotate(VAR Root: AVLTree);
VAR New: AVLTree;
BEGIN
  New := Root^.Left;
  Root^.Left := New^.Right;
  New^.Right := Root;
  New^.Right^.Bal := 0;
  Root := New;
END RightRotate;

PROCEDURE LeftRotate(VAR Root:AVLTree);
VAR New: AVLTree;
BEGIN
  New := Root^.Right;
  Root^.Right := New^.Left;
  New^.Left := Root;
  New^.Left^.Bal := 0;
  Root := New;
END LeftRotate;

PROCEDURE LeftRightRotate(VAR Root:AVLTree);   (* double rotation *)
VAR New, Left: AVLTree;
BEGIN
  Left := Root^.Left;
  New := Left^.Right;
  Left^.Right := New^.Left;
  Root^.Left := New^.Right;
  New^.Left := Left;
  New^.Right := Root;
  IF New^.Bal = -1 THEN
    Root^.Bal := +1;
  ELSE
    Root^.Bal := 0;
  END;
  IF New^.Bal = +1 THEN
    Left^.Bal := -1;
  ELSE
    Left^.Bal := 0;
  END;
  New^.Bal := 0;
  Root := New;
END LeftRightRotate;
```

```
PROCEDURE RightLeftRotate(VAR Root:AVLTree);   (* double left rotation *)
VAR New, Right: AVLTree;
BEGIN
  Right := Root^.Right;
  New := Right^.Left;
  Right^.Left := New^.Right;
  Root^.Right := New^.Left;
  New^.Right := Right;
  New^.Left := Root;
  IF New^.Bal = +1 THEN
    Root^.Bal := -1;
  ELSE
    Root^.Bal := 0;
  END;
  IF New^.Bal = -1 THEN
    Right^.Bal := +1;
  ELSE
    Right^.Bal := 0;
  END;
  New^.Bal := 0;
  Root := New;
END RightLeftRotate;
```

The insertion operation will then be defined by procedure InsertNode.

```
PROCEDURE InsertNode(VAR Tree: AVLTree; VAR Elt: ElementType; Comp: CompProc);
VAR Change: BOOLEAN;

  PROCEDURE CreateNode(VAR NewPtr: AVLTree);
  BEGIN
    ALLOCATE(NewPtr, SIZE(NodeType));
    NewPtr^.Element := Elt;
    NewPtr^.Left := NIL;
    NewPtr^.Right := NIL;
    NewPtr^.Bal := 0;
  END CreateNode;

  PROCEDURE Insertion(VAR Node: AVLTree; VAR HeightIncreased: BOOLEAN);
  VAR Compare:INTEGER;
  BEGIN
    IF Node = NIL THEN
      CreateNode(Node);
      HeightIncreased := TRUE;
    ELSE
      Compare:= Comp(Elt.Key, Node^.Element.Key);
      IF Compare = -1 THEN
        Insertion(Node^.Left, HeightIncreased);
```

```
      IF HeightIncreased THEN    (* Left subtree HeightIncreased *)
        IF Node^.Bal = 1 THEN
          Node^.Bal := 0;
          HeightIncreased := FALSE; (* rebalanced *)
        ELSIF Node^.Bal = 0 THEN
          Node^.Bal := -1;
        ELSE (* Bal = -1 *)
          IF Node^.Left^.Bal = -1 THEN
            RightRotate(Node);   (* single right rotation *)
          ELSE
            LeftRightRotate(Node);   (* double right rotation *)
          END; (* IF *)
          Node^.Bal := 0;    (* Node = New root *)
          HeightIncreased := FALSE;
        END; (* IF *)
      END; (* IF *)
    ELSIF Compare = 1 THEN
      Insertion(Node^.Right, HeightIncreased);
      IF HeightIncreased THEN    (* Right subtree HeightIncreased *)
        IF Node^.Bal = -1 THEN
          Node^.Bal := 0;
          HeightIncreased:=FALSE; (* rebalanced *)
        ELSIF Node^.Bal = 0 THEN
          Node^.Bal:= +1;
        ELSE (* Bal= +1 *)
          IF Node^.Right^.Bal = 1 THEN
            LeftRotate(Node);   (* single left rotation *)
          ELSE
            RightLeftRotate(Node);   (* double left rotation *)
          END; (* IF *)
          Node^.Bal := 0;   (* Node = New root *)
          HeightIncreased:=FALSE;
        END; (* IF *)
      END; (* IF *)
    ELSE (* Compare = 0: already exists *)
      HeightIncreased:= FALSE
    END; (* IF *)
  END; (* IF *)
END Insertion;
BEGIN
  Insertion(Tree, Change);
END InsertNode;
```

In each case where an insertion occurs, we check whether rebalancing is necessary and update the node's balance factor. Figure 10-4 illustrates the two cases of single rotation, while Figure 10-5 illustrates the two cases of double rotation.

Figure 10-4
Insertion with
Single Rotations

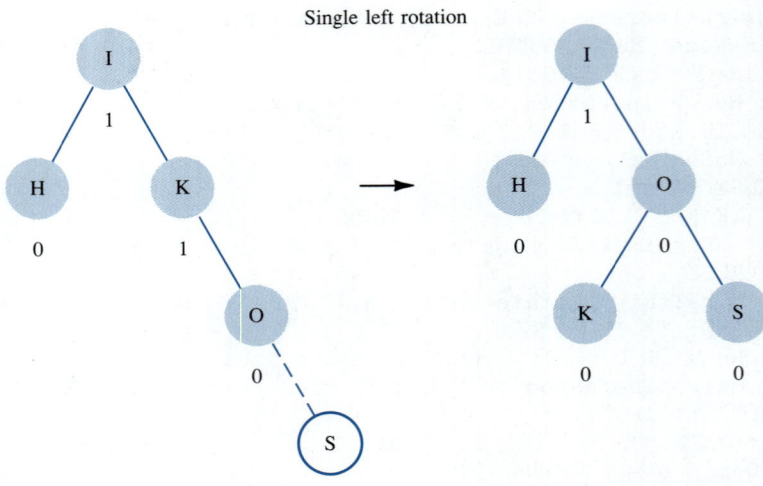

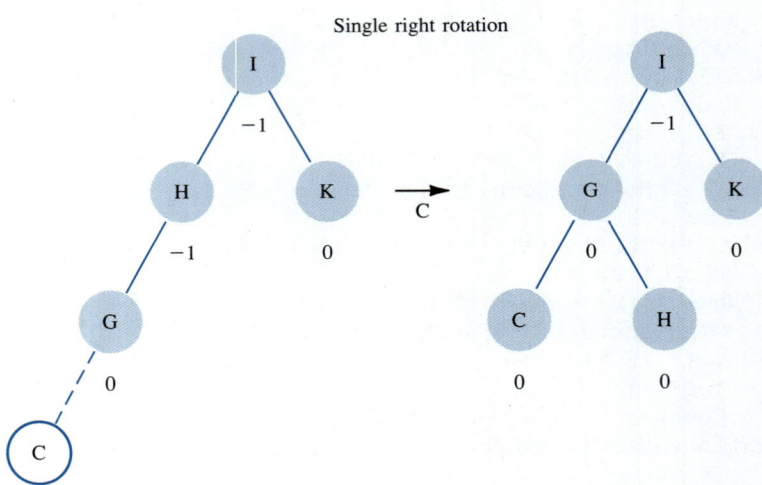

The deletion operation is implemented by procedure DeleteNode. Like deletion operations with simpler tree implementations, this deletion operation is more complicated than the corresponding insertion operation. First we present the code and then explain its operation.

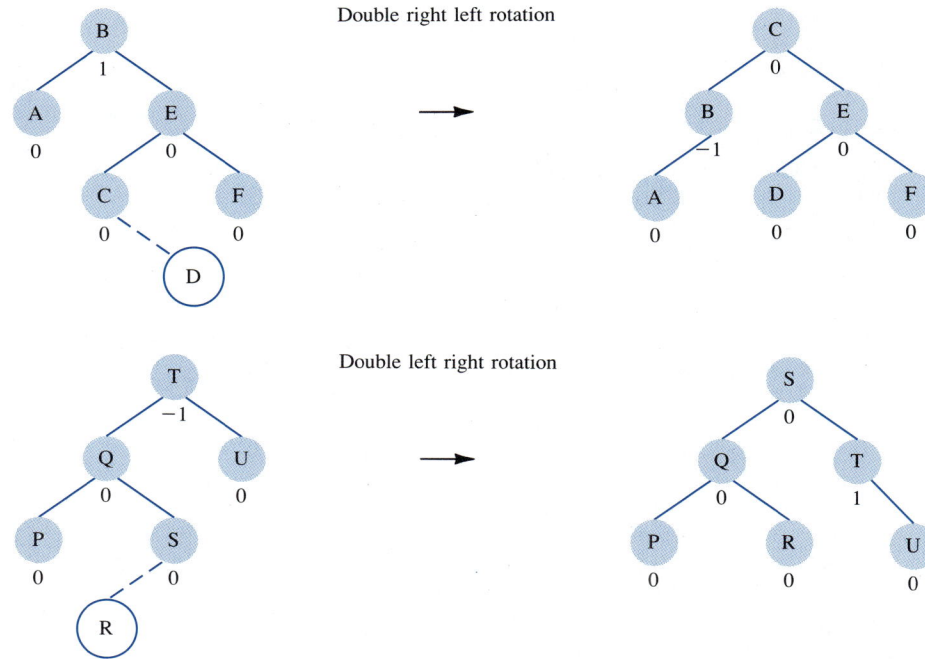

Figure 10-5
Insertion with Double Rotations

```
PROCEDURE DeleteNode(VAR Tree: AVLTree; Key: KeyType; Comp: CompProc);
VAR Change: BOOLEAN;

  PROCEDURE SearchAndDelete(VAR Node:AVLTree; VAR HeightReduced:BOOLEAN);
  VAR Compare: INTEGER;
      ToDispose: AVLTree;
    PROCEDURE RightBalance(VAR Node:AVLTree; VAR HeightReduced:BOOLEAN);
    VAR NewBal:INTEGER;
    BEGIN
      IF Node^.Bal = 1 THEN
        Node^.Bal := 0;
      ELSIF Node^.Bal = 0 THEN
        Node^.Bal := -1;
        HeightReduced := FALSE;
      ELSE
        NewBal := Node^.Left^.Bal;
        IF NewBal <= 0 THEN
          RightRotate(Node);
          IF NewBal = 0 THEN
            Node^.Bal := +1;
            Node^.Right^.Bal := -1;
            HeightReduced := FALSE;
          ELSE
            Node^.Bal := 0;
            Node^.Right^.Bal := 0;
          END;
```

```
      ELSE (* NewBal=1 *)
        LeftRightRotate(Node);
      END; (* IF *)
    END; (* IF *)
END RightBalance;

PROCEDURE LeftBalance(VAR Node: AVLTree; VAR HeightReduced: BOOLEAN);
VAR NewBal: INTEGER;
BEGIN
  IF Node^.Bal = -1 THEN
    Node^.Bal := 0;
  ELSIF Node^.Bal = 0 THEN
    Node^.Bal := +1;
    HeightReduced := FALSE;
  ELSE
    NewBal := Node^.Right^.Bal;
     IF NewBal >=0 THEN
        LeftRotate(Node);
        IF NewBal = 0 THEN
           Node^.Left^.Bal := +1;
           Node^.Bal := -1;
           HeightReduced := FALSE;
        ELSE
           Node^.Bal := 0;
           Node^.Left^.Bal := 0;
        END;
     ELSE (* NewBal= -1 *)
        RightLeftRotate(Node);
     END; (* IF *)
   END; (* IF *)
END LeftBalance;

PROCEDURE ExchangeAndDelete(VAR Replace: AVLTree; VAR HeightReduced: BOOLEAN);
(* Replace by rightmost Node of left subtree *)
BEGIN
  IF Replace^.Right # NIL THEN
    ExchangeAndDelete(Replace^.Right, HeightReduced);
    IF HeightReduced THEN
      RightBalance(Replace, HeightReduced)
    END;
  ELSE
    ToDispose^.Element := Replace^.Element;
    ToDispose := Replace;
    Replace := Replace^.Left;
    HeightReduced := TRUE;
  END; (* IF *)
END ExchangeAndDelete;
```

```
BEGIN    (* SearchAndDelete *)
  IF Node = NIL THEN
    HeightReduced:= FALSE;
    RETURN;
  END;    (* NOT FOUND *)
  Compare:=Comp(Key, Node^.Element.Key);
  IF Compare = -1 THEN
    SearchAndDelete(Node^.Left, HeightReduced);
    IF HeightReduced THEN
      LeftBalance(Node,HeightReduced);
    END;
  ELSIF Compare = 1 THEN
    SearchAndDelete(Node^.Right, HeightReduced);
    IF HeightReduced THEN
      RightBalance(Node,HeightReduced);
    END;
  ELSE              (* Key FOUND *)
    ToDispose:=Node;
    IF Node^.Left = NIL THEN
      Node := Node^.Right;
      HeightReduced := TRUE;
    ELSIF Node^.Right = NIL THEN
      Node := Node^.Left;
      HeightReduced:= TRUE;
    ELSE (* both Right and Left have non-empty subtrees *)
      ExchangeAndDelete(ToDispose^.Left, HeightReduced);
      IF HeightReduced THEN
        LeftBalance(Node, HeightReduced);
      END;
    END;
    DEALLOCATE(ToDispose, SIZE(Node));
  END;
END SearchAndDelete;
BEGIN
  SearchAndDelete(Tree, Change);
END DeleteNode;
```

The SearchAndDelete procedure searches the tree by following a path through the left and right subtrees of the visited node. After the node to delete has been found, it is deleted if it has one empty subtree and then an indication that the tree height was reduced is returned. If the node to delete has two nonempty subtrees, procedure ExchangeAndDelete is called, which replaces the node by the rightmost node of its left subtree (its predecessor). After the node has been deleted and the subtree height has been reduced, either LeftBalance or RightBalance is called to rebalance the tree. These two balancing procedures are symmetric, and call the same single or double rotation procedures used by InsertNode.

Figure 10-6 shows a tree example that will be used in the three following figures to illustrate a sequence of deletion operations.

Figure 10-6
Original Tree Before Deletion

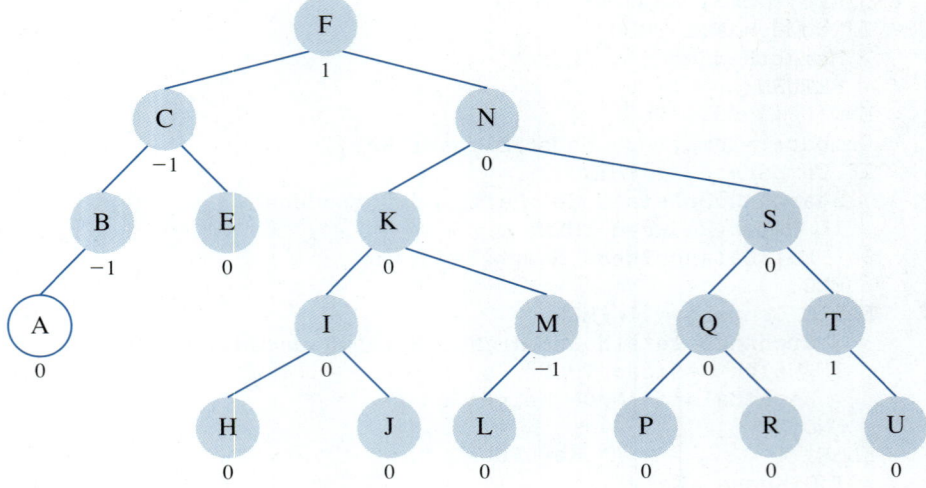

Figure 10-7 shows the tree example after deletion of node A and restructuring by single left rotation of nodes F and N. To delete node A, SearchAndDelete was called four times, as shown below.

SearchAndDelete call #1: Node = F, go left
  SearchAndDelete call #2: Node = C, go left
    SearchAndDelete call #3: Node = B, go left
      SearchAndDelete call #4: Node = A
        Node A is deleted, HeightReduced is True
      Call LeftBalance on node B
        Reset node balance factor to zero
    Call LeftBalance on node C
      Reset node balance to zero
  Call LeftBalance on node F
    NewBal is zero
    Call LeftRotate on node F and adjust balance factors

Figure 10-8 shows the example tree after two additional deletions: deletion of node T, which caused no restructuring, and deletion of node U, which caused restructuring by single right rotation of nodes S and Q. With the tree of Figure 10-7, where node T has been deleted, SearchAndDelete was called three times, as illustrated at the bottom of the following page.

Figure 10-7
Tree After Deletion of Node A

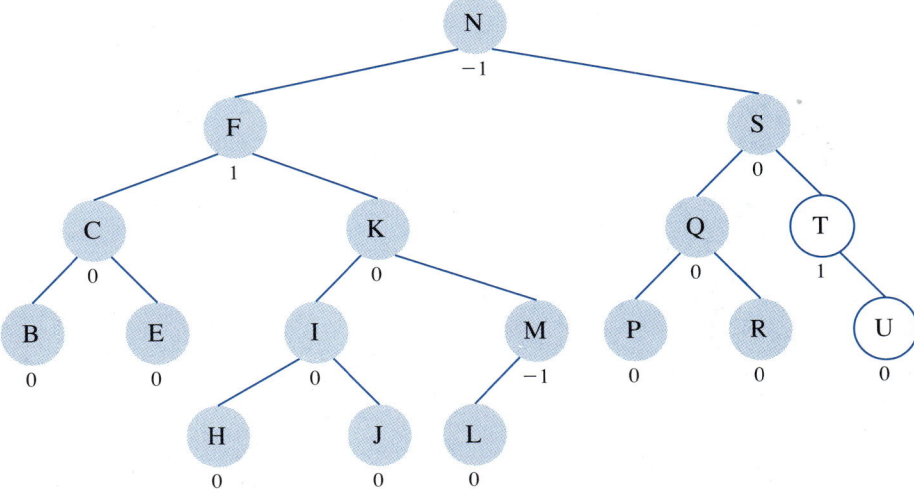

Figure 10-8
Tree After Deletion of Nodes T and U

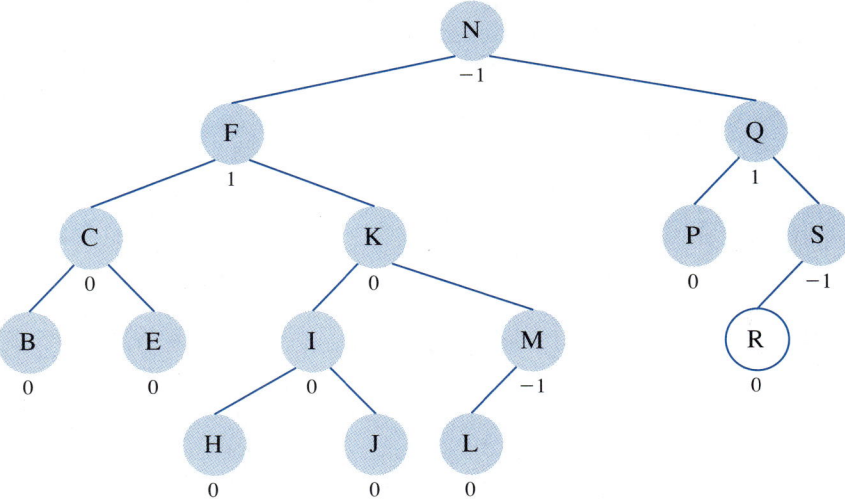

SearchAndDelete call #1: Node = N, go right
  SearchAndDelete call #2: Node = S, go right
    SearchAndDelete call #3: Node = U
      Node U is deleted, HeightReduced is True
    Call RightBalance on node S (balance factor = −1)
      NewBal is zero
      Call RightRotate on node S and adjust balance factors
      Set HeightReduced to False

Figure 10-9

Tree After Deletion of Node R

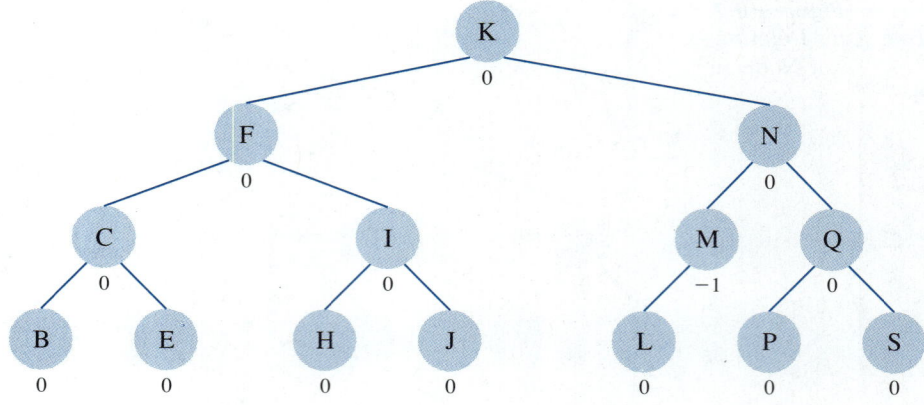

Figure 10-9 shows the example tree after the additional deletion of node R and restructuring by double left right rotation of nodes N, F, and K. For the deletion of node R, SearchAndDelete was called four times, as shown below.

SearchAndDelete call #1: Node = N, go right
  SearchAndDelete call #2: Node = Q, go right
    SearchAndDelete call #3: Node = S, go left
      SearchAndDelete call #4: Node = R
        Node R is deleted, HeightReduced is True
      Call LeftBalance on node S
        Reset node balance factor to zero
    Call RightBalance on node Q
      Reset node balance to zero
  Call RightBalance on node N
    NewBal is one
    Call LeftRightRotate on node N

The mathematical analysis of these two algorithms is complicated and has yet to be done, but empirical measures indicate that the height of the AVL tree built by InsertNode is equal to log n plus a small constant, and that rebalancing is done approximately once for every other insertion. Thus, the behavior of AVL trees is almost as good as that of perfectly balanced trees. Note that the rebalancing in InsertNode requires at most one rotation involving two or three nodes. Although DeleteNode is more complex than InsertNode, empirical tests have shown that its complexity is also O(log n). The rebalancing of an AVL tree after deletion of a node may require a rotation at every node along the search path, but surprisingly, empirical tests have shown that rebalancing is needed only once for every five deletions.

10.2 B-Trees

Although we have concentrated on binary trees up to now, some applications are better served by general trees, introduced in Chapter 8, which are also called multiway trees. Each node in such a tree may contain elements and may have many descendants. Depending on the criteria used to produce balanced multiway trees, balancing such trees might require too much overhead.

B-trees are a special type of well-balanced trees with very short search path lengths for accessing very large collections of elements. In a B-tree, every node contains between n and 2n elements, and the search path length is $\log_{n+1} N$ in the worst case, if there are N nodes in the B-tree.

In a B-tree of order n:

- The root node may contain between 1 and 2n elements.
- Each node besides the root node contains between n and 2n elements.
- Each node has either 0 descendants or m + 1 descendants, where m is the number of elements in that node.
- All leaves appear at the same level.

A B-tree node has the form shown in Figure 10-10. The elements are kept in increasing order from left to right, and each element is between two pointers.

To implement this B-tree node, we use the following type declarations:

```
TYPE BTree = POINTER TO NodeType;
     Item = RECORD
              Element: ElementType;
              NextPointer: BTree;
            END;
     NodeType = RECORD                    (* Multi-key node of a tree *)
                  FirstPointer: BTree;    (* far left pointer *)
                  Items: ARRAY [1..MaxKeys] OF Item;
                  LastKey: CARDINAL;      (* 0..MaxKeys: last used key position *)
                END;
```

with the following constant declarations for a B-tree of order 2:

```
CONST MinKeys = 2;              (* B-tree order: minimum number of keys *)
      MaxKeys = MinKeys * 2;    (* maximum number of keys in a node *)
```

Figure 10-10
A B-Tree Node

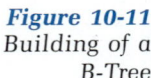

Figure 10-11
Building of a
B-Tree

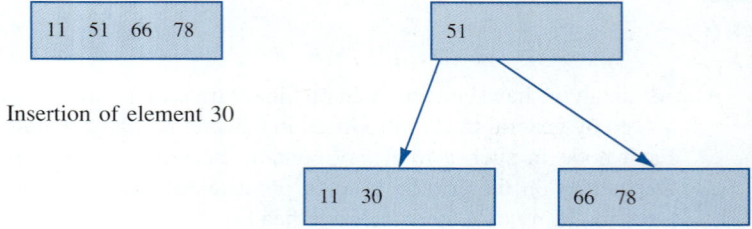

Insertion of element 30

As an example, let's take the building of a B-tree of order 2 created by inserting a sequence of elements in a tree initially empty. Figure 10-11 shows the tree after inserting elements 11, 66, 78, and 51, and then after inserting element 30, which causes the tree height to increase. There is not enough room for 30 in a node with four elements, so 51, the middle value of the sequence 11, 30, 51, 66, 78, is passed up to form a new root node and the four remaining values are split into two half-filled nodes that are the descendants of the new root node.

Continuing to build the B-tree by inserting the elements 2, 7, 12, 15, 22, 41, 35, 53, 54, 68, 69, 63, and 71 produces the B-tree of Figure 10-12. Note that the tree height has not changed, since each time a leaf node split and passed up the middle value, the root node was able to accept the value without splitting.

Then the insertion of element 79 will increase the tree height, as the leaf where 79 must be inserted is full. The middle value, 71, is passed up to the root, which is also full. So this node is split and 51 is passed up to form the new root node. The insertion of elements 84 and 93 does not affect the height of the tree. The resultant B-tree is shown in Figure 10-13.

Searching

Searching for an element x in a B-tree is very simple. For each node, one of the following holds:

- The desired element x occurs in the node and searching is over.
- $x < e_1$ and the search continues with node p_0.
- $x > e_m$ and the search continues with node p_m.
- $e_i < x < e_{i+1}$ and the search continues with node p_i.

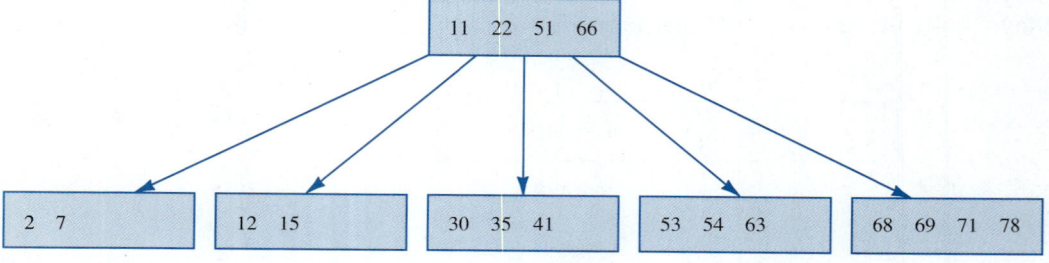

Figure 10-12 Further Building of a B-Tree

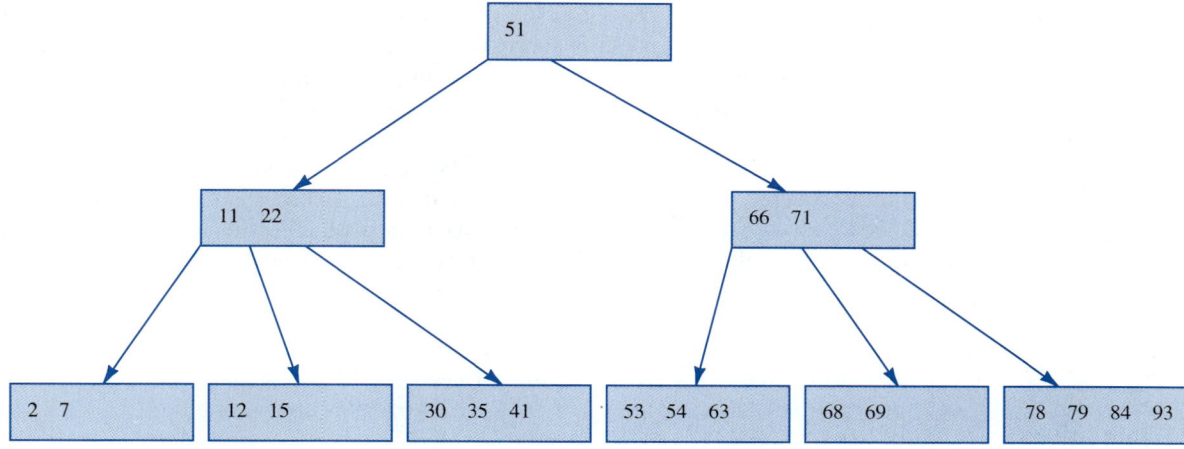

Figure 10-13 B-Tree of Order 2

If a pointer is NIL, there is no descendant and the search fails. Depending on the size of a node (or the order of the B-tree), searching a node can be done sequentially or by using a binary search (see Chapter 3). Procedure SearchKey illustrates this method.

```
PROCEDURE SearchKey(Tree: BTree; Key: KeyType;
                    VAR Element: ElementType; Comp: CompProc): BOOLEAN;
(* Search Key in Tree. If found return TRUE and Element value, otherwise
   return FALSE *)
VAR SubTree: BTree;
    Pos: CARDINAL;
BEGIN     (* efficient non-recursive search *)
  SubTree := Tree;
  LOOP
    IF SubTree = NIL THEN   (* Key NOT FOUND *)
      RETURN FALSE;
    END; (* IF *)
    IF SearchInNode(SubTree, Key, Pos, Comp) THEN   (* Key FOUND *)
      Element := SubTree^.Items[Pos].Element;
      EXIT
    END; (* IF *)
    IF Pos = 0 THEN
      SubTree := SubTree^.FirstPointer;
    ELSE (* try child *)
      SubTree := SubTree^.Items[Pos].NextPointer;
    END; (* IF *)
  END; (* LOOP *)
  RETURN TRUE;
END SearchKey;
```

Procedure SearchKey starts at a given node. It examines the node and if the desired element is present, the search is successful and the node element is returned. If the desired element is not present, the search continues at the next level in the B-tree. To examine a node, the procedure calls utility procedure SearchInNode, which compares the desired key to all the elements in the node. If the key is found, then the search is successful and the position of the element in the node is returned. The elements in a node are ordered, and as soon as it is known that the desired element is not present in the node, the position of the element with the largest value less than the key's value is returned. The following procedure is an example of a sequential implementation of SearchInNode.

```
PROCEDURE SearchInNode(Node: BTree; Key: KeyType;
                VAR Pos: CARDINAL; Comp: CompProc):BOOLEAN;
(* Return TRUE if Key was found at position Pos, otherwise Key was
   not found and Pos precedes Key position *)
VAR Compare:INTEGER;
BEGIN
  Pos:=1;
  LOOP
    Compare := Comp(Key, Node^.Items[Pos].Element.Key);
    IF Compare = 0 THEN
      RETURN TRUE;                        (* found *)
    ELSIF Compare = -1 THEN
      DEC(Pos);
      RETURN FALSE; (* less *)
    ELSE (* Comp=1 *)                     (* greater *)
      IF Pos = Node^.LastKey THEN
        RETURN FALSE                      (* past last node *)
      ELSE
        INC(Pos)                          (* try next Key *)
      END; (* IF *)
    END; (* IF *)
  END; (* LOOP *)
END SearchInNode;
```

Insertion

Insertion in a B-tree is relatively simple. To insert element X in a B-tree:

- Search the tree to find the leaf node where the element should be inserted.
- If the node is not full, the element is inserted. (An example would be the insertion of element 60 in the B-tree of Figure 10-13.)
- If the node is full (2n elements), it must be split and a new node added. The n smallest elements are stored in the first node, the n largest elements are stored in the new node, and the middle element is inserted in the parent node. If the latter overflows, it must be split, and the splitting may propagate upwards to the root. This is, in fact, the only way for the B-tree to increase its height.

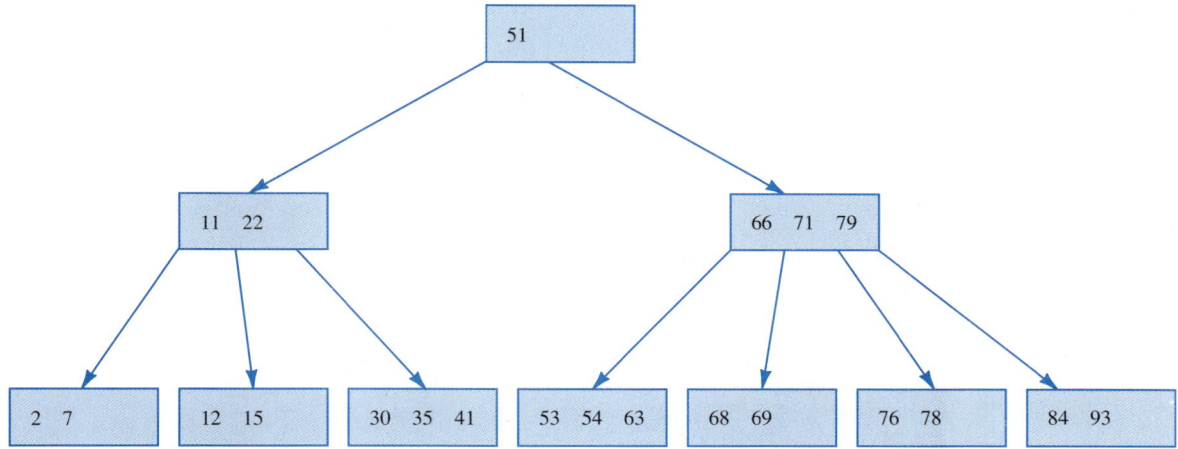

Figure 10-14 B-Tree After the Insertion of Element 76

The actual insertion process can be described by the following pseudocode.

```
Store and Split
    If there is room in node     { less than 2n elements }
        Insert in node
        Reset upper level insertion flag
    Else     { 2n+1 elements }
        Create new node
        Keep the middle element for upper level
        Keep the first n elements in old node
        Copy the last n elements in new node
    End if
End Store and Split
```

Figure 10-14 illustrates the result of the insertion of element 76 in the B-tree of Figure 10-13. The rightmost leaf was full and has been split, while an element was put in the parent node.

Procedure InsertElement implements this strategy.

```
PROCEDURE InsertElement(VAR Tree: BTree; VAR Element: ElementType; Comp: CompProc);
(* Insert Element in Tree, using Comp to find position *)
VAR Root: BTree;
    NewRoot: BOOLEAN;
    NewData: Item;

  PROCEDURE Place(Node: BTree; VAR PassUp: BOOLEAN; VAR NewData: Item);
  VAR Pos: CARDINAL;
      CurrentData: Item;
```

Chapter 10 Special Purpose Trees

```
PROCEDURE StoreAndSplit;
(* Insert CurrentData in Node, splitting Node if necessary *)
VAR Index: CARDINAL;
    NewNode: BTree;
BEGIN
  WITH Node^ DO
    IF LastKey < MaxKeys THEN    (* there is room in Node *)
      INC(LastKey);
      PassUp := FALSE;                 (* reset flag *)
      FOR Index := LastKey TO Pos+2 BY -1 DO
        Items[Index] := Items[Index-1];
      END; (* FOR *)
      Items[Pos+1] := CurrentData;
    ELSE   (* Node is full, split and assign middle item to NewData *)
      ALLOCATE(NewNode, SIZE(NodeType));   (* create new Node *)
      IF Pos <= MinKeys THEN
        IF Pos = MinKeys THEN
          NewData := CurrentData;          (* middle Element *)
        ELSE
          NewData := Items[MinKeys];       (* middle Element *)
          FOR Index := MinKeys TO Pos+2 BY -1 DO    (* shift right *)
            Items[Index] := Items[Index-1];         (* to make room *)
          END; (* FOR *)
          Items[Pos+1] := CurrentData;     (* insert Element *)
        END; (* IF *)
        FOR Index:= 1 TO MinKeys DO  (* copy second half to new Node *)
          NewNode^.Items[Index] := Node^.Items[Index+MinKeys];
        END; (* FOR *)
      ELSE (* insert CurrentData in new Node *)
        Pos := Pos - MinKeys;
        NewData := Items[MinKeys+1];       (* middle Element *)
        FOR Index := 1 TO Pos-1 DO  (* copy second half to new Node *)
          NewNode^.Items[Index] := Node^.Items[Index+MinKeys+1];
        END; (* FOR *)
        NewNode^.Items[Pos] := CurrentData;   (* insert Element *)
        FOR Index := Pos+1 TO MinKeys DO   (* finish copy *)
          NewNode^.Items[Index] := Node^.Items[Index+MinKeys]
        END; (* FOR *)
      END; (* IF *)
      LastKey := MinKeys;            (* two half full nodes *)
      NewNode^.LastKey := MinKeys;
      NewNode^.FirstPointer := NewData.NextPointer;
      NewData.NextPointer := NewNode;
    END; (* IF *)
  END; (* WITH *)
END StoreAndSplit;
```

```
BEGIN  (* Place *)
  IF Node = NIL THEN    (* found leaf where Element should go *)
    PassUp := TRUE;     (* send Element back up for insertion *)
    NewData.Element := Element; (* create Element *)
    NewData.NextPointer:=NIL;
  ELSE
    WITH Node^ DO
      IF SearchInNode(Node, Element.Key, Pos, Comp) THEN
        PassUp := FALSE;  (* Element already in Tree *)
      ELSE   (* find position in lower levels *)
        IF Pos = 0 THEN     (* Element precedes first Node Element *)
          Place(FirstPointer, PassUp, CurrentData);
        ELSE (* next descendant *)
          Place(Items[Pos].NextPointer, PassUp, CurrentData);
        END; (* IF *)
        IF PassUp THEN StoreAndSplit END;
      END; (* IF *)
    END; (* WITH *)
  END; (* IF *)
END Place;

BEGIN (* InsertElement *)
  Place(Tree, NewRoot, NewData);
  IF NewRoot THEN           (* root was split, so create new one *)
    ALLOCATE(Root, SIZE(NodeType));
    WITH Root^ DO
      LastKey := 1;
      FirstPointer := Tree;
      Items[1] := NewData;
    END; (* IF *)
    Tree:=Root;
  END; (* IF *)
END InsertElement;
```

Procedure InsertElement calls Place to do the insertion of Element. Upon returning from that call, InsertElement checks to see whether or not the insertion has resulted in the splitting of the old root node, and, if this is the case, a new root node is created.

Procedure Place finds the leaf where the element should be stored. It uses function SearchInNode to search a node for an element and to return the position of the element if it finds it. If the element is not found, Place is called recursively until either the element is found or a leaf is found where the element should be inserted. Upon return from the recursive calls, Place calls procedure StoreAndSplit to do the actual insertion.

StoreAndSplit checks to see if there is room in the node, and if it is the case, the element is inserted in its proper position, and the PassUp flag is set to FALSE in order to stop the process. Otherwise the node is full and must be split. A new node is created in which the second half of the full node is copied and the middle element is carried up to the next level, where the same process is repeated.

Deletion

Deletion in a B-tree is not complicated in principle, but its implementation details can be difficult. If the element to be deleted belongs to a leaf node, the deletion is simply done as long as the number of elements in the node remains greater than or equal to the order of the B-tree: the node elements are only compacted. If the number of elements in the leaf becomes too small, the leaf must be combined with a neighbor, as shown in Figure 10-15, where element 15 has been deleted from the B-tree of Figure 10-13, and where the deletion has caused a minor reorganization of three nodes.

The merging of two nodes pulls down an element of the parent node and may reduce that parent node to a size that is too small. In this case the merging process must be continued, possibly up to the root. This is the only way the height of a B-tree might be reduced. If we start with the B-tree of Figure 10-15 and we delete element 7, we cause a major reorganization of the whole tree, as most of the nodes have the minimum number of elements. The leaves are combined, but the parent node is left with one element and must be combined with its neighbor. The result is the B-tree of Figure 10-16, which has lost one level.

In the case where the element to be deleted belongs to an internal node, its immediate predecessor is in a leaf and can replace the deleted element, and then be deleted in the leaf. The immediate predecessor of an element is found by locating the rightmost element of its left subtree. If the leaf contains the minimum number of elements, we must combine it with a neighbor, as we have seen above. The following pseudocode defines this process.

```
Remove
   If node exists
      If element has been found
         If leaf
            Eliminate element in leaf
            Set underflow flag if necessary
         Else
            Replace element with predecessor
            If underflow Combine node with neighbor
         End if
      Else
         Remove element starting at next level
         If underflow Combine node with neighbor
      End if
   Else     { element to delete absent }
      Reset underflow flag
   End if
End Remove
```

Procedure DeleteElement implements this method.

10.2 B-Trees   385

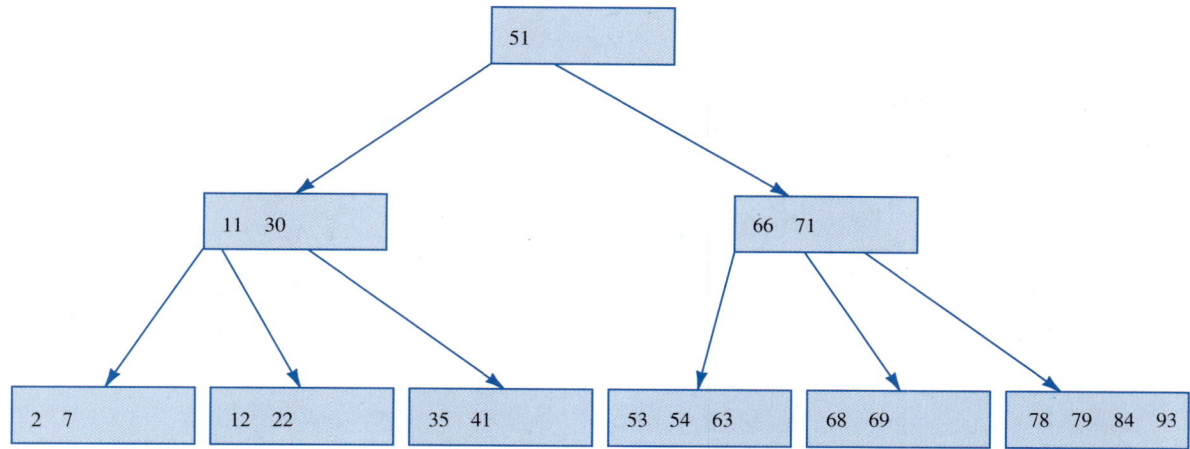

Figure 10-15   Result of Deleting Element 15

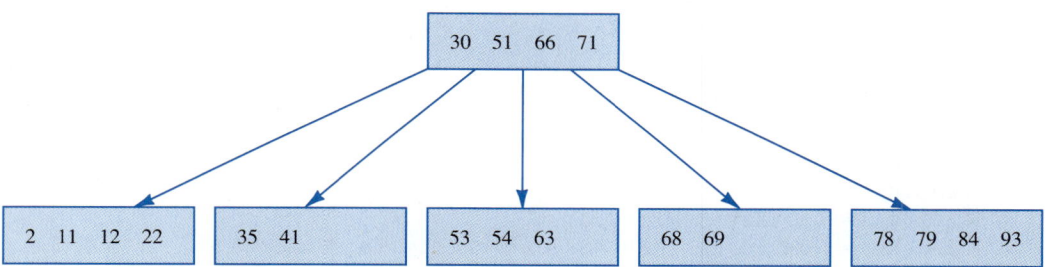

Figure 10-16   Result of Deleting Element 7

```
PROCEDURE DeleteElement(VAR Tree: BTree; Key: KeyType; Comp: CompProc);
VAR OldRoot:BTree;
    Underflow:BOOLEAN;

  PROCEDURE Remove(VAR Node: BTree; VAR Underflow: BOOLEAN);
  VAR Index, Pos, Left: CARDINAL;
      Next: BTree;

    PROCEDURE Replace(Locnode: BTree; VAR Underflow: BOOLEAN);
    (* Descend rightmost pointers and replace item to delete by
       rightmost item on leaf *)
    VAR Point: BTree;    (* global Node, Pos *)
    BEGIN
      WITH Locnode^ DO
        Point := Items[LastKey].NextPointer;
```

```
          IF Point # NIL THEN
            Replace(Point, Underflow);
            IF Underflow THEN
              Combine(Locnode, Point, LastKey, Underflow);
            END; (* IF *)
          ELSE   (* replace item to delete by closest inferior Element *)
            Locnode^.Items[LastKey].NextPointer:=Node^.Items[Pos].NextPointer;
            Node^.Items[Pos] := Locnode^.Items[LastKey];
            DEC(LastKey);        (* delete rightmost item in leaf *)
            Underflow := LastKey < MinKeys;
          END; (* IF *)
      END; (* WITH *)
    END Replace;

BEGIN (* Remove *)
    IF Node = NIL THEN   (* not in Tree *)
      Underflow := FALSE;
    ELSE
      WITH Node^ DO
        IF SearchInNode(Node, Key, Pos, Comp) THEN    (* found *)
          Left := Pos - 1;
          IF Left = 0 THEN
            Next := FirstPointer
          ELSE
            Next := Items[Left].NextPointer;
          END; (* IF *)
          IF Next = NIL THEN   (* leaf *)
            DEC(LastKey);
            Underflow := LastKey < MinKeys;
            FOR Index := Pos TO LastKey DO   (* shift Items Left *)
              Items[Index] := Items[Index+1];
            END; (* FOR *)
          ELSE      (* not leaf, find replacement from a leaf *)
            Replace(Next, Underflow);
            IF Underflow THEN
              Combine(Node, Next, Left, Underflow);
            END; (* IF *)
          END; (* IF *)
        ELSE   (* continue search *)
          IF Pos = 0 THEN
            Next := FirstPointer;
          ELSE
            Next := Items[Pos].NextPointer;
          END; (* IF *)
          Remove(Next, Underflow);   (* search subtree *)
```

```
            IF Underflow THEN
              Combine(Node, Next, Pos, Underflow);
            END; (* IF *)
          END; (* IF *)
        END; (* WITH *)
      END; (* IF *)
    END Remove;
BEGIN
  Remove(Tree, Underflow);
  IF Underflow THEN
    IF Tree^.LastKey = 0 THEN    (* remove empty Node *)
      OldRoot := Tree;
      Tree := OldRoot^.FirstPointer;
      DEALLOCATE(OldRoot, SIZE(NodeType));
    END; (* IF *)
  END; (* IF *)
END DeleteElement;
```

Procedure DeleteElement is similar to InsertElement, as it calls recursive procedure Remove and then deletes the tree root if necessary. Procedure Remove looks repeatedly in the tree until it finds the element to delete. It then deletes it if the node is a leaf, or replaces it by its immediate predecessor by calling procedure Replace. When necessary, procedure Combine is called to merge two nodes together. The merging of two nodes is accomplished by the following algorithm.

> Combine
>   If there is an adjacent node to the right of underflowing node
>   Copy element from parent into underflowing node
>   If adjacent node has enough elements
>   Move elements from adjacent to underflowing node
>   Copy middle element into parent node
>   Reset underflow flag
>   Else
>   Copy adjacent node into underflowing node
>   Reduce the parent node
>   Release adjacent node
>   Set underflow flag if parent node too small
>   End if
>   Else
>   Take left neighbor of underflowing node as adjacent node
>   If adjacent node has enough elements
>   Make room in underflowing node by shifting elements
>   Move parent element to underflowing node
>   Move elements from adjacent to underflowing node
>   Copy middle element into parent node
>   Reset underflow flag

Chapter 10 Special Purpose Trees

> Else
>   Copy parent element into adjacent node
>   Copy underflowing elements into adjacent node
>   Reduce the parent node
>   Release underflowing node
>   Set underflow flag if parent node too small
>   End if
> End if
> End Combine

The following procedure implements this algorithm.

```
PROCEDURE Combine(Parent, Underflowing: BTree; Pos: CARDINAL;
                  VAR Underflow: BOOLEAN);
(* Node Underflowing will be merged with another descendant of node
   Parent. Pos is Parent element pointing to Underflowing *)
VAR Adjacent: BTree;    (* Adjacent node *)
    Index, Count, AdjacentLast, ParentLast: CARDINAL;
BEGIN
  ParentLast := Parent^.LastKey;
  IF Pos < ParentLast THEN
    (* combine with adjacent node to right of Underflowing node *)
    INC(Pos);
    Adjacent := Parent^.Items[Pos].NextPointer;
    AdjacentLast := Adjacent^.LastKey;
    (* compute number of Items available on adjacent page *)
    Count := (AdjacentLast - MinKeys + 1) DIV 2;
    (* copy item from Parent node *)
    Underflowing^.Items[MinKeys] := Parent^.Items[Pos];
    Underflowing^.Items[MinKeys].NextPointer := Adjacent^.FirstPointer;
    IF Count > 0 THEN    (* move Count Items from Adjacent to Underflowing *)
      FOR Index := 1 TO Count-1 DO
        Underflowing^.Items[Index+MinKeys] := Adjacent^.Items[Index];
      END; (* FOR *)
      Parent^.Items[Pos] := Adjacent^.Items[Count];
      Parent^.Items[Pos].NextPointer := Adjacent;
      Adjacent^.FirstPointer := Adjacent^.Items[Count].NextPointer;
      DEC(AdjacentLast, Count);
      FOR Index := 1 TO AdjacentLast DO   (* shift left remaining elements *)
        Adjacent^.Items[Index] := Adjacent^.Items[Index+Count];
      END; (* FOR *)
      Adjacent^.LastKey := AdjacentLast;
      Underflowing^.LastKey := MinKeys - 1 + Count;
      Underflow := FALSE;
    ELSE       (* merge nodes Underflowing and Adjacent *)
      FOR Index := 1 TO MinKeys DO (* copy Adjacent into Underflowing *)
        Underflowing^.Items[Index+MinKeys] := Adjacent^.Items[Index];
      END; (* FOR *)
```

```
        FOR Index := Pos TO ParentLast-1 DO   (* shift left Parent elements *)
          Parent^.Items[Index] := Parent^.Items[Index+1];
        END; (* FOR *)
        Underflowing^.LastKey := MaxKeys;
        Parent^.LastKey := ParentLast - 1;
        DEALLOCATE(Adjacent, SIZE(NodeType));   (* free Node *)
        Underflow := Parent^.LastKey < MinKeys;
      END; (* IF *)
    ELSE    (* combine with Adjacent Node on left of Underflowing Node *)
      IF Pos = 1 THEN
        Adjacent := Parent^.FirstPointer;
      ELSE
        Adjacent := Parent^.Items[Pos-1].NextPointer;
      END; (* IF *)
      AdjacentLast := Adjacent^.LastKey + 1;
      Count := (AdjacentLast - MinKeys) DIV 2;
      IF Count > 0 THEN       (* move Count Items from Adjacent to Underflowing *)
        FOR Index := MinKeys-1 TO 1 BY -1 DO    (* shift right to make room *)
          Underflowing^.Items[Index+Count] := Underflowing^.Items[Index];
        END; (* FOR *)
        Underflowing^.Items[Count] := Parent^.Items[Pos]; (* move Parent item down *)
        Underflowing^.Items[Count].NextPointer := Underflowing^.FirstPointer;
        DEC(AdjacentLast, Count);
        FOR Index := Count-1 TO 1 BY -1 DO     (* copy from Adjacent Node *)
          Underflowing^.Items[Index] := Adjacent^.Items[Index+AdjacentLast];
        END; (* FOR *)
        Underflowing^.FirstPointer := Adjacent^.Items[AdjacentLast].NextPointer;
        Parent^.Items[Pos] := Adjacent^.Items[AdjacentLast];
        Parent^.Items[Pos].NextPointer := Underflowing;
        Adjacent^.LastKey := AdjacentLast - 1;
        Underflowing^.LastKey := MinKeys - 1 + Count;
        Underflow:= FALSE;
      ELSE    (* merge nodes together *)
        Adjacent^.Items[AdjacentLast] := Parent^.Items[Pos];
        Adjacent^.Items[AdjacentLast].NextPointer := Underflowing^.FirstPointer;
        FOR Index :=1 TO MinKeys-1 DO    (* copy Underflowing to Adjacent *)
          Adjacent^.Items[Index+AdjacentLast] := Underflowing^.Items[Index];
        END; (* FOR *)
        Adjacent^.LastKey := MaxKeys;
        Parent^.LastKey := ParentLast - 1;
        DEALLOCATE(Underflowing, SIZE(NodeType));   (* free node *)
        Underflow := Parent^.LastKey < MinKeys;
      END; (* IF *)
    END; (* IF *)
END Combine;
```

Procedure Combine is given a node parameter, Underflowing, whose number of elements is too small, and its parent, parameter Parent. It selects an adjacent node, trying right, then left, either to merge it with the underflowing node or to transfer elements from it to the underflowing node. If the adjacent node has more than n elements, the extra elements are copied into the underflowing node; otherwise, the two nodes are merged into a full node. If elements are transferred from the adjacent node to the underflowing node, the upper element in the parent node is adjusted. In the case where the nodes are merged, the in-between element from the parent node is removed and included in the merged node.

Complexity

Except for traversals, the required operations for B-trees consist of at most visiting the nodes on the path from the root to the leaves. If the B-tree is of order n and contains N nodes, it can be shown that the height of the B-tree is $O(\log_{n+1} N)$. For instance, the height of a B-tree of order 100 with one million elements is only 3! We can see that B-trees are interesting structures to store large collections of data. Furthermore, at least 50 percent of memory of a B-tree is always utilized.

One application of B-trees is their use to represent data sets that are so large that they cannot fit in central memory. Such B-trees are stored in secondary storage. Each node of the B-tree is large and it is usually called a *page*. A search will thus access the root node and all the nodes on the path from the root to the desired element. Since an access to a node requires an access to secondary storage (a very slow operation), B-trees allow for good performance by minimizing the number of such accesses. In some operating systems, B-trees are used to represent the file system directories.

10.3 Optimal Search Trees

Until now we have assumed that the frequency of access to the tree nodes is the same for all nodes. In other words, we have considered that it was equally likely that each of the key elements stored in a tree would be used as a search argument. This hypothesis is obviously the best one if we have no information on access distribution. However, in some applications there are cases where some information on the probabilities of access to the keys stored in the tree is available. We will assume the tree keys do not change and the tree is used only for searching, as there are no insertions or deletions.

An example of such an application is the lexical analyzer of a compiler. Here each identifier must be checked to see if it belongs to the reserved words set. If statistical information can be collected on a large number of programs written in the language to be compiled, it is possible to obtain information on the frequency of access to the reserved words. In turn, this information can be used to organize the reserved word search tree so that searching becomes optimal. However, few programming languages have enough reserved words to make this extra effort worthwhile.

To build an optimal tree, a weight is associated with each node: the nodes that are used more often have greater weights. Given a search tree, we compute its *weighted path length* (WPL), the sum of all paths from the root to each node, multiplied by that node's weight.

$$\text{WPL} = \sum_{i=1}^{n} w_i \, l_i$$

where w_i is the weight of node i
       l_i is the level of node i

Given a search tree with n nodes, our objective will be to find a tree organization that produces the minimum WPL.

For instance, suppose we have a three-node search tree to build with weights (or probabilities) associated with each of the three nodes as follows:

$$w_A = 2/11 \quad w_B = 3/11 \quad w_C = 6/11$$

Figure 10-17 shows different ways of placing these nodes in a search tree.

The WPL of each of the search trees in Figure 10-17 would then be:

$\text{WPL}_1 = (2 \times 3 + 3 \times 2 + 6 \times 1)/11 = 18/11$
$\text{WPL}_2 = (2 \times 2 + 3 \times 3 + 6 \times 1)/11 = 19/11$
$\text{WPL}_3 = (2 \times 2 + 3 \times 1 + 6 \times 2)/11 = 19/11$
$\text{WPL}_4 = (2 \times 1 + 3 \times 3 + 6 \times 2)/11 = 23/11$
$\text{WPL}_5 = (2 \times 1 + 3 \times 2 + 6 \times 3)/11 = 26/11$

In this example, the optimal structure would be the first tree that is a degenerate binary search tree.

If we want to find an optimal search tree by building all possible trees and picking the one with the minimum WPL, we face a hopeless task, as the number of possible configurations for n nodes grows exponentially with n. However, if we note that all the subtrees of an optimal tree are also optimal, we see that it is possible to build an optimal tree from the leaves to the root. There exists a number of algorithms to build optimal trees whose complexities are $O(n^2)$ or even $O(n \log n)$ for near optimal trees. The Huffman code tree discussed in Section 8.3 is an example of building an optimal tree in which the most frequently used letters have the shortest path lengths and, thus, the shortest encoding string.

While building optimal trees, it is also possible to take into account statistical information about the searches that fail. In our earlier compiler example, unsuccessful

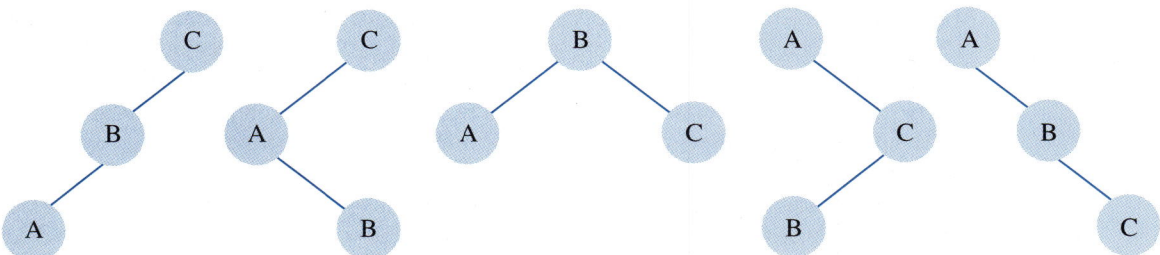

Figure 10-17 Three-Node Search Trees

searches are more numerous than successful searches, and can be considered to access a nonexisting node situated between two keys. If the probability that a search argument is situated between two adjacent keys is known, this information can be used to influence the structure of the optimal search tree.

10.4 Heaps and Priority Queues

A *heap* is a special kind of tree. A heap is defined as a sequence of elements h_1, h_2, h_3, . . . , h_{Max}, whose values (or keys) are such that $h_i \leq h_{2i}$ and $h_i \leq h_{2i+1}$, for i = 1 to Max/2. In particular, h_1 represents the minimum value of the sequence, and h_{2i} and h_{2i+1} are said to be the children of h_i. A heap can also be defined as a partially ordered tree, as shown in Figure 10-18. Although the partially ordered tree of Figure 10-18 is a full binary tree, note that a heap is not necessarily a full binary tree because the last internal node might have only one descendant.

The definition indicates that a heap can also be represented by an array, and therefore the heap of Figure 10-18 can be represented by the sequence 5, 7, 11, 9, 8, 11, 15, 15, 20, 10, 11. We should note that such a representation is very efficient but only applies to binary trees where all levels above the lowest level are full and the leaves at the lowest level appear to the left as far as possible. In other words, this representation cannot be used if there are holes in the middle of the tree, unless a special value is used to indicate the absence of a value. We will use this array representation in the following heap implementation for priority queues and in the Heapsort algorithm in the "Internal Sorting" section in the next chapter.

As mentioned in Chapter 7, first-in/first-out queues sometimes do not match the needs of the application and should be replaced by *priority queues*. The hospital emergency room provides an example in which a priority (the seriousness of injury or illness) is used to take the next patient off the queue.

Priority queues will have the same operations as regular queues, and their elements will have an extra field to store the element's priority. Priority queues can be implemented by ordered linear lists, and the difference between priority and regular queues will appear either in the implementation of the operation Dequeue, or in the implementation of operation Enqueue. In the first case, for a Dequeue operation, the whole queue must be inspected to find the element with the highest priority and take it out of the queue. There is no change to operation Enqueue, as elements are queued in the order of their arrival. The complexity of operation Dequeue becomes O(n). In the second case, the queue is kept as a list ordered on the element's priority values: enqueuing an element requires inserting it in order and has a complexity of O(n), while removal of an element involves only the first element and has constant complexity.

Priority queues can be implemented more efficiently by heaps. Even though the highest priority element is always at the top of the heap, operation Dequeue will have a complexity of O(log n), as the heap must always be reorganized after its first element is taken away. Such a reorganization is restricted to a path between the root of the heap and a heap node: the operation has complexity O(log n). The Enqueue operation will have the same complexity, O(log n), for the same reason.

Figure 10-18
A Heap

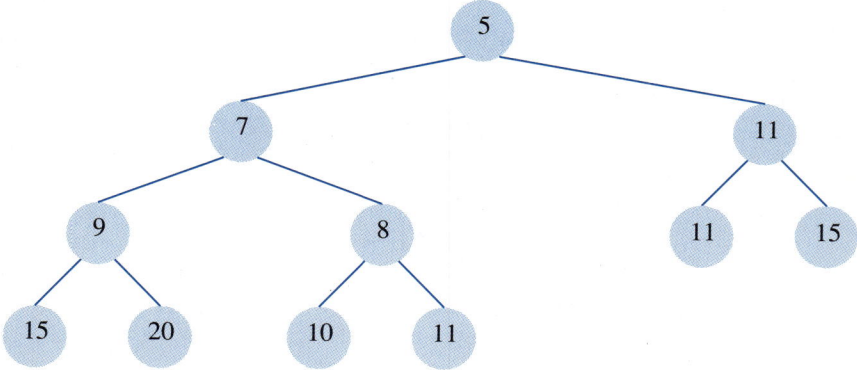

We will show here an implementation of priority queues, which uses a heap defined by the following declarations.

```
TYPE Node = RECORD
              Priority: CARDINAL;
              Element: ElementType;
            END;
     Position = [0..Max];
     PriorityQueue = RECORD
                       Size: Position;
                       QueueElements: ARRAY Position OF Node;
                     END;
```

Procedure Enqueue will then be defined as follows.

```
PROCEDURE Enqueue(VAR Q: PriorityQueue; Elt: ElementType;
                  Prior: CARDINAL);
(* Add Element with Priority to Priority queue Q *)
VAR Parent, Child: Position;
BEGIN
  IF Q.Size < Max THEN
    INC(Q.Size);
    Q.QueueElements[Q.Size].Priority := Prior;   (* add at end *)
    Q.QueueElements[Q.Size].Element := Elt;
    (* move Element up to its place in heap *)
    Q.QueueElements[0] := Q.QueueElements[Q.Size]; (* sentinel *)
    Child := Q.Size;
    Parent := Child DIV 2;
    WHILE Q.QueueElements[Parent].Priority < Prior DO
      (* find proper position for last Element *)
      Q.QueueElements[Child] := Q.QueueElements[Parent];
      Child := Parent;
      Parent := Parent DIV 2;
    END; (* WHILE *)
```

```
                        (* copy Element in its proper place *)
                        Q.QueueElements[Child] := Q.QueueElements[0];
                    END; (* IF *)
                END Enqueue;
```

We start with a priority queue of n elements that satisfy the heap conditions. We add the new element as the last element in the heap, and we rearrange elements so that all of them satisfy the heap conditions. In procedure Enqueue, the new element is moved up from a leaf towards the root. We examine all the elements that are ancestors of the last element, and move them down if they have a lower priority than the new element. The process stops when a parent is encountered that has greater priority or when the new element has migrated all the way to the root. When the correct position is found, the new element is inserted there.

Procedure Dequeue will be defined as follows.

```
PROCEDURE Dequeue(VAR Q: PriorityQueue; VAR Elt: ElementType;
                  VAR Prior: CARDINAL);
(* Retrieve Element with lowest Priority *)
VAR Parent, Child: Position;
    Finished: BOOLEAN;
    Saved: Node;
BEGIN
  IF Q.Size > 0 THEN
    Prior := Q.QueueElements[1].Priority;  (* copy first Element *)
    Elt := Q.QueueElements[1].Element;
    Q.QueueElements[1] := Q.QueueElements[Q.Size]; (* replace it *)
    DEC(Q.Size);
    Parent := 1;     (* rebuild heap by moving first Element *)
    Child := 2;      (* down to proper position for heap *)
    Saved := Q.QueueElements[1];
    Finished := FALSE;
    WHILE (Child <= Q.Size) AND NOT Finished DO    (* inspect children *)
      IF Child < Q.Size THEN
        IF Q.QueueElements[Child].Priority
           < Q.QueueElements[Child+1].Priority THEN
          INC(Child);              (* select smaller of two children *)
        END; (* IF *)
      END; (* IF *)
      IF Saved.Priority > Q.QueueElements[Child].Priority THEN
        Finished := TRUE;          (* position found *)
      ELSE
        Q.QueueElements[Parent] := Q.QueueElements[Child]; (* move up one level *)
        Parent := Child;
        Child := 2 * Parent;
      END; (* IF *)
    END; (* WHILE *)
    Q.QueueElements[Parent] := Saved;
  END; (* IF *)
END Dequeue;
```

We start with n elements in the priority queue that satisfy the heap conditions. We remove the first element of the heap, replace it with the last element, and rearrange elements so that all elements satisfy the heap conditions. In procedure Dequeue, the element placed at the root may be moved down from the root towards the leaves until it satisfies the heap conditions. When the priorities of the children are examined, the child with the highest priority greater than the saved node is moved up into the position of the parent and the process is repeated. Notice that this process will eventually stop either because the saved node has higher priority than its children or because it reaches a leaf position. Once the process stops, the element is copied in its final position.

10.5 Case Study: Global Rebalancing

In the height-balanced tree algorithms we studied, a tree can be slightly out of balance, but if it becomes too far out of balance, it is rebalanced by a *local* rotation. We can call this an *incremental* solution to the balancing problem, since the tree is continually being rebalanced. Another approach to the same problem would allow the tree to get out of balance, but would provide a procedure to globally rebalance the tree by rebuilding it to be optimally balanced.

Design

In this case study we will develop an algorithm to rebuild a binary search tree with optimal balancing. In order to help us test our rebalancing algorithm, we will also develop a utility algorithm that builds unbalanced test trees.

Definition of the Problem We shall consider a tree to be optimally balanced if it retains the binary search tree property, and if, at every level, all the nodes have two descendants, except for the last and possibly next-to-last level. Our algorithm should be able to accept any binary search tree as input and build an optimally balanced search tree with the same data.

In order to test our algorithm, we will need a utility routine that will build a binary search tree that is out of balance, including a worst-case, degenerate binary search tree that is linear.

Design of a Solution Our solution will have three steps:

Traverse the binary search tree inorder and copy the data into an array.
Dispose of the original tree (to conserve memory space).
Rebuild the tree from the array data by inserting elements in the proper sequence.

We will assume that we have enough memory space to hold two copies of the data, as we will need this space at the end of the first and the third step. Of course, after we exit from the rebalancing procedure, the array used for temporary storage will be automatically discarded. It should be noted that this rather simple solution will not involve any comparison operations on the data, since an inorder traversal of a binary search tree visits the data in sorted order.

Our utility routine to build a binary search tree for testing needs to be carefully designed. We may first be tempted to design a binary search tree builder that inserts nodes in a randomly generated order, but such a routine would not be good for testing limiting cases, such as a degenerate search tree. Our approach will use tree elements with a two-part key, made of a character followed by a number. The characters will be selected from a parameter string, such as "ABC". The numbers start at 0 and are incremented up to a specified maximum value. If we use the input string characters from the first to the last, and for each character generate all the possible numbers, then using "ABC" and 0 through 2, our key values are: A0, A1, A2, B0, B1, B2, C0, C1, C2. If the keys are inserted in the binary search tree in this order, we would obtain a tree with maximum imbalance, shown as Tree #1 in Figure 10-19. We will call this ordering *number sequencing* because the number part of the key changes most rapidly. An alternative would be to change the characters most rapidly when holding the number fixed; we will refer to this scheme as *letter sequencing*. Using "ABC" and 0 through 2, letter sequencing would produce the following key sequence: A0, B0, C0, A1, B1, C1, A2, B2, C2. The tree resulting from this order of insertion is shown as Tree #2 in Figure 10-19. If we alter the input string to "BCA" and use letter sequenc-

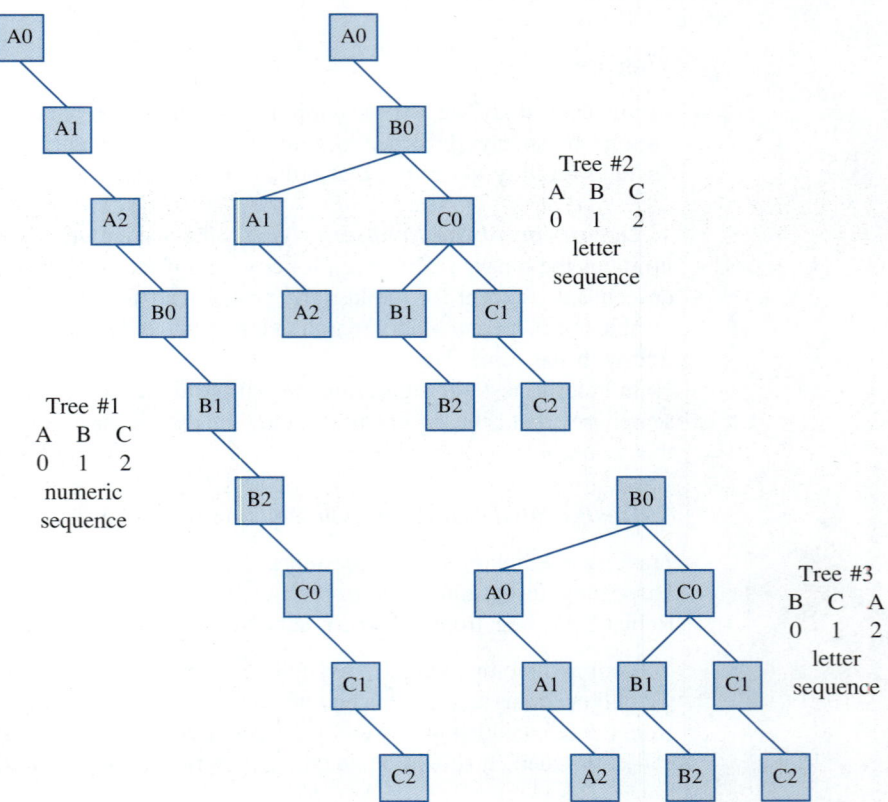

Figure 10-19
Sample Trees from Tree Builder

ing, then the order of insertion would be B0, C0, A0, B1, C1, A1, B2, C2, A2 and the result would be Tree #3 in Figure 10-19. The variety of trees offered by this simple sequencing method will be sufficient for testing our rebalancing algorithm.

In order to examine the results of our procedures to build a tree and rebalance a tree, we will include an inorder traversal procedure and a display tree procedure in our rebalancing module. Our complete definition module is shown below.

```
DEFINITION MODULE Rebalancing;
FROM Strings IMPORT String;

TYPE BinarySearchTree;
PROCEDURE ReBalance(Tree: BinarySearchTree): BinarySearchTree;
(* Given a binary search Tree, return a balanced binary search tree *)

PROCEDURE BuildTree(Keys: String; NumOrder: BOOLEAN;
                    MaxNum: CARDINAL;  VAR Tree: BinarySearchTree);
(* Build a binary search tree with a two part key: a character taken
   sequentially from Keys and a number from 0 to MaxNum.
   If NumOrder is TRUE, keys are inserted with numeric values changing
   most rapidly; if FALSE character values change most rapidly.
   For example, given Keys of ''ABC'' and MaxNum = 2, then for
   NumOrder TRUE the order of insertion is A0, A1, A2, B0, B1, B2, C0,
   C1, C2. If NumOrder is false, the order of insertion is A0, B0, C0,
   A1, B1, C1, A2, B2, C2. *)

PROCEDURE InOrder(Tree: BinarySearchTree);
(* Perform an inorder traversal of Tree and print out the key
   for each node *)

PROCEDURE DisplayTree(Tree: BinarySearchTree);
(* Display entire Tree from left to right with the root at the left *)

END Rebalancing.
```

Refine the Solution Our rebuild procedure involves three steps: traverse the tree and store the nodes in an array (we will call this the flatten step), dispose of the tree, and rebuild the tree by selecting data from the array and inserting the data in the new tree. The pseudocode for the flatten procedure is:

> Flatten
>   If the left subtree is not empty
>   Flatten left subtree
>   End if
>   Copy data from root into data array
>   Increment index for data array
>   If the right subtree is not empty
>   Flatten right subtree
>   End if
> End Flatten

Notice that we have modified our normal traversal technique to guard against calling the Flatten routine in the event the subtree is empty. This style of traversal cuts down on the levels of recursion, but it also assumes that the initial tree is not empty. For the Dispose algorithm, we will use the DeleteTree algorithm that has been presented in Chapter 9; we will not duplicate it here. Rebuilding the tree will be done recursively using the following scheme: put the middle element of the subarray being processed at the root, and then build the left subtree from the subarray that comes before the root, and finally build the right subtree from the subarray that comes after the root. Here is the corresponding pseudocode:

>Rebuild Tree
>   Allocate a new node
>   Set Mid to the index midway between Low and High
>   Transfer the data at the Mid index of data array to the new node
>   If the left subarray from Low to Mid−1 has one or more elements
>   Set the left subtree to Rebuild Tree left subarray
>   Else
>   Set the left subtree to nil
>   End if
>   If the right subarray from Mid+1 to High has one or more elements
>   Set the right subtree to Rebuild Tree right subarray
>   Else
>   Set the right subtree to nil
>   End if
>   Return the new node
>End Rebuild Tree

The rebalance algorithm just invokes the algorithms Flatten, Dispose, and Rebuild Tree.

>Rebalance
>   If tree is not empty
>   Set Count to 0
>   Flatten tree in data array
>   Dispose tree
>   Set Low to 0 and High to Count − 1
>   Return Rebuild Tree with data array
>   Else
>   Return nil
>   End if
>End Rebalance

Our next task is to develop a build tree algorithm that will accept a string of characters, a Boolean flag to indicate the order of insertion (numeric sequence or letter sequence), and a maximum for the number sequence, and then return the appropriate binary search tree. To accomplish this task, we will develop three utility procedures. Recall that our key data will comprise a primary key of a character and a secondary key of a number in a range from 0 to a given maximum. We need a Less Than procedure to test the relationship between two keys.

```
Less Than
    If Ch of Key1 is less than Ch of Key2
        Return true
    Elsif Ch of Key1 is greater than Ch of Key2
        Return false
    Else { character values are equal }
        Return Num of Key1 is less than Num of Key2
    End if
End Less Than
```

We also need a procedure to generate the next logical key value, given the flag indicating numeric or letter sequencing and the string of characters. If the string is "ABC" and numeric sequencing is desired, then, assuming a maximum number value of 2, the logical sequencing of key values is

A0, A1, A2, B0, B1, B2, C0, C1, C2

If letter sequencing is desired, then the sequence is

A0, B0, C0, A1, B1, C1, A2, B2, C2

The current values for the letter and number along with our flag, called NumSequence, will determine the next logical key. We assume that this procedure will not be called after the last key has been generated.

```
Next Key
    If NumSequence
        If Num is less than MaxNum
            Increment Num
        Else
            Set Num to 0
            Set Ch to next character from string Keys
        End if
    Else { letter sequencing }
        If Ch is not at the end of Keys
            Set Ch to the next character from Keys
        Else
            Set Ch to the first character from Keys
            Increment Num
        End if
    End if
End Next Key
```

The Insert algorithm uses the Less Than procedure developed above to recursively search the binary search tree for the key to be inserted, and to insert a new node when a nil tree has been reached. This algorithm was presented as InsertNode in Chapter 9 and will not be repeated here. Finally, the algorithm for building the tree is:

```
Build Tree
    Set Tree to nil
    Set Ch to the first character from Keys
    Set Num to 0
    Loop
        Insert node with values Ch, Num into Tree
        Exit if last key
        Next Key
    End loop
End Build Tree
```

Our library module is completed by developing an inorder traversal algorithm and a display tree algorithm, as already given in Chapter 9 (TraverseTree and PrintTree, respectively).

Develop a Testing Strategy We will test our rebalance procedure for a variety of trees, including

The empty tree
The tree built with Keys "A" and MaxNum of 0
The trees built with all permutations of "AB" and MaxNum of 9
The trees built with all permutations of "ABCD" and MaxNum of 1
A few large trees with a long Keys string and a MaxNum of 99

For each of the "small" trees, the tree will be built and displayed. Then the tree will be rebalanced and displayed. Using InOrder on the original and the rebalanced trees should also give us the same key list. Once we have confidence the algorithm is basically correct, we can try to automate this testing process for larger trees, since it will not be feasible to inspect displays of large trees. Instead, we can modify our InOrder procedure to store the traversals of the unbalanced and the balanced trees. Then we only need to develop an array equality procedure to ensure that the two trees produced the same inorder traversal. This automated testing is left as an exercise (see problem 17).

Implementation

Code and Test the Program Our code follows directly from the pseudocode and is presented on the next page.

10.5 Case Study: Global Rebalancing

```
IMPLEMENTATION MODULE Rebalancing;

FROM Storage IMPORT ALLOCATE, DEALLOCATE;
FROM Strings IMPORT String,InitString,FetchChar,Pos,Length,ToString;
FROM InOut IMPORT Write, WriteCard, WriteString, WriteLn;

CONST MaxNode = 100;      (* maximum number of nodes in tree *)

TYPE BinarySearchTree = POINTER TO TreeNode;
     TreeNode = RECORD
                   Ch: CHAR;
                   Num: CARDINAL;
                   Left, Right: BinarySearchTree;
                END;

     Buffer = ARRAY [0..MaxNode] OF RECORD
                                       Ch: CHAR;
                                       Num: CARDINAL;
                                    END;

PROCEDURE ReBalance(Tree: BinarySearchTree): BinarySearchTree;
(* Given a binary search Tree, return a balanced binary search tree *)

  PROCEDURE DisposeTree(VAR Tree: BinarySearchTree);
  (* Delete Tree and free used memory *)
  BEGIN
    IF Tree # NIL THEN
      DisposeTree(Tree^.Left);
      DisposeTree(Tree^.Right);
      DEALLOCATE(Tree, SIZE(TreeNode));
    END; (* IF *)
  END DisposeTree;

  PROCEDURE FlattenTree(Tree: BinarySearchTree; VAR Table: Buffer;
                        VAR Count: CARDINAL);
  (* Move all elements of Tree into sorted array Table *)
  BEGIN
    IF Tree^.Left # NIL THEN
      FlattenTree(Tree^.Left, Table, Count);
    END; (* IF *)
    Table[Count].Ch := Tree^.Ch;
    Table[Count].Num := Tree^.Num;
    INC(Count);
    IF Tree^.Right # NIL THEN
      FlattenTree(Tree^.Right, Table, Count);
    END; (* IF *)
  END FlattenTree;
```

```
    PROCEDURE ReBuild(Table: Buffer;
                     VAR Low, High: INTEGER): BinarySearchTree;
    (* Given sorted array Table, return a balanced binary search tree *)
    VAR NewTree : BinarySearchTree;
        NewLow, Mid, NewHigh : INTEGER;
    BEGIN
      ALLOCATE(NewTree, SIZE(TreeNode));   (* build root *)
      Mid := Low + (High - Low) DIV 2;
      NewTree^.Ch := Table[Mid].Ch;
      NewTree^.Num := Table[Mid].Num;
      IF Low <= (Mid - 1) THEN     (* build left subtree *)
        NewHigh := Mid - 1;
        NewTree^.Left := ReBuild(Table, Low, NewHigh);
      ELSE
        NewTree^.Left := NIL;
      END; (* IF *)
      IF (Mid + 1) <= High THEN  (* build right subtree *)
        NewLow := Mid + 1;
        NewTree^.Right := ReBuild(Table, NewLow, High);
      ELSE
        NewTree^.Right := NIL;
      END; (* IF *)
      RETURN NewTree;
    END ReBuild;

VAR Table : Buffer;
    Counter: CARDINAL;
    Low, High : INTEGER;
BEGIN (* ReBalance *)
  Counter := 0;    (* keep track of the number of nodes in the tree *)
  IF Tree # NIL THEN      (* rebalance *)
    FlattenTree(Tree, Table, Counter);
    DisposeTree(Tree);
    Low := 0;  High := Counter - 1;
    RETURN ReBuild(Table, Low, High);
  ELSE                 (* empty tree *)
    RETURN NIL;
  END; (* IF *)
END ReBalance;

PROCEDURE BuildTree(Keys: String; NumOrder: BOOLEAN;
                    MaxNum: CARDINAL;  VAR Tree: BinarySearchTree);
(* Build a binary search Tree *)
```

```
PROCEDURE LessThan(Ch1: CHAR; Num1: CARDINAL;
                   Ch2: CHAR; Num2: CARDINAL): BOOLEAN;
(* Key comparison *)
BEGIN
  IF Ch1 < Ch2 THEN
    RETURN TRUE;
  ELSIF Ch1 > Ch2 THEN
    RETURN FALSE;
  ELSE
    RETURN Num1 < Num2;
  END; (* IF *)
END LessThan;

PROCEDURE NextKey(Keys: String; NumOrder: BOOLEAN;
                  VAR Ch: CHAR; VAR Num: CARDINAL);
(* Build next key *)
VAR ChStr: String;
BEGIN
  InitString(ChStr);
  ToString(Ch, ChStr);
  IF NumOrder THEN (* A0, A1, A2, ... *)
    IF Num < MaxNum THEN
      INC(Num);
    ELSE
      Num := 0;
      Ch := FetchChar(Keys, Pos(ChStr, Keys)+1);
    END; (* IF *)
  ELSE            (* A0, B0, C0, ... *)
    IF Pos(ChStr, Keys) < Length(Keys)-1 THEN
      Ch := FetchChar(Keys, Pos(ChStr, Keys)+1);
    ELSE
      Ch := FetchChar(Keys, 0);
      INC(Num);
    END; (* IF *)
  END;  (* IF *)
END NextKey;

PROCEDURE Insert(Ch: CHAR; Num: CARDINAL; VAR Tree: BinarySearchTree);
(* Insert node with values Ch, Num in BinarySearchTree *)
BEGIN
  IF Tree = NIL THEN   (* build node *)
    ALLOCATE(Tree, SIZE(TreeNode));
    Tree^.Ch := Ch;
    Tree^.Num := Num;
    Tree^.Left := NIL;
    Tree^.Right := NIL;
```

```
      ELSIF LessThan(Ch, Num, Tree^.Ch, Tree^.Num) THEN  (* left *)
        Insert(Ch, Num, Tree^.Left);
      ELSIF LessThan(Tree^.Ch, Tree^.Num, Ch, Num) THEN  (* right *)
        Insert(Ch, Num, Tree^.Right);
      END; (* IF *)
  END Insert;

VAR Ch: CHAR;
    Num: CARDINAL;

BEGIN       (* BuildTree *)
  Tree := NIL;
  Ch := FetchChar(Keys, 0); Num := 0;
  LOOP
    Insert(Ch, Num, Tree);
    IF (Ch = ...MaxNum) THEN
        EXIT;
    END (* IF *)
  END;  (* LOOP *)
END BuildTree;

PROCEDURE InOrder(Tree: BinarySearchTree);
(* Perform an inorder traversal of Tree and print out the key for
   each node *)
BEGIN
  IF Tree # NIL THEN
    InOrder(Tree^.Left);
    Write(Tree^.Ch); WriteCard(Tree^.Num,1); Write(' ');
    InOrder(Tree^.Right);
  END;   (* IF *)
END InOrder;

PROCEDURE PrintTree(Tree: BinarySearchTree; Indentation: CARDINAL);
(* Utility procedure that actually prints the Tree *)
VAR Indent: CARDINAL;
BEGIN
  IF Tree # NIL THEN
    IF Tree^.Right # NIL THEN
      PrintTree(Tree^.Right, Indentation+1);
    END;
    FOR Indent := 1 TO Indentation DO
      WriteString("   ");
    END; (* FOR *)
    Write(Tree^.Ch); WriteCard(Tree^.Num,1); WriteLn;
    IF Tree^.Left # NIL THEN
      PrintTree(Tree^.Left, Indentation+1);
    END;
  END; (* IF *)
END PrintTree;
```

```
PROCEDURE DisplayTree(Tree: BinarySearchTree);
(* Display entire Tree from left to right with the root at the left;
   interface supplying indentation value to PrintTree *)
BEGIN
  PrintTree(Tree, 0);
END DisplayTree;

END Rebalancing.
```

We tested our BuildTree and ReBalance procedures with a number of different trees of various sizes, and they worked as expected.

Complete the Documentation The documentation should include a careful statement of the problem and an explanation of the BuildTree procedure, as described in the "Design of a Solution" section. The pseudocode solution might also be included, but this is optional because the program is fairly short and reasonably self-documenting. The test cases and their output should be part of the documentation. A user's manual is not required for this application, as the information necessary for using the procedures is already included in the definition module.

Summary

In this chapter we have completed our presentation of trees by introducing special purpose trees. AVL trees are balanced binary trees, which guarantee good performance for the insertion and deletion operations, and eliminate extreme cases such as degenerate binary trees (trees which are, in fact, linear lists). The insertion and deletion operations for AVL trees are more complicated, but empirical tests have shown that their performance is close to the performance of perfectly balanced trees.

B-trees offer good solutions for storing large quantities of data elements and for efficiency of access. B-trees are multiway trees in which all the leaves are at the same level. Their definition is such that they remain balanced at all times with minimum effort. The maximum height of a B-tree of order n with N elements is $O(\log_{n+1} N)$, which means the maximum search path length is of the same order. A B-tree is always at least 50 percent full, giving a good utilization of memory. B-trees are sometimes used to implement file system directories.

Optimal trees can be built and used in cases where the frequency of access to various elements is known. These cases are the exception rather than the rule, though. Priority queues may be implemented by partially ordered trees or heaps that allow enqueing and dequeueing operations with a complexity of $O(\log n)$.

Exercises

1. Which of the binary search trees shown are AVL trees? If not AVL, what nodes violate the AVL property?

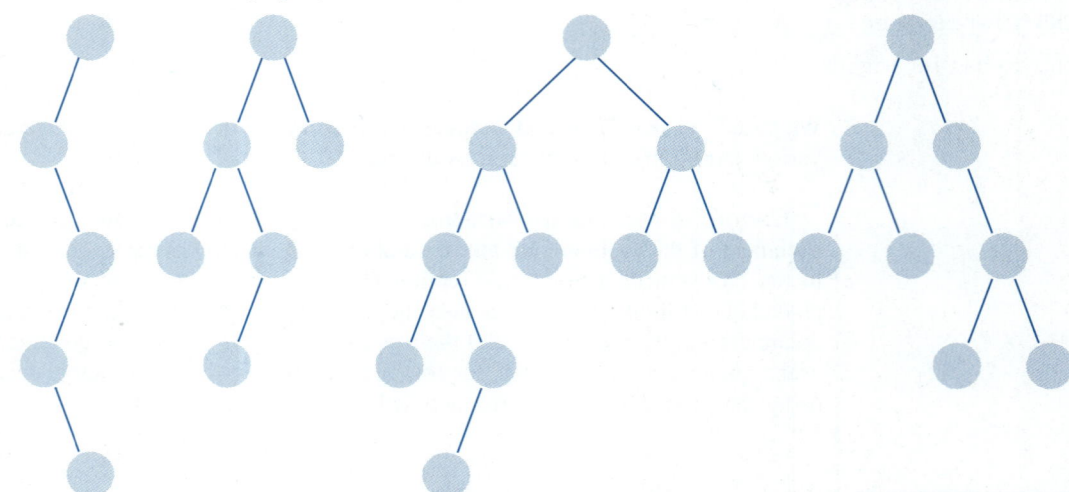

2. Show an AVL tree after inserting elements, A, B, C, D, E, F, G, H, I, J, one by one in that order, and then after inserting elements K, L, M, N, O, P, Q, R, S, T, one by one in that order.

3. For n = 1, 2, 3, . . . , draw an AVL tree with maximum height. (These are known as Fibonacci trees; see problem 31 in the Exercises section of Chapter 8.) It has been shown that the height of an AVL tree never exceeds 1.45 log n. Compute that value for all your trees and compare it to the tree height.

4. Show as well as you can that the number of single or double rotations done in deleting one element from an AVL tree cannot exceed half the height of the tree.

5. Insert the following values, in the order given, into an empty B-tree of order: a) 2, b) 3, c) 7.

    1, 7, 6, 2, 11, 4, 8, 13, 10, 5, 19, 9, 18, 23, 3, 12, 14, 20, 21, 16.

    Draw each B-tree after all insertions.

6. What is the smallest number of keys that, when inserted in an empty B-tree of order 4, will force it to have height 2 (3 levels).

7. If an element in a B-tree is not in a leaf, prove that both its immediate predecessor and immediate successor are in leaves.

8. In a B-tree, does the insertion of an element that was just deleted restore the tree as it was before the deletion? Explain.

9. Given a B-tree of order 2, elements 1, 2, 3, 4, . . . are inserted in that order. What elements cause a split? What elements cause an increase of the tree height? If the elements are deleted in the same order, what are the elements that cause merges, and those that cause a decrease of the tree height?

10. Given a heap with n elements, where e_k is the element in position k for $1 \leq k \leq n$, prove that the height of the subtree rooted at e_k is $\lfloor \log(n/k) \rfloor$ for $1 \leq k \leq n$. Use induction on k, starting with the leaves and working back up toward the root, e_1.

Programming Problems

11. Write and test a main program and modify the AVL tree insertion operation to compute the number of rotations of each kind needed for insertion of an item in an AVL tree. Use your program to produce statistical information on the average number of rotations for this AVL tree operation. Are your results in agreement with the conclusions in the text?

12. Write and test a main program and modify the AVL tree deletion operation to compute the number of rotations of each kind needed for deletion of an item in an AVL tree. Use your program to produce statistical information on the average number of rotations for this AVL tree operation. Do your results agree with the empirical results presented in the text?

13. B-trees of order 1 are also called binary B-trees or 2–3 trees. Define and implement the ADT BBTree.

14. Write and test a main program that creates random B-trees and measures the path length for each insertion and search operation. Use your program to produce statistical information on the average path length for these two operations.

15. Write and test a program that uses a random number generator to generate priorities for elements to insert in a priority queue. Compute the number of moves and comparisons for operations Enqueue and Dequeue as defined in the text. Compare these values with log(priority queue size).

16. Write a test program for the Rebalancing module and test the algorithms using small trees.

17. Automate the testing process for the Rebalancing module and test the algorithms using larger trees.

*18. Write a program that builds an optimal tree, given the keys and their frequencies.

19. Rewrite procedures Enqueue and Dequeue for the linear list implementation of priority queues. Then write a program that will compare the efficiency of these two procedures with the efficiency of the same procedures based on a heap.

Note: Problems marked with an asterisk (*) have a higher level of difficulty.

Internal and External Sorting

INTRODUCTION

In Chapter 3 we introduced several simple sorting algorithms, and we analyzed their time complexity. Then, we introduced two other well-known sorting procedures, Quicksort and merge sort, which are significantly faster than those simple sorting algorithms when there is a large number of data items. In this chapter we will introduce several other sorting algorithms.

Internal sorting includes all sorting algorithms in which the data to be sorted are stored in central memory; for example, all algorithms discussed in Chapter 3 were internal sorting algorithms. We will present here three new internal sorting algorithms. When the volume of data to sort is too large to fit in central memory, we must use external sorting techniques that use secondary memory to store the temporary results of the sorting process. We present two external sorting algorithms. The chapter concludes with a case study that shows yet another internal sorting algorithm.

11.1 Internal Sorting

Internal sorting methods are applied to data collections that can be stored entirely in central memory. All the algorithms that have been presented in Chapter 3 are internal sorting algorithms. We present here three additional algorithms, all of which are very efficient.

Shell Sort

The sorting method invented in 1959 by D. L. Shell is more efficient than the simple sorting methods discussed previously. Given a sequence of unsorted values, the Shell sort will sort separate subsequences of values. These subsequences will contain every kth element of the original sequence, and each one of them can be sorted using a simple sorting method like insertion sort. For instance, if we are sorting an array A, and if k has value 5, the subsequence A[1], A[6], A[11], A[16], . . . is sorted first. Then subsequence A[2], A[7], A[12], A[17], . . . is sorted, followed by subsequence A[3], A[8], A[13], A[18], . . . then subsequence A[4], A[9], A[14], A[19], . . . and finally the subsequence A[5], A[10], A[15], A[20], ...

After the first k subsequences are sorted, a smaller value is chosen for k, and new subsequences are sorted in the same manner. This process is repeated until the value of k is 1. Figure 11-1 illustrates the Shell sort method on a 12-element array.

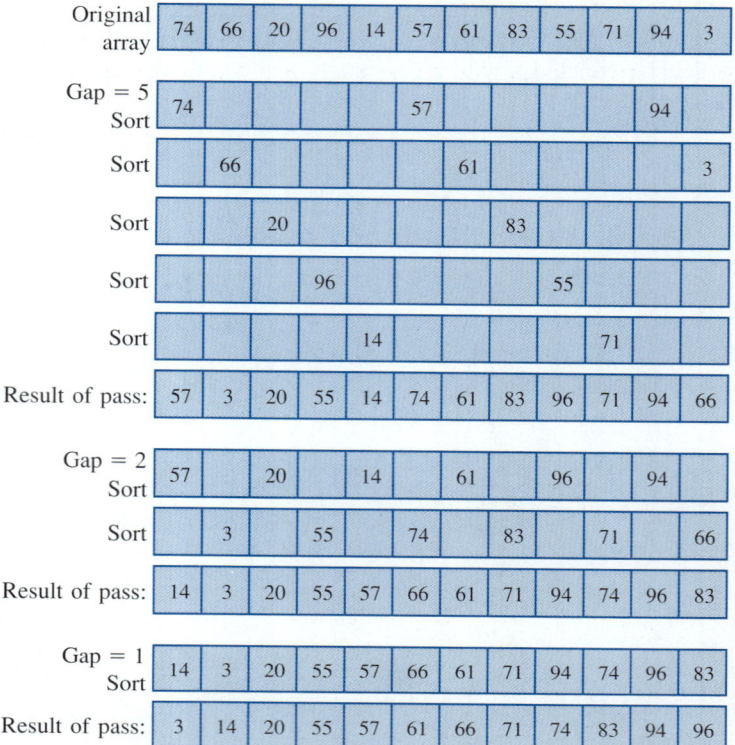

Figure 11-1
Shell Sort

Since the first increment used by the Shell sort is large, the individual subsequences are small, so that a simple insertion sort on these subsequences is fast enough. Each sorting of a subsequence causes the entire subsequence to come closer to being completely ordered. Successive passes use smaller increments—larger subsequences—but these subsequences are almost completely sorted because of the preceding passes, and so a simple insertion sort is still efficient. The following procedure implements the Shell sort. It uses the same parameters as the other sorting procedures developed earlier. Thus we can sort in any order, provided we define a comparison procedure (see Chapter 3).

```
TYPE KeyType = INTEGER;
     SomeRecord = RECORD
                     Key: KeyType;
                     Info: ARRAY [1..Max] OF CHAR;
                  END;
     Order = (Ascending, Descending);
     CompareProc = PROCEDURE(SomeRecord, SomeRecord, Order): BOOLEAN;
PROCEDURE ShellSort(VAR Table: ARRAY OF SomeRecord;
                    Number: CARDINAL; SortingOrder: Order;
                    Ordered: CompareProc);
(* Sort vector Table in given order *)
VAR Copy: SomeRecord;
    Low, High, Gap, Last: INTEGER;
BEGIN
  Last := Number-1;
  Gap := Last;
  WHILE Gap > 1 DO
    Gap := Gap DIV 2;
    FOR High := Gap TO Last DO
      Low := High - Gap;
      Copy := Table[High];      (* new value to check *)
      LOOP
        IF Low < 0 THEN EXIT END;
        IF Ordered(Copy, Table[Low], SortingOrder) THEN
          Table[Low + Gap] := Table[Low];
          Low := Low - Gap;     (* check back *)
        ELSE
          EXIT;
        END; (* IF *)
      END; (* LOOP *)
      Table[Low + Gap] := Copy;   (* final position *)
    END; (* FOR *)
  END; (* WHILE *)
END ShellSort;
```

In the ShellSort procedure, the first value used for the gap is Number/2, and then the gap is halved during each successive pass. The outer WHILE loop controls the number of passes. The FOR loop controls the comparisons of elements in a subsequence: High and Low are the indices of the vector elements being compared. The nested LOOP compares the high element, Copy, with the preceding element in the subsequence, and if they are not in order, it moves the lower element up. The elements are not really exchanged at this time, since it will be more efficient to copy the high element only in its final position. The loop goes back in the subsequence and compares the elements with Copy. As long as it is necessary, elements are moved up. The loop is ended when the final position of Copy has been found, that is, when the two elements being compared are in order, or when the end of the vector is reached (Low becomes negative). When the nested LOOP ends, the value of Copy is placed in its final position.

For instance, in Figure 11-1, the last comparisons of pass 2 are done on the following subsequence:

In that subsequence, 83 and 66 are not in order. Value 83 is moved up and the subsequence temporarily becomes 3, 55, 71, 74, 83, 83. Value 66 is not lost, as it is kept in Copy, and must be compared to 74. The result of the comparison moves 74 up, and the subsequence temporarily becomes 3, 55, 71, 74, 74, 83. Next, the value of Copy is compared to 71, which is moved up, giving a subsequence of 3, 55, 71, 71, 74, 83. Copy is then compared to the previous element, 55, and that comparison indicates that the subsequence is ordered. Copy is then inserted in its final position and the subsequence becomes 3, 55, 66, 71, 74, 83.

It is very difficult to analyze the complexity of this algorithm mathematically, since the choice of the values to be used for Gap affects the complexity. It has been shown by D. E. Knuth that a reasonable choice of values for Gap could be:

$$\begin{array}{ll} & 1, 4, 13, 40, 121, \ldots \quad (\text{Gap}_k = 3\text{Gap}_{k-1} + 1) \\ \text{or also:} & 1, 3, 7, 15, 31, \ldots \quad (\text{Gap}_k = 2\text{Gap}_{k-1} + 1) \end{array}$$

Mathematical analysis shows the complexity of the Shell sort to be as low as $O(n^{1.2})$, which is certainly much better than $O(n^2)$, but, in general, it is not as good as the Quicksort algorithm for large n.

Heapsort

The Heapsort method was invented in 1964 by J. Williams, and is similar to the selection sort discussed in Chapter 3, in that it selects successive elements and then exchanges them into sorted order. Heapsort uses a more efficient data structure than does a selection sort, but a selection sort would be more efficient for smaller sets of elements.

Heapsort uses a heap (see Chapter 10), defined as a sequence of elements $h_1, h_2, h_3, \ldots h_{\text{Max}}$, whose values (or keys) are such that $h_i \leq h_{2i}$ and $h_i \leq h_{2i+1}$, for i = 1 to Max/2. We say that h_{2i} and h_{2i+1} are the children of h_i. Notice that h_1 represents the minimum value of the sequence. Heapsort can be described simply by the following pseudocode.

> Heapsort
>   Form a heap from the original sequence of elements
>   Repeat
>   Exchange first and last elements of heap
>   Push the new first element down until it finds its proper place
>   in the new heap
>   Until no element left
> End Heapsort

Figure 11-2 illustrates this process for a descending order sort. Boldface type shows elements in their final position and that are not part of the heap anymore.

A new heap is obtained by putting an element in front of the others and letting this new element sift down into place by following the path of smaller values that move up

Figure 11-2
Heapsort

Original array:	74	66	20	96	14	57	61	83	55	71	94	3
First heap:	3	14	20	55	66	57	61	83	96	71	94	74
New heap:	14	55	20	74	66	57	61	83	96	71	94	**3**
New heap:	20	55	57	74	66	94	61	83	96	71	**14**	**3**
New heap:	55	66	57	74	71	94	61	83	96	**20**	**14**	**3**
New heap:	57	66	61	74	71	94	96	83	**55**	**20**	**14**	**3**
New heap:	61	66	83	74	71	94	96	**57**	**55**	**20**	**14**	**3**
New heap:	66	71	83	74	96	94	**61**	**57**	**55**	**20**	**14**	**3**
New heap:	71	74	83	94	96	**66**	**61**	**57**	**55**	**20**	**14**	**3**
New heap:	74	94	83	96	**71**	**66**	**61**	**57**	**55**	**20**	**14**	**3**
New heap:	83	94	96	**74**	**71**	**66**	**61**	**57**	**55**	**20**	**14**	**3**
New heap:	94	96	**83**	**74**	**71**	**66**	**61**	**57**	**55**	**20**	**14**	**3**
New heap:	96	**94**	**83**	**74**	**71**	**66**	**61**	**57**	**55**	**20**	**14**	**3**
Final array:	**96**	**94**	**83**	**74**	**71**	**66**	**61**	**57**	**55**	**20**	**14**	**3**

at the same time. For instance, in Figure 11-2, in step one, 3 and 74 are exchanged, and then 74 is sifted down so that the heap property is preserved.

The following procedure implements this algorithm. Like ShellSort, it uses procedure parameters to make it possible to sort in any order.

```
PROCEDURE HeapSort(VAR Table: ARRAY OF SomeRecord;
                   Number: CARDINAL; SortingOrder: Order;
                   Ordered: CompareProc);
(* Sort Table in specified order *)
  PROCEDURE Swap(VAR X, Y: SomeRecord);
  VAR Copy: SomeRecord;
  BEGIN
    Copy := X;
    X := Y;
    Y := Copy;
  END Swap;

  PROCEDURE SiftDown(VAR Arr: ARRAY OF SomeRecord; First, Last: CARDINAL);
  (* Arr[First]..Arr[Last] obey heap property except possibly for Arr[First].
     The procedure will sift down Arr[First] until the heap property is
     restored *)
  VAR Pos: CARDINAL;   (* Current position of Arr[First] *)
  BEGIN
    Pos := First;
    LOOP
      IF 2 * Pos + 1 > Last THEN (* no children *) EXIT END;
      IF 2 * Pos + 1 = Last THEN    (* Pos has one child at 2*Pos+1 *)
        IF Ordered(Arr[2 * Pos + 1], Arr[Pos], SortingOrder) THEN
          Swap(Arr[Pos], Arr[2 * Pos + 1]);
        END; (* IF *)
        EXIT;
      ELSIF    (* Pos has 2 children at 2*Pos+1 and 2*Pos+2 *)
          Ordered(Arr[2 * Pos + 1], Arr[Pos], SortingOrder) AND
          Ordered(Arr[2 * Pos + 1], Arr[2 * Pos + 2], SortingOrder) THEN
        (* Swap Pos with first child, which has the extreme value *)
        Swap(Arr[Pos], Arr[2 * Pos + 1]);
        Pos := 2 * Pos + 1;
      ELSIF Ordered(Arr[2 * Pos + 2], Arr[Pos], SortingOrder) AND
            Ordered(Arr[2 * Pos + 2], Arr[2 * Pos + 1], SortingOrder) THEN
        (* Swap Pos with second child, which has the extreme value *)
        Swap(Arr[Pos], Arr[2 * Pos + 2]);
        Pos := 2 * Pos + 2;
      ELSE (* the heap property is respected *)
        EXIT;
      END; (* IF *)
    END; (* LOOP *)
  END SiftDown;
```

```
VAR Index, LastIndex: CARDINAL;
BEGIN
  (* Create heap *)
  LastIndex := Number - 1;
  FOR Index := LastIndex DIV 2 TO 0 BY -1 DO
    SiftDown(Table, Index, LastIndex);
  END; (* FOR *)
  FOR Index := LastIndex TO 1 BY -1 DO
    (* Remove minimum from front of heap *)
    Swap(Table[0], Table[Index]);
    (* Re-establish heap property *)
    SiftDown(Table, 0, Index-1);
  END; (* FOR *)
END HeapSort;
```

Intuitively, it is not obvious that this method will give good results. It turns out that for large numbers of elements HeapSort is very efficient, and that it becomes better as the number of elements increases. In the worst case, the LOOP in procedure SiftDown is executed $\log_2 n$ times, where n is the number of elements in the heap. In procedure HeapSort, SiftDown is called n/2 times to build the original heap, and then (n − 1) times. This leads us to a maximum of $(3n/2 \log_2 n)$ compares or moves. It should be obvious that this is a very conservative bound, as SiftDown is often called on heaps with much less than n elements. We can see that the complexity of Heapsort is $O(n \log n)$.

There are variations of this heapsort algorithm. Changing the relationship that forms the heap ($h_i > h_{2i}$ and $h_i > h_{2i+1}$) results in an ascending order sort. We can accomplish this reversal of order by changing our comparison procedure. We formed the initial heap by applying the SiftDown operation to the elements in the first half of the array, working towards the first element. It is also possible to form the heap by starting at the first element and applying a SiftUp operation to the children.

Radix Sort

Radix sorting is a different sorting method that has some historical significance since it was initially implemented on mechanical card sorters. These machines, which are now obsolete, were used to sort stacks of punched cards and place each card in an output slot determined by the value in a selected column. By the use of these card sorters, it is possible to sort the cards in any desired way by sorting repeatedly on different columns and stacking the contents of the various slots.

A radix sort makes no comparisons and possibly produces no data movement, depending on the data structures used. Therefore it is a promising approach, as it is known that no sorting algorithm based on comparing pairs of elements can require fewer than $O(n \log n)$ comparisons for random data. We will illustrate the radix sort method by way of a simple example. Let's suppose we have to sort a sequence of three-digit integers (if an integer requires less than three digits, it is extended with leading zeros). The first step is to distribute the integers into sequences based on the value of the least significant digit, as shown in Figure 11-3, and then to concatenate the

Figure 11-3
Radix Sort of Three-Digit Numbers

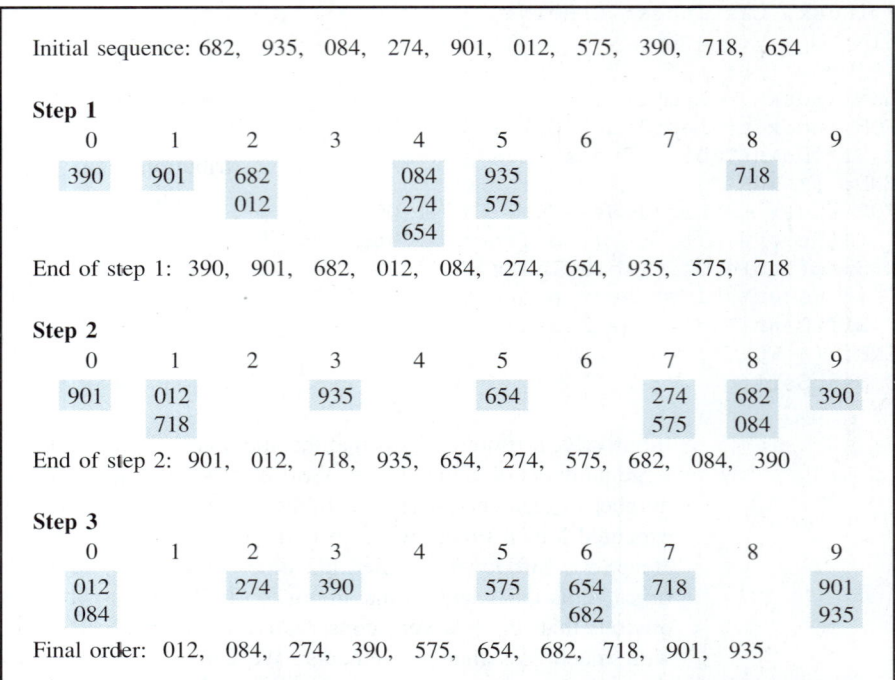

integer sequences. The second step repeats this process based on the second digit, and the third step is a repetition of the previous steps based on the most significant digit.

Based on this example, we will develop a sorting algorithm. We assume here that each element is characterized by an m-character key, and that character values are ordinal numbers (our preceding example used three-digit keys).

We can define our radix sort algorithm with the following pseudocode.

```
RadixSort
    Set Index to index of last character
    Repeat
        Add each element of the sequence to sort to a character sequence
            based on the value of the character at position index
        Form a new sequence by concatenating the character
            sequences in order from the first to the last
        Decrement Index
    Until Index < index of first character
End RadixSort
```

The data structures used to implement the radix sort are important for the efficiency of the algorithm, as it is obviously better to avoid any unnecessary data movement. Using arrays makes data movement necessary; the arrays must also be large, as any sequence must be able to contain all the keys. Moreover, if there are m possible values for each character, then the sort requires m arrays, each of the size of the original list. Therefore radix sort is usually implemented using linked lists, as shown in Figure 11-4.

We have used an array of linked lists for the bins 0 through 9 shown after the distribution phase on step 1 in Figure 11-3. Each array element contains a head and tail pointer, which are set to nil before the distribution begins. Data are added to the end of the appropriate list, but since we have tail pointers, this is a constant time operation. Notice that the data are not actually moved, only the pointer values are changed. The concatenation process is also facilitated by using the tail pointers: one simply changes the nil link at the end of each nonempty list to the head pointer of the next nonempty list. Assuming the number of items to be sorted is larger than the number of bins, the radix sort algorithm is O(n), as the formation of sequences involves all the elements, and is repeated a constant number of times (equal to the number of characters in the keys).

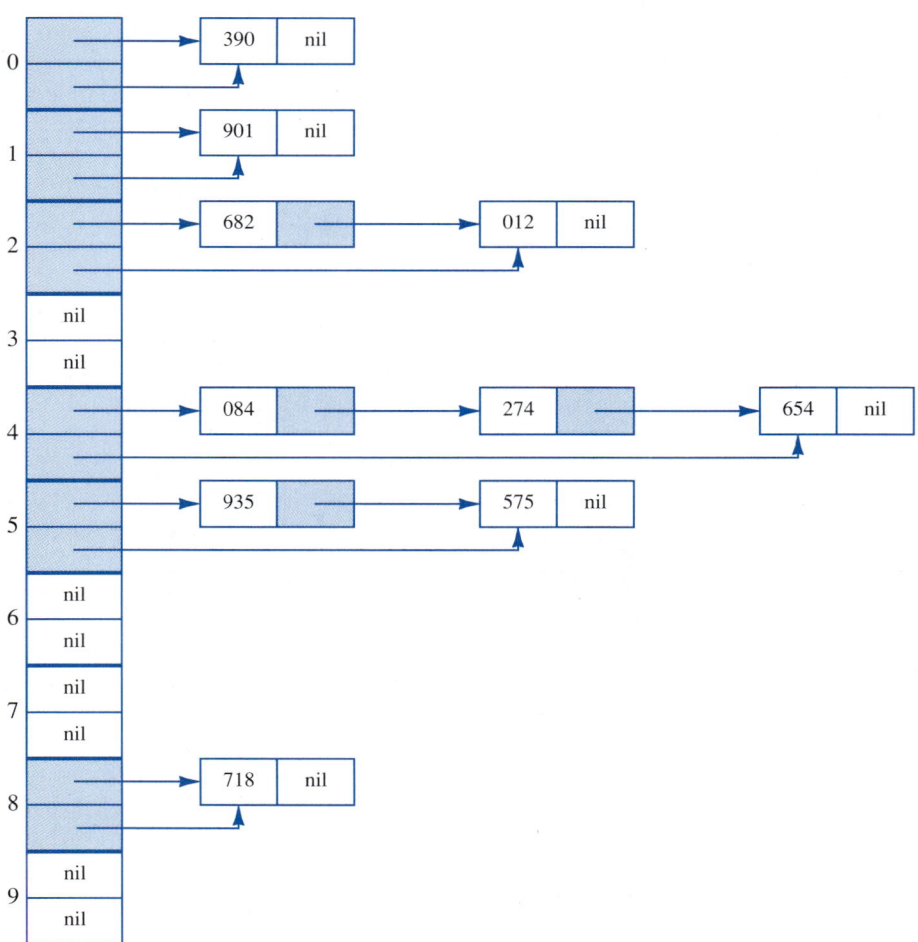

Figure 11-4
A Linked List Structure for Radix Sort

For fixed length keys and very large n, radix sort is faster than any of the other sort algorithms, but it is not simple to determine the value of n at which the radix sort becomes better than sorts with complexity O(n log n). Radix sort is not used all the time for two reasons: it is less efficient with keys having many characters, and the splitting of keys into their component characters might not be efficient. For instance, decomposing the key into single "characters" might require some extra operations: a three-digit key would require three Modula-2 statements involving operations MOD and DIV. For real numbers with finite precision (as is the case for all numbers in a computer), a radix sort is possible, but rarely practical. The value of n for which radix sort surpasses O(n log n) sorts might also be very large, depending on the structure of the key, the programming language, the compiler, and the computer used.

11.2 External Sorting

The sorting algorithms we have seen so far cannot be used if the amount of data to sort is so large that it cannot fit into the computer main memory. In such cases, the data to be sorted are kept in a sequential file, where at a given time, one and only one element is accessible. This imposes restrictions on the methods we can use to sort the data, as we can no longer access random data elements as we could by indexing an array. This type of sorting is called external sorting because we have to use external (or secondary) memory to perform the sort.

Merge Sort

The most common external sort is the merge sort, where we use merging as an auxiliary operation for sequential sorting. As we have seen in Chapter 1 and in Chapter 3, merging is a much simpler operation than sorting. Let's give an example of the external merge sort method.

We start with an unordered file of data. In order to be able to merge two sequences of data, we first split the data into two temporary files, and we consider that each of these files comprises a series of ordered runs (see the case study in Chapter 3).

The original input file can be considered to be a series of runs of length 1. While splitting this input file, it is easy to read elements two at a time and to create runs of length 2. The first pass of merge sort will combine pairs of runs of length 2 and create runs of length 4, which will be stored in two other temporary files. These two files will then be used as input files for the next pass, which will build runs of length 8 and store them in the previous two temporary files. The process will be repeated until we obtain a final run containing all elements in sorted order. Figure 11-5 illustrates the merge sort process, with an input file, and four temporary files.

In the example of Figure 11-5, we start with 14 elements in the original file to be sorted. First, the file is split into two temporary files in such a way that each temporary file contains a set of runs of length 2: Temporary 1 contains four runs of length 2, while Temporary 2 contains three of them. The first pass of merge sort combines runs of

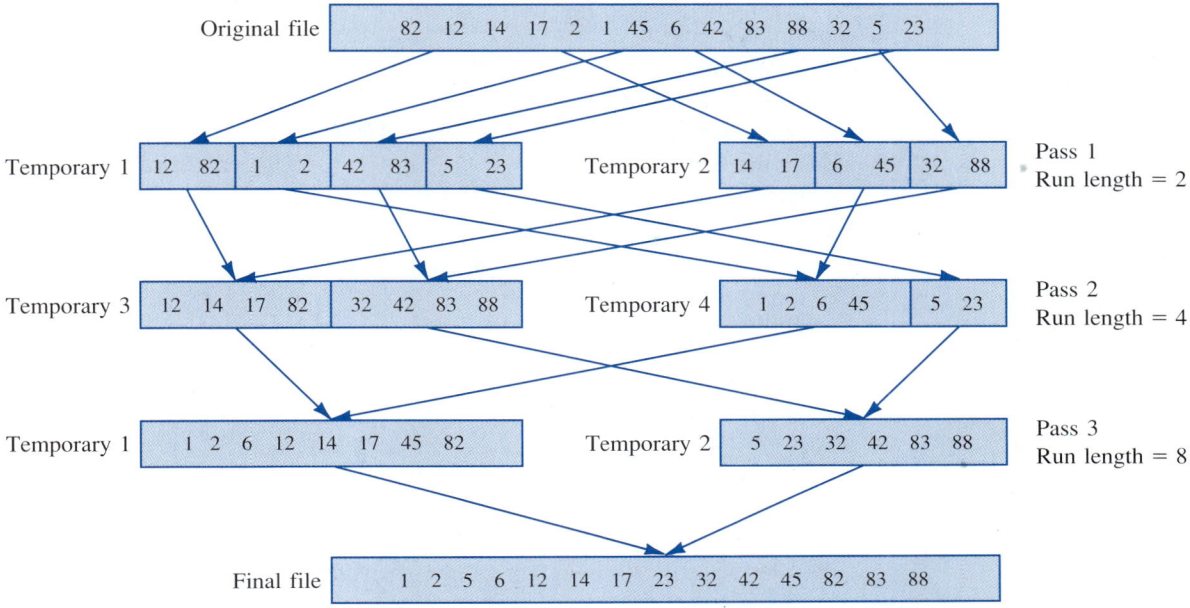

Figure 11-5 Example of Merge Sort

length 2 into runs of length 4, alternately distributed on temporary files 3 and 4. At the end of pass 1, Temporary 3 contains two runs of length 4, and Temporary 4 contains one run of length 4 and one run of length 2 (left over from the preceding pass because it could not be merged with any other). Pass 2 combines runs of length 4 into runs of length 8 distributed on temporary files Temporary 1 and Temporary 2 (which, at this time, are free to be used again). At the end of pass 2, Temporary 1 contains one run of length 8 and Temporary 2 contains one run of length 6 (obtained by merging one run of length 4 and one run of length 2). Pass 3 is the last pass and combines the two runs into a single run of length 14 in temporary file Temporary 3. This final result can be transferred to a permanent file or we may simply rename Temporary 3 to the permanent file name. Note that Temporary 4 still exists, but is empty, as it has not been used in pass 3 for lack of runs.

This solution can be described in more detail by the following pseudocode.

```
Distribute Input
    Set Number of records to 0
    Define current output file
    Loop {  read input file and write to output files  }
        Read 2 records from input file
        Exit if end of input file
```

```
         Update Number of records
         Write two records in order on current output file
         Switch to other output file
      End loop
   End Distribute Input
   Merge Sort
      Set Length to 2
      Repeat {   sort by merging runs of increasing size   }
         Set Limit to Number of records
         Switch temporary input and output files
         Read a record from input file 1
         Read a record from input file 2
         Repeat {   merge all runs from file 1 and file 2   }
            Switch output file
            Set Length1 to length of runs in file 1
            Set Length2 to length of runs in file 2
            Reduce Limit by these two lengths
            While Length1 and Length2 not zero {   combine 2 runs   }
               Write record with smallest key
               Read a record from file whose record was output
               Decrease length of file just read
            End while
            While still elements in run of file 1 {   empty file 1   }
               Write record
               Read record
            End while
            While still elements in run of file 2 {   empty file 2   }
               Write record
               Read record
            End while
         Until Limit = 0
         Set Length to 2 * Length {   double run length   }
      Until Length >= Number of records
   End Merge Sort
```

The corresponding Modula-2 program uses types Items and FileArray, defined as:

```
TYPE Items = RECORD
                Key:  ARRAY [0..KeyLength-1] OF CHAR;
                Info: ARRAY [1..InfoLength] OF CHAR;
             END;
     FileArray = ARRAY[0..3] OF File;
```

The sorting procedure follows directly from the pseudocode.

```
PROCEDURE MergeSort(VAR F: FileArray; VAR ResFile: CARDINAL;
                    NumberOfRecords: CARDINAL);
(* Sorting of a file of records on the Key field.
   Sorting is done by combining (merging) runs of length
   2, 4, 8 ... using 4 temporary files F[0],F[1],F[2],F[3].
   Initially runs of length 2 are in files F[0] and F[1].
   Sorting is done in several passes, each pass combining
   runs of given length until the length of runs exceeds
   the file size. The sorted records will be in temporary
   file F[ResFile] when sorting is over. *)

VAR Input, Output,          (* Designate input and output files *)
    Limit,                  (* Number of records left to sort *)
    Length,                 (* Length of current run *)
    Length1,Length2: CARDINAL;(* Lengths of run1 and run2 *)
    FlipFlop: BOOLEAN;      (* Flags which files are used *)
    Item1, Item2: Items;    (* Temporary records *)
BEGIN
  FlipFlop := TRUE;
  Length := 2;              (* Start with runs of length 2 *)
  REPEAT                    (* Sort runs *)
    Limit := NumberOfRecords;
    IF FlipFlop THEN  (* First files unsorted, second files to store *)
      Input := 0;
      Output := 3;
      Reset(F[0], "MFile1.dat"); Reset(F[1], "MFile2.dat");
      Rewrite(F[2], "MFile3.dat"); Rewrite(F[3], "MFile4.dat");
    ELSE              (* Second files to sort, first files to store *)
      Input := 2;
      Output := 1;
      Reset(F[2], "MFile3.dat"); Reset(F[3], "MFile4.dat");
      Rewrite(F[0], "MFile1.dat"); Rewrite(F[1], "MFile2.dat");
    END; (* If *)
    ReadRecord(F[Input], Item1);
    ReadRecord(F[Input + 1], Item2);
    REPEAT          (* Merge runs from input files to output files *)
      IF ODD(Output) THEN  (* Distribute on two output files *)
        Output := Output - 1;(* Switch from 1 to 0, or from 3 to 2 *)
      ELSE
        Output := Output + 1;(* Switch from 0 to 1 or from 2 to 3 *)
      END; (* If *)
```

```
        IF Limit >= Length THEN    (* Compute lengths in each file *)
          Length1 := Length;
        ELSE
          Length1 := Limit;
        END; (* If *)
        Limit := Limit - Length1;   (* Updates limit *)
        IF Limit >= Length THEN
          Length2 := Length;
        ELSE
          Length2 := Limit;
        END; (* If *)
        Limit := Limit - Length2;
        ResFile := Output;          (* Last file written *)
        WHILE (Length1 # 0) AND (Length2 # 0) DO   (* Actual merge *)
          IF CompareStr(Item2.Key, Item1.Key) > 0 THEN
            WriteRecord(F[Output], Item1);
            ReadRecord(F[Input], Item1);
            Length1 := Length1 - 1;
          ELSE
            WriteRecord(F[Output], Item2);
            ReadRecord(F[Input+1], Item2);
            Length2 := Length2 - 1;
          END; (* If *)
        END; (* While *)
        (* Copy tail of second file *)
        WHILE Length2 # 0 DO
          WriteRecord(F[Output], Item2);
          ReadRecord(F[Input+1], Item2);
          Length2 := Length2 - 1;
        END; (* While *)
        (* Copy tail of first file *)
        WHILE Length1 # 0 DO
          WriteRecord(F[Output], Item1);
          ReadRecord(F[Input], Item1);
          Length1 := Length1 - 1;
        END; (* While *)
      UNTIL Limit=0;
      FlipFlop := NOT FlipFlop; (* Switch input and output files *)
      Length := 2 * Length;      (* Increment runs length *)
    UNTIL Length >= NumberOfRecords;
END MergeSort;
```

The outer REPEAT loop in procedure MergeSort controls the number of passes made on the data by starting with a run length of 2, and doubling this length until it equals or exceeds the number of records in the original input file. Each pass will alternate pairs of temporary files as input files and output files. During the first pass, F[0] and F[1] will be the two input files, while F[2] and F[3] will be the output files. The next pass will take F[2] and F[3] as input files and F[0] and F[1] as output files, and so on. Variable FlipFlop controls this alternation.

The nested REPEAT loop processes a pair of runs from the two input files. Variable Limit gives the number of records left to sort. Normally, Length1 and Length2 are equal to Length (the length of the current run), but towards the end of the input files we might be left with runs of different lengths. We make sure we do not try to sort more records than were present in the original file. Merging two runs is done simply by comparing the first elements of each run and writing the record with the smallest key. When all records of one run have been written, we copy the tail of the other run. Note that only one of the last two WHILE loops will write records. Every time a pair of runs has been processed, the output file is changed so that output is alternated between the two output files. Once all records are in one temporary file, the sort is completed and the temporary output file index is returned, so that the file can be renamed and made permanent.

Some procedures like Reset and Rewrite might not be available on all systems, but it is a small task to define such procedures using whatever tools are provided by your system's input/output library modules. Procedures ReadRecord and WriteRecord can also be adapted to use your system's input/output tools.

The analysis of MergeSort is simple: each pass doubles Length, and the sort is done when Length $\geq$ NumberOfRecords. The total number of passes is therefore equal to $\log_2 n$, where n is the number of records. Now, each pass will copy exactly once the entire set of records, and will involve n data moves. So the overall complexity of MergeSort is $O(n \log n)$.

The efficiency of MergeSort can be improved in two ways:

- First, instead of using a two-way merge with four files for each pass, we can use an N-way merge with 2N files. This will have the effect of reducing the number of passes from $\log_2 n$ to $\log_N n$ (see problem 9).
- Second, we can merge the two longest possible runs during any given pass instead of merging runs of fixed length (the *k*th pass would normally merge runs of length 2^k). This is called a natural merge sort, as it uses the existing natural runs, so that two ordered runs of lengths m and n will be merged into a run of length m + n. However, this will add a number of comparisons in order to detect the end of the natural runs and might be interesting only with data sets where it is known that long natural runs do exist (see problem 8).

Polyphase Sort

There are other external sorting methods, but one specific method offers a better performance than merge sort: the polyphase sort. Assuming that we can keep N files open at one time, the idea behind polyphase sorting is that it might be more efficient to abandon the rigid division of files into N/2 source files and N/2 destination files, and instead merge N − 1 files into a single file in a given pass. This method was invented by R. L. Gilstad in 1960.

We will illustrate the method on two examples, the first one using three files and the second one using five files. In our first example, each pass will merge two files into a third one, but the two source files will not necessarily have the same length (or number of runs). Figure 11-6 illustrates the method by showing the number of runs in each of

Figure 11-6
Polyphase Sort of 34 Runs with 3 Files

f_1	f_2	f_3	
21^1	13^1	0	Initial Distribution
8^1	0	13^2	Result of pass 1
0	8^3	5^2	Result of pass 2
5^5	3^3	0	Result of pass 3
2^5	0	3^8	Result of pass 4
0	2^{13}	1^8	Result of pass 5
1^{21}	1^{13}	0	Result of pass 6
0	0	1^{34}	Result of pass 7

the three files, the exponent indicating the run lengths. We have assumed that initially the two input files contain 21 and 13 runs of length 1: the first pass merges 13 runs from f_1 and f_2 to f_3, the second pass merges 8 runs from f_1 and f_3 to f_2, and so on. The last pass leaves the sorted sequence as a run of length 34 in f_3.

Keep in mind that the notation in Figures 11-6 and 11-7 is to indicate the number of runs (main number), and their length (superscript). So 3^8 means there are three runs, each of length eight. The number of elements is constant; so after the fourth pass in Figure 11-6, we have $3 \times 8 = 24$ elements plus $5 \times 2 = 10$ elements, the same as the original 34 elements. The second example illustrates the polyphase method on 5 files, as shown in Figure 11-7.

In our two examples, the initial distribution of the runs was carefully chosen in order to lead to the intended result. In particular, in the polyphase sort each pass, except for the last pass, results in exactly one empty file, so that the remaining files may be partially merged into it.

To find what the distribution should be, we can work our way backwards from the final distribution. If we look at the numbers of runs of our first example, we have the series: 0, 1, 1, 2, 3, 5, 8, 13, 21, which we can recognize as the Fibonacci series. In this series, each number is the sum of the two preceding numbers, with the Fibonacci numbers defined by:

$$f_0 = 0$$
$$f_1 = 1$$
$$f_i = f_{i-1} + f_{i-2} \quad \text{for } i > 1$$

For the polyphase sort to work, the initial distribution of runs must be based on consecutive Fibonacci numbers.

The second example is a little more complex. Here we will see that the initial distribution must be based on Fibonacci numbers of order p. These Fibonacci numbers are defined by:

$$f_i = 0 \quad \text{for } i < p - 1$$
$$f_{p-1} = 1$$
$$f_i = f_{i-1} + f_{i-2} + f_{i-3} + \cdots + f_{i-p} \quad \text{for } i \geq p$$

Figure 11-7
Polyphase Sort of 49 Runs with 5 Files

f_1	f_2	f_3	f_4	f_5	
15^1	14^1	12^1	8^1	0	Initial Distribution
7^1	6^1	4^1	0	8^4	Result of pass 1
3^1	2^1	0	4^7	4^4	Result of pass 2
1^1	0	2^{13}	2^7	2^4	Result of pass 3
0	1^{25}	1^{13}	1^7	1^4	Result of pass 4
1^{49}	0	0	0	0	Result of pass 5

In the case of our second example, we deal with Fibonacci numbers of order 4:

$$f_i = 0 \text{ for } i < 3$$
$$f_3 = 1$$
$$f_i = f_{i-1} + f_{i-2} + f_{i-3} + f_{i-4} \text{ for } i \geq 4$$

which gives the sequence:

0, 0, 0, 1, 1, 2, 4, 8, 15, 29, 56, ...

This gives us the number of runs on the first file, which has the greatest number of runs. The number of runs on the other files can be computed in a similar way, by replacing the starting sequence (0, 0, 0, 1) in turn by (0, 0, 1, 0), (0, 1, 0, 0), and (1, 0, 0, 0):

0, 0, 1, 0, 1, 2, 4, 7, 14, ...
0, 1, 0, 0, 1, 2, 3, 6, 12, ...
1, 0, 0, 0, 1, 1, 2, 4, 8, ...

Looking at Figure 11-7, we find these sequences by cyclically shifting files one position to the left at each pass.

When merging has to be done, it is very unlikely that the number of runs will be exactly the number of runs needed for a perfect Fibonacci distribution. It is still possible to proceed with the merge by adding "dummy" runs as needed, and by distributing them as uniformly as possible. Merging dummy runs from all the files involves no actual merge operation, but only the recording of a dummy run on the output file.

The first part of the polyphase algorithm will be the distribution of the original runs to the (n − 1) files. In order to distribute the runs, we will use two tables to help us reach the Fibonacci distribution. Table 11-1 contains the values of the above computed sequences, which correspond to the example of Figure 11-7.

Table 11-2 contains differences between each level of Table 11-1, except for level 0. Diff will indicate how many runs must be distributed in order to reach the next level. Each time an actual run is copied, the corresponding Diff element will be decreased, as Diff can be considered to represent the number of dummy runs necessary to reach the distribution of a specific level.

Table 11-1 Fibonacci Distribution

Level	$Fibo_1$	$Fibo_2$	$Fibo_3$	$Fibo_4$
0	1	0	0	0
1	1	1	1	1
2	2	2	2	1
3	4	4	3	2
4	8	7	6	4
5	15	14	12	8

Table 11-2 Numbers of Runs to Distribute

Level	$Diff_1$	$Diff_2$	$Diff_3$	$Diff_4$
1	1	1	1	1
2	1	1	1	0
3	2	2	1	1
4	4	3	3	2
5	7	7	6	4

The distribution algorithm will need to use the following ComputeDistribution procedure in order to know on which file to copy the next available run. The procedure returns the next file or, if need be, computes the next row of tables Fibo and Diff.

```
PROCEDURE ComputeDistribution(VAR Diff, Fibo: ArrFileNo;
                              VAR File: FileNo; VAR level: CARDINAL);
(* Select the File for the next run.
   File: current file
   Fibo: ideal distribution for level
   Diff: dummy runs for this level (Diff[i] decreases as i increases
         and Diff[N] = 0 *)
VAR Index, Old: CARDINAL;
BEGIN
  IF Diff[File] < Diff[File+1] THEN    (* next file *)
    INC(File);
  ELSE
    IF Diff[File] = 0 THEN              (* new level *)
      INC(level);
      Old := Fibo[1];
      FOR Index := 1 TO N-1 DO
      (* compute next row for tables Diff and Fibo *)
        Diff[Index] := Old + Fibo[Index+1] - Fibo[Index];
        Fibo[Index] := Old + Fibo[Index+1];
      END; (* FOR *)
    END; (* IF *)
    File := 1;                          (* start at file 1 *)
  END; (* IF *)
  DEC(Diff[File]);                      (* replace dummy run by actual run *)
END ComputeDistribution;
```

The ComputeDistribution procedure as well as the sort procedure use the following declarations.

```
CONST N = 6;

TYPE FileNo = [1..N];
     CurrentArray = ARRAY FileNo OF INTEGER;
     FileArray = ARRAY FileNo OF FileDescr;
     ArrFileNo = ARRAY FileNo OF CARDINAL;
     String = ARRAY [0..9] OF CHAR;
     NameArray = ARRAY FileNo OF String;
     FileNoArr = ARRAY FileNo OF FileNo;
```

The distribution part of the polyphase algorithm will first distribute one run onto each of the (n − 1) files. Then, the remaining runs will be distributed by alternate calls to ComputeDistribution and to CopyRun, which can be defined by:

```
PROCEDURE CopyItem(InFile: FileDescr; VAR InCurrent: INTEGER;
                   OutFile: FileDescr; VAR OutCurrent: INTEGER);
(* Copy an item from file InFile to file OutFile and update
   current item values *)
VAR Done: BOOLEAN;
BEGIN
  OutCurrent := InCurrent;
  WriteWord(OutFile, OutCurrent);
  Done := ReadWord(InFile, InCurrent);
END CopyItem;

PROCEDURE CopyRun(InFile: FileDescr; F: FileArray; FileNumber: FileNo;
                  VAR Current: INTEGER; VAR CurrentF: CurrentArray);
(* Copy an ascending run from file InFile to file F[FileNumber] *)
BEGIN
  REPEAT
    CopyItem(InFile, Current, F[FileNumber], CurrentF[FileNumber])
  UNTIL Eof(InFile) OR (Current < CurrentF[FileNumber]);
END CopyRun;
```

However, it will be necessary to consider the possibility that two runs arriving consecutively on a given file may turn out to constitute a single run. In that case, we must keep track of the exact number of runs on each file, and process correctly such coincidental merges. This distribution algorithm will be implemented by local procedure InitialRuns, in procedure PolyphaseSort.

Once the initial distribution has been made and the original source file is empty, we can proceed to the actual polyphase merge sort. We will still use the Fibo and Diff arrays, but this time in the reverse order. The values in Fibo will be used to control the necessary repetitions, while the values in Diff will indicate the dummy runs. If $Diff_i > 0$, then its value is the number of dummy runs for file i. An actual merge is done for all files with $Diff_i = 0$, while $Diff_i$ is decreased for all other files (one dummy run is taken off). After each pass the files are rotated; this rotation will be done by using an array of indices. The following procedure implements the polyphase algorithm.

```
PROCEDURE PolyphaseSort(VAR InFile: FileDescr; Input: String;
                       VAR F: FileArray; Name: NameArray;
                       VAR ResultFile: FileNo);
(* Sorting of a file of integers, InFile named Input. Runs of various
   lengths are first distributed to files F[1],F[2], ... ,F[N-1].
   Sorting is done by combining (merging) these runs first onto F[N],
   and then the remaining runs from F[N],F[1], ... ,F[N-2] to F[N-1],
   and so on. Sorting is done in several such passes. The sorted
   integers will be in file F[ResultFile] when sorting is over. *)
  PROCEDURE InitialRuns(VAR Ideal, Diff: ArrFileNo;
                        VAR Level: CARDINAL);
  (* Initialize Ideal and Diff tables for level 1. Open files F[Index]
     and distribute initial runs from InFile *)
  VAR Index, File: FileNo;
      Current: INTEGER;
      CurrentElt: CurrentArray;       (* current elements of each File *)
      Done: BOOLEAN;                  (* read indicator *)
  BEGIN
    FOR Index := 1 TO N-1 DO     (* initialize and open all files *)
      Ideal[Index] := 1;
      Diff[Index] := 1;
      Rewrite(F[Index], Name[Index]);
    END; (* FOR *)
    Level := 1;
    File := 1;
    Ideal[N] := 0;
    Diff[N] := 0;
    Reset(InFile, Input); (* open input file and read first item *)
    Done := ReadWord(InFile, Current);
    REPEAT                 (* distribute initial N-1 runs *)
      ComputeDistribution(Diff, Ideal, File, Level);
      CopyRun(InFile, F, File, Current, CurrentElt);
    UNTIL Eof(InFile) OR (File = N-1);
    (* distribute rest of runs *)
    WHILE NOT Eof(InFile) DO
      ComputeDistribution(Diff,Ideal,File,Level);
      (* CurrentElt[File] is last item written to F[File] *)
      IF CurrentElt[File] <= Current THEN
        (* new run can be integrated with previous run *)
        CopyRun(InFile, F, File, Current, CurrentElt);
        IF Eof(InFile) THEN
          INC(Diff[File]);
        ELSE (* copy a new run anyhow *)
          CopyRun(InFile, F, File, Current, CurrentElt);
        END; (* IF *)
```

```
      ELSE (* new run *)
        CopyRun(InFile, F, File, Current, CurrentElt);
      END; (* IF *)
  END; (* WHILE *)
END InitialRuns;
PROCEDURE MergeRuns(VAR Ideal, Diff: ArrFileNo; VAR Level: CARDINAL;
                    VAR FileIndex: FileNoArr; VAR CurrentElt: CurrentArray);
(* Merge files FileIndex[1]...FileIndex[N-1] into File FileIndex[N] *)
VAR Index, MinIndex: FileNo;
    AvailIndex, Old: CARDINAL;
    Element, Min: INTEGER;
    AvailFiles: FileNoArr; (* indices of rotating files *)
BEGIN
  Old := Ideal[N-1];
  REPEAT (* merge one run *)
    AvailIndex := 0;
    FOR Index := 1 TO N-1 DO
      IF Diff[Index] > 0 THEN (* ignore dummy runs *)
        DEC(Diff[Index]);
      ELSE
        INC(AvailIndex);
        AvailFiles[AvailIndex] := FileIndex[Index]; (* keep available files *)
      END; (* IF *)
    END; (* FOR *)
    IF AvailIndex = 0 THEN
      INC(Diff[N]);
    ELSE
      (* merge first runs from files AvailFiles[1]...AvailFiles[AvailIndex]
         to file FileIndex[N] *)
      REPEAT
        Index := 1;
        MinIndex := 1;
        Min := CurrentElt[AvailFiles[1]];
        WHILE Index < AvailIndex DO (* look for minimum item *)
          INC(Index);
          Element := CurrentElt[AvailFiles[Index]];
          IF Element < Min THEN
            Min := Element;
            MinIndex := Index;
          END; (* IF *)
        END; (* WHILE *)
        CopyItem(F[AvailFiles[MinIndex]], CurrentElt[AvailFiles[MinIndex]],
                F[FileIndex[N]], CurrentElt[FileIndex[N]]);
        IF Eof(F[AvailFiles[MinIndex]]) OR
           (CurrentElt[AvailFiles[MinIndex]] < CurrentElt[FileIndex[N]]) THEN
          (* eliminate available File with exhausted run *)
          AvailFiles[MinIndex] := AvailFiles[AvailIndex];
          DEC(AvailIndex);
        END; (* IF *)
```

```
            UNTIL AvailIndex = 0;
        END; (* IF *)
        DEC(Old);
    UNTIL Old = 0;
  END MergeRuns;

VAR Index, FileIndexN: FileNo;
    Diffn, Old, Level: CARDINAL;
    Ideal,                          (* ideal distribution *)
    Diff: ArrFileNo;                (* differences between previous and current levels *)
    FileIndex: FileNoArr;           (* indices of rotating files *)
    CurrentElt: CurrentArray;       (* current elements of each File *)
    Done: BOOLEAN;                  (* read indicator *)
BEGIN
  InitialRuns(Ideal, Diff, Level);
  FOR Index := 1 TO N-1 DO          (* open initial files *)
    FileIndex[Index] := Index;
    Reset(F[Index], Name[Index]);
    Done := ReadWord(F[Index], CurrentElt[Index]);
  END; (* FOR *)
  FileIndex[N] := N;
  REPEAT     (* merge N-1 files into the Nth file *)
    Diff[N] := 0;
    Rewrite(F[FileIndex[N]], Name[FileIndex[N]]);
    MergeRuns(Ideal, Diff, Level, FileIndex, CurrentElt);
    (* Rotate files so that next step merges F[N], F[1], ... ,F[N-2] into F[N-1] *)
    Reset(F[FileIndex[N]], Name[FileIndex[N]]); (* newest file *)
    Done := ReadWord(F[FileIndex[N]], CurrentElt[FileIndex[N]]);
    FileIndexN := FileIndex[N];
    Diffn := Diff[N];
    Old := Ideal[N-1];
    FOR Index := N TO 2 BY -1 DO
      (* rotate files and compute distribution for previous level *)
      FileIndex[Index] := FileIndex[Index-1];
      Diff[Index] := Diff[Index-1];
      Ideal[Index] := Ideal[Index-1] - Old;
    END; (* FOR *)
    FileIndex[1] := FileIndexN;
    Diff[1] := Diffn;
    Ideal[1] := Old;
    (* Prepare next output File *)
    Rewrite(F[FileIndex[N]], Name[FileIndex[N]]);
    DEC(Level);
  UNTIL Level = 0;
  ResultFile := FileIndex[1];
END PolyphaseSort;
```

Local procedure InitialRuns initializes and opens all the files. It then distributes the first N − 1 runs into the first N − 1 files by calling ComputeDistribution and CopyRun. Then it distributes the remaining runs to the N − 1 files by repeatedly calling ComputeDistribution and either creating a new run in the file or, if possible, integrating that run with the previous one in the file.

Local procedure MergeRuns does the actual merging of runs from files 1 to N − 1 into file N by repeating the following process until all runs have been merged. The procedure checks array Diff for dummy runs that will be ignored and keeps track of the files actually involved in the merge process. The merging of runs is done by finding the smallest value of the runs and outputting it, using a call to CopyItem.

Procedure Polyphase calls InitialRuns to distribute the runs from the input file to the other N − 1 files. Then it repeatedly merges N − 1 files into the Nth file by calling MergeRuns, and rotating the files (new file 2 is old file 1, new file 3 is old file 2, . . . , new file N is old file N − 1 and, finally, new file 1 is old file N).

Polyphase sort is an efficient sort because, given N files, it always operates with an (N − 1) merge. The number of required passes is approximately equal to $\log_{N-1} n$, where N is the number of files, and n is the total number of elements to be sorted. Contrary to merge sort, polyphase sort does not move all n elements in one pass, but only a portion of them. For this reason, the complexity of the polyphase sort is still O(n log n), but better than merge sort. This algorithm can still be improved by using a heap for the distribution part (see problem 12 of the Exercises section).

11.3 Case Study: Implementing the Tournament Sort

Let's now take as an example the design of a new internal sorting algorithm.

Design

We will design a new sorting procedure based on what is known as the tournament-elimination technique.

Definition of the Problem The problem is to design a sorting procedure based on the tournament method. In a tournament players (or teams) are paired to play a match. The loser is eliminated from the tournament, while the winner moves up and plays against a new opponent. This process of elimination is repeated until only one player remains, who wins the tournament. Figure 11-8 illustrates this method.

We will design a tournament sort procedure that applies this method using a tree structure. (Note that Figure 11-8 represents a binary tree.) The procedure will take an unsorted array of elements and sort them in decreasing order on a given key field.

Design of a Solution The original data are kept in an array and will have to be inserted in a binary tree in order to build a tree similar to Figure 11-8. To represent our binary tree, we will use the technique used in the HeapSort procedure shown earlier in

Figure 11-8
A Tournament

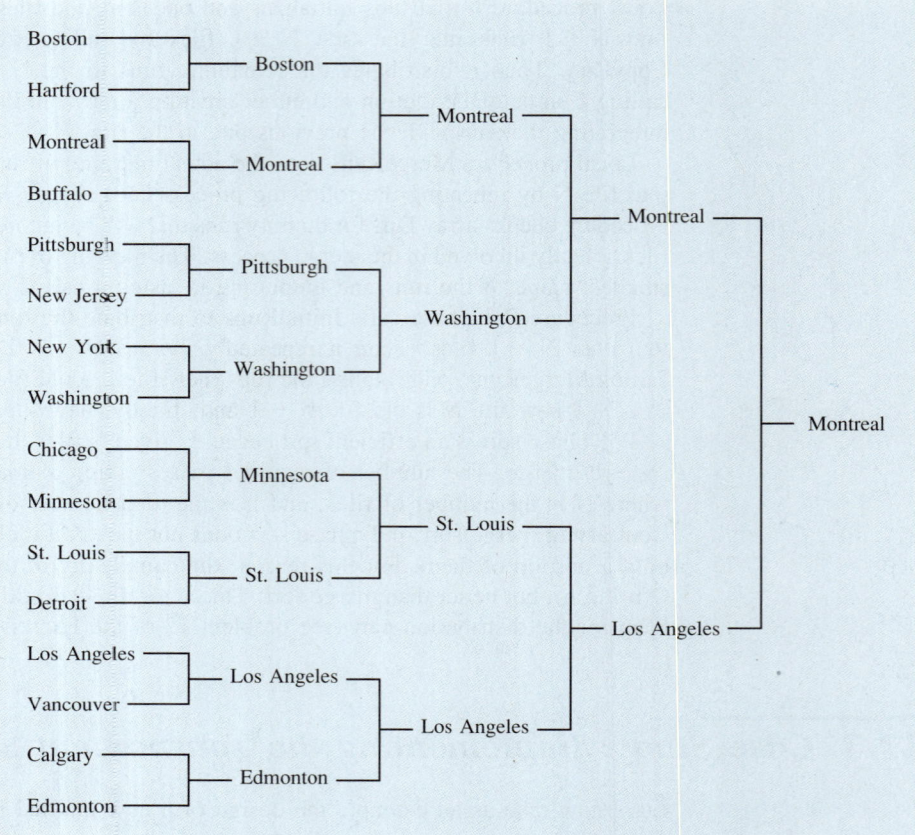

this chapter: the tree will be represented by an array. The leaves of the tree will contain the original data and the internal nodes will contain indices to that data, as illustrated by Figure 11-9.

In Figure 11-9, the boldface figures represent the data elements in the tree leaves, while the internal nodes are indices corresponding to the numbered leaves of the tree. The tree root, 12, indicates that element 543 is the largest element. The bottom of Figure 11-9 shows the array used to represent the tree with the actual indices going from 1 to 31, the leaves being in array elements 16 to 29. Note that we have added two dummy elements (30 and 31 with minimum values) in order to have a complete binary tree.

From this example we can see that our procedure will need to build the original tree from the unsorted data, then to repeatedly eliminate the largest element and readjust the tree structure. In order to build the tree we will need to start with the leaves and to construct the upper levels one by one up to the tree root. This leads us to the structure chart in Figure 11-10. We have included a comparison function for data items, since we have left to the user the definition of the type of data to be sorted.

11.3 Case Study: Implementing the Tournament Sort   433

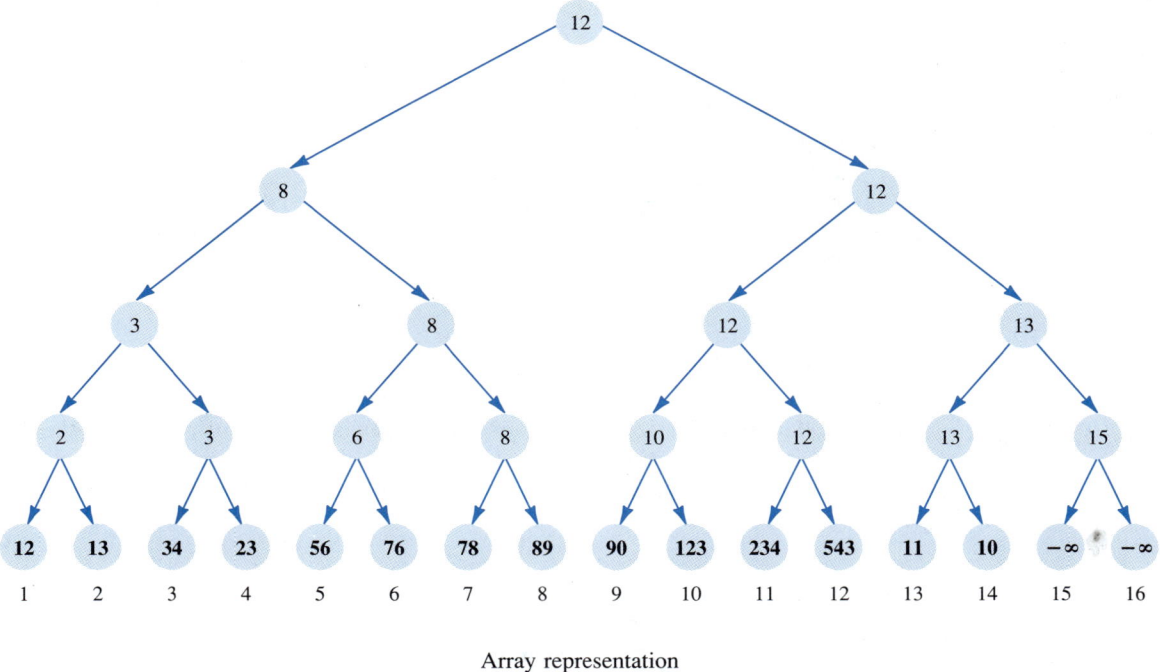

Figure 11-9   The Tournament Sort Tree

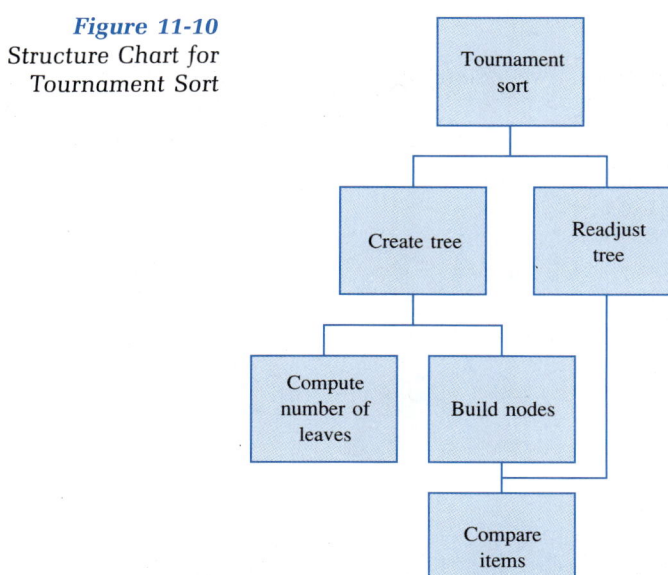

Figure 11-10
Structure Chart for
Tournament Sort

Refine the Solution   We can develop the pseudocode solution from our structure chart.

```
Tournament Sort
    Create tree from unsorted data
    For all data items
        Copy root element to sorted array
        Readjust tree
    End for
End Tournament Sort
```

The tree creation algorithm must copy the unsorted data into the leaves of the tree. To do this it must first compute the number of leaves needed to accommodate the unsorted data, and then the tree size. (The number of leaves is a power of two, since the tree must be complete.) The tree creation algorithm fills the tree leaves with data, making sure to add the correct number of dummy elements, with minimum values, in the extra leaves.

```
Create Tree
    Compute the number of leaves and the tree size
    Pad the unsorted array with dummy elements
    Copy unsorted data in the tree leaves
    Build first level of internal nodes above the leaves
    For all levels up to the root
        Build a level of internal nodes above the last level
    End for
End Create Tree
```

To compute the number of leaves, we look for the first power of two greater than the number of data elements.

```
Compute Number of Leaves
    Set Number of Leaves to 1
    Repeat
        Multiply Number of leaves by 2
        Divide Number of Items by 2
    Until Number of Items is zero
End Compute Number of Leaves
```

Building a new level of internal nodes is a simple process.

> **Build Nodes**
>   For all element pairs in level
>   Set parent node to index of largest element of the pair
>   End for
> End Build Nodes

To readjust the tree after a leaf has been taken off, first we replace that leaf's parent with the other child, and then we move up the tree, reassigning the parent index based on the values associated with the children.

> **Readjust Tree**
>   Replace parent index by other element in pair
>   For all upper levels up to root
>   Reassign parent index based on values associated with children
>   End for
> End Readjust Tree

Develop a Testing Strategy As we have seen in Chapter 3, in testing sorting procedures it is important to consider extreme cases: empty array, full array, data without duplicate values, data with duplicate values, array already sorted, array already sorted in reverse order, random array. For our Tournament Sort procedure, we will assume that the original array has at least one element, and our test cases will include the following:

1. An array in which all elements have the same value
2. An array of random data with no duplicates
3. An array of random data with some duplicates
4. An array in which the data are already sorted
5. An array in which the data are initially sorted in reverse order
6. An array whose number of elements is a power of 2
7. An array whose number of elements is not a power of two
8. An array of one element
9. A full array

Case 1 is easy to cover. Cases 6 and 7 can be combined with other cases. To illustrate case 2, we can use a testing program that will generate random entries in the array before calling the Tournament Sort procedure. Once the results from that sort have been checked, they can be used as data for case 4. We can combine case 9 with one of the previous cases. Our test data sets will be built to cover the following cases:

Data set 1: cases 1 and 7
Data set 2: cases 2 and 6
Data set 3: cases 3 and 6

Data set 4: cases 4 and 7 and 9
Data set 5: cases 5 and 7
Data set 6: case 8

Implementation

The implementation will be simple, as we only have to implement a sorting procedure. The procedure will use the following constants and types, type ItemType and procedure Greater being user-defined.

```
CONST MaxItem = 1000;    (* The size of array to store items *)
      Marker = MIN(INTEGER);

TYPE UnSortedType = ARRAY [0..MaxItem-1] OF ItemType;
     NodeType = RECORD
                    Index: CARDINAL;
                    Value: ItemType;
                END;
     TreeType = ARRAY [1..2*MaxItem-1] OF NodeType;
```

In the tree, field Index will be used only by internal nodes, while field Value will be used only by leaf nodes.

Code and Test the Program   The following Modula-2 procedure follows the pseudocode defined earlier.

```
PROCEDURE TournamentSort(VAR Table: ARRAY OF ItemType;
                        NumberOfItems: CARDINAL);
(* Apply tournament sort to Table array; Table contains unsorted
   data when call is made, and sorted data at end of procedure.
   The Tree is initialized with the Table data, the largest
   element is output, the tree is readjusted, and the process is
   repeated until the tree is empty. *)

  PROCEDURE ComputeNumberOfLeaves(NumberOfItems: CARDINAL;
                                  VAR NumberOfLeaves: CARDINAL);
  (* Compute number of leaves of the minimum tree able to store
     NumberOfItems elements *)
  BEGIN
    NumberOfLeaves := 1;
    REPEAT
      NumberOfLeaves := NumberOfLeaves * 2;
      NumberOfItems := NumberOfItems DIV 2;
    UNTIL NumberOfItems = 0;
  END ComputeNumberOfLeaves;
```

```
PROCEDURE BuildNodes(VAR Tree: TreeType; Leaf: BOOLEAN;
                    Left, Right: CARDINAL);
(* Build the parent nodes of a level of Tree nodes.
   The leaf nodes contain actual element values,
   while the internal nodes contain indices to other
   Tree nodes *)
VAR Position: CARDINAL;

BEGIN
  IF Leaf THEN     (* compare leaf level *)
    FOR Position := Left TO Right BY 2 DO
      IF Greater(Tree[Position].Value,Tree[Position+1].Value) THEN
        Tree[Position DIV 2].Index := Position;
      ELSE
        Tree[Position DIV 2].Index := Position+1;
      END; (* IF *)
    END; (* FOR *)
  ELSE    (* compare nonleaf level *)
    FOR Position := Left TO Right BY 2 DO
      IF Greater(Tree[Tree[Position].Index].Value,
                 Tree[Tree[Position+1].Index].Value) THEN
        Tree[Position DIV 2] := Tree[Position];
      ELSE
        Tree[Position DIV 2] := Tree[Position+1];
      END; (* IF *)
    END; (* FOR *)
  END; (* IF *)
END BuildNodes;

PROCEDURE CreateTree(VAR Tree: TreeType; NumberOfItems: CARDINAL;
                     UnSorted: ARRAY OF ItemType);
(* Compute the number of leaves and the Tree size. Copy
   elements from UnSorted array into the Tree leaves. Then
   build the Tree from the leaves up to the root. *)
CONST Leaves = TRUE;
VAR Position, ItemNumber, NumberOfLeaves, TreeSize: CARDINAL;

BEGIN
  ComputeNumberOfLeaves(NumberOfItems, NumberOfLeaves);
  TreeSize := NumberOfLeaves * 2 -1;
  Position := NumberOfItems ;
  WHILE Position <= NumberOfLeaves-1 DO (* fill with markers *)
    UnSorted[Position] := Marker;
    INC(Position);
  END; (* WHILE *)
```

```
      Position := NumberOfLeaves;        (* copy data array in tree leaves *)
      FOR ItemNumber := 0 TO NumberOfLeaves-1 DO
        Tree[Position].Value := UnSorted[ItemNumber];
        Tree[Position].Index := 0;
        INC(Position);
      END; (* FOR *)
      (* build first level of nodes above leaves *)
      BuildNodes(Tree, Leaves, NumberOfLeaves, TreeSize-1);
      ItemNumber := NumberOfLeaves;
      WHILE ItemNumber > 1 DO (* build next level of nodes *)
        BuildNodes(Tree, NOT Leaves, ItemNumber DIV 2, ItemNumber-2);
        ItemNumber := ItemNumber DIV 2;
      END; (* WHILE *)
    END CreateTree;

    PROCEDURE ReadjustTree(VAR Tree: TreeType; Position: CARDINAL);
    (* Element at Position has just been deleted; readjust Tree upper
       nodes by bringing neighbor of deleted node up *)

    VAR Place: CARDINAL;

    BEGIN
      IF (Position MOD 2) = 0 THEN                  (* replace parent by *)
        Tree[Position DIV 2].Index := Position+1; (*   right neighbor    *)
      ELSE                                          (*          or       *)
        Tree[Position DIV 2].Index := Position-1; (*    left neighbor    *)
      END; (* IF *)
      Place := Position DIV 2;
      WHILE Place > 1 DO
        (* bring index of largest value up by comparing
           neighbor (even-odd) pairs *)
        IF (Place MOD 2) = 0 THEN       (* Place even, Place+1 odd *)
          IF Greater(Tree[Tree[Place].Index].Value,
                     Tree[Tree[Place+1].Index].Value) THEN
            Tree[Place DIV 2].Index := Tree[Place].Index;
          ELSE
            Tree[Place DIV 2].Index := Tree[Place+1].Index;
          END; (* IF *)
        ELSE                            (* Place-1 even, Place odd *)
          IF Greater(Tree[Tree[Place-1].Index].Value,
                     Tree[Tree[Place].Index].Value) THEN
            Tree[Place DIV 2].Index := Tree[Place-1].Index;
          ELSE
            Tree[Place DIV 2].Index := Tree[Place].Index;
          END; (* IF *)
        END; (* IF *)
        Place := Place DIV 2;           (* go up the tree *)
      END;        (* WHILE *)
    END ReadjustTree;
```

```
VAR ItemNumber : CARDINAL;
    Position : INTEGER;
    Tree: TreeType;
BEGIN (* TournamentSort *)
  CreateTree(Tree, NumberOfItems, Table);
  FOR ItemNumber := 0 TO NumberOfItems-1 DO
    (* copy tree element into Table array *)
    Position := Tree[1].Index;
    Table[ItemNumber] := Tree[Position].Value;
    Tree[Position].Value := Marker; (* delete copied item *)
    ReadjustTree(Tree, Position);
  END; (* FOR *)
END TournamentSort;
```

The code for procedure TournamentSort is very similar to its pseudocode. The same is true of local procedure ComputeNumberOfLeaves. Procedure CreateTree is not very different from its pseudocode, although a couple of pseudocode lines have been expanded into loops.

Procedure BuildNodes has been divided into two parts: the first part deals with the building of the first level of internal nodes above the leaves, while the second part deals with the building of a new level of internal nodes above a level of internal nodes. This building procedure is necessary because the leaves comprise data values, while internal nodes comprise only indices to the leaves. The differences can be seen in two places: at the point at which the comparison procedure is called directly on the values of the leaves or at the point it is called indirectly on the leaf values indicated by the internal node index. Also, the index kept in the new parent nodes is either the explicit leaf index or the index provided by the internal nodes.

Procedure ReadjustTree follows the model of its pseudocode, but includes more details. Pairs of elements in the tree are defined by a pair of even–odd indices (for instance, 2–3, 8–9, 12–13). The procedure checks the index of the deleted element: if it is even, its neighbor is indicated by the next odd index; if it is odd, its neighbor's index is the preceding even index. Once the neighbor is identified, it replaces the deleted element in the parent node. The same technique is used as the procedure goes up in the tree.

The procedure was called on the data sets identified in the preceding section; in each case it returned an ordered array.

To determine the time complexity of procedure TournamentSort, we must consider two stages. The first stage is the initial building of the binary tree: after copying the n unsorted elements, procedure BuildNodes is called once for each level of the tree. We know there are $\log_2 n$ such levels, and in procedure BuildNodes a loop is executed n/4 times during the first call, n/8 times the second call, and so on. We can conclude that the time complexity of the building of the tree is no more than O(n log n). The second stage copies the n elements from the tree to the sorted array. Each time an element is copied, procedure ReadjustTree is called; this procedure follows a path going from the leaf to the tree root. We know the length of such a path is $\log_2 n$. Thus the complexity of the second stage is also $O(n \log n)$. The time complexity of TournamentSort is $O(n \log n)$, which makes it an efficient sort.

However, we can easily see that procedure HeapSort will have a better efficiency, because most of the time in HeapSort, procedure SiftDown does not follow the whole path from the root to a leaf—an element will often find its place in an internal node. In contrast, in procedure TournamentSort, the paths from leaf to root are completed all the time.

The space complexity of procedure TournamentSort requires that we keep two copies of the data, one in the data array (unsorted or sorted), and one in the binary tree. This space requirement is another drawback compared to procedure HeapSort. However, TournamentSort works by copying indices rather than data, a technique that may be beneficial for large data items.

Complete the Documentation Since we have only developed one procedure, it is not deemed necessary to provide a user's manual. However, the documentation will always include a discussion of some of the design decisions, as well as the various structure charts and example figures, and all the test data and the test results.

Summary

Shell sort has complexity $O(n^{1.2})$, a complexity that is good for small n but not as good as $O(n \log n)$ for large n. Heapsort and tournament sort have a time complexity of $O(n \log n)$, which is very good. It can be shown that any sort based solely on the comparison of keys can, in general, be no better than $O(n \log n)$. Radix sort involves processing keys in other ways, such as forming 26 bins for the letters of the alphabet, and so it can reduce the theoretical time complexity to $O(n)$.

External sorting was also introduced and two examples were given: merge sort and polyphase sort. Both external sorts were efficient, with a complexity of $O(n \log n)$, but required more complicated algorithms and much more space for data storage.

■ Exercises

1. Given the following 20 integers: 472, 623, 161, 322, 767, 278, 624, 310, 139, 757, 456, 268, 790, 66, 365, 222, 754, 116, 193, 970, sort them showing each pass using:
   (a) ShellSort
   (b) HeapSort
   (c) RadixSort

2. Figure 11-7 shows an example of polyphase sorting in which each pass has a maximum order merge, i.e., four files are merged at each pass. Build a table that will show the number of initial runs for polyphase sorting necessary for every pass to have a maximum order merge (like the first line of Figure 11-7), and show this for orders up to and including 10.

3. Show that if an array is partially ordered using a gap g in the Shell sort, it remains partially sorted on that gap after it is partially sorted on another smaller gap value.

4. Modify procedure TournamentSort so that it can sort in ascending as well as descending order, as procedures ShellSort and HeapSort do.

■ Programming Problems

5. Write and test a procedure RadixSort that applies the radix sort method to an array of elements using linked list techniques to minimize the data movements. The data will be copied in an array of elements with a next field. Sorting will link elements in a number of lists. (To accelerate processing, keep a list head for concatenating the lists at the end of each pass and a list tail for inserting elements during a pass.)

6. Modify the internal sort procedure ShellSort so that it computes the number of moves and the number of comparisons done. Generate sequences of random numbers, sort these, and plot the number of moves and of comparisons as a function of n. Draw your own conclusions.

7. Repeat problem 6 for HeapSort.

8. Modify procedure MergeSort so that it does what is called a "natural merge." This sort will merge any two ordered runs of lengths L_1 and L_2, into a single run of length $L_1 + L_2$. So at any time, the two longest possible runs will be merged, and the method will take advantage of data that are already partially sorted.

9. Modify the MergeSort procedure so that, instead of always merging runs from two files into a third, it uses an N-way merge scheme. The runs are first equally distributed on N files; then each pass merges them onto N other files, and the process continues by continually reversing the input and output files.

*10. The Cascade sort is a sorting method similar to the polyphase sort. Write a Cascade procedure to implement this algorithm. With six files, the Cascade sort starts with a perfect distribution on $f_1, \ldots, f_5$, and performs a five-way merge onto f_6, until f_5 is empty. Then, without using f_6, Cascade performs a four-way merge onto f_5, then a three-way merge onto f_4, a two-way merge onto f_3, and a copy from f_1 to f_2. The next pass is similar and starts with a five-way merge onto f_1, etc. Even though it uses some copy operations and does not involve all files all the time, the Cascade algorithm is superior to polyphase sorting for very large files and for a number of files greater than 6.

11. Write and test a procedure to merge n ordered input files into a single output file using a heap. The files are in ascending order, and each element of the heap will comprise two pieces of data: a file number and a key value used to order the data. Initially a value is read from each input file and placed in the heap, along with its file number. The smallest value is then output. The next value is read from the corresponding file, and then sifted down the heap. This process is repeated until all input files are exhausted.

12. Use the procedure from problem 11 for the distribution part of the polyphase sort.

Note: Problems marked with an asterisk (*) have a higher level of difficulty.

Tables

INTRODUCTION

How best to store, retrieve, and delete specific information from a large mass of data is not a new problem. Even before computers existed, information was organized for efficient manipulation and presentation. Although searching for information may appear simple, the speed with which it can be done will determine whether a method is practical or not. Since the choice of data structures influences algorithm design and efficiency, this chapter will examine the Table and its various implementations with respect to searching efficiency. Searching a table normally involves comparing record keys to a given search key with the intent of finding a record with that search key or determining that no such record is present in the table.

In this chapter we will introduce the abstract data type Table as well as some of its applications. Then we will examine some of the possible implementations for it, in relation to various searching algorithms.

12.1 Abstraction: The Table

A *table* can be simply defined as a set of pairs of the form (x, F(x)) for some function F and some finite domain. For instance, Figure 12-1 illustrates the table concept with function sine (where x is in degrees).

In computer science, a table is a group of elements, usually called records (collections of information). Associated with each record is a key, which is used to differentiate among various records. Oftentimes, a key is chosen so as to identify a particular record uniquely in a table, but this is not always the case.

The abstract data type Table can be defined as a set of records of a given record type, with keys of a given key type. The basic operations needed for a table are defined as part of the following Tables definition module.

Figure 12-1
Sine Function Table

x	F(x)
0.0	0.00000
0.1	0.00175
0.2	0.00349
0.3	0.00524
0.4	0.00698
0.5	0.00873
0.6	0.01047
0.7	0.01222
0.8	0.01396
0.9	0.01571
1.0	0.01745

```
DEFINITION MODULE Tables;
FROM TableElements IMPORT KeyType, ElementType;

TYPE Table;

PROCEDURE Create(VAR T: Table);
(* Create a new table T.
   Pre-condition:   table T does not exist
   Post-condition:  table T exists and is empty *)
PROCEDURE Search(T: Table; Key: KeyType; VAR Elt: ElementType;
                 VAR Found: BOOLEAN);
(* Search table T for element with Key. If an element
   is found in table then return it in Elt and Found
   is True, otherwise Found is False.
   Pre-condition:   table T exists
   Post-condition:  Found' is False if Key not in T
                    or Found' is true and
                    Elt' = table T element with Key *)
```

```
PROCEDURE Insert(VAR T: Table; Elt: ElementType;
                 VAR Success: BOOLEAN);
(* Insert element Elt in table T. Success is true if
   insertion was successful, false otherwise.
   Pre-condition:   table T exists
   Post-condition:  Success' is True and table T includes Elt
                    or Success' is False and table T was not changed *)
PROCEDURE Delete(VAR T: Table; Key: KeyType;
                 VAR Success: BOOLEAN);
(* Delete element with Key from table T. If element
   was successfully deleted Success is set to True,
   otherwise it is set to False.
   Pre-condition:   table T exists
   Post-condition:  Success' is True and table T does not include Key
                    or Success' is False and table T was not changed *)
PROCEDURE DisplayKeys(T: Table);
(* Display all the keys of table T elements.
   Pre-condition:   table T exists
   Post-condition:  all keys of elements present in
                    table T are displayed *)
END Tables.
```

We should note here that no relation is presumed to exist among the table elements; that is, there are no assumptions about ordering of the elements.

12.2 Applications

Tables are used in a great many applications: in compilers, in operating systems, in assemblers, in databases, in telecommunication systems, in management systems, in information systems, and so forth. Tables are defined in a wide variety of ways; however, the operations are similar on all tables and independent of the chosen representation. Consequently, the abstract data type we just defined can be used in most applications.

A Name Server

The large variety of applications for tables makes it difficult to choose one or two that can be truly representative of all applications. We will introduce the name server application. A name server is usually a small system which, given a name, returns some information associated with the name. For instance, given a user's identification, a name server might return the corresponding user's name, or full address, or simply telephone number. Let's develop such a name server using the abstract data type Tables we defined earlier and based on the element type declaration from the TableElements module:

```
TYPE KeyType = String;
     ElementType = RECORD
                      Key: KeyType;
                      Name: String;
                      Address: String;
                      Password: String;
                      Telephone: String;
                   END;
```

Our name server will provide the user with operations that will check if a user exists, get the user's name, address, telephone number, check a user's password, and eliminate a user from the user table. The following definition module gives a more precise definition of all operations.

```
DEFINITION MODULE NameServer;
FROM TableElements IMPORT KeyType, ElementType;
FROM Strings IMPORT String;

PROCEDURE IsUser(Id: KeyType): BOOLEAN;
(* Return True if Id identifies an existing user *)

PROCEDURE GetName(Id: KeyType; VAR Name: String;
                  VAR Found: BOOLEAN);
(* If Id identifies an existing user then Found' = True
   and Name' = user's name, else Found' = False *)

PROCEDURE ValidPassword(Id: KeyType; Password: String): BOOLEAN;
(* Return True if Id identifies an existing user
   with password Password *)

PROCEDURE GetPhone(Id: KeyType; VAR Phone: String;
                   VAR Found: BOOLEAN);
(* If Id identifies an existing user then Found' = True
   and Phone' = user's phone number else Found' = False *)

PROCEDURE GetAddress(Id: KeyType; VAR Address: String;
                     VAR Found: BOOLEAN);
(* If Id identifies an existing user then Found' = True
   and Address' = user's address else Found' = False *)

PROCEDURE Eliminate(Id: KeyType): BOOLEAN;
(* Eliminate user identified by Id from the users table.
   Return True if user has been eliminated, False otherwise *)

END NameServer.
```

Figure 12-2 shows the modular diagram of the name server application. The user will write a program calling on the NameServer module.

The corresponding NameServer implementation module is based on our ADT Table and is shown on the following page.

12.2 Applications   447

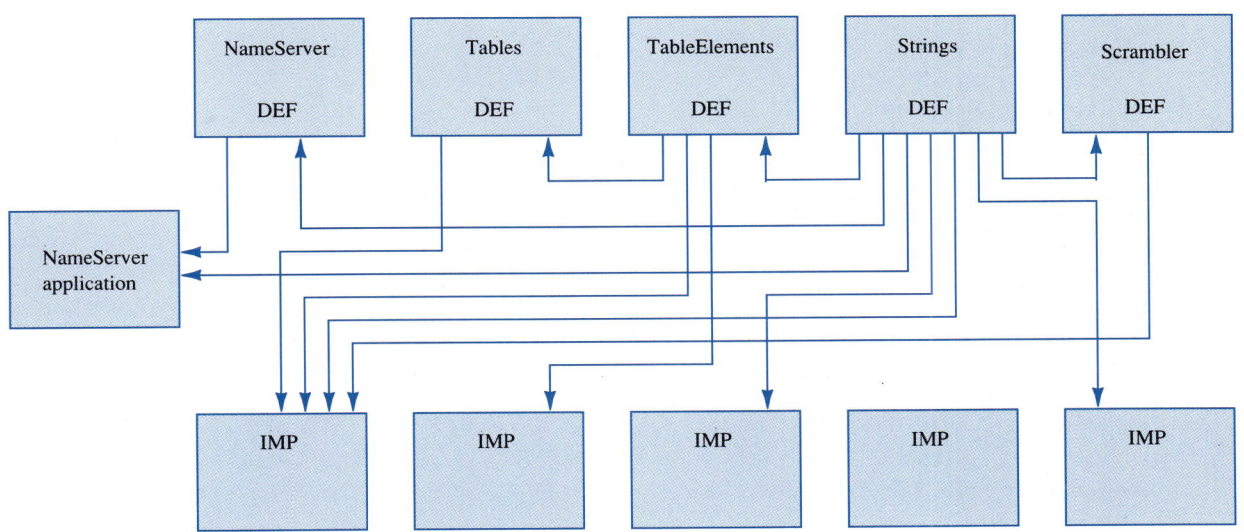

Figure 12-2 Modular Diagram of the Name Server Application

```
IMPLEMENTATION MODULE NameServer;
FROM TableElements IMPORT KeyType, ElementType, InitElement;
FROM Strings IMPORT String, Assign, StringEqual, InitString,
                    InputString, AssignConst;
FROM Tables IMPORT Search, Table, Create, Insert, DisplayKeys, Delete;
FROM Scrambler IMPORT Scramble;
FROM InOut IMPORT OpenInput, CloseInput, WriteString, ReadString;

VAR UserTable: Table;

PROCEDURE Initialize(VAR NameTable: Table);
VAR Elt: ElementType;
    Done: BOOLEAN;
    EndString: String;
BEGIN
  InitElement(Elt);
  InitString(EndString);
  WriteString("Initializing user table...");
  OpenInput("dat");
  AssignConst(EndString, "END");
```

```
      LOOP
        InputString(Elt.Key);
        IF StringEqual(Elt.Key, EndString) THEN EXIT END;
        InputString(Elt.Name);
        InputString(Elt.Address);
        InputString(Elt.Telephone);
        InputString(Elt.Password);
        Scramble(Elt.Password);
        Insert(NameTable, Elt, Done);
      END; (* LOOP *)
      CloseInput;
    END Initialize;

    PROCEDURE IsUser(Id: KeyType): BOOLEAN;
    VAR Elt: ElementType;
        Done: BOOLEAN;
    BEGIN
      Search(UserTable, Id, Elt, Done);
      RETURN Done;
    END IsUser;

    PROCEDURE GetName(Id: KeyType; VAR Name: String;
                     VAR Found: BOOLEAN);
    (* Get user name *)
    VAR Elt: ElementType;
    BEGIN
      Search(UserTable, Id, Elt, Found);
      IF Found THEN
        Assign(Name, Elt.Name);
      ELSE
        AssignConst(Name, "    ");
      END; (* IF *)
    END GetName;

    PROCEDURE ValidPassword(Id: KeyType; Password: String): BOOLEAN;
    VAR Elt: ElementType;
        Done: BOOLEAN;
    BEGIN
      Scramble(Password);
      Search(UserTable, Id, Elt, Done);
      RETURN Done AND
             StringEqual(Password, Elt.Password);
    END ValidPassword;
```

```
PROCEDURE GetPhone(Id: KeyType; VAR Phone: String;
                   VAR Found: BOOLEAN);
(* Get user phone number *)
VAR Elt: ElementType;
BEGIN
  Search(UserTable, Id, Elt, Found);
  IF Found THEN
    Assign(Phone, Elt.Telephone);
  ELSE
    AssignConst(Phone, "     ");
  END; (* IF *)
END GetPhone;

PROCEDURE GetAddress(Id: KeyType; VAR Address: String;
                     VAR Found: BOOLEAN);
(* Get user address *)
VAR Elt: ElementType;
BEGIN
  Search(UserTable, Id, Elt, Found);
  IF Found THEN
    Assign(Address, Elt.Address);
  ELSE
    AssignConst(Address, "     ");
  END; (* IF *)
END GetAddress;

PROCEDURE Eliminate(Id: KeyType): BOOLEAN;
VAR OK: BOOLEAN;
    Password: String;
BEGIN
  WriteString("Give Password of user you want to eliminate: ");
  InitString(Password);
  InputString(Password);
  IF ValidPassword(Id, Password) THEN
    Delete(UserTable, Id, OK);
    DisplayKeys(UserTable);
  ELSE
    OK := FALSE;
  END; (* IF *)
  RETURN OK;
END Eliminate;

BEGIN
  Create(UserTable);
  Initialize(UserTable);
  DisplayKeys(UserTable);
END NameServer.
```

Examining the implementation of the various operations shows that it has been very simple to define them using the Tables primitives. We have also included an automatic table initialization procedure, which is invoked only once at module import time, as we have not deemed it necessary to give it to the user. The data read are directly stored in the user's table, except for the password, which is stored in scrambled form using an external Scramble routine imported from module Scrambler. We will discuss data encryption in the next chapter, Section 13.2.

```
DEFINITION MODULE Scrambler;
FROM Strings IMPORT String;

PROCEDURE Scramble(VAR S: String);
(* Scramble string S for ciphered representation *)

END Scrambler.
```

This example illustrates one possible application of the ADT Table. We could design a different name server adapted to another set of rules for accessing and storing data, but conceptually, the name server would not change much.

Another type of widely used application for tables is the "symbol table." Compilers, loaders, assemblers, and lexical analyzers use symbol tables to store associations between names and values. Names are usually identifiers, operation codes, or keywords, while values may be single items or multiple-value items such as types, relative addresses, pointers, or sizes. In general, we can view a symbol table as a set of n-tuples of the form:

(Id, v_1, v_2, . . . , v_n)

where Id is a name, where v_i represents values associated with the name, and where n is a constant. The names, which are used to access the table elements, must be unique. We can see that symbol tables are not very different from name servers. The organization chosen for representing symbol tables will depend heavily on the intended use of the table. Some symbol tables might be static and ordered—such as a keywords table in a compiler or an operation codes table in an assembler. Some symbol tables might be dynamic—such as user-defined identifier tables in compilers. Static tables have a fixed size; they usually do not allow insertion or deletion operations, and allow only look-up operations. On the other hand, dynamic tables allow for insertions and deletions of elements. Table organization is part of implementation, but as we saw briefly here, we will also have to consider the impact of organization on system performance as we cover table implementations.

12.3 Implementations

Tables can be represented in a number of ways, using some of the data structures presented earlier. A table can be represented by an array of records, as in the following Tables implementation module. A table may also be represented by a linear list (using either the array representation or the dynamic representation) or by a binary tree. Algorithms for implementation of the various table operations will vary, depending on the chosen table representation. However, we can already see that table insertion and deletion algorithms, for instance, will be very similar to insertion and deletion algorithms used for the underlying representation. Let's look now at an example of the Tables implementation module that uses the following user-defined table elements.

```
DEFINITION MODULE TableElements;
FROM Strings IMPORT String;

TYPE KeyType = String;
     ElementType = RECORD
                      Key: KeyType;
                      Name: String;
                      Address: String;
                      Password: String;
                      Telephone: String;
                   END;

PROCEDURE WriteKey(Key: KeyType);
(* Display Key value *)

PROCEDURE InitElement(VAR Elt: ElementType);
(* Initialize all fields of Elt *)

PROCEDURE AssignElement(VAR Dest: ElementType; Source: ElementType);
(* Assign Dest := Source *)

PROCEDURE CompareKeys(Key1, Key2: KeyType): INTEGER;
(* Return 1 if Key1 > Key2, 0 if Key1 = Key2, -1 if Key1 < Key2 *)

END TableElements.
```

Using the above TableElements definition module, we define the Tables implementation module.

```
IMPLEMENTATION MODULE Tables;
FROM TableElements IMPORT KeyType, ElementType, WriteKey,
                          InitElement, AssignElement, CompareKeys;
FROM Storage IMPORT ALLOCATE;
FROM InOut IMPORT WriteLn;

CONST TableSize = 25;
TYPE Table = POINTER TO RecordType;
     IndexType = [1..TableSize];
     RecordType = RECORD
                     NumberOfElements: CARDINAL;
                     Elements: ARRAY IndexType OF ElementType;
                  END;
```

```
PROCEDURE Create(VAR T: Table);
(* Create table T *)
VAR Index: IndexType;
BEGIN
  ALLOCATE(T, SIZE(RecordType));
  FOR Index := 1 TO TableSize DO   (* set elements to empty *)
    InitElement(T^.Elements[Index]);
  END; (* FOR *)
  T^.NumberOfElements := 0;         (* no elements *)
END Create;

PROCEDURE Search(T: Table; Key: KeyType;
                 VAR Elt: ElementType;
                 VAR Found:   BOOLEAN);
(* Search table T for element with Key *)
VAR Index: IndexType;
BEGIN
  Index := 1;
  WHILE (Index <= T^.NumberOfElements)
        AND (CompareKeys(Key, T^.Elements[Index].Key) = 1) DO
    INC(Index);              (* Key not in positions 1..Index *)
  END; (* WHILE *)
  IF (Index <= T^.NumberOfElements) AND
        (CompareKeys(Key, T^.Elements[Index].Key) = 0) THEN   (* found *)
    AssignElement(Elt, T^.Elements[Index]);
    Found := TRUE;
  ELSE          (* not in table *)
    Found := FALSE;
  END; (* IF *)
END Search;

PROCEDURE Insert(VAR T: Table; Elt: ElementType;
                 VAR Success: BOOLEAN);
(* Insert element Elt in table T *)
VAR Index, Place: IndexType;
BEGIN    (* keep T ordered *)
  Index := 1;
  WHILE (Index <= T^.NumberOfElements) AND
        (CompareKeys(Elt.Key, T^.Elements[Index].Key) = 1) DO
    INC(Index);           (* Elt.Key not in positions 1..Index *)
  END; (* WHILE *)
  (* Index indicates where Elt.Key should be placed *)
  IF (CompareKeys(Elt.Key, T^.Elements[Index].Key) # 0) AND
     (T^.NumberOfElements < TableSize) THEN (* insert *)
    FOR Place := T^.NumberOfElements TO Index BY -1 DO (* make room *)
      T^.Elements[Place+1] :=T^.Elements[Place];
    END; (* FOR *)
    AssignElement(T^.Elements[Index], Elt);
    INC(T^.NumberOfElements);
    Success := TRUE;
```

```
    ELSE
      Success := FALSE;   (* Key already present *)
    END; (* IF *)
  END Insert;

  PROCEDURE Delete(VAR T: Table; Key: KeyType;
                   VAR Success: BOOLEAN);
  (* Delete element with Key from table T *)
  VAR Index, Place: IndexType;
  BEGIN
    Index := 1;
    WHILE (Index <= T^.NumberOfElements) AND
          (CompareKeys(Key, T^.Elements[Index].Key) = 1) DO
      INC(Index);          (* find Key position in table *)
    END; (* WHILE *)
    IF (CompareKeys(Key, T^.Elements[Index].Key) = 0) THEN
      FOR Place := Index TO T^.NumberOfElements-1 DO
        (* delete by compacting table *)
        T^.Elements[Place] := T^.Elements[Place+1];
      END; (* FOR *)
      DEC(T^.NumberOfElements);
      Success := TRUE;
    ELSE
      Success := FALSE;   (* element is not present *)
    END; (* IF *)
  END Delete;

  PROCEDURE DisplayKeys(T: Table);
  VAR Index: IndexType;
  BEGIN
    FOR Index := 1 TO T^.NumberOfElements DO    (* display keys *)
      WriteKey(T^.Elements[Index].Key); WriteLn;
    END; (* FOR *)
  END DisplayKeys;

END Tables.
```

The Tables implementation module is straightforward. Table is an opaque type, and this forces us to use a pointer to the record structure. There we use an array to hold the table elements, and a cardinal for the number of elements in the table. The Create procedure allocates space for the table structure, all the elements are initialized using procedure InitElement imported from the TableElements module, and the count is set to zero.

All the following procedures assume that the elements in the table are stored in increasing order of their keys. They also use procedures CompareKeys and AssignElement imported from the TableElements module. Procedure Search examines sequentially the table elements until the key is found, or the end of the table is reached. Once the key is found in the table, information associated with this key is returned. Procedure Insert searches the table sequentially until either the key is found, in which case nothing is done, or the correct position for insertion is found. In this case, the rest of the table is moved down one position, and the new element is inserted. Procedure Delete follows a pattern similar to Insert: the position of the key is found, then the elements of the table are moved up one position. Procedure DisplayKeys will display the keys kept in the table in the order they are stored, using procedure WriteKey imported from the TableElements module.

The search operation is the main operation for tables and its efficiency is important. Implementations of the search algorithm are based on the type of table used. We can consider three types of tables: unordered, ordered, and hash tables.

Searching Tables

Unordered Tables The simplest form of a table is an unordered table into which elements can be added very easily. Such tables can be organized either as arrays or as linear lists. Insertion and deletion algorithms will be very similar to the insertion and deletion algorithms related to the chosen representation. For such cases, the searching operation will be implemented using the simplest form of a search: the sequential search as seen in Chapter 3. Whatever the keys distribution, sequential search algorithms will always be $O(n)$, although the performance can be much improved if the most frequently used keys are placed at the front of the table.

Ordered Tables The simplest and most efficient method of searching an ordered sequential table is the binary search. The search key is compared to the middle element of the table. If the keys match, then the search is over; otherwise, the same method is applied either to the first half or to the second half of the table. We have seen an implementation of this algorithm in Chapter 3.

Fibonacci Search A Fibonacci search is a method of searching similar to the binary search, based on the Fibonacci numbers:

$$F(0) = 0$$
$$F(1) = 1$$
$$F(n) = F(n-1) + F(n-2) \quad \text{for } n \geq 2$$

If the table contains $F(n) - 1$ elements, then the first element inspected is element $F(n-2)$, and the table is split such that the first part contains $F(n-2) - 1$ elements and the second part contains $F(n-1) - 1$ elements. The two parts, added to the inspected element make up the whole table:

$$F(n-2) - 1 + 1 + F(n-1) - 1 = F(n) - 1 \quad \text{elements.}$$

The following algorithm implements the method.

12.3 Implementations

```
PROCEDURE FibonacciSearch(T: TableType; K: KeyType): INTEGER;
VAR Found: BOOLEAN;
    Item: KeyType;
    F0, F1, F2, Middle: INTEGER;
    Index: INTEGER;
BEGIN
  F0 := 0;
  F1 := 1;
  F2 := 1;
  WHILE F2 < TableSize DO
     (* compute corresponding Fibonacci number *)
     F0 := F1;
     F1 := F2;
     F2 := F0 + F1;
  END; (* WHILE *)
  Index := F0;
  Middle := TableSize + 1 - F1;
  Found := FALSE;
  F2 := F1 - F0;            (* previous Fibonacci numbers *)
  F1 := F0 - F2;
  IF K > Key(T[Index]) THEN
     INC(Index, Middle);
  END; (* IF *)
  WHILE (Index # 0) AND NOT Found DO
     Item := Key(T[Index]);
     IF K = Item THEN        (* found *)
        RETURN Index;
     ELSIF K < Item THEN     (* first part of table *)
        IF F1 = 0 THEN       (* finished *)
           Index := NotFound;
        ELSE
           Index := Index - F1;
           F0 := F2;
           F2 := F1;
           F1 := F0 - F1;    (* previous Fibonacci numbers *)
        END; (* IF *)
     ELSIF F2 = 1 THEN       (* finished *)
        Index := NotFound;
     ELSE
        Index := Index + F1; (* second part of table *)
        F2 := F2 - F1;
        F1 := F1 - F2;
     END; (* IF *)
  END; (* WHILE *)
END FibonacciSearch;
```

The number of comparisons in a Fibonacci search is, on the average, slightly higher than that for a binary search, as the binary search tree modeling the search is not a complete binary search tree. A slight advantage of the Fibonacci search is that it uses only addition and subtraction. It can also be shown that the worst-case search time in a Fibonacci search is O(log n).

Interpolation Search Binary search does not make use of any information we might possess on the table. Sometimes many things are known about the table, such as, in rare instances, key distribution or, more often, extreme values for the keys. If we take a telephone book search as an example, we observe that most people looking for a telephone number use an interpolation search because they know that some letters have only a few entries while others have many. The interpolation search is not sophisticated: it assumes only that the distance of a given key K to the beginning of the table is proportional to a function of the total range of all the keys. Keys are kept in lexicographic order but possess equivalent numerical values. If mini and maxi are the addresses for the minimum key MinKey and the maximum key MaxKey then:

$$\frac{\text{Address of K} - \text{mini}}{\text{maxi} - \text{mini}} = \frac{K - \text{MinKey}}{\text{MaxKey} - \text{MinKey}}$$

which provides us with a possible address for K:

$$\text{Address of K} = \text{mini} + \text{Ceiling}\left(\frac{(\text{maxi} - \text{mini} - 1)(K - \text{MinKey})}{\text{MaxKey} - \text{MinKey}}\right)$$

For instance, if our example is looking for "Chandler" in a telephone book, then:

MinKey = "A A Amco"
MaxKey = "ZZ Fashions Inc"
mini = 1
maxi = 820,000

$$\text{address of Chandler} = 1 + \text{Ceiling}\left(\frac{819998 \, (\text{``Chandler''} - \text{``A A Amco''})}{\text{``ZZ Fashions Inc''} - \text{``A A Amco''}}\right)$$

where the difference of alphabetic keys has to be defined precisely.

Once this address is obtained, K is compared to the corresponding key. If the latter is too large, maxi is replaced by the computed address and MaxKey by the corresponding key. Then a new address is computed with the same formula. Otherwise, if the key is too small, mini is replaced by the computed address and MinKey by the corresponding key before a new address is recomputed. This process is repeated until the key is found. The interpolation search algorithm follows.

```
PROCEDURE Ceiling(c, d: INTEGER): INTEGER;
BEGIN
   IF (c MOD d) = 0 THEN
     RETURN c DIV d;
   ELSE
     RETURN c DIV d + 1;
   END;
END Ceiling;
```

```
PROCEDURE InterpolationSearch(T: TableType; Mini, Maxi: INTEGER;
                              MinKey, MaxKey, K: KeyType): INTEGER;
VAR Index: INTEGER;
BEGIN
  Index := Maxi;
  WHILE (K # T[Index].key) AND ((Maxi - 1) > Mini) DO
    Index := Mini + Ceiling((Maxi - Mini - 1)*(K - MinKey), (MaxKey-MinKey));
    IF T[Index].key < K THEN         (* continue in second half *)
      Mini := Index;
      MinKey := T[Mini].key;
    ELSIF T[Index].key > K THEN      (* continue in first half *)
      Maxi := Index;
      MaxKey := T[Maxi].key;
    END; (* IF *);
  END; (* WHILE *)
  IF T[Index].key # K THEN           (* not found *)
    RETURN NotFound;
  ELSE                               (* found *)
    RETURN Index;
  END; (* IF *)
END InterpolationSearch;
```

This example assumes that the key type is a numerical type whose values can be used in computations. If this were not the case, operations on the key type would have to be devised in order to apply the interpolation search concepts. The expected number of comparisons for interpolation search for a random distribution of keys is $O(\log \log n)$, which is better than binary search. However, this performance decreases quickly if the keys are not uniformly distributed, with a worst-case performance similar to sequential search. The extra computation time required by the method may also be substantial.

12.4 Hash Tables

As we have seen so far, searching for an entry in a table involves inspecting several other entries according to some systematic method. It is obvious that a better search method could be found if we could simply derive an entry position in the table by computing it from the value of its key. It would be even simpler if we could just use the key as an index in the table, as we may do in Modula-2 for example:

```
TYPE StdType = (Undef, Bool, Char, Card, Int, Enum, LCard,
                Double, Range, Real, LongReal, Pointer, Set,
                ProcType, Opaque, String, Array, Record);
     TableType = ARRAY StdType OF EntryType;
VAR Table: TableType;
```

In this example, Table[Enum] directly accesses the element corresponding to "key" Enum. In such a case, it is not necessary to store the key in the table. The table search consists of a direct access to one of the table entries, followed by the checking of the presence or absence of the element.

Unfortunately, such cases are rare in practice, as the set of possible keys is usually much larger than the table that must be used. Just take as an example the symbol table used by a compiler, where identifiers must start with a letter followed by letters or digits with at most 10 characters (which is more limited than Modula-2). Then the set of all possible identifiers contains 26×36^9 or 2,640,558,873,378,816 different identifiers! Even though computer memory is inexpensive nowadays, we cannot afford to reserve enough memory to store all the possible symbols. As a matter of fact, the number of symbols in a program is not overly large and a table with 1,000 entries would usually suffice. Compiler tables are not the only examples; tables of student names or tables of student id numbers will offer the same problem.

Since we cannot use direct indexing, we will have to use a mapping function of the keys to the table indices. Such a function is usually called a *hash function* or a key-to-index (address) transformation function. Given a key K, h(K) produces the corresponding index i. We will discuss hash functions in more detail later; for now it is sufficient to note that the computations are usually done in a constant time, which means that, given a transformation, a table index can be computed in O(1) time. This sounds too good to be true, and, to a degree, it is. Since there are many more possible keys than there are locations in the table, the hash function h(K) cannot be a one-to-one function, but must be a *many-to-one* function. It is therefore expected that we will have situations where two different keys, K1 and K2, hash to the same index:

$$h(K1) = h(K2) = i$$

and that, potentially, many elements will compete for the same position in the table. We say that K1 and K2 have a *collision* at index i under mapping function h.

The design of a good hash table meets the following two requirements:

1. The design will define a mapping function h(K) that produces a low number of collisions by spreading items around the table as evenly and uniformly as possible.
2. The design will define a collision-resolution method that stores or finds a record with a given key among all the records whose keys collide at the same table position.

Hash Functions

There is no best hash function, as the choice of a function h depends very much on the definition of the keys in the table, their degree of randomness, and the size of the table. Actually, it can only be said that some hash functions can turn out to be extremely bad and give extremely poor performance. **A given hash function must always be tried on real data in order to find out whether it is effective or not.** Care must be exercised whenever choosing a hash function.

All hash functions manipulate keys as if they were integers. In the case the keys are alphanumeric, the internal bit representation of the key may be interpreted as a binary number. This method has the disadvantage that bit representations of all letters are very similar. If the keys are made of letters only, each letter is given a sequential number from 1 to 26, but that means that every other digit is 0, 1, or 2. Another way of solving this problem is to consider an alphabetic key as a number expressed in base 26, and to compute its value using positional notation:

ALLO becomes $1 \times 26^3 + 12 \times 26^2 + 12 \times 26 + 15 = 26015$.

Division In this method, we let h(K) be the remainder of K after division by the table size S:

$$h(K) = K \text{ MOD } S.$$

This method is very commonly used, although some precautions must be taken. For one thing, S must be a prime number, but must not be of the form $r^k \pm a$, where r is the radix of the key character set, if the key is alphanumeric (128 for ASCII, 256 for EBCDIC), and where k and a are small integers. Similarly, if r MOD S equals 1, then the hash function key MOD m is actually the sum of the binary codes for the characters: two keys that are simple character permutations will hash into the same value, thus promoting collisions. If we take precautions to avoid such cases, this method gives good results.

Truncation Another method consists in taking only a few of the first or last characters of the key as the hash code. Depending on the set of keys that are used, the method gives acceptable or disastrous results. For instance, a national credit card organization might distribute its customer numbers by state, and for a given state, the first three digits might be the same or very similar: picking those digits as hash code would probably produce only 20% of the possible table positions. On the other hand, picking the last three digits might be a good idea, provided they are uniformly distributed. Picking the three middle digits might also prove a bad choice, as they might identify a particular bank branch and again prove to be far from uniformly distributed.

A good hash function must be able to generate all the positions in the table. To determine if it does, the set of possible keys must be examined closely to detect any possible bias in the distribution of the keys.

Mid-Square In this method, the key is squared and the middle digits of the result are used as hash code. This method ensures that all the elements of the key are used in hash code computation. Also, if some parts of the key are biased, this method tends to diminish their effect on the hash code. For instance:

```
K = 123456
K * K = 15241383936 → 138
```

Folding Another popular method, folding, helps in randomizing the key elements. The key is partitioned into several pieces, and the pieces are used to produce the hash code, sometimes simply by addition, sometimes by reversing them before addition. For instance:

```
K = 123456
      12      or      21
      34              43
      56              65
      ___             ___
→     102             120
```

Besides these four methods, there are many others. We can even combine some methods to obtain new ones. However, no simple method is generally superior, as each method might be more suited for use with a given set of keys. Among the four methods presented above, the truncation method is probably the fastest, as it can be programmed very easily in assembly language. Because of arithmetic manipulations, the folding and mid-square methods might not be as fast if they deal with long keys.

One disadvantage of hash functions is that they do not preserve the order of the keys: if $K1 > K2$, then it does not follow that $h(K1) > h(K2)$. However, order-preserving hash functions are usually far from uniform and lead to a high rate of collisions.

Perfect Hash Functions Normally, as we have already stated, a hash function will return the same value for a number of different key values. There exist some hash functions for which $h(K_i) \neq h(K_j)$ for all distinct i and j. They are called perfect hash functions, as no collision will occur. It is usually extremely difficult to find a perfect hash function for a given set of keys. Even if one can be found, any change to the original set of keys transforms the perfect hash function into a nonperfect hash function. Therefore perfect hash functions can only be used in situations where the set of keys is not changed. They are usually costly and should be reserved for cases requiring very frequent searches.

Collision Resolution

Because of the nature of hash functions, collisions will occur. A method has to be devised to resolve these collisions. When a collision occurs, we must search for an alternative location in a systematic and repeatable manner. It is important that the chosen method will consistently produce the same indices for the same keys. That way, the table is searched in the same order as the order in which it was created, and we can know quickly whether or not an item is in the table.

Several methods can be used. They all rely on a probing function which, given a hash index (not a key) produces a new hash index. After a collision occurs, the probing function is used to obtain another hash index. If the corresponding location is also full, then the probing function is used again to generate a new index from it, and the process is repeated until an open location is found, or it is determined the table is full. In most cases, an item can be placed in the table with only a few probes. Searching for an item works in the same way. However, we must be able to tell whether or not a position in the table is used. This can be easily done by initializing the table with an "empty" flag. But it turns out that, if we allow deletions, we need to be able to distinguish between "never used" and "no longer in use."

We can identify three kinds of collision resolutions: open addressing, chaining, and bucket hashing.

Open Addressing To resolve collisions in open addressing, once a collision occurs, we search for an empty table location at an index other than Hash(Key). A typical search and insert function is given below.

```
PROCEDURE SearchAndInsert(VAR Table: TableType;
                    Key: KeyType; Rec: RecordType): IndexType;
VAR Index: IndexType;
BEGIN
   Index := Hash(K);
   WHILE (Table[Index].Key # Key) AND (Table[Index].Flag = InUse) DO
     Index := Probe(Index);
   END; (* WHILE *)
   IF Table[Index].Flag # InUse THEN
     Table[Index] := Rec;
   END; (* IF *)
   RETURN Index;
END SearchAndInsert;
```

Function SearchAndInsert uses the hash function Hash, as well as the Probe function and a Flag field indicating whether or not a table entry is occupied. The WHILE loop is exited in one of two ways: either `Index` is the index of the entry with key Key, or `Index` is the index of an entry that has not been used. In the first case, the search is successful; in the second case, an empty position is found and the record is inserted into the table.

However, it is possible for the loop to execute forever because if the table is full, we keep looking for an empty spot. This case can be detected by using a counter of the number of entries. It is also possible to loop indefinitely even if there are some empty positions in the table. For instance, suppose the Probe function is defined as:

`Probe(i) = (i+2) mod TableSize.`

In this case, if the initial hash computation gives an even index, only even positions will be inspected: all even positions of the table might be occupied, while many odd positions might be empty.

This example shows that the probe function should ideally cover all of the integers between 0 and the table size. The probe function:

`Probe(i) = (i + 1) mod TableSize`

does that. This method is usually called *linear probing*. It is a simple method, but also causes *primary clustering*, a condition in which a number of "synonyms" (different keys having the same hash index) are stored in adjacent positions and mixed with other keys. Figure 12-3 illustrates primary clustering. Key3 hashes into index 94, which is occupied, so it is stored in the next free position, 95. In Figure 12-3 the sign "→"

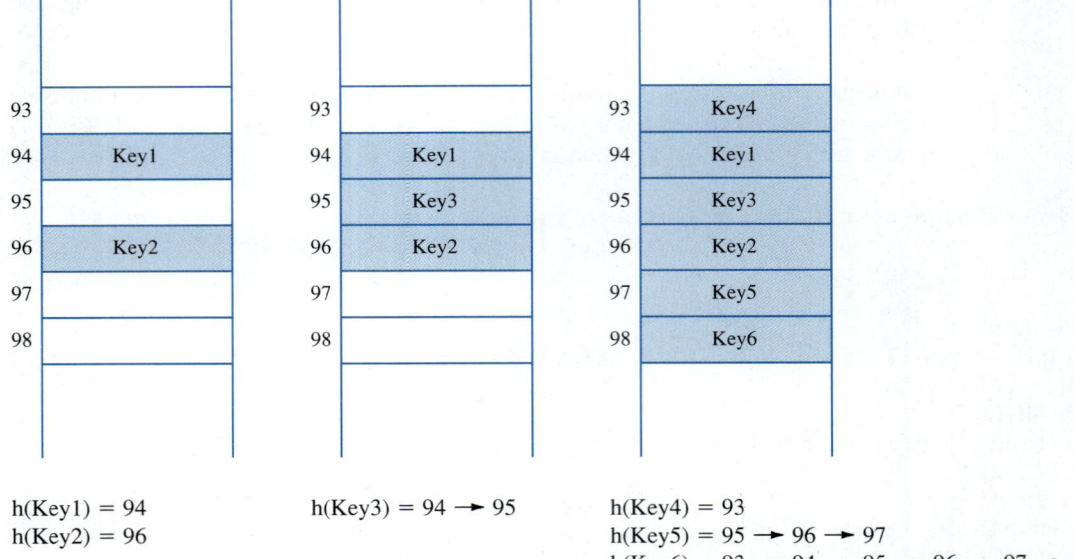

Figure 12-3 Primary Clustering

indicates that a collision has occurred; it is followed by the index of the next try. Key4 is hashed into position 93 and stored there. Key5 is hashed into index 95, which is occupied, so it is stored in the next available position, 97, after three tries. If we now hash Key6 into index 93, it will have to be stored in position 98 after 6 tries. This example shows that large clusters will grow faster than small clusters, making the table unbalanced, a situation to be avoided. This clustering phenomenon greatly increases retrieval and insertion times when the table is nearly full.

It can be shown that the average number of probes necessary for a successful search with the linear probing method is approximately:

$$0.5[1 + (1 - a)^{-1}]$$

where a = N/TableSize represents the load factor for the table. Similarly the average number of probes for an unsuccessful search is:

$$0.5[1 + (1 - a)^{-2}]$$

An improvement over linear probing is to have:

```
Probe(i) = (i + c) mod TableSize
```

where c is a constant relatively prime to TableSize. This is sometimes called *pseudorandom probing,* as the same effect can be obtained by using a random permutation of integers 0 through TableSize − 1. The average number of probes remains the same as before, but the technique does reduce primary clustering. We will investigate the approach of using a random permutation of table indices in our case study at the end of the chapter.

Quadratic probing is another method that spreads the keys more uniformly than linear probing, while still only involving a simple computation. The sequence of indices for probing is (all mod the table size):

$$h(K), \quad h(K) + 1, \quad h(K) + 2^2, \quad h(K) + 3^2, \quad \cdots \quad h(K) + j^2$$

The method solves the primary clustering problem, but creates a problem called *secondary clustering*, in which two keys that collide then will follow the same probe sequence. Analysis of this method leads to an average number of probes in the case of a successful search equal to:

$$1 - \ln(1 - a) - 0.5\, a$$

and in the case of an unsuccessful search:

$$(1 - a)^{-1} - a - \ln(1 - a)$$

Double hashing is yet another method for resolving collisions in open addressing; it eliminates the effect of primary and secondary clustering. This method uses two hash functions: h1, the primary hash function is first used, as before, to find the position in the table. If the position is already full, the secondary hash function h2 is used in the probe function:

$$\text{Probe}(i) = (i + h2(K)) \mod \text{TableSize}.$$

In the case of a collision, we know that $h1(K1) = h1(K2)$, but it is unlikely that $h2(K1) = h2(K2)$. The probe function depends on the original index and also on the key. Ideally h1 and h2 should distribute the computed indices uniformly over the table while minimizing clustering, but such functions are not always easy to find. Note that h2(K) is computed only once, even if it takes several probes. The average number of probes for a successful search with this method is shown to be:

$$a^{-1} \ln[(1 - a)^{-1}]$$

while the average number of probes for an unsuccessful search is:

$$(1 - a)^{-1}$$

Table 12-1 shows various values derived from the given formulas for the average number of probes in successful and unsuccessful searches as a function of the table load factor.

Table 12-1 Average Number of Probes

Method	Successful searches			Unsuccessful searches		
Load factor	50%	80%	90%	50%	80%	90%
Linear probing	1.5	3.0	5.5	2.5	13.0	50.5
Quadratic probing	1.4	2.2	2.9	2.2	5.8	11.4
Double hashing	1.4	2.0	2.6	2.0	5.0	10.0

As this table shows, the number of probes required to locate an item in a hash table is low, even with the poorest method of collision handling. This is true as long as the table is not too full. However, before jumping to the conclusion that hash tables are superior to all other methods, we should consider three major disadvantages.

1. The size of the table is fixed and must be guessed a priori; it should be at least 10% larger than the actual maximum number of entries.
2. Deletions in a hash table with open addressing are extremely cumbersome and should be avoided.
3. If the table must be listed in order, then a sort is necessary, as the elements are not even in hash key order.

Chaining Another method of resolving collisions is called chaining. It keeps a distinct linked list for all elements whose keys have the same hash index. Figure 12-4 illustrates this concept.

A key K hashes to position h(K); the entry at this position is either empty or contains an element. This element might itself be the head of a linked list containing all elements having keys for which the hash function produces the same index. If the table has m entries, and if there is a total of n elements in the table, then the average number of elements in a list is $a = n/m$. The average list length is usually short, which reduces the time needed for list search once a collision occurs.

The chaining method has the advantage of being dynamic: if the number of elements grows, so does the hash table. It is also possible to remove elements from the table without difficulty. The primary disadvantage of chaining is the extra space needed for the pointers. Also, if the individual lists become long, then the objective of hashing, constant access time, is defeated.

The average number of probes required to locate an existing item is approximately

$$1 + 0.5(a - 1)$$

while an unsuccessful search will require $(e^{-a} + a)$ probes. We should note that the load factor a can be greater than 1, as n/m can be greater than 1. For instance, if there are four times as many keys as entries in the hash table, the average number of probes for a successful search is $1 + 1.5 = 2.5$.

Figure 12-4
Hash Table with Chaining

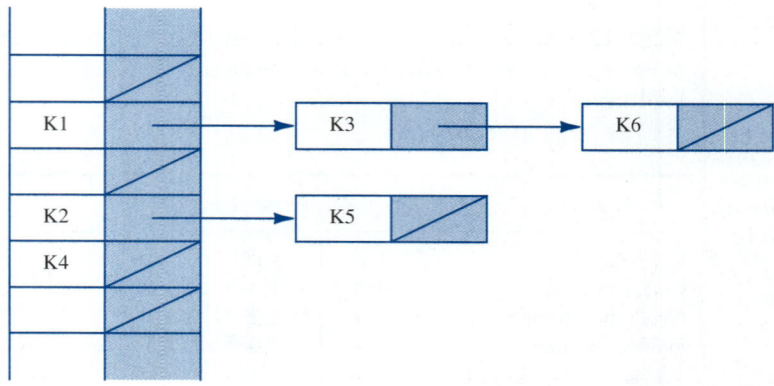

We can improve the search time for individual lists if we keep these ordered by key. Then the average number of probes for an unsuccessful search is

$$1 + 0.5a - (1 - e^{-a})a^{-1} + e^{-a}$$

Buckets Let's modify the preceding method so that we store in the hash table only pointers to the first elements of the list of all entries whose keys hash in the same index value. Each entry in the hash table is then called a bucket. The space required to store all the elements is increased by the memory required for the buckets. However the search algorithm is slightly simpler to write.

```
PROCEDURE SearchBuckets(VAR T: TableType; Key: KeyType;
                       Rec: RecordType): EntryPtr;
VAR Index: INTEGER;
    Last, Current: EntryPtr;
BEGIN
  Index := h(Key);
  Last := NIL;
  Current := T[Index];
  WHILE (Current # NIL) AND (Current.Key # Key) DO (* search list *)
    Last := Current;
    Current := Current^.Next;
  END; (* WHILE *)
  IF Current = NIL THEN     (* key was absent *)
    GetNode(Current);
    Store(Rec, Current);
    IF Last = NIL THEN      (* first element in bucket *)
      T[Index] := Current;
    ELSE                    (* attach at end of list *)
      Last^.Next := Current;
    END; (* IF *)
  END; (* IF *)
  RETURN Current;
END SearchBuckets;
```

One technique to improve the search time in the individual lists is to replace linked lists by binary search trees. However, this requires more space, as two pointers must now be kept with each element. Since the chains are usually small (if they are not, the hash table size should be increased), the added algorithm complexity coupled to the added memory space makes it more difficult to justify using the technique.

Historically, buckets had a different definition: the records of the hash table were divided into a number, say G, of groups. Each group contained the same number of records, R, and was called a bucket. The hash function applied to a given key h(K) computed a bucket number, and the record with key K was retrieved or stored in bucket h(K). If a bucket overflowed, it could be chained to an overflow bucket. The concept is roughly the same as the one presented earlier; however, the applications of these buckets are limited to external searching, in which records are kept in secondary storage. A read operation retrieves a whole bucket from secondary memory into main memory. A binary search on the bucket can locate the record of interest. A good choice of bucket size minimizes the overflow problem, and Knuth has shown that the number of accesses required as a function of the load factor is quite good—less than three accesses for small bucket sizes.

12.5 Case Study: Collision Resolution in a Closed Hash Table

The collision resolution strategies presented in the previous section dealt with two types of table structure: those of fixed size, often called closed tables, and those that can grow as new elements are added, often called open tables. We want to investigate here alternative strategies for collision resolution in a closed hash table and to come up with a comparison of these methods and the linear probing method.

Design

Definition of the Problem When the table starts to become full, the performance of hashing techniques is critically dependent on the collision resolution strategy. Linear probing is the easiest strategy, but it is susceptible to primary clustering and performs poorly as the load factor increases beyond fifty percent. We will develop here two other strategies for collision resolution: pseudorandom probing and coalesced chaining. Pseudorandom probing was already discussed briefly, but we will examine it in more detail. Coalesced chaining, another approach to collision resolution for closed hash tables, borrows some of the ideas of chaining. We will develop a test program to collect empirical data for these two techniques and compare them with linear probing for table load factors of 50%, 75%, 90%, 95% and 99%. We will focus on the probe length for an unsuccessful search, since this will always be greater than the probe length for a successful search.

Design of a Solution *Pseudorandom Probing* Pseudorandom probing is based on a probe sequence that is determined by a "random" permutation of the locations in the table. We will use the operations of "shift" and "exclusive or" (XOR) applied to binary values, to generate this random permutation. Since both of these operations are built into the instruction set of most machine architectures, this generation can be done very rapidly. We will assume that the table has elements numbered from 1 to $B - 1$, where B is a power of 2.

Let's illustrate this technique with two examples. For our first example, suppose B is 8, so the table has 7 entries and the index can be represented by three bits. Suppose also that we choose our "exclusive or" constant K to be 5. Let's assume that our initial probe is at index 6 and that this results in a collision. Our strategy is to shift the current index value left by one bit. If there is overflow (in which a bit 1 is shifted left outside the three-bit index) our strategy is to delete the leading bit and do an exclusive or of the result with K. The probe sequence for this specific example is as shown in Table 12-2.

Table 12-2
Probe Sequence

Explanation	Resulting value
initial value	110 = 6
shift, delete leading 1, XOR with 101	001 = 1
shift	010 = 2
shift	100 = 4
shift, delete leading 1, XOR with 101	101 = 5
shift, delete leading 1, XOR with 101	111 = 7
shift, delete leading 1, XOR with 101	011 = 3
shift	110 = 6 (initial value)

The value of K we have chosen for this example has produced a permutation of the indices 1 through 7. For a particular value of B, not every value of K will produce a permutation of all possible index values. For a given B, it is necessary to find a correct value for K through testing. For instance, if B = 8, the value K = 3 also works, but other values of K fail to produce a permutation of all the index values.

To illustrate the effects of a bad value for K, let's consider a slightly larger example. Suppose that B = 16 (we need four bits for the index) and that K is equal to 5 again. If the initial index value resulting in a collision is 7, let's try our method, as shown in Table 12-3.

Clearly this value of K did not produce an exhaustive search of the table. With this table size, it turns out that K = 9 does work and produces the following probe sequence when starting at 7:

7, 14, 5, 10, 13, 3, 6, 12, 1, 2, 3, 8, 9, 11, 15, 7 (initial value)

Fortunately, it is only necessary to find a value of K that produces an exhaustive search for a particular value of B once during the design phase. This search for a suitable value of K can also be automated by writing a small program that exhaustively checks all possible values of K from 1 to B − 1. We wrote such a program, tested it for B = 1024, and found 60 values of K that worked:

9, 27, 39, 45, 101, 111, 129, 139, 197, 215, 231, 243, 255, 269, 281, 291, 305, 317, 323, 343, 363, 389, 399, 407, 417, 455, 485, 503, 507, 531, 533, 549, 567, 579, 591, 603, 633, 639, 649, 693, 705, 723, 735, 765, 791, 797, 801, 825, 839, 845, 853, 857, 867, 893, 909, 915, 945, 987, 1011, 1017

Writing such a program is left as an exercise (see problem 24).

Table 12-3
Incomplete Probe Sequence

Explanation	Resulting value
initial value	0111 = 7
shift	1110 = 14
shift, delete leading 1, XOR with 0101	1001 = 9
shift, delete leading 1, XOR with 0101	0111 = 7 (initial value)

Coalesced Chaining The second technique we will examine is called coalesced chaining. It is conceptually similar to the chaining technique presented in Figure 12-4, but has two different characteristics:

- Coalesced chaining uses a closed hash table, where all the elements of the chain are stored in the table and are connected together by links that are indices to other table locations.
- Since a new entry may hash to a location that is already part of a chain, it is possible for two or more chains to share common data (thus the name coalesced chaining).

The table is an array of records where each record contains the key value, any related data, and a link field. The table is indexed from 1 to some maximum value; if the link value is in that range, then it is the index of the next item in the chain. Otherwise, we will use a link value of 0 to represent the empty link. A pointer into the table, called `free`, will be used to search for the next available empty location if the item is not in the table and the initial position was not empty. Initially, `free` is set to point past the last position of the table. The general strategy is the following:

Apply the hash function to the key to find the initial position to be checked; if that position is empty, then the item is not in the table and could be inserted at that location.

If the position is occupied, follow the chain of entries either until the item is found or the empty link is encountered (indicating that the item is not in the table). In the latter case, using `free`, we will search sequentially from the last location where an item was inserted towards the top of the table; if `free` becomes zero while searching for an empty position, then the table is full.

To better understand this collision-resolution strategy, let's look at a simple example, illustrated by Figure 12-5. Our table indices vary from 1 to 7, so `free` is initially set to 8 and all links are set to 0, the empty link. Assume that key k1 hashes to index 4, where it is inserted, and then that key k2 hashes to index 6, where it is inserted. Suppose now that key k3 hashes to index 4, a location already occupied by k1. Since the link field at index 4 is 0, there are no more elements in this chain, so we use `free` to find the next empty location. Free is decremented to 7, the highest index of an empty location. Key k3 is inserted at location 7, and the link field of location 4 is set to point to entry 7. Next, key k4 hashes to index 7, which is occupied and has no other items in its chain. So `free` is decremented to 5, k4 is inserted there, and the link of location 7 is set to 5. Finally, key k5 hashes to index 4, which is occupied. The chain is searched at locations 7 and 5, and k5 is not found. Therefore, `free` is decremented to 3, k5 is put in at location 3, and the link of the last item in the chain, location 5, is set to location 3.

Searching for an item already in the table involves checking the original hash position and, if the item is not there, traversing the chain until the item is found. With a

12.5 Case Study: Collision Resolution in a Closed Hash Table

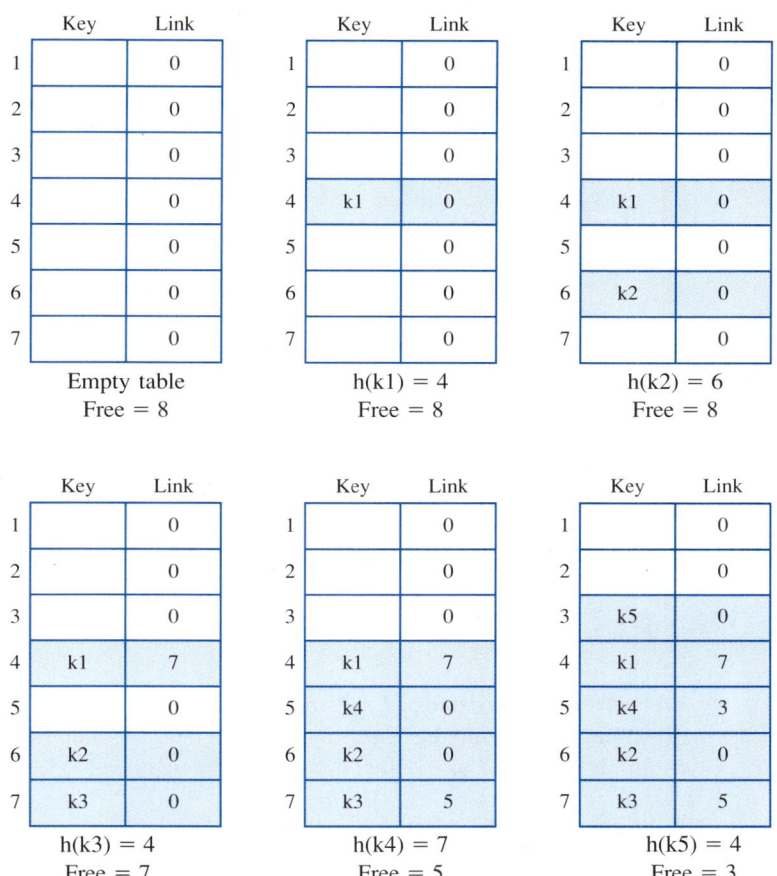

Figure 12-5 Collision Resolution by Coalesced Chaining

good hash function that spreads the initial probes throughout the table indices, this technique produces fairly short chains and has good performance even when the table is almost full, as our measures will show.

Refine the Solution *Pseudorandom Probing* Now that we have a technique for generating a "random" permutation of the numbers 1 through $B - 1$, where B is a power of 2, we modify our probing to use this information. We use the initial hash function value as the starting point and generate a sequence of "random" table locations to check for an empty location if a collision with another value occurs. If we come back to the initial location without finding the desired item or without finding an empty location, then the table must be full and insertion is impossible. Since the generated sequence is a permutation of all possible locations, we know the search must have been exhaustive.

```
Hash Random
   If the number of entries equals the table size
      Table overflow error
   Else
      Set Location to Hash(Key)
      Loop
         If Location is empty
            Insert Key at Location
         Elsif Location key matches Key value then
            Item is found
         Else     { collision resolution }
            Shift Location left by one bit
            If Location is greater than table size
               Remove leading 1 bit
               Exclusive Or Location with K
            End if
         End if
      End Loop
   End if
End Hash Random
```

We will leave the details of shifting, deleting the leading 1 bit, and the exclusive or operation until coding because the implementation will depend on the choice of using assembly language or the facilities of Modula-2.

Coalesced Chaining Our algorithm for coalesced chaining follows directly from the discussion of the algorithm in the design section. In the pseudocode below, we assume that Free has been initialized to the table size plus 1.

```
Hash Coalesced
   Set Address to the hash of Key
   If entry at Address is not empty
      Search the chain until Key is found or the chain is exhausted
            and set Previous to the end of the chain
   End if
   If Key was not found
      If location Address is empty
         Insert the item at location Address
      Else
         Decrement Free until an empty location is found or the table
            is exhausted
```

> If the table is exhausted
>   Generate an overflow error condition
>   Else
>   Link location Previous to Free
>   Insert Key at location Free
>   End if
>   End if
> End if
> End Hash Coalesced

Develop a Testing Strategy We will compare the performance of the pseudorandom probing algorithm and the coalesced chaining algorithm with linear probing by inserting the same sequence of "random" key values into a hash table until the table is completely filled. The table indices will vary from 1 to 1,023, which is $2^{10} - 1$, as required for the pseudorandom approach. We will generate alphabetic keys in lowercase characters. We will assume identifiers will have a maximum of eight characters. Since the character values will be generated randomly, the key itself need not have any meaning in terms of natural language. With this flexibility in key generation, it will be very unlikely that keys will be duplicated in the process of filling the table.

We will set checkpoints when the table is 50%, 75%, 90%, 95%, 99% and 100% full. At each of these checkpoints we will record the following information:

- The average probe length for all keys inserted so far
- The average probe length for the last ten keys inserted
- The time used for inserting all keys so far

The calculations for probe lengths involve simple averages based on counting probe sequences. The timing data will be implementation dependent and should only be judged relative to the other timing results. Our test program is relatively straightforward and will not be presented here.

Implementation

Code and Test the Program The structure of the table we will use includes all the fields necessary for the three methods we will measure (fields `Next` and `Free` are only needed by the coalesced chaining method) and is defined by:

```
TYPE Element = ARRAY[1..IdLength] OF CHAR;
     NodeType = RECORD
                  Identifier : Element;
                  Next : CARDINAL;   (* link field for coalesced chaining *)
                END;
```

```
HashTable = POINTER TO HTable;
HTable = RECORD
            Elements: ARRAY[1..MaxNodes] OF NodeType;
            Size: CARDINAL;
            Free: CARDINAL;
         END;
```

Our hash function uses the ordinal values of the first three characters of the key weighted by their position.

```
PROCEDURE HashFunction (Node: NodeType): CARDINAL;
(* This procedure takes in a Node and gives
   a value from 1 to MaxNodes in return. *)
VAR Value:CARDINAL;
    Elt:Element;
BEGIN
  Elt:= Node.Identifier;
  Value:= ((ORD(Elt[1]) * 26 * 26 + ORD(Elt[2]) * 26
          + ORD (Elt[3])) MOD MaxNodes)+1;
  RETURN Value;
END HashFunction;
```

The code for the collision-resolution techniques follows the detailed design closely. The algorithm has been augmented by the collection of data. It is unlikely that two keys will have the same value, but if they do, the algorithms generate a node with a new key value and insert it instead through a recursive call. We initialized the table with all key values equal to "+" to represent an empty node.

For pseudorandom probing, we have used a multiplication by 2 to accomplish a left shift, subtraction of (table size + 1) to delete the leading 1-bit, and the set operations on a BITSET to accomplish the exclusive or. The two set differences eliminate the bits in Bits and K with the same value, and the union of the differences returns the XOR result. Because of Modula-2's strong type checking, we have to use type transfer functions to be able to manipulate cardinal value Location as a BITSET.

```
PROCEDURE HashRandom(VAR NodeType: NodeType; VAR Table: HashTable;
                    VAR Trials: CARDINAL);
(* This procedure takes in a Node and the Table to place the Node in. It returns
   the updated Table and the number of collisions encountered while inserting
   the Node. -- special case -- if the Node is a repeat, a new Node is
   created and inserted as per specifications. The new
   Node is returned for use in the other hash functions. *)
VAR Location: CARDINAL;
    Bits, K: BITSET;
BEGIN
  IF Table^.Size < MaxNodes THEN
    Trials := 0;
    Location := HashFunction(NodeType);
    K := BITSET(9);  (* XOR number *)
```

```
      LOOP
        INC(Trials);
        IF Table^.Elements[Location].Identifier[1] = "+" THEN
          (* empty slot *)
          Table^.Elements[Location] := NodeType;
          INC(Table^.Size);
          EXIT;
        ELSIF StringEqual(Table^.Elements[Location].Identifier,
                                        NodeType.Identifier) THEN
          (* already here try another one *)
          GenerateNode(NodeType);
          HashRandom(NodeType, Table, Trials);
          EXIT;
        ELSE
          Location := Location * 2;  (* shift left one bit *)
          IF Location > MaxNodes THEN (* delete first bit and XOR *)
            Location := Location - (MaxNodes + 1);
            Bits := BITSET(Location);
            Location := CARDINAL((Bits - K) + (K - Bits));
          END;  (* IF *)
        END;  (* IF *)
      END;  (* LOOP *)
    ELSE
      WriteString("Shift Table overflow, no operations performed");
      WriteLn;
    END;  (* IF *)
END HashRandom;
```

For coalesced chaining, we assume a table from 1 to 1,023 (maxnodes) and a link value of 0 to represent an empty link. When the variable Free reaches 0, the table is full.

```
PROCEDURE HashCoalesced (VAR Node: NodeType; VAR Table: HashTable;
                         VAR Trys: CARDINAL);
(* This procedure inserts a Node into a hash table using the coalesced method of
   collision resolution. Note if duplicate Node found, a new Node is created
   and inserted *)
VAR Index, Address, Previous: CARDINAL;
    Found: BOOLEAN;
BEGIN
  IF Table^.Size < MaxNodes THEN
    Trys := 0;
    Address := HashFunction(Node);
    Found := FALSE;
    IF Table^.Elements[Address].Identifier[1] # "+" THEN
      (* occupied *)
      Index := Address;
```

```
          REPEAT
            INC(Trys);
            IF StringEqual(Table^.Elements[Index].Identifier,
                                         Node.Identifier) THEN
               Found := TRUE;     (* node already there, try another *)
               GenerateNode(Node);
               HashCoalesced(Node,Table,Trys);
            ELSE
               Previous := Index;                (* for future linking *)
               Index := Table^.Elements[Index].Next;
            END; (* IF *)
          UNTIL Found OR (Index = 0);
       END; (* IF *)
       IF Found = FALSE THEN
          IF Table^.Elements[Address].Identifier[1] = "+" THEN
             (* store it in empty slot *)
             Table^.Elements[Address] := Node;
             INC(Trys);
             INC(Table^.Size);
          ELSE
             REPEAT       (* find free slot *)
               INC(Trys);
               DEC(Table^.Free);
             UNTIL Table^.Elements[Table^.Free].Identifier[1] = "+";
             IF Table^.Free # 0 THEN
                Table^.Elements[Previous].Next := Table^.Free;
                Table^.Elements[Table^.Free] := Node;
                Table^.Elements[Table^.Free].Next := 0;
                INC(Table^.Size);
             END;(* IF *)
          END; (* IF *)
       END; (* IF *)
    ELSE
       WriteString("Coalesced table overflow, no operations performed");
       WriteLn;
    END;(* IF *);
END HashCoalesced;
```

We ran our tests on a Sun 3/60 workstation running under Berkeley Unix 4.2. The timing facilities were able to time separate processes within a program and were independent of machine usage by other users. Our results fluctuated slightly since the generation of keys is not truly random. In general, the pseudorandom probing performed slightly better than linear probing, while coalesced chaining performed remarkably well, even when the table was filled. The data on the following page is for the average of the last ten probes, which have been averaged for three test runs.

Load factor	Linear	Pseudorandom	Coalesced
0.50	2.1	2.4	2.0
0.75	8.5	8.1	2.8
0.90	47.3	27.1	3.8
0.95	154.2	106.5	5.2
0.99	411.5	311.1	5.3
0.9999	311.8	468.8	4.1

Since a small number of probes is used for each average, there is some statistical fluctuation, as seen in the figures for 0.9999 being lower than for 0.99 in linear probing and coalesced chaining. Despite these fluctuations, the trends are clear. Pseudorandom probing is a small improvement over linear probing, while coalesced chaining is significantly better than either of the other two techniques. This advantage is particularly noticeable when the table is near full capacity. But don't forget—there is a price to pay for coalesced chaining: each entry in the hash table needs an extra link field to form the coalesced chains.

We timed each algorithm for insertion of all 1,023 keys on a Sun 3/60. We obtained the following results, averaged for three sets of data (where a tick is 1/60th of a second).

Linear probing	370.3 ticks
Pseudorandom probing	346.7 ticks
Coalesced chaining	20.7 ticks

Complete the Documentation The documentation should include a careful statement of the collision-resolution techniques, as described in the "Design of a Solution" section on page 466. The pseudocode solution might also be included, since it is much simpler and independent of data collection facilities and of any machine-dependent code. The test cases and the resultant analysis should be part of the documentation. A user's manual is not required for this application.

Summary

Conceptually, tables are very simple, as the abstract data type examples have shown. The ADT Table supports value-oriented operations such as retrieval of all or part of the information associated with an element. From an implementation point of view, however, we are faced with a number of possible choices, and, as usual, the best choice depends on the application.

Searching is the main operation on tables. The simplest method for searching is the sequential search, which does not require that the table elements be ordered. This is all right for small dynamic tables, but is not very efficient for large tables. In the case of static tables, the binary search and its variants are the best methods available, even though they require that the table elements be ordered.

When faced with a large set of keys, we must use hashing techniques for storing and retrieving table elements. These methods work well if the hash functions are chosen with care and are well-adapted to the particular applications. However, they introduce problems of collisions when several keys hash to the same table index. Some techniques for resolving collisions are open addressing, chaining (both in open and closed tables), and the use of buckets.

■ Exercises

1. Although our definition of the ADT Table did not mention duplicates, it might be wise to test for them rather than just assume they won't occur. Why? What are the implications of inserting duplicate items? Modify our implementation so that it disallows any duplicates.

2. What search method would you use to locate all elements in a table between keys K1 and K2?

3. If there is a large quantity of information associated with each key, this information should not be kept in the hash table. Explain why, and define a method to represent such a collection of data.

4. Prove that if a and b are relatively prime integers, the sequence of a numbers of the form $(i * b)$ MOD a for $1 \leq i \leq a$ forms a permutation of the numbers 0 to $a - 1$.

5. Suppose that a key is equally likely to be any integer between low and high. Suppose that the mid-square hash method is used to produce an integer between 0 and $2^{(k-1)}$. Is the result equally likely to be an integer in that range? Why or why not?

6. A hash function is selected, which is h(K) = K MOD M. M is chosen to be 1,024. Prove that this function maps even keys onto even hash indices, and odd keys onto odd indices. Is this a good hash function?

7. Compare the efficiency of searching an ordered table of size N and searching an unordered table of the same size for a given key:
   (a) if the key is absent.
   (b) if the key is present.
   (c) if the key appears several times, but only the first instance is wanted.
   (d) if the key appears several times and all elements with the same key are wanted.

8. Apply the mid-square method to a set of identifiers. Are the computed indices uniformly distributed in the chosen domain?

9. Assume a hash table has 13 entries and that the following keys are to be stored in the table:

   23, 61, 45, 58, 71, 48, 16, 42, 270, 135, 0

   (a) Find the hash indices and the number of collisions when the hash function is MOD TableSize.

(b) Find the hash indices and the number of collisions for a hash function in which the keys are folded by adding their digits together and then taking the result MOD TableSize.
(c) repeat (a) and (b) with TableSize = 11.

10. Another method for resolving collisions with open addressing is to keep a separate overflow table in which all items that collide are kept. Discuss the advantages and disadvantages of that method.

11. In a chained hash table, suppose that the elements in each chain are kept in key order. Then a search can be terminated as soon as it passes the place where the key should be if it was in the table. How many fewer probes will be done, on the average, for a successful and an unsuccessful search? How many probes are needed, on the average, to insert a new element? Compare your answers with those obtained from the formulas in the text, which are for unordered chains.

12. Define a simple hash function for mapping three-letter words to integers between 0 and $n - 1$. Find the values of your function for the words: ART, BIT, CAT, FIG, GET, JUG, MAN, NOT, PIT, RAP, TAR for $n = 7, 11, 13, 17$. Try to have as few collisions as possible.

13. Write an algorithm to delete identifier X from a hash table with linear collision-resolution. Show that setting to zero the position occupied by X is not sufficient. What has to be done to the search algorithm to allow for deletions? Where is it possible to insert a new element?

■ Programming Problems

14. Given a set of keys $\{1..16\}$, apply procedures BinarySearch from Chapter 3 and Fibonacci-Search to search for keys 2, 10, and 15. For each search find the number of comparisons used.

15. Define and program algorithms for insertion and deletion in an ordered table.

16. Add a Replace operation to our implementation of the ADT Table. (That operation can already be accomplished with Search and Delete, but define a more efficient operation.)

17. Take as the set of keys, the name appearing first on 50 consecutive pages of your phone book. (If your phone book is too small, pick two or three names per page). With these keys, write and test a program to build a hash table with:

a = 80%
linear method for collision
several hash functions (modulo, mid-square, folding)

Compare the actual search time with the theoretical one. What method gives the best key distribution?

18. Write and test a procedure that lists all identifiers in a hash table in lexicographic order. Assume that $h(X)$ = first character of X and that collisions are solved by a linear method.

19. Write and test a procedure for the deletion of an element in a chained hash table.

20. Write a function procedure Search(Table, Key) that searches a hash table for an element with key Key. The table is defined as:

```
TYPE ElementType = RECORD
                     K: KeyType;
                     R: RecordType;
                     Occupied: BOOLEAN;
                   END;
VAR Table: ARRAY [1..TableSize] OF ElementType;
```

The Occupied flag indicates if a table position is empty or not. The function returns an integer index in the table, or -1 if the element is not in the table. Suppose the two hashing functions h1 and h2 producing an integer value between 1 and TableSize from a given key are available, and that the probe function used is:

Probe(i) = (i + h2(Key)) MOD TableSize

21. Suppose that an ordered table is stored as a linked list. Write a function procedure Search(Table, Item, Key) that returns the pointer to the retrieved item, or returns NIL in case of failure. Item is initially equal to Table, but is reset after each search to the last retrieved item (or to Table if the search is not successful). It is used to reduce the number of comparisons in a search.

22. Suppose the implementation chosen for an ordered table makes it possible to search sequentially either backwards or forwards. Suppose that a given pointer P always points to the last element successfully retrieved and that the search always begins at the element pointed by P. Write a function Search(Table, P, Key) that returns the retrieved element. Compare the number of key comparisons in a successful and an unsuccessful search with the method of problem 21.

*23. Given a hash function h for a table of size N, write a simulation program to first generate enough keys (six-digit integers) to fill the table to 80 percent. Then compute the following quantities:
   (a) the percentage of integers between 0 and $N - 1$ that do not equal h(key) for any generated key
   (b) the percentage of integers between 0 and $N - 1$ that equal h(key) for more than one generated key
   (c) the maximum number of keys that hash into a single value between 0 and $N - 1$
   (d) the average number of keys that hash into values between 0 and $N - 1$, not including the values into which no key hashes
   Run the program to test the uniformity of the following hash functions:
   (a) h(key) = key MOD N for N prime
   (b) h(key) = key MOD N for N a power of 2
   (c) the folding method producing five-bit indices with N = 64
   (d) the mid-square method producing four-digit indices with N = 5,000.

Note: Problems marked with an asterisk (*) have a higher level of difficulty.

24. Write a program that, given B, a power of 2, finds all values K from 1 to B − 1 that generate a permutation of the numbers from 1 to B − 1 using the pseudorandom probing technique presented in the case study.

25. Complete the case study by writing a main test program and the necessary utility procedures to compare the algorithms for linear probing, pseudorandom probing, and coalesced chaining. How did your results compare with those presented at the end of the case study?

26. Add the techniques of quadratic probing and double hashing to your program from problem 25. How did these two techniques compare with the others?

Character Strings

INTRODUCTION

Character strings are used in all computer science applications. As a matter of fact, strings are used to represent the programs we submit to the computer for compilation and execution. Strings are also used to represent program data as well as program results. In some cases, these data are texts that will be used by text editors and publication software. Character strings are found in text files and databases. They are found in programming languages to name variables and procedures, and in symbol tables and various operating system tables. In short, character strings are an integral part of computer science, so much so, that they are often taken for granted.

Because of the widespread use of character strings, it is important to be able to choose a representation that is appropriate for the given application and that takes into account the usual compromises between time efficiency, memory space, and ease of programming. This chapter will address these issues as it covers string representations and algorithms.

13.1 Abstraction: The String

Let's first give a number of definitions. An *alphabet* is a finite and nonempty set of symbols. Set A = {a, b, c, . . . , x, y, z} is a familiar alphabet; similarly, set {$, @, X, Y, Z} is an alphabetic set of five characters. The *concatenation* of two alphabetic characters "x" and "y" is their juxtaposition to form a sequence of two characters "xy". Concatenation can also involve multicharacter sequences like "xy" and "uvw"; the result is "xyuvw" after concatenation. Single or double quotation marks are normally used to enclose and delimit character string literals. A *character string* on alphabet A is either one of the letters of alphabet A or a sequence made of concatenated letters from alphabet A. If A = {X, Y, Z}, the following are character strings on A: "X", "YZ", "YXZZ". An empty character string contains no characters and is denoted by " ".

Generally, in computer applications the alphabet used for strings is the character set used on the particular computer. The ASCII character set is used on most computers (see Appendix C), although some other character sets, like the EBCDIC on IBM mainframe computers, are also used. In our discussion we will use the ASCII character set, so we can refine our string definition: a *string* is a finite sequence of characters $c_1 c_2 c_3 \ldots c_n$ with $n \geq 0$, taken from the ASCII character set. The value of n represents the length of the string. If $n = 0$, then the string is said to be empty.

In Modula-2, there is no built-in String type, however string constants (or literals) do exist. They are represented as sequences of characters enclosed within single or double quotes (the delimiter may not be included in the string). Within a string, all characters (including spaces and other punctuation marks) are significant. They all contribute to the string's length (but the enclosing quotes for string literals do not). The types of string literals are taken to be ARRAY [0..n] OF CHAR. It is therefore possible to use similar types to declare string variables to which string constants may be assigned, by using the regular Modula-2 assignment statement. For instance:

```
VAR MyString: ARRAY [0..54] OF CHAR;
      .
      .
      .
MyString := "This is Pat's string constant";
```

Such an assignment always appends an additional null character (designated as 0C in Modula-2) after the last character of the string constant to mark the end of the string. In the case of our example, it puts the null character in MyString[29]. Note that such an assignment puts the first character in MyString[0], the second in MyString[1], and so on: the strings are said to be zero-based. Standard module InOut offers procedures ReadString and WriteString to manipulate these objects.

The ADT String will include the type String and the following operations: string creation, string length, string assignment, deletion of a substring in a string, making a string empty, extraction of a substring from a string, insertion of a substring in a string,

string concatenation, string comparisons, string search, access to string elements, string input/output.

Without even thinking yet of implementation details, we are faced with implementation questions as we try to define the ADT string and produce a definition module for it. If we do as we have done so far and define String as an opaque type, all the objects of type String will *not* be compatible with Modula-2 string literals. In particular, we will not be able to use the Modula-2 assignment statement as we have done for variable MyString in the example above. We will also not be able to use procedures ReadString and WriteString from module InOut on objects of type String. However, redefining such operations is not difficult and we will go ahead and use an opaque type, as seen in the following definition module.

```
DEFINITION MODULE Strings;

CONST MaxString = 256;      (* maximum string size *)
      EndOfString = 0C;

TYPE String;    (* a string is a sequence of at most MaxString
                    characters, ended by the EndOfString character
                    and where characters are numbered starting
                    with index 0 *)

PROCEDURE InitString(VAR S: String);
(* Initialize a string; this operation is absolutely necessary.
   before using string S.
   Pre-condition: none
   Post-condition: S' is an empty string *)

PROCEDURE Length(S: String): CARDINAL;
(* Give length of a string.
   Pre-condition: S is an initialized string
   Post-condition: Return the number of characters in S not
                   counting the EndOfString character *)

PROCEDURE Assign(VAR Dest: String; Source: String);
(* Assign value of string Source to string Dest.
   Pre-condition: Dest and Source are initialized strings
   Post-condition: Dest' = Source *)

PROCEDURE AssignConst(VAR Dest: String; Source: ARRAY OF CHAR);
(* Assignment of a Modula-2 string constant Source to String Dest.
   If Source is longer than MaxString, it is truncated.
   Pre-condition: Dest and Source are initialized strings
   Post-condition: Dest' = Source *)

PROCEDURE Copy(Source: String; Index, Count: CARDINAL;
               VAR Dest: String);
(* Copy part of string Source into string Dest.
   Pre-condition: Index + Count - 1 < Length(Source)
   Post-condition: Dest' = Source [Index..Index+Count-1] *)
```

```
PROCEDURE Delete(VAR Source: String; Index, Count: CARDINAL);
(* Delete Count characters of string Source starting at Index.
   Deleted substring is lost.
   Pre-condition: Index + Count - 1 < Length(Source)
   Post-condition: Source' = Source [0..Index-1] |
                   Source [Index+Count .. Length(Source)-1] *)

PROCEDURE Insert(Source: String; VAR Dest: String;
                 Index: CARDINAL);
(* Insert substring Source into string Dest at position Index.
   Pre-condition: Index <= Length(Dest)
                  Length(Dest) + Length(Source) <= MaxString
   Post-condition: Dest' = Dest [0..Index-1 ] | Source |
                   Dest[Index .. Length(Dest)-1]
                   If Index = Length(Dest), Source is
                   concatenated to Dest *)

PROCEDURE Concat(Str1, Str2: String; VAR Dest: String);
(* Concatenate Str1 and Str2 and store result in Dest.
   Pre-condition: Length(Str1) + Length(Str2) <= MaxString
   Post-condition: Dest' = Str1 | Str2   *)

PROCEDURE StringGreater(Str1, Str2: String): BOOLEAN;
(* Compare strings Str1 and Str2 in lexical order according
   to character set.
   Pre-condition: Str1 and Str2 are initialized strings
   Post-condition: TRUE if Str1 > Str2 otherwise FALSE *)

PROCEDURE StringEqual(Str1, Str2: String): BOOLEAN;
(* Compare strings Str1 and Str2 in lexical order according
   to character set.
   Pre-condition: Str1 and Str2 are initialized strings
   Post-condition: TRUE if Str1 = Str2 otherwise FALSE *)

PROCEDURE FetchChar(Source: String; Index: CARDINAL): CHAR;
(* Extract a character from position Index of string Source.
   Pre-condition: Index < Length(Dest)
   Post-condition: Return Source[Index]
                   or EndOfString if Index out of string *)

PROCEDURE AssignChar(Ch: CHAR; VAR Dest: String; Index: CARDINAL);
(* Store a character at position Index of string Dest.
   Pre-condition: Index <= Length(Dest)
   Post-condition: Dest[Index]' = Ch
                   or not changed if Index out of string *)

PROCEDURE Pos(Sub, Source: String): CARDINAL;
(* Search string Source for substring Sub and return index
   of leftmost occurrence of Sub or Length(Source) if not found.
   Pre-condition: Sub and Source are initialized strings
   Post-condition: Return Length(Source) if there is no match,
                   otherwise 0 <= Pos < Length(Source) and
                   Source[Pos..Pos+Length(Sub)-1] = Sub
                   and there is no match before Pos *)
```

```
PROCEDURE DisposeString(VAR S: String);
(* Delete string S.
   Pre-condition: S is an initialized string
   Post-condition: S' is empty  *)

PROCEDURE ToString(Ch: CHAR; VAR Str: String);
(* Convert character Ch to string Str.
   Pre-condition: Str is an initialized string
   Post-condition: Str' = Ch *)

PROCEDURE InputString(VAR Str: String);
(* Read string Str from standard input, string will be terminated
   by a blank, a return or any other control character.
   Pre-condition: Str is an initialized string
   Post-condition: Str' = typed in string *)

PROCEDURE OutputString(Str: String);
(* Write string Str on standard output
   Pre-condition: Str is an initialized string
   Post-condition: Str' is output *)

PROCEDURE ReadLine(VAR Str: String);
(* Input a string which may contain spaces from standard input.
   End of string indicated by EOL or control character.
   Pre-condition: Str is an initialized string
   Post-condition: Str' = sequence of characters from current input
                   device *)
END Strings.
```

Note that, as in Chapter 4, we have used the "|" character in the comments to indicate string concatenation. If we had decided to remain entirely compatible with Modula-2 string constants, the String type would have had to be transparent and defined as:

```
TYPE String = ARRAY [0..MaxString] OF CHAR;
```

and all value parameters of our procedures would have had to be of the open array type ARRAY OF CHAR.

Because of the fact that type String is opaque, we need to have two assignment operators, one to assign a Modula-2 string literal to objects of type String and another one to assign a value of type String to a variable of type String. We cannot use the Modula-2 assignment statement because opaque types are implemented by pointers and an assignment of opaque types would result in aliases pointing to the same string structure rather than give the intended result of copying the string value.

Whenever a structured type is defined, it is necessary to provide access to its components, and the string type is no exception. This access has been achieved here by defining the two operations FetchChar and AssignChar that make it possible to retrieve and to store individual characters in strings. The individual characters must be indicated by an index value representing the position of the character in the string, the first character being at position 0.

13.2 Applications

As we mentioned earlier, applications of character strings are numerous. We will only describe here two simple examples of string applications.

Text Formatting

Word or text processing is a widespread application of character strings. Word processing is used for editing and formatting of newspaper articles, books, reports, as well as program and data preparation. Entire texts are stored in permanent files instead of on paper; text processing may include text addition, text deletion, text modification as well as text formatting for printing. In general, text processing applications are divided into two categories: *text editors,* which process texts (additions, deletions, modifications), and *text formatters,* which prepare texts for printing. Modern publication software that is "what you see is what you get" (*WYSIWYG*) combines these two activities, at least from a user perspective.

We will limit ourselves here to text formatters. These process text contain formatting commands, which are usually placed at the beginning of a line and are preceded by some special character. These commands help control page numbering, text centering, left or right text justifying, page-margins definition, text underlining, page-size or line-gaps definition, line skipping, page-header title definition, and so forth. Developing a text formatter is a major task and we will limit ourselves here to a very simple text formatting application.

Our formatter uses text from a file one line at a time. Leading spaces and tabs are eliminated and output lines are edited one word at a time (the end of a word is either a blank, a tab, or the end of a line). Once an output line is full, it is right-justified and printed. This process is repeated as long as the input is not exhausted. The following program implements this approach. An explanation of the program follows the code.

```
MODULE TextJustify;
(* Right justification of a text *)
FROM InOut IMPORT WriteLn, Write, OpenInput, OpenOutput,
                  CloseInput, CloseOutput, Done, WriteString;
FROM Strings IMPORT String, InitString, FetchChar, AssignChar, Length,
                    Insert, ReadLine, Copy, AssignConst,
                    OutputString, DisposeString;
```

13.2 Applications

```
CONST Space =' ';
      Tab = 11C;
      LineWidth = 60;     (* must be less than MaxString *)
      EndOfString = 0C;
PROCEDURE Output(VAR Line: String; VAR OutPos, WordsCount: CARDINAL);

(* Display output buffer and reset counters and buffer *)
BEGIN
  IF OutPos > 0 THEN
    AssignChar(EndOfString, Line, OutPos);
    OutputString(Line);
    WriteLn;
    OutPos := 0;
    WordsCount := 0;
    DisposeString(Line); (* empty line *)
  END; (* IF *)
END Output;

PROCEDURE GetWord(Text: String; VAR Index: CARDINAL; VAR Word: String);
(* Copy a word from Text at Index into Word *)
VAR WordIndex: CARDINAL;
BEGIN
  DisposeString(Word); (* empty string *)
  WHILE (FetchChar(Text, Index) = Space) OR
        (FetchChar(Text, Index) = Tab) DO    (* skip spaces and tabs *)
    INC(Index);
  END; (* WHILE *)
  WordIndex := 0;
  WHILE NOT ((FetchChar(Text, Index) = Space) OR
             (FetchChar(Text, Index) = Tab) OR
             (FetchChar(Text, Index) = EndOfString)) DO
    AssignChar(FetchChar(Text, Index), Word, WordIndex);
    INC(Index);
    INC(WordIndex);
  END; (* WHILE *)
  AssignChar(EndOfString, Word, WordIndex);  (* end of word *)
  IF FetchChar(Text, Index) = EndOfString THEN
    Index := 0;          (* flag end of input line *)
  END; (* IF *)
END GetWord;

PROCEDURE Justify(VAR Buffer: String;
                  OutPos, SpacesLeft, WordsCount: CARDINAL;
                  VAR PadRight: BOOLEAN);
(* Right justify Buffer if more than one word in it. Expand line by
   inserting blanks in spaces between words, alternatively adding
   more blanks on right side or on left side of line. *)
CONST Empty = "                                                            ";
VAR LastNonBlank, Last, NBlanks, NGaps: CARDINAL;
    Extension, EmptyString: String;
    Ch: CHAR;
```

```
BEGIN
  InitString(EmptyString); AssignConst(EmptyString, Empty);
  InitString(Extension);
  (* expand Buffer to LineWidth *)
  Copy(EmptyString, 0, SpacesLeft, Extension);
  Insert(Extension, Buffer, Length(Buffer));
  PadRight := NOT PadRight;     (* change direction of blank insertion *)
  NGaps := WordsCount - 1;      (* number of gaps between words *)
  LastNonBlank := OutPos - 2;           (* back up over last space *)
  Last := LastNonBlank + SpacesLeft;
  WHILE LastNonBlank < Last DO
    (* move last word to end of line and insert blanks at each gap *)
    Ch := FetchChar(Buffer, LastNonBlank);
    AssignChar(Ch, Buffer, Last);
    IF Ch = Space THEN          (* insert blanks *)
      IF PadRight THEN   (* larger gaps at right *)
        NBlanks := (SpacesLeft - 1) DIV NGaps + 1;
      ELSE                      (* larger gaps at left *)
        NBlanks := SpacesLeft DIV NGaps;
      END; (* IF *)
      DEC(SpacesLeft, NBlanks);
      DEC(NGaps);
      WHILE NBlanks > 0 DO      (* insert blanks *)
        DEC(Last);
        AssignChar(Space, Buffer, Last);
        DEC(NBlanks);
      END; (* WHILE *)
    END; (* IF *)
    DEC(LastNonBlank);
    DEC(Last);
  END; (* WHILE *)
END Justify;

PROCEDURE OutputWord(VAR Word, EditedLine: String;
                     VAR OutPos, WordsCount: CARDINAL;
                     VAR PadRight: BOOLEAN);
(* Store Word in EditedLine starting at OutPos *)
VAR WordLength, SpacesLeft, Last: CARDINAL;
BEGIN
  WordLength := Length(Word);
  Last := WordLength + OutPos + 1; (* new end of EditedLine *)
  IF (OutPos > 0) AND (OutPos + WordLength >= LineWidth) THEN
    (* EditedLine is full, justify and output it *)
    Last := Last - OutPos;      (* reset Last for next line *)
    SpacesLeft := LineWidth - OutPos + 1;
```

```
      IF (SpacesLeft > 0) AND (WordsCount > 1) THEN
        Justify(EditedLine, OutPos, SpacesLeft, WordsCount, PadRight);
        OutPos := OutPos + SpacesLeft;
      END; (* IF *)
      Output(EditedLine, OutPos, WordsCount);
    END; (* IF *)
    Insert(Word, EditedLine, OutPos);
    OutPos := Last;
    AssignChar(Space, EditedLine, Last-1);         (* add a space after Word *)
    INC(WordsCount);
  END OutputWord;

VAR InputText, Word, EditedLine: String;
    OutputPosition, WordsCount, InputIndex: CARDINAL;
    PadRight: BOOLEAN;

BEGIN
  OutputPosition := 0;
  WordsCount := 0;
  PadRight := FALSE;
  OpenInput("dat")
  OpenOutput("ftd");
  InitString(InputText); InitString(Word); InitString(EditedLine);
  LOOP     (* for each input line *)
    ReadLine(InputText);
    IF NOT Done THEN EXIT END;       (* terminate if no more input *)
    IF Length(InputText) = 0 THEN  (* empty line *)
      Output(EditedLine, OutputPosition, WordsCount); (* output buffer *)
      WriteLn;
    ELSE
      InputIndex := 0;
      REPEAT
        GetWord(InputText, InputIndex, Word);
        IF Length(Word) > 0 THEN    (* actual word *)
          OutputWord(Word, EditedLine, OutputPosition, WordsCount, PadRight);
        END; (* IF *)
      UNTIL InputIndex = 0;    (* end of input line *)
    END; (* IF *)
  END; (* LOOP *)
  Output(EditedLine, OutputPosition, WordsCount);  (* empty last buffer *)
  WriteLn;
  CloseInput;
  CloseOutput;
  WriteString("Formatting completed"); WriteLn;
END TextJustify.
```

A "word" is taken as any sequence of characters not including a space, a tab, or an end of line. Procedure GetWord finds the next word in the input line and returns it along with the updated input text index (which is set to zero if the end of the input line has been reached). To accomplish this, first Word is set to the empty string. Then the procedure skips all blanks and tabs in the input line. It then accumulates all the characters in string Word, updating Index as it goes, and stops when it reaches a blank, a tab, or the end of the input line. It adds an end-of-string character at the end of Word, and if the end of the input line was reached, Index is set to zero before returning.

Procedure OutputWord places a word in the edited line. If the space left in the edited line is insufficient for the word, the edited line is right-justified and output, and the word is stored at the beginning of the next edited line. Otherwise, the word is stored in the edited line, followed by a space, and counter WordsCount and index OutPos are updated. To right-justify the edited line, the number of spaces left in the line is computed. If there are extra spaces, then Justify is called and OutPos is updated before calling Output.

Procedure Justify is called whenever an edited line must be right-justified prior to being output. First, the edited line is extended to the line width by addition of extra spaces at its end. After this is done, some extra spaces (equal in number to the value of SpacesLeft) will be inserted in the NGaps gaps between words. The space insertion is alternately done in two ways in order to avoid an accumulation of spaces on one of the sides of the text. Variable PadRight controls this alternation. The larger gaps are inserted at right for a line, then at left for the next line and again at right for a third line, and so on. Starting from the last word in Buffer, characters are copied to the right end of Buffer. For each gap (space) encountered while backing up in Buffer, the number of spaces to insert, NBlanks, is computed and the spaces are inserted.

Procedure Output displays the contents of the output buffer and updates counter WordsCount, index OutPos, and the output buffer.

Given the following text:

```
  Any technical revolution has, in the past, caused an intensive
reorganization of the economy and of society. It can be at the same
time the occasion of a crisis and the way out of it. This invention of
the steam engine, the building of the railroads, and the harnessing of
electricity were technical advances that had significant impact on the
entire society.

The "computer revolution" will have even broader consequences.
Computing is the major technological innovation of the last few years;
it is the common factor that allows and accelerates all other technical
changes. Because of the way in which it changes the processing and
conservation of information, it will modify the communications
system - the nervous system of organizations and of the entire society.

Until recently, computing was expensive and inefficient. It was also
esoteric; its use was limited to a restricted number of organizations.
Because it was elitist, it remained the monopoly of the powerful. Now
mass computing is emerging. Where before there were only large computers, now
many inexpensive, small but powerful machines are in existence,
interconnected through networks. Like electrical networks, they will
permeate society and transform it.
```

TextJustify produces the following output:

```
Any   technical   revolution  has,  in  the  past,  caused   an
intensive  reorganization  of the economy and of society.  It
can be at  the  same  time  the  occasion of  a   crisis  and   the
way  out   of   it.   The   invention  of   the steam  engine,  the
building   of   the   railroads,   and   the   harnessing   of
electricity   were   technical   advances   that had significant
impact on the entire society.

The   "computer     revolution"  will    have    even    broader
consequences.   Computing   is   the   major  technological
innovation  of  the  last  few  years; it is   the   common   factor
that   allows   and   accelerates   all other technical changes.
Because of the way  in which  it changes   the   processing   and
conservation    of     information,    it    will    modify    the
communications system — the nervous system of  organizations
and of the entire society.

Until    recently, computing was  expensive  and  inefficient.  It
was  also  esoteric;  its   use   was   limited   to   a   restricted
number    of    organizations.    Because   it   was   elitist,  it
remained the monopoly of the powerful.   Now   mass  computing
is   emerging.   Where before there were only large computers,
now many inexpensive,  small but   powerful   machines   are   in
existence,    interconnected  through  networks. Like electrical
networks, they will permeate society and transform it.
```

Even though this example was relatively simple, several procedures were needed. It is easy to see that the size of a general formatter can be very large. Since these programs are used frequently, they must be efficient despite their size. Text editors have also become extremely important, especially since the advent of microcomputers. Their diverse operations include pattern matching, which will be covered in Section 13.4.

Data Encryption

Enciphering and deciphering messages has historically been limited to military applications for which the secrecy of messages is of vital importance. Recently, however, civilian applications of cryptography have appeared, in particular, to ensure the security of computer files and electronic fund transfers. The owner of a file wants the information stored in that file to be as secure as if it were stored in a safe. Banks want their electronic fund transfers to be as safe as if made by armored trucks. For this degree of security, it is necessary to have means to encipher character strings and to decipher them. Through computers, there are now greatly enhanced methods for working in cryptography. We will briefly present some of the methods of cryptography, seen here as processing methods intended for character strings, in messages, or in computer files.

One of the oldest and simplest enciphering methods is known as Caesar's cipher, so called because it was used by Julius Caesar to code military messages. Each character in the alphabet is replaced by the character three places to the right (A is considered to be following Z). For instance "ATTACK MONDAY" becomes "DWWDFN PRQGDB." The method is weak, because even with its generalization where we replace character n by character n + k, the decipherer only has to try 26 possible choices in order to decipher the message.

A better method would be to use a *keyed alphabet* or *substitution table*. The following example of this method is based on the key "the quick brown fox jumped over the lazy dog":

```
ABCDEFGHIJKLMNOPQRSTUVWXYZ
THE QUICKBROWNFXJMPDVLAZYDG
```

The key is copied under the alphabet, but characters that have already appeared are not repeated (for instance, the space after QUICK, the "O" in FOX, etc). With this substitution table, our preceding message becomes "TDDTERGWFN TY." This is better than Caesar's cipher, as the decipherer must try 27! tables to be sure to decipher the message.

However, such enciphering methods based on substitutions are easy to solve because they do not hide the frequency of use of the letters in a given language. For example, in English, the most frequently occurring letters and their approximate frequencies, as computed on a large number of varied texts* is given by Table 13-1.

Note that punctuation marks are usually ignored, as are blanks, even though blanks occur more frequently than any single letter. Natural languages other than English will show somewhat different frequencies than those in Table 13-1, but each has a specific profile. By knowing the message language, it is therefore not difficult to replace the most-often-used character in the message by the most frequently occurring letter of the language, and so on. This approach helps to avoid having to try each of the 26 letters, but there is still some uncertainty.

Table 13-1
Most Frequently Occurring Letters in English

Letter	Frequency of occurrence (%)
E	13.1
T	10.5
A	8.2
O	8.0
N	7.1
I	6.8
R	6.3
S	6.1
H	5.3

*Griswold, R. E. "String and List Processing in SNOBOL4," Prentice Hall, 1975, p. 153.

In order to complicate the deciphering, it is sufficient to use more than one substitution table: this is called *polyalphabetic substitution*. One way of doing polyalphabetic substitution is to use a Vigenère square, where there are as many alphabets as there are characters in the original alphabet. Each alphabet might be a keyed alphabet, but sometimes it is sufficient to use a single key and to obtain the other alphabets by successive rotations, as in the following example based on the key NAPOLEON-BONAPARTE. Eliminating repetitions in the key, we obtain the character sequence: NAPOLEBRT. We define 26 alphabets, and start by defining the first alphabet, which will start with the key, and continue with the unused letters of the complete alphabet, in our case:

N A P O L E B R T C D F G H I J K M Q S U V W X Y Z

From that alphabet we build the other alphabets starting in order with letters A, P, O, L, E, B, R, T, C, D, etc. Each alphabet is obtained by rotating the original alphabet cyclically one position left. The 26 alphabets built in this manner are given in Table 13-2.

We can use alphabet 1 to encode the first character of the message, alphabet 2 to encode the second character, etc. For instance, PREPOSTEROUS becomes

Table 13-2
Alphabets for Polyalphabetic Substitution

```
 1   A P O L E B R T C D F G H I J K M Q S U V W X Y Z N
 2   B R T C D F G H I J K M Q S U V W X Y Z N A P O L E
 3   C D F G H I J K M Q S U V W X Y Z N A P O L E B R T
 4   D F G H I J K M Q S U V W X Y Z N A P O L E B R T C
 5   E B R T C D F G H I J K M Q S U V W X Y Z N A P O L
 6   F G H I J K M Q S U V W X Y Z N A P O L E B R T C D
 7   G H I J K M Q S U V W X Y Z N A P O L E B R T C D F
 8   H I J K M Q S U V W X Y Z N A P O L E B R T C D F G
 9   I J K M Q S U V W X Y Z N A P O L E B R T C D F G H
10   J K M Q S U V W X Y Z N A P O L E B R T C D F G H I
11   K M Q S U V W X Y Z N A P O L E B R T C D F G H I J
12   L E B R T C D F G H I J K M Q S U V W X Y Z N A P O
13   M Q S U V W X Y Z N A P O L E B R T C D F G H I J K
14   N A P O L E B R T C D F G H I J K M Q S U V W X Y Z
15   O L E B R T C D F G H I J K M Q S U V W X Y Z N A P
16   P O L E B R T C D F G H I J K M Q S U V W X Y Z N A
17   Q S U V W X Y Z N A P O L E B R T C D F G H I J K M
18   R T C D F G H I J K M Q S U V W X Y Z N A P O L E B
19   S U V W X Y Z N A P O L E B R T C D F G H I J K M Q
20   T C D F G H I J K M Q S U V W X Y Z N A P O L E B R
21   U V W X Y Z N A P O L E B R T C D F G H I J K M Q S
22   V W X Y Z N A P O L E B R T C D F G H I J K M Q S U
23   W X Y Z N A P O L E B R T C D F G H I J K M Q S U V
24   X Y Z N A P O L E B R T C D F G H I J K M Q S U V W
25   Y Z N A P O L E B R T C D F G H I J K M Q S U V W X
26   Z N A P O L E B R T C D F G H I J K M Q S U V W X Y
```

KXHZSOEMEODW. The first letter, P, is letter number 16 and is replaced by K, the 16th letter from the first alphabet, the second letter, R, is letter number 18 and is replaced by X, the 18th letter of alphabet 2, the third letter, E, is the 5th letter and is replaced by H, the fifth letter of alphabet 3, and so on.

A better way to use the Vigenère square is to use a secondary key that indicates what alphabet is used for each character of the message. For instance, the secondary key

TWENTYTHOUSANDLEAGUESUNDERTHESEA

and the message

ENEMYWILLATTACKSUNDAYATDAWNWITHALLFORCES

produce the cipher

GCCGBUKYIUGUNGIXVZXEMUSHEOVCHGGASRDIZNGE

The first character is picked from alphabet T (or 20), the second from alphabet W (or 23), the third from alphabet E (or 5), and so on. The following procedure creates a Vigenère square from a primary key.

```
TYPE Alphabet = ['A'..'Z'];
     Square = ARRAY Alphabet, Alphabet OF Alphabet;
PROCEDURE CreateSquare(VAR Vigenere: Square; Key: String);
VAR Chosen: ARRAY Alphabet OF BOOLEAN;
    First, Last, Second, Ch, Column: CHAR;
    Index: CARDINAL;
BEGIN
  FOR Ch := 'A' TO 'Z' DO     (* no character has been picked *)
    Chosen[Ch] := FALSE;
  END; (* FOR *)
  First := FetchChar(Key, 0);
  Second := 'A';
  FOR Index := 0 TO Length(Key)-1 DO (* start of first alphabet = key *)
    Ch := FetchChar(Key, Index);
    IF NOT Chosen[Ch] THEN     (* pick character *)
      Vigenere[First, Second] := Ch;
      INC(Second);
      Chosen[Ch] := TRUE;
    END; (* IF *)
  END; (* FOR *)
  FOR Ch := 'A' TO 'Z' DO     (* rest of first alphabet *)
    IF NOT Chosen[Ch] THEN
      Vigenere[First, Second] := Ch;
      INC(Second);
      Chosen[Ch] := TRUE;
    END; (* IF *)
  END; (* FOR *)
```

```
  Last := First;
  FOR Ch := 'B' TO 'Z' DO          (* all other alphabets *)
    Second := Vigenere[First, Ch];
    FOR Column := 'A' TO 'Y' DO    (* rotate Second from Last *)
      Vigenere[Second, Column] := Vigenere[Last, CHR(ORD(Column)+1)];
    END; (* FOR *)
    Vigenere[Second, 'Z'] := Vigenere[Last, 'A'];
    Last := Second;
  END; (* FOR *)
END CreateSquare;
```

The following procedure encodes a message using a secondary key and a Vigenère square.

```
PROCEDURE Encode(VAR Message: String; Key: String; Vigenere: Square);
(* Encode Message using Key and Vigenere square *)
VAR KeyLength, Index, KeyIndex: CARDINAL;
BEGIN
  KeyLength := Length(Key);
  KeyIndex := 0;
  FOR Index := 0 TO Length(Message)-1 DO
    AssignChar(Vigenere[FetchChar(Key, KeyIndex), FetchChar(Message, Index)],
               Message, Index);
    INC(KeyIndex);
    IF KeyIndex >= KeyLength THEN
      KeyIndex := 0;
    END; (* IF *)
  END; (* FOR *)
END Encode;
```

Since this example has only touched upon the field of cryptography, a few more remarks are needed to put things in a better perspective. If a message and its key are binary coded, then it is easy to obtain the cipher by doing an Exclusive OR of the message and its key. An Exclusive OR of the cipher and the key produces the message, while an Exclusive OR of the cipher and the message gives the key. This property, which is well known in cryptography, means the key may be found if the message and the cipher are known.

All the modifications defined by enciphering methods can be applied to character strings, whatever their meaning. However, when numerous character strings must be transmitted through an unsafe network, a ciphering machine is used. The sender provides a key for the machine, which uses it to produce a long string of bits. An Exclusive OR of the message and this string of bits is made before sending. The receiver has a similar machine, which uses the same key to produce the same long string of bits, then does an Exclusive OR on the received cipher to obtain the original message.

In commercial applications like electronic fund transfers, public keys are used: the keys are known by all. Each person also has a secret deciphering key. The sender uses the public key to send, the receiver uses a secret key to decipher. In order for the system to work, the secret key applied to the public key cipher must produce the original message. The two keys must be distinct and the discovery of the secret key by using the public key must be extremely difficult. The enciphering and deciphering must be efficient. This leads to a complex field whose scope of investigation is beyond our objectives. However, we note that this field directly uses character strings and, with the extensive use of computer networks, has become extremely important.

13.3 Implementation

As with other abstract data types, we find two classes of implementation, one based on a static representation and the other based on a dynamic representation of strings.

Static Implementation

Various implementations of character strings are based on arrays of characters. As we have already mentioned, an implementation of strings compatible with Modula-2 string literals must declare a transparent type string in the following manner.

TYPE String = ARRAY [0..MaxString] OF CHAR;

This representation is zero-based; that is, the first character has index zero, the second character has index one, and so on. As always with static representations we must define a maximum size (here MaxString, as the last character is always null).

Character strings are normally of variable length and some Pascal strings implementations use the array element with index zero to store the string length. In that case, the maximum length of the string is 255, as this is the largest integer that can fit in the byte used to store a character. As Modula-2 string literals are zero-based, this same approach cannot be used. In Modula-2, instead of keeping the string length, the null character (0C) is used to indicate the end of the string.

Our ADT String offers an opaque type String, and we can still implement strings with arrays, as the following implementation module shows. We have elected not to store the string length; rather, we mark the end of the string by the leftmost occurrence of the null character. Operation StringLength is thus a little slower, as its complexity is O(n), but we do not have to update the string length after each operation.

```
IMPLEMENTATION MODULE Strings;
FROM Storage IMPORT ALLOCATE, DEALLOCATE;
FROM InOut IMPORT Read, Write, Done, EOL;

TYPE String = POINTER TO CharSequence;      (* opaque type *)
     CharSequence = ARRAY [0..MaxString] OF CHAR;

(* This type of string is provided for applications where a maximum
   of MaxString characters is appropriate. The string is
   terminated by a null character (EndOfString). *)
```

```
PROCEDURE InitString(VAR S: String);
(* Initialize S to empty string *)
BEGIN
  S := NIL;
END InitString;

PROCEDURE Length(S: String): CARDINAL;
(* Return the current length of S *)
VAR Count: CARDINAL;
BEGIN
  Count := 0;
  IF S # NIL THEN
    WHILE S^[Count] # EndOfString DO
      INC(Count);
    END; (* WHILE *)
  END; (* IF *)
  RETURN Count;
END Length;

PROCEDURE Assign(VAR Dest: String; Source: String);
(* Assignment of Source to Dest *)
BEGIN
  IF Source = NIL THEN
    IF Dest # NIL THEN       (* empty string *)
      DEALLOCATE(Dest, SIZE(CharSequence));
      Dest := NIL;
    END; (* IF *)
  ELSE
    IF Dest = NIL THEN       (* allocate space *)
      ALLOCATE(Dest, SIZE(CharSequence));
    END; (* IF *)
    Dest^ := Source^;   (* copy character array *)
  END; (* IF *)
END Assign;

PROCEDURE Delete(VAR Source: String; Index, Count: CARDINAL);
(* Delete a substring of Source *)
VAR Deleted, Last, SourceLength: CARDINAL;
BEGIN
  SourceLength := Length(Source);
  IF (Index+Count-1 < SourceLength) AND (Count > 0) THEN
    Last := Index;
    FOR Deleted := Index+Count TO SourceLength DO
      (* shift end of string left over deleted substring *)
      Source^[Last] := Source^[Deleted];
      INC(Last);
    END: (* FOR *)
```

```
      FOR Deleted := Last TO MaxString DO    (* pad end of array *)
        Source^[Deleted] :=EndOfString;
      END; (* FOR *)
    END; (* IF *)
END Delete;
PROCEDURE DisposeString(VAR S: String);
(* Delete string S *)
BEGIN
  IF S # NIL THEN
    DEALLOCATE(S, SIZE(CharSequence));
    S := NIL;
  END; (* IF *)
END DisposeString;
PROCEDURE Copy(Source: String; Index, Count: CARDINAL; VAR Dest: String);
(* Copy Count characters from Source starting at position Index
   into Dest *)
VAR Intermediate: String;
BEGIN
  InitString( Intermediate );  (* the use of pointers as value parameters
  does not protect the source string, so we must make a working copy of it *)
  Assign(Intermediate, Source );
  IF (Index+Count-1 < Length(Intermediate))        (* valid substring *)
      AND (Count <= MaxString) THEN                (* fits into Dest *)
        (* delete characters preceding and following substring *)
      Delete(Intermediate, 0, Index);
      Delete(Intermediate, Count, Length(Intermediate)-Count);
      Assign(Dest, Intermediate);   (* keep substring *)
    ELSE
      DisposeString(Dest);     (* no extraction possible *)
    END; (* IF *)
    DisposeString( Intermediate );
END Copy;
PROCEDURE AssignConst(VAR Dest: String; Source: ARRAY OF CHAR);
(* Assignment of a Modula-2 string constant, Source, to String Dest *)
VAR High, Index: CARDINAL;
BEGIN
  IF Dest = NIL THEN
    ALLOCATE(Dest, SIZE(CharSequence));
  END; (* IF *)
  High := HIGH(Source);
  Index := 0;     (* Source is zero-based *)
  WHILE (Index <= High) AND (Index < MaxString)
      AND (Source[Index] # EndOfString) DO         (* copy characters *)
    Dest^[Index] :=Source[Index];
    INC(Index);
  END; (* WHILE *)
  Dest^[Index] := EndOfString;
END AssignConst;
```

```
PROCEDURE Insert(Source: String; VAR Dest: String;
                 Index: CARDINAL);
(* Insert string Source into string Dest at Index *)
VAR SourceLength, DestLength, LastDest, Current: CARDINAL;
BEGIN
  SourceLength := Length(Source);
  DestLength := Length(Dest);
  IF (SourceLength + DestLength <= MaxString)
       AND (Index <= DestLength) THEN
    IF Dest = NIL THEN
      ALLOCATE(Dest, SIZE(CharSequence));
    END;
    LastDest := DestLength - 1;
    FOR Current := DestLength + SourceLength - 1
           TO Index + SourceLength BY -1 DO
      (* shift end of string right to make room for substring *)
      Dest^[Current] := Dest^[LastDest];
      DEC(LastDest);
    END; (* FOR *)
    DestLength := DestLength + SourceLength;
    Dest^[DestLength] := EndOfString;
    LastDest := 0;
    FOR Current := Index TO Index + SourceLength - 1 DO  (* copy substring *)
      Dest^[Current] := Source^[LastDest];
      INC(LastDest);
    END; (* FOR *)
  END; (* IF *)
END Insert;

PROCEDURE Concat(Str1, Str2: String; VAR Dest: String);
(* Concatenate Str1 and Str2 and store result in Dest *)
VAR Length1, Length2, DestIndex, Index2: CARDINAL;
BEGIN
  Length1 := Length(Str1);
  Length2 := Length(Str2);
  IF Length1 + Length2 <= MaxString THEN
    Assign(Dest, Str1);    (* copy Str1 *)
    Index2 := 0;
    FOR DestIndex := Length1 TO Length1 + Length2 - 1 DO
      (* copy Str2 *)
      Dest^[DestIndex] := Str2^[Index2];
      INC(Index2);
    END; (* FOR *)
    Dest^[Length1 + Length2] := EndOfString;
  END; (* IF *)
END Concat;
```

```
PROCEDURE StringGreater(Str1, Str2: String): BOOLEAN;
(* String comparison in lexical order according to character set *)
VAR Length1, Length2, Current: CARDINAL;
BEGIN
  Length1 := Length(Str1);
  Length2 := Length(Str2);
  IF (Length1 > 0) AND (Length2 > 0) THEN
    Current := 0;
    WHILE (Current < Length1) AND (Current < Length2)
          AND (Str1^[Current] = Str2^[Current]) DO
      INC(Current);
    END; (* WHILE *)
    IF (Current <= Length1) AND (Current <= Length2)
          AND (Str1^[Current] > Str2^[Current]) THEN
      RETURN TRUE;
    ELSIF (Current = Length2) AND (Length2 < Length1) THEN
      (* Str2 shorter *)
      RETURN TRUE;
    ELSE
      RETURN FALSE;
    END; (* IF *)
  ELSIF (Length1 # 0) AND (Length2 = 0) THEN
    (* Str2 empty *)
    RETURN TRUE;
  ELSE
    RETURN FALSE;
  END; (* IF *)
END StringGreater;

PROCEDURE StringEqual(Str1, Str2: String): BOOLEAN;
(* String comparison in lexical order according to character set *)
VAR Length1, Length2, Current: CARDINAL;
BEGIN
  Length1 := Length(Str1);
  Length2 := Length(Str2);
  IF (Length1 > 0) AND (Length2 > 0) THEN
    Current := 0;
    WHILE (Current < Length1) AND (Current < Length2)
          AND (Str1^[Current] = Str2^[Current]) DO
      INC(Current);
    END; (* WHILE *)
    RETURN (Current = Length1) AND (Current = Length2);
  ELSE
    RETURN (Length 1 = 0) AND (Length 2 = 0)
  END (* IF *)
END StringEqual;
```

```
PROCEDURE FetchChar(Source: String; Index: CARDINAL): CHAR;
(* Extract a character from a string *)
VAR Res: CHAR;
BEGIN
  IF Index < Length(Source) THEN
    Res := Source^[Index];
  ELSE                    (* outside string *)
    Res := EndOfString;
  END; (* IF *)
  RETURN Res;
END FetchChar;

PROCEDURE AssignChar(Ch: CHAR; VAR Dest: String; Index: CARDINAL);
(* Store a character into a string *)
BEGIN
  IF Index < Length(Dest) THEN
    Dest^[Index] := Ch;
  ELSIF (Index = Length(Dest)) AND (Index < MaxString) THEN
    (* add to end *)
    IF Dest = NIL THEN       (* empty string *)
      ALLOCATE(Dest, SIZE(CharSequence));
    END; (* IF *)
    Dest^[Index] := Ch;
    Dest^[Index + 1] := EndOfString;
  END; (* IF *)
END AssignChar;

PROCEDURE Pos(Sub, Source: String): CARDINAL;
(* Search a string for a substring *)
VAR Length1, Length2, SubIndex, SourceIndex, Res: CARDINAL;
BEGIN
  Length1 := Length(Sub);
  Length2 := Length(Source);
  Res := Length2;                   (* failure result *)
  IF Length1 <= Length2 THEN
    SubIndex := 0;
    SourceIndex := 0;
    WHILE (SubIndex < Length1) AND (SourceIndex < Length2) DO
      IF Sub^[SubIndex] = Source^[SourceIndex] THEN
        INC(SubIndex);
        IF Res = Length2 THEN
          Res := SourceIndex;       (* match start *)
        END; (* IF *)
```

```
        ELSIF Res # Length2 THEN      (* incomplete match, reset *)
          SourceIndex := Res;         (* reset in string *)
          SubIndex := 0;              (* start again substring *)
          Res := Length2;             (* failure flag *)
        END; (* IF *)
        INC(SourceIndex);
      END; (* WHILE *)
      IF NOT ((SubIndex = Length1) AND (SourceIndex = Length2)) THEN
        Res := Length2;  (* failure *)
      END;
    END; (* IF *)
    RETURN Res;
  END Pos;

  PROCEDURE ToString(Ch: CHAR; VAR Str: String);
  (* Conversion between type CHAR and type String *)
  BEGIN
    IF Str = NIL THEN
      ALLOCATE(Str, SIZE(CharSequence));      (* create string *)
    END; (* IF *)
    Str^[0] := Ch;
    Str^[1] := EndOfString;
  END ToString;

  PROCEDURE InputString(VAR Str: String);
  (* Input string Str from standard input, string will be terminated
     by a blank, a return or any other control character. Use
     InOut and reset InOut.Done *)
  VAR Index: CARDINAL;
      Ch: CHAR;
  BEGIN
    IF Str = NIL THEN
      ALLOCATE(Str, SIZE(CharSequence));      (* create string *)
    END; (* IF *)
    REPEAT                   (* skip blanks *)
      Read(Ch);
    UNTIL (Ch > ' ') OR NOT Done;
    IF Done THEN
      Index := 0;
      WHILE Done AND (Ch > ' ')
            AND (Index < MaxString) DO  (* store characters *)
        Str^[Index] := Ch;
        Read(Ch);
        INC(Index);
      END; (* WHILE *)
      Str^[Index] := EndOfString;
      WHILE Ch > ' ' DO  (* skip superfluous characters *)
        Read(Ch);
      END; (* WHILE *)
```

```
    ELSE                        (* empty string *)
      Str^[0] := EndOfString;
    END; (* IF *)
END InputString;

PROCEDURE OutputString(Str: String);
(* Output string Str on standard output *)
VAR Index: CARDINAL;
BEGIN
  IF Str # NIL THEN
    Index := 0;
    WHILE Str^[Index] # EndOfString DO
      Write(Str^[Index]);
      INC(Index);
    END; (* WHILE *)
  END; (* IF *)
END OutputString;

PROCEDURE ReadLine(VAR Str: String);
(* Input a string which may contain spaces. The end of the
   string is indicated by the end of the line. If the line is
   longer than MaxString the rest of the line is skipped *)
VAR Length2: CARDINAL;
    Ch: CHAR;
BEGIN
  IF Str = NIL THEN
    ALLOCATE(Str, SIZE(CharSequence));    (* create string *)
  END; (* IF *)
  Length2:= 0;
  LOOP
    Read(Ch);
    IF (Ch = EOL) OR NOT Done THEN    (* end of line or end of file *)
      IF Length2 <= MaxString THEN Str^[Length2] := EndOfString END;
      EXIT;
    ELSIF Length2 < MaxString THEN              (* keep *)
      Str^[Length2]:= Ch;
      INC(Length2);
    ELSE                       (* skip *)
      INC(Length2);
    END; (* IF *)
  END; (* LOOP *)
END ReadLine;

END Strings.
```

The implementation of the various operations is straightforward. Almost all the operations have a complexity of $O(n)$, as most have to scan the array of characters. The exceptions are operations InitString, FetchChar, AssignChar, DisposeString, and ToString, which are $O(1)$.

When dealing with a number of character strings that are kept concurrently in memory during the execution of an application, it is possible to use yet another sequential representation. A very large array of characters is declared, for instance:

```
VAR Buffer: ARRAY [0..32000] OF CHAR,
```

and the strings are stored sequentially in it. There are two possible representations, as shown in Figure 13-1: each string is defined by its starting index in Buffer and followed by an end-of-string character, or each string is defined by its starting index in Buffer and its length.

With such a sequential string representation use of memory space is optimal; however, insertions and deletions will be slow. In fact, if the value of a string changes, it is more convenient to create a new string. This representation is often used in applications where strings are stored and used but not modified. For instance, it might be used to store all the identifiers of a program being compiled or assembled.

Dynamic Implementation

A string may be represented by a linear list of characters, as shown in Figure 13-2. With such a representation, memory use is poor, as most of the memory is used to store pointers. To increase memory efficiency each element is extended to store a sequence of characters, as shown in Figure 13-3.

Any unused space in a block is filled with null characters (shown as "°"). With this representation, these null characters will only appear in the last block of the string. Memory management is not difficult, but character insertion and deletion will be complex. If the block size increases, so does the unused space in the last block. On the other hand, if the block size decreases, we come closer to the list of single characters shown in Figure 13-2.

To speed up insertions and deletions, a variation of this representation is used that makes it possible to use blocks only partially filled. For instance, suppose we want to

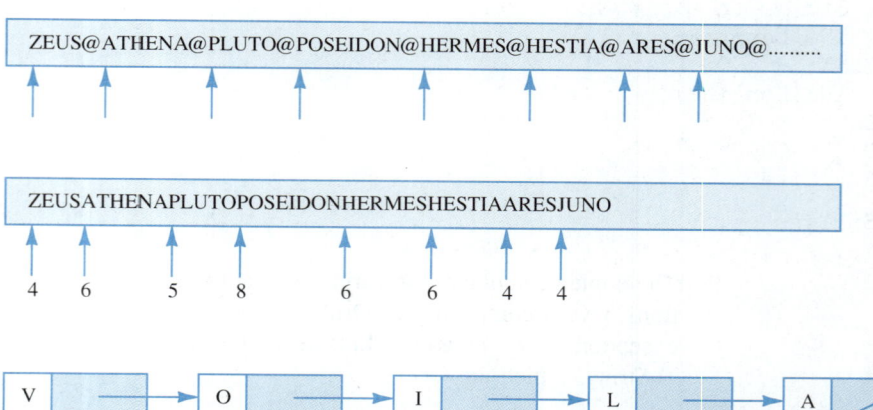

Figure 13-1 Sequential String Representation

Figure 13-2 A Linear List of Characters

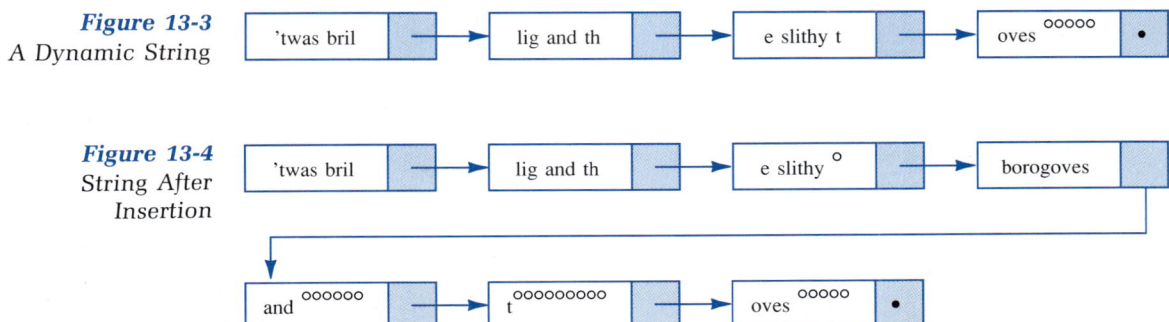

Figure 13-3
A Dynamic String

Figure 13-4
String After
Insertion

insert the words "borogoves and " after the word "slithy" in the example of Figure 13-3. This will save processing time but use more memory space for null characters ("o").

The following code is the beginning of the implementation based on a representation similar to Figure 13-3. Most operations are not very different from what was seen in the static implementation. The main difference is that here the string is sliced in blocks of BlockLength characters, and now we must allow access to individual characters by locating the block in which they appear.

```
IMPLEMENTATION MODULE Strings;
FROM Storage IMPORT ALLOCATE, DEALLOCATE;
FROM InOut IMPORT WriteLn, Read, Write, Done, EOL;

CONST BlockLength = 10;

TYPE String = POINTER TO Block;   (* opaque types must be pointers *)
     Block = RECORD
               CharSequence: ARRAY [0..BlockLength-1] OF CHAR;
               Next: String;
             END;
(* This type of string is provided for applications where unlimited
   strings are appropriate. If the working length of the string is
   not a multiple of BlockLength characters, then the string is terminated
   by the EndOfString character (0C). *)

PROCEDURE InitString(VAR S: String);
(* Initialize S to empty string *)
BEGIN
  S := NIL;
END InitString;

PROCEDURE Length(S: String): CARDINAL;
(* Return the current length of S *)
VAR Count, Index: CARDINAL;
BEGIN
  IF S # NIL THEN
    Count := 0;
```

```
      WHILE S^.Next # NIL DO    (* count full blocks *)
        INC(Count, BlockLength);
        S := S^.Next;
      END; (* WHILE *)
      Index := 0;
      WHILE (Index < BlockLength) AND (S^.CharSequence[Index] # 0C) DO
        (* count characters in last block *)
        INC(Index);
      END; (* WHILE *)
      RETURN Count+Index;
    ELSE
      RETURN 0;
    END; (* IF *)
  END Length;
```

Procedure Length is rather simple: if the string exists, the character counter is set to zero and the number of full blocks is counted. When the procedure reaches the last allocated block, the characters are counted individually.

```
PROCEDURE AssignConst(VAR Dest: String; Source: ARRAY OF CHAR);
(* Assignment of Modula-2 character string Source to Dest *)
VAR LastIndex, Current, Index: CARDINAL;
    BlockPointer: String;
BEGIN
  DisposeString(Dest);
  ALLOCATE(Dest, SIZE(Block));
  Dest^.Next := NIL;
  BlockPointer := Dest;
  LastIndex := HIGH(Source);      (* last index of Source *)
  Index := 0; Current := 0;
  WHILE (Index <= LastIndex) AND (Source[Index] # 0C) DO
    IF Current >= BlockLength THEN    (* add new block *)
      ALLOCATE(BlockPointer^.Next, SIZE(Block));
      BlockPointer := BlockPointer^.Next;
      BlockPointer^.Next := NIL;
      Current := 0;
    END; (* IF *)
    BlockPointer^.CharSequence[Current] := Source[Index]; (* copy char. *)
    INC(Index); INC(Current);
  END; (* WHILE *)
  WHILE Current < BlockLength DO        (* fill with nulls *)
    BlockPointer^.CharSequence[Current] := EndOfString;
    INC(Current);
  END; (* WHILE *)
END AssignConst;
```

Procedure AssignConst is obviously more complicated than with the static implementation, although the basic algorithm remains the same. A first block is allocated to string Dest and characters are copied from Source; whenever a block is filled, a new block is allocated and linked to the previous block. If necessary, the last block is filled with end-of-string characters.

```
PROCEDURE Assign(VAR Dest: String; Source: String);
(* Assigns value of string Source to string Dest *)
VAR BlockPointer: String;
BEGIN
  DisposeString(Dest);
  IF Source # NIL THEN
    ALLOCATE(Dest, SIZE(Block));      (* first block *)
    Dest^.Next := NIL;
    BlockPointer := Dest;
    WHILE Source # NIL DO    (* copy blocks *)
      BlockPointer^.CharSequence := Source^.CharSequence;
      Source := Source^.Next;         (* next block *)
      IF Source = NIL THEN
        BlockPointer^.Next := NIL;    (* end of block list *)
      ELSE
        ALLOCATE(BlockPointer^.Next, SIZE(Block));   (* new block *)
        BlockPointer := BlockPointer^.Next;
        BlockPointer^.Next := NIL;
      END; (* IF *)
    END; (* WHILE *)
  END; (* IF *)
END Assign;
```

Procedure Assign follows a pattern similar to AssignConst: a first block is allocated to Dest, then the blocks of string Source are copied one by one. After the copy of a block, the Source pointer moves to the next block and a new block is allocated and linked to the previous block in Dest.

```
PROCEDURE Copy(Source: String; Index, Count: CARDINAL;
               VAR Dest: String);
(* Extract Count characters from Source starting at position Index
   store them into Dest *)
VAR Intermediate: String;
BEGIN
  InitString(Intermediate);
  (* The use of pointers as value parameters does not protect the
     Source string, so we must make a working copy of it *)
  Assign(Intermediate, Source);
  DisposeString(Dest);
```

```
  IF Index+Count < Length(Intermediate) THEN    (* valid substring *)
    Delete(Intermediate, 0, Index);             (* preceding characters *)
    Delete(Intermediate, Count,
           StringLength(Intermediate)-Count);   (* end *)
    Assign(Dest, Intermediate);
  END; (* IF *)
  DisposeString(Intermediate);
END Copy;
```

Procedure Copy follows the same pattern as in the static implementation, since it relies on calls to other string operations.

Operations Delete (about 50 lines) and Insert (about 90 lines) are much more complex than was the case with the static implementation. Here, we will only give their pseudocode.

> Delete
>   Find block and index in that block of first character following substring to delete
>   Locate substring start
>   Shift part of string following substring to delete leftover substring
>   Pad last block with end of string characters
>   Free the last blocks no more in use
> End Delete
>
> Insert
>   If insertion is possible
>   If destination is empty allocate first block
>   Set last index to length of destination
>   Locate last block and index of destination
>   Compute number of blocks to add to destination and add them
>   Find last block and index of expanded destination
>   Shift part of destination following insertion point right to new end
>   Insert all the characters of source at insertion point
>   End if
> End Insert

Apart from operations InitString and ToString, which are $O(1)$, all operations are $O(n)$, although they have different proportionality constants than in the case of the static implementation. For instance, in the case of long strings, Length will be faster, as it skips characters 10 by 10. On the other hand, Delete and Insert will be slower than with a static implementation, but are still $O(n)$.

13.4 Pattern Matching

When using character strings, it is very often necessary to search the string for occurrences of a given substring. We can see the need demonstrated in operation POS in our ADT String, and in the design of text editors, which always provide such a feature. When dealing with long texts, a search operation must be implemented as efficiently as possible. We will concentrate here on various pattern-matching algorithms that search for a given substring.

Simple Search

The implementation of operation SearchString we have seen earlier illustrates the simplest pattern-matching algorithm. Figure 13-5 illustrates this algorithm. During the search for substring xyz in string xyxyz, character "|" marks the position in the pattern and in the string where a comparison is made. We start at the beginning of the string and the substring (or pattern), and the first characters are compared. They match, so the second characters are compared; they match, so the third characters are compared. Since the third characters do not match, we back up to the second character of the string and the first character of the pattern, and we repeat the process.

This algorithm is simple and easy to program, as seen in procedure Pos in our Strings ADT. The following procedure SimpleSearch illustrates the algorithm again.

Figure 13-5
Pattern Matching

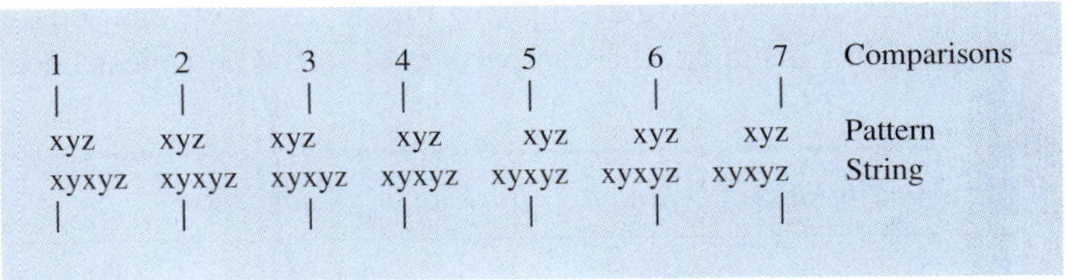

1	2	3	4	5	6	7	Comparisons
|	|	|	|	|	|	|	
xyz	xyz	xyz	xyz	xyz	xyz	xyz	Pattern
xyxyz	xyxyz	xyxyz	xyxyz	xyxyz	xyxyz	xyxyz	String
|	|	|	|	|	|		

```
PROCEDURE SimpleSearch(Pattern, Text: String): CARDINAL;
(* Search for Pattern in Text and return index of pattern start in text
   or Length(Text) if not found *)
VAR StringIndex, PatternIndex, PatternLength, TextLength: CARDINAL;
BEGIN
  StringIndex := 0;
  PatternIndex := 0;
  PatternLength := Length(Pattern);
  TextLength := Length(Text);
```

```
  REPEAT
    IF FetchChar(Text, StringIndex) = FetchChar(Pattern, PatternIndex) THEN
      INC(StringIndex);
      INC(PatternIndex);
    ELSE
      StringIndex := StringIndex - PatternIndex + 1;   (* back up in text *)
      PatternIndex := 0;                     (* beginning of pattern *)
    END; (* IF *)
  UNTIL (PatternIndex >= PatternLength) OR (StringIndex >= TextLength);
  IF (PatternIndex >= PatternLength) THEN    (* found *)
    RETURN StringIndex - PatternLength;
  ELSE                                       (* not found *)
    RETURN TextLength;
  END; (* IF *)
END SimpleSearch;
```

Characters from the string and the pattern are systematically compared in the REPEAT loop, which backs up in the string and restarts the pattern each time a mismatch occurs. In the worst case, where the pattern cannot be found in the string, each of the p characters of the pattern will be compared with the s characters of the string, as for example, if we search for "plus" in the string "pluaplubplucpludpluepluf." The algorithm complexity is thus O(ps).

Knuth-Morris-Pratt Algorithm

In the pattern matching example of Figure 13-5, we can see that some comparisons are useless. For instance, the comparison of step 4 is useless because the second character

Figure 13-6
Backup Table

Mismatch position j	Match	Backup[j]	Comments
1	none	0	Restart pattern and advance to next character in string.
2	f	1	Not i, could be f. Backto 1 in pattern. Stay on same character in string.
3	fi	0	Not f. Start over and advance to next character in string.
4	fif	2	Not o, could be i. Backto 2 in pattern. Stay on same character in string.
5	fifo	0	Not f. Start over and advance to next character in string.
6	fifof	1	Not i, could be f. Backto 1 in pattern. Stay on same character in string
7	fifofi	0	Not f. Start over and advance to next character in string.
8	fifofif	4	Not u, could be o. Backto 4 in pattern. Stay on same character in string.
9	fifofifu	1	Not m, could be f. Backto 1 in pattern. Stay on same character in string.

in the string has already been inspected and could be skipped. The basic idea of the Knuth-Morris-Pratt algorithm is to take advantage of the information obtained before a mismatch occurs. If a mismatch occurs on the nth character of the pattern, the first $n - 1$ characters did match. Completely skipping past the matched portion of the pattern will not work, because the pattern could match itself at the point where the mismatch occurs. For instance, if we search "fifofifum" in "fifofifofifum," the first mismatch will be detected at the eighth character, but we should back up to the fifth character of the string. If we do not, we will miss the match. The "best" backup depends only on the pattern matching itself and can be computed ahead of time and stored in vector Backup, as shown in Figure 13-6.

Procedure KnuthMorrisPratt below does pattern matching by advancing in a normal way as long as the characters match; otherwise, it shifts the pattern by a value taken from table BackupTable. If the value is zero, the process advances to the next character in the string and starts again at the start of the pattern. Figure 13-7 on page 513 illustrates the shifting process at places where there is some matching. A star indicates the end of a match.

After the first 11 mismatches on the first character of the pattern, the pattern is tried again from its start before a mismatch is found on the fifth character of the pattern. The comparisons start again in the string at the last mismatched character in the string. We then get mismatches on the first character of the pattern until a mismatch occurs on the fourth character of the pattern. The pattern is shifted two positions for the next try, which ends again in a mismatch. Three mismatches on the first character are followed by a complete match.

```
PROCEDURE KnuthMorrisPratt(Pattern, Text: String): CARDINAL;
(* Search for Pattern in Text.  Return index of pattern in text if found
   else return Length(Text) *)
TYPE Table = ARRAY [0..MaxPattern-1] OF INTEGER;

  PROCEDURE ComputeBackup(Pattern: String;
                         VAR BackupTable: Table);
  (* Compute skip table for pattern characters *)
  VAR PatternLength, Pat1, Pat2: INTEGER;
  BEGIN
    PatternLength := Length(Pattern);
    Pat1 := 0;
    Pat2 := -1;
    BackupTable[0] := -1;
    REPEAT     (* match pattern with itself *)
      IF (Pat2 = -1) OR
         (FetchChar(Pattern, Pat1) = FetchChar(Pattern, Pat2)) THEN
        INC(Pat1);
        INC(Pat2);
```

```
          IF FetchChar(Pattern, Pat1) # FetchChar(Pattern, Pat2) THEN
            BackupTable[Pat1] := Pat2;
          ELSE
            BackupTable[Pat1] := BackupTable[Pat2];
          END; (* IF *)
        ELSE
          Pat2 := BackupTable[Pat2];
        END; (* IF *)
    UNTIL Pat1 >= PatternLength;
  END ComputeBackup;
VAR StringIndex, PatternIndex, PatternLength, TextLength: CARDINAL;
    BackupTable : Table;
BEGIN
  ComputeBackup(Pattern, BackupTable);
  TextLength := Length(Text);
  PatternLength := Length(Pattern);
  StringIndex := 0;
  PatternIndex := 0;
  REPEAT
    IF (PatternIndex = 0) OR
       (FetchChar(Text, StringIndex) = FetchChar(Pattern, PatternIndex)) THEN
      INC(StringIndex);
      INC(PatternIndex);
    ELSE     (* take shortcut *)
      PatternIndex := BackupTable[PatternIndex];
    END; (* IF *)
  UNTIL (PatternIndex >= PatternLength) OR (StringIndex >= TextLength);
  IF PatternIndex >= PatternLength THEN (* success *)
    RETURN StringIndex - PatternLength;
  ELSE    (* failure *)
    RETURN TextLength;
  END; (* IF *)
END KnuthMorrisPratt;
```

The ComputeBackup procedure is very similar to the KnuthMorrisPratt procedure, as it tries to match the pattern with itself and uses the same pattern-matching method. Procedure KnuthMorrisPratt has a complexity of $O(s)$, but this does not include the BackupTable creation, whose complexity is $O(p)$. The total complexity is $O(p + s)$, which is better than $O(ps)$. However, these procedures might not prove to be significantly faster than the simple search method when they are used in actual applications because they do not often involve searching for a highly repetitive pattern in a highly repetitive string. This comparison will be discussed in detail in our case study in Section 13.5.

Boyer-Moore Algorithm

It is still possible to improve the search by scanning the pattern from right to left and deciding what to do on the first nonmatching character. Suppose we consider the same

Figure 13-7 Searching for "fifer"

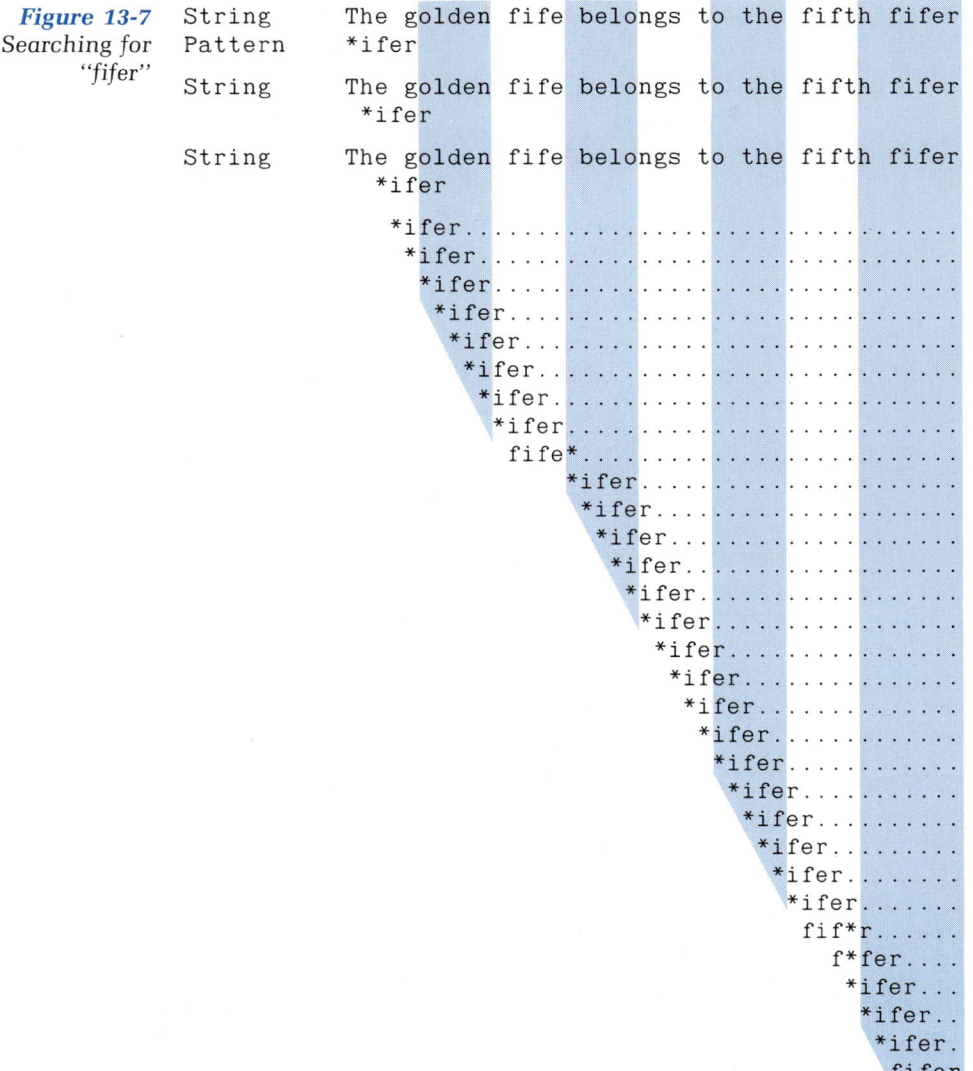

example as previously, searching "fifer" in the string "the golden fife belongs to the fifth fifer." In this algorithm, we start by comparing the r of the pattern with the g of the string. There is no match, but since g does not appear in the pattern, we can advance in the string by the length of the pattern. The next comparison is then between r and n, and we advance again to compare r and e. Since e appears in the pattern, it is shifted right one position so that we compare r and a space. As there is no space in the pattern, we advance five positions and repeat the comparisons, as shown in Figure 13-8.

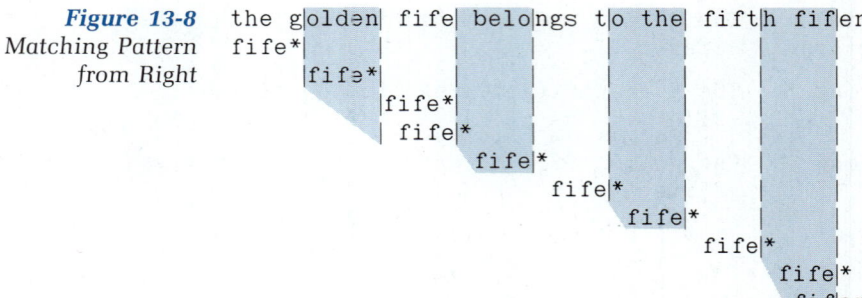

Figure 13-8
Matching Pattern
from Right

We have compared 14 characters from the text, including 5 to determine matching. The corresponding algorithm is implemented by procedure SimpleBoyerMoore, whose code follows. It uses a vector SkipTable, which gives for each character in the alphabet the number of characters to skip if this character is in the string and causes a mismatch. All characters that do not appear in the pattern give a jump of the pattern length, whereas characters that appear in the pattern show a jump from zero to the pattern length minus one, from right to left. For our example, pattern ''fifer'' gives 0 for letter r, 1 for letter e, 2 for letter f, and 3 for letter i. (There is no 4, as the first letter is repeated in the pattern.) Procedure ComputeSkip sets up the skip table.

```
PROCEDURE SimpleBoyerMoore(Pattern, Text: String): CARDINAL;
(* Search for Pattern in Text. Return index of pattern in text or
   Length(Text) if not found *)

TYPE CharArray = ARRAY [' '..'~'] OF CARDINAL;

  PROCEDURE ComputeSkip(Pattern: String;
                        VAR SkipTable: CharArray);
  (* Initialize skip table *)
  VAR Index, PatternLength: CARDINAL;
      Ch: CHAR;
  BEGIN
    PatternLength := Length(Pattern);
    FOR Ch := ' ' TO '~' DO
      SkipTable[Ch] := PatternLength;
    END; (* FOR *)
    FOR Index := 0 TO PatternLength-1 DO
      SkipTable[FetchChar(Pattern, Index)] := PatternLength-Index-1;
    END; (* FOR *)
  END ComputeSkip;

VAR StringIndex, PatternLength, TextLength: CARDINAL;
    SkipTable: CharArray;
    PatternIndex: INTEGER;
```

```
BEGIN
  ComputeSkip(Pattern, SkipTable);
  PatternLength := Length(Pattern);
  TextLength := Length(Text);
  StringIndex := PatternLength-1;
  PatternIndex := PatternLength-1;
  REPEAT
    IF FetchChar(Text, StringIndex) = FetchChar(Pattern, PatternIndex) THEN
      DEC(StringIndex);
      DEC(PatternIndex);
    ELSE
      StringIndex := StringIndex + SkipTable[FetchChar(Text, StringIndex)];
      PatternIndex := PatternLength - 1;
    END; (* IF *)
  UNTIL (PatternIndex < 0) OR (StringIndex >= TextLength);
  IF PatternIndex < 0 THEN
    RETURN StringIndex + 1;
  ELSE
    RETURN TextLength;
  END; (* IF *)
END SimpleBoyerMoore;
```

Procedure SimpleBoyerMoore tries matching the pattern from right to left. When a mismatch is discovered the procedure advances in the string using jump values from the skip table. This algorithm is actually a simplified version of a complete Boyer-Moore algorithm. The complete Boyer-Moore algorithm chooses the largest jump between values computed by the method we presented and another more complex method not discussed in this book. This complete Boyer-Moore algorithm is the fastest known pattern-matching algorithm: with a large alphabet and short patterns, the algorithm's complexity is approximately $O(s/p)$.

Rabin-Karp Algorithm

The Rabin-Karp method uses a transformation function, also called a hash function, to compute a numerical value for the pattern. The method computes the hash value for each of the possible p character sections of the text, and checks to see if it is equal to the pattern hash function. This approach is not very different from that of our first simple search method, except that here the computation of the hash function for position i is based on the previous hash value for position $i - 1$.

The p characters are taken to represent an integer; that is, each character is taken to be a digit in a given base b, where b is the number of different possible characters. The value corresponding to the p characters between indices k and $k + p - 1$ is expressed by:

$$n = s_k b^{p-1} + s_{k+1} b^{p-2} + \cdots + s_{k+p-1}$$

If we shift one position right in the text, the new value is:

$$(n - s_k b^{p-1})b + s_{k+p}$$

Chapter 13 Character Strings

We take the hash function to be h(n) = n mod t, where t is a large prime number. Knowing that taking the remainder when dividing by t after each arithmetic operation gives the same result as taking the remainder when dividing by t after all arithmetic operations have been done, we can program our search procedure in the following manner.

```
PROCEDURE RabinKarp(Pattern, Text: String): CARDINAL;
(* Search for Pattern in Text. Return index of pattern in text or
   Length(Text) if not found *)
CONST Prime = LONGCARD(10000019);
      Base  = LONGCARD(128);
VAR PatternHash, TextHash, Power: LONGCARD;
    Index, TextLength, PatternLength: CARDINAL;
BEGIN
  PatternLength := Length(Pattern);
  TextLength := Length(Text);
  Power := 1;
  FOR Index := 1 TO PatternLength-1 DO
    (* compute Base to the (PatternLength-1)th Power *)
    Power := (Power * Base) MOD Prime;
  END; (* FOR *)
  PatternHash := 0;
  FOR Index := 0 TO PatternLength-1 DO
    (* compute hash value of pattern *)
    PatternHash := (PatternHash * Base
        + LONGCARD(ORD(FetchChar(Pattern, Index)))) MOD Prime;
  END; (* FOR *)
  TextHash := 0;
  FOR Index := 0 TO PatternLength-1 DO
    (* compute hash value of beginning of text *)
    TextHash := (TextHash * Base
        + LONGCARD(ORD(FetchChar(Text, Index)))) MOD Prime;
  END; (* FOR *)
  Index := 0;
  WHILE (PatternHash # TextHash) AND
        (Index <= TextLength - PatternLength) DO
    (* compute new hash value of text slice *)
    TextHash := (TextHash + Base * Prime -
            LONGCARD(ORD(FetchChar(Text, Index))) * Power) MOD Prime;
    TextHash := (TextHash * Base +
            LONGCARD(ORD(FetchChar(Text, Index + PatternLength)))) MOD Prime;
    INC(Index);
  END; (* WHILE *)
  IF Index <= TextLength - PatternLength THEN
    RETURN Index;
  ELSE
    RETURN TextLength;
  END; (* IF *)
END RabinKarp;
```

We have taken Base as 128 (assuming the whole ASCII character set) and Prime as the first prime number after ten millions. When choosing base and prime, we must make sure that [(base + 1) × prime] doesn't cause an overflow. The procedure first computes the hash value of the pattern as well as b^{p-1}, and then the hash value of the first p characters of the text. From then on, the procedure repeatedly computes the hash value of the next text section using the method outlined above, until a hash value equal to the pattern hash value is found. When a match is found, it is still necessary to do a direct comparison of the pattern and the text, since it is possible that different strings produce the same hash value. However, a large value for Prime makes this extremely unlikely. In the first step of computation of the new value of TextHash, an extra (base × prime) is added so that the subtraction produces a positive result as required by the MOD operation. This algorithm will have a complexity of $O(p + s)$.

13.5 Case Study: Performance of Pattern-Matching Algorithms

We have studied four pattern-matching algorithms: Simple Search, Knuth-Morris-Pratt, Boyer-Moore and Rabin-Karp. The choice of algorithm will probably depend on the application. It is true that the worst-case complexity for a Simple Search is $O(n^2)$ if you are searching for the pattern aaaaaaaaab in the string aaaaaaaaaaaaaaaaaaa, but one might wonder how often this happens. If the search is for bit patterns made up of only 0's and 1's where the 0's and 1's tend to be clustered, then the simple search may actually exhibit this worst-case behavior. However, given a string of characters that appear with the same frequency as characters in English, then this worst-case scenario would be unlikely to happen. In this case study, we will study the performance of these four pattern-matching algorithms using strings of alphabetic characters.

Design

Because pattern matching is a critical factor in a software product, it would probably be worthwhile to code all the alternative algorithms and measure the system's performance in each case. Our goal here is less ambitious; we will simulate searching for patterns in a text that has letter frequencies similar to those observed in English.

Definition of the Problem In general, the frequencies of the alphabetic characters in typical English text are as given in Table 13-3.

These frequencies are based on a large body of modern prose. The frequencies may not be the same for other material, such as technical writing or, even worse, for computer programs, and the letter frequencies may be different for other forms of English literature or for writings in other time periods. We will use the frequencies in Table 13.3 in our case study. Our text to be searched should be made up of character sequences, which we will call "words," separated by a single space. There will be no punctuation or any other characters besides the 26 lowercase letters and a space.

Table 13-3
Frequencies of Letters in English

a	0.0856	j	0.0013	s	0.0607
b	0.0139	k	0.0042	t	0.1045
c	0.0279	l	0.0339	u	0.0249
d	0.0378	m	0.0249	v	0.0092
e	0.1304	n	0.0707	w	0.0149
f	0.0289	o	0.0797	x	0.0017
g	0.0199	p	0.0199	y	0.0199
h	0.0528	q	0.0012	z	0.0008
i	0.0627	r	0.0677		

The distribution of word lengths in our text should be:

```
lengths 1 to  7 : 12.5% each
lengths 3 to 10 :  4.166% each
```

These distributions are arbitrary and do not match any actual data for word lengths in English.

The program should generate a text string of length 999, based on the data given above, and use the four pattern-matching algorithms to search for patterns with lengths varying from 2 to 15 characters. The patterns will not contain spaces. As we want to measure worst-case behavior, we will perform the timing on patterns that are not present in the text string. The program should print a table of timing results based on averaging the data for 10 different patterns of each length.

After we collect and print out the performance data, we will try to account for this data in terms of the four algorithms tested. We will add this discussion component to our case study.

It should be noted that the text and patterns will not be actual English text. Letter frequencies alone cannot generate English, as letter combinations are more important than individual frequencies in natural language. Some ways of generating more "realistic" text will be discussed at the end of the case study and left as exercises.

Design of a Solution The top-level design, as shown in Figure 13-9, is straightforward:

- Generate a text string.
- Apply each algorithm to 10 patterns, each of lengths 2 through 15.
- Print a table of the average results.

Accomplishing these tasks will require a variety of utility procedures to:

- generate random integers within a specified range
- generate random letters with the desired frequency distribution
- generate random letter sequences ("words") that can form text or patterns
- time each search algorithm

13.5 Case Study: Performance of Pattern-Matching Algorithms

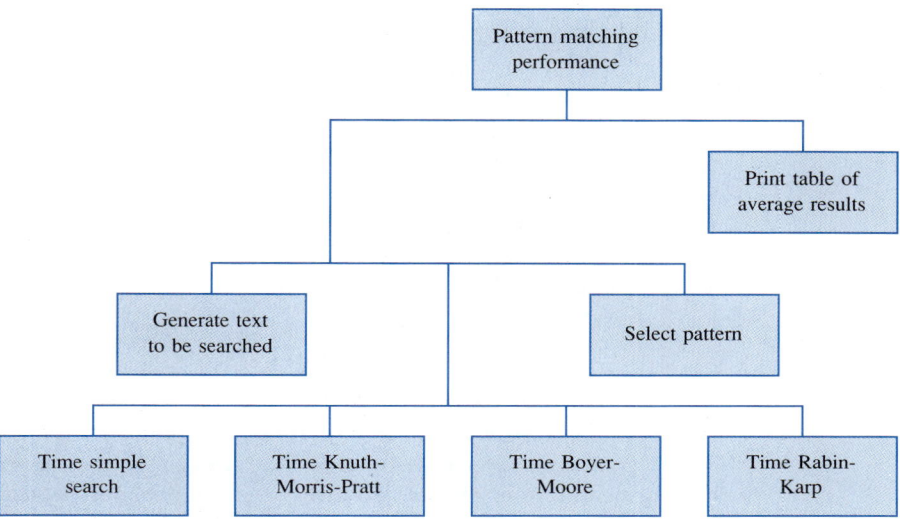

Figure 13-9
Structure of the Performance Analysis Program

Refine the Solution Procedures to generate random real numbers and random integers appeared in the queueing simulation presented in Section 7.2 and will not be repeated here. Generating random letters with the desired frequency distribution will be accomplished by generating a random integer from 0 to 1000 and using that value to return the appropriate character. For example, there would be 86/1000 chance for an A, 14/1000 for a B, 28/1000 for a C, etc. So integers from 0 to 85 would correspond to an A, 86 to 99 to a B, 100 to 127 to a C, and so forth. A large IF statement could detect each of these cases and return the appropriate letter.

To form words, we need to generate a length with the appropriate frequency distribution and then generate that number of random characters. Generating a text string will involve generating words, separated by spaces, until the desired text length is attained. Generating the search patterns will call the random letter procedure until a pattern of the desired length is obtained.

Timing each search will involve system-dependent procedures that will start a timer and then return the time elapsed since the timer started. The units of time will vary between systems, but we will want to make sure that we only time the search routine itself and not any other activity.

We will store the data in a three-dimensional array indexed by the search type, the pattern length, and the trial number.

The following pseudocode algorithm will print our table of averages.

```
Display Average Results
    Display the header data
    For each word length
        Display the word length
```

> For each type of search
>   Set the total time to 0
>   For each trial
>   Add the search time to the total time
>   End for
>   Display the average of all the trials
> End for
> Terminate current line
> End for
> End Display Average Results

Develop a Testing Strategy Since this program is designed to collect data on performance analysis, the testing strategy is "built-in." It must be pointed out that this program is designed to test unsuccessful searches only and does not validate the searching algorithms in general. For that type of validation we would want to supplement our random data with carefully contrived data for limiting cases. Examples might be:

pattern	text
empty	empty
non-empty	empty
empty	non-empty
aaaaaaaab	aaaaaaaaaaaaaaaaaaa
aaaaaaaab	aaaaaaaaaaaaaaaaaab

Since the focus of this case study is timing performance of searches with random data, we will not pursue these limiting cases any further.

Implementation

Code and Test the Program The program itself is fairly simple; we present it with explanatory comments interspersed between procedures. We have not included the code for the pattern-matching procedures, as it has already been presented and discussed earlier. The test results are the critical output of the program; they will be presented and discussed in detail. This section includes a discussion of ways to make this simulation more realistic.

```
MODULE PatternMatches;

FROM InOut IMPORT WriteCard, WriteString, WriteLn, WriteReal;
FROM Strings IMPORT String, Length, FetchChar, Pos, InitString, Assign,
    AssignConst, Delete, ToString, Insert, OutputString, DisposeString;
(* the following module is nonstandard and system dependent *)
FROM CStandard IMPORT Time, CProcessTimeSet, CProcessTimeSince;
```

13.5 Case Study: Performance of Pattern-Matching Algorithms

The location and form of a WriteReal procedure is system dependent. The timing functions are highly dependent on the individual Modula-2 compiler and the operating system that are used. The system on which this testing was performed was a Sun 3/60 workstation running Berkeley Unix 4.2. The timing routines themselves were written in C. The process time options noted above only include time for the individual process and do not include input/output wait time. Since Unix is a multiprocessing system, it is important to avoid using CPU time, since that would include the total time from start to end and could include time for other processes and for input/output. Whenever you make performance measurements on your system, you need to be aware of all these timing issues.

```
CONST MinPattern = 2;
      MaxPattern = 15;
      MaxTrial = 10;
      Display = FALSE;
TYPE SearchType = (Simple_Search, Knuth_Morris_Pratt, Boyer_Moore, Rabin_Karp);
     PatternLen = [MinPattern..MaxPattern];
     Trial = [1..MaxTrial];
     DataArray = ARRAY SearchType, PatternLen, Trial OF CARDINAL;
     StrSearch = PROCEDURE(String, String): CARDINAL;

MODULE PseudoRandom;
(* local module for generation of random real numbers and integers *)
EXPORT Random, RandomInt, ReSeed;
VAR Seed: REAL;

PROCEDURE ReSeed(NewSeed: REAL);
(* allows the seed value to be reset at any time *)
BEGIN
  Seed := NewSeed;
END ReSeed;

PROCEDURE Random() : REAL;
(* Return pseudo-random real value where 0.0 <= value < 1.0 *)
BEGIN
  Seed := 27.182313 * Seed + 34.415917;
  Seed := Seed - FLOAT(TRUNC(Seed));
  RETURN Seed;
END Random;

PROCEDURE RandomInt(Min, Max: INTEGER) : INTEGER;
(* Returns a pseudo-random integer value where Min <= value <= Max *)
BEGIN
  RETURN Min + TRUNC( Random() * FLOAT(Max - Min + 1));
END RandomInt;

BEGIN
  Seed := 0.0;   (* default initial value *)
END PseudoRandom;
```

This PseudoRandom local module is similar to the one presented in Section 7.2. We have added a "reseed" procedure that allows the user to restart the number generation process. Although we do not use the Random procedure that generates random reals directly, it is still necessary as the basis for the RandomInt procedure.

```
PROCEDURE RandomLetter(): CHAR;
(* Generate a lowercase letter from "a" to "z" based on its frequency in
   English usage *)
VAR RandomValue: INTEGER[0..1000];
BEGIN
  RandomValue := RandomInt(0,1000);
  IF RandomValue < 86 THEN RETURN "a"
  ELSIF RandomValue < 100 THEN RETURN "b"
  ELSIF RandomValue < 128 THEN RETURN "c"
  ELSIF RandomValue < 166 THEN RETURN "d"
  ELSIF RandomValue < 296 THEN RETURN "e"
  ELSIF RandomValue < 325 THEN RETURN "f"
  ELSIF RandomValue < 345 THEN RETURN "g"
  ELSIF RandomValue < 398 THEN RETURN "h"
  ELSIF RandomValue < 460 THEN RETURN "i"
  ELSIF RandomValue < 462 THEN RETURN "j"
  ELSIF RandomValue < 466 THEN RETURN "k"
  ELSIF RandomValue < 500 THEN RETURN "l"
  ELSIF RandomValue < 525 THEN RETURN "m"
  ELSIF RandomValue < 595 THEN RETURN "n"
  ELSIF RandomValue < 675 THEN RETURN "o"
  ELSIF RandomValue < 696 THEN RETURN "p"
  ELSIF RandomValue < 697 THEN RETURN "q"
  ELSIF RandomValue < 765 THEN RETURN "r"
  ELSIF RandomValue < 825 THEN RETURN "s"
  ELSIF RandomValue < 930 THEN RETURN "t"
  ELSIF RandomValue < 955 THEN RETURN "u"
  ELSIF RandomValue < 964 THEN RETURN "v"
  ELSIF RandomValue < 979 THEN RETURN "w"
  ELSIF RandomValue < 981 THEN RETURN "x"
  ELSIF RandomValue < 999 THEN RETURN "y"
  ELSE RETURN "z";
  END; (* IF *)
END RandomLetter;
```

We have elected to implement the RandomLetter procedure with a large IF statement. We were able to avoid the testing for an explicit range of values by testing the values in increasing order. Although it is tempting to use a CASE statement, it is best to avoid this approach because of the large number of possible values for the test variable, RandomValue. CASE statements should only be used when the range of possible values is relatively small.

```
PROCEDURE RandomWord(VAR Word: String);
(* Generate a sequence of random letters, based on English letter frequencies,
   of the following lengths:
   1 letter to 7 letters  : each with a frequency of 0.125
   8 letters to 10 letters : each with a frequency of 0.04166 *)
VAR RandomValue: INTEGER[0..7];
    ChStr: String;
    Count: CARDINAL;
BEGIN
  RandomValue := RandomInt(0,7);
  IF RandomValue = 0 THEN
    WordLength := RandomInt(8,10);
  ELSE
    WordLength := RandomValue;
  END; (* IF *)
  InitString(Word);
  InitString(ChStr);
  FOR Count := 1 TO WordLength DO
    ToString(RandomLetter(), ChStr);
    Insert(ChStr, Word, Length(Word));
  END; (* FOR *)
  DisposeString(ChStr);
END RandomWord;
```

A random number in the range of 0 to 7 is generated, so each number should have a frequency of 12.5%. We use the 0 value to indicate a length longer than 7, which is selected by another call to RandomInt with the range 8 to 10. Notice that the random letter generated has to be converted to a string and then concatenated at the end of the word by calling Insert with a position value of the word length. We call DisposeString to free the memory space that was allocated to local string variable ChStr. That space was not allocated on the system stack and therefore will not be released upon exit from the procedure. Not disposing of it would unnecessarily clutter memory, and small systems would not be able to complete the execution of this program, as RandomWord is called often.

```
PROCEDURE GenerateString(StrLength: CARDINAL; VAR Str: String);
(* Generate a sequence of random "words" separated by a single space so that
   Str has a length of StrLength *)
VAR Temp, Space: String;
BEGIN
  InitString(Str);
  InitString(Temp);
  InitString(Space);
  ToString(" ", Space);
  WHILE Length(Str) < StrLength DO
    RandomWord(Temp);
    Insert(Temp, Str, Length(Str));
    Insert(Space, Str, Length(Str));
  END; (* WHILE *)
```

```
    IF Length(Str) > StrLength THEN
      Delete(Str, StrLength, Length(Str)-StrLength);
    END; (* IF *)
    DisposeString(Temp);
    DisposeString(Space);
END GenerateString;
```

Random words, followed by a single space, are added on the end of the text string until the desired length is reached. If the last word added makes the string too long, then delete is used to truncate the string to the desired length.

```
PROCEDURE VerifyAbsence(VAR Pattern: String; Text: String): BOOLEAN;
(* Verify that Pattern is not a substring of Text; if it is, then reset
   Pattern to the empty string *)
VAR Found: BOOLEAN;
BEGIN
  Found := Pos(Pattern, Text) < Length(Text);
  IF Found THEN
    AssignConst(Pattern, "");
  END; (* IF *)
  RETURN NOT Found;
END VerifyAbsence;

PROCEDURE SelectPattern(PatLength:CARDINAL; VAR Pattern:String; Text:String);
(* Generate a pattern of length PatLength that is NOT present in Text;
   to avoid infinite loops, the pattern length should be at least two
   characters *)
VAR Count : CARDINAL;
    ChStr : String;
BEGIN
  InitString(Pattern);
  InitString(ChStr);
  REPEAT
    FOR Count := 1 TO PatLength DO
      ToString(RandomLetter(), ChStr);
      Insert(ChStr, Pattern, Length(Pattern));
    END; (* FOR *)
  UNTIL VerifyAbsence(Pattern, Text);
  DisposeString(ChStr);
END SelectPattern;
```

We generate a pattern as a sequence of random letters and then verify that the pattern is not in the string, as we want to test our algorithms for an unsuccessful search. We have used the function Pos from the Strings module to do this pattern-matching search. Pattern lengths of 1 should be avoided because most large text strings will contain every character and the select-pattern procedure would generate patterns forever in a fruitless search for one that is not present in the string.

```
PROCEDURE TimeSearch(SearchIndex: SearchType; PatternLength, Trial: CARDINAL;
          VAR Data: DataArray; Search: StrSearch; Pattern, Text: String;
          TextLength: CARDINAL; Display: BOOLEAN; SearchName: ARRAY OF CHAR);
(* Apply the function parameter Search to find Pattern in Text. Since Pattern
   was generated so that it is not in text, report an error if it is actually
   found. Record the search time in the array Data. If Display is TRUE,
   then print the search name, the index returned by the search, and the
   elapsed time. *)
VAR Result, ElapsedTime: CARDINAL;
    T: Time;
BEGIN
  IF Display THEN
    WriteString(SearchName);
  END; (* IF *)
  CProcessTimeSet(T);
  Result := Search(Pattern, Text);
  ElapsedTime := CProcessTimeSince(T);
  Data[SearchIndex, PatternLength, Trial] := ElapsedTime;
  IF Result # TextLength THEN
    WriteString("PATTERN MATCH ERROR !!! ");
    WriteString(SearchName); WriteLn;
    WriteString("pattern causing error : ");
    OutputString(Pattern); WriteLn;
  END; (* IF *)
  IF Display THEN
    WriteString(": position = "); WriteCard(Result, 8);
    WriteString(", Time = "); WriteCard(ElapsedTime, 8); WriteLn;
  END; (* IF *)
END TimeSearch;
```

Notice that each pattern-matching function has the same form: it has two String value parameters for the pattern and the text, and it returns a CARDINAL value. Therefore, TimeSearch uses the procedure parameter Search to apply the procedure passed in at the time of call. There are two options: to simply collect the timing values in the data array with or without a display of the timing values. Additional parameters Search-Index, PatternLength, and Trial are supplied to indicate the proper indexing within Data, the data array, and parameter SearchName is used for the display messages.

```
VAR Pattern, Text : String;
    WordLength, TextLength, Count, TotalTime: CARDINAL;
    Data: DataArray;
    Search: SearchType;
    AverageTime: REAL;
BEGIN
  (* generate text to be searched *)
  GenerateString(999, Text);
  TextLength := Length(Text);
  IF Display THEN
    OutputString(Text); WriteLn;
  END; (* IF *)
```

```
   (* generate search data *)
   FOR WordLength := MinPattern TO MaxPattern DO
     FOR Count := 1 TO MaxTrial DO
       SelectPattern(WordLength, Pattern, Text);
       IF Display THEN
         WriteCard(WordLength, 2);
         WriteString(" pattern = "); OutputString(Pattern); WriteLn;
       END; (* IF *)
       FOR Search := Simple_Search TO Rabin_Karp DO
         CASE Search OF
           Simple_Search :
             TimeSearch(Search, WordLength, Count, Data, SimpleSearch,
               Pattern, Text, TextLength, Display, "Simple Search ");
         | Knuth_Morris_Pratt :
             TimeSearch(Search, WordLength, Count, Data, KnuthMorrisPratt,
               Pattern, Text, TextLength, Display, "KnuthMorrisPratt ");
         | Boyer_Moore :
             TimeSearch(Search, WordLength, Count, Data, SimpleBoyerMoore,
               Pattern, Text, TextLength, Display, "Simple BoyerMoore ");
         | Rabin_Karp :
             TimeSearch(Search, WordLength, Count, Data, RabinKarp,
               Pattern, Text, TextLength, Display, "Rabin Karp ");
         END; (* CASE *)
       END; (* FOR *)
     END; (* FOR *)
     DisposeString(Pattern);
   END; (* FOR *)

   (* display average results *)
   WriteLn; WriteLn;
   WriteString("Unsuccessful search with a text length of ");
   WriteCard(TextLength, 6); WriteLn;
   WriteString("Average results based on ");
   WriteCard(MaxTrial, 3); WriteString(" trials."); WriteLn; WriteLn;
   WriteString(
   "Pattern_Length Simple_Search KnuthMorrisPratt Boyer_Moore    Rabin_Karp");
   WriteLn;
   FOR WordLength := MinPattern TO MaxPattern DO
     WriteCard(WordLength, 8);
     FOR Search := Simple_Search TO Rabin_Karp DO
       TotalTime := 0;
       FOR Count := 1 TO MaxTrial DO
         TotalTime := TotalTime + Data[Search, WordLength, Count];
       END; (* FOR *)
       AverageTime := FLOAT(TotalTime) / FLOAT(MaxTrial);
       WriteReal(AverageTime, 15, 1);
     END; (* FOR *)
     WriteLn;
   END; (* FOR *)
   WriteLn; WriteLn;
END PatternMatch.
```

13.5 Case Study: Performance of Pattern-Matching Algorithms

The main program follows our structure chart in Figure 13-9. The text string is generated, the pattern length is varied from the minimum to the maximum value, and the search is performed for the four algorithms for the required number of trials. The averages of the results are computed and printed in a compact table. This program could be put into a loop allowing the user to specify a new seed value for each iteration of the loop; however, since 10 patterns were generated for each length, the results presented below should be fairly representative.

Before examining the table of results, we should look at the text string that was generated.

```
rae tolrnot ug du n ef domooe tpy rit inmontt sel tfairih d oa
atpsec tarlr evisese h nyh n bt tttw lesoosn etiooe doea m iri
tmasghdte hioain n adpalo ncoled wode etnrdtl taace r yia rnwr
e dmirsftg tp e s sla tge zn iom pad ai glfure frnpd u tehae
fentnr uwtnrrr ei tadtoo bagihwsf i agpaors miidtctae obc toyc
r efnm ehsvitsf tfoaah teso euaf lttepas rr ttooeo teo nstltip
lteaiel hn htny uee eruteej tuthrog it teehreeapt leih nerpttr
h ilhatt peeow pcmep ex ilnalneom ttw orsaos jthhm iit sionht
rotrin pbteba tferine tbttd aetittt el ihafs nygia oaes d lups
ig utgh oa o rebs itndra nrvl vi ee yiinx vmehlfutim e co cglr
sf toebtav tmb eauacts ait eh niiomhp haisglfu epfrn deurt h
sfentnru wtnrrrh it adtooaf gihwsfei agpaors miidtctae obc toyc
r efnm ehsvitsf tfoaah teso euaf lttepas rr ttooeo teo nstltip
lteaiel hn htny uee eruteej tuthrog it teehreeapt leih nerpttr
h ilhatt peeow pcmep ex ilnalneom ttw orsaos jthhm iit sionht
rotrin pbteba tferine tbttd aetittt el ihafs nygia oaes d
```

This hardly looks like English! It is clear that it would take a monkey hitting keys on a typewriter an extremely long time to generate a meaningful English sentence, let alone all of Shakespeare. It is an interesting challenge to try to generate real English words using random processes. Letter sequences in English are not random; some sequences, such as "ing," appear frequently whereas most other sequences never appear. The study of cryptography has developed extensive tables of two-grams (frequencies of two-letter sequences) and three-grams (frequencies of three-letter sequences) to help "break" simple coding schemes. For example, some of the more frequent two-grams are: th (3.21%), he (3.05%), in (2.30%), and er (2.13%). Most entries in a two-gram table have probabilities at or near zero. The use of such data will help generate words that look much more like English, but even this technique is a long way from generating meaningful English sentences.

One alternative strategy would involve putting sentences together by randomly choosing words from a list of known English words. Or one could simply input several large textual passages from English prose and select the text passage randomly. However, such efforts go beyond the scope of this case study, whose results we present in tabular form in Table 13-4 and in graphical form in Figure 13-10.

Table 13-4

Output of the Pattern-Matching Timing Program

Unsuccessful search with a text length of 999
Average results based on 10 trials.

Pattern_Length	Simple_Search	KnuthMorrisPratt	Boyer_Moore	Rabin_Karp
2	529.7	691.5	795.2	1016.0
3	530.7	690.4	554.0	1016.5
4	558.7	710.1	424.9	1015.4
5	545.1	708.9	350.7	1013.4
6	557.3	711.8	300.9	1013.8
7	545.9	705.2	253.8	1013.4
8	554.3	718.4	235.9	1012.2
9	542.4	695.7	215.3	1011.7
10	564.5	729.0	202.7	1010.8
11	551.4	703.0	183.1	1011.9
12	541.8	705.8	169.1	1012.1
13	549.3	712.4	164.1	1009.9
14	546.9	702.3	152.8	1009.2
15	546.2	708.7	146.6	1009.3

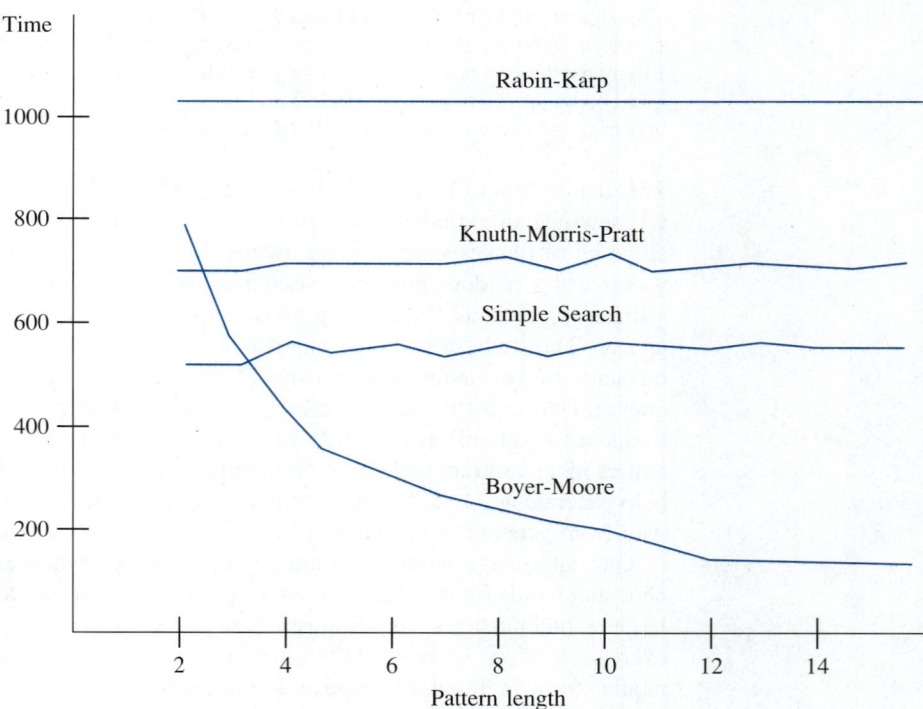

Figure 13-10

Graph of Pattern-Matching Performance

These times include preprocessing, such as building the tables for Knuth-Morris-Pratt and Boyer-Moore. Three of the techniques, Rabin-Karp, Simple Search, and Knuth-Morris-Pratt, perform relatively consistently for all pattern lengths, while Boyer-Moore performs better as the pattern becomes longer. This result should not be surprising since the search going from right to left can leave more characters unexamined as the pattern becomes longer. The behavior can actually become sublinear.

Rabin-Karp was the slowest algorithm, a result that is not surprising, given the amount of numeric computation. The performance is also virtually "flat" since the computation on the text is the same regardless of the pattern. Rabin-Karp might perform better for a more restricted alphabet. In particular, for a binary choice of 0 or 1, the numeric computation would be much simpler and the performance should improve dramatically.

Simple Search outperformed Knuth-Morris-Pratt, a performance that at first may seem surprising. However, the generation of data should be considered in analyzing these results. Simple Search performs poorly if the first mismatch occurs after the first few characters. As the earlier discussion on two-grams and three-grams indicated, certain sequences appear relatively frequently in actual English text, whereas most sequences never or rarely occur. This means that, for real English text, Simple Search would probably have some initial matches more often than for the randomly generated data we have used. We would expect the performance of Simple Search to degrade when used with actual English text, while this change of text should have little effect on Knuth-Morris-Pratt. We would also expect the performance of Simple Search to be much poorer for a more restricted set of characters and be particularly bad if there are only two characters, such as 0 and 1.

For patterns of more than a few characters, Boyer-Moore is a clear winner, as the performance becomes sublinear with increasing pattern length. It should be noted that Boyer-Moore, like Simple Search, is benefiting from the randomness and variety of the data to produce the first mismatch quickly. This performance would probably degrade with a more restricted set of characters or with actual English text.

Complete the Documentation The program code should be supplemented with a discussion of the generation of test data. The test results should be supplemented with a discussion of the validity of these results, similar to the brief discussion above.

Summary

Character strings are used in practically all computer applications. However Modula-2 does not include a string type and offers only string literals that can be assimilated to zero-based arrays of characters. All Modula-2 implementations offer some Strings module, but the definitions vary. Most implementors choose to remain compatible with Modula-2 string constants and make type String a transparent type.

We have defined a complete and independent ADT Strings with all the necessary operations, including access to the elementary components of a string. Implementations of strings can be based on arrays of characters or on linear lists of character blocks. The flexibility of a dynamic implementation makes the implementation of some operations like Insert or Delete more difficult.

Pattern matching is a specific operation on strings used in many applications. There exist several efficient algorithms for this operation, the complexity of the best algorithm known, Boyer-Moore, is $O(s/p)$, where s is the string length and p the pattern length.

■ Exercises

1. Write a search algorithm to find in a character string *all* occurrences of a given pattern. For instance searching for the pattern "my" in the string "Oh, my! what an eponymy!" would return indices 4 and 21.

2. Choose and define a representation for a character string type "String" assuming:
   (a) a fixed length string
   (b) a string whose length may vary up from 1 to 8
   (c) a variable length string

3. We use a computer with byte and word addressing capabilities to implement a character-string manipulation system. Each word may contain up to four characters or a pointer and a single character. Most strings are more than four characters long. Compare the following representations with respect to the efficiency of memory use, the ease of scanning a given string, the ease and speed of character insertion and character deletion.
   (a) sequential representation, one character per byte
   (b) linked representation, each element comprising a character and a pointer
   (c) linked representation, each element comprising a word and a pointer
   (d) linked representation, one character per byte, consecutive bytes followed by a pointer

4. Define algorithms for operations StringGreater and Concat for the dynamic implementation discussed in Section 13.3.

5. Using the static representation for strings, define a procedure Cut that eliminates all the spaces at the end of a string.

6. Using the static representation for strings, define a procedure Duplicate that, from a string S and an integer N, produces a new string by concatenation of N strings S.

7. Using an array representation for strings, define a string-compression algorithm in which all sequences of more than two spaces are replaced by two characters @n, where n is the number of spaces.

8. Compute the values of BackupTable for the following patterns:

   babarbarbados, chouchoutrain, hiphiphip.

9. Our TextJustify program is not quite safe, as it does not validate the input strings. Add the necessary validation statements.

10. Write a procedure Center that could replace our Justify procedure, and which centers the text of a line between the right and left margins.

Programming Problems

11. Write a Decode procedure to decipher messages by using the Vigenère square of Section 13.2.

12. Complete the dynamic implementation of strings using the results of problem 4 and the operations given in the text.

13. Modify the static implementation of strings given in the text so that the representation of a string is a zero-based array of characters, where the first character is used to store the string length.

14. Write a Modula-2 program to delete in a given string all occurrences of each of the characters of a second string. For instance, with the string "HUGO FLUCHY CAB BUKCITED" and "BCDHU," we obtain "GO FLY A KITE."

15. Write a Modula-2 program to search a given text for all occurrences of each member of a set of strings and display all positions in the text where each string occurs.

16. Write a Modula-2 program to find and display the longest substring common to two strings, S1 and S2.

17. Write two procedures to convert a string of decimal digits to a string of roman numerals, and to convert a string of roman numerals to a string of decimal digits.

18. In your library, find a book on cryptography that contains the frequency data for two-grams in English. Write a Modula-2 program to generate random words using this data.

19. Adapt the program in the case study to use whatever timing routines are available on your system. Did you obtain similar results?

20. Expand the program in the case study to include timing for successful searches. You might want to write a procedure that randomly selects a word from the text by starting at a random position and taking the first following full word.

21. Test the pattern-matching algorithms on lengthy passages of actual English prose. How do the results compare with those in the case study?

22. Study the behavior of the pattern-matching algorithms when both the pattern and the text being searched are made up of 0's and 1's.

23. A concordance list is a list that gives the position of each word of the text as well as the context surrounding the word (this is also called a KWIC index, for KeyWord In Context). Write a program to establish a concordance list for a given text (the context will be the line in which the word appears). Some common words found in an omission list will be skipped: "the," "a," "an," "its," "his," "her," "their," "and," "or," "not," "from," "of," "our," "your."

24. Some programming languages require composite characters made of several characters typed on top of each other, for instance the sign $\neq$ is made of sign $=$ followed by a backspace and sign /. Write a program that takes as input a character sequence from alphabet A (including backspace) and that converts this sequence into a sequence from alphabet B, where B does not include a backspace and where individual characters can be equivalent to sequences of characters from A.

Generalized Lists

INTRODUCTION

The linear list, which was introduced in Chapter 5, was defined to be a sequence of elements, and the structures used to implement such a list were all simple structures. Although it is possible to use some of the linear list concepts with other abstract data types or data structures, linear lists cannot be used to implement either trees or graphs (see Chapter 15) because these two abstract data types are too complex.

However, there exist more general list structures which make implementation of trees or graphs possible. In this chapter we will introduce the concept of a *generalized list,* and briefly present one of its best known applications, the Lisp programming language. We will also discuss the implementation of generalized lists, both from the point of view of the structural representation and of the algorithms. Since generalized lists can have very complex and recursive structures, we will spend more time discussing their representations. Finally, in a case study, we will introduce techniques known as *garbage collection,* related to memory management in dynamic systems.

14.1 Definition and Abstraction: The Generalized List

A generalized list is a finite sequence of zero or more elements, the elements being either atoms or generalized lists. An *atom* is a member of a given set and is considered to be indivisible. It will be necessary to be able to distinguish between atoms and generalized lists (simply called lists in the rest of this chapter). Note that the definition of lists is recursive. This means that lists themselves can be recursive, which greatly increases the power and complexity of this structure.

In order to simplify the notation we will use, atoms will be represented by lowercase letters, while lists will be represented by uppercase letters. List elements will be enclosed in parentheses and separated by commas as in:

$$L = (e_1, e_2, e_3, \ldots, e_n)$$

where e_i represents an element of the list. Let's take a few examples.

A = ( )   Empty list
B = (a, (b, c), d) List with three elements, the second one being a list
C = (n, C)   Recursive list of two elements, corresponding to the infinite list (n, (n, (n, (n, . . .)))).

Figure 14-1 shows other ways of representing the above three lists by means of a graphical representation.

Each node in the figure is either an atom (round node) or a list (square node). This implementation may lead us to think that trees can always be used to represent lists. This conjecture is true in some particular cases, but not in general. List C in the above examples shows why, in general, trees cannot be used to represent lists. Lists may be recursive (a list may be a member of itself), whereas trees are not. Thus, not all lists can be represented by trees, whereas all trees can be represented by lists.

Lists possess three properties:

- Order: List elements are ordered and cannot be moved without the list becoming another list. List (a, b, c) is different from list (c, b, a).
- Depth: The depth of a list is the maximum level of all the list elements. The level of an element shows its degree of nesting in the list. In list B = (a, (b, c), d) the level of "a" and "d" is 1, while the level of "b" and "c" is 2. B's depth is thus 2. Depth is even more apparent when using the graphical representation of Figure 14-1.
- Length: The length of a list is the number of elements occupying the first level of the list. Thus the length of list B is 3.

We can define an abstract data type List based on our first definition with the following operations:

- Creation of a List
- Insertion of an element in a List

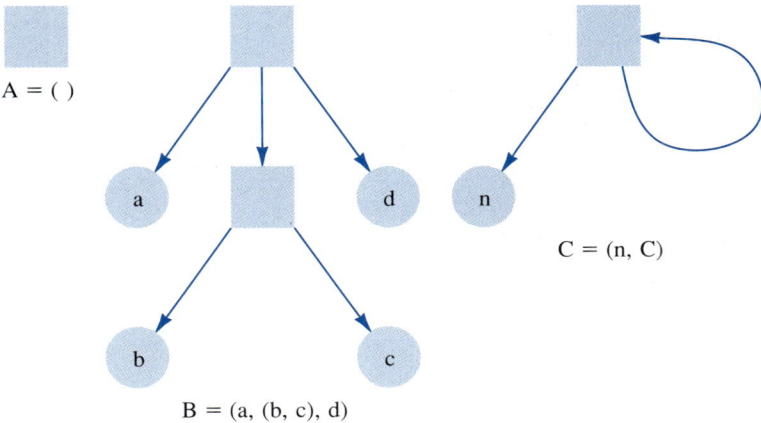

Figure 14-1
Graphical Representation of Lists

- Deletion of an element in a List
- Concatenation of two Lists
- Copy of a List
- Display of a List
- Traversal of a List
- Counting the elements in a List
- Deletion of a List

14.2 Application: The Lisp Programming Language

There are several programming languages that are specialized in list processing. The most important and the most powerful is the Lisp language, which evolved from LISP 1.5 defined in 1959 by John McCarthy. Lisp strongly influenced the design of the Logo programming language used in teaching computer programming to pupils in elementary schools. We will present here a short introduction to the Lisp language and system.

Lisp is a programming language for handling symbolic data. It has been used in mathematical logic, symbolic calculus, linguistics, and artificial intelligence. This language is a representation system for partial recursive functions of a class of symbolic expressions called *S-expressions*. Lisp is based on the theoretical foundations of lambda calculus. The syntax of the Lisp language is very simple, although a little cumbersome because of the large number of parentheses used. Its main advantage is that there exists a very simple matching between a Lisp program and its internal representation as S-expressions. In Lisp, programs and data have the same internal representation. From this it follows that a Lisp program may easily build another program, which can then be executed. This characteristic of Lisp contributes to its power and explains its use in artificial intelligence applications where this dynamic capability is of prime importance.

Definitions

Lisp primitive objects are called atoms because they cannot be divided or decomposed. There are three kinds of atoms:

- Atomic symbols (character strings whose first character is a letter)
   Examples: quantity, Modula2, Variable, U235
- Numbers (integers or reals)
   Examples: 1234, 1.31415
- Truth values: T for true, and NIL for false

An S-expression is either an atom or a dotted pair made of an opening parenthesis, an S-expression, a period, another S-expression and a closing parenthesis. Examples of S-expressions are A, (A.B) or (A.(B.C)).

The NIL symbol is used to indicate the absence of an element, as in (A.(B.NIL)), which is different from (A.B). A list notation is used, which helps represent S-expressions more simply. Thus, the following S-expression:

$$(e_1.(e_2.(e_3.(\ldots (e_n.NIL)) \ldots)))$$

is equivalent to the following list:

$$(e_1 \; e_2 \; e_3 \; \ldots \; e_n),$$

Also, for instance, (A) is equivalent to (A.NIL).

With this notation it is possible to consider that the primitive data type in Lisp is the list. Conversion of lists to dotted pairs is always possible: a list made of a single atom is transformed into a dotted pair made of this atom and NIL.

From the programmer's point of view, a list will be either empty or made of elements (atoms or lists) within parentheses and separated by spaces, as for instance (A B C), a list of three elements A, B, and C. The empty list will be represented either by ( ) or by NIL. The list (A (B C) D) is a list of three elements, the second of these being a list.

Operations

A number of functions are defined in Lisp, five of them constituting what is called "pure Lisp": all the other functions can be defined by using these five functions. As already mentioned, Lisp programs are lists (also called *forms*), which are interpreted in the following way: The first element of the list is taken as the function to perform. All the other elements of the list are the function's arguments, which are evaluated, and then the function is applied to the evaluated elements, returning a value.

In order to avoid argument evaluation, it is possible to use the QUOTE operator on the arguments that are not to be evaluated. QUOTE is used so frequently it has a short form:

(QUOTE A B) is written as '(A B).

The principal functions are the following:

(CAR X)   Returns the first element of list X, which can be a either a list or an atom. CAR applied to a dotted pair returns the left element in the pair.
(CAR '(A.B)) = A   (CAR '((A B) C D) = (A B)
(CDR X)   Returns the list obtained by removing the first element of X. If list X contains only one element, CDR returns the empty list.
(CDR '(A.B)) = B   (CDR '((A B) C D) = (C D)
CAR and CDR may be combined a number of times; thus we may simply write:
(CADR '(A B C)) = (CAR (CDR '(A B C))) = B
(CADDR '(A B C)) = (CAR (CDR (CDR '(A B C)))) = C
(CADADR '(A (B C) D) =
(CAR (CDR (CAR (CDR '(A (B C) D)))) = C
(CONS X Y)   Returns a dotted pair whose CAR is X and whose CDR is Y.
(CONS 'A '(B C)) = (A B C)
(CONS (CAR L) (CDR L)) = L
(ATOM X)   Returns a Boolean value: returns T if X is an atom, NIL otherwise.
(EQ X Y)   Returns a Boolean value: returns T if X and Y refer to the same object, NIL otherwise.

We use here the traditional Lisp notation, although nowadays Common Lisp, a "pseudo-standard" for Lisp based on a union of several Lisp dialects, uses a newer notation. For instance, CAR is replaced by FIRST, and CDR by REST, while CADR is SECOND, CADDR is THIRD, etc.

Other Lisp functions include the following.

(NULL X)   Returns a Boolean value indicating whether or not X is the NIL atom.
(NUMBERP X)   Returns a Boolean value indicating whether or not X is a number.
(GREATERP X Y)   Returns a Boolean value indicating whether or not X is greater than Y (">" in Common Lisp).
(LESSP X Y)   Returns a Boolean value indicating whether or not X is less than Y ("<" in Common Lisp).
(PLUS X_1 X_2 . . . X_n)   Returns the sum of arguments $X_1 + X_2 + \cdots + X_n$ ("+" in Common Lisp).
(DIFFERENCE X Y)   Returns the difference $X - Y$ ("−" in Common Lisp).
(TIMES X_1 X_2 . . . X_n)   Returns the product of arguments $X_1 * X_2 * \cdots * X_n$ (" * " in Common Lisp).
(DIVIDE X Y)   Returns the quotient X / Y ("/" in Common Lisp).
(PLUS1 X)   Returns the value of X incremented by 1 ("1+" in Common Lisp).
(SUB1 X)   Returns the value of X decremented by 1 ("1−" in Common Lisp).

There also exists an important special form:

(COND (P_1 S_1) (P_2 S_2) (P_3 S_3) ... (P_n S_n))

which checks successively the predicates P_i and returns the value of expression S_i corresponding to the first P_i that is true (or non-nil). The effect of COND is similar to the conditional expression:

IF P_1 THEN S_1
ELSIF P_2 THEN S_2
ELSIF P_3 THEN S_3
.
.
.
ELSIF P_n THEN S_n
END;

We call COND a special form because it uses *lazy evaluation:* the predicates P_i and the S-expressions S_i are only evaluated on an "as-needed" basis.

A Lisp programmer is expected to define functions in order to solve the problem at hand. The following examples illustrate various useful functions; they use the DEFUN operator to DEfine a FUNction.

```
(DEFUN FIRSTATOM (L)
        (COND    ((ATOM L) L)
                 (T (FIRSTATOM (CAR L)))))
```

returns the first atom in list L, or NIL, if the list is empty. If L is an atom, its value is returned; otherwise, the first atom of the first element of L is sought recursively. Notice that the final predicate to be checked, T, will always cause its corresponding S-expression to be executed if all other predicates evaluate to NIL. This is similar to a final ELSE clause in an IF statement.

```
(DEFUN MEMBER (X SET)
        (COND ((NULL SET) NIL)
              ((EQ X (CAR SET)) T)
              (T (MEMBER X (CDR SET)))))
```

returns true if atom X is one of the elements of list SET. (The function does not check to see whether X is a member of a possible sublist of SET.)

```
(DEFUN ERASE (Y LIST)
        (COND ((NULL LIST) NIL)
              ((EQ Y (CAR LIST)) (CDR LIST))
              (T (CONS (CAR LIST) (ERASE Y (CDR LIST))))))
```

returns a copy of LIST in which the first occurrence of atom Y as an element of LIST has been eliminated.

```
(DEFUN FACT (N)
       (COND ((ZEROP N) 1)
             (T (TIMES N (FACT (SUB1 N))))))
```

computes Factorial N recursively using predicate ZEROP to determine the base case when the argument is zero.

```
(DEFUN UNION (S1 S2)
       (COND ((NULL S1) S2)
             ((MEMBER (CAR S1) S2) (UNION (CDR S1) S2))
             (T (CONS (CAR S1)(UNION (CDR S1) S2)))))
```

returns a list representing the union of the two lists S1 and S2. If the first list is empty, the second list is returned. Otherwise, if the first element of the first list is a member of the second list, then UNION is called recursively on the rest of the first list, or else in all other cases, that first element is added to the union of the rest of the list and the second list.

```
(DEFUN INTERSECTION (S1 S2)
    (COND ((NULL S1) NIL)
          ((MEMBER (CAR S1) S2)
             (CONS(CAR S1) (INTERSECTION (CDR S1) S2)))
          (T (INTERSECTION (CDR S1) S2))))
```

returns a list representing the intersection of the two lists S1 and S2. Function CONS is used to build the resulting list. If the first list is empty, then the result is NIL. Otherwise, if the first element of the first list is a member of the second list, it is added to the intersection of the rest of the first list and the second list, or else in all other cases, the result is the intersection of the rest of the first list and the second list.

```
(DEFUN COUNTATOMS (S-EXPR)
    (COND ((NULL S-EXPR) 0)
          ((ATOM S-EXPR) 1)
          (T (PLUS (COUNTATOMS (CAR S-EXPR))(COUNTATOMS (CDR S-EXPR))))))
```

returns the number of atoms in the S-EXPR. Atoms are counted at all levels and each occurrence is counted. This function illustrates the use of recursion on the CAR and the CDR to reach all nested levels of a list structure. If the S-expression is empty, the function returns zero; if it is an atom, then 1 is returned. Otherwise, the S-expression must be a list, in which case the number returned is the sum of the number of atoms in the first element of the list and the number of atoms in the rest of the list.

These functions, although small, give some idea of Lisp programming. Programs in Lisp are usually interpreted, but present day systems make it possible to compile them and thus reduce execution time. Most Lisp applications consist of large programs whose debugging would be a very difficult task without the tools offered by most Lisp implementations: tracing, setting breakpoints, single-stepping through a program, examining or changing the environment at breakpoints, and so on.

14.3 Implementations

Any Lisp implementation system constitutes a complete implementation of the generalized list abstract data type.

Lisp Representation

The nodes used to represent lists in Lisp are made of two parts: the dotted pair (B.C) would usually be shown as in Figure 14-2. However, atoms are not directly kept in the nodes; instead the nodes contain pointers to atoms, as shown in Figure 14-3.

An atom is represented by a node containing a flag (we will use -1) and a pointer to the atom's property list. This list normally includes the atom's name, its value, its type, etc. Each property on the list is introduced by an indicator: PNAME for the name, VALUE for the value, and so on. Figure 14-4 represents atom MONTHYEAR with a value of 1290. Integer 1290 is itself an atom.

A value can also be a list that will be represented using the same method. Condensed representations are generally used, as shown in Figure 14-5 for various lists.

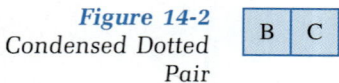

Figure 14-2 Condensed Dotted Pair

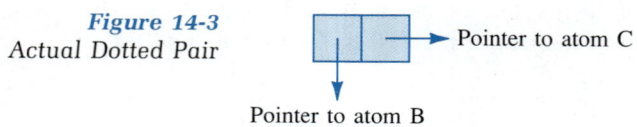

Figure 14-3 Actual Dotted Pair

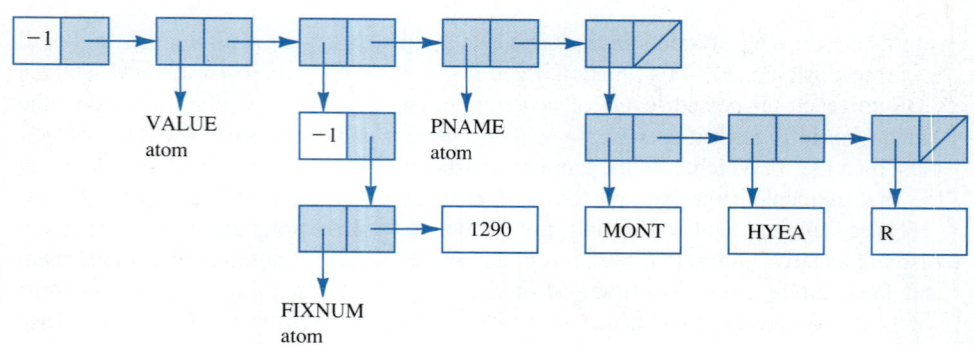

Figure 14-4 Atom MONTHYEAR

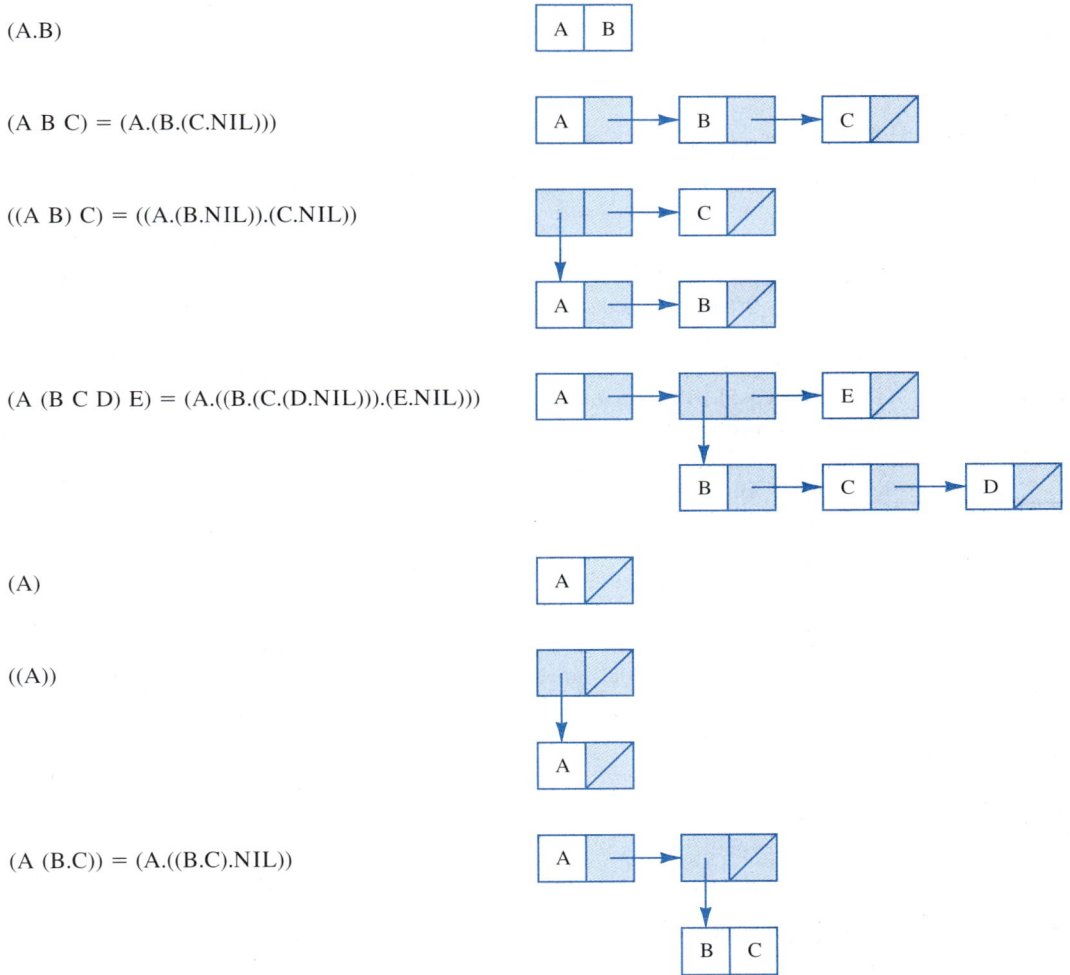

Figure 14-5 Condensed Representation of Lisp Lists

List Representations

List applications are primarily based on symbol manipulations found in artificial intelligence or mathematics. For all these applications, the memory size that will be needed is not known in advance and data manipulation is intensive. Thus it is necessary to choose structures that allow memory to be used efficiently in handling algorithms and with maximum problem-solving capability. For these reasons, the representations must be based on pointers because of their dynamic allocation of elements, easy manipulation, and possibility of sublist sharing.

As shown in Figure 14-6, nodes must have at least three fields: Type is a simple flag to differentiate between atoms and lists (a or ℓ), Data includes an atom (or a pointer to an atom) or a pointer to a list, and Pointer is a pointer to the next element in the list.

Figure 14-6
Node of a List

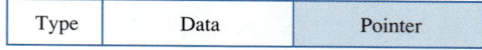

Figure 14-7 shows list L = (P, s, (P, P)) with P = (t, u, v).

This representation of a generalized list is simple but has one major drawback—if list P is changed it may be necessary to modify the pointers to it. This might be the case if the first element is deleted or if a new element is inserted at the beginning of P. However, this drawback can be avoided if a header is used for each list. When a header is used, there is no need to update the list representation if a sublist is modified, as only the sublist would be changed. Figure 14-8 shows the same list as Figure 14-7; note that changing the first element of list P does not require updating the pointer.

List headers add to the memory size needed to represent a list, but they can also include useful information on the list: number of elements, pointer to the end of the list, name of the list, reference counter (number of pointers to the list), a field for marking a visit during traversal, and so on. List headers also improve the representation of recursive lists, as shown in Figure 14-9.

Although our figures have shown the value of an atom directly in the node, normally there would be only a pointer to the atom's value. The distinction between atoms and lists may seem somewhat arbitrary; however, it is of prime importance because it is part of our definition of generalized lists. Atoms are not handled in the same manner as lists; atomic nodes can lead to more information, such as to property lists.

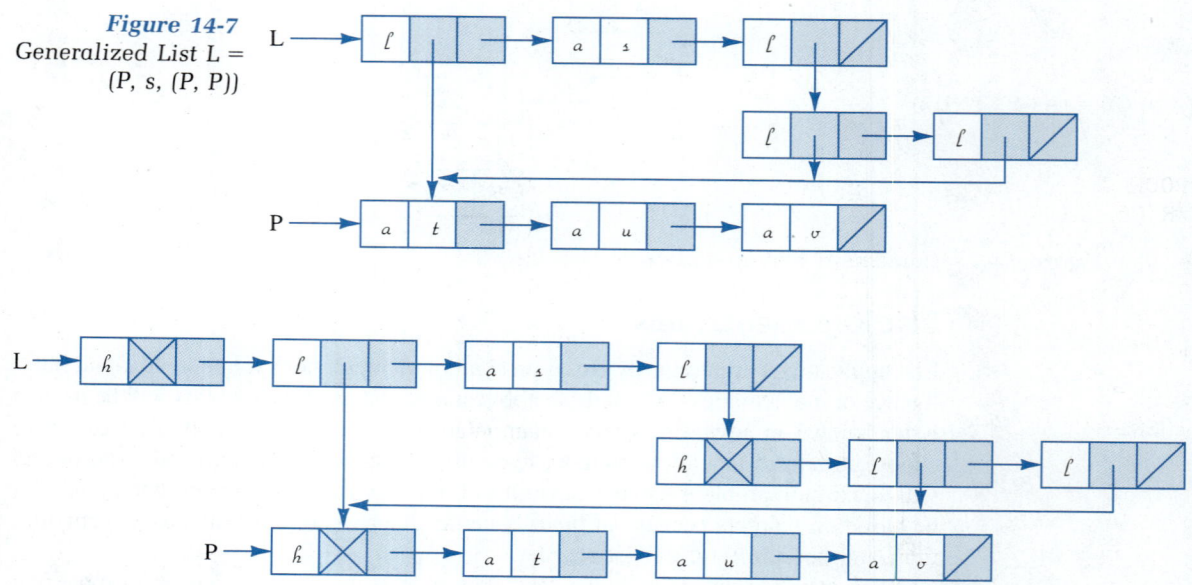

Figure 14-7
Generalized List L = (P, s, (P, P))

Figure 14-8 List L with List Headers

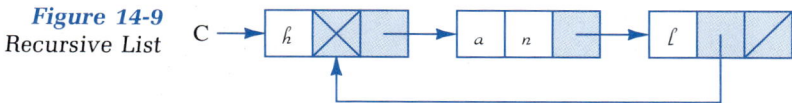

Figure 14-9
Recursive List

Here we can use the representation techniques we used for linear lists. It is possible to use circular lists by replacing all NIL pointers by pointers to the list headers. Similarly, the lists can be doubly linked, at the cost of an extra pointer in each element. The chosen representation will chiefly depend on the particular applications, but in most cases, a simple representation like the one in Figure 14-8 will be used.

We will illustrate three of the operations on generalized lists based on the following representations.

```
TYPE List = POINTER TO Element;
     Element = RECORD
                 Next: List;                (* Next element at same level *)
                 CASE Atomic: BOOLEAN OF
                   FALSE: SubLevel: List;   (* sublist pointer *)
                 | TRUE: Atom: CHAR;        (* atom value *)
                 END;
               END;
```

Each element has three fields: a pointer to the next element at the same level, a Boolean flag to indicate whether the element is an atom or not, and, in the case of an atom, a value field (a character for our simple examples), or, in the case of a list node, a pointer to a sublist. Our implementation will use list headers: nodes of type Element where Atomic will be false, field SubLevel will be NIL, and Next will point to the list itself.

Procedure CreateList is called to create a new list based on the input of the parenthesized representation of the list. It returns a pointer to a new list header.

```
PROCEDURE CreateList(VAR NewList: List);
VAR Ch: CHAR;
(* Create a new list NewList from parenthesized input list
   like: (a, (b), c, (d, e)) where atoms are single lowercase
   characters *)
  PROCEDURE BuildList(L: List);
  (* Recursive building of the list L whose header exists *)
  VAR New: List;
  BEGIN
    LOOP
      Read(Ch);
      IF Done THEN
```

```
            CASE Ch OF
              '(': ALLOCATE(New, SIZE(Element));  (* pointer node to sublist *)
                   New^.Next := NIL;
                   New^.Atomic := FALSE;
                   L^.Next := New;
                   L := New;
                   ALLOCATE(New, SIZE(Element));  (* sublist header *)
                   New^.Atomic := FALSE;
                   New^.Next := NIL;
                   New^.SubLevel := NIL;
                   L^.SubLevel := New;
                   BuildList(New);
            | ')': EXIT;                          (* end of list *)
            | ',', ' ':                           (* ignore separators *)
            | 'a'..'z': ALLOCATE(New, SIZE(Element));  (* atom *)
                    New^.Atomic := TRUE;
                    New^.Next := NIL;
                    New^.Atom := Ch;
                    L^.Next := New;
                    L := New;
            ELSE
               EXIT;                              (* stop on other characters *)
            END; (* CASE *)
          ELSE
            EXIT;                                 (* stop if no more characters *)
          END; (* IF *)
      END; (* LOOP *)
    END BuildList;

BEGIN
  Read(Ch);
  WHILE Done AND (Ch = ' ') DO                    (* skip blanks *)
    Read(Ch);
  END; (* WHILE *)
  IF Ch = '(' THEN                                (* create header *)
    ALLOCATE(NewList, SIZE(Element));
    NewList^.Atomic := FALSE;
    NewList^.SubLevel := NIL;
    NewList^.Next := NIL;
    BuildList(NewList);                           (* build rest of list *)
  ELSE
    NewList := NIL;
  END; (* IF *)
END CreateList;
```

In Procedure CreateList, input characters are read and blanks are skipped. If the first nonblank character is a left parenthesis, a list header is created and procedure BuildList is called to build the rest of the list. Input characters are then processed. Lowercase letters represent atoms for which a node is created and linked to the list. A left parenthesis indicates the beginning of a sublist: two nodes are created, one element attached to the list and pointing to the second node, which is a sublist header. To process the

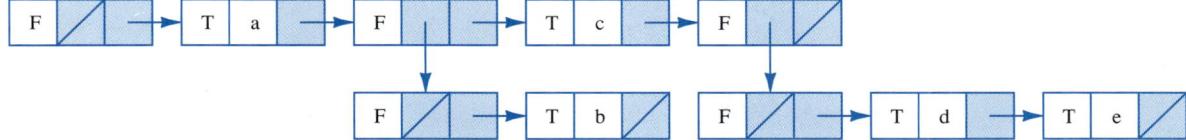

Figure 14-10 List (a, (b), c, (d, e))

elements of the sublist, BuildList is called recursively. A right parenthesis indicates the end of the list.

Figure 14-10 shows the list built by CreateList when the input is

(a, (b), c, (d, e))

```
PROCEDURE CAR(L: List): List;
(* Return first element of list L *)
VAR New: List;
BEGIN
  IF L = NIL THEN
    Error("Nonexisting list");
    RETURN NIL;
  ELSIF L^.SubLevel # NIL THEN
    Error("Badly formed list");
    RETURN NIL;
  ELSIF L^.Next = NIL THEN           (* empty list *)
    RETURN NIL;
  ELSIF L^.Next^.Atomic THEN   (* return atom's copy *)
    CopyList(L^.Next, New);
    RETURN New;
  ELSE                            (* return sublist's copy *)
    CopyList(L^.Next^.SubLevel, New);
    RETURN New;
  END; (* IF *)
END CAR;
```

Procedure CAR returns a pointer to a copy of the first element of the list. If the list is empty, the procedure returns NIL; otherwise, it returns a copy of the first element, which is either an atom or a list.

```
PROCEDURE CDR(L:List): List;
(* Return tail of list L *)
VAR Elt: List;
BEGIN
  IF L = NIL THEN
    Error("Nonexisting list");
    RETURN NIL;
  ELSIF L^.SubLevel # NIL THEN
    Error("Badly formed list");
    RETURN NIL;
```

```
      ELSIF L^.Next = NIL THEN          (* return empty list *)
        ALLOCATE(Elt, SIZE(Element));   (* header *)
        Elt^.Atomic := FALSE;
        Elt^.Next := NIL;
        Elt^.SubLevel := NIL;
        RETURN Elt;
      ELSE            (* return copy of list minus first element *)
        CopyList(L, Elt);
        Elt^.Next := Elt^.Next^.Next;
        RETURN Elt;
      END; (* IF *)
    END CDR;
```

Procedure CDR returns either an empty list or a copy of the original list where the first element has been discarded. Both procedures CAR and CDR call procedure CopyList. (Its structure is more complex and similar to the CopyList algorithm to be discussed in Section 14.5.) In order to make it easier to understand this CopyList algorithm, we first present a case study dealing with the management of memory in a dynamic system, an approach known as *garbage collection*.

14.4 Case Study: Garbage Collection

Among the operations on generalized lists, the deletion operation is more complex than the others. It is not possible to simply link the deleted list to the free list, as other lists might still refer to it. Since a list can contain other lists or be contained inside yet other lists, it is difficult to know when it is possible to free the memory space allocated to the list. In this case study, we will discuss some methods for allocating and freeing generalized list memory space.

Design

Definition of the Problem Before defining our memory management problem, we will discuss some of the difficulties associated with the management of dynamic structures. The growth of dynamic structures makes it necessary to have a memory allocation mechanism. Memory allocation is easily done by the system when entering a block where some structures are declared or when calling a procedure creating a given structure.

Freeing unused memory is more difficult to do. When exiting a block, the system may free the memory space that was allocated for declarations inside the block—this causes no problem. However, memory space dynamically allocated for structure growth (list nodes, tree nodes, character strings) is more difficult to manage. It is, in fact, easy to know when more space is needed, whereas it is hard to know when a structure is no longer in use. The simplest way of solving this problem is just to let the programmer bear the memory management responsibility. Modula-2 has a standard module, Storage, with operations ALLOCATE and DEALLOCATE. This approach assumes that the programmer will take care of freeing the memory that is not used anymore. However, this places a heavy responsibility on the programmer, as it is easy for a person to forget some temporary structures and it is difficult to have a complete vision of all structures used.

This complex responsibility may lead in turn to a false reference problem: there might exist, in the structures currently in use, a pointer to a block of memory that has been freed. If this block is allocated again, this pointer will refer to a structure used for a different purpose, which has no relation with the original structure. The effects of this may be extremely unpleasant. Such a false reference might very easily occur in a program where space was allocated for a given structure by a call like ALLOCATE(P, Size). During program execution, pointer P might be copied into another pointer variable, as in T := P. Later on, some space might be released by DEALLOCATE(P, Size), but there still remains in the system a pointer T referring to the freed block; this block can be reallocated to other structures later on. Whether it is reallocated or not, a false reference has been created.

Many languages, such as Lisp, that allow creation and handling of dynamic structures, maintain responsibility of allocating and freeing memory space rather than burdening the programmer with these tasks. Allocation is relatively simple; it is handled on a demand basis as long as there is sufficient memory available. Deallocation of memory space no longer in use is more challenging, since it is difficult to know when a structure is no longer referenced in a program. There are two methods used for deallocating memory space used in list processing, as discussed in the design of our algorithms.

Design of a Solution One approach to deallocation is to free each memory block as soon as it is not used any more. This seems to be the most efficient plan, but it requires extra checking during processing. To implement this method, reference counters are used; these show, for a given block, how many pointers refer to it. When a new block is allocated, its reference count is 1, and each time a new pointer refers to it, the reference count is incremented by 1, while each time a link to the block is removed, the reference count is decremented by 1. When the reference count becomes zero, the block cannot be accessed, as no pointer refers to it. Thus, the block is released and attached to the free space.

There are several disadvantages to this approach. It will not work with circular or recursive structures, as the reference count will never be zero even if no external pointers refer to them. To solve this problem, it is possible to simply forbid circular or recursive structures, but this solution is not acceptable because recursive structures might be most appropriate for some applications. Other possible solutions might be to flag recursive structures for special treatment, or to use special list headers with a reference count including only external references. Even if the problem of circular or recursive structures is solved, others remain. Every node must contain space for a count field; if this count field ever overflows, it may "wrap around" to zero and cause premature collection. If it is made large enough to insure no overflow, the amount of memory space may be unacceptable. Another major disadvantage of this method is the significant increase in normal processing time that occurs with updating the reference count. All processing will need to check and update reference counters. Thus, just to assign a new value to a pointer P, it will be necessary to:

- access the structure pointed to by P and decrement its reference count
- free the structure if the new reference count is zero
- evaluate the address to assign to P, access the corresponding structure, and increment its reference count
- assign the address to pointer P

From this list we see that the extra operations are not negligible and that the reference count maintenance costs may become excessive. Because of these problems, we will not develop this technique. Rather, we will discuss another method based on marking and gathering.

The *mark-and-gather* approach does not reclaim any unused space until there is almost no free space left. All the allocated blocks are then checked, and those of them that are no longer in use are freed. The method is commonly called *garbage collection:* the free memory space decreases constantly until either a certain level is reached or an allocation request cannot be satisfied. When this happens, normal processing is suspended and the garbage collection process is started. Once memory reclamation is complete, normal processing resumes. This method proceeds in two phases, marking and gathering. In the marking phase, all the allocated blocks that can be accessed through the program's and the system's variables are accessed and marked. In the gathering phase, all the memory blocks are inspected. If the block is marked, then it is unmarked, otherwise if the block is unmarked, then it is placed in the free list.

When marking the used blocks, the program follows all the pointers from the accessible structures to find the blocks in use. This implies that during the marking process all pointers have their normal value. This might seem obvious, but there are algorithms that temporarily modify various structures, for instance by reversing pointers in order to be able to backtrack. It will be impossible to correctly mark structures if some of them are being used by such temporary modification algorithms. Such algorithms should be avoided, or the marking should be started only after these algorithms are not in use.

The cost of storage reclamation grows with the degree of use of memory: if there remains little free memory then the reclamation must be done more often. Furthermore, if the memory is almost full, the number of structures is high and marking becomes long, as there are many things to mark. In order to improve efficiency, garbage collection is often started when memory utilization is not too high (for instance, at fifty percent). It can also be decided that if garbage collection does not reduce memory utilization below a given level, the memory will be considered to be full and processing will stop. This criterion seems extreme, but it avoids repeated calls to garbage collection when memory is almost full. The system is said to be *thrashing* when it is always doing background work, such as garbage collection, and never making any real progress on the problem at hand.

Marking

The objective of this phase is to mark all the blocks that can be accessed by following chains of pointers that start from known variables. This means that a list of all variables pointing to the dynamic memory area must exist: a symbol table may be used. If a variable points to a dynamic block, this block must be marked as well as all the other blocks that can be reached from this first block, and all the blocks that can be accessed from these other blocks, and so on. Once all the blocks accessible from a given variable have been so marked, the process is repeated for the next variable. Once all variables have been processed in that manner, marking is finished, and the gathering phase can begin. The marking algorithm may be illustrated by the following pseudo-code.

```
Mark
    If the first block contains no pointers
        Mark it and finish
    Else
        Push its address on stack
    End if
    While the stack is not empty
        Pop a block address from stack
        For all pointers in the block
            If the block pointed to is not marked
                If the block contains no pointers
                    Mark it
                Else
                    Push its address on stack
                End if
            End if
        End for
    End while
End Mark
```

Such an algorithm will have a complexity of O(n), where n is the number of blocks that are marked. However, the use of a stack is a major disadvantage, because the storage reclamation process is started when the memory space left is small. Therefore, if the structures are complex and intertwined, the stack can become too large for the remaining storage space. Thus, it is necessary to define marking algorithms that do not use extra memory and therefore use no stack. These algorithms also cannot be recursive (because they would use stacks indirectly). Most marking algorithms use an elegant technique discovered independently by H. Schorr and W. M. Waite, and by Peter Deutsch in 1967. We will develop this technique in the next section.

Gathering

The gathering phase may simply examine all the nodes that are in memory and link all those which are not marked to the free list. This gathering is done by a linear sweep through memory, as shown in the following pseudocode.

```
Gather
    For each node in dynamic memory
        If the node is not marked
            Add the node to the free list
        Else
            Set the node to unmarked
        End if
    End for
End Gather
```

It is possible to perform a compaction of memory in which all the marked nodes are copied into consecutive storage positions from the beginning of memory storage. We will develop a compacting algorithm when we refine this solution.

Refine the Solution Using the Schorr-Waite-Deutsch approach to marking, we use the list structure itself to build a "stack" for backtracking by reversing links. Starting at the root of the structure, the algorithm follows one type of link (left link, for instance). For each link followed, the pointer is reversed to indicate the preceding node and to allow backtracking. When encountering an atom or a null pointer, the algorithm follows the other type of link (right link, for instance) and marks the node to indicate that the right link contains a backtracking pointer. During backtracking, pointers are reset to their previous values and the unmarked nodes are marked. We will use three pointers, Last, Current, and Temp, as we move through the structure. The operation "descend left" means: set Temp to left pointer of Current, reverse the left pointer of Current to Last, set Last to Current, and set Current to Temp. Operation "descend right" is similar, except that the right pointer is reversed.

```
Mark
    Set Current and Last to the list Root
    If Current is an atom
        Mark Current as visited
        Set Finished to True
    Else
        Set Finished to False
    End if

    While not Finished
        Set Left and Right to the left and right pointers of Current
        Mark Left as visited if atomic
```

> If Left is not empty and not atomic and not marked
>   Descend left
> Elsif Right is not empty and not atomic and not marked
>   Descend Right
> Else
>   Mark Right node as visited if not empty
>   Mark Current node as visited
>   If Current is the list root
>   Set Finished to True
>   Elsif Last is marked   { ascending from Right }
>   Set Temp to the Right pointer of Last
>   Set the Right pointer of Last to Current { restore link }
>   Else   { ascending from Left }
>   Set Temp to Left pointer of Last
>   Set the Left pointer of Last to Current { restore link }
>   End if
>   Set Current to Last
>   Set Last to Temp
> End if
> End while
> End Mark

If the list root is not an atom, a loop is repeated in which atoms are marked and left links are followed as far as possible, then right links as far as possible. Then the algorithm backtracks up to the root, resetting left and right pointers on the way. When the program is advancing left, the left pointer is reversed, and when advancing right, the node is marked and the right pointer is reversed. When advancing is no longer possible, it is necessary to backtrack, marking the nodes and resetting left and right pointers. To know which way to backtrack, nodes are marked only when advancing right. Since each node is visited at most three times, the algorithm's complexity is O(n), where n is the number of nodes.

Figure 14-11 illustrates the execution of the algorithm Mark on a given list structure. It shows the structure at the end of the main loop. Each iteration marks an atom, or goes left, or goes right, or backtracks. Procedure Mark must be called for each variable in the program that points to a dynamic structure. The marking phase will be over when all the calls to Mark are done. The mark field is the second Boolean field in the structure of Figure 14-11, the first Boolean field indicating whether or not the node is atomic.

We now refine our gathering algorithm to compact memory space by copying nodes in use to the start of memory. The copied pointers point, in general, to nodes that will be copied—their values must be updated. This problem of copying and updating is solved in a simple way by making two passes. During the first pass, the new address of each node is found (and kept in the node itself); during the second pass, the pointers to moved nodes will be adjusted by using the new address kept in the old nodes they point

552 Chapter 14 Generalized Lists

Initial structure

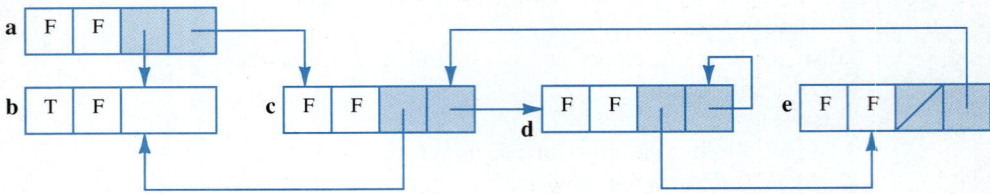

Atom **b** marked

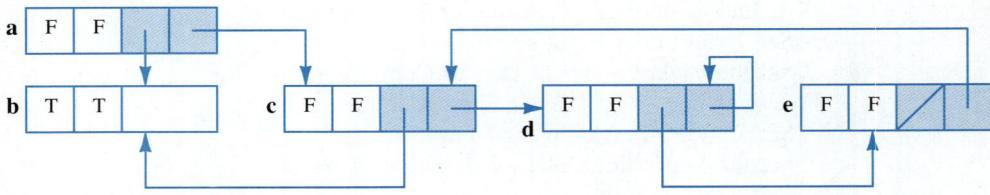

Element **a** marked and modified

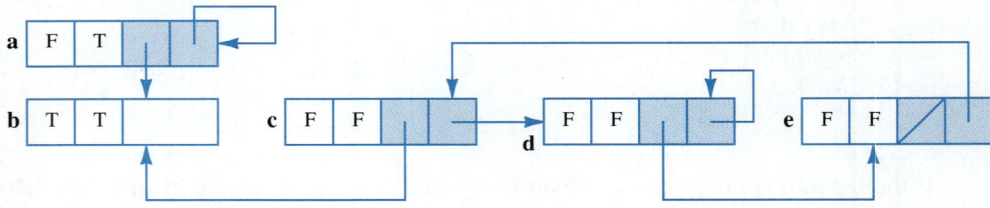

Element **c** marked and modified

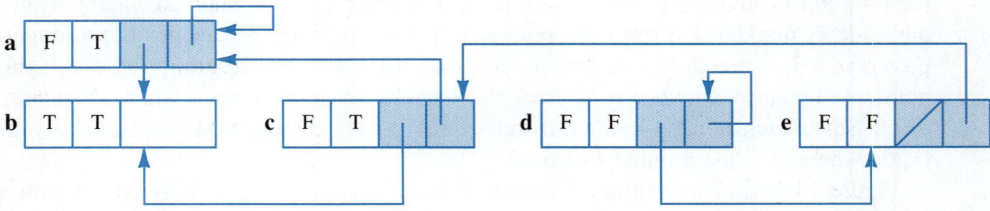

Element **d** modified

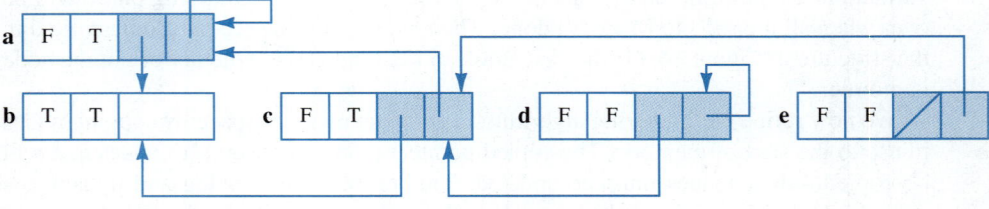

Figure 14-11   Trace of the Marking Algorithm

14.4 Case Study: Garbage Collection 553

Element **d** restored and element **e** marked

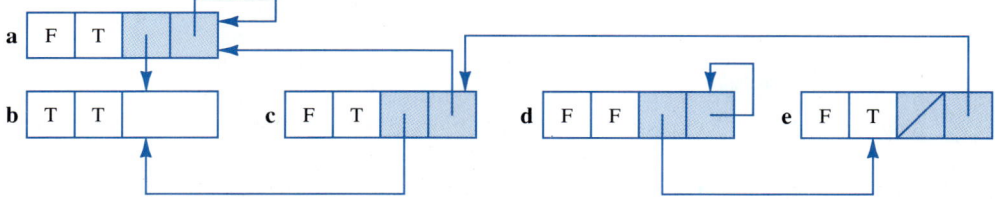

Element **d** modified again

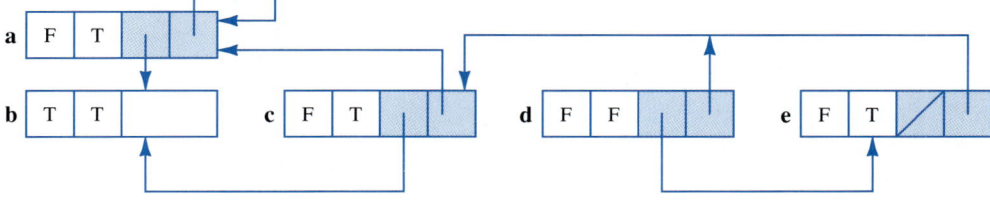

Element **d** restored

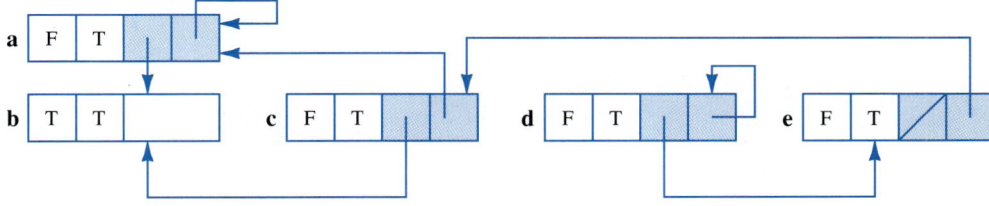

Element **c** restored

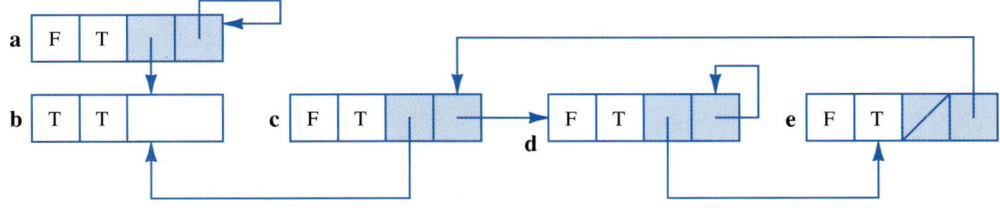

Element **a** restored

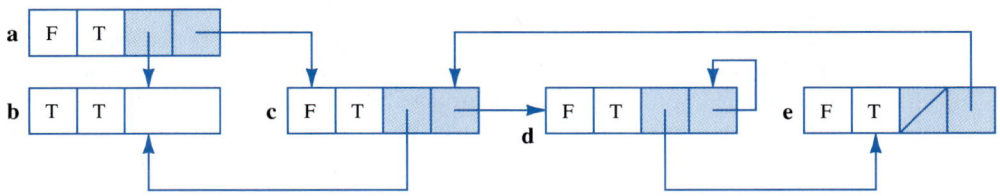

Figure 14-11 (Continued)

to. The complexity of such an algorithm will be O(n). Figure 14-12 shows the marked storage space before and after compaction. (For simplicity, pointers in unmarked nodes are not shown.)

Procedure Compact uses two indices "Low" and "High" to indicate the first free position in memory and the last node used in memory. The algorithm copies all marked nodes so that they occupy consecutive positions at the beginning of the storage space.

```
Compact
    Set Low to 0 and High to the maximum memory location + 1
    Mark the location Low and unmark the location High
    While Low <= High
        Increment Low until an unmarked location is found
        Decrement High until a marked location is found
        If Low < High
            Copy node from location High to location Low
            Set the left pointer of location High to location Low
            Unmark the location High
        End if
    End while

    For Low going from 1 to High
        Unmark the location Low
        If Location Low is not atomic
            If the left pointer of Low is greater than High
                { points to old location }
                Set left pointer of Low to left pointer of old location
            End if
            If the right pointer of Low is greater than High
                { points to old location }
                Set right pointer of Low to left pointer of old location
            End if
        End if
    End for
End Compact
```

The first While loop corresponds to the first pass: Low is advanced to the first unmarked node. The High node is copied into the Low position, is unmarked, and its new address (Low) is copied into its left pointer. When the first pass is finished, all the copied nodes' pointers must be adjusted. This is done by a sequential examination of all the nodes situated at the beginning of storage. If some nodes have pointers to the freed storage (beyond index High), these must be modified by using the new address stored in the old node to which they are still pointing. Once this second pass is done, all the nodes in use are at the beginning of storage (up to index High) and the rest of storage is free.

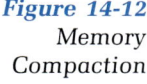
Figure 14-12
Memory
Compaction

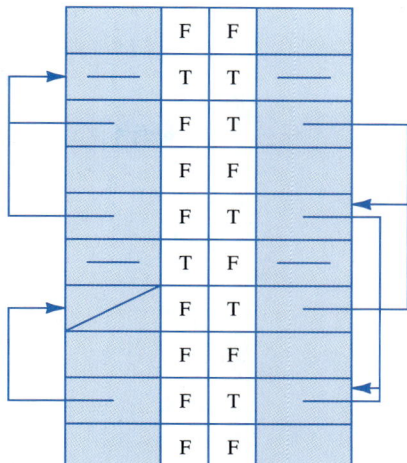
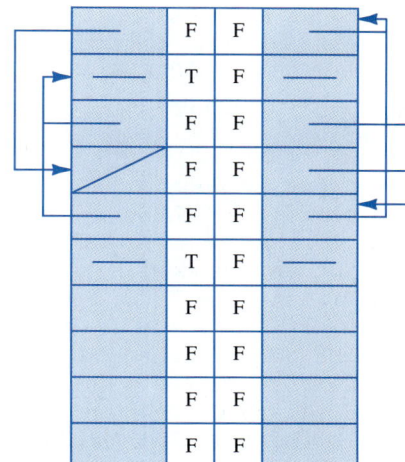

Develop a Testing Strategy We should test our marking and gathering with compaction algorithms with a variety of list structures, including many cases of lists with cycles. We should include tests for the following cases:

an empty list
a list with a single atomic node
a recursive list of the form C = (n, C)
a linear list with no cycles

To test these procedures we will need a driver program and a display procedure to evaluate their correctness. The writing of such a program is left as an exercise (see problem 19).

Implementation

Code and Test the Program We first must define our data type for a node so that we can implement our algorithm.

```
TYPE NodePointer = POINTER TO Node;
     Node = RECORD
              Marked: BOOLEAN;
              CASE Atomic: BOOLEAN OF
                FALSE: LeftNode,RightNode: NodePointer;(* sublist pointers *)
              | TRUE: Atom: CHAR;                      (* atom value *)
              END;
            END;
```

Procedure Mark applies our marking algorithm to a generalized list Root; even though Root is not modified, it is passed as a variable parameter to indicate that temporary changes will be made to the structure to which it points.

```
PROCEDURE Mark(VAR Root: NodePointer);
(* Mark elements of list Root *)
VAR Finished: BOOLEAN;
    Last, Current, Left, Right, Temp: NodePointer;
BEGIN
  Last := Root;
  Current := Root;
  Finished := FALSE;
  IF Current^.Atomic THEN          (* mark atomic root and stop *)
    Current^.Marked := TRUE;
    Finished := TRUE;
  END; (* IF *)
  WHILE NOT Finished DO            (* traverse and mark *)
    Left := Current^.LeftNode;
    Right := Current^.RightNode;
    IF (Left # NIL) AND Left^.Atomic THEN    (* mark atom *)
      Left^.Marked := TRUE;
    END; (* IF *)
    IF NOT ((Left = NIL) OR Left^.Atomic OR Left^.Marked) THEN (* go left *)
      Temp := Left;
      Current^.LeftNode := Last;
      Last := Current;
      Current := Temp;
    ELSIF NOT ((Right = NIL) OR Right^.Atomic OR Right^.Marked) THEN (* go right *)
      Current^.Marked := TRUE;
      Temp := Right;
      Current^.RightNode := Last;    (* reverse pointer *)
      Last := Current;
      Current := Temp;
    ELSE                           (* come back up *)
      IF Right # NIL THEN
        Right^.Marked := TRUE;
      END; (* IF *)
      Current^.Marked := TRUE;
      IF Current = Root THEN  (* all done *)
        Finished := TRUE;
      ELSIF Last^.Marked THEN   (* came from right *)
        Temp := Last^.RightNode;
        Last^.RightNode := Current;
      ELSE                         (* came from left *)
        Temp := Last^.LeftNode;
        Last^.LeftNode := Current;
      END; (* IF *)
      Current := Last;
      Last := Temp;
    END; (* IF *)
  END; (* WHILE *)
END Mark;
```

14.4 Case Study: Garbage Collection

To implement our gathering with compaction algorithm in a simple way, we assume memory is an array of nodes and modify our previous declarations in the following manner (pointers are replaced by indices).

```
CONST Maxi = 100;
      MaxiPlusl = Maxi + 1;

TYPE Index = [0..MaxiPlusl];
     Node = RECORD
              Marked: BOOLEAN;
              CASE Atomic: BOOLEAN OF
                FALSE: LeftNode, RightNode: Index;      (* sublist pointers *)
              | TRUE: Atom: CHAR;                       (* atom value *)
              END;
            END;
     Memory = ARRAY Index OF Node;
```

Our compaction algorithm follows directly from the pseudocode solution.

```
PROCEDURE Compact(VAR Mem: Memory; VAR High: Index);
(* Compact Marked elements in bottom of memory *)
VAR Low: Index;
BEGIN
  Low := 0;                          (* initialize extremes *)
  High := MaxiPlusl;
  Mem[Low].Marked := TRUE;           (* sentinels *)
  Mem[High].Marked := FALSE;
  (* copy Marked elements from top into nonmarked elements at bottom
     original elements point to new position through LeftNode pointer *)
  WHILE Low <= High DO
    WHILE Mem[Low].Marked DO         (* skip marked elements *)
      INC(Low);
    END; (* WHILE *)
    WHILE NOT Mem[High].Marked DO    (* skip unmarked elements *)
      DEC(High);
    END; (* WHILE *)
    IF Low < High THEN
      Mem[Low] := Mem[High];         (* copy marked element at bottom *)
      Mem[High].LeftNode := Low;     (* pointer to new position *)
      Mem[High].Marked := FALSE;     (* erase mark *)
    END; (* IF *)
  END; (* WHILE *)
  (* adjust pointers of copied elements *)
  FOR Low := 1 TO High DO
    Mem[Low].Marked := FALSE; (* erase marks *)
    IF NOT Mem[Low].Atomic THEN
      IF Mem[Low].LeftNode > High THEN    (* pointer to old place *)
        Mem[Low].LeftNode := Mem[Mem[Low].LeftNode].LeftNode; (* adjust left *)
      END; (* IF *)
```

```
        IF Mem[Low].RightNode > High THEN  (* pointer to old place *)
          Mem[Low].RightNode := Mem[Mem[Low].RightNode].LeftNode;  (* adjust right *)
        END;  (* IF *)
      END;  (* IF *)
    END;  (* FOR *)
END Compact;
```

We tested these procedures for a small group of list structures corresponding to the various cases identified in our testing strategy and in the example list of Figure 14-11; we found they worked as expected.

Complete the Documentation   The documentation should include a careful statement of the problem and explanations of the Marking and Compacting algorithms, as described in the "Refine the Solution" section. The pseudocode solution might also be included, but this is optional because the program is fairly short and reasonably self-documenting. The test cases and their output should be part of the documentation. A user's manual is not required for this application.

14.5 Copying a List Structure

In addition to the method shown in the Compact algorithm, there are other ways to compact memory. For instance, it is possible to copy the structures to be kept in a consecutive area of storage. We will develop here a list copying algorithm that copies an original list into a new memory area. The marking algorithm just discussed avoided recursion and the use of a stack by reversing links to build an "internal stack" for backtracking. The following algorithm to copy a list structure uses a similar technique; its complexity is O(n).

```
PROCEDURE Move(VAR Original, Copy, Next: NodePointer);
(* Copy of Original list into a new memory space Copy *)
VAR SubList: BOOLEAN;
    Stack, Current, Left, Right, Temp: NodePointer;
BEGIN
  Current := Original;
  Next := Copy;
  SubList := TRUE;
  Stack := NIL;
  LOOP
    WHILE SubList DO
      Left := Current^.LeftNode;
      Right := Current^.RightNode;
      Current^.LeftNode := Next;           (* left link of original points to copy *)
      IF (Left # NIL) AND NOT Left^.Atomic THEN
        Current^.RightNode := Stack;       (* add left sublist to stack *)
        Stack := Current;                  (* current node for stack *)
      END;  (* IF *)
```

```
        Next^.LeftNode := Left;           (* left link of copy points to original *)
        IF (Right = NIL) OR Right^.Atomic OR Mem(Right^.LeftNode) THEN
          (* end of SubList *)
          IF (Right = NIL) OR Right^.Atomic THEN
            Next^.RightNode := Right;                  (* because of atomic *)
          ELSE
            Next^.RightNode := Right^.LeftNode;        (* because already copied list *)
          END; (* IF *)
          SubList := FALSE;
        ELSE                                           (* continue copying segment *)
          Next^.RightNode := Increment(Next);          (* next cell *)
          Current := Right;
        END; (* IF *)
        Next := Increment(Next);
      END; (* WHILE *)
      IF Stack = NIL THEN
        EXIT;
      ELSE                                             (* new sublist to copy *)
        Current := Stack^.LeftNode^.LeftNode;
        Temp := Stack;
        Stack := Stack^.RightNode;                     (* pop stack *)
        IF Mem(Current^.LeftNode) THEN
          Temp^.LeftNode^.LeftNode := Current^.LeftNode;
        ELSE
          Temp^.LeftNode^.LeftNode := Next;
          SubList := TRUE;
        END; (* IF *)
      END; (* IF *)
    END; (* LOOP *)
END Move;
```

Procedure CopyList copies list Original into a consecutive storage area Copy. To do this copying, the algorithm follows a chain of pointers (right pointers) until it finds an atom or a pointer to a node already processed. During this traversal, left pointers to sublists that must be traversed later are stacked in "Stack." Note that the stack requires no extra storage space, as nodes of the Original list are linked together to make up the stack. When the end of a sublist is reached, the stack is popped and the process is repeated until the stack is empty. At the end of the algorithm execution, Next points to the next node to use in the new storage area.

Two special functions are used by procedure CopyList. Mem(P) is a Boolean function returning True if P points to the new storage area. Increment(Q) is a function returning a pointer to the next memory cell. After procedure CopyList has been executed, the nodes in the original list have a left pointer indicating their replacements. This and function Mem make it possible to avoid copying shared elements several times. Procedure CopyList does not copy atomic nodes that are assumed to be kept in a separate storage area. Figure 14-13 illustrates various stages of the copy of a given list into a new storage area.

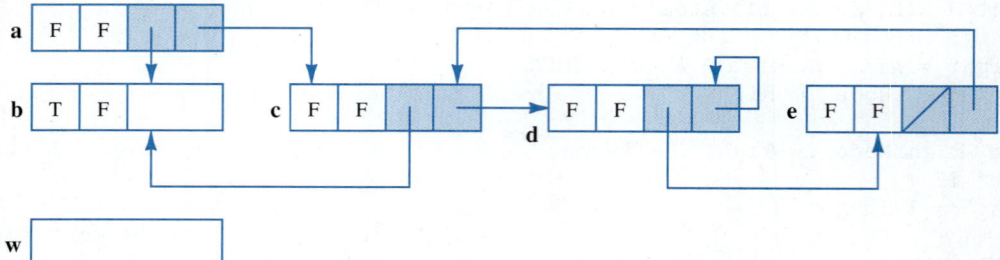

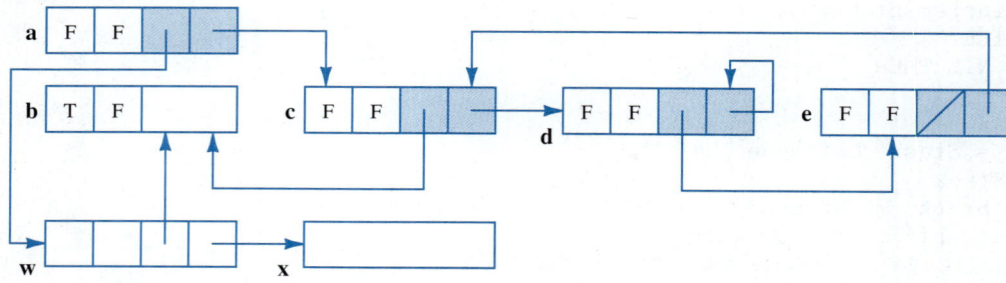

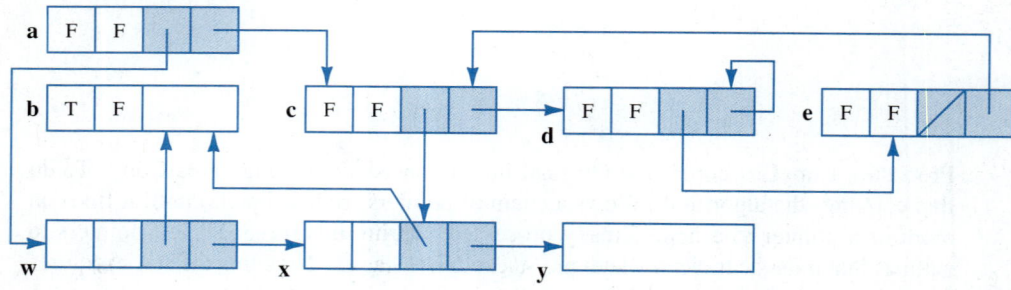

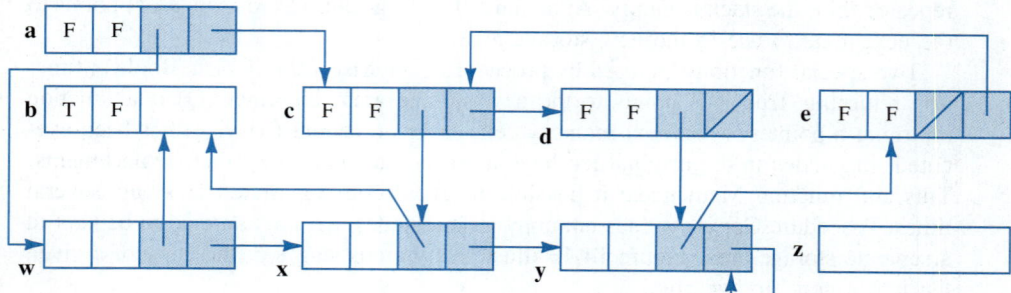

Figure 14-13 Copying a List

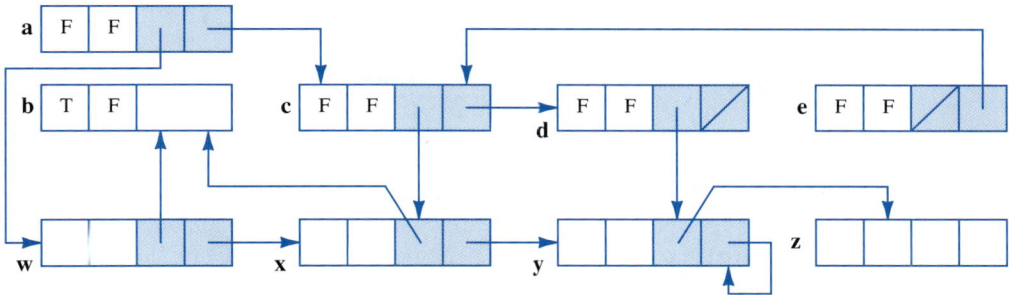

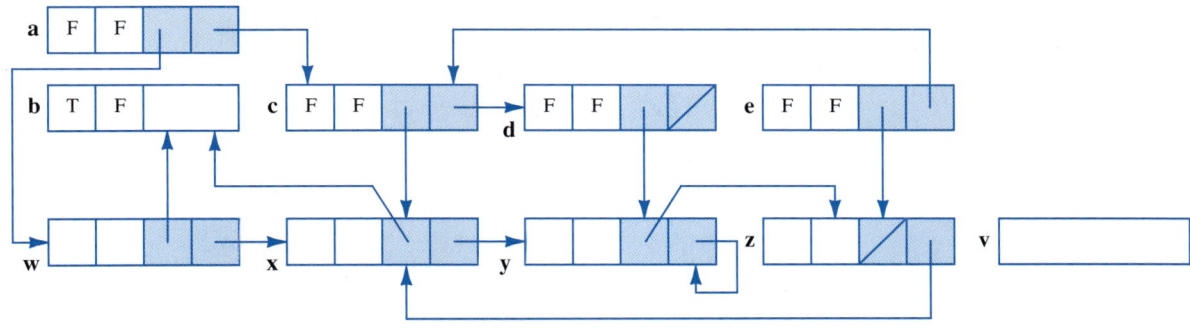

Figure 14-13 (Continued)

Notice that this copy algorithm compacts the list, making it possible to use it as a basis for memory management. Thus, it is possible to divide memory in two parts. The free list is, in fact, a big block of storage and allocation is done if there is enough space. This only requires keeping a pointer to the free block. Storage space is reclaimed periodically and the pointer is updated accordingly. Despite its simplicity, this method is not always used, in large part because of the inefficiency of the first compaction algorithms.

Summary

The generalized list extends the concepts of the linear list and of the tree structures. The generalized list data type is more powerful than any other data type we have discussed so far. However, the implementation of generalized lists is also more complex than for the other data types. For that reason we have considered representations for the generalized lists in a more detailed manner, since they strongly influence the algorithms that can be implemented and their efficiency as well.

The Lisp programming language is an implementation of generalized lists and, as such, offers all the needed operations and more. Implementations of Lisp systems use very simple nodes to build complex structures.

As generalized lists are complex structures that can be recursive and intertwined, the problem of memory management becomes very acute. Because of the complexity of the structures involved, some means of automatic storage reclamation is needed. This reclamation is accomplished by garbage collection techniques based on marking and gathering. The structures used are marked and, either following this or after compaction of the storage space, the unmarked nodes are gathered and added to the free space as a list. Garbage collection is done periodically, suspending normal processing.

■ Exercises

1. Using the representation of Figure 14-8, draw a representation for the following lists.
   (a) (x, (y, (z, w)), t)
   (b) ((x), y, L, (z)) with L = (k, (l, m), n)
   (c) (((a, b), c), d)

2. Represent the following structure by using the lists internal representation seen in Figure 14-7 in the text.

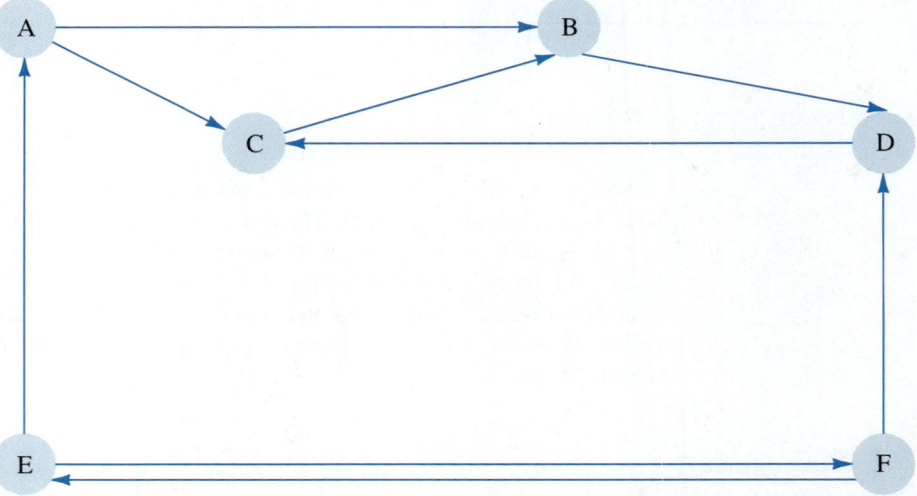

3. Write an algorithm which, given an S-expression, will decide whether or not the S-expression is well built.

4. Give the algorithm for a Lisp function EQ that will determine whether two atomic arguments are equal.

5. Modify the Lisp function MEMBER to check for the specified structure at all levels of the list being searched. (*Hint:* This is most easily done by recursing on both the CAR and the CDR of the list.)

6. Modify the ERASE function to remove *all* occurrences of the specified item at the top level of the list structure.

7. Modify the ERASE function to remove *all* occurrences of the specified item at *all* levels of the list structure.

8. Write a Lisp function REVERSE that reverses a given list as well as its sublists. For instance, (REVERSE '(A B (C D))) returns ((D C) B A)

9. Two lists are said to be equal if they have the same structure and the same data in corresponding fields. Give the algorithm for function EQUAL to determine if the two lists are equal.

10. Define a function DEPTH that computes and returns the depth of a given list. The depth is zero if the list is empty or is an atom; otherwise, it is 1 plus the maximum of the depth of its elements. For instance, (DEPTH '((((A))))) returns 4.

11. Write a Modula-2 procedure CopyList that copies a nonrecursive list with no shared sublists.

12. Write a Modula-2 procedure DisplayList that displays a nonrecursive list with no shared sublists.

13. Write a Modula-2 recursive marking procedure using the same nodes as procedure Mark in the text.

■ *Programming Problems*

14. Complete our implementation example by writing and testing Modula-2 procedures CONS, ATOM, and EQ as they are defined for Lisp.

15. After you have implemented the procedures of problem 14, use them to program in Modula-2 the Lisp functions defined in the text (FirstAtom, Member, Erase, Fact, Union, Intersection, CountAtoms).

16. Rewrite procedure Mark for lists and sublists having a special header. Assume field "RightNode" is free and can be used to point to the top of a stack whose elements are the list elements, as in procedure CopyList.

17. Test the procedure CopyList and modify it as necessary to handle the copy of recursive lists.

18. Write and test a procedure DisplayList that is able to list recursive lists.

19. Write a driver program to test the Mark and Compact procedures. You might find the CreateList procedure useful for creating some initial list structures.

*20. Generalized lists can be represented by nodes with two pointer fields and a symbol table comprising all the atom and list names, as well as pointers to lists. Field left of the nodes points either to another node at a lower level or at an element in the symbol table. Field right in a node points to the next node at the same level or is NIL.

Note: Problems marked with an asterisk (*) have a higher level of difficulty.

Chapter 14 Generalized Lists

```
TYPE Pointer = POINTER TO Node;
     Node = RECORD
                   CASE SubList: BOOLEAN OF
                     TRUE: Left: Pointer;
                   | FALSE: Symbol: Index;
                   END;
                   Right: Pointer;
            END;
     Element = RECORD
                   Name: String;
                   Atom: Boolean;
                   Address: Pointer;
               END;
     Table = ARRAY Index OF Element;
```

List L = (A (D E) L) could have the following list representation.

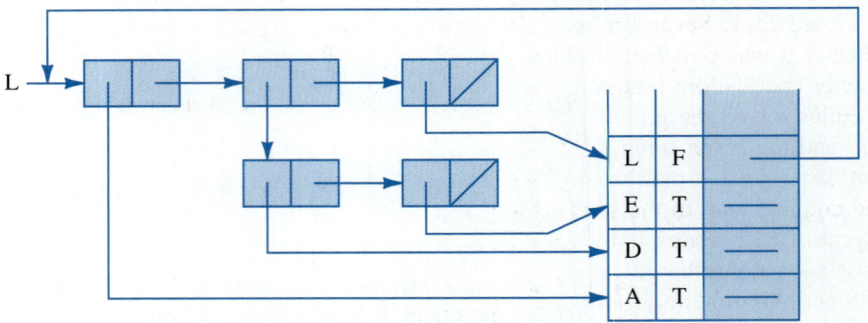

Write a procedure to read a list in parenthesized notation and create the corresponding structure. The algorithm may use the following procedures, which must then be declared.

Search(X, P)   Searches the symbol table for X and returns the element position P, or returns zero if the element is absent.

Place(X, T, P) Places X in the symbol table at position P. If T is zero, X is an atom; otherwise, T is the address of X.

Token   Returns the next token in the input string: name, parenthesis, or special symbol at end of string.

NewNode   returns a new node.

Graphs

INTRODUCTION

One of the earliest developments in graph theory goes back to 1736, when Euler, a renowned mathematician, solved the problem of the Königsberg bridges. As a short introduction, let's describe this problem and its solution. The city of Königsberg, in eastern Prussia, was crossed by the river Pregel, which flowed around an island, and then divided into two branches, as shown in Figure 15-1. Seven bridges crossed the river. The problem was to decide whether it was possible, starting from a given point, to cross all seven bridges exactly once before returning to the starting point.

Euler solved the problem by representing the four land points by graph vertices, and the seven bridges by graph edges, as shown in Figure 15-2. He proved that there exists a path from any vertex going through all edges exactly once and coming back to the starting vertex if and only if the degree (number of edges) of each vertex is even. This means that no such path exists for the bridges of Königsberg.

Since this first application, graphs have become of considerable importance and are being used to analyze many problems in computer science.

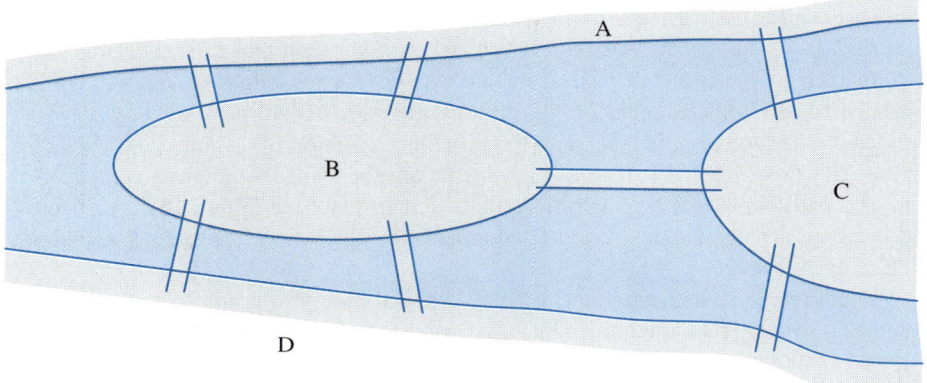

Figure 15-1 Königsberg Bridges

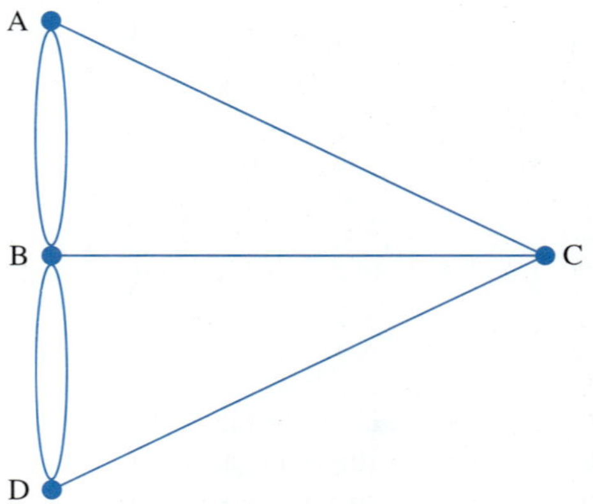

Figure 15-2
Euler's Solution

15.1 Definitions and Abstraction

A graph G is made of a finite nonempty set of *vertices* (or *nodes*) and of a set of *edges* E. Edges are represented by pairs of vertices. If these pairs are ordered pairs, the graph is a *directed graph;* otherwise, the pairs are unordered and the graph is said to be an *undirected graph*. Figure 15-3 represents a directed graph with the set of vertices {A, B, C, D} and the set of edges {(A, B), (B, C), (D, C), (C, A), (A, A)}.

Two vertices, u and v, are said to be *adjacent* if they are distinct and there is an edge connecting them. The neighbors of a vertex are all vertices that are adjacent to it. Two edges are said to be adjacent to each other if they share a common vertex.

A *path* is a sequence of vertices, $v_1, v_2, v_3, \ldots v_n$, such that each successive pair is connected by an edge, that is, such that (v_i, v_{i+1}) is an edge for $1 \leq i < n$. The *length* of a path is the number of edges along the path. A path is a *simple path* if all vertices on the path are distinct, with the possible exception of v_1 and v_n. A *cycle* is a simple path in which the first and last vertices are the same. A graph is *connected* if there is a path between every pair of vertices. For instance, in Figure 15-3, vertices A and B are adjacent, whereas A and D are not. Edge CA is *incident* to A. The path C, A, B, C is a cycle.

We can note here that a tree is, in fact, a special case of a graph that is connected and has no cycles. As a matter of fact, if a connected graph has n vertices and (n − 1) edges, it cannot have any cycle and thus is a tree. A *weighted graph* is a graph in which each edge possesses an associated value. Given a connected graph, weighted or not, it is possible to remove edges in order to eliminate cycles until a tree is obtained. Such a tree is called a *spanning tree* for the original graph. Figure 15-4 gives an example of a weighted graph and an associated spanning tree.

Figure 15-3
A Directed Graph

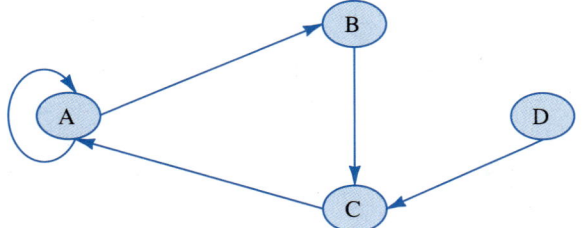

Figure 15-4
Weighted Graph
and Spanning Tree

(a) a weighted graph

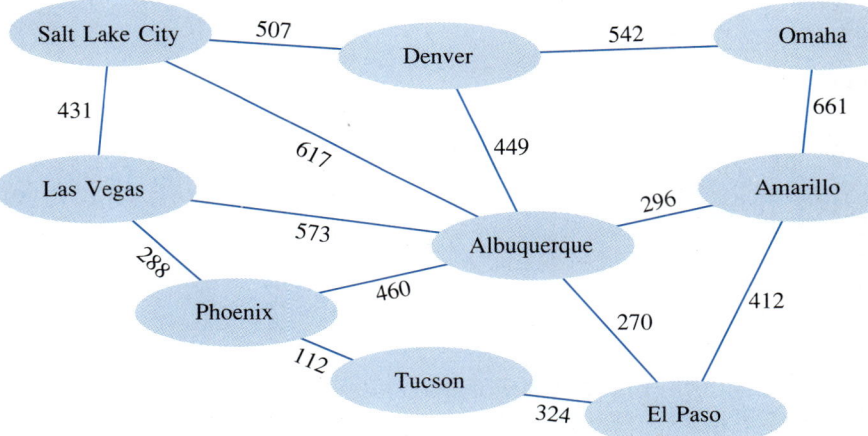

(b) an associated spanning tree

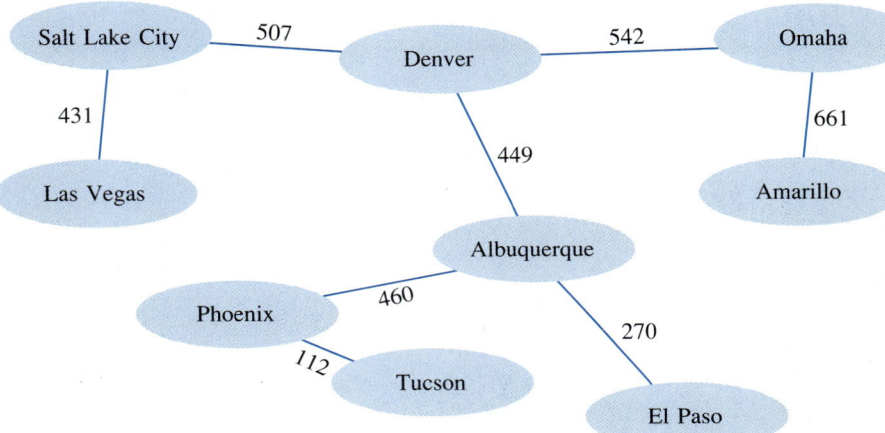

Our ADT Graph will comprise the type Graph, but will import types "KeyType" (used to identify vertices) and "ElementType" (associated with graph vertex values) from user-defined module GraphElements. The operations needed will include the creation of a graph, the addition or deletion of a vertex or an edge to or from a graph, the search for a vertex or an edge, the update of a vertex element, the fetching of an edge's weight, and the search for vertices adjacent to a given vertex. The following definition module defines completely our ADT Graphs.

```
DEFINITION MODULE Graphs;
FROM GraphElements IMPORT ElementType, KeyType;

TYPE Graph;

PROCEDURE Create(VAR G: Graph);
(* Create a new graph. This operation MUST be called before
   any other operation.
    Precondition: graph G does not exist
    Postcondition: G' exists and is empty *)

PROCEDURE Clear(VAR G: Graph);
(* Eliminate all vertices and edges from graph G.
    Precondition: graph G exists
    Postcondition: graph G' is empty *)

PROCEDURE VertexCount(G: Graph): CARDINAL;
(* Count the number of vertices in graph G.
    Precondition: graph G exists
    Postcondition: return the number of vertices in G. *)

PROCEDURE InsertVertex(VAR G: Graph; Key: KeyType; Elt: ElementType);
(* Insert a new vertex in graph G identified by Key and with value Elt.
    Precondition: graph G doesn't contain a Key vertex
    Postcondition: vertex Key of graph G' has value Elt and is not
                   adjacent to any other vertex *)

PROCEDURE InsertEdge(VAR G: Graph; Key1, Key2: KeyType;
                     Weight: INTEGER);
(* Insert a new edge with Weight in graph G between vertices
   Key1 and Key2.
    Precondition: graph G contains vertices Key1 and Key2, and
                  doesn't contain an edge between these vertices
    Postcondition: graph G' contains an edge between vertices
                   Key1 and Key2, and with weight Weight. *)

PROCEDURE DeleteVertex(VAR G: Graph; Key: KeyType);
(* Delete vertex Key from graph G.
    Precondition: there exists a vertex Key in graph G
    Postcondition: vertex Key is no longer part of graph G,
                   neither are edges previously connected
                   to this vertex *)
```

```
PROCEDURE DeleteEdge(VAR G: Graph; Key1, Key2: KeyType);
(* Delete the edge between vertices Key1 and Key2 in graph G.
   Precondition: there exists an edge between vertices Key1
                 and Key2
   Postcondition: the edge is no longer part of graph G' *)
PROCEDURE FindVertex(G: Graph; Key: KeyType; VAR Elt: ElementType;
                     VAR Found: BOOLEAN);
(* Search graph G for vertex Key and return the vertex' value.
   Precondition: graph G exists
   Postcondition: if graph G contains a vertex Key,
                  then Elt' has the value of the vertex element,
                  and Found is TRUE, otherwise Found is FALSE *)
PROCEDURE UpdateVertex(VAR G: Graph; Key: KeyType; Elt: ElementType;
                       VAR Done: BOOLEAN);
(* Update vertex Key's value in graph G.
   Precondition: there exists a vertex Key in graph G
   Postcondition: vertex Key' has value Elt and Done is TRUE,
                  otherwise Done is FALSE *)
PROCEDURE Weight(G: Graph; Key1, Key2: KeyType): INTEGER;
(* Return the weight associated with the edge between vertices
   Key1 and Key2 in graph G.
   Precondition: there exist an edge in graph G between vertices
                 Key1 and Key2
   Postcondition: return the weight associated with the
                  corresponding edge *)
PROCEDURE GetAdjacent(G: Graph; Key: KeyType; N: CARDINAL;
                      VAR Adjacent: KeyType);
(* Return the Nth adjacent vertex to vertex Key in graph G.
   Adjacent nodes are numbered sequentially as the graph is built.
   Precondition: there exists a Key vertex in graph G
   Postcondition: Adjacent' is the Nth adjacent vertex to Key,
                  or 0 if none exists. *)
END Graphs.
```

Operations on graphs can be classified into utility operations (Create, Clear), basic operations (VertexCount, InsertVertex, InsertEdge, DeleteVertex, DeleteEdge), and selection operations (FindVertex, FindEdge, UpdateVertex, Weight, GetAdjacent). We have not included traversal operations in our ADT, as these can be implemented using the operations provided. Our ADT provides operations for weighted graphs, but it should be noted that it can be used for unweighted graphs as well by just using a zero weight in calls to InsertEdge, and never using operation Weight.

15.2 Applications

Applications involving graphs are numerous. We will select a few in order to illustrate some of the most common uses of graphs.

Topological Sort

Directed acyclic graphs (digraphs or dags) are directed graphs with no cycles. They are often used to represent some kind of ordering between the vertices of the digraph. For instance, a digraph can represent the order of tasks in a project. Here the vertices can represent the tasks to be performed for the project, while the edges indicate the fact that a task must be completed before another one can begin. Or a digraph can represent the various courses of a given curriculum and the prerequisite relationships of these courses. The topological order of the tasks, or of the courses, is a linear relationship among the vertices of the associated graph, such that, if there exists an edge from vertex i to vertex j, then i will appear before j in the linear ordering. There is always at least one such topological ordering and usually more than one. Figure 15-5 shows a digraph and the three possible topological orders for that digraph. From the graph it should be obvious that A must precede all other nodes, and that D must always precede C, and that E must be preceded by all other nodes.

The topological sort algorithm can be implemented in a variety of ways. Using our ADT Graphs, the following procedure produces a list of vertices in reverse topological order.

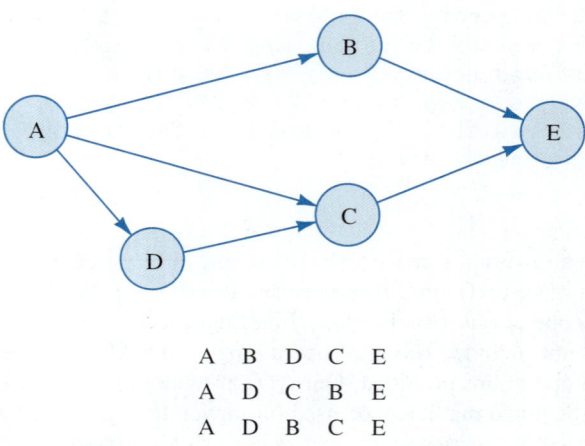

Figure 15-5
Topological Orders

```
A   B   D   C   E
A   D   C   B   E
A   D   B   C   E
```

```
PROCEDURE TopoSort(G: Graph; Vertex: CARDINAL; VAR Visited: BITSET);
(* Topological sort of a directed acyclic graph. This procedure
   produces a list of the graph vertices in reverse topological order.
   Vertex is a vertex number, and Visited a set of all visited vertices
   (note that using a BITSET might unduly limit the graph size). *)
VAR Next, N: KeyType;
BEGIN
  INCL(Visited, Vertex);
  N := 1;
  GetAdjacent(G, Vertex, N, Next);
  (* apply TopoSort to all vertices adjacent to Vertex *)
  WHILE (Next # 0) AND (N <= MaxVertices) DO
    IF NOT(Next IN Visited) THEN
      TopoSort(G, Next, Visited);
    END; (* IF *)
    INC(N);
    GetAdjacent(G, Vertex, N, Next);
  END; (* WHILE *)
  WriteCard(Vertex, 3);
END TopoSort;
```

The starting vertex is marked as visited, and the process is applied to all its adjacent vertices. After this is done, the vertex is displayed (which explains why the displayed order is the *reverse* topological order). A call example might be:

```
Marked := {};
TopoSort(G, 1, Marked);
```

If we apply TopoSort to the graph of Figure 15-6, we obtain the following reverse order.

8 5 2 7 9 6 3 4 1

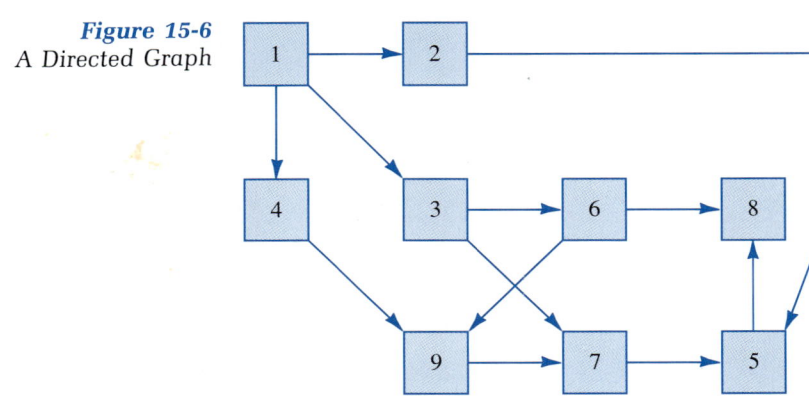

Figure 15-6
A Directed Graph

For a graph with n vertices and e edges, the time complexity of the topological sort algorithm is O(n + e). TopoSort is called only once for each vertex, as the first thing we do is mark the vertex as visited, and we never call TopoSort on a vertex that has already been visited. The total time spent in the WHILE loop is proportional to the number of vertices adjacent to vertex K, that is, to the number of edges connected to K. Thus, the total time spent is O(n + e). If we assume that n is much smaller than e, a relationship that is usually true for digraphs, the complexity may be considered to be O(e).

Graph Traversal

Numerous applications involve graph searching or examining all vertices of a given graph. Algorithms for graph traversal are therefore very useful. There are two techniques used for graph traversal: depth-first traversal or breadth-first traversal. Both techniques start at a given vertex and reach all other vertices by following edges out of that vertex.

The depth-first search (or traversal) is a generalization of the preorder traversal of a tree: the start vertex is marked as visited, then each unvisited vertex adjacent to the start vertex is searched, in turn, using recursion. This technique is called "depth first" because it continues in the forward (or deeper) direction as long as possible. The previous topological sort algorithm used a similar technique. If we want the depth-first traversal to work on graphs that are totally or partially disconnected, we must make sure we inspect all vertices because the method we just described will only work on a connected graph. The following procedure traverses a graph that may be disconnected.

```
PROCEDURE DepthFirstTraversal(G: Graph);
(* Apply depth-first method to traversal of graph G which
   might not be a connected graph *)
VAR Vertex: KeyType;
    Elt: ElementType;
    Found: BOOLEAN;
    Visited: BITSET;             (* might limit the graph size *)

  PROCEDURE DepthFirst(Vertex: KeyType);
  (* Traverse recursively all vertices accessible from vertex Vertex *)
  VAR Adjacent: KeyType;
      OtherVertex: CARDINAL;
  BEGIN
    INCL(Visited, Vertex);
    FOR OtherVertex := 1 TO MaxVertices DO
    (* apply depth-first to all vertices adjacent to Vertex *)
      GetAdjacent(G, Vertex, OtherVertex, Adjacent);
```

```
        IF (Adjacent # 0) AND NOT(Adjacent IN Visited) THEN
          DepthFirst(Adjacent);
          (* display edge *)
          WriteCard(Vertex, 2); WriteString("--");
          WriteCard(Adjacent, 2); WriteLn;
        END; (* IF *)
     END; (* FOR *)
  END DepthFirst;
BEGIN
  Visited := {};
  FOR Vertex := 1 TO VertexCount(G) DO   (* traverse all vertices *)
    FindVertex(G, Vertex, Elt, Found);
    IF NOT (Vertex IN Visited) AND Found THEN
      (* Vertex exists and not visited *)
      WriteString("Node "); WriteCard(Vertex, 3); WriteLn;
      DepthFirst(Vertex);
    END; (* IF *)
  END; (* FOR *)
END DepthFirstTraversal;
```

This algorithm applied to the connected graph of Figure 15-7 produces the following output:

```
Node   1
 3-- 6
 8-- 3
 5-- 8
 7-- 5
 9-- 7
 4-- 9
 2-- 4
 1-- 2
```

Figure 15-7
A Connected Graph

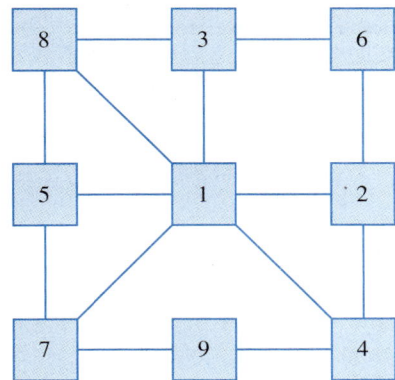

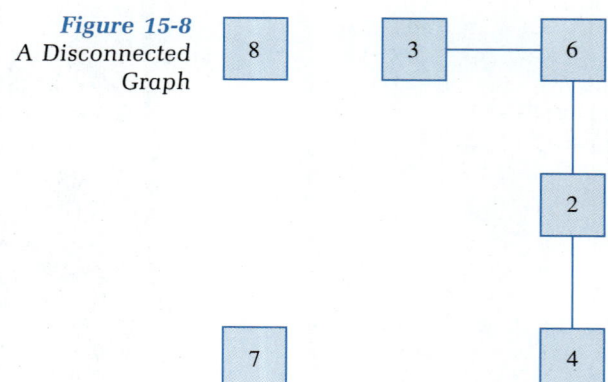

Figure 15-8
A Disconnected Graph

In this connected graph, it was possible to reach all the nodes from node 1: from 1 to 2 to 4 to 9 to 7 to 5 to 8 to 3 to 6. The output is actually a reverse trace of the encountered nodes.

If we remove vertices 1, 5, 9 and the edge between nodes 8 and 3 from this graph, we obtain the graph of Figure 15-8. If we apply DepthFirstTraversal to it, we obtain the following output:

```
Node    2
 2--    4
 6--    3
 2--    6
Node    7
Node    8
```

The other systematic way of visiting the vertices of a graph is called breadth-first traversal because, for each vertex visited, we traverse as broadly as possible by next visiting all vertices adjacent to it. The traversal procedure below illustrates this technique applied to graphs that may be disconnected.

```
PROCEDURE BreadthFirstTraversal(G: Graph);
(* Visit all vertices of graph G using breadth-first method.
   Graph G might not be a connected graph. *)
VAR Visited: BITSET;           (* might limit the graph size *)
    Vertex: KeyType;
    Elt: ElementType;
    Found: BOOLEAN;
    Q: Queue;
```

```
PROCEDURE BreadthFirst(Vertex: KeyType);
(* Traverse all vertices accessible from Vertex using
   breadth-first method. *)
VAR Adjacent, Next: KeyType;
BEGIN
   INCL(Visited, Vertex);                (* start with Vertex *)
   Enqueue(Q, Vertex);
   WHILE CountQueue(Q) # 0 DO
      Dequeue(Q, Vertex);
      Next := 1;
      GetAdjacent(G, Vertex, Next, Adjacent);
      (* visit all vertices adjacent to Vertex *)
      WHILE (Adjacent # 0) AND (Next <= MaxVertices) DO
        IF NOT (Adjacent IN Visited) THEN
           INCL(Visited, Adjacent);
           Enqueue(Q, Adjacent);
           (* display edge *)
           WriteCard(Vertex, 2); WriteString("--");
           WriteCard(Adjacent, 2); WriteLn;
        END; (* IF *)
        INC(Next);
        GetAdjacent(G, Vertex, Next, Adjacent);
      END; (* WHILE *)
   END; (* WHILE *)
END BreadthFirst;

BEGIN
   Visited := {};
   CreateQueue(Q);                       (* initialize *)
   FOR Vertex := 1 TO VertexCount(G) DO  (* traverse *)
      FindVertex(G, Vertex, Elt, Found); (* if vertex exists and not visited *)
      IF NOT (Vertex IN Visited) & Found THEN
         WriteString("Node "); WriteCard(Vertex, 3); WriteLn;
         BreadthFirst(Vertex);
      END; (* IF *)
   END; (* FOR *)
END BreadthFirstTraversal;
```

Procedure BreadthFirst uses a queue and operations Enqueue and Dequeue. Visited vertices are enqueued in order to process their adjacent vertices later. This algorithm applied to the connected graph of Figure 15-7 produces the following output:

```
Node    1
 1-- 2
 1-- 3
 1-- 4
 1-- 5
 1-- 7
 1-- 8
 2-- 6
 4-- 9
```

As nodes 2, 3, 4, 5, 7, and 8 can be reached from node 1, they appear first. Then the remaining nodes that can be reached from these are listed. If we apply BreadthFirstTraversal to the graph of Figure 15-8, we obtain:

```
Node    2
 2-- 4
 2-- 6
 6-- 3
Node    7
Node    8
```

The time complexity of breadth-first traversal is similar to the time complexity of the depth-first method used in procedure TopoSort, that is, $O(n + e)$, where n is the number of vertices and e is the number of edges of the graph. If we assume that e is much larger than n, the complexity is $O(e)$.

We can also note here a difference between depth-first traversal and breadth-first traversal: the queue for a "broad" graph (one where each vertex has numerous adjacent vertices) may need to be very large, while the stack used in depth-first is never very large. For an average breadth of B and a number of levels N, the worst-case size can be B^N for breadth-first and only $B \times N$ for depth-first.

Minimum-Cost Spanning Tree

Recall from the definitions that a spanning tree for a connected graph reaches all vertices of the graph and has no cycles. Given a weighted graph, the cost of the corresponding spanning tree is the sum of the costs of the edges in the tree. A minimum-cost spanning tree has a total less than or equal to all other spanning trees, but is not necessarily unique. Minimum-cost spanning trees are used to design communication networks in which we represent cities as vertices and communication links as edges, as shown in Figure 15-4. A minimum-cost spanning tree for such a graph will then represent a communication network connecting all cities at minimum cost.

The simplest method to construct a minimum cost spanning tree, MCST, is known as Prim's algorithm. If the graph vertices belong to the set $\{1, 2, \ldots, n\}$, the algorithm can be described by the following pseudocode.

> Set MCST to { }
> Set Used to {1}
> While Used # Vertices do
>   Set (v_1, v_2) to the lowest cost edge such that
> v_1 is in Used and v_2 is in the set (Vertices − Used)
>   Include (v_1, v_2) in MCST
>   Include v_2 in Used
> End while

The set MCST will comprise all edges for the minimum-cost spanning tree. Prim's algorithm is an example of a "greedy" algorithm where local conditions determine the path to the solution. Procedure Prim implements this algorithm using two vectors of integers: Closest, which gives the vertex in Used currently closest to a vertex in Vertices−Used, and LowCost, which gives the cost of the edge between a vertex and its closest vertex.

```
TYPE Vector = ARRAY [1..MaxVertices] OF INTEGER;

PROCEDURE Prim(Cost: Graph; VAR LowCost, Closest: Vector; N: CARDINAL);
(* Gives the edges of a minimum cost spanning tree for graph Cost
   with vertices {1,2,...,N}. The MCST starts at vertex 1 and grows
   from there *)
VAR Vertex, Neighbor, Low: CARDINAL;    (* indices *)
    Min: INTEGER;                       (* lowest cost found *)
BEGIN
  FOR Vertex := 2 TO N DO      (* initialize *)
    LowCost[Vertex] := Weight(Cost, 1, Vertex);
    Closest[Vertex] := 1;
  END; (* FOR *)
  FOR Vertex := 2 TO N DO      (* find vertex Low closest to Vertex *)
    Min := LowCost[2];
    Low := 2;
    FOR Neighbor := 3 TO N DO
      IF LowCost[Neighbor] < Min THEN
        Min := LowCost[Neighbor];
        Low := Neighbor;
      END; (* IF *)
    END; (* FOR *)
    (* display edge *)
    WriteInt(LowCost[Low],5); WriteCard(Low, 5);
    WriteInt(Closest[Low], 5); WriteLn;
    LowCost[Low] := Infinity;        (* Low is added to MST *)
```

```
      FOR Neighbor := 2 TO N DO       (* adjust costs *)
        IF (Weight(Cost, Low, Neighbor) < LowCost[Neighbor])
          AND (LowCost[Neighbor] < Infinity) THEN
          LowCost[Neighbor] := Weight(Cost, Low, Neighbor);
          Closest[Neighbor] := Low;
        END; (* IF *)
      END; (* FOR *)
    END; (* FOR *)
END Prim;
```

At each step, LowCost is searched for the vertex in Vertices–Used that is closest to Used. The corresponding edge is displayed and the arrays LowCost and Closest are updated to reflect the fact that a vertex has been added to Used. We use a constant "Infinity" to represent a value larger than any actual cost. This value helps mark a vertex as a member of Used. Figure 15-9 shows the minimum-cost spanning tree obtained by applying procedure Prim to the graph of Figure 15-4(a).

The time complexity of Prim's algorithm is $O(n^2)$, since we make $(n - 1)$ iterations in the outer loop, and each iteration is itself $O(n)$ because of the inner loops.

Activity Graph

Some applications in project planning consist of network flow problems; in these, it is desired to find a network path that satisfies certain specified conditions. We will consider here schedules constructed by the critical-path method (CPM) or the program evaluation review technique (PERT), both of which use data in the form of an acyclic graph.

Let us consider data in the form of an event-vertex network, as shown in Figure 15-10. Vertices represent events and edges represent activities and their duration. The network has to be topologically ordered: our example graph in Figure 15-10 is already ordered; otherwise, a topological sort would be required before proceeding.

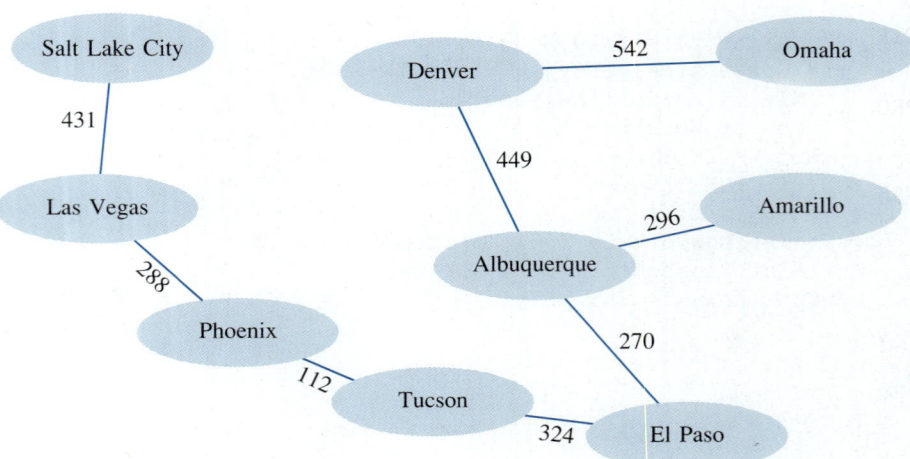

Figure 15-9
Minimum-Cost
Spanning Tree

Figure 15-10
An Event-Vertex Network

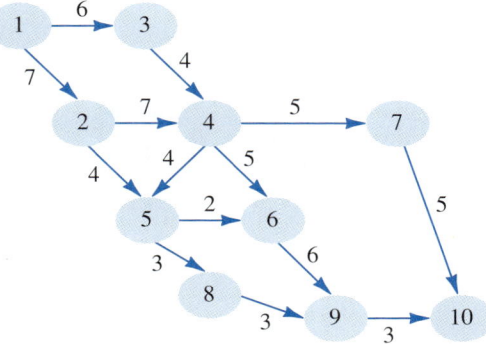

To find the critical path we must compute two values for each event: the earliest time and the latest time. The earliest time for an event without predecessors is always zero. For an event with predecessors, it is the maximum of all the sums of the earliest time of its predecessors and the activity duration between them. For instance, in the example of Figure 15-10, the earliest time (et) of event 5 is the maximum of ($et_4 + 4$) and ($et_2 + 4$), that is to say, the maximum of (14 + 4) and (7 + 4), or 18. The shortest time for a project is given by et_m if m is the index of the last event. The latest time (lt) of an event is computed backwards from the last event and is the minimum of the differences between the latest time of its successors and the activity duration. For instance, in the example of Figure 15-10, the latest time for event 4 is the minimum of ($lt_7 - 5$), ($lt_6 - 5$), and ($lt_5 - 4$), that is to say, the minimum of (24 - 5), (20 - 5), and (18 - 4), or 14.

After these times have been computed for each event, the critical path is found by noting events whose earliest and latest times are identical. (This obviously indicates that these events cannot be delayed without delaying the whole project.) The critical path for the example of Figure 15-10 is 1, 2, 4, 5, 6, 9, 10. The following procedure applies the process by using an array for the event times and displays the critical path.

```
TYPE TimeType = (Early, Late);
     TimeTable = ARRAY [1..MaxVertices], TimeType OF INTEGER;

PROCEDURE CriticalPath(VAR G: Graph; VAR Times: TimeTable;
                      Vertices, Edges: CARDINAL);
(* From a given graph, find the critical vertices *)
VAR Vertex, Edge: CARDINAL;
    Destination: KeyType;
    More: BOOLEAN;
BEGIN
  (* Compute Early values for each vertex *)
  Vertex := 1;
  WHILE Vertex < Vertices DO
    Edge := 1;
    More := TRUE;
```

```
      WHILE (Edge <= MaxVertices) AND More DO
        GetAdjacent(G, Vertex, Edge, Destination);
        IF Destination = 0 THEN
          More := FALSE;
        ELSE
          Times[Destination, Early] := Max(Times[Destination, Early],
                  Times[Vertex, Early] + Weight(G, Vertex, Destination));
          INC(Edge);
        END; (* IF *)
      END; (* WHILE *)
      INC(Vertex);
    END; (* WHILE *)
    (* Compute Late values for each vertex *)
    Times[Vertex, Late] := Times[Vertex, Early];
    Vertex := Vertices;
    WHILE Vertex >= 1 DO
      Edge := 1;
      More := TRUE;
      WHILE (Edge <= MaxVertices) AND More DO
        GetAdjacent(G, Vertex, Edge, Destination);
        IF Destination = 0 THEN
          More := FALSE;
        ELSE
          Times[Vertex, Late] := Min(Times[Vertex, Late],
                  Times[Destination, Late] - Weight(G, Vertex, Destination));
          INC(Edge);
        END; (* IF *)
      END; (* WHILE *)
      DEC(Vertex);
    END; (* WHILE *)
    (* Output critical vertices *)
    WriteString("Critical path: ");
    FOR Vertex := 1 TO Vertices DO
      IF Times[Vertex, Early] = Times[Vertex, Late] THEN
        Write('-'); WriteCard(Vertex,3); Write('-');
      END; (* IF *)
    END; (* FOR *)
    WriteLn;
END CriticalPath;
```

The algorithm works as follows: the earliest time for each event is computed, then all the latest times are computed, and finally, by comparison of the earliest and latest times, the critical path is determined and displayed. In the case of the example of Figure 15-10, the Times table is:

```
 1:   0    0
 2:   7    7
 3:   6   10
 4:  14   14
 5:  18   18
 6:  20   20
 7:  19   24
 8:  21   23
 9:  26   26
10:  29   29
```

and the critical path displayed is:

-1-- 2-- 4-- 5-- 6-- 9--10-

This will end our presentation of graph applications. You should note, however, that there are many more interesting graph applications, including graph-matching or network problems, and the well-known traveling salesman problem.

15.3 Implementation

There are two basic approaches for graph representation: using adjacency matrices and using adjacency lists. We will concentrate on these basic representations here, although there exist other ways of representing graphs that involve combinations of the basic representations.

Adjacency Matrix

The adjacency matrix for a graph G with vertices in {1, 2, 3, . . . n} is an n × n matrix (we will call it A) of Boolean values, where A[i, j] is True if and only if there exists an edge from vertex i to vertex j. This representation is very useful in applications in which we frequently need to know whether or not a given edge is present, since the time required to access an element is independent of the number of vertices or edges. In addition, this representation may be used for directed as well as undirected graphs. In the latter case, the matrix will be symmetrical, as an edge between two vertices may be considered as going both ways. Figure 15-11 gives an example of a graph and of its adjacency matrix. Sometimes, in adjacency matrices, True and False values are replaced by numerical values 0 and 1.

A variation on the adjacency matrix representation is what is often called the labeled adjacency matrix, or the weighted adjacency matrix. Here the matrix elements are not Boolean, but are values associated with edges. A special value must be used to indicate the absence of an edge.

Figure 15-11
Adjacency Matrix

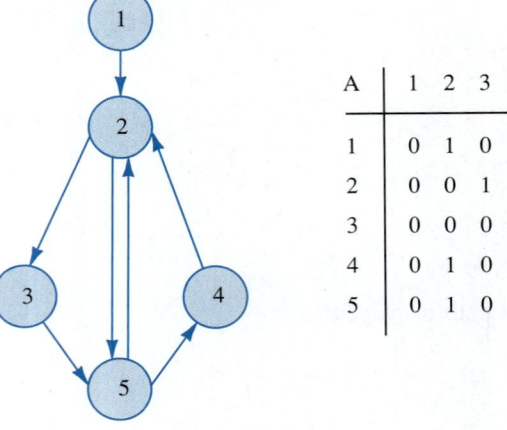

A	1	2	3	4	5
1	0	1	0	0	0
2	0	0	1	0	1
3	0	0	0	0	1
4	0	1	0	0	0
5	0	1	0	1	0

The main disadvantage of the adjacency matrix representation is the fact that it requires memory space proportional to n^2, even if the graph has far fewer edges than n^2. Algorithms to examine the matrix would be $O(n^2)$, even if the graph had only n edges.

We now present an implementation module based on this representation. In fact, we will represent a graph by a record structure, with (1) a cardinal indicating the number of vertices (assuming vertices are in order {1, 2, 3, . . . n}), and (2) an adjacency matrix, where elements represent labels or weights associated with edges, the value zero indicating the absence of an edge, and (3) a vector of values, each value associated with a vertex.

```
IMPLEMENTATION MODULE Graphs;
FROM GraphElements IMPORT ElementType, KeyType, MaxVertices;
FROM Storage IMPORT ALLOCATE, DEALLOCATE;

TYPE Graph = POINTER TO Struct;     (* opaque type *)
     Struct = RECORD
                N: KeyType;
                Matrix: ARRAY [1..MaxVertices], [1..MaxVertices]
                         OF INTEGER;  (* edges *)
                Value: ARRAY [1..MaxVertices] OF ElementType;
              END;              (* vertex values *)

PROCEDURE Create(VAR G: Graph);
(* Create graph G *)
BEGIN
  ALLOCATE(G, SIZE(Struct));
  Clear(G);
END Create;
```

```
PROCEDURE Clear(VAR G: Graph);
(* Empty graph G *)
VAR Row, Column: CARDINAL;
BEGIN
  FOR Row := 1 TO MaxVertices DO
    G^.Value[Row] := 0;            (* no value *)
    FOR Column := 1 TO MaxVertices DO
      G^.Matrix[Row,Column] := 0;  (* no edges *)
    END;
  END;
  G^.N := 0;
END Clear;

PROCEDURE VertexCount(G: Graph): CARDINAL;
(* Return the number of vertices in G *)
BEGIN
  RETURN G^.N;
END VertexCount;

PROCEDURE InsertVertex(VAR G: Graph; Key: KeyType;
                       Elt: ElementType);
(* Create new vertex Key of graph G with value Elt and
   not connected to any other vertex *)
BEGIN
  IF G^.N = Key-1 THEN    (* sequential insertion *)
    G^.Value[Key] := Elt;
    INC(G^.N);
  END;
END InsertVertex;

PROCEDURE InsertEdge(VAR G: Graph; Key1, Key2: KeyType; Weight: INTEGER);
(* Insert a weighted edge in graph G between vertices Key1 and Key2 *)
BEGIN
  IF (Key1 <= G^.N) AND (Key2 <= G^.N) THEN
    G^.Matrix[Key1, Key2] := Weight;
  END;
END InsertEdge;

PROCEDURE DeleteVertex(VAR G: Graph; Key: KeyType);
(* Delete vertex Key *)
VAR Index: CARDINAL;
BEGIN
  FOR Index := 1 TO G^.N DO
    G^.Matrix[Key, Index] := 0;
    G^.Matrix[Index, Key] := 0;
  END;
  G^.Value[Key] := 0;
END DeleteVertex;
```

```
PROCEDURE DeleteEdge(VAR G: Graph; Key1, Key2: KeyType);
(* Delete edge between Key1 and Key2 the edge is no longer
   part of graph G *)
BEGIN
  G^.Matrix[Key1, Key2] := 0;
  G^.Matrix[Key2, Key1] := 0; (* only for undirected graphs *)
END DeleteEdge;

PROCEDURE FindVertex(G: Graph; Key: KeyType; VAR Elt: ElementType;
                     VAR Found: BOOLEAN);
(* Search graph G for vertex Key, return Elt *)
BEGIN
  IF (Key < G^.N) & (G^.Value[Key] # 0) THEN
    Elt := G^.Value[Key];
    Found := TRUE;
  ELSE
    Found := FALSE;
  END;
END FindVertex;

PROCEDURE UpdateVertex(VAR G: Graph; Key: KeyType; Elt: ElementType;
                       VAR Done: BOOLEAN);
(* Update vertex Key with value Elt *)
BEGIN
  IF Key < G^.N THEN
    G^.Value[Key] := Elt;
    Done := TRUE;
  ELSE
    Done := FALSE;
  END;
END UpdateVertex;

PROCEDURE Weight(G: Graph; Key1, Key2: KeyType): INTEGER;
(* Return the weight associated with edge *)
BEGIN
  RETURN G^.Matrix[Key1, Key2];
END Weight;

PROCEDURE GetAdjacent(G: Graph; Key: KeyType; N: CARDINAL;
                      VAR Adjacent: KeyType);
(* Return the Nth adjacent vertex to Key *)
VAR Neighbor, Index: CARDINAL;
BEGIN
  Adjacent := 0;
  Neighbor := 0;
  FOR Index := 1 TO G^.N DO
    IF G^.Matrix[Key, Index] # 0 THEN   (* count vertices *)
      INC(Neighbor);
```

```
      IF Neighbor = N THEN
        Adjacent := Index;
        RETURN;
      END;
    END;
  END;
END GetAdjacent;

END Graphs.
```

Our previous applications have all been tested with this implementation.

With the adjacency matrix representation, we can also introduce two more graph algorithms, both of which were designed to work specifically with this representation: Warshall's algorithm and Floyd's algorithm.

Transitive Closure In some applications it is necessary to determine if there exists a path of length 1 or more from a given vertex to another vertex. Starting with the adjacency matrix A for a given graph, we know that A[i, j] is True if there is an edge from vertex i to vertex j. This gives us all the paths of length 1 in the graph. If the matrix values are not Boolean but rather 0 and 1 and if A[i, k] and A[k, j] both have value 1, then there exists a path of length 2 between vertices i and j. Thus, if the product A[i, k] $\times$ A[k, j] is 1, then there exists a path between vertices i and j, going through vertex k. Furthermore, A[i, 1] $\times$ A[1, j] + A[i, 2] $\times$ A[2, j] + $\cdots$ + A[i, n] $\times$ A[n, j] will give the number of paths of length 2 between vertices i and j. This expression actually computes the value of an element of the square of matrix A. In order to know the number of paths of length 2 in a graph, it is sufficient to compute the square of the adjacency matrix. For instance, the square of the adjacency matrix for the graph of Figure 15-11 is:

```
0  0  1  0  1
0  1  0  1  1
0  1  0  1  0
0  0  1  0  1
0  1  1  0  1
```

which, for instance, indicates that a path exists between vertices 2 and 5 (2–3–5). The cube of the adjacency matrix will give us the number of paths of length 3, and so forth.

Usually, though, we only want to know whether or not a path exists, and we don't need information on paths of various lengths. We often wish to compute a matrix T where T[i, j] will be True if there is a path of length 1 or more from vertex i to vertex j. Matrix T is called the *transitive closure* of the adjacency matrix A. Procedure Warshall below implements an algorithm to produce the transitive closure of adjacency matrix A and is named after the discoverer of the algorithm, S. Warshall.

```
PROCEDURE Warshall(G: BMatrix; VAR TransClos: BMatrix; N: CARDINAL);
(* Find the transitive closure of the adjacency matrix G *)
VAR Vertex, Neighbor, Next: CARDINAL;
BEGIN
  FOR Vertex := 1 TO N DO      (* initialize by copying adjacency matrix *)
    FOR Neighbor := 1 TO N DO
      TransClos[Neighbor, Vertex] := G[Neighbor, Vertex];
    END; (* FOR *)
  END; (* FOR *)
  FOR Vertex := 1 TO N DO
    FOR Neighbor := 1 TO N DO
      IF TransClos[Neighbor, Vertex] THEN
        FOR Next := 1 TO N DO
          IF TransClos[Vertex, Next] THEN
            TransClos[Neighbor, Next] := TRUE;
          END; (* IF *)
        END; (* FOR *)
      END; (* IF *)
    END; (* FOR *)
  END; (* FOR *)
END Warshall;
```

where

```
BMatrix = ARRAY [1..N], [1..N] OF BOOLEAN;
```

Here is the basic idea of Warshall's algorithm: If there is a path from vertex j to vertex i, and another from vertex i to vertex k, then there is one from vertex j to vertex k. Procedure Warshall applies this idea with a pass over the adjacency matrix. Nevertheless, Warshall's algorithm complexity is $O(n^3)$. Actually this is rather good, as an alternative method of computing the transitive closure would involve raising the adjacency matrix to powers from 1 to n. Since the computation of a matrix product has a complexity of $O(n^3)$, this would produce an overall time complexity of $O(n^4)$.

With the following adjacency matrix (where * represents True and − represents False), the procedure creates the transitive closure shown in Figure 15-12. Original paths have been kept and others added: for instance, in A there is a path from 9 to 7, and also paths from 7 to 5 and from 5 to 8, so two paths from 9 to 5 and from 9 to 8 have been added in T.

All-Pairs Shortest–Path Given a weighted graph representing cities and distances between cities as in Figure 15-4, we often need to construct a table giving the shortest distance from any city to any other. Determining how to calculate the table entries is known as the all-pairs shortest-path problem. Procedure ShortestPath below implements Floyd's algorithm as a solution to this problem. It uses an n × n matrix ShortPath in which to compute the lengths of the shortest paths. Initially this matrix is a copy of the weighted adjacency matrix A. In this matrix, all weights are nonnegative, and the absence of an edge is represented by a large constant. Matrix PathPoint is

Figure 15-12
Transitive Closure

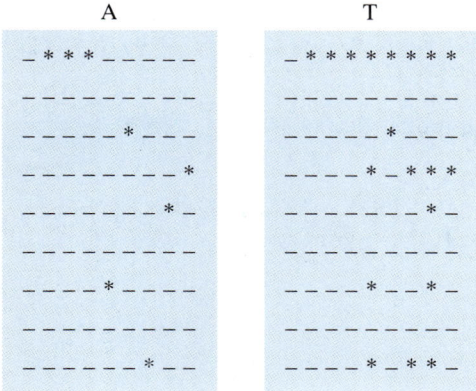

initially set to zero and will hold vertices on the shortest path: PathPoint[i, j] = k, if k is on the shortest path from i to j. PathPoint will allow us to reconstruct the complete shortest path, once all the shortest paths between intermediate points have been found.

Floyd's algorithm makes N iterations over the ShortPath matrix. For an element (i, j), if we find a vertex k such that the cost of (i, k) added to the cost of (k, j) is less than the cost of the current shortest path from i to y, we keep it as a shorter path.

```
PROCEDURE ShortestPath(G: CMatrix; VAR ShortPath, PathPoint: CMatrix;
                       N: CARDINAL);
(* Solve the all-pairs shortest paths problem for graph G, using
   Floyd's algorithm. Graph G is represented by a matrix where each
   element represents a path length between the vertices corresponding
   to its indices, or has value infinity if there is no path.
   PathPoint[Vertex, Neighbor] will show an intermediate point of the path
   ShortPath[Vertex, Neighbor], and can be used to find the complete
   shortest path. *)
VAR Vertex, Neighbor, Next: CARDINAL;
BEGIN
   FOR Vertex := 1 TO N DO        (* initialize by making a copy *)
     FOR Neighbor := 1 TO N DO
       ShortPath[Vertex, Neighbor] := G[Vertex, Neighbor];
       PathPoint[Vertex, Neighbor] := 0;
     END; (* FOR *)
   END; (* FOR *)
   FOR Vertex := 1 TO N DO        (* length of path to self is zero *)
     ShortPath[Vertex, Vertex] := 0;
   END; (* FOR *)
```

```
    FOR Vertex := 1 TO N DO
      FOR Neighbor := 1 TO N DO
        FOR Next := 1 TO N DO
          IF ShortPath[Neighbor, Vertex] + ShortPath[Vertex, Next]
                < ShortPath[Neighbor, Next] THEN
            (* keep shorter path *)
            ShortPath[Neighbor, Next] :=
                ShortPath[Neighbor, Vertex] + ShortPath[Vertex, Next];
            PathPoint[Neighbor, Next] := Vertex;
          END; (* IF *)
        END; (* FOR *)
      END; (* FOR *)
    END; (* FOR *)
END ShortestPath;
```

where

CMatrix = ARRAY [1..N], [1..N] OF CARDINAL;

The complexity of Floyd's algorithm is $O(n^3)$, since the procedure is essentially three nested loops. Once this algorithm has been applied to a given graph, the matrix Path-Point can be used to find the complete shortest path between two vertices i and j, using the following procedure.

```
PROCEDURE PrintPath(Path: CMatrix; Vertex, Neighbor: CARDINAL;
                   VAR First: BOOLEAN);
(* Print shortest path between vertices Vertex and Neighbor *)
VAR Next: CARDINAL;
BEGIN
  Next := Path[Vertex, Neighbor];
  IF Next = 0 THEN RETURN END;
  PrintPath(Path, Vertex, Next, First);
  IF First THEN
    WriteString(" through");
    First := FALSE;
  ELSE
    WriteString(" and");
  END; (* IF *)
  WriteCard(Next, 3);
  PrintPath(Path, Next, Neighbor, First);
END PrintPath;
```

The graph of Figure 15-4(a), corresponds to the adjacency matrix of Figure 15-13. Applied to this graph, ShortestPath produces the following shortest paths (we have omitted paths of length 1, as well as symmetric paths like Path from 3 to 2 through 1, which is the same as the path from 2 to 3).

Figure 15-13
Adjacency Matrix

∞	296	449	270	573	∞	460	617	∞
296	∞	∞	412	∞	661	∞	∞	∞
449	∞	∞	∞	∞	542	∞	507	∞
270	412	∞	∞	∞	∞	∞	∞	324
573	∞	∞	∞	∞	∞	288	431	∞
∞	661	542	∞	∞	∞	∞	∞	∞
460	∞	∞	∞	288	∞	∞	∞	112
617	∞	507	∞	431	∞	∞	∞	∞
∞	∞	∞	324	∞	∞	112	∞	∞

```
Path from 1 to 6 through 2
Path from 1 to 9 through 7
Path from 2 to 3 through 1
Path from 2 to 5 through 1
Path from 2 to 7 through 1
Path from 2 to 8 through 1
Path from 2 to 9 through 4
Path from 3 to 4 through 1
Path from 3 to 5 through 8
Path from 3 to 7 through 1
Path from 3 to 9 through 1 and 7
Path from 4 to 5 through 9 and 7
Path from 4 to 6 through 2
Path from 4 to 7 through 9
Path from 4 to 8 through 1
Path from 5 to 6 through 8 and 3
Path from 5 to 9 through 7
Path from 6 to 7 through 2 and 1
Path from 6 to 8 through 3
Path from 6 to 9 through 2 and 4
Path from 7 to 8 through 5
Path from 8 to 9 through 5 and 7
```

Adjacency List

In this representation, the n rows of the adjacency matrix are replaced by n linear lists. For each vertex in the graph there is a list of adjacent vertices, which may be empty. Figure 15-14 shows how the graph of Figure 15-11 will be represented with adjacency lists. Each list element will carry two or three pieces of information: a vertex number indicating the end of an edge, an optional weight associated with the edge, and a pointer to the next element of the adjacency list. For adjacency lists, the memory space used is no more than what is necessary, with, of course, a pointer for each list element. If a graph with n vertices has few edges, then the memory space is proportional to the number of edges, whereas with the adjacency matrix it would be proportional to n^2.

Figure 15-14
Adjacency List

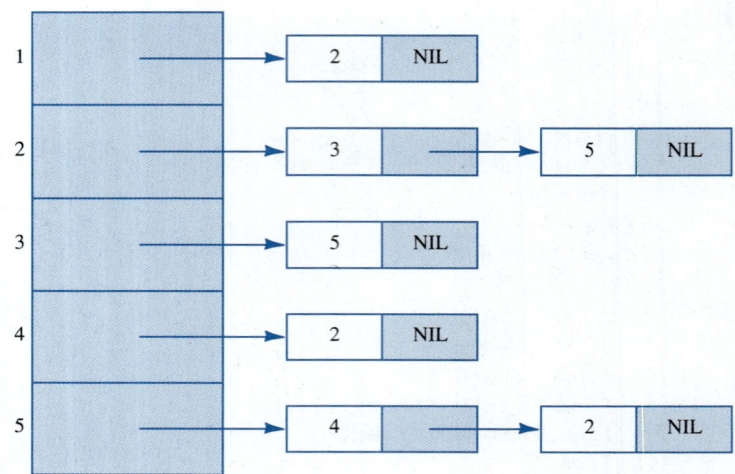

Using this representation, we can redefine the implementation module for our ADT Graphs, as follows.

```
IMPLEMENTATION MODULE Graphs;
FROM GraphElements IMPORT ElementType, KeyType, MaxVertices;
FROM Storage IMPORT ALLOCATE, DEALLOCATE;

TYPE Graph = POINTER TO Struct;
     EdgePointer = POINTER TO Edge;
     Edge = RECORD
              Key: KeyType;
              WeightValue: INTEGER;
              Next: EdgePointer;
            END;
     Vertex = RECORD
                Value: ElementType;
                Point: EdgePointer;
              END;
     Struct = RECORD
                N: KeyType;
                Vector: ARRAY [1..MaxVertices] OF Vertex;
              END;
PROCEDURE Create(VAR G: Graph);
(* Create graph G *)
BEGIN
  ALLOCATE(G, SIZE(Struct));
  Clear(G);
END Create;
```

```
PROCEDURE Clear(VAR G: Graph);
(* Empty graph G *)
VAR Index: CARDINAL;
BEGIN
  FOR Index:=1 TO MaxVertices DO
    G^.Vector[Index].Point := NIL;
    G^.Vector[Index].Value := 0;
  END; (* FOR *)
  G^.N := 0;
END Clear;
PROCEDURE VertexCount(G: Graph): CARDINAL;
(* Return the number of vertices in G. *)
BEGIN
  RETURN G^.N;
END VertexCount;
PROCEDURE InsertVertex(VAR G: Graph; Key: KeyType; Elt: ElementType);
(* Insert Key in graph G with value Elt not connected to any
   other vertex *)
BEGIN
  IF G^.N = Key-1 THEN
    INC(G^.N);
    G^.Vector[Key].Value := Elt;
  END; (* IF *)
END InsertVertex;
```

Procedures Create, Clear, and VertexCount are straightforward. Procedure InsertVertex just inserts a new value for the given vertex in the Vertices array.

```
PROCEDURE InsertEdge(VAR G: Graph; Key1, Key2: KeyType;
                    Weight: INTEGER);
(* Insert edge in graph G between vertices Key1 and Key2 *)
VAR New, Current, Previous: EdgePointer;
BEGIN
  IF (Key1 <= G^.N) AND (Key2 <= G^.N) THEN
    Current := G^.Vector[Key1].Point;    (* first edge *)
    Previous := NIL;
    WHILE (Current # NIL) AND (Current^.Key < Key2) DO  (* find spot *)
      Previous := Current;
      Current := Current^.Next;
    END; (* WHILE *)
    IF Current^.Key = Key2 THEN  (* already here *)
      Current^.WeightValue := Weight;
    ELSE
      ALLOCATE(New, SIZE(Edge));
      New^.WeightValue := Weight;
      New^.Key := Key2;
      New^.Next := Current;
```

```
          IF Previous = NIL THEN
            G^.Vector[Key1].Point := New;
          ELSE
            Previous^.Next := New;
          END; (* IF *)
        END; (* IF *)
    END; (* IF *)
END InsertEdge;
```

Procedure InsertEdge checks that Key1 and Key2 exist. Then it follows the edge list of node Key1, in order to find where to insert the new edge. Note that edge lists are ordered on the ending vertex of the edge. If the edge already existed, then its weight value is updated. Otherwise, a new edge node is created and inserted in the list.

```
PROCEDURE DeleteVertex(VAR G: Graph; Key: KeyType);
(* Delete vertex Key *)
VAR Index: CARDINAL;
    Current, Previous: EdgePointer;
BEGIN
  IF Key <= G^.N THEN
    Current := G^.Vector[Key].Point;
    WHILE Current # NIL DO     (* eliminate edge list *)
      Previous := Current;
      Current := Current^.Next;
      DEALLOCATE(Previous, SIZE(Edge));
    END; (* WHILE *)
    G^.Vector[Key].Point := NIL;
    G^.Vector[Key].Value := 0;    (* mark as absent *)
    FOR Index := 1 TO G^.N DO  (* search for edges involving vertex Key *)
      IF G^.Vector[Index].Point # NIL THEN
        Current := G^.Vector[Index].Point;
        Previous := NIL;
        WHILE (Current # NIL) AND (Current^.Key # Key) DO
          Previous := Current;
          Current := Current^.Next;
        END; (* WHILE *)
        IF (Previous # NIL) AND (Current # NIL) THEN
          Previous^.Next := Current^.Next;
          DEALLOCATE(Current, SIZE(Edge));
        ELSIF Current # NIL THEN
          G^.Vector[Index].Point := Current^.Next;
          DEALLOCATE(Current, SIZE(Edge));
        END; (* IF *)
      END; (* IF *)
    END; (* FOR *)
  END; (* IF *)
END DeleteVertex;
```

Procedure DeleteVertex must inspect all edges in order to eliminate those that involve the deleted vertex. First the edge list of the deleted vertex is deleted one element at a time. Then the vertex is marked as absent. Finally, all the edge lists of all the existing vertices are inspected to eliminate the edges leading to the deleted vertex.

```
PROCEDURE DeleteEdge(VAR G: Graph; Key1, Key2: KeyType);
(* Delete the edge between Key1 and Key2 *)
VAR Current, Previous: EdgePointer;
BEGIN
  Current := G^.Vector[Key1].Point;
  Previous := NIL;
  WHILE (Current # NIL) AND (Current^.Key # Key2) DO  (* look for edge *)
    Previous := Current;
    Current := Current^.Next;
  END; (* WHILE *)
  IF (Current # NIL) AND (Previous # NIL) THEN    (* eliminate *)
    Previous^.Next := Current^.Next;
    DEALLOCATE(Current, SIZE(Edge));
  ELSIF Current # NIL THEN     (* first element *)
    G^.Vector[Key1].Point := Current^.Next;
    DEALLOCATE(Current, SIZE(Edge));
  END; (* IF *)
END DeleteEdge;
```

Procedure DeleteEdge is simpler, as we only have to inspect the edge list of vertex Key1. Once found, the edge leading to vertex Key2 is eliminated from the edge list.

```
PROCEDURE FindVertex(G: Graph; Key: KeyType; VAR Elt: ElementType;
                    VAR Found: BOOLEAN);
(* Find vertex Key, return value in Elt *)
BEGIN
  Found := FALSE;
  IF (Key < G^.N) & (G^.Vector[Key].Value # 0) THEN
    Elt := G^.Vector[Key].Value;
    Found := TRUE;
  END; (* IF *)
END FindVertex;

PROCEDURE UpdateVertex(VAR G: Graph; Key: KeyType; Elt: ElementType;
                      VAR Done: BOOLEAN);
(* Update vertex Key with Elt *)
BEGIN
  Done := FALSE;
  IF Key < G^.N THEN
    G^.Vector[Key].Value := Elt;
    Done := TRUE;
  END; (* IF *)
END UpdateVertex;
```

Procedures FindVertex and UpdateVertex are simple, as they just access the vertices vector and check that the vertex has not been eliminated.

```
PROCEDURE Weight(G: Graph; Key1, Key2: KeyType): INTEGER;
(* Return the weight associated with edge *)
VAR Current: EdgePointer;
BEGIN
  Current := G^.Vector[Key1].Point;
  WHILE (Current # NIL) AND (Current^.Key # Key2) DO (* look for edge *)
    Current := Current^.Next;
  END; (* WHILE *)
  IF Current # NIL THEN
    RETURN Current^.WeightValue;
  ELSE
    RETURN 0;
  END; (* IF *)
END Weight;
```

Procedure Weight inspects the edge list of vertex Key1. When the edge leading to vertex Key2 is found, its weight is returned.

```
PROCEDURE GetAdjacent(G: Graph; Key: KeyType; N: CARDINAL;
                     VAR Adjacent: KeyType);
(* Precondition: there exists a vertex in graph G with Key
   Postcondition: Adjacent' is the Nth adjacent vertex to Key,
                  or 0 if none exists *)
VAR Neighbor: CARDINAL;
    Current: EdgePointer;
BEGIN
  Adjacent := 0;
  Neighbor := 0;
  Current := G^.Vector[Key].Point;
  WHILE Current # NIL DO
    INC(Neighbor);
    IF Neighbor = N THEN (* found *)
      Adjacent := Current^.Key;
      RETURN;
    END; (* IF *)
    Current := Current^.Next;
  END; (* WHILE *)
END GetAdjacent;

END Graphs.
```

Procedure GetAdjacent counts the edges in the edge list of vertex Key and returns the edge for which the count is equal to N.

All our previous applications were tested with this new implementation without any changes, and produced the same results. The adjacency list representation can also be implemented with arrays, as we have seen in Chapter 5 in the discussion on linear lists.

15.4 Case Study: Dijkstra's Algorithm

Floyd's algorithm, presented in Section 15.3, solves the all-pairs shortest-path problem assuming an adjacency matrix representation. There is a simpler problem—finding the shortest path from a single vertex to all other vertices in a directed graph—that was first solved by Edsger Dijkstra. Dijkstra's algorithm can be repeated for all vertices in a graph as a way to solve the all-pairs shortest-path problem. It is instructive to develop this approach for two reasons:

- This algorithm is a classic example of the "greedy" method.
- Unlike Floyd's algorithm, Dijkstra's algorithm can be used with both an adjacency matrix representation and an adjacency list representation.

Design

Definition of the Problem We want first to develop a procedure to implement Dijkstra's algorithm to find the shortest path from a single vertex to all other vertices in a directed graph. We will use our implementation of Dijkstra's algorithm to implement a solution to the all-pairs shortest-path problem. Then Dijkstra's algorithm can be compared to Floyd's. Our objective is to run Floyd's and Dijkstra's algorithms solving the all-pairs shortest-path problem on the same set of graphs and to come up with a measure of their relative efficiency.

Since Dijkstra's algorithm can be implemented with an adjacency matrix representation for the graph, as well as an adjacency list representation, we will complete two implementations of the algorithm based on each representation. We will then compare the efficiency of both these implementations with Floyd's algorithm.

Dijkstra's algorithm solves the single-source shortest-path problem. We will illustrate its method on the graph of Figure 15-15 in the design section that follows.

For the graph of Figure 15-15, Dijkstra's algorithm gives the following results. Starting from vertex 1, the shortest path to vertex 2 has a cost of 9 (via vertices 3 and 4), while the shortest path to vertex 3 has a cost of 2. The shortest path to vertex 4 has a cost of 5 (via vertex 3), while the shortest path to vertex 5 has a cost of 7 (via vertices 3 and 4).

After we have solved the single-source shortest-path problem, we can apply the algorithm to all vertices in the graph and thereby solve the all-pairs shortest-path problem.

Figure 15-15
A Graph with Five Vertices

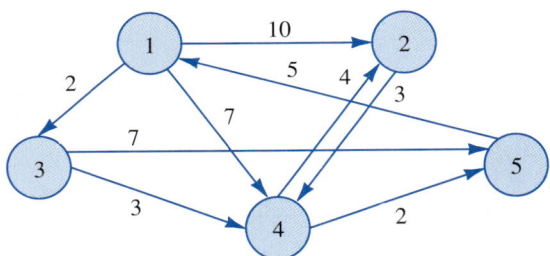

Design of a Solution Dijkstra's algorithm is a classic example of a "greedy" algorithm because it uses local conditions to determine the course of the solution. We will use a set of vertices that initially only contains the source vertex, and we will add vertices to the set one at a time, until all the vertices in the graph are in the set. At each step of the algorithm, we will store in a distance vector the current shortest path from the source vertex to the other vertices, using only the vertices in the set. The vertex added to the set at each step is the vertex not yet in the set that currently has the shortest path from the source.

The distance vector corresponding to the graph of Figure 15-15 will be D with indices going from 1 to 5, although we will not use D[1] as 1 is the source vertex. Table 15-1 shows a trace of the values stored in D at each step of the algorithm.

Initially, only 1 is in the set of vertices, so the minimum distance stored in D for each of the other vertices is the weight of the edge between each of the vertices and vertex 1, or an infinite value if no edge exists.

During the first step, since D[3] is minimum in the first row of the table, we add 3 to the set of vertices. The vertices with edges starting at vertex 3 are now potential candidates for lowering the path distance value, since we can now use paths that pass through vertex 3. There is an edge from vertex 3 to vertex 4 with a weight of 3. The path from vertex 1 to vertex 3 to vertex 4 has a total weight of 5; this is less than the direct path from vertex 1 to vertex 4, which has weight 7, and the value of D[4] is changed from 7 to 5. The edge from vertex 4 to vertex 5 gives a possible path from vertex 1 to vertex 3 to vertex 5 with a weight of 8, so D[5] is changed from infinity to 8. No other distances change their values at this time.

During the second step, D[4] is found to be the minimum distance for the vertices not in the set, so vertex 4 is added to the set. Vertex 4 has edges to vertex 2 and vertex 5 and it turns out that these arcs will lower the total distance of vertex 1 to vertex 2 from 10 to 9, and the total distance from vertex 1 to vertex 5 from 8 to 7.

In the third step, vertex 5 has the minimum distance amongst the vertices not in the set, and is added to the set. Vertex 5 has only one outgoing edge to vertex 1, the source vertex, so it cannot change any of the distances.

In step 4, vertex 2 is the only remaining vertex and is added to the set. There is an edge from vertex 2 to vertex 4, but because the path from vertex 1 to vertex 2 to vertex 4 has a total weight of 13, which is greater than the current minimum weight of 5, the value of D[4] is not changed. The final row of Table 15-1 represents the shortest distances from vertex 1 to all of the other vertices.

Table 15-1
Trace of the Distance Values

Step	Set	D[2]	D[3]	D[4]	D[5]
initial	{1}	10	2	7	infinity
1	{1, 3}	10	2	5	8
2	{1, 3, 4}	9	2	5	7
3	{1, 3, 4, 5}	9	2	5	7
4	{1, 3, 4, 5, 2}	9	2	5	7

Although Table 15-1 gives us the distances, it does not give us the paths responsible for the distance values. We can record this information by maintaining a path vector, P. Each time a vertex is added to the set that reduces a total distance, we will enter that vertex number in the path vector. Table 15-2 shows our path vector for the data given above.

Suppose that we want to find the shortest path from vertex 1 to vertex 2. P[2] is 4, so vertex 4 is on the path prior to vertex 2. P[4] is 3, so vertex 3 precedes vertex 4. P[3] is 1, which get us back to the source vertex. So the path is 1 to 3 to 4 to 2. Other paths are constructed in a similar way.

Refine the Solution Our pseudocode algorithm follows directly from the solution presented in the design section. We will use the notation C(i, j) to represent the weight of the edge connecting vertex i to vertex j. If there is no such edge, the value is assumed to be infinite. We will assume the graph has n vertices.

```
Single Source Shortest Path
    Add the source vertex, s, to the set of vertices
    Initialize the D values to C(s, i) for all i except s
    Initialize the P values to s
    For n − 1 iterations
        Find the vertex w such that w is not in the set of vertices and
            D[w] is the minimum distance for all D[i] where i is not in
            the set of vertices
        Include w in the set of vertices
        For every vertex i not in the set of vertices
            If D[w] + C[w, i] < D[i]      { new shorter path }
                Set D[i] to D[w] + C[w,i]
                Set P[i] to w
            End if
        End for
    End for
End Single Source Shortest Path
```

We will first analyze the complexity of this algorithm for an adjacency matrix representation. The initialization steps before the main For loop have complexity O(n). The

Table 15-2
Trace of the Path Vector

Step	P[2]	P[3]	P[4]	P[5]
initial	1	1	1	1
1	1	1	3	3
2	4	1	3	4
3	4	1	3	4
4	4	1	3	4

main loop iterates (n − 1) times. The inner For loop executes (n − 2) times, then (n − 3) times, and so forth down to 1 time for the final iteration of the outer loop. So the inner loop has complexity O(n), which means the outer loop has a complexity of $O(n^2)$. Combining this with an initialization of complexity O(n) means that the overall algorithm has a complexity of $O(n^2)$.

Now, if we assume to have an adjacency list representation, and if we assume that there are e edges in the graph, the initialization phase is still O(n). If we maintain the vertices that are not in the set of vertices as a priority queue, then operations on this set can be done in log n time. The inner FOR loop can be implemented by traversing all vertices in the adjacency list for vertex w and updating the distances in the priority queue, as needed. Since there are a total of at most e vertices in all adjacency lists, each of which is being updated in (log n) time, the total complexity of the inner FOR loop for all iterations of the outer FOR loop is O(e log n). Since the vertices not in the set are organized in a priority queue, finding the minimum distance takes log n time, and this is done (n − 1) times. The number of edges in a graph can range from 0 to n^2 (if we allow edges from a vertex to itself). If the number of edges is greater than n, which is typically the case, then Dijkstra's algorithm using an adjacency list has complexity O(e log n). If e is less than n, then the complexity is O(n log n). If e is significantly smaller than n^2, then an adjacency list representation may be more efficient than an adjacency matrix.

We can apply Dijkstra's algorithm to every vertex in the graph to solve the all-pairs shortest-path problem, increasing the complexity by a factor of n. For an adjacency matrix, this would result in an $O(n^3)$ algorithm, the same complexity class as Floyd's algorithm. For an adjacency list representation where e is in the range from n to n^2, the complexity is O(n e log n).

Develop a Testing Strategy We will test our algorithm on a graph with 100 vertices where, for each vertex, seven edges are selected randomly to connect to other vertices. This means that we will have a value of 700 out of a possible 10,000 edges, so we may see some improvement in performance for the adjacency list representation. Weights will be generated randomly in the range of 1 to 100. We will generate our random graphs by filling in an adjacency matrix until each row and each column contains seven weights indicating edges. We will then construct an adjacency list representation for the same data.

In addition to the random graphs discussed above, we should test our algorithm with graphs that represent limiting cases, such as

- a graph with no edges,
- a graph with n^2 edges, and
- a graph with several disconnected components

Implementation

Code and Test the Program We first present the data types to define our graph structure, which could be found in an implementation module for graphs including Floyd's and Dijkstra's algorithms as operations.

```
TYPE NodeRange = [1..MaxNumNodes];
     NodeSet = SET OF NodeRange;
     EdgeRange = [0..MaxNumEdges];
     Vertex = RECORD
                 Key: [0..MaxNumNodes];
                 (* other information associated with vertex *)
              END;
     Edge = RECORD
               Weight: CARDINAL;
               (* other information associated with edge *)
            END;
     Graph = POINTER TO GraphRecord;
     GraphRecord = RECORD
                      NumNodes : NodeRange;
                      NumEdges : EdgeRange;
                      Vertices : ARRAY NodeRange OF Vertex;
                      Edges : ARRAY NodeRange,NodeRange OF Edge;
                   END;
     NodeArray = ARRAY [1..MaxNumNodes], [1..MaxNumNodes] OF CARDINAL;
     NodeVector = ARRAY [1..MaxNumNodes] OF CARDINAL;
```

Notice that for each vertex and each edge, we have provided a record structure that can include all information necessary to the application. The following implementation of Dijkstra's algorithm assumes we have access to this internal structure.

```
PROCEDURE Dijkstra(VAR G: Graph; V: Vertex;
                   VAR Weights, Paths: NodeVector);
(* Given a graph, G, and a specific vertex, V, this procedure
   returns an array of the minimum path Weights from the specified
   vertex to the vertex indicated by the index position and a Paths
   array which can be used to recover the path from V to any other
   vertex, if such a path exists. *)

  PROCEDURE FindMinVertex(Weights: NodeVector; Set: NodeSet;
                          NumNodes: NodeRange; VAR Small: CARDINAL);
  (* Return as Small the node not in Set that has the smallest
     value of Weights *)
  VAR Scan: NodeRange;
      Min: CARDINAL;
  BEGIN
    Small := MaxNumNodes+1;
    Min := MAX(CARDINAL);
    FOR Scan := 1 TO NumNodes DO    (* check all vertices *)
      IF NOT(Scan IN Set) THEN
        IF Weights[Scan] < Min THEN
          Small := Scan;
          Min := Weights[Scan];
        END; (* IF *)
      END; (* IF *)
    END; (* FOR *)
  END FindMinVertex;
```

```
VAR Set: NodeSet;
    Scan1, Scan2: NodeRange;
    Mini: CARDINAL;
    TestWeight: CARDINAL;
BEGIN  (* Dijkstra *)
  FOR Scan1 := 1 TO G^.NumNodes DO  (* initialize *)
    Weights[Scan1] := G^.Edges[V.Key,Scan1].Weight;
    Paths[Scan1] := V.Key;
    EXCL(Set,Scan1);
  END; (* FOR *)
  Paths[V.Key] := 0;
  INCL(Set,V.Key);
  FOR Scan1 := 1 TO G^.NumNodes DO  (* new shortest paths *)
    IF Scan1 # V.Key THEN           (* for vertices not in set *)
      FindMinVertex(Weights, Set, G^.NumNodes, Mini);
      IF (Mini-1) # MaxNumNodes THEN    (* avoid overflow *)
        INCL(Set,Mini);
        FOR Scan2 := 1 TO G^.NumNodes DO
          IF NOT(Scan2 IN Set) THEN
            IF (MAX(CARDINAL) - Weights[Mini]) >= G^.Edges[Mini,Scan2].Weight THEN
              TestWeight := Weights[Mini] + G^.Edges[Mini, Scan2].Weight;
            ELSE
              TestWeight := MAX(CARDINAL);
            END; (* IF *)
            IF TestWeight < Weights[Scan2] THEN   (* smaller value *)
              Weights[Scan2] := TestWeight;
              Paths[Scan2] := Mini;
            END; (* IF *)
          END; (* IF *)
        END; (* FOR *)
      END; (* IF *)
    END; (* IF *)
  END; (* FOR *)
END Dijkstra;
```

Since we have elected to use MAX(CARDINAL) to represent the absence of an edge, we must handle this possibility as a special case before we perform the summation of the previous distance with the current edge. We use this technique in order to avoid an arithmetic overflow.

To find the shortest path between all vertex pairs and to collect information on the paths, we need a matrix structure to hold all the results.

```
Matrix = ARRAY[1..MaxNumNodes],[1..MaxNumNodes] OF CARDINAL;
```

The following procedure DijkstraAll applies procedure Dijkstra to every vertex of graph G and collects results in AllWeights and AllPaths. It uses function GetVertex, which returns a vertex having the parameter as key.

```
PROCEDURE DijkstraAll(VAR G: Graph; VAR NumNodes: CARDINAL;
                     VAR AllWeights, AllPaths: NodeArray);
(* Given a graph G, this algorithm applies Dijkstra's algorithm from
   every possible source vertex and returns a two dimensional matrix
   of weights, AllWeights, for all pairs of vertices and a matrix of
   paths, AllPaths, corresponding to the minimum weights. *)
VAR Paths, Weights: NodeVector;
    Scan1, Scan2: NodeRange;
BEGIN
  NumNodes := G^.NumNodes;
  FOR Scan1 := 1 TO G^.NumNodes DO
    Dijkstra(G, GetVertex(G, Scan1), Weights, Paths);
    FOR Scan2 := 1 TO G^.NumNodes DO      (* keep results *)
      IF Scan1 = Scan2 THEN
         AllWeights[Scan1, Scan2] := 0;
         AllPaths[Scan1, Scan2] := 0;
      ELSIF Weights[Scan2] = MAX(CARDINAL) THEN
         AllWeights[Scan1, Scan2] := MAX(CARDINAL);
         AllPaths[Scan1, Scan2] := MAX(CARDINAL);
      ELSE
         AllWeights[Scan1, Scan2] := Weights[Scan2];
         AllPaths[Scan1, Scan2] := Paths[Scan2];
      END; (* IF *)
    END; (* FOR *)
  END; (* FOR *)
END DijkstraAll;
```

We now present a version of Dijkstra's algorithm that works on graphs based on an adjacency list representation. Let's first give the declarations for the structures we use. Notice that field Edges is an array of vertices containing pointers to edges that are organized as a linked list. In order to avoid confusion with the preceding representation we have prefixed the various types with an "L" (for linked representation).

```
TYPE EdgePtr = POINTER TO LEdge;
     LEdge = RECORD
               Weight: CARDINAL;
               EndVertex : CARDINAL;
               Next : EdgePtr;
             END;
     LVertex = POINTER TO Vertex;
     LGraph = POINTER TO LGraphRecord;
     LGraphRecord = RECORD
                      NumNodes : NodeRange;
                      NumEdges : EdgeRange;
                      Vertices : ARRAY NodeRange OF LVertex;
                      Edges : ARRAY NodeRange OF EdgePtr;
                    END;
```

Chapter 15 Graphs

In this version (procedure LDijkstra), the most significant change to the previous Dijkstra algorithm is that here edges are processed by traversing a list using a WHILE loop, rather than by sequencing through an array component with a FOR loop. It should be noted that the vertices not in the set S have not been put into a priority queue, as suggested during the design phase. This improvement is left as an exercise (see problem 20 in the Exercise section).

```
PROCEDURE LDijkstra(VAR G: LGraph; V: LVertex;
                    VAR Weights, Paths: NodeVector);
(* Given a graph, G, and a specific vertex, V, this procedure returns
   an array of weights, the minimum path Weights from the specified
   vertex to the vertex indicated by the index position. The Paths
   array can be used to recover the path from the vertex V to any
   other vertex, if such a path exists. *)

  PROCEDURE FindMinVertex(Weights : NodeVector; Set: NodeSet;
                          NumNodes : NodeRange; VAR Low: CARDINAL);
    VAR Scan: NodeRange;
        Min: CARDINAL;
    BEGIN
      Low := MaxNumNodes+1;
      Min := MAX(CARDINAL);
      FOR Scan := 1 TO NumNodes DO    (* check all vertices *)
        IF NOT(Scan IN Set) THEN
          IF Weights[Scan] < Min THEN
            Low := Scan;
            Min := Weights[Scan];
          END; (* IF *)
        END; (* IF *)
      END; (* FOR *)
    END FindMinVertex;

  VAR Set : NodeSet;
      Scan1, Scan2: NodeRange;
      TestWeight, Mini: CARDINAL;
      Ptr: EdgePtr;
  BEGIN (* LDijkstra *)
    FOR Scan1 := 1 TO G^.NumNodes DO   (* initialize *)
      Weights[Scan1] := MAX(CARDINAL);
      Paths[Scan1]   := V^.Key;
      EXCL(Set,Scan1);
    END; (* FOR *)
    Ptr := G^.Edges[V^.Key];
    WHILE Ptr # NIL DO                  (* initialize weights *)
      IF Ptr^.EndVertex > 0 THEN
        Weights[Ptr^.EndVertex] := Ptr^.Weight;
      END; (* IF *)
      Ptr := Ptr^.Next;
    END; (* WHILE *)
```

```
      Paths[V^.Key] := 0;
      INCL(Set,V^.Key);
      FOR Scanl := 1 TO G^.NumNodes DO  (* check all nodes *)
         IF Scanl # V^.Key THEN
            FindMinVertex(Weights, Set, G^.NumNodes, Mini);
            IF (Mini-1) # MaxNumNodes THEN    (* avoid overflow *)
               INCL(Set, Mini);
               Ptr := G^.Edges[Mini];
               WHILE ((Ptr # NIL) AND (Ptr^.EndVertex # 0)) DO
                  (* check all edges *)
                  IF NOT(Ptr^.EndVertex IN Set) THEN
                     IF (MAX(CARDINAL) - Weights[Mini]) >= Ptr^.Weight THEN
                        TestWeight := Weights[Mini] + Ptr^.Weight;
                     ELSE
                        TestWeight := MAX(CARDINAL);
                     END; (* IF *)
                     IF TestWeight < Weights[Ptr^.EndVertex] THEN
                        Weights[Ptr^.EndVertex] := TestWeight;
                        Paths[Ptr^.EndVertex] := Mini;
                     END; (* IF *)
                  END; (* IF *)
                  Ptr := Ptr^.Next;          (* next edge *)
               END; (* WHILE *)
            END; (* IF *)
         END; (* IF *)
      END; (* FOR *)
   END LDijkstra;
```

The all-pairs shortest-path algorithm for adjacency list graph implementations is identical to procedure DijkstraAll already given, except that procedure LDijkstra is called in place of procedure Dijkstra. We tested both versions of Dijkstra's algorithm and Floyd's algorithm with 100 vertex graphs, each vertex having seven incident edges. All three algorithms produced the same results. We also measured the execution time in ticks (1/60th of a second) for each algorithm. The system on which these measures were taken was a Sun 3/60 workstation running Berkeley Unix 4.2. Our results for one test run were:

```
Dijkstra all pairs for adjacency matrix        590  ticks
Dijkstra all pairs for adjacency list          439  ticks
Floyd's algorithm for adjacency matrix         759  ticks
```

These figures fluctuated with the random graph selected, but Dijkstra's algorithm with an adjacency list always performed better than the same algorithm for an adjacency matrix, which was only slightly better than Floyd's algorithm. These results were not surprising, since 93% of all possible edges were nonexistent, and these edges did not have to be examined for the adjacency list implementation.

Complete the Documentation This documentation should include a careful statement of the single-vertex shortest-path problem and an outline of the solution, as described in the "Design of a Solution" section. The pseudocode solution might also be included, since it is more concise than the actual code and relatively independent of the choice of data structure. The test cases and the resultant analysis should be part of the documentation. A user's manual is not required for this application.

Summary

In this chapter, we have introduced graphs and some of their applications. We have shown a few of the many operations on graphs. Besides the graph algorithms presented here, there are numerous other important ones. Thus, this chapter should be viewed as an introduction to graphs rather than as a complete treatment.

We have seen that there are two main representations for a graph: the adjacency matrix and the adjacency list. Applications of graphs are very diverse and this makes the definition of a complete ADT Graphs more difficult. Very often algorithms on graphs do exist that are bound to some particular representation, for instance, Warshall's algorithm. Our presentation of graph algorithms has shown that their time complexity can be relatively low for simple traversals. But the time complexity can also grow sharply for algorithms like Prim's or Warshall's and can become very costly if care is not exercised.

■ Exercises

1. Given the following graph define the corresponding adjacency matrix. Find all paths of length 1, 2, and 3 from vertex 1 to vertex 2. Check your results by computing the square and the cube of the adjacency matrix.

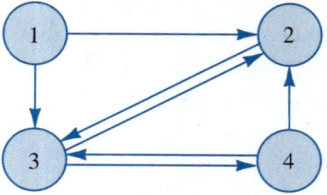

2. Represent the following graph with a list structure.

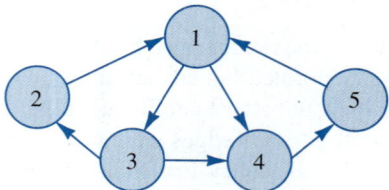

*3. Given the following grammar, represent it as a graph.

A ::= a | b | (A + B)
B ::= C | (B)
C ::= A = A

4. Draw the directed graph corresponding to the following arithmetic expression, taking care that the common subexpressions are shared. Vertices will include operands (v, w, x, y, z) or operators (+, *). The representation should preserve the inherent order of evaluation.

((x + y) * z + ((x + y) + w) * (w + v)) * ((x + y) * z)

5. Given the following activity graph, compute Early and Late for each of its vertices. What is the minimum duration of the project? What activities are critical? Is there an activity whose speeding up would reduce the total duration of the project?

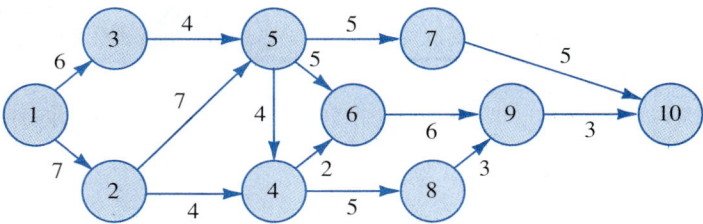

6. In procedure Warshall, if we change after the initialization loop the outer "FOR i:=1 TO n DO" to "FOR i:=n TO 1 BY -1 DO", will the modified procedure still compute the transitive closure of A? Explain how the new algorithm works and what it produces.

7. The following table represents the planning for replacing a mainframe computer. Find the critical path and the minimum duration of the whole operation.

Number	Activity	Duration	Predecessors
1	Remove old computer	1	none
2	Remove old wiring, dividers	1	1
3	Install new electrical wiring	2	none
4	Install floor	1	2,3
5	Build partitions	2	4
6	Install lighting	2	5,3
7	Install acoustical ceiling	1	5,6
8	Paint	2	7
9	Install air conditioning	2	5
10	Install fire protection	1	7
11	Install computer & furniture	2	8
12	Install security system	1	5
13	Install transmission cables	2	11
14	Verification of system	3	13

Note: Problems marked with an asterisk (*) have a higher level of difficulty.

Programming Problems

8. Rewrite the Graph implementation module using an array representation based on two arrays. The main array will have a row for each vertex, and each row will have three columns: vertex number, number of edges from this vertex, index of first edge in second array. The secondary array will have two columns, one for the edge weight and the other one for the end vertex of the edge. Each row of the secondary array will define an edge.

*9. Write an implementation module for Graphs in which the vertices are part of a vertex list, and comprise the vertex value, a pointer to the next vertex, and two pointers to edge lists. The first pointer is used for the vertex's edge list, the second pointer points to an edge belonging to another vertex's edge list but involving the current vertex. Similarly, each edge comprises two vertex keys, K_1 and K_2, and two edge list pointers. Each edge belongs to two lists: the edge list of vertex K_1 and the edge list of vertex K_2. This representation ensures that an edge appears only once. For instance, in Figure 15-4 the edge Albuquerque–El Paso is represented by one element belonging both to Albuquerque's edge list and to El Paso's edge list.

10. Modify the implementation of problem 9 by replacing the vertex list by a binary search tree.

11. In the ADT Graphs, implement and test a new procedure Traversal that uses the depth-first approach.

12. Implement and test a procedure to build a minimum-cost spanning tree, which first orders the edges according to their weights, then, starting with an empty tree, adds each edge and the vertices it connects, as long as the resulting graph is acyclic, and stops when all vertices have been added.

13. The root of a directed graph is a vertex V such that all other vertices of the graph can be reached from V. Write a procedure that will decide whether or not a given graph has a root.

14. Write a procedure that will list all simple cycles of a graph.

15. The radius of a tree is the maximum distance from the root to a leaf. Write an algorithm that, from a symmetrical graph, determines a partial tree with minimum radius by using a breadth-first search.

*16. In a semantic network, an inference is a statement whose truth can be checked by using inference rules from propositional calculus, and a fact is a relation between given concepts. What data must be associated with the network so as to obtain an efficient way to check and state inferences? Define an algorithm to determine the truth of a given inference. For instance, the semantic network in the following illustration corresponds to these facts:

Kitty Kat is a cat
A cat is an animal
A cat has four legs
A cat has a tail
Kitty Kat is grey
A cat eats fish
Kitty Kat meows

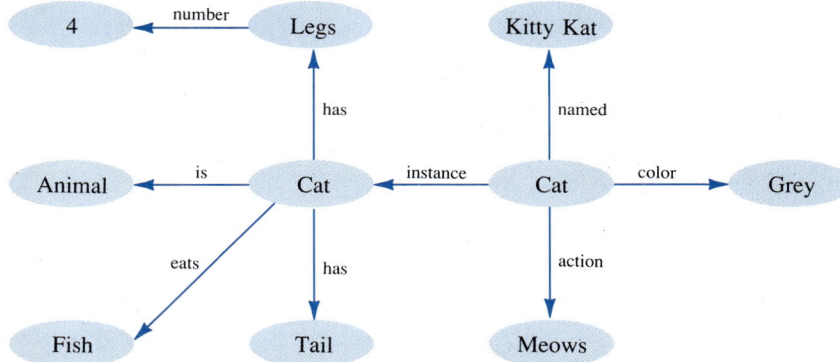

Check your algorithm by determining the truth of the following facts:

Kitty Kat has four legs
Animals eat fish

*17. Design and program a prototype system for the reservation of seats on the flights of an airline company. Data for a given flight are the following:

flight number
origin and time of departure
destination and time of arrival
number of seats
list of passengers

Possible operations will be:

Reserve a seat for a passenger.
Cancel a reservation.
Print the list of passengers for a given flight.
Print the flights where there is still room.
Print the waiting list for a given flight.

18. Develop and test a driver program for Dijkstra's algorithm as given in the case study.

19. Add Floyd's algorithm to your program in problem 18 and then see if you obtain similar results, in relative terms, to the data given in the case study.

20. Improve Dijkstra's algorithm for adjacency lists by organizing the vertices not yet in the set of vertices into a priority queue.

Sets

INTRODUCTION

A large number of applications use set types and operations. The reason is simple: the set is a basic structure of mathematics and, as such, is frequently used in mathematical methods. In practice, a large number of representations based on the various structures we have studied can be used for sets. As we have seen before, one particular representation is usually more appropriate for a given application and there is no representation general enough to satisfy all applications.

16.1 Definitions and Abstraction

A set is a collection of *elements* (or *members*); each set element may itself be a set or a primitive element called an *atom*. All members of a set are different; that is, a set cannot contain two copies of the same element.

Although mathematical sets are unordered, in computer science applications there usually exists a linear order relation on the elements of a set. For instance, when sets contain integers, characters or enumerated values, the order relation is already defined in the underlying programming language. A linear ordering may be defined for elements of other types.

Notations used for sets include curly braces, { and }, the membership symbol $\in$, the empty set symbol $\emptyset$, inclusion symbols $\subseteq$ and $\supseteq$, and operators $\cup$, $\cap$, and $-$. Curly braces are used to represent a set constant as A = {a, b, c}, and B = {c, d}, and then $a \in A$ and $a \notin B$ (a is a member of A and is not a member of B). In a like manner {a, b} $\subseteq$ A indicates the first set {a, b} is a *subset* of set A, or that set A is a *superset* of {a, b}: A $\supseteq$ {a, b}. Any set is included in itself, and the empty set { } is included in every set. The *union* of two sets A and B includes all elements that are members of set A or of set B or of both: A $\cup$ B = {a, b, c, d}. The *intersection* of two sets A and B comprises all elements that belong to both sets: A $\cap$ B = {c}. The *difference* of two sets A and B comprises all elements from the first set that do not belong to the second set: A $-$ B = {a, b}. The *symmetric difference* of two sets, A and B, comprises all elements in one set or the other set but not both: A/B = {a, b, d}.

In Modula-2, there is a standard set type called BITSET, defined as a set of positive integers. Constants of that type are denoted in the usual mathematical notation, as in

{ }
{1,2,3,4}
{0,2,4,6,8,10}

Several set operators and relational operators can be used with BITSET. The maximum number of elements in a BITSET is system dependent, but it should be at least as large as the word size of the computer.

Relational operators

Symbol	Meaning	Example
=	equality	{2,4}={4,2} is true
#	inequality	{1,2}#{1,2} is false
IN	membership	2 IN {1,2,3,4} is true
<=	subset	{2,3}<={1,2,3,4} is true
>=	superset	{2,4}>={2,4} is true

Set operators

Symbol	Meaning	Usage	Definition
+	union	S1+S2	Set of elements in either S1 or S2 (or both)
*	intersection	S1*S2	Set of elements common to both S1 or S2
−	difference	S1 − S2	Set of elements in S1, but not in S2
/	symmetric difference	S1/S2	Set of elements either in S1 or in S2, but not in both

Examples:

$\{1,2,3,4\} + \{3,4,5\} = \{1,2,3,4,5\}$
$\{1,2,3\} * \{2,4,6\} = \{2\}$
$\{1,2,3,4\} - \{3,4,5\} = \{1,2\}$
$\{1,2,3,4\} / \{3,4,5\} = \{1,2,5\}$

In addition to these operators, there are two standard procedures to manipulate sets.

INCL(S, x) Include element x in set S.
EXCL(S, x) Exclude element x from set S.

In Modula-2, BITSET is the only standard set type, but it is also possible to define and use sets based on enumeration or subrange types. For instance, the declarations:

```
TYPE Toys = (TeddyBear, Doll, Lego, Skates, Tricycle, Ball);
     Gifts = SET OF Toys;
```

make it possible to manipulate objects of type Gifts, which are sets of Toys. Toys is said to be the *base type* of type Gifts. Type Gifts has 64 values, since, using the six values of Toys, it is possible to define 64 (2^6) different sets.

Values of type Gifts are denoted by lists of values from the base type enclosed in braces and preceded by the name of the set type:

```
Gifts{ Lego, Tricycle, Ball }
```

All the operators that can be used with BITSET can also be used with other set types. Unfortunately, in Modula-2 the size of sets is limited to the size of the computer memory word or a small multiple of it, usually 16 or 32. Some implementations allow sets with 1,024 or even 65,536 elements while keeping BITSET limited to 16 elements, but this creates a software portability problem.

Under these circumstances, it is usually better to define a distinct ADT for sets. Our ADT set will define type Set and use type ElementType from a user-defined module SetsElements.

```
DEFINITION MODULE SetsElements;
CONST ElementsInASet = 256;   (* 0..255 *)
TYPE ElementType = ...;
     CompProc = PROCEDURE(ElementType, ElementType): BOOLEAN;
END SetsElements.
```

The operations needed include the creation of a set, the assignment of a set value to a set, the inclusion and exclusion of an element in a set, the union, intersection and difference of two sets, Boolean operations (to check whether an element is a member of a set, whether two sets are equal, whether a set is a subset of another set, or whether a set is empty), operations to make a set empty, and to count the number of elements in a set. If a linear ordering exists for the elements of a set, then we can add two operations to find the minimum or maximum elements in a set. These operations will require a comparison function that can be defined by the user and passed as a parameter of type CompProc defined above. The following definition module provides all these operations.

```
DEFINITION MODULE Sets;
FROM SetsElements IMPORT ElementsInASet, ElementType, CompProc;

TYPE Set;

PROCEDURE CreateSet (VAR S: Set);
(* Create a set variable and initialize it to the empty set.
   Pre-condition: S does not exist
   Post-condition: S' exists and is empty *)

PROCEDURE Include (VAR S: Set; Element: ElementType);
(* Include Element into S.
   Pre-condition: S exists
   Post-condition: S' includes Element *)

PROCEDURE Exclude (VAR S: Set; Element: ElementType);
(* Exclude Element from S.
   Pre-condition: S exists
   Post-condition: S' does not include Element *)

PROCEDURE Union (VAR Result: Set; S1, S2: Set);
(* Return set Result containing all elements in either
   S1 or S2.
   Pre-condition: S1 and S2 exist
   Post-condition: Result' includes elements from S1 and S2 *)

PROCEDURE Intersection (VAR Result: Set; S1, S2: Set);
(* Return set Result containing all elements in
   both S1 and S2.
   Pre-condition: S1 and S2 exist
   Post-condition: Result' includes elements common to S1 and S2 *)

PROCEDURE Difference (VAR Result: Set; S1, S2: Set);
(* Return set Result containing all elements in
   S1 that are not in S2.
   Pre-condition: S1 and S2 exist
   Post-condition: Return' includes elements from S1 that
                   are not members of S2 *)

PROCEDURE Equal (S1, S2: Set): BOOLEAN;
(* Return TRUE, if both sets contain the same elements,
   FALSE otherwise.
   Pre-condition: S1 and S2 exist
   Post-condition: return True if sets S1 and S2 are equal,
                   False otherwise *)
```

```
PROCEDURE Subset (SubSet, S: Set): BOOLEAN;
(* Return TRUE, if all the elements in SubSet
   are in S, FALSE otherwise.
   Pre-condition: S and SubSet exist
   Post-condition: return True if SubSet is a subset of
                   set S, False otherwise *)
PROCEDURE Member (Element: ElementType; S: Set): BOOLEAN;
(* Return TRUE, if  Element is in set S, FALSE otherwise.
   Pre-condition: S exists
   Post-condition: return True if S includes Element,
                   False otherwise *)
PROCEDURE MakeEmpty(VAR S: Set);
(* Make the empty set be the value for S.
   Pre-condition: S exists
   Post-condition: S' is the empty set *)
PROCEDURE Assign(VAR S1: Set; S2: Set);
(* Set the value of S1 to be equal to the value of S2.
   Pre-condition: S1 and S2 exist
   Post-condition: S1' has the same value as S2 *)
PROCEDURE Empty(S: Set): BOOLEAN;
(* Empty returns TRUE if the value of S is the empty set.
   Pre-condition: S exists
   Post-condition: return True if S is the empty set,
                   False otherwise *)
PROCEDURE Cardinality(S: Set): CARDINAL;
(* Return the number of elements in S.
   Pre-condition: S exists
   Post-condition: return the number of elements in S *)
PROCEDURE Min(S: Set; VAR Element: ElementType;
              Less: CompProc);
(* Return the least Element in S or ElementsInASet
   if empty.
   Pre-condition: S exists
   Post-condition: Element' is the least element in set S *)
PROCEDURE Max(S: Set; VAR Element: ElementType;
              Greater: CompProc);
(* Return the maximum Element in S or ElementsInASet
   if empty.
   Pre-condition: S exists
   Post-condition: Element' is the maximum element in set  S *)
END Sets.
```

This gives us an ADT that can be used in most applications. However, we should note that some applications do not require all these operations. In those cases it is possible to adapt the ADT to the particular application, as we will see in the following section.

16.2 Applications

Dictionary

Some set applications do not need all the power of our ADT Sets, but instead will require only three operations: insertion, deletion, and membership verification. Such an ADT is usually called a *dictionary*. Based on our ADT Sets, we see it is very easy to define such an ADT dictionary. Adding a creation operation, to initialize the data structure used for a dictionary, we can define our ADT Dictionaries in the following manner.

```
DEFINITION MODULE Dictionaries;
FROM Sets IMPORT Set;
FROM SetsElements IMPORT ElementType;

TYPE Dictionary = Set;

PROCEDURE CreateDictionary(VAR Dict: Dictionary);
(* Create an empty dictionary. *)

PROCEDURE Insert(VAR Dict: Dictionary; Element: ElementType);
(* Insert Element in dictionary. *)

PROCEDURE In(Dict: Dictionary; Element: ElementType): BOOLEAN;
(* Return TRUE if Element is in dictionary. *)

PROCEDURE Delete(VAR Dict: Dictionary; Element:ElementType);
(* Delete Element from dictionary. *)

END Dictionaries.
```

The implementation can even be done directly by using the set operations already defined.

```
IMPLEMENTATION MODULE Dictionaries;
FROM SetsElements IMPORT ElementType;
FROM Sets IMPORT Set, CreateSet, Include, Exclude, Member;

PROCEDURE CreateDictionary(VAR Dict: Dictionary);
(* Create an empty dictionary. *)
BEGIN
  CreateSet(Dict);
END CreateDictionary;

PROCEDURE Insert(VAR Dict: Dictionary; Element: ElementType);
(* Insert Element in dictionary. *)
BEGIN
  Include(Dict, Element);
END Insert;
```

```
PROCEDURE In(Dict: Dictionary; Element: ElementType): BOOLEAN;
(* Return TRUE if Element is in dictionary. *)
BEGIN
  RETURN Member(Element, Dict);
END In;

PROCEDURE Delete(VAR Dict: Dictionary; Element:ElementType);
(* Delete Element from dictionary. *)
BEGIN
  Exclude(Dict, Element);
END Delete;

END Dictionaries.
```

Obviously, even though this is an easy way to define an ADT Dictionaries, it might not be the best way in terms of performance, depending on the implementation of the ADT Set. Besides, type Dictionary might be defined in a different manner, since the element type should be based on character strings.

Finding a Set of Distinct Representatives

The problem of distinct representatives involves sets; it can be stated this way:

> Given a collection of nonempty subsets s_i (i = 1, 2, . . . , n) of a set S, we want to know if it is possible to choose an element e_i in each subset s_i such that $e_i \neq e_k$ for i $\neq$ k. If so, we want to find these elements.

A practical example could be seen in the choosing of the chairpersons of the various committees of an academic department when the following rules are in effect. The departmental committees have overlapping memberships (that is, a faculty member may belong to several departmental committees), each committee must have a chairperson, and no faculty member may be the chairperson of more than one committee.

The problem can be solved only if for all k $\leq$ n, the union of any k subsets contains at least k members. The algorithm to solve the problem can be described by the following pseudocode.

> Set Representatives to { }
> Set NoRepresentatives to {1,2,3, . . . ,n}
> Repeat
>   Select the set in NoRepresentatives with the smallest cardinality
>   Select a member of this set
>   Include this member in Representatives
>   Exclude the chosen set from NoRepresentatives
>   Exclude the latest chosen representative for all the
>   remaining sets in NoRepresentatives
> Until NoRepresentatives = { } or some sets with no representative
>   are empty

616 Chapter 16 Sets

> If there are no remaining sets in NoRepresentatives then display the Representatives elements, otherwise indicate the problem cannot be solved

To implement this algorithm, we have decided to use type BITSET for the set of subsets NoRepresentatives, even though we assume this limits us to a maximum of 16 subsets. This decision required us to define a Cardinality function for BITSET, as none exists. ElementType is defined in SetsElements as:

```
TYPE ElementType = RECORD
                     First, Second: [0..15];
                   END;
```

The following procedure implements the distinct representatives algorithm.

```
PROCEDURE DistinctReps(MaxSets: CARDINAL; S: ARRAY OF BITSET);

  PROCEDURE Cardinality(SmallSet: BITSET): CARDINAL;
  VAR Count, Index: CARDINAL;
  BEGIN
    Count := 0;
    FOR Index := 0 TO Maximum DO
      IF Index IN SmallSet THEN
        INC(Count);
      END; (* IF *)
    END; (* FOR *)
    RETURN Count;
  END Cardinality;

VAR Index, Minimum, SetNumber, Value, NumberInSet: CARDINAL;
    Continue: BOOLEAN;
    Representatives: Set;
    NoRepresentatives: BITSET;
    Pair: ElementType;
BEGIN
  CreateSet(Representatives);
  NoRepresentatives := { };
  FOR Index := 0 TO MaxSets-1 DO
    INCL(NoRepresentatives, Index);     (* all the subsets *)
  END; (* FOR *)
  REPEAT
    Minimum := Maximum + 1;
    FOR Index := 0 TO MaxSets-1 DO
      (* select set with no representative and with smallest cardinality *)
      IF Index IN NoRepresentatives THEN
        NumberInSet := Cardinality(S[Index]);
```

```
          IF NumberInSet < Minimum THEN
            Minimum := NumberInSet;
            SetNumber := Index;
          END; (* IF *)
        END; (* IF *)
      END; (* FOR *)
      (* choose a member in the set with the smallest number of elements *)
      Index := 0;
      Continue := TRUE;
      WHILE (Index <= Maximum) AND Continue DO
        IF Index IN S[SetNumber] THEN
          Value := Index;
          Continue := FALSE;
        END; (* IF *)
        INC(Index);
      END; (* WHILE *)
      (* create pair *)
      Pair.First := SetNumber;
      Pair.Second := Value;
      Include(Representatives, Pair);        (* keep new representative *)
      EXCL(NoRepresentatives, SetNumber);    (* eliminate chosen set *)
      FOR Index := 0 TO MaxSets - 1 DO (* eliminate value from remaining sets *)
        IF Index IN NoRepresentatives THEN
          EXCL(S[Index], Value);
        END; (* IF *)
      END; (* FOR *)
    UNTIL (NoRepresentatives = { }) OR (Minimum = 0);
    (* Minimum is zero if some sets with no representative are empty *)
    IF NoRepresentatives = { } THEN
      Display(Representatives);
    ELSE
      WriteString(" no distinct representatives possible ");
    END; (* IF *)
END DistinctReps;
```

With the following five subsets: {1,2,3,4,5}, {1,4}, {4,3,2}, {5,4}, {1,3} as input data, the procedure displays the following result:

<1,1><4,3><2,2><0,4><3,5>

where each pair gives the subset number and the chosen representative: <4, 3> indicates that the representative for subset number 4 (the last one as they are numbered from zero) is 3. The result shows that the representatives of the subsets are:

Subset 0	{1,2,3,4,5}	4
Subset 1	{1,4}	1
Subset 2	{4,3,2}	2
Subset 3	{5,4}	5
Subset 4	{1,3}	3

Kruskal's Algorithm

In the last chapter, we have seen that a graph could be defined as a set of vertices and a set of edges. We have also shown a procedure to build a minimum-cost spanning tree for a graph, based on Prim's algorithm. Kruskal's algorithm achieves the same result in a different and possibly more efficient manner. It considers a graph to be defined by two sets, and, using mostly set operations, it produces the set of edges defining a minimum-cost spanning tree.

Starting with the set of vertices V and the set of edges E, we progressively build MCST, our resulting set of edges. We start with Components, a set of the vertices. In this set, each vertex is considered to be a connected component by itself. (Recall that a graph is *connected* if every pair of its vertices is connected.) Let's illustrate the method on the communication graph from the preceding chapter.

Figure 16-1 presents the communication graph for our example. We extract edges from E in order of increasing cost: if the edge connects two vertices that belong to two different components, then it is added to MCST; if it connects two vertices in the same component, it would add a cycle and is therefore discarded. For instance, for the example of Figure 16-1, the first edge is the one with cost 112, involving vertices Phoenix and Tucson. The edge is extracted and both vertices are made part of the same component. The second edge to be extracted has cost 270 and places vertices Albuquerque and El Paso in the same component. The third edge has cost 288 and adds Las Vegas to our first component. This process is repeated until all vertices are in the same component. Figure 16-2 illustrates the application of our algorithm to the graph of Figure 16-1.

To implement this algorithm, we will need to be able to define sets of vertices and sets of edges. We will also need to be able to define a set of components, where components are themselves sets, and where we only need operations to merge two components into a single component, and, given an element, to find the component it belongs to.

Figure 16-1
A Communication Graph

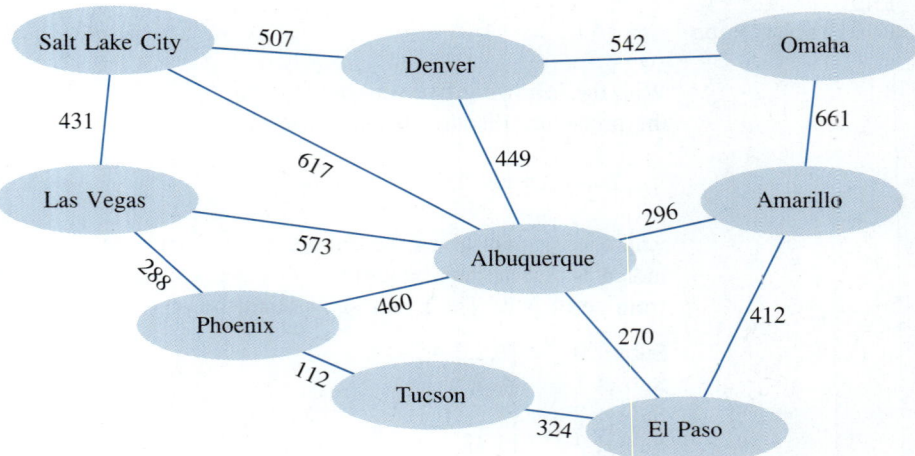

Figure 16-2
Construction of
Minimum-Cost
Spanning Tree

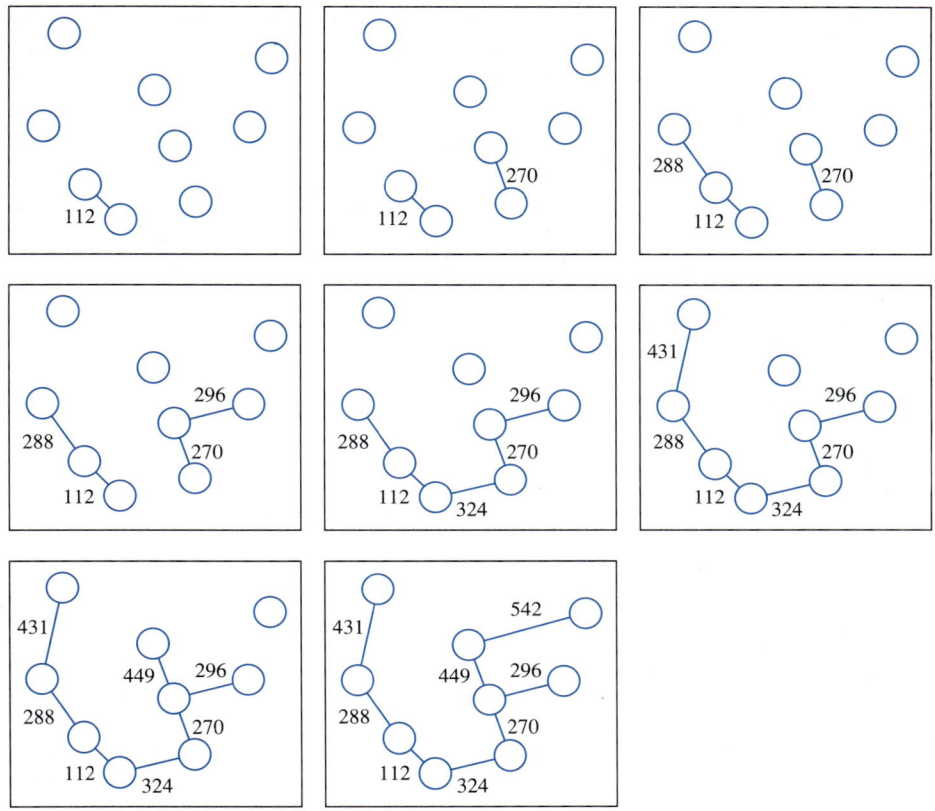

In Kruskal's algorithm, the vertices are used as elements in Components. If we number our vertices from 1 to n, the set of vertices is then identified by n. An edge will be fully defined by an identification, two vertices, and a cost. Our ADT Sets will represent sets of edges after we define ElementType in module SetsElements in the following way.

```
TYPE ElementType = RECORD
                       Id: CARDINAL;
                       Cost: CARDINAL;
                       V1, V2: [0..Max];
                   END;
```

We can note here that the operations available in our ADT Sets make it possible to use a set as a priority queue, using operations Min or Max in connection with Include and Exclude. Thus we need not define yet another ADT in order to implement Kruskal's algorithm.

In our algorithm, we start with a collection of vertices, each in a set by itself. We then will combine sets, and will need to find in which set a particular vertex is contained. Similar problems occur in a number of applications, and can be handled using only Merge and Find. The result of Merge is the union of its two set arguments provided they are disjoint, while Find returns the set of which its argument is a member. Merge-Find sets are a special kind of sets specifically designed for these operations. We can thus define an ADT MFSETs in the following definition module. We will study the implementation of MFSETs in the case study at the end of the chapter.

```
DEFINITION MODULE MFSETs;

CONST N = 15;
TYPE MFSET;
     NameType = [1..N];
     ElementType = [1..N];

PROCEDURE MFSCreate(VAR Components: MFSET);
(* Create set Components.
   Pre-condition: none
   Post-condition: set Components is empty *)

PROCEDURE Initial(Comp: NameType; Elt: ElementType; VAR Components: MFSET);
(* Initialize Comp to a set containing Elt only.
   Pre-condition: set Components exists
   Post-condition: Comp is the name of a component in Components
                   of which Elt is a member *)

PROCEDURE Merge(Comp1, Comp2: NameType; VAR Components: MFSET);
(* Merge Comp1 and Comp2 calling the result Comp1 or Comp2 arbitrarily.
   Pre-condition: set Components exists
                  components Comp1 and Comp2 are disjoint
   Post-condition: components Comp1 and Comp2 are merged in the set
                   of connected components Components, the result
                   being called Comp1 or Comp2 arbitrarily *)

PROCEDURE Find(Elt: ElementType; Components: MFSET): NameType;
(* Return the name of the set of which Elt is a member.
   Pre-condition: Elt belongs to only one component
   Post-condition: return the name of the component in Components
                   of which Elt is a member *)

PROCEDURE Clear(VAR Components: MFSET);
(* Clear set Components
   Pre-condition: set Components exists
   Post-condition: set Components is empty *)

END MFSETs.
```

With the tools we have defined, we can implement Kruskal's algorithm in the following manner.

```
PROCEDURE Kruskal(Vertices: CARDINAL; Edges: Set; VAR MST: Set);
VAR EdgeSet: Set;         (* edges priority queue *)
    Components: MFSET;
    ComponentsNumber, NewComponent, Vertex1: CARDINAL;
    Elt: ElementType;
    Comp1, Comp2: CARDINAL;
BEGIN
  (* initialize various sets *)
  MFSCreate(Components);
  CreateSet(MST);
  CreateSet(EdgeSet);
  NewComponent := 0;
  ComponentsNumber := Vertices;
  FOR Vertex1 := 1 TO Vertices DO
  (* put each vertex in a component by itself *)
    INC(NewComponent);
    Initial(NewComponent, Vertex1, Components);
  END; (* FOR *)
  Assign(EdgeSet, Edges);      (* copy edge set *)
  WHILE ComponentsNumber > 1 DO
    Min(EdgeSet, Elt, Less);   (* get edge with minimum cost *)
    Exclude(EdgeSet, Elt);
    Comp1 := Find(Elt.V1, Components);
    Comp2 := Find(Elt.V2, Components);
    IF Comp1 # Comp2 THEN      (* edge between different components *)
      Merge(Comp1, Comp2, Components);
      DEC(ComponentsNumber);
      Include(MST, Elt);       (* keep it *)
    END; (* IF *)
  END; (* WHILE *)
END Kruskal;
```

Execution of this procedure on the graph of Figure 16-1 produces the results shown in Figure 16-2.

The time complexity of Kruskal's algorithm depends heavily on the implementation of the various tools we have to use. In particular, note that the WHILE loop is executed once for each edge. If the Min, Exclude, and Include operations are based on a binary search tree representation, then the time complexity of these operations would be $O(\log e)$. (We know this because we already know the time complexity of a tree search is $O(\log e)$, where e is the number of edges.) Thus, with that representation, the time complexity of Kruskal's algorithm would be $O(e \log e)$.

16.3 Implementation

Sets can be implemented using many of the data structures we have discussed in the preceding chapters. We will not attempt to examine here all possible set implementations, but will only show some of the most frequently used ones.

Bit Vector

The most efficient way of representing sets of positive integers from a memory-space point of view, is to use a bit to represent each set element. In fact, Modula-2 already offers such a representation in a very limited way in the BITSET type, which is predefined as:

TYPE BITSET = SET OF [0..W-1];

where W is the computer memory word length (usually 16 or 32).

In microcomputer implementations, BITSETs have 16 elements. This size is usually not enough to be able to use these sets in most applications. The implementation of type BITSET on any computer is straightforward: each set element is represented by a specific bit in a computer memory word. Let's number the bits in a word from right to left starting at zero, and let bit 0 represent value 0, bit 1 represent value 1, bit 2 value 2, and so on. Then, the following sets will be represented by the corresponding binary values.

bit positions	15	14	13	12	11	10	9	8	7	6	5	4	3	2	1	0
{ }	0	0	0	0	0	0	0	0	0	0	0	0	0	0	0	0
{1,2,3}	0	0	0	0	0	0	0	0	0	0	0	0	0	1	1	1	0
{2,4,6,8,10,12,14}	0	1	0	1	0	1	0	1	0	1	0	1	0	1	0	0

The set operations available in Modula-2, union (+), intersection (*), difference (−), symmetric difference (/), set membership (IN), and set inclusion (⊆ or ⊇) can all be implemented by machine language logical operations like OR, NOT, AND, XOR, and SHIFT. This way, the BITSET implementation is efficient in the use of memory space, as well as in execution speed. As a matter of fact, BITSETs are often used in order to be able to manipulate bits from Modula-2 programs, as we saw in the case study of Chapter 12.

Because of their limited size, BITSETs cannot be directly used as representations for larger sets; however, it is possible to combine a number of BITSETs to obtain much larger sets. The following implementation of our ADT Sets is based on an array of BITSETs, where each BITSET is considered to be a piece of a very large BITSET. The first BITSET in our array is used to represent values [0..15], the second BITSET is used to represent values [16..31], the third BITSET [32..47], and so on. A given element n < ElementsInASet will be represented by a BITSET element: n DIV 16 will provide us with the index of the BITSET in the array, and n MOD 16 will give the element value in the chosen BITSET. For example, element 40 is part of BITSET number 2 (40 DIV 16), where it is represented by bit 8 (40 MOD 16). The following implementation illustrates this method and uses the following definition of Element-Type.

```
TYPE ElementType = [0..ElementsInASet-1];
```

```
IMPLEMENTATION MODULE Sets;
FROM SetsElements IMPORT ElementType, ElementsInASet, CompProc;
FROM Storage IMPORT ALLOCATE;

(* The purpose of this module is to implement set operations on sets
   whose members are positive integers: 0, 1, 2, ... *)

CONST BitsInAWord = 16;
      SetMax = (ElementsInASet+BitsInAWord-1) DIV BitsInAWord - 1;

TYPE Set = POINTER TO SetTable;
     SetTable = ARRAY [0..SetMax] OF BITSET;

PROCEDURE CreateSet(VAR S: Set);
(* Create an S variable and initialize it to the empty S *)
BEGIN
  ALLOCATE(S, SIZE(SetTable));
  MakeEmpty(S);
END CreateSet;

PROCEDURE Exclude(VAR S: Set; Element: ElementType);
(* Exclude Element from S *)
VAR Word, Bit: CARDINAL;
BEGIN
  Word := Element DIV BitsInAWord;(* find position *)
  Bit := Element MOD BitsInAWord;(* include element *)
  EXCL(S^[Word], Bit);
END Exclude;

PROCEDURE Include(VAR S: Set; Element: ElementType);
(* Include Element into S *)
VAR Word,Bit: CARDINAL;
BEGIN
  Word := Element DIV BitsInAWord;(* find position *)
  Bit := Element MOD BitsInAWord;(* include element *)
  INCL(S^[Word], Bit);
END Include;

PROCEDURE Union (VAR Result: Set; S1, S2: Set);
(* Return set Result containing all elements in either S1 or S2 *)
VAR Word: CARDINAL;
BEGIN
  FOR Word := 0 TO SetMax DO   (* union of each BITSET *)
    Result^[Word] := S1^[Word] + S2^[Word];
  END;
END Union;
```

```
PROCEDURE Intersection (VAR Result: Set; S1, S2: Set);
(* Return set Result containing all elements in both S1 and S2. *)
VAR Word: CARDINAL;
BEGIN
  FOR Word := 0 TO SetMax DO    (* intersection of each BITSET *)
    Result^[Word] := S1^[Word] * S2^[Word];
  END;
END Intersection;

PROCEDURE Difference (VAR Result: Set; S1, S2: Set);
(* Return set Result containing all elements in
   S1 that are not in S2. *)
VAR Word: CARDINAL;
BEGIN
  FOR Word := 0 TO SetMax DO    (* difference of each BITSET *)
    Result^[Word] := S1^[Word] - S2^[Word];
  END;
END Difference;

PROCEDURE Equal (S1, S2: Set): BOOLEAN;
(* Return TRUE, if both sets contain the same elements, FALSE otherwise. *)
VAR Word: CARDINAL;
BEGIN
  FOR Word := 0 TO SetMax DO    (* compare each BITSET *)
    IF S1^[Word] # S2^[Word] THEN
      RETURN FALSE;
    END; (* IF *)
  END; (* FOR *)
  RETURN TRUE;
END Equal;

PROCEDURE Subset (SubSet, S: Set): BOOLEAN;
(* Return TRUE, if SubSet contains all the elements
   that are in S, FALSE otherwise. *)
VAR Word: CARDINAL;
BEGIN
  FOR Word := 0 TO SetMax DO    (* check each BITSET *)
    IF (SubSet^[Word] - S^[Word]) # { } THEN
      RETURN FALSE;   (* at least one element not in set *)
    END; (* IF *)
  END; (* FOR *)
  RETURN TRUE;   (* all differences empty *)
END Subset;

PROCEDURE Member (Element: ElementType; S: Set): BOOLEAN;
(* Return TRUE, if  Element is in the S, FALSE otherwise. *)
VAR Word,Bit: CARDINAL;
BEGIN
  Word := Element DIV BitsInAWord;   (* find position *)
  Bit := Element MOD BitsInAWord;
  RETURN Bit IN S^[Word];              (* check membership *)
END Member;
```

```
PROCEDURE MakeEmpty(VAR S: Set);
(* Make the empty set be the value for S *)
VAR Word: CARDINAL;
BEGIN
  FOR Word := 0 TO SetMax DO    (* empty BITSETs *)
    S^[Word] := { };
  END;
END MakeEmpty;

PROCEDURE Assign(VAR S1: Set; S2: Set);
(* Set the value of S1 to be equal to the value of S2. *)
VAR Word: CARDINAL;
BEGIN
  FOR Word := 0 TO SetMax DO    (* assign all BITSETs *)
    S1^[Word] := S2^[Word];
  END;
END Assign;

PROCEDURE Empty(S: Set): BOOLEAN;
(* Empty returns true if the value of S is the empty set *)
VAR Word: CARDINAL;
BEGIN
  FOR Word := 0 TO SetMax DO    (* check all BITSETs *)
    IF S^[Word] # { } THEN
      RETURN FALSE;
    END;
  END;
  RETURN TRUE;
END Empty;

PROCEDURE Cardinality(S: Set): CARDINAL;
(* Return the number of elements in a set *)
VAR Index, Count: CARDINAL;
BEGIN
  Count := 0;
  FOR Index := 0 TO ElementsInASet-1 DO  (* count elements *)
    IF Member(Index, S) THEN
      INC(Count);
    END; (* IF *)
  END; (* FOR *)
  RETURN Count;
END Cardinality;
```

```
PROCEDURE Min(S: Set; VAR Element: ElementType; Less: CompProc);
(* Return the least element in S. Less is a dummy as
   BITSET elements are automatically ordered *)
VAR Index: CARDINAL;
BEGIN
  FOR Index:= 0 TO ElementsInASet-1 DO
    IF Member(Index, S) THEN
      Element := Index;      (* found *)
      RETURN;
    END; (* IF *)
  END; (* FOR *)
  Element := ElementsInASet;  (* empty set *)
END Min;

PROCEDURE Max(S: Set; VAR Element: ElementType; Greater: CompProc);
(* Return the maximum element in S. Greater is a dummy as
   BITSET elements are automatically ordered *)
VAR Index: CARDINAL;
BEGIN
  FOR Index := ElementsInASet-1 TO 0 BY -1 DO
    IF Member(Index, S) THEN
      Element := Index;      (* found *)
      RETURN;
    END; (* IF *)
  END; (* FOR *)
  Element := ElementsInASet;  (* empty set *)
END Max;

END Sets.
```

With this implementation, we can see that the time complexity of the Min operation is $O(e)$. Thus, if we use this representation in Kruskal's algorithm, its time complexity would become $O(e^2)$ since the Min operation is applied e times.

Some applications require sets of characters. Using BITSET, it might not be possible to define sets of characters, because 128 elements or 256 elements are needed, depending on the character code. Given the previous implementation, it is easy to transform it into a SetOfCHAR implementation where:

```
TYPE SetOfCHAR    = POINTER TO BitSets;
     BitSets      = ARRAY [0..SetSize] OF BITSET;
     ElementType  = CHAR;
```

and where BITSET element values are obtained by using ORD(element).

Linked List

As with other abstract data types, whenever there is an implementation based on arrays, there is an alternative implementation based on dynamic structures. Using linked lists, we can implement sets with list nodes comprising two pieces of information: the element value and a pointer to the next element of the set. For example, the set {1, 5, 7} could be represented by the list of Figure 16-3.

The linked lists may be ordered by element values or unordered. In the following code sequence we will show part of an ordered linked list implementation of our ADT set. The comparison operations are imported from module SetsElements along with type ElementType and constant ElementsInASet. Our implementation uses linked lists that are in increasing order of the element values. The insertion operation is therefore more time-consuming than it would be with an unordered list, but other operations like Exclude, Member, Union, Intersection, Difference, Equal, and Min are more efficient.

Figure 16-3
A Linked List Representing a Set

```
IMPLEMENTATION MODULE Sets;
FROM Storage IMPORT ALLOCATE, DEALLOCATE;
FROM SetsElements IMPORT ElementsInASet, ElementType, LessThan, Equal;

(* Dynamic implementation of sets *)

TYPE Set = POINTER TO SetElement;
     SetElement = RECORD
                    Element: ElementType;
                    Next: Set;
                  END;

PROCEDURE CreateSet(VAR S: Set);
(* Create a set variable and initialize it to the empty set *)
BEGIN
  S := NIL;
END CreateSet;

PROCEDURE Include(VAR S: Set; Elt: ElementType);
(* Include element Elt into S. *)
VAR New, Current, Previous: Set;
BEGIN
  ALLOCATE(New, SIZE(SetElement));   (* create new element *)
  New^.Element := Elt;
  IF S = NIL THEN                     (* first and only element *)
    S := New;
    S^.Next := NIL;
  ELSE
    Current := S; Previous := NIL;
```

```
      WHILE (Current # NIL) AND LessThan(Current^.Element, Elt) DO
        (* search ordered list for position where to insert *)
        Previous := Current;
        Current := Current^.Next;
      END; (* WHILE *)
      IF (Previous = NIL) AND NOT Equal(Current^.Element, Elt) THEN
        (* insert in first position *)
        New^.Next := S;
        S := New;
      ELSIF (Current = NIL) (* last *) OR (* middle *)
            (Current # NIL) AND NOT Equal(Current^.Element, Elt) THEN
        Previous^.Next := New;
        New^.Next := Current;
      END; (* IF *)
    END; (* IF *)
END Include;
```

Procedure Include creates the element to include and, if the list is empty, inserts it as the first and only element. Otherwise, the list is scanned for the position where to insert (by determining if the current element is greater than the element to insert), and the insertion is done between the previous and the current element.

```
PROCEDURE Intersection (VAR Result: Set; S1, S2: Set);
(* Return set Result containing all elements in both S1 and S2 *)
VAR Current1, Current2, CurrentResult, New: Set;
BEGIN
  Current1 := S1;
  Current2 := S2;
  CurrentResult := NIL;
  Result := NIL;
  WHILE (Current1 # NIL) AND (Current2 # NIL) DO
    IF Equal(Current1^.Element, Current2^.Element) THEN (* add to intersection *)
      ALLOCATE(New, SIZE(SetElement));
      New^.Element := Current1^.Element;
      IF CurrentResult # NIL THEN
        CurrentResult^.Next := New;
      ELSE (* first Element *)
        Result := New;
      END; (* IF *)
      CurrentResult := New;
      Current1 := Current1^.Next;
      Current2 := Current2^.Next;
    ELSIF LessThan(Current1^.Element, Current2^.Element) THEN (* skip S1 Element *)
      Current1 := Current1^.Next;
    ELSE                    (* skip S2 Element *)
      Current2 := Current2^.Next;
    END; (* IF *)
  END; (* WHILE *)
```

```
      IF CurrentResult # NIL THEN
        CurrentResult^.Next := NIL;
      END; (* IF *)
END Intersection;
```

Procedure Intersection scans the two lists. When it finds two identical elements, it adds it to the resulting list, setting Result to point to the first element. Because the two lists are ordered, it is simple to advance in the list with the smallest value (thus ignoring that element) and to then repeat the comparison until one list has been exhausted.

```
PROCEDURE Member (Elt: ElementType; S: Set): BOOLEAN;
(* Return TRUE, if the element is in set S, FALSE otherwise. *)
VAR Current: Set;
    Continue: BOOLEAN;
BEGIN
  Current := S;
  Continue := TRUE;
  WHILE (Current # NIL) AND Continue DO   (* search ordered list *)
    IF LessThan(Current^.Element, Elt) THEN
      Current := Current^.Next;
    ELSE
      Continue := FALSE; (* either found or not there *)
    END; (* IF *)
  END; (* WHILE *)
  IF (Current # NIL) AND Equal(Current^.Element, Elt) THEN
    RETURN TRUE;
  ELSE
    RETURN FALSE;
  END; (* IF *)
END Member;
```

Procedure Member inspects all the elements of the ordered list until it finds element Elt or until it reaches a place in the list with an element greater than Elt. The procedure then returns the corresponding value.

```
PROCEDURE Min(S: Set; VAR Elt: ElementType);
(* Return the least element in S, i.e. the first element in the list *)
BEGIN
  Elt := S^.Element;
END Min;
```

The list representing S is ordered, so it is sufficient to return the first element of the list as the minimum value in the set.

The other procedures will follow similar models; the rest of this implementation module is left as problem 11 in the Exercises.

With such an implementation, we realize that the time complexity of the Min operation is $O(1)$, while that of the Include operation is $O(e)$. If we use this implementation for Kruskal's algorithm, then its time complexity would be $O(e^2)$.

Binary Search Tree

Binary search trees, studied in Chapter 9, can be used to represent sets whose elements are ordered according to some linear order. The type definition for our implementation module would then be:

```
TYPE Set = POINTER TO Node;
     Node = RECORD
              Element: ElementType;
              LeftSet, RightSet: POINTER TO Node;
            END;
```

Like the binary search tree operations, set operations Include, Exclude, Member, and Min based on this representation all have a time complexity of O(log n), where n is the number of elements in the set. We will give here only two examples of these operations, as they are very similar to the tree operations we have seen in Chapter 9.

```
PROCEDURE Include(VAR S: Set; Elt: ElementType);
BEGIN
  IF S = NIL THEN                          (* include here *)
    ALLOCATE(S, SIZE(Node));
    S^.Element := Elt;
    S^.LeftSet := NIL;
    S^.RightSet := NIL;
  ELSIF LessThan(Elt, S^.Element) THEN     (*include in left subtree *)
    Include(S^.LeftSet, Elt);
  ELSIF Greater(Elt, S^.Element) THEN      (* include in right subtree *)
    Include(S^.RightSet, Elt);
  END; (* IF *)
END Include;

PROCEDURE Member(Elt: ElementType; S: Set): BOOLEAN;
BEGIN
  IF S = NIL THEN
    RETURN FALSE;
  ELSIF Equal(Elt, S^.Element) THEN        (* found *)
    RETURN TRUE;
  ELSIF LessThan(Elt, S^.Element) THEN     (* look in left subtree *)
    RETURN Member(Elt, S^.LeftSet);
  ELSE                                     (* look in right subtree *)
    RETURN Member(Elt, S^.RightSet);
  END; (* IF *)
END Member;
```

With such an implementation, the time complexity of operations Min and Include is normally O(log e). Using it, Kruskal's algorithm time complexity would be O(e log e).

Binary search trees may sometimes degenerate into linear lists, with a marked decrease of efficiency. To avoid this situation, it is also possible to use balanced trees, as seen in Chapter 10, to represent sets. The use of balanced trees will guarantee that the worst case time complexity of operations Min and Include is still O(log e).

Table

It is also possible to implement sets using the hashing techniques that we have discussed in Chapter 12. The primary advantage is that hashing requires constant time per operation, or, in the worst case, time proportional to the size of the set. Using open hashing, we can define the following types and procedures.

```
TYPE Node = RECORD
              Element: ElementType;
              Next: POINTER TO Node;
            END;
     BucketType = [0..Max];
     Set = ARRAY BucketType OF POINTER TO Node;
```

An object of type Set is actually a vector of pointers to linear lists. Let's give here, as an example, the implementation of operations Include and Exclude.

```
PROCEDURE Include(VAR S: Set; Elt: ElementType);
VAR Bucket: BucketType;
    Old: POINTER TO Node;
BEGIN
  IF NOT Member(Elt, S) THEN
    Bucket := Hash(Elt);
    Old := S[Bucket];
    ALLOCATE(S[Bucket], SIZE(Node));
    S[Bucket]^.Element := Elt;
    S[Bucket]^.Next := Old;
  END; (* IF *)
END Include;

PROCEDURE Exclude(VAR S: Set; Elt: ElementType);
VAR Current: POINTER TO Node;
    Bucket: BucketType;
BEGIN
  Bucket := Hash(Elt);
  IF Equal(S[Bucket]^.Element, Elt) THEN
    S[Bucket] := S[Bucket]^.Next;   (* remove first element *)
  ELSE
    Current := S[Bucket];
```

```
          WHILE Current^.Next # NIL DO
            IF Equal(Current^.Next^.Element, Elt) THEN
              Current^.Next := Current^.Next^.Next;     (* remove it *)
              RETURN;
            ELSE
              Current := Current^.Next;
            END; (* IF *)
          END; (* WHILE *)
        END; (* IF *)
      END Exclude;
```

Other operations will follow the same pattern. We should note that operations like Min will not be very efficient, as only a sequential search of the table can be used.

16.4 Case Study: Merge-Find Sets

Design

Definition of the Problem In the discussion of Kruskal's algorithm in Section 16.2, a Merge-Find set ADT was introduced and the definition module was given. We will not duplicate that discussion here. Instead, in this case study we will discuss alternative designs for this ADT and then implement one of two possible approaches.

Design of a Solution MFSETs have to deal with three types: the components, the set names, and the members of these sets. In this section we will investigate two different approaches to MFSETs: an array implementation and a tree implementation. We will then select one of these approaches and refine the solution.

An Array Implementation One easy way to implement MFSETs is to define an array for the components, where the indices are the element values, and where the array elements are the set names. For instance, Components[x] will contain the name of the set that contains x. Such a representation is simple and leads to extremely simple implementations of Initial and Find but will require that the Merge operation check all components to change the name of some.

We can improve on this representation and the corresponding algorithms if we link all the elements belonging to the same component. The linking is easily done with two arrays, the first one to identify the components (number of elements and pointer to their first element), and the second one to represent the members (name of the set they belong to, and next element in the component). The components and the members are identified by the indices in the two arrays. Figure 16-4 illustrates such an organization. For instance, component 4 contains three members, the first one being 1, the second one being 4, and the last one being 3. A summary of all components for Figure 16-4 is:

Figure 16-4
An Array Representation for MFSETs

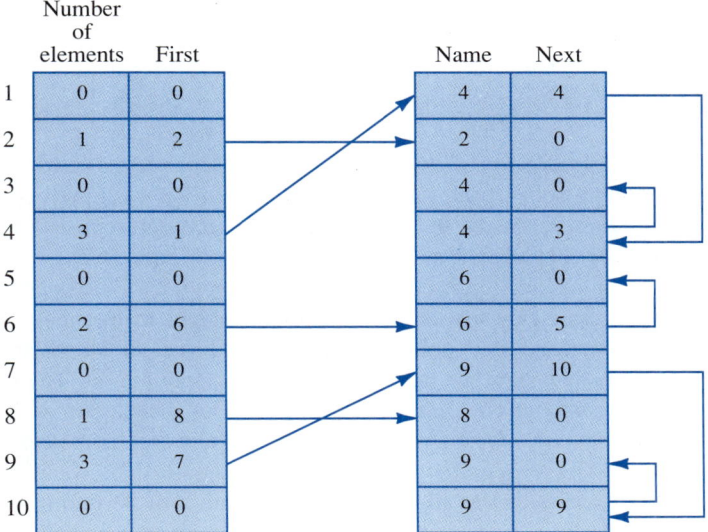

2 with elements {2}
6 with elements {5, 6}
4 with elements {1, 3, 4}
8 with elements {8}
9 with elements {7, 9, 10}

With this representation, the Find operation is very easy. We simply index the right-hand array with the element name and return the set name that is stored in the name field.

The Merge operation involves combining two linked lists and changing the set names for one of the components to the name of the other component. In Kruskal's algorithm, we start out with each vertex being a singleton in a set and then merge sets together until all vertices are in a single set. We are interested here in the total complexity of all the Merge operations. Let's try to discover the worst-case behavior for all the merges using the array representation of Figure 16-4. Suppose we link together sets S and T by changing the set names for all of the components of S to the name T and changing the link at the end of the S chain to point to the start of the T chain. If S is of size k and T is of size 1, then this single Merge has complexity $O(k)$, since k elements have their set name changed. Initially k will be 1, but if we then merge a set of size 2 into a set of size 1, then k will be 2. In the next step, k may be 3. If this worst-case behavior continues until we merge a set of size $(n - 1)$ into a set of size 1, then the total complexity of all merges is $1 + 2 + 3 + \cdots + (n - 1) = n(n - 1)/2$.

There is a simple way to improve this worst-case behavior: keep track of the set size, as we have done in the left-hand array, and always merge the smaller set into the larger set. Since only the set names in the smaller set will be changed, and since these elements will now be in a set at least twice as large, any individual element will change its name at most (1 + log n) times. Since there are n elements, the worst-case total complexity will be n(1 + log n), a value which is much better than for the previous worst-case behavior. Therefore, using this representation, we will always merge the smaller set into the larger set.

Tree Implementation We could represent sets as trees, with the root of the tree being the name of the set. We will allow our trees to have any number of children, so we are not restricted to binary trees. The sets represented in Figure 16-4 using arrays could be represented as trees, as shown in Figure 16-5.

With this tree representation, the first step of the Find operation is to look up—in an array indexed by the element name—a pointer to the node containing that element. Notice that the links point to the root of the tree, so we can traverse up the links until we find the root of the tree, which is the name of the set. To merge two sets, we let the root of one set be a child of the root of other set. For example, if we merge the components 4 and 9 above, then the resultant tree is as shown in Figure 16-6.

The Merge operation takes constant time, so it is clear that a sequence of Find-Merge operations as in Kruskal's algorithm will be dominated by the times for the Find. Again, it is instructive to consider worst-case behavior. In the example above, the complexity of the Find operation for all of the elements in component 9 increased by one since the path length is one greater than before the merge. The worst-case behavior would be a tree of n nodes that is a chain of nodes. The Find operations would have complexities of 1, 2, . . . , n, so that the total complexity of all Finds would be $O(n^2)$.

We can reduce this overall complexity by keeping a count of the number of elements in the set at the root and by always merging the smaller tree as a child of the root of the larger tree. Since every time an element is moved into another component the height increases by one, we must find the worst-case number of moves to find the worst-case height. After merging the smaller tree into the larger tree, the resultant tree will be at least twice as large. So each node can be moved at most (log n) times, resulting in a Find operation of complexity O(log n). Combining the Find operations for n nodes gives a worst-case complexity of O(n log n).

Path compression is another technique for speeding up the Find operations. Every time a Find operation is performed, the nodes that are traversed on the way to the root will become direct children of the root. For example, when a Find is done on node 7, every node on the path from 7 to the root that is not already a child of the root will be made a child of the root. The result of doing a Find with path compression on node 7 for the tree in Figure 16-6 is shown in Figure 16-7.

Figure 16-5
A Tree Representation for MFSETs

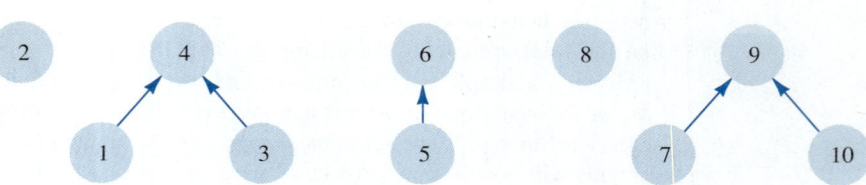

Figure 16-6
The Result of Merging Components 4 and 9

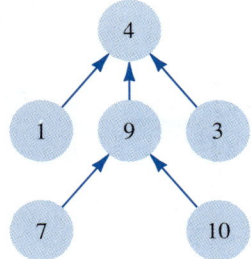

Figure 16-7
Path Compression After Doing a Find on Node 7

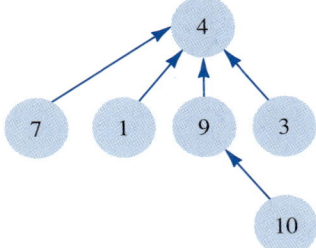

This path compression will shorten the paths on successive Find operations. It can be shown that the total number of Finds is now n × f(n), where the function f(n) is not constant, but grows incredibly slowly. This analysis is beyond the scope of this book.

Refine the Solution The array representation is easier to implement and, providing we always merge the smaller set into the larger set, its performance is acceptable. Let's name the arrays in Figure 16-4: Headers will be the left-hand array and Elements the right-hand array. For the moment, we will deal with them as separate structures, but in the actual implementation we will combine them into a single record structure. Let's define the various MFSETs operations.

Operation Find simply looks up the set name out of Elements.

```
Find
    Return the name of Element x
End Find
```

Our Merge operation will assume that the set S is smaller than the set T.

```
Merge
    Rename all elements of S with the name of T
    Link the next field of the last element in S to the first
        element in T
```

> Change field first in Headers for T to point where field
>   first of S points
> Change the number of elements for T to the sum of elements
>   in S and T
> Set the number of elements of S to zero and set the first
>   field to empty
> End Merge

With this version of Merge, we will use an If statement to call Merge with the proper ordering of sets.

> If set S is larger than set T
>   Merge(T, S)
> Else
>   Merge(S, T)
> End if

Develop a Testing Strategy We will use Kruskal's algorithm performed on a variety of graphs to test our MFSETs implementation. We will also test the operations separately with some limiting cases, such as:

- merging an empty set into a nonempty set
- merging two empty sets
- finding the set name for an element that does not exist in any set

Implementation

Code and Test the Program The following is an implementation of the MFSETs ADT using an array representation.

```
IMPLEMENTATION MODULE MFSETs;
FROM Storage IMPORT ALLOCATE;

TYPE Pointer = [0..N];
     MFSET = POINTER TO Structure;
     Structure = RECORD
                   Components: ARRAY[1..N] OF RECORD
                                 NumberOfElements: Pointer;
                                 FirstElement: Pointer;
                               END;
                   Elements: ARRAY[1..N] OF RECORD
                               SetName: NameType;
                               NextElement: Pointer;
                             END;
                 END;
```

```
PROCEDURE MFSCreate(VAR Components: MFSET);
(* Create set Components *)
BEGIN
  ALLOCATE(Components, SIZE(Structure));
  Clear(Components);
END MFSCreate;

PROCEDURE Initial(Comp: NameType; Elt: ElementType; VAR Components: MFSET);
(* Initialize Comp to a set containing Elt only *)
BEGIN
  Components^.Elements[Elt].SetName := Comp;
  Components^.Elements[Elt].NextElement := 0;
  Components^.Components[Comp].NumberOfElements := 1;
  Components^.Components[Comp].FirstElement := Elt;
END Initial;

PROCEDURE Merge(Comp1, Comp2: NameType; VAR Components: MFSET);
(* Merge Comp1 and Comp2 calling the result Comp1 or Comp2 arbitrarily *)
  PROCEDURE MergeInto(S1, S2: NameType);
  (* Merge S1 into S2, S1 and S2 are members of Components *)
  VAR Index: [0..N];
  BEGIN
    Index := Components^.Components[S1].FirstElement;
    REPEAT        (* attach S1 elements to S2 name *)
      Components^.Elements[Index].SetName := S2;
      IF Components^.Elements[Index].NextElement # 0 THEN
        (* next element *)
        Index := Components^.Elements[Index].NextElement;
      END; (* IF *)
    UNTIL Components^.Elements[Index].NextElement = 0;
    (* append list S2 to list S1 and call result S2 *)
    Components^.Elements[Index].SetName := S2;      (* last element of S1 *)
    Components^.Elements[Index].NextElement :=
                      Components^.Components[S2].FirstElement;
    Components^.Components[S2].FirstElement :=
                      Components^.Components[S1].FirstElement;
    Components^.Components[S2].NumberOfElements :=
                      Components^.Components[S2].NumberOfElements +
                      Components^.Components[S1].NumberOfElements;
    Components^.Components[S1].NumberOfElements := 0;
    (* S1 does not exist anymore *)
    Components^.Components[S1].FirstElement := 0;
  END MergeInto;
BEGIN
  IF Components^.Components[Comp1].NumberOfElements >
              Components^.Components[Comp2].NumberOfElements THEN
    MergeInto(Comp2, Comp1);  (* merge Comp2 into Comp1 *)
  ELSE
    MergeInto(Comp1, Comp2);  (* merge Comp1 into Comp2 *)
  END; (* IF *)
END Merge;
```

```
PROCEDURE Find(Elt: ElementType; Components: MFSET): NameType;
(* Return the name of the set of which Elt is a member *)
BEGIN
  RETURN Components^.Elements[Elt].SetName;
END Find;

PROCEDURE Clear(VAR Components: MFSET);
(* Clear set Components *)
VAR Index: CARDINAL;
BEGIN
  WITH Components^ DO
    FOR Index := 1 TO N DO
      Components[Index].NumberOfElements := 0;
      Components[Index].FirstElement := 0;
      Elements[Index].SetName := 1;
      Elements[Index].NextElement := 0;
    END; (* FOR *)
  END; (* WITH *)
END Clear;

END MFSETs.
```

Our previously defined Kruskal procedure was executed using this implementation; it worked as expected.

Complete the Documentation Since we have developed a library module to be used by other programmers, it is not necessary to prepare a user's manual. The internal documentation in the definition module is sufficient for proper use of the ADT and the internal documentation in the implementation module is sufficient to aid the programmer making small modifications to the module. It is wise to document some of the design decisions, such as the array representation of the Merge-Find sets. The complexity analysis might also be included in order to explain merging the smaller set into the larger set.

Summary

In this chapter, we have introduced the set data type based on the set structure of mathematics. We have defined a complete ADT Sets, which was used to implement some applications. Some set types do not require all of the operations defined in our set ADT. These constitute particular set types, like the dictionary or the priority queue.

Sets can be implemented using many of the data structures we have presented in this book. Some implementations are better suited to given applications than others, and here again, the choice of the set representation and implementation will be influenced by considerations from the applications themselves.

Sets can be represented by bit vectors, which provide efficient memory utilization and efficient execution at the machine level. They can also be represented by linked

Exercises

1. If X = {1,2,3,4} and Y = {3,4,5,6} what are the results of the following operations?
   (a) Member(2, X)
   (b) Include(X, 4)
   (c) Exclude(Y, 4)
   (d) Min(Y)
   (e) Union(Z, X, Y)
   (f) Intersection(Z, X, Y)
   (g) Difference(Z, X, Y)

2. Write a procedure DisplaySet to display all members of a given set without destroying the set.

3. We can use the bit vector representation whenever the universal set can be translated into integers in [1..N]. How would this translation be made in the following cases?
   (a) integers a through b where a $\leq$ b
   (b) characters 'a' through 'z'
   (c) integers a, a + 3, a + 6, . . . , a + 3 * k, for any a and k
   (d) pairs of lowercase letters

4. Given the following dictionary representation, define procedures In, Insert, and Delete.

   ```
   TYPE Dictionary = RECORD
                       Data: ARRAY[1..Max] OF NameType;
                       Last: CARDINAL;
                     END;
   ```

5. Write procedure Exclude corresponding to the binary search tree representation introduced in the text.

6. Write procedure Assign corresponding to the binary search tree representation introduced in the chapter.

7. Write procedure Member for the hash table representation introduced in the text.

Programming Problems

8. Modify the bit vector implementation of sets to implement SetOFCHARs, as defined in the text.

9. The following set representation, based on multilists, is used in an application involving university students and their courses.

```
TYPE Kind = (Student, Course, List);
     Pointer = POINTER TO Element;
     Element = RECORD
                 CASE What: Kind OF
                   Student:  Name: String;
                             Courses: Pointer;
                 | Course:   Title: String;
                             Students: Pointer;
                 | List:     NextCourse, NextStudent:
                                         Pointer;
                 END;
               END;
```

Items of type List comprise lists of courses taken by a given student, and lists of students taking a particular course. These lists are circular lists, so that starting from a student record, the courses the student has taken are obtained by following pointers Courses and NextCourse, which return to the original student record. Similarly, from a course record, by following pointers Students and NextStudent, we obtain the list of students who have taken this course, before returning to the original course record.

(a) Write and test a procedure ListStudents that, given a course name, lists all students registered for the course.

(b) Write and test a procedure ListCourses that, given a student name, lists all courses for which the student is registered.

(c) Write and test a procedure ListAllCourses that lists all courses along with the students registered for each course.

10. Modify the representation used in problem 9, to give each enrollment record a direct pointer to its student and to its course. Rewrite the procedures of problem 9 to use this new structure.

11. Complete the implementation module for Sets based on an ordered linked list representation, whose beginning was given in Section 16.3.

12. Modify the linked list implementation of the ADT Sets, so that lists of elements are not kept in sorted order.

13. Use the examples given in the text and problem 7 to implement the ADT Sets using a hash table representation.

14. Use the examples given in the text as well as problems 5 and 6 to implement the ADT Sets using a binary search tree representation.

*15. Implement the Merge-Find sets using a tree representation. Each component is a tree. Each node corresponds to a set member and points to its parent. The root of a tree holds a set member as well as the set name. Two arrays are used to define the correspondence between set members and tree nodes, and also between set names and tree roots. The Merge operation will make the root of one tree the child of the root of another tree. The Find operation will start by finding the node corresponding to an element and then will follow the path from that node to the root of the tree, and then to its name.

16. Add path compression, as discussed in the case study, to the Merge-Find sets implemented as trees in problem 15.

Note: Problems marked with an asterisk (*) have a higher level of difficulty.

Appendixes

Appendix A Programming Methodology

Computer science includes the study of computer methods in solving problems. Problem solving with a computer comprises the complete process of formulating the problem statement, designing a solution, implementing this solution as a computer program, and verifying the correctness of the solution through testing.

Such a computer solution contains two parts: algorithms (precise descriptions of methods to solve problems) and data structures (means of representing data). Niklaus Wirth, designer of the programming languages Pascal and Modula-2, entitled his classic data structures book *Algorithms + Data Structures = Programs*. Actually, this division is not clear cut; abstract data structures usually include algorithms to perform operations on their data. When developing a computer solution, both algorithms and data structures should be developed in parallel, as they influence each other.

In this appendix, we will review several fundamental principles that constitute the basis for dealing with the complexities of large programs, while introducing a useful six-step problem solving method. We will also apply this method to the development of a complete programming example.

Modula-2 offers tools that make it possible to solve complex problems. However, when solving such large problems, we must be very careful about designing our solutions. The biggest mistake you can make is to rush into coding a program before the solution has been carefully thought out. The problems you have tackled in your first programming course have been relatively simple. For very small programs, if you coded an ill-advised solution, you could simply discard it and start over since no great amount of effort was involved. This will be less true as you attempt to solve more complex problems. You must learn to resist the overwhelming urge to rush to the computer and start coding. We introduce here a six-step problem solving method which will help you make sure your solutions are well designed before you start programming them.

The six steps of the method are:

1. Define the problem
2. Design a solution
3. Refine the solution
4. Develop a testing strategy
5. Code and test the program
6. Complete the documentation

The first four steps usually constitute what is commonly called design, while the last two steps constitute implementation. During this initial discussion we will discuss each of these steps in detail in the following sections and give short examples of problems, sometimes unrelated, and their solutions. In the section Application of the Method on page A15 we will review the entire method by applying it to solve a single, important problem.

Design

Define the Problem   There is no substitute for understanding the problem to be solved. If the definition of a problem is vague or ambiguous, it is impossible to develop a solution without running into difficulties. Thus, vague parts must be made precise and ambiguities must be resolved. We can do this as we develop the solution, but the overall development will be much smoother and quicker if we make the problem definition as precise as possible before starting the development.

If the problem is one that you have originated, then you must get your own thoughts in good order so that the definition can be made precise. If the problem was originated by someone else, then you must study the specification to identify parts that are vague or ambiguous, and thoroughly discuss all these trouble spots, in order to come up with a mutually satisfactory and precise definition.

In all problems there will be a need for input/output operations. In order to include these operations in our design, we must define precisely all the input and the output of the planned system. In particular input/output formats must be completely defined at this stage. For example, if we want to develop a program for computing students grades, the input format for adding a student record could be defined as the student name followed by three real numbers representing the grades, as in:

```
Abigail Van Cliff     60.0 70.0 80.0
```

while the output format for displaying class grades might be the student name followed by a real number expressing the final grade, as in:

```
Pooh Bear             83.5
```

The result of this step is a precise problem specification, including a careful description of the input to be provided and the output that is expected.

Design a Solution   In this step we develop a description of the structure of the solution by using the powerful problem solving technique of "divide and conquer." We do this by analyzing the problem and decomposing it into its major subproblems; the solutions to these subproblems will be the major components of our final program. Then we decompose each subproblem itself into its major subproblems, and continue this decomposition until we have subproblems whose solutions seem fairly obvious. We use a structure chart to depict the decomposition, and this entire step is sometimes called *structural design*.

As an example of this decomposition process, let's assume we are designing a grading system for your class. We try to define all the tasks that will have to be done in

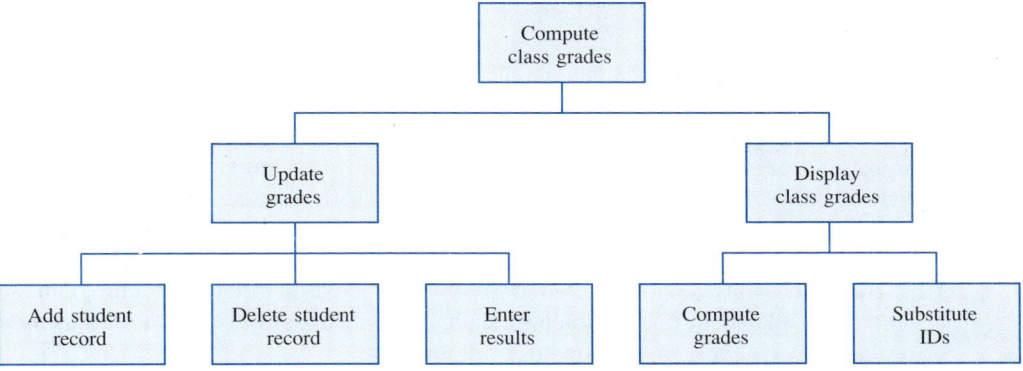

Figure A-1   Example of a Structure Chart

order to accomplish the main task. This first decomposition is simple: the system will have to update the students records, and to print the results. Updating students records calls for addition of a student record, deletion of a student record, or entering the results of an exam or a homework. Printing the results calls for computing the final grades. If the results are to be posted, we might need to replace students' names by student ID numbers so as to protect the students' privacy. Such a method is called *top-down design*, and leads to the outline of a solution, which can be illustrated by the structure chart shown in Figure A-1. A structure chart illustrates the hierarchy of the solution's various parts.

This design might still be refined by subdividing each of the lower level components into their major components, if this is possible. For instance "Enter results" might be subdivided further as shown in Figure A-2. This is sometimes called *stepwise refinement*.

In effect, a structure chart is a skeleton of the structure of the final program, where the solutions to the subproblems will be the components which fill out this skeleton. There will be some communication between these components, so we also develop general specifications, called *interfaces*, for the data that will be transmitted between these components, as well as final specifications for the input and output. We might want to do some *rapid prototyping* of the human/computer interface to insure that the appearance of the final product will match the user's expectations.

In this step it is wise to consider various alternatives for doing the decomposition, and consider the relative advantages and disadvantages of each alternative. Initially, it

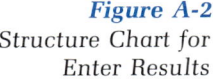

Figure A-2
Structure Chart for
Enter Results

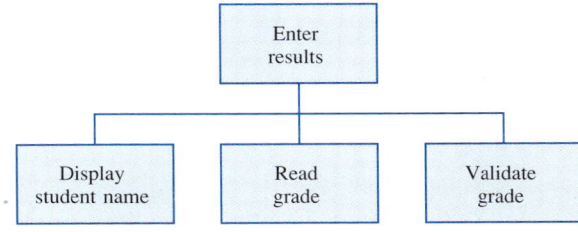

may be hard to judge the advantages and disadvantages, but your judgement will improve with experience.

In addition to decomposing the problem into subproblems to determine an appropriate structure for the program, you should also try to identify groups of related operations that could be used throughout the program to make implementation easier. If a group of operations all deal with a certain kind of data structure, then it may be desirable to include them in a separate module as part of an abstract data type. For example, a program that deals with Cartesian coordinates could use a module that defines a data type for a point in the Cartesian plane, and operations, such as the distance between two points. Often utility routines are used throughout a program, so rather than add them to the structure chart, we will document their design using a *modular design chart*, as illustrated in Figure A-3.

In our grades problem, we can anticipate the need for procedures to do input/output and processing of numbers and strings, so we will need to import objects from the InOut, RealInOut and Strings modules.

Our planned use of modules can be documented as shown in Figure A-3, which is called a modular design chart. The chart shows the various interconnections of the modules we intend to use for this solution, but it is not complete because we don't know exactly which procedures we will need from InOut, and RealInOut, and Strings. We will be able to complete the chart after we refine the solution in the next step.

The result of the design step should include documents that describe design decisions, structure charts, and modular design charts. The detailed example in the section Application of the Method on page A15 will show you how this documentation is developed.

Refine the Solution Starting with a skeletal solution developed in the previous step, we refine the solution by adding more detail, which is why this step is sometimes

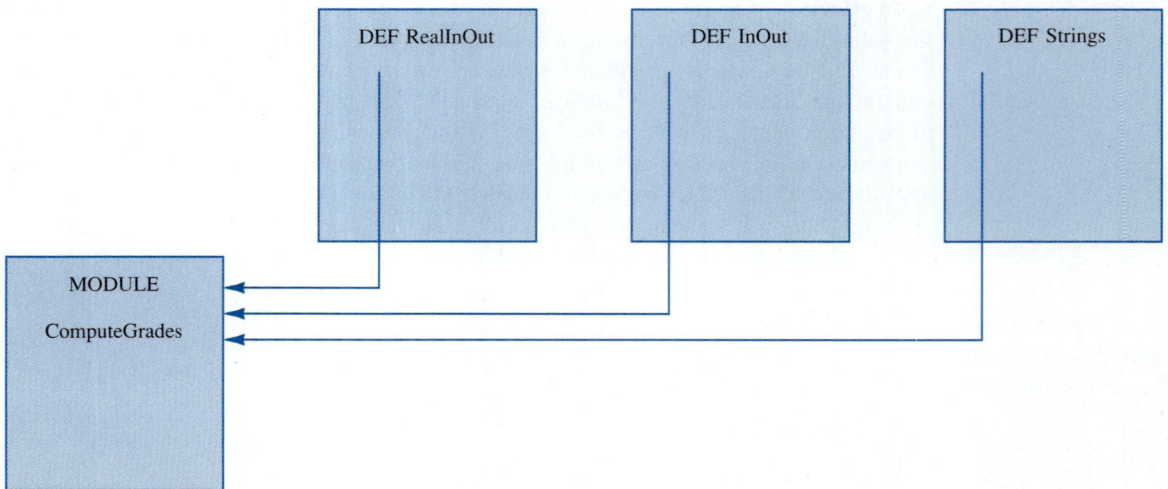

Figure A-3   Modular Design Chart for Grade Computation

called detailed design. Algorithms that provide solutions to the subproblems (the boxes in our structure charts) are developed in *pseudocode*, and the specification of our data interfaces are made more detailed by giving precise descriptions of the data and using parameter lists for our algorithms. Pseudocode is a language used to provide a description of the algorithms. As a language, it uses concise imperative sentences as well as simple mathematical notations, and is simpler than English.

As your programs become larger and your knowledge of programming more extensive, you will find your pseudocode becomes more abstract, with one pseudocode statement representing several programming language statements or even entire procedures. Consider the following example of the development of the grade computation of our Class Grades example; we have included the implementation in Modula-2 so that you can compare the pseudocode solution and the actual program code.

Pseudocode

> Compute Grades
>   For all students
>   Compute final grade by assigning weights 20% to first grade,
>   30% to second grade and 50% to last grade
>   End for
>   Compute total of all grades
> End Compute Grades

Implementation

```
PROCEDURE ComputeGrades(VAR Class: ClassType;
                           StudentCount: CARDINAL;
                       VAR GradesTotal: REAL);
CONST Weight1 = 0.20;
      Weight2 = 0.30;
      Weight3 = 0.50;
VAR i: CARDINAL;
BEGIN
  GradesTotal := 0.0;
  (* for all students *)
  FOR i := 1 TO StudentCount DO  (* compute final grade *)
    WITH Class[i] DO
      FinalGrade := Grade1 * Weight1 +
                    Grade2 * Weight2 +
                    Grade3 * Weight3;
      (* update total of all grades *)
      GradesTotal := GradesTotal + FinalGrade;
    END; (* WITH *)
  END; (* FOR *)
END ComputeGrades;
```

The pseudocode should be *language independent*: it can be translated into most programming languages, particularly imperative languages such a Modula-2, Pascal, C, Ada, etc.

Program Verification

At this stage, we are designing algorithms and we should make every effort to ascertain that the algorithms we design are correct. One way of doing it is to include assertions in our pseudocode as we write it. An assertion is a statement that must be true when execution of the algorithm reaches the point at which the assertion is given. Assertions are not really pseudocode, but rather comments on the pseudocode giving information about the values of the variables or about the relationships between variables. Assertions are usually placed at the beginning and end of procedures and control structures. Assertions placed inside loops are called *loop invariants*, as they are true for every iteration of the loop, regardless of the number of iterations or of the changes in values of individual variables. Remember, it is usually the relationship between variables that we are asserting to remain invariant, not the variables themselves.

Assertions can be used to give formal proofs of correctness for parts of the program. A complete proof of correctness must prove the final assertion when that part of the program terminates (called partial correctness) and also show that the program will eventually terminate. There are well known techniques for proving assertions on a statement-by-statement basis. Proof of termination is often established using *mathematical induction*, a method to demonstrate the validity of a formula by proving it holds for integer zero, and that if it holds for all integers preceding a given integer then it must hold for that integer. For example, given the program fragment:

```
ReadCard(N);
WHILE N > 0 DO
   (* body of the loop *)
   DEC(N);
END; (* WHILE *)
```

we would use induction to show that for any CARDINAL value N, if we decrement N each time the loop executes, then N will eventually reach zero and the loop would terminate.

The purpose of an assertion is to represent the state of the computation at a certain point in the program. Stating assertions and loop invariants is not always easy. However, it sometimes leads to the simplification of the algorithm, which in turn makes the algorithm correctness easier to check. Algorithm verification is a complex subject and correctness proofs are difficult to produce for complex algorithms.

Even if our goal is not a formal proof of correctness, when writing an algorithm, it is always very useful to include assertions as we go along, since they help us informally "prove" that the code we are writing is correct. Assertions are tools for program verification.

To illustrate the concept of assertions, let's take the example of a loop:

> While (Index # Max + 1) and (the key at Index # Search Key)
>   { Search Key is not in table elements before Index }
>   Increment Index
> End while
> { Index = Max + 1 or Search Key = the key at Index }

The assertion in the loop is the loop invariant, while the assertion after the loop is the final assertion that states the condition which is true on loop exit.

Algorithm Analysis

In designing algorithms we also need methods to evaluate algorithms and to help us choose between several possible ways of accomplishing the same task. The analysis of algorithms makes it possible to compare methods from the standpoint of efficiency, and constitutes an important topic in computer science.

One crude way of analyzing an algorithm is to count the number of statements executed upon completion. This gives us a basis for comparing two algorithms: a measure of the time necessary for their execution. However, the comparison must usually include other aspects, like the programming effort necessary to implement the algorithms. A given program might be 10 times slower than a second program solving the same problem, but might also be short, easy to write and to debug, and simple to understand. The second program might be longer, based on subtleties and might require complex reasoning to make sure it is correct. The comparison must also consider the memory space requirements of both programs, as computer algorithms usually offer substantial trade-offs between time and space: an algorithm requiring more memory space usually takes less time, and vice versa.

To determine the *complexity* of an algorithm, we must find an expression that gives us an estimate of the execution time of the algorithm. This expression is usually a function of a variable representing the size of the task that the algorithm has to perform. For instance, the size of a search would be the length of the sequence to be searched, say n. When we say that the run time for a searching algorithm is proportional to n, or that the complexity of the searching algorithm is $O(n)$, we are expressing a functional relationship between the size of the searching job and the amount of work required to complete the job. The mathematical notation used to express such relationships is called the Big-O notation. Common algorithm complexities are used to define complexity classes like $O(\log n)$, $O(n)$, $O(n^2)$, etc. It is usually sufficient to interpret this notation as meaning that the algorithm complexity is proportional to log n, n, or n^2, but you will find a precise definition of the Big-O notation and more on the analysis of algorithms in Chapter 3.

In selecting an algorithm, one should always check to see if there is an existing algorithm which is suitable. A solution may be available from a library module or another program. Sometimes a solution to a similar problem can be adapted to solve the current problem. A good computer scientist tries to reuse code whenever it is feasible. If you have to design an algorithm "from scratch", keep the algorithm as simple as possible, consider the space and time trade-offs, and don't be afraid to start over if things get too complex.

Choice of Data Structures

The ease of coding an algorithm, and sometimes its complexity, are affected by the choice of data structure (the way data are organized). Consider the following classic problem: is there any way to place eight queens on a chess board so that no queen can be taken by any other queen? Remember that a chessboard is 8 by 8 and that queens can capture other pieces across rows, along columns, and on all diagonals. Here is one solution to the eight queens problem:

Q	–	–	–	–	–	–	–
–	–	–	–	–	–	Q	–
–	–	–	–	Q	–	–	–
–	–	–	–	–	–	–	Q
–	Q	–	–	–	–	–	–
–	–	–	Q	–	–	–	–
–	–	–	–	–	Q	–	–
–	–	Q	–	–	–	–	–

It turns out that there are 92 solutions (disregarding symmetric solutions) to the eight queens problem. To write a computer program to solve this problem, one of the first decisions to be made is the data structure to represent the chess board shown above. A first attempt might be :

TYPE   ChessBoard = ARRAY [1..8], [1..8] OF ChessPiece;

where ChessPiece is a record that contains a status (black or white or empty) and a piece (king, queen, bishop, knight, rook, pawn). This would be a fine representation for an entire chessboard filled with the normal chess pieces, but it is more complex than we need to solve the eight queens problem.

Our next attempt at a data structure might be:

TYPE   ChessBoard = ARRAY [1..8], [1..8] OF BOOLEAN;

where the Boolean value indicates the presence or absence of a queen. It turns out that even this data structure is more complex than we need for this problem. Consider the following one dimensional array:

```
TYPE   ChessBoard = ARRAY [1..8] OF CARDINAL;
```

This simple data structure is sufficient. We will use the index to the array to indicate the board column under consideration and the element value to be the row number for the queen. A zero entry would mean that no queen has been placed in the column. If the variable Board was of type ChessBoard, then the following assignments would produce the board shown above:.

```
Board[1] := 1;    Board[2] := 5;
Board[3] := 8;    Board[4] := 6;
Board[5] := 3;    Board[6] := 7;
Board[7] := 2;    Board[8] := 4;
```

Using this data structure, the algorithm to solve the eight queens problem becomes very compact and efficient.

The major products of the refinement step are the data specifications and the pseudocode algorithms. When it is appropriate, we will also produce Definition Modules in this step.

Develop a Testing Strategy We must test a program to give us confidence that it gives correct results before we put the program into regular use. It is important to develop a plan for testing before we do the actual coding, because developing the test cases may cause us to recognize errors in the design. Correcting these errors at this stage will be *much* easier than correcting erroneous programs. In effect, developing the testing strategy tests the design steps, and the testing strategy itself is subsequently used to test the implementation of the design.

Another advantage of developing a testing strategy before coding is that we are usually much more objective before the coding is done. If we develop a testing strategy after coding, we may end up testing what was actually implemented rather than what was desired.

In developing a testing strategy for smaller programs, it is usually sufficient to specify the input data and the corresponding expected results for a wide variety of test cases. Remember, it is very important to test "extreme" cases and erroneous cases. For example, test cases for a payroll program should include negative hours worked, an erroneous value, to insure that the program produces an appropriate error message. A procedure involving string processing should be tested using extreme cases such an the empty string or a string of the maximum allowed length (if applicable). Test cases should also be chosen to make sure that every statement in the program is executed at least once.

For large programs, we need a plan for doing the testing along with the coding. We may choose a top-down approach, a bottom up approach or a combination of both approaches. *Top-down testing* means to start by coding and testing the main program first and then the subprograms. In terms of a structure chart, it means to start developing the program component at the top of the chart and working down, thus the name "top down". We will often have to design program *stubs* for the lower level components during the initial stages of development. These stubs may simply print a message or they may supply artificial data. For example, the structure chart given in Figure A-1 shows that the main program component, Compute class grades, will have two major subcomponents: Update grades and Display class grades. We could start a top-down development by coding the main program and these two major procedures, but the procedures at the lower level could merely be stubs. A stub for the AddStudentRecord procedure might be:

```
PROCEDURE AddStudentRecord(VAR Class: Table;
                          NStudents: CARDINAL): BOOLEAN;
(* A stub *)
BEGIN
  WriteString("AddStudentRecord"); WriteLn;
  RETURN TRUE;
END AddStudentRecord;
```

A message indicating that the procedure has been called is displayed, and a value is returned. This procedure would later be replaced by a procedure that actually does the desired processing, but meanwhile the program can be run to make sure that:

1. procedures are called in the right order, and
2. the interfaces between procedures are correct (i.e., the actual parameter lists in the calls match the formal parameter lists in the declaration).

Bottom-up development means that we code and test the components at the bottom of the structure chart first and then integrate these tested components into the next higher level working our way up the structure chart. Since these bottom level components usually cannot function as stand alone programs, it is necessary to write *driver* programs to test the components.

For the sake of illustration, assume that we have just developed a function procedure to compute the natural logarithm of positive real values. Also, assume that we have determined that our function is faster than the "ln" function in the MathLib library module, and so we want to use it in a program where execution speed is very important. We should write a small testing program to check the function before we incorporate it into the larger program. If our procedure is named Log, an interactive testing program might include the following program segment:

```
LOOP
  WriteString(
       "Argument for logarithm function (0.0 will exit) > ");
  ReadReal( X ); WriteLn;
  IF X = 0.0 THEN EXIT END; (* IF *)
  WriteString("The result of Log is: "); WriteReal(Log(X), 16);
  WriteString(" and the result of ln is: ");
  WriteReal(ln(X), 16);
  WriteLn; WriteLn;
END; (* LOOP *)
```

This would allow you to test a variety of arguments and compare the results to the results given by the function from the standard library. You could even write a more sophisticated testing program, which generated test arguments, compared the results, and provided a message when the results did not agree to some desired accuracy. The logarithm test program would be a part of a much larger process of testing the large program.

Often both bottom-up and top-down approaches are used. Utility routines that are used throughout a program might be coded and tested independently using a bottom-up approach. Then development will switch to a top-down approach with stubs being used for major program components. As development continues down the structure chart, the programmer has confidence that the utility routines can be integrated smoothly since they have been tested independently.

The major product of this step is an outline of the testing strategy, specific input with corresponding output for test cases, and, when appropriate, pseudocode for stubs and drivers.

Implementation

Program Coding, Programming Style, and Testing

In this step we use our pseudocode algorithms and our testing strategy to code and test the actual computer program. For large programs, this coding will be done little by little, coding the various components with the necessary stubs and drivers, so that the program components can be tested systematically. It is not uncommon to encounter difficulties in coding, due to errors in design or to peculiarities of the programming language, which prevent a certain aspect of the design from being implemented. If this happens, we must return to the design step and consider alternative design strategies. This step is completed when all coding has been done and all test data has been successfully processed.

The final program should adhere to generally accepted guidelines for good programming style.

Some Programming Style Guidelines

1. Programs should be well structured, with procedures of reasonable size (not longer than a page or two) and no large monolithic blocks of code.
2. The flow of control should be as straightforward as possible.
3. There should be no coding "tricks" that make the program difficult to understand.
4. The program should be made readable by choosing meaningful identifiers, using blank lines to separate components, and using indentation to indicate the flow of control that will be followed at run time.
5. Meaningful comments, which explain the program should be included. The main program should have an extensive preface, which includes a brief statement of the problem, appropriate references to external documents, name of the original programmer or team, date of the original implementation, and a change log. The

change log should have an entry for each significant alteration of the program, including the date of the change, the name of the person who made the change, and a brief description of the change. Each procedure should have a small preface describing its function. Difficult sections of code should contain explanatory comments. The pseudocode developed earlier may sometimes be used as comments.
6. Information should be transferred to procedures via parameters and use of global data should be avoided when practical.
7. Functions should avoid side effects, such as returning VAR parameters or changing global values.
8. Objects should be declared as local as possible.

The program in the section Application of the Method on page A15 provides an example that adheres to these guidelines.

If a program has been well structured during the design steps and the design has been faithfully coded using good programming style, program testing should not be inordinately difficult.

As mentioned during the algorithm design step, it is a good practice to include assertions in the code in the form of comments. If the pseudocode algorithms already included assertions, they can be included in the code; otherwise, assertions should be inserted at the appropriate places as the code is developed. The example we saw earlier would then be coded as:

```
WHILE (Index # Max+1) AND (Object[Index].Key # SearchKey) DO
    (* SearchKey is not in Object[Min]..Object[Index] *)
    INC(Index);
END; (* WHILE *)
(* Index=Max+1 or SearchKey=Object[Index].Key *)
```

However, even if we use assertions, some semantic errors (the program does not perform the desired task) nearly always occur, and the debugging necessary to find and correct the errors can be demanding. We offer some guidelines to make the debugging process less onerous.

Some Debugging Guidelines

1. Make sure that the expected results for your test cases really are correct. In other words, make sure that the result given by the program is really an error before expending the effort to find the error.
2. Do a mental trace with the input data to see if you can locate the error quickly.
3. Try to isolate the error to a small segment of the program by inserting write statements at key points in the program. For example, if you suspect that a certain procedure may be the source of the error, insert write statements at the beginning of the procedure to print arguments passed to the procedure and at the end of the procedure to print the results computed by the procedure. If assertions have been used in the program, the values printed out can be substituted in the assertions to determine if the state of the computation is erroneous at this point in the program.
4. If your efforts to isolate the error fail, create and test a simplified version of the

> program. This version should be a copy of the program that does not contain segments of code which are inessential to the computation of the test case under consideration. Naturally, this approach requires careful thought and sometimes considerable effort, so is usually only a last resort.

Many program development environments include a symbolic debugger. If your system contains such a tool, it will be well worth your time to learn how to use it effectively. In general, a symbolic debugger will allow you to carefully control the execution of a program and to examine the state of the program. During the debugging session, the source program will be displayed so that you will know exactly where the program is executing. You can set breakpoints in the program; this means that execution will halt when a breakpoint is encountered. You can examine values of any variables visible at that point in the program. You might even be allowed to change these values if you wish. Execution breaks can also be associated with a change in value of a specified variable. You can also single step through a program; that is, execute one statement at a time. These are only some of the features available with a sophisticated symbolic debugger. If such a tool is available on your system you should invest some time in learning how to use it, as this knowledge will improve markedly your programming efficiency.

The results of this coding and testing step are a readable program and information on the testing that has been performed. The program itself, including comments, is called *internal documentation*, whereas the testing information is part of the *external documentation* (all documentation other than the program listing).

Complete the Documentation   If a program is to be used by others, it must be documented; a naive user must have instructions for running the program, someone wishing to alter the program must have information about design decisions, implementation, and testing. Documentation is even necessary for the original programmer, who may be asked to change the program long after it has been developed. It is surprising how quickly design decisions and the reasons they were made are forgotten.

> *"The palest ink is better than the best memory."*
> — A CHINESE PROVERB

Program documentation begins in the first step of program development and continues throughout the lifetime of the program. Documentation of various forms is produced at each step of the program development process:

Define the Problem—The problem specification, including a general description of the input and output.
Design a Solution—Textual description of the design, structure charts, and modular design charts.
Refine the Solution—Data specifications, pseudocode, and definition modules.
Develop a Testing Strategy—Outline of testing strategy, test data and expected results, pseudocode for drivers and stubs.
Code and Test the Program—The program code (internal documentation), test data and results.

All relevant documentation should be collected into a comprehensible form. This documentation should be kept current throughout the lifetime of the software. In addition to the documentation generated during development, we may need additional user documentation. The user should be provided with enough information to make full use of the program and its functions, but should not be burdened with implementation details. A preliminary version of user documentation may be developed during problem definition and then refined after coding and testing is finished.

Summary of the Program Development Method

We will often refer to the first four steps of the method as design, and the last two steps as implementation. With the simple programs you have developed in your preceding course, it is often difficult to see the differences between design and implementation or to appreciate the need for design. When you are designing a program, you are producing *abstractions*, which are precursors of programs. These abstractions contain the essential elements of the design, without implementation details. They are at a higher level than a particular programming language and are usually produced on paper. There are many commercial packages, often called CASE tools (Computer Assisted Software Engineering), that can automate part of this process. When you are implementing, you are producing an actual physical realization of a software system. Implementation involves translating abstractions into operational and tested programs on a particular computer, operating within a particular software environment.

When developing algorithms in pseudocode, you might have felt it was simpler to code directly in Modula-2. This may be true for the simple programs you have written previously, but, as your programs become larger and more complex, you will find design to be an indispensable step in the development of software. Studies have shown that the earlier flaws in a program are detected, the less expensive they are to correct. These expenses can be "orders of magnitude" different. You will find this true of the longer programs you will develop later on, where inadequate or sloppy design will result in great difficulty in the implementation phase. In fact, if you are having a difficult time with implementation, it is often wise to reconsider your design.

Maintenance

The topic of program maintenance needs special emphasis, as it is not directly part of the original design and implementation process. Maintenance refers to all activities that occur after the program first becomes operational. Large programs have long lifetimes often exceeding the lifetime of the hardware. The cost of maintaining the programs over this lifetime will usually exceed the total development costs.

Program maintenance includes:

locating and fixing previously undetected program bugs
modifying the program, often to improve performance or to adapt to a new hardware/software environment

adding new features and capability to the program
keeping the documentation current

Maintenance is also important from a documentation standpoint, since changes to a program may render the previous documentation obsolete. Maintenance documentation may include many of the results of the program development steps: design documents, the program code, and information about testing. As maintenance is performed, any program changes should be reflected in the documentation. External documentation should be updated, and a *change log* should be kept in the program preface. The change log should contain the name of the programmer who made the change, the date of the change, and a brief description of the change.

Application of the Method

Let's apply the six step method to a specific example.

As part of the current efforts of the World Hockey League to publicize its teams and games, we are asked to develop a program that will read in the WHL current standings, read in the latest results, and update the current standings. These will then be transmitted electronically to all newspapers in the country. Although the program will not be very large, it will illustrate our problem solving method. As indicated earlier, the first four steps of our method will comprise the design phase and the last two steps the implementation phase.

Design

Define the Problem Write a program to read the WHL current standings from a file, to read the latest results from another file, to update the standings with these results, and to produce a new file with the new standings, while displaying the new standings on the screen.

The current standings file and new standings file have one line per team (current number of teams: 10), and the teams are ordered by number of points. Each line of the standings file includes the following:

name of team (includes no space), number of games played, number of wins, number of losses, number of ties, number of goals for, number of goals against, number of points.

The format of the standings file is made of a character string followed by 7 integers, as in the following example:

```
Flying_Dutchmen 13   9   2   2   51   41   20
```

Team names will include no spaces (the underline character will be used for clarity).

The output format to the screen will be identical to the standings file format except for a header (played, won, lost, tied, goals for, goals against, points):

```
                       P    W   L   T   GF   GA   PTS
Red_Barons_____    14   11   2   1   61   47   23
```

The results file has a variable number of lines, where each line includes:

name of first team, number of goals it scored, name of second team, number of goals it scored,

The input format of the results file comprises a string followed by an integer, another string followed by another integer, as in the following example:

```
Skating_Bulls__ 2 Flying_Dutchmen 3
```

WHL rules for computing points awarded to a team are that a win gives two points, a tie gives only one point, while a loss gives no point.

The current standings input file data will be checked for consistency: the number of wins, losses and ties should be equal to the number of games played, the number of points should correspond to the number of wins, losses, and ties. If the current standings file is in error, processing will be stopped with an appropriate message.

The results file will be checked to make sure the team names correspond to the team names in the current standings, and also that the number of goals scored is positive and less than 25. Any error condition will result in the display of an error message on the screen, and the corresponding results will be ignored.

Design of a Solution We use the "divide and conquer" strategy and decompose the problem into subproblems. A reasonable decomposition is shown as a structure chart in Figure A-4.

In this structure chart the left to right order indicates a probable order of execution, although this is not always the case because of unseen loops and condition testing.

The subproblem "Initialize Standings" is relatively simple: current standings are read from the input file.

The subproblem "Sort Standings" is straightforward: we have to sort the updated standings on the number of points.

The subproblem "Output Standings" is also straightforward; the standings are written to the standard output device. We will use output redirection in the main program to write the new standings into a new file, and also to display them on the screen.

The subproblem "Update Standings" in Figure A-4 will be easier to implement if we have a function, let's call it Rank, to find the position of a team in the standings table. This leads to the more detailed structure chart shown in Figure A-5.

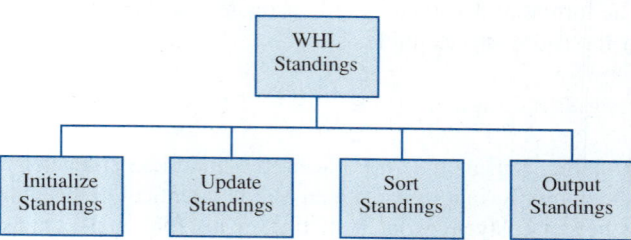

Figure A-4
Structure Chart for WHL Standings

Figure A-5
Complete Structure Chart for WHL Standings

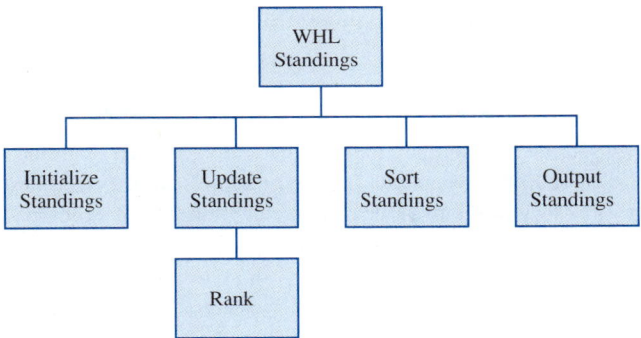

As already pointed out, the choice of data structures for a problem usually has a substantial impact on the design of a solution, so we should think carefully about a structure for the standings table that comprise the data in this problem. The team names are represented by character strings which will be stored in a simple table along with the numeric data. A line of the standings table will thus be a record.

We will need procedures for input/output, and also for processing of strings. Thus, we will need to import objects from the InOut standard module.

Our planned use of modules is documented in the modular design chart of Figure A-6. This chart is not complete because we don't know exactly which procedures we will need from InOut. We will be able to complete the chart after we refine the solution in the next step.

Refine the Solution We refine the solution designed in the previous step by developing pseudocode for each of the parts of the structure chart.

Figure A-6
Modular Design Chart for WHL Standings

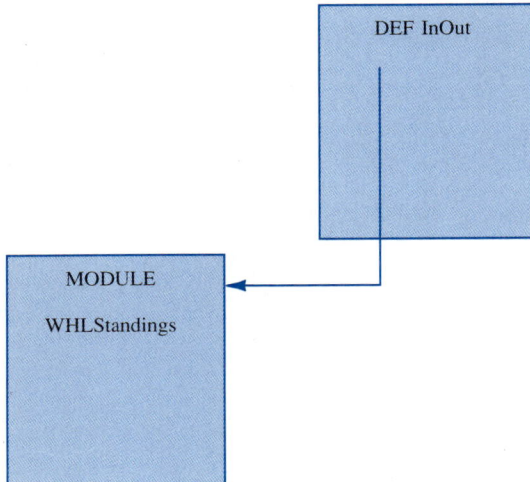

The Initialize Standings component must read the data for all teams in the league.

> Initialize Standings
>   For each team in the league
>   Read team name, number of games played, number of games won,
>   number of games lost, number of games tied, number of goals
>   for, number of goals against, number of points
>   Check consistency of data
>   End for
> End Initialize Standings

The Update Standings component must read result data and use them to update the statistics of the teams involved.

> Update Standings
>   Loop
>   Read first name, first number of goals, second name,
>   second number of goals
>   Exit if no more input
>   Find rank of first team and second team in table
>   If both teams are found in the table
>   Update number of games played, number of goals for,
>   number of goals against for both teams
>   Else
>   Display "Error in team name"
>   End if
>   End loop
> End Update Standings

Function Rank finds the position of a given team in the standings table.

> Rank
>   Set index to 1
>   While name of Table[index] ≠ team name
>   Increment index
>   End while
>   Return index
> End Rank

Sort Standings must sort the updated standings table

```
Sort Standings
   For each team in table
      Among remaining teams find team with maximum points
      Exchange team with maximum points with current team
   End for
End Sort Standings
```

Output Standings must output the standings to the standard output.

```
Output Standings
   For each team
      Write on standard output
         team name, number of games played, number of games won, number
         of games lost, number of games tied, number of goals for,
         number of goals against, number of points
   End for
End Output Standings
```

The main program simply calls the major components, so we choose not to develop it in pseudocode.

The pseudocode given above appears very similar to an actual program, particularly since it is shown in typewritten form. In actual practice, pseudocode is often written by hand and may be less formal.

From the pseudocode, we can determine which procedures we will need to import from library modules, and thus complete the modular design chart we started earlier in Figure A-6. The complete chart is shown in Figure A-7.

Figure A-7
Modular Design Chart for WHL Standings

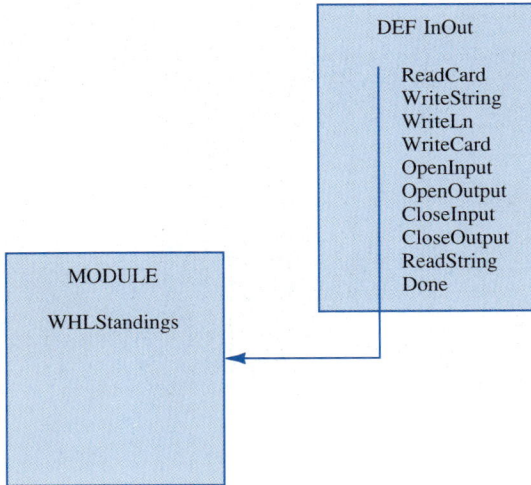

The lines showing the interconnections in such a diagram are called the *software bus* and indicate the importation of objects (constants, types, variables, procedures) into the various modules. Of course, the lines must originate at the exporting module; however, the lines are determined by specific IMPORT lists, not by what is available to import. A more complex problem would lead to a greater number of modules, including many user-defined modules.

Develop a Testing Strategy Before we start translating our algorithm into Modula-2, we must plan our program testing. Experience has shown that when testing is not well planned, it takes an enormous amount of time. Furthermore, when testing is planned early, it can lead to modifications of the solution by uncovering forgotten cases or unexpected combinations of data. Such modifications are much easier to make before implementation, since no actual programming has been done. Therefore the testing strategy should be defined before implementation begins and should lead to the definition of a set of test data that is as comprehensive as feasible. A testing strategy should be such that every part of the program will be executed at least once. Even when this has been done, we must be aware that subtle errors may remain. Such bugs may show up later, when the program is in regular use, and must be corrected by the programmer responsible for maintenance. This is the basis for one of the most well known sayings in programming:

> **Testing can show the presence of bugs, but cannot guarantee their absence.**

For our program, we will use current standings including 10 teams. We will then enter results including:

a) a win by the first team of the pair
b) a loss by the first team of the pair
c) a tie
d) a mistyped team name, to check our error detection
e) a team scoring more than 25 goals

We can use the following standings, stored in the current standings file:

```
Blue_Bombers____ 14 10 2 2 56 42 22
Red_Barons_____ 13 10 2 1 55 44 21
Eskimos_____ 14  9 3 2 64 55 20
Flying_Dutchmen 13  9 2 2 51 41 20
Skating_Bulls__ 13  9 3 1 49 40 19
Coyotes_____ 13  8 3 2 55 45 18
Gliders_____ 13  8 4 1 42 33 17
Roadrunners_____ 13  7 4 2 40 35 16
Black_Swans_____ 13  6 6 1 35 36 13
Zig-Zags_____ 13  4 5 4 32 42 12
```

and the following results, stored in the current results file:

```
Red_Barons_____     6 Zig-Zags_____   3
Skating_Bulls__      2 Flying_Dutchmen   3
Sloping_Fulls__      1 Eskimos_____ 5
Coyotes_____     26 Roadrunners_____  1
Coyotes_____      0 Roadrunners_____  1
Gliders_____      2 Black_Swans_____  2
```

The expected output is:

```
                         P    W    L    T    GF    GA    PTS
Red_Barons_____        14   11    2    1    61    47    23
Blue_Bombers____        14   10    2    2    56    42    22
Flying_Dutchmen         14   10    2    2    54    43    22
Eskimos_____        14    9    3    2    64    55    20
Skating_Bulls__         14    9    4    1    51    43    19
Coyotes_____        14    8    4    2    55    46    18
Gliders_____        14    8    4    2    44    35    18
Roadrunners_____        14    8    4    2    41    35    18
Black_Swans_____        14    6    6    2    37    38    14
Zig-Zags_____        14    4    6    4    35    48    12
```

along with the message

```
Error in team name: Sloping_Fulls__ Eskimos_____
Error in goals scored: Coyotes_____ Roadrunners_____
```

during program execution.

We should also have two extra test data sets: one where a team has a number of games different from the total of wins, losses, and ties, and another one where a team has a number of points which is wrong.

This set of test cases is the minimum we would recommend and more cases would be desirable, including, for example, the standings at the beginning of the season (all teams with zero values).

Implementation

The design phase is now over and we can concentrate on the implementation of the solution we have developed.

Code and Test the Program From the pseudocode solution previously defined we develop the following program.

```
MODULE WHLStandings;
(* This program reads in the World Hockey League standings: name of teams,
   number of games played, number of wins, losses and ties, goals for and
   goals against and points. Teams are ranked according to their points
   total. The program updates the standings according to the latest results
   (pairs of teams and goals scored), and writes the new standings to a
   file, and displays them on the screen as well.
                        Ph. Gabrini      December 1991 *)
FROM InOut IMPORT ReadCard, WriteCard, WriteLn, Done, OpenInput, CloseInput,
                  OpenOutput, CloseOutput, ReadString, WriteString;

CONST MaxTeams = 10;
      MaxGames = 25;
      NameLength = 15;
      MaxPoints = 2*MaxGames;
      MaxGoals = 25;

TYPE TeamRank = [1..MaxTeams];
     NameString = ARRAY [1..NameLength] OF CHAR;
     TeamStats = RECORD
                    Name: NameString;
                    Played, Won, Lost, Ties,
                    GoalsFor, GoalsAgainst,
                    Points: CARDINAL;
                 END;
     Table = ARRAY TeamRank OF TeamStats;

PROCEDURE InitializeStandings(VAR League: Table;
                              VAR Success: BOOLEAN);
(* Read in current standings from file; if errors are detected
   in input data Success is set to FALSE *)
VAR Team: CARDINAL;
BEGIN
  Success := TRUE;
  FOR Team := 1 TO MaxTeams DO
    WITH League[Team] DO
      ReadString(Name);
      ReadCard(Played); ReadCard(Won);
      ReadCard(Lost); ReadCard(Ties);
      IF Played # Won + Lost + Ties THEN
        WriteString("Error in games number for team ");
        WriteString(Name); WriteLn;
        Success := FALSE;
      END; (* IF *)
```

```
          ReadCard(GoalsFor); ReadCard(GoalsAgainst); ReadCard(Points);
          IF Points # 2 * Won + Ties THEN
             WriteString("Error in points for team ");
             WriteString(Name); WriteLn;
             Success := FALSE;
          END; (* IF *)
       END; (* WITH *)
    END; (* FOR *)
END InitializeStandings;

PROCEDURE UpdateStandings(VAR League: Table);
(* Read in the latest results from an input file:
       Name of first team, goals they scored
       Name of second team, goals they scored
    and update the current standings with them.
    A win brings 2 points, a tie brings 1 point and
    a loss brings no point *)

PROCEDURE EqualNames(Name1, Name2: NameString): BOOLEAN;
(* Character string comparison *)
VAR Character: CARDINAL;
BEGIN
   Character := 1;
   WHILE (Character <= NameLength)
         AND (Name1[Character] = Name2[Character]) DO
      INC(Character);
   END; (* WHILE *)
   IF (Character > NameLength) THEN      (* all alike *)
      RETURN TRUE;
   ELSE
      RETURN FALSE;
   END; (* IF *)
END EqualNames;

PROCEDURE Rank(NameOfTeam: NameString; TeamTable: Table): CARDINAL;
(* Find current position of team in standings *)
VAR Team: CARDINAL;
BEGIN
   Team := 1;
   WHILE (Team <= MaxTeams)
         AND NOT EqualNames(TeamTable[Team].Name, NameOfTeam) DO
      (* NameOfTeam is not in TeamTable[1]..TeamTable[Team] *)
      INC(Team);
   END; (* WHILE *)
   (* Team=MaxTeams+1 or NameOfTeam=TeamTable[Team].Name *)
   IF Team <= MaxTeams THEN
      RETURN Team;
   ELSE
      RETURN 0;
   END; (* IF *)
END Rank;
```

```
VAR Name1, Name2: NameString;
    Team1, Team2, Goals1, Goals2: CARDINAL;
BEGIN  (* UpdateStandings *)
  LOOP
    ReadString(Name1); ReadCard(Goals1);
    IF NOT Done THEN        (* no more data *)
      EXIT;
    END; (* IF *)
    ReadString(Name2); ReadCard(Goals2);
    IF (Goals1 < MaxGoals) AND (Goals2 < MaxGoals) THEN
      Team1 := Rank(Name1, League);
      Team2 := Rank(Name2, League);
      IF (Team1 # 0) AND (Team2 # 0) THEN      (* update common data *)
        WITH League[Team1] DO
          INC(Played);
          INC(GoalsFor, Goals1);
          INC(GoalsAgainst, Goals2);
        END; (* WITH *)
        WITH League[Team2] DO
          INC(Played);
          INC(GoalsFor, Goals2);
          INC(GoalsAgainst, Goals1);
        END; (* WITH *)
        IF Goals1 > Goals2 THEN                (* Team 1 won *)
          WITH League[Team1] DO
            INC(Won);
            INC(Points, 2);
          END; (* WITH *)
          INC(League[Team2].Lost);
        ELSIF Goals2 > Goals1 THEN             (* Team 2 won *)
          INC(League[Team1].Lost);
          WITH League[Team2] DO
            INC(Won);
            INC(Points, 2);
          END; (* WITH *)
        ELSE                                   (* tie *)
          WITH League[Team1] DO
            INC(Ties);
            INC(Points);
          END; (* WITH *)
          WITH League[Team2] DO
            INC(Ties);
            INC(Points);
          END; (* WITH *)
        END; (* IF *)
```

```
          ELSE
            WriteString("Error in team name: ");
            WriteString(Name1); WriteString(" "); WriteString(Name2);
          END; (* IF *)
        ELSE
          WriteString("Error in goals scored: ");
          WriteString(Name1); WriteString(" "); WriteString(Name2);
        END; (* IF *)
    END; (* LOOP *)
END UpdateStandings;

PROCEDURE SortStandings(VAR League: Table);
(* Given the updated current standings, sort the teams by points *)
VAR Team, OtherTeam, MaxRank: CARDINAL;
    Maximum: [0..MaxPoints];
    TempStats: TeamStats;
BEGIN
  FOR Team := 1 TO MaxTeams-1 DO              (* sort teams *)
    Maximum := League[Team].Points;
    MaxRank := Team;
    FOR OtherTeam := Team+1 TO MaxTeams DO    (* look for maximum *)
      IF League[OtherTeam].Points > Maximum THEN
        Maximum := League[OtherTeam].Points;
        MaxRank := OtherTeam;
      END; (* IF *)
    END; (* FOR *)
    IF MaxRank # Team THEN                    (* exchange *)
      TempStats := League[Team];
      League[Team] := League[MaxRank];
      League[MaxRank] := TempStats;
    END; (* IF *)
    (* League[Team] >= League[Team+1]..League[MaxTeams] *)
  END; (* FOR *)
END SortStandings;

PROCEDURE OutputStandings(League: Table);
(* Print the sorted standings *)
VAR Team: CARDINAL;
BEGIN
  FOR Team := 1 TO MaxTeams DO
    WITH League[Team] DO                      (* Write results file *)
      WriteString(Name); WriteCard(Played, 3);
      WriteCard(Won, 4); WriteCard(Lost, 4);
      WriteCard(Ties, 4); WriteCard(GoalsFor, 5);
      WriteCard(GoalsAgainst, 5); WriteCard(Points, 5); WriteLn;
    END; (* WITH *)
  END; (* FOR *)
END OutputStandings;

VAR WHL: Table;
    NoError: BOOLEAN;
```

```
BEGIN
  WriteString("Give current standings file name (ex: Standings.cur)");
  WriteLn;
  OpenInput("cur");              (* Standings.cur *)
  InitializeStandings(WHL, NoError);
  CloseInput;
  IF NoError THEN
    WriteString("Give new results file name (ex: Results.new)");
    WriteLn;
    OpenInput("new");            (* Results.new *)
    UpdateStandings(WHL);
    CloseInput;
    SortStandings(WHL);
    WriteString("Give new standings file name (ex: Standings.new)");
    WriteLn;
    OpenOutput("new");           (* Standings.new *)
    OutputStandings(WHL);           (* Save results in file *)
    CloseOutput;
    WriteString("            P    W    L    T   GF   GA   PTS");
    WriteLn;
    OutputStandings(WHL);           (* Display results on screen *)
  ELSE
    WriteString(
        "Errors made it impossible to compute new standings");
    WriteLn;
  END; (* IF *)
END WHLStandings.
```

Notice the formatting that has been done to make the program readable. We have used blank lines to set off the procedures that form the major structural components of the program. Indentation has been used to emphasize the flow of control aspects of the program: the bodies of procedures, the statements to be repeated inside a loop, and the alternatives in selection statements.

Also, notice that the comments, which *we have kept to a very minimum*, are an important part of the internal documentation of the program. The preface at the beginning of the program gives its objectives, its author, and the date of its completion. The prefaces of the procedures give brief statements of their function, and their names have been chosen to suggest functionality as well. Some names have been abbreviated, such as WHLStandings, but remain intelligible. Variable names have been chosen to suggest the contents of the variable. Some comments are assertions in procedure Rank, and also in procedure SortStandings.

A function should produce only one result and should not have any *side effects* (that is, it does not change any nonlocal value and does not do input or output). The function Rank in our program satisfies these criteria. A function should also be self-contained and, as such, should not be accessing any nonlocal variables. Adhering to these stylistic guidelines can be beneficial in debugging large programs, since it helps us isolate the parts of the program that we feel may contain the error. For example, if we suspect that the value of a variable is being altered inadvertently, we can concentrate on examining proper procedures (that are not functions) since they may have a side effect which cause the undesired alteration.

Once the program is written, we compile it. We might have to correct a few syntactical errors before being able to run the program. This is normal since we may mistype or be careless in other ways. The first time we ran our WHL program using the previously defined test data, it stopped with a "range error" message. This led us to modify function Rank to include a check that we do not go beyond the end of the League table. This is why function Rank listed above is different from its earlier pseudocode solution. Once this modification was completed, the program ran and produced the expected results.

If we run into trouble (program execution stops before the end of the data, wrong results, or various run time errors), we will have to find and correct the errors (debugging). The first thing to do is simply to mentally trace the execution to see if the error can be found quickly. If this is unsuccessful the trace can be done more carefully, or debugging statements may be added at appropriate points in the program. One simple way of doing this, is to add statements of the form:

```
IF Debug THEN
   WriteString(-- a message   --);
   Write--(-- a variable  --); WriteLn;
   ...
END; (* IF *)
```

where Debug is a BOOLEAN constant and the write statements are appropriate for the types of the variables we wish to print. The write statements will be executed only when Debug is TRUE, so if we declare Debug by "CONST Debug = TRUE", then the write statements will be executed when the program is run. When we are finished with our testing, we can replace the constant declaration with "CONST Debug = FALSE", and then the write statements will be ignored when the program is run. Thus when we are not debugging, the program runs as designed, but when Debug is TRUE, the debugging statements will produce a series of messages which enable us to trace program execution. Using this technique, we can easily switch back and forth between a normal mode of execution and a debugging mode by simply changing a single constant and recompiling our program.

As a simple example, assume that one of the first statement in procedure UpdateStandings in program WHLStandings had been incorrectly entered as:

```
Team2 := Rank(Name1);
```

When the results of the test cases are carefully examined, we should observe that the results are erroneous. If we fail to notice the error in our quick mental trace, we could put the following statement at the end of the procedure:

```
IF Debug THEN
   WriteString( "Team1 = " ); WriteCard( Team1, 15 ); WriteLn;
   WriteString( "Team2 = " ); WriteCard( Team2, 15 ); WriteLn;
END; (* IF *)
```

After running the altered program, the results will be checked and the error will be discovered.

> **The use of debugging statements allows us to see precisely what the program IS doing, rather than what we THINK it is doing.**

The technique of using debugging statements is so effective that many programmers include them in their programs at the very beginning, in anticipation of their need in testing.

Many language implementations are supplied with special debugging packages that can simplify the process of tracing or observing intermediate results. If such a package is available, it is wise to spend some time learning to use it effectively, as its use will accelerate the debugging process.

Finding errors is very much like detective work: looking for clues and traces. We have to use our reasoning and deductive power to find the culprits (erroneous statements, incorrect declarations, etc.). We may have to add debugging statements at different places in the program and delete other debugging statements as we narrow the search for errors.

For relatively simple programs, such as this example, the coding and testing process described above is usually adequate. When dealing with larger programs, it is imperative to use a structured approach to coding and testing. We will illustrate how a top-down approach might have been done on our example. Referring back to the structure chart of our solution in Figure A-5, we could begin our development at the top level; this makes it possible to make sure the overall logic design is correct and that the interfaces between procedures work.

In the present case, we would write the main program with stubs for InitializeStandings, UpdateStandings, and OutputStandings. For example, the stub for InitializeStandings could be:

```
PROCEDURE InitializeStandings(VAR League: Table;
                              VAR Success: BOOLEAN);
BEGIN
  WriteString("InitializeStandings called"); WriteLn;
  Success := TRUE;
END InitializeStandings;
```

Stubs may have to supply values for VAR parameters or return a value in the case of functions. This version of InitializeStandings might be used once to check interfaces, and then modified to include actual initialization of the League table.

After the program runs correctly with the stubs, the next step is to replace one of the stubs, InitializeStandings, for instance, by the actual procedure and test it; then one by one replace the other stubs by the actual procedures and test them. Although this testing process may not be required for a small program like WHLStandings, this example illustrates the top-down testing method.

As already mentioned, another testing method is the bottom up testing method, whereby the lowest level procedures are tested first. This approach of testing a module separately is very useful for critical components where an error would have significant (and disastrous) effects on other components, and also in programming teams where each component is implemented by a different person. It will be necessary to write special programs called drivers to run and test these low-level procedures. It is also possible to combine top down and bottom up methods: critical procedures are tested first, then a top down approach is used.

Note that all the testing methods require extra work: creating stubs or creating drivers. Those extra programs must also be written and tested. In large projects, the team of programmers assigned to testing may be totally separate from the development team. This helps maintain an objective attitude, since the testing team does not have the protective attitude to the program that the development team might have.

Complete the Documentation   The level of documentation may vary widely depending on how extensively the program is used. At the very least, the final version of the source code should be documented, as described below. Additional external documentation, such as discussion of the design, structure charts and modular design charts, might be maintained so that it is clear why certain design decisions were made and what alternatives were considered.

When we wrote the program we started our internal documentation. As we have previously stated, the internal documentation includes comments, meaningful identifier names, and program formatting to make the code as self-documenting as possible.

Comments should help others understand what your program does, but should not belabor the obvious, as with:

```
K := 1;          (* Initialize to one *)
```

This would clutter the program and render it less clear and legible.

Comments should always be used to construct explanatory prefaces for programs and procedures. They should also help clarify declarations if the identifier names are not sufficient. Finally, they should explain code that is not obvious.

We should emphasize once more the importance of program formatting. An unformatted program would be like a book without paragraph or chapter breaks; it might work but it certainly would not be easy to read. Extra blank spaces and lines make it possible to see at a glance the main structure of the program and indentation helps to trace the flow of control that will be followed when the program is executed.

Your code will be much clearer if you choose your identifier names carefully:

```
GrossPay := Hours * Rate;
```

is certainly clearer than:

```
C := A * B;
```

Figure A-8 presents a procedure that is definitely not self-documenting code. It is functionally correct but difficult to read and understand.

Figure A-8
An Example of Poorly Documented Code

```
PROCEDURE R(NT: String; T: Table): CARDINAL;
VAR I: CARDINAL;
BEGIN
I:=1; WHILE (I<=10) AND (EqualNames(T[I].N, NT) # Equal) DO
INC(I) END;
IF I <= 10 THEN RETURN I ELSE RETURN 0 END;
END R;
```

This procedure is the equivalent of our function Rank shown in the complete program. Comparing the two procedures shows how important the choice of identifier names and program formatting are.

In general, the use of constants makes code more readable and also much easier to modify. For example, the following declarations are used in program WHLStandings:

```
CONST    MaxTeams = 10;
         MaxGames = 25;
         MaxPoints = 2 * MaxGames;
```

If these constants were to be changed, we would only have the constant declarations to modify, without having to inspect all our statements to find and modify occurrences of the actual values, as would have been the case with function R above.

The external documentation of a program is, of course, external to the program code. It usually includes the problem definition, the design documents, a description of the testing performed, a history of the program's development and its different versions, and possibly a user's manual. In the case of our example, we still have to produce a user's manual that will describe to a naive user how to use the program. The manual for our program is relatively simple.

WHLStandings User's Manual

WHLStandings is a program to read in the current standings in the World Hockey League, and then to read in the latest results which are used to update the standings. Current standings are read from a file (normally Standings.cur), while results are read from another file (normally Results.new).

An example of current standings file input data is:

```
Blue_Bombers____ 14 10 2 2 56 42 22
Red_Barons_____ 13 10 2 1 55 44 21
Eskimos_____ 14  9 3 2 64 55 20
Flying_Dutchmen 13  9 2 2 51 41 20
Skating_Bulls__ 13  9 3 1 49 40 19
Coyotes_____ 13  8 3 2 55 45 18
Gliders_____ 13  8 4 1 42 33 17
Roadrunners_____ 13  7 4 2 40 35 16
Black_Swans_____ 13  6 6 1 35 36 13
Zig-Zags_____ 13  4 5 4 32 42 12
```

Note that team names do not contain spaces, and that these have been replaced by the underline character: this is to ensure that the resulting new standings table columns are aligned. Also note that numeric data are positive integers representing in order: the number of games played, the number of victories, the number of losses, the number of tied games, the number of goals scored by the team, the number of goals allowed by the team and the number of points. If there is an inconsistency in a team's data (number of games played different from the sum of the number of wins, losses and ties, or number of points not corresponding to wins and ties), an error message is printed and processing will stop once the input file is read.

An example of results input data is:

```
Red_Barons_____ 6 Zig-Zags_____ 3
Skating_Bulls__ 2 Flying_Dutchmen 3
Coyotes_____ 0 Roadrunners_____ 1
Gliders_____ 2 Black_Swans_____ 2
```

Team names are followed by a positive integer representing the number of goals scored by the team. If a team name is misspelled in the results file, a message is displayed and the corresponding result line is not considered. If the number of goals scored is greater than 25, a message is displayed and the corresponding result line is not considered.

Once the data are read in, the program updates the standings and writes the updated standings to a file (normally Standings.new), and displays them on the screen as well.

To run the program, prepare the current standings file, as well as the results file, insert disk WHL, and run the program WHLStandings. You will be asked to specify the current standings file name, then the results file name, and the new standings file name.

Summary

Based on our six step problem solving method we have given a fairly complete example of program design and implementation:

Design

Define the Problem
Design a Solution (Structural Design)
Refine the Solution (Detailed Design)
Develop a Testing Strategy

Implementation

Code and Test the Program
Complete the Documentation

The design of algorithms should be done in an orderly manner, using assertions to help document the program's operation. Algorithms should also be analyzed to ensure that their performance is acceptable.

You should adapt the style used in the example to meet your own needs, and use it to develop the larger programs that you will subsequently have to do. In developing larger programs you should also design to facilitate maintenance. Even though the programs you do to solve this book's exercises may not be changed after they are completed, this is usually not true of programs developed to solve actual problems. Even more importantly, you must practice clarity in design and documentation, critically important traits of any good scientific work.

Appendix B Modula-2 Syntax (Using EBNF)

To describe the syntax of a given language, one must use a language. It is possible to use the given language to describe its own syntax, just as you can describe the syntax of the English language in English. The language used to describe syntax is often called a meta-language. In order to describe the syntax of Modula-2, we will use a meta-language known as EBNF (Extended Backus Naur Form).

The EBNF meta-language uses meta-symbols = , |, [,], {, }, ", ', parentheses, and the period. The equal sign and the period are used for the definition of terms, as in

T = X Y.

where T is defined to be the concatenation of X and Y.

The vertical bar indicates a choice between alternatives, as in

T = X | Y.

which defines T as either X or Y.

The square brackets indicate an optional part, as in

T = X [Y].

which defines T as either X or XY.

The braces indicate any number of repetitions of their contents (including none), as in

T = X {Y}

which defines T as X, XY, XYY, XYYY, and so forth.

Parentheses are used to group terms as in

T = X (Y | Z).

which defines T as XY or XZ.

In the following definition of the syntax of Modula-2, quotation marks (single or double) are used to indicate symbols which should be used as they appear. These are called *terminal symbols*. Terminal symbols include reserved works, which are written in uppercase letters and are used without any modification. A list of reserved words for Modula-2 follows.

AND	ELSIF	LOOP	REPEAT
ARRAY	END	MOD	RETURN
BEGIN	EXIT	MODULE	SET
BY	EXPORT	NOT	THEN
CASE	FOR	OF	TO
CONST	FROM	OR	TYPE
DEFINITION	IF	POINTER	UNTIL
DIV	IMPLEMENTATION	PROCEDURE	VAR
DO	IMPORT	QUALIFIED	WHILE
ELSE	IN	RECORD	WITH

Reserved words will appear directly in the syntax definition without being enclosed in quotation marks. The complete syntax definition of Modula-2 follows.

1. Compilation Units

1.1   `CompilationUnit = DefinitionModule |`
       `[IMPLEMENTATION] ProgramModule.`

1.2   `DefinitionModule = DEFINITION MODULE Ident ";" {Import}`
       `{Definition} END Ident ".".`

1.3   `ProgramModule =`
       `MODULE Ident [Priority] ";" {Import} Block Ident ".".`

2. Declarations

2.1   `Definition = CONST {ConstantDeclaration ";"} |`
       `TYPE {Ident ["=" Type] ";"} |`
       `VAR {VariableDeclaration ";"} |`
       `ProcedureHeading ";".`

2.2   `Block = {Declaration} [BEGIN StatementSequence] END.`

2.3   `Declaration = CONST {ConstantDeclaration ";"} |`
       `TYPE {TypeDeclaration ";"} |`
       `VAR {VariableDeclaration ";"} |`
       `ProcedureDeclaration ";" | ModuleDeclaration ";".`

2.4   `ConstantDeclaration = Ident "=" ConstExpression.`

2.5   `TypeDeclaration = Ident "=" Type.`

2.6   `VariableDeclaration = IdentList ":" Type`

2.7   `ProcedureDeclaration = ProcedureHeading ";" Block Ident.`

2.8   `ProcedureHeading = PROCEDURE Ident [FormalParameters].`

2.9   `FormalParameters =`
       `"(" [FPSection {";" FPSection}] ")" [":" Qualident].`

2.10 FPSection = [VAR] IdentList ":" FormalType.

2.11 ModuleDeclaration =
      MODULE Ident [Priority] ";" {Import} [Export] Block Ident.

2.12 Priority = "[" ConstExpression "]".

2.13 Import = [FROM Ident] IMPORT IdentLIst ";".

2.14 Export = EXPORT [QUALIFIED] IdentList ";".

3. Types

3.1 Type = SimpleType | ArrayType | RecordType | SetType |
     PointerType | ProcedureType.

3.2 SimpleType = Qualident | Enumeration | SubrangeType.

3.3 Enumeration = "(" IdentList ")".

3.4 SubrangeType = [Qualident]
     "[" Constexpression ".." ConstExpression "]".

3.5 ArrayType = ARRAY SimpleType {"," SimpleType} OF Type.

3.6 RecordType = RECORD FieldListSequence END.

3.7 FieldListSequence = FieldList {";" FieldList}.

3.8 FieldList = [IdentList ":" Type |
     CASE [Ident] ":" Qualident OF Variant {"|" Variant}
     [ELSE FieldListSequence] END].

3.9 Variant = [CaseLabelList ":" FieldListSequence].

3.10 SetType = SET OF SimpleType.

3.11 PointerType = POINTER TO Type.

3.12 ProcedureType = PROCEDURE [FormalTypeList].

3.13 FormalTypeList = "(" [[VAR] FormalType
      {"," [VAR] FormalType}] ")" [":" Qualident].

3.14 FormalType = [ARRAY OF] Qualident.

4. Statements

4.1 StatementSequence = Statement {";" Statement].

4.2 Statement = [Assignment | ProcedureCall |
     IfStatement | CaseStatement | WhileStatement |
     RepeatStatement | LoopStatement | ForStatement |
     WithStatement | EXIT | RETURN [Expression]].

4.3 Assignment = Designator ":=" Expression.

4.4   ProcedureCall = Designator [ActualParameters].

4.5   IfStatement = IF Expression THEN StatementSequence
         {ELSIF Expression THEN StatementSequence}
         [ELSE StatementSequence] END.

4.6   CaseStatement = CASE Expression OF Case {"|" Case}
         [ELSE StatementSequence] END.

4.7   Case = [CaseLabelList ":" StatementSequence].

4.8   CaseLabelList = CaseLabels {"," CaseLabels}.

4.9   CaseLabels = ConstExpression [".." ConstExpression].

4.10 LoopStatement = LOOP StatementSequence END.

4.11 WhileStatement = WHILE Expression DO StatementSequence END.

4.12 RepeatStatement = REPEAT StatementSequence UNTIL Expression.

4.13 ForStatement = FOR Ident ":=" Expression TO Expression
         [BY ConstExpression] DO StatementSequence END.

4.14 WithStatement = WITH Designator DO StatementSequence END.

5. Expressions

5.1   ExpList = Expression {"," Expression}.

5.2   ConstExpression = Expression.

5.3   Expression = SimpleExpression [Relation SimpleExpression].

5.4   SimpleExpression = ["+" | "−"] Term {AddOperator Term}.

5.5   Term = Factor {MulOperator Factor}.

5.6   Factor = Number | String | Set |
         Designator [ActualParameters] |
         "(" Expression ")" | NOT Factor.

5.7   Relation = "=" | "#" | "<" | "<=" | ">" | ">=" | IN.

5.8   AddOperator = "+" | "−" | OR.

5.9   MulOperator = "*" | "/" | DIV | MOD | AND.

5.10 Set = [Qualident] "{" [Element {"," Element}] "}".

5.11 Element = Expression [".." Expression].

5.12 Designator = Qualident {"." Ident | "[" ExpList "]" | "^"}.

5.13 ActualParameters = "(" [ExpList] ")".

6. Names and Literals

6.1   IdentList = Ident {"," Ident}.

6.2   Qualident = Ident {"." Ident}.

6.3   Ident = Letter {Letter | Digit}.

6.4   Number = Integer | Real.

6.5   Integer = Digit {Digit} |
       OctalDigit {OctalDigit} ("B" | "C") |
       Digit {HexDigit} "H".

6.6   Real = Digit {Digit} "." {Digit} [ScaleFactor].

6.7   ScaleFactor = "E" ["+" | "−"] Digit {Digit}.

6.8   HexDigit = Digit | "A" | "B" | "C" | "D" | "E" | "F".

6.9   Digit = OctalDigit | "8" | "9".

6.10   OctalDigit = "0" | "1" | "2" | "3" | "4" | "5" | "6" | "7".

6.11   String = "'" {Character} "'" | '"' {Character} '"'.

Cross References

```
"     6.11
#     5.7
'     6.11
(     2.9, 3.3, 3.13, 5.6, 5.13
)     2.9, 3.3, 3.13, 5.6, 5.13
*     5.9
+     5.4, 5.8, 6.7
,     3.5, 3.13, 4.8, 5.1, 5.10, 6.1
−     5.4, 5.8, 6.7
/     5.9
:     2.6, 2.9, 2.10, 3.8, 3.9, 3.13, 4.7
:=    4.3, 4.13
;     1.2, 1.3, 2.1, 2.3, 2.7, 2.9, 2.13, 2.14, 3.7, 4.1
<     5.7
<=    5.7
=     2.1, 2.4, 2.5, 5.7
>     5.7
>=    5.7
[     2.12, 3.4, 5.12
]     2.12, 3.4, 5.12
^     5.12
```

{ 5.10
| 3.8, 4.6
} 5.10
ActualParameters (5.13) 4.4, 5.6
AddOperator (5.8) 5.4
AND 5.9
ARRAY 3.5, 3.14
ArrayType (3.5) 3.1
Assignment (4.3) 4.2
BEGIN 2.2
Block (2.2) 1.3, 2.7, 2.11
BY 4.13
CASE 3.8, 4.6
Case (4.7) 4.6
CaseLabelList (4.8) 3.9, 4.7
CaseLabels (4.9) 4.8
CaseStatement (4.6) 4.2
Character 6.11
CompilationUnit (1.1)
CONST 2.1, 2.3
ConstantDeclaration (2.4) 2.1, 2.3
ConstExpression (5.2) 2.4, 2.12, 3.4, 4.9, 4.13
Declaration (2.3) 2.2
Definition (2.1) 1.2)
DEFINITION 1.2
DefinitionModule (1.2) 1.1
Designator (5.12) 4.3, 4.4, 4.14, 5.6
Digit (6.9) 6.3, 6.5, 6.6, 6.7, 6.8
DIV 5.9
DO 4.11, 4.13, 4.14
Element (5.11) 5.10
ELSE 3.8, 4.5, 4.6
ELSIF 4.5
END 1.2, 2.2, 3.6, 3.8, 4.5, 4.6, 4.10, 4.11, 4.13, 4.14
Enumeration (3.3) 3.2
EXIT 4.2
ExpList (5.1) 5.12, 5.13
Export (2.14) 2.11
EXPORT 2.14
Expression (5.3) 4.2, 4.3, 4.5, 4.6, 4.11, 4.12, 4.13, 5.1, 5.2, 5.6, 5.11
Factor (5.6) 5.5, 5.6
FieldList (3.8) 3.7
FieldListSequence (3.7) 3.6, 3.8, 3.9
FOR 4.13
FormalParameters (2.9) 2.8
FormalType (3.14) 2.10, 3.13

FormalTypeList (3.13) 3.12
ForStatement (4.13) 4.2
FPSection (2.10) 2.9
FROM 2.13
HexDigit (6.8) 6.5
Ident (6.3) 1.2, 1.3, 2.1, 2.4, 2.5, 2.7, 2.8, 2.11, 2.13, 3.8, 4.13, 5.12, 6.1, 6.2
IdentList (6.1) 2.6, 2.10, 2.13, 2.14, 3.3, 3.8
IF 4.5
IfStatement (4.5) 4.2
IMPLEMENTATION 1.1
Import (2.13) 1.2, 1.3, 2.11
IMPORT 2.13
IN 5.7
Integer (6.5) 6.4
Letter 6.3
LOOP 4.10
LoopStatement (4.10) 4.2
MOD 5.9
MODULE 1.2, 1.3, 2.11
ModuleDeclaration (2.11) 2.3
MulOperator (5.9) 5.5
Number (6.4) 5.6
NOT 5.6
OctalDigit (6.10) 6.5, 6.9
OF 3.5, 3.8, 3.10, 3.14, 4.6
OR 5.8
POINTER 3.11
PointerType (3.11) 3.1
Priority (2.12) 1.3, 2.11
PROCEDURE 2.8, 3.12
ProcedureCall (4.4) 4.2
ProcedureDeclaration (2.7) 2.3
ProcedureHeading (2.8) 2.1, 2.7
ProcedureType (3.12) 3.1
ProgramModule (1.3) 1.1
Qualident (6.2) 2.9, 3.2, 3.4, 3.8, 3.13, 3.14, 5.10, 5.12
QUALIFIED 2.14
Real (6.6) 6.4
RECORD 3.6
RecordType (3.6) 3.1
Relation (5.7) 5.3
REPEAT 4.12
RepeatStatement (4.12) 4.2
RETURN 4.2
ScaleFactor (6.7) 6.6
Set (5.10) 5.6

SET 3.10
SetType (3.10) 3.1
SimpleExpression (5.4) 5.3
SimpleType (3.2) 3.1, 3.5, 3.10
Statement (4.2) 4.1
StatementSequence (4.1), 2.2, 4.5, 4.6, 4.7, 4.10, 4.11, 4.12, 4.13, 4.14
String (6.11) 5.6
SubrangeType (3.4) 3.2
Term (5.5) 5.4
THEN 4.5
TO 3.11, 4.13
Type (3.1) 2.1, 2.5, 2.6, 3.5, 3.8, 3.11
TYPE 2.1, 2.3
TypeDeclaration (2.5) 2.3
UNTIL 4.12
VAR 2.1, 2.3, 2.10, 3.13
VariableDeclaration (2.6) 2.1, 2.3
Variant (3.9) 3.8
WHILE 4.11
WhileStatement (4.11) 4.2
WITH 4.14
WithStatement (4.14) 4.2

Appendix C Modula-2 Syntax Diagrams

1. Compilation Units

1.1 **CompilationUnit**

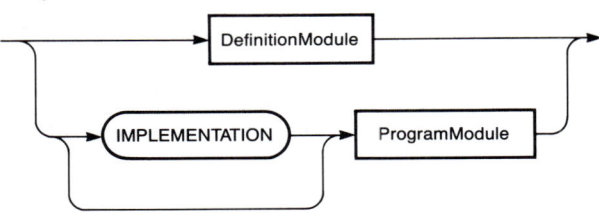

1.2 **DefinitionModule**

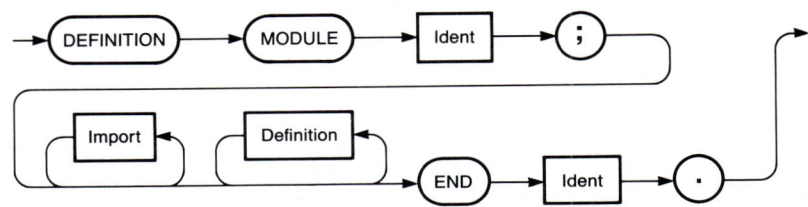

1.3 **ProgramModule**

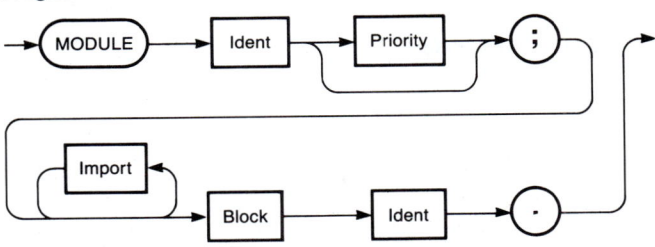

2. Declarations

2.1 Definition

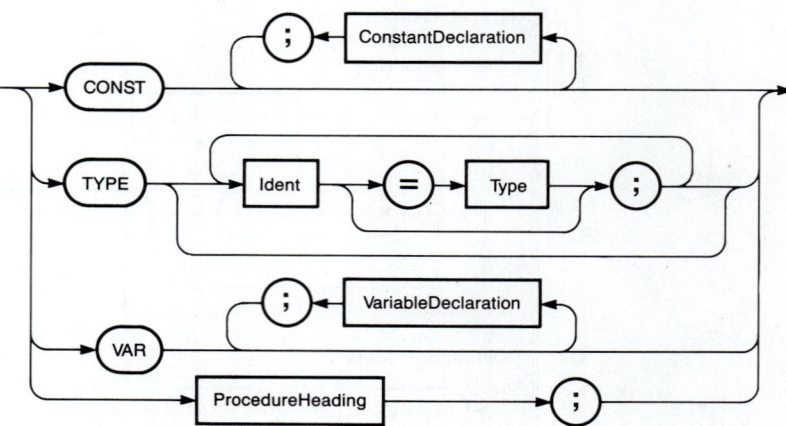

2.2 Block

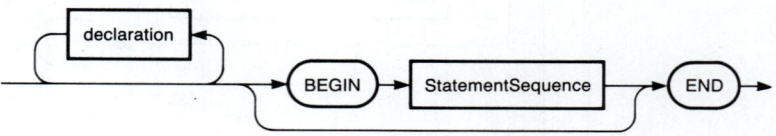

2.3 Declaration

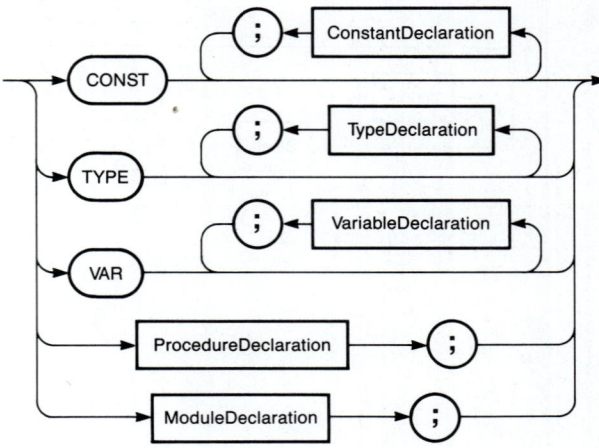

Appendix C   A43

2.4   ConstantDeclaration

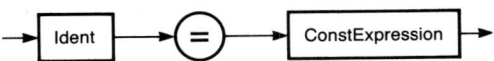

2.5   TypeDeclaration

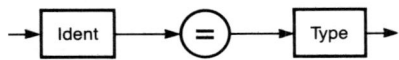

2.6   VariableDeclaration

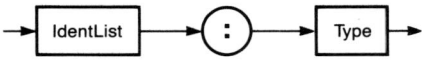

2.7   ProcedureDeclaration

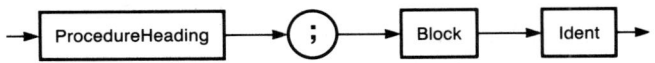

2.8   ProcedureHeading

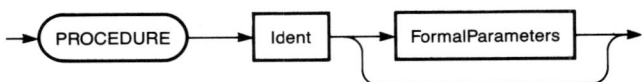

2.9   FormalParameters

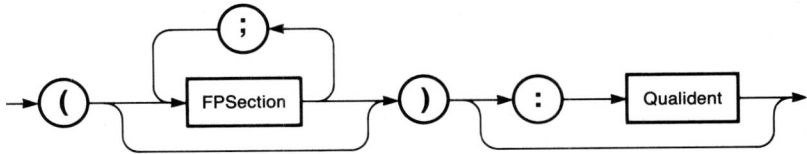

2.10   FPSection

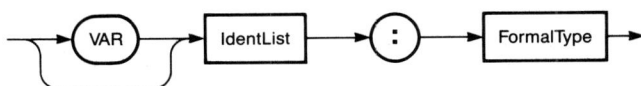

2.11 ModuleDeclaration

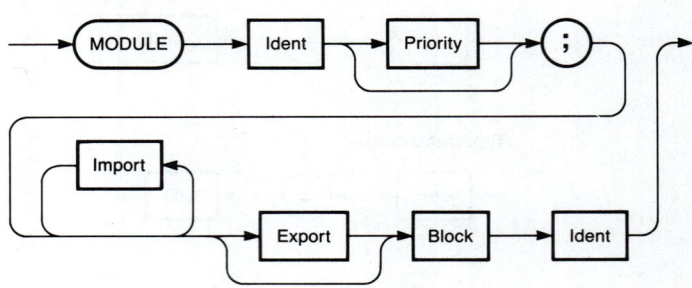

2.12 Priority

2.13 Import

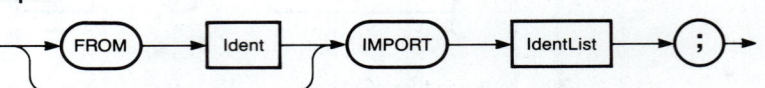

2.14 Export

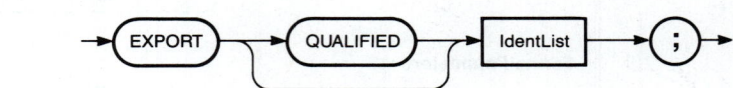

3. Types

3.1 Type

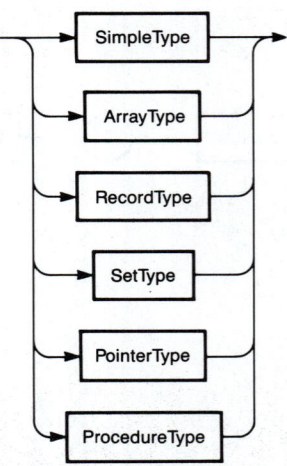

Appendix C   **A45**

3.2   SimpleType

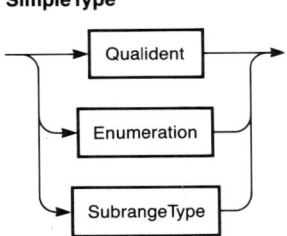

3.3   Enumeration

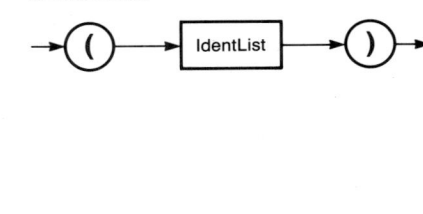

3.4   SubrangeType

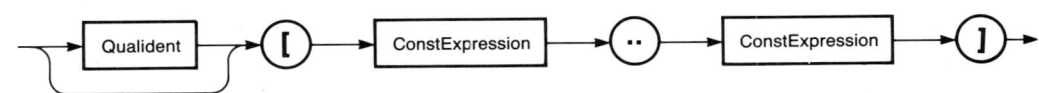

3.5   ArrayType

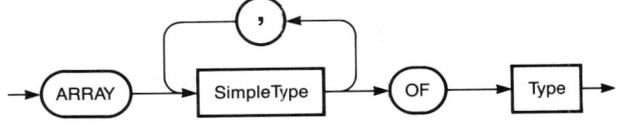

3.6   RecordType

3.7   FieldListSequence

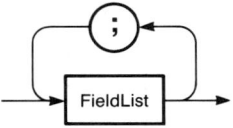

3.8   FieldList

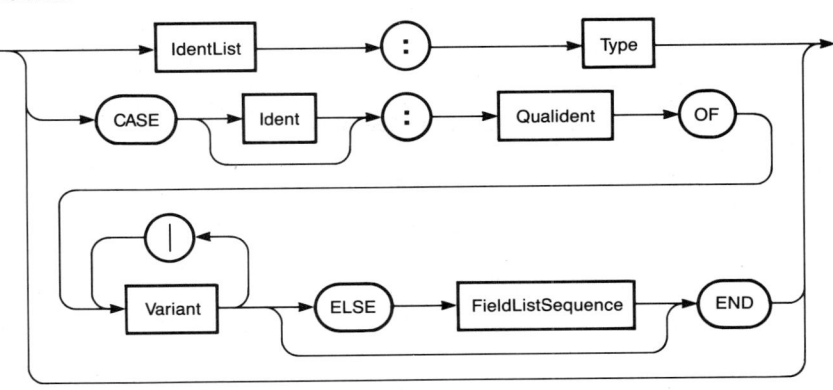

3.9   **Variant**

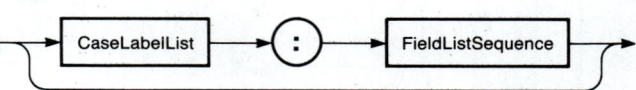

3.10 **SetType**

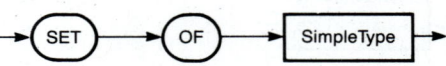

3.11 **PointerType**

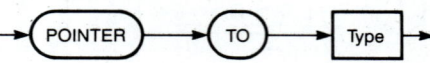

3.12 **ProcedureType**

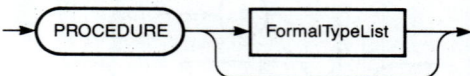

3.13 **FormalTypeList**

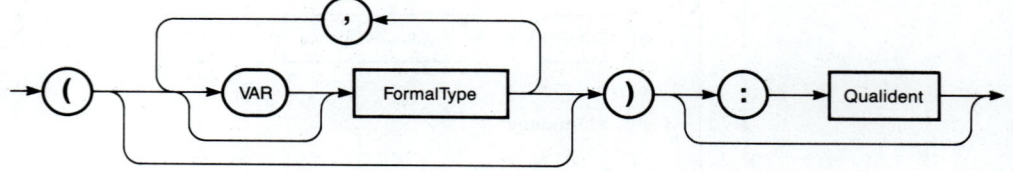

3.14 **FormalType**

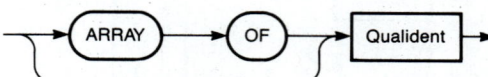

4. Statements

4.1   **StatementSequence**

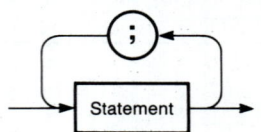

4.2 Statement

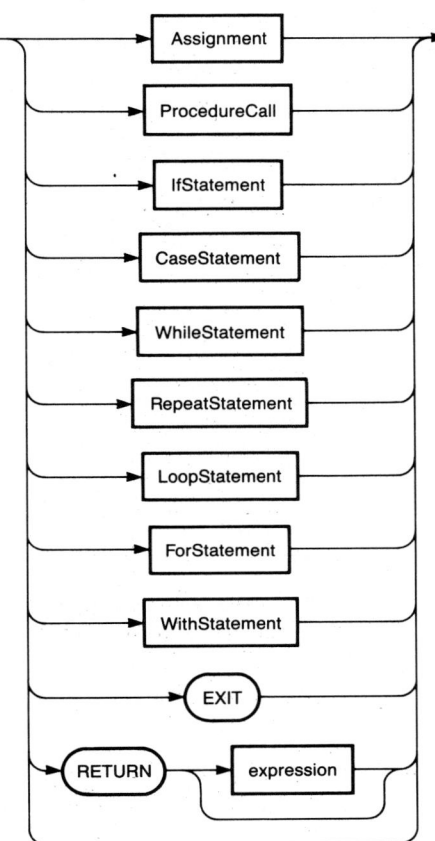

4.3 Assignment

4.4 ProcedureCall

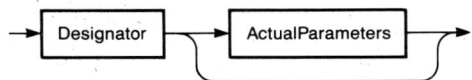

4.5 IfStatement

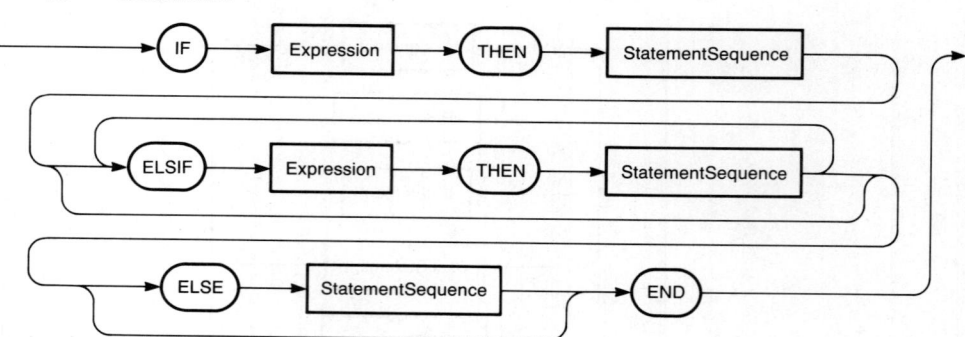

4.6 CaseStatement

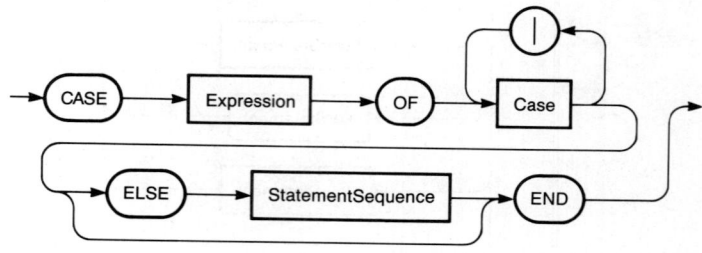

4.7 Case

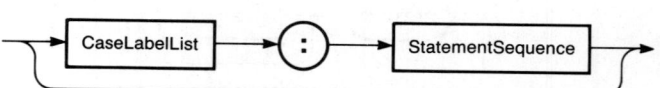

4.8 CaseLabelList

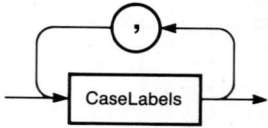

4.9 CaseLabels

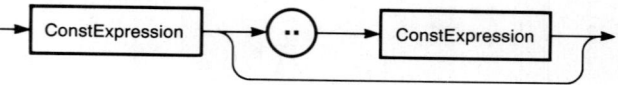

4.10 LoopStatement

4.11 WhileStatement

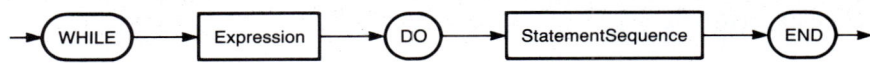

4.12 RepeatStatement

4.13 ForStatement

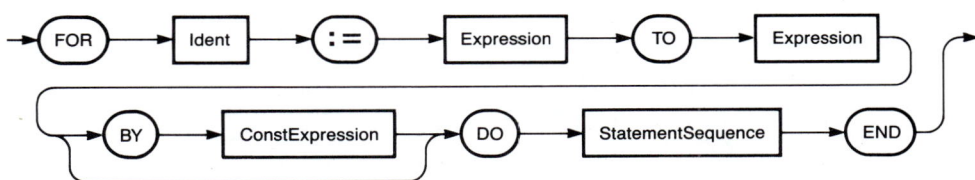

4.14 WithStatement

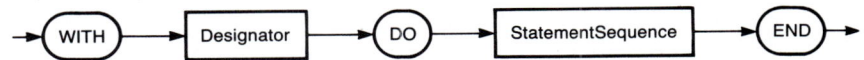

5. Expressions

5.1 ExpList

5.2 ConstExpression

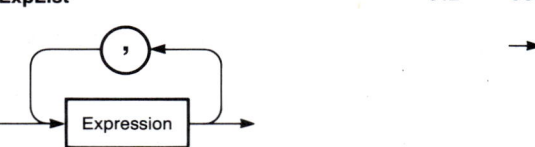

5.3 Expression

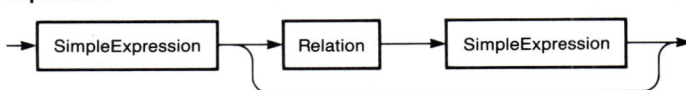

5.4 SimpleExpression

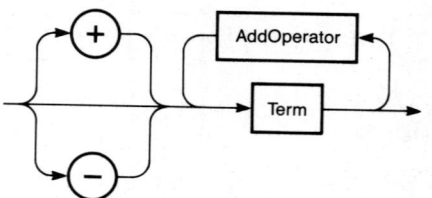

5.5 Term

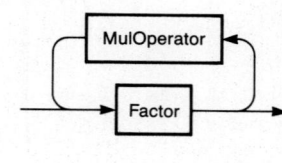

5.6 Factor

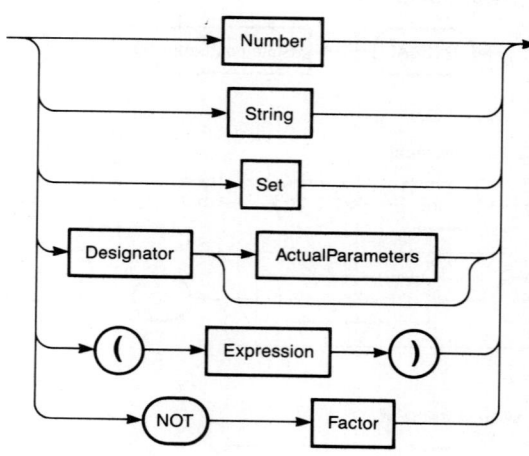

5.7 Relation

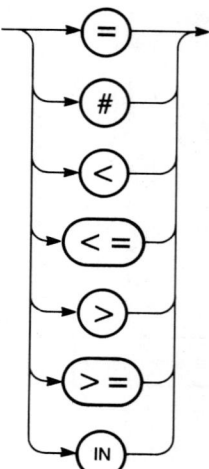

Appendix C   A51

5.8 AddOperator

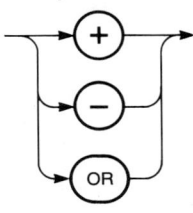

5.9 MulOperator

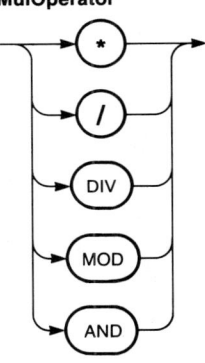

5.10 Set

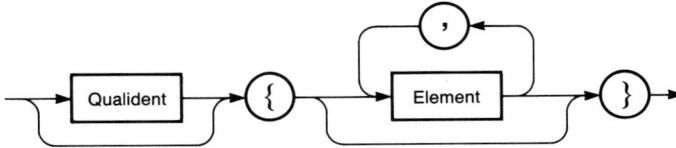

5.11 Element

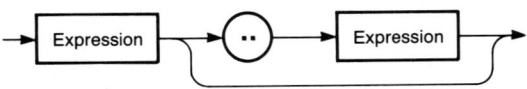

5.12 Designator

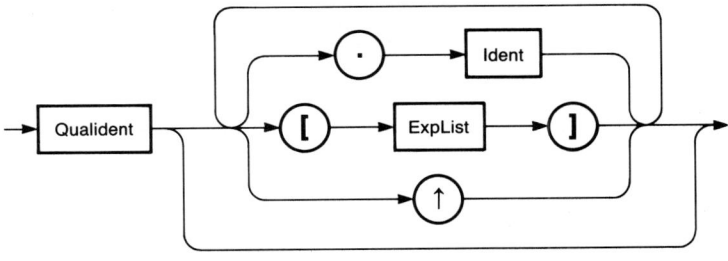

5.13 ActualParameters

6. Names and Literals

6.1 IdentList

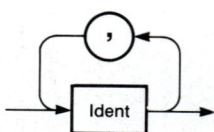

6.2 Qualident

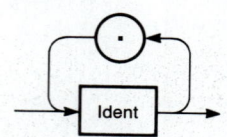

6.3 Ident

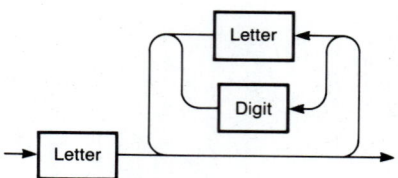

6.4 Number

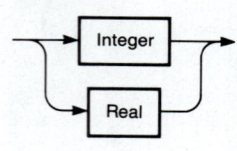

6.5 Integer

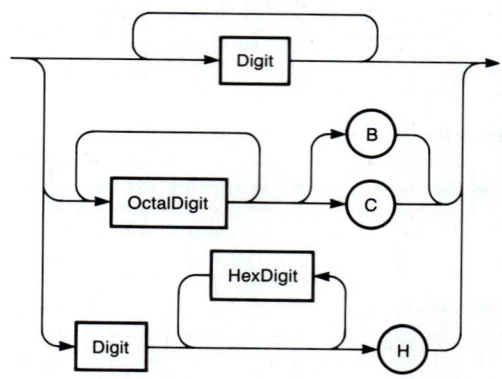

6.6 Real

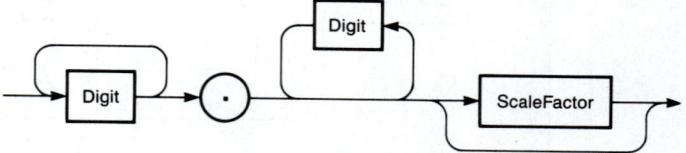

6.7 ScaleFactor

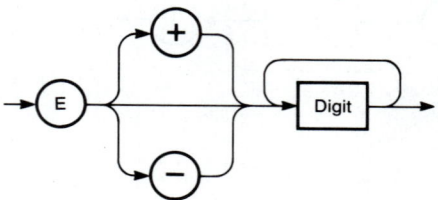

Appendix C A53

6.8 HexDigit

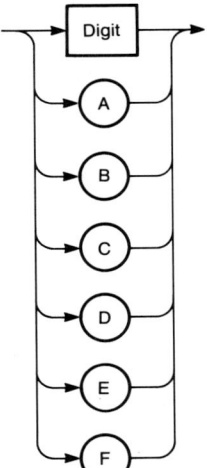

6.9 Digit

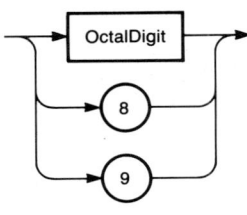

6.10 OctalDigit

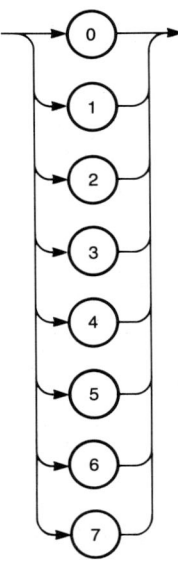

6.11 String

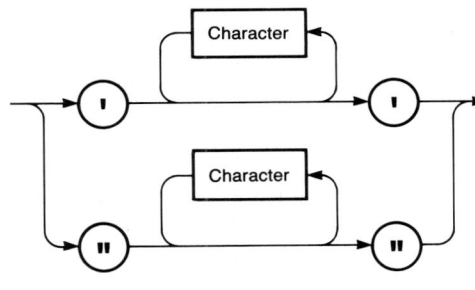

Appendix D From Pascal to Modula-2

This appendix gives a short introduction to Modula-2 for persons who are familiar with Pascal. Even though Modula-2 was designed by Pascal's author, Niklaus Wirth, there are many differences between the two languages.

Compilation Units

One of the basic differences between Modula-2 and Pascal is that Modula-2 offers separate compilation. Each portion of a program is called a module. The main program is a module that has only one part. Other modules have two parts: a definition part and an implementation part. Each part may be compiled separately.

A Modula-2 main program is introduced by the reserved word MODULE and is similar to a Pascal program, except that there is no list of program parameters following the program name. The main module is terminated by the reserved word END, the module name, and a period.

```
MODULE Example;
   :
END Example.
```

A definition module is introduced by the reserved words DEFINITION MODULE, and declares all objects that can be accessed from outside the module.

An implementation module is introduced by the reserved words IMPLEMENTATION MODULE, and completes the definition of objects that are partially declared in the corresponding definition module. Additional objects may be declared and used in the implementation module. However, only what is declared in the corresponding definition module is visible from the outside, the rest being hidden. The definition module can be considered a prefix to the implementation module.

In order to use objects declared in an external module, one must import them with an import statement introduced by the reserved word IMPORT. Modular design charts (*see* Sincovec and Wiener *Software Engineering with Modula-2 and Ada,* Wiley) describe the relationships between modules, by specifying what objects are imported from other modules. Figure D-1 gives an example of modular design chart.

The definition modules from which the current module imports must be compiled before the current module. In our example, the order of compilation must be: DEF B, DEF A, (Main Prog, IMP B, IMP A). The order of compilation for the elements inside the parentheses is not important, but all modules must be compiled before linking them to produce the executable program.

A good example of external modules is provided by Modula-2 input and output facilities. In Modula-2, input/output statements are not part of the language, and in order to do input/output operations, it is necessary to import procedures from standard external modules like InOut and RealInOut.

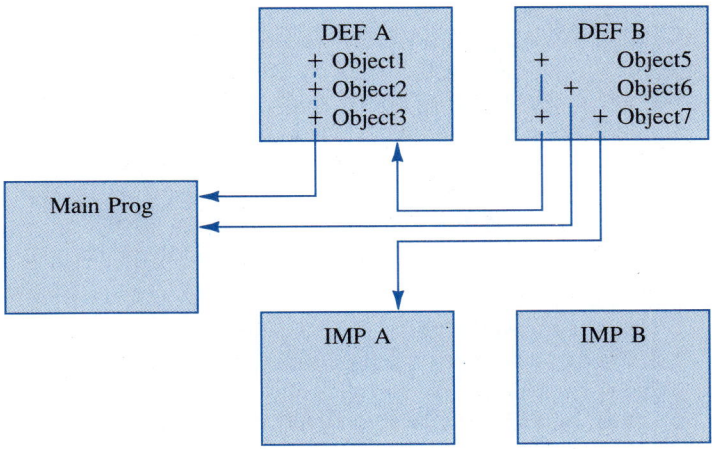

Figure D-1
An example of a Modular Design Chart

General Syntactic Differences

Reserved Words and Standard Identifiers Modula-2 has reserved words, which do not exist in Pascal:

BY, DEFINITION, ELSIF, EXIT, EXPORT, FROM, IMPLEMENTATION, IMPORT, LOOP, MODULE, POINTER, QUALIFIED and RETURN.

In turn, Pascal has a few reserved words which do not exist in Modula-2:

FILE, FUNCTION, GOTO, LABEL, NIL, PACKED, PROGRAM.

Modula-2 has a number of standard identifiers which do not exist in Pascal:

BITSET, CAP, CARDINAL, DEC, EXCL, FLOAT, HALT, HIGH, INC, INCL, LONGCARD, LONGINT, LONGREAL, MAX, MIN, NIL, PROC, SIZE, VAL.

A number of Pascal standard identifiers do not exist in Modula-2:

ARCTAN, COS, DISPOSE, EOF, EOLN, EXP, GET, LN, NEW, PACK, PAGE, PRED, PUT, READ, READLN, RESET, REWRITE, ROUND, SIN, SQR, SQRT, SUCC, TEXT, UNPACK, WRITE, WRITELN.

Some of the standard identifiers that we have listed as missing in Modula-2 are not part of the language itself but are available for importation from library modules.

Identifiers

While in Pascal the case of the letters used to write a program is not significant. This is not true in Modula-2. Reserved words in Modula-2 must appear in upper case letters. In identifiers the case of the letters is significant: "WordCount" is an identifier which is not the same as "WORDCOUNT" or as "wordcount". The number of significant characters in identifiers is limited in Pascal, while in Modula-2 all characters are significant.

Modula-2 uses the following characters in particular ways:

"{" and "}" are used as set brackets
"|" is used to separate the various cases in a CASE statement
"#" and "<>" are both used to test for not equal
"&" is used as a synonym for AND
"~" is used as a synonym for NOT.

Characters and Character Strings Constants

In Modula-2, character constants are enclosed in single or double quotes:

```
"a"
'd'
```

It is also possible to define characters by their octal character code followed by the capital letter C (indicating a constant of type CHAR):

```
CONST CR = 15C;
      Space = 40C;
```

Likewise, character strings are enclosed in double or single quotes:

```
"Here is one"
'and another one!'
```

It is not possible to have single and double quotes within the same string:

```
'He said "I have enough"'
"that's it".
```

Character strings of N characters are of type ARRAY[0..N] OF CHAR, as a null character is used to terminate the string. In Modula-2 it is possible to assign a string constant to any such "string" variable of equal or greater length. However, Modula-2 does not allow the use of the relational operators with "strings", thus most implementations provide a strings library module which usually contains the comparison procedures.

Comments

In Modula-2 they are enclosed between "(*" and "*)" only. They can also be nested, which is not the case in Pascal.

Declarations and Types

In Modula-2 declarations appear in any order and can be repeated, which is not the case in Pascal. There are declarations for constants (CONST), types (TYPE), variables (VAR), and procedures (PROCEDURE). Modula-2 allows us to use a constant expression at any place where a constant is required, for instance:

CONST Maximum = Minimum + 2*N;

where N is a constant.

In Modula-2, it is possible to use both octal and hexadecimal numbers. Octal numbers must be suffixed by letter B: 12757B. Hexadecimal numbers must not begin with a letter and must be suffixed by letter H, as in 0B12D7H. In Modula-2, real numbers must contain a decimal point, and at least one digit must precede it.

Besides the regular Pascal elementary types, we find several new types in Modula-2.

CARDINAL	unsigned integers
LONGREAL	long real numbers
LONGCARD	long positive integers
LONGINT	long integers
BITSET	bit access type
PROC	parameterless procedure type
POINTER TO t	instead of ^t

Subrange types must be declared with brackets as in:

TYPE Month=[1..12];

A procedure can be a value assigned to a variable having a procedure type, whereas in Pascal procedure types are restricted to procedure parameters.

In an array declaration the brackets are part of subranges used for index types, and not part of the array declaration.

ARRAY Color OF REAL;
ARRAY [1..10], CHAR, [1..2*N − 1] OF INTEGER;

Set declarations are similar in both languages, but there are several differences. The base type of a Modula-2 set must be an enumeration type, or a subrange of CARDINAL, with at most N values, where N is usually the memory word size. The definition of set constants is allowed in Modula-2, which is not the case in Pascal. Set constants are enclosed in braces, and, apart from standard set type BITSET, must be prefixed by their type name.

set type	TYPE Gift = SET OF Toys;
set constant	Gift {TeddyBear, Tricycle, Ball}
set constant	{2,4..8,10}

In addition to set operations +, −, *, Modula-2 also provides operator / (symmetric difference), and standard procedures INCL and EXCL.

In Modula-2 type CHAR is compatible with type ARRAY[0..1] OF CHAR, a one character string, and the empty string is allowed.

Module SYSTEM exports type WORD (or BYTE) which is compatible with any type taking up a word (or a byte) of memory. It also exports type ADDRESS which is compatible with all pointer types, and with type CARDINAL (or LONGCARD) for arithmetic operations.

Modula-2 record types are equivalent to Pascal record types, except for variants which can be multiple and appear anywhere in the record. Each variant declaration ends with its own END, and its syntax is similar to the CASE statement syntax, using | to separate variants, and possibly including an ELSE clause. Within a variant part, parentheses do not enclose field lists. Variants may be empty. If the tag field of a variant part is omitted, then the colon that normally follows it must remain.

Type compatibility is stricter in Modula-2 which does not allow mixing of real and integer values in expressions.

In Modula-2, there is no file types. These are usually provided by library modules.

Procedures and Functions

Proper procedures are declared in Modula-2 in the same way as in Pascal, however the procedure END must be followed by the procedure name. Parameterless procedure declarations and calls may include or omit the parentheses.

```
PROCEDURE Try (P1, P2: CARDINAL; VAR P3: REAL);
BEGIN
   :
END Try;
```

In Modula-2 the reserved word FUNCTION does not exist, PROCEDURE is used instead, and the rest of the function heading is similar to Pascal. However, parameterless functions must include in their declaration heading a pair of empty parenthesis, and the function calls must also include the pair of empty parenthesis.

```
Declaration:   PROCEDURE Func( ): CHAR;
               BEGIN
                  :
                 IF Cond THEN
                   RETURN "?";
                 ELSE
                   RETURN "!";
                 END;
               END Func;
Call:          Func( )
```

At least one RETURN statement must be present in a function procedure to indicate the value returned by the function. A RETURN not followed by an expression can also be used to exit a proper procedure.

In Modula-2 procedures can have one dimensional arrays of varying length as formal parameters, called open array parameters whose form is:

```
ARRAY OF Type
```

(the index type is omitted). The index used inside the procedure is a cardinal whose lower bound is zero, and whose upper bound can be obtained by a call to standard function HIGH, with the open array as its argument.

Statements

Consecutive statements must be separated by semicolons. However, programmers may use the semicolon as a statement terminator for most implementations.

Assignment statements are similar in both languages. However, Modula-2 does not allow the assignment of an integer value to a real variable.

```
x := {1, 2, 3};
y := Gift{TeddyBear};
z := z + Sqrt (Number*123.25);
```

Structured statements include other statements and all end with END, except REPEAT which, like in Pascal, ends with an UNTIL clause. Consequently, compound statements do not exist in Modula-2 as there is no need for them.

IF statements may include a number of ELSIF clauses.

```
IF Condition1 THEN
   a :=1;
ELSIF Condition2 THEN
   a := 2;
ELSIF Condition3 THEN
   a := 3;
ELSE
   a := 4;
END; (* IF *)
```

CASE statements use the character "|" to separate the various cases, and they may have an ELSE part. Case label lists contain constant expressions and may contain ellipses (..).

```
CASE Month OF
   1..4,10: WriteString ("one, two, three, four, ten");
 | 5,7:     WriteString("five, seven");
 | 2*N:     WriteString("2*N");
   ELSE     WriteString("otherwise");
END;  (* CASE *)
```

FOR statements may specify a step value which may be negative (there is no DOWNTO as in Pascal).

```
FOR i := 1 TO 10 DO          (* write 10 numbers *)
  WriteCard(i,5); WriteLn;
END;  (* FOR *)
FOR c := "z" TO "a" BY -2 DO (* write every other letter *)
  Write(c); WriteLn;
END;  (* FOR *)
```

LOOP statements have no equivalent in Pascal. They produce infinite repetitions unless they are combined with EXIT statements.

```
LOOP
    :
  IF Cond THEN EXIT END;
    :
END; (* LOOP *)
```

There is no GOTO statement in Modula-2, as the EXIT and RETURN statements usually cover the cases where GOTOs are used in Pascal.

In WITH statements only a single record variable may appear between WITH and DO, but it is possible to nest WITH statements.

Expressions

Expressions in Modula-2 are very much like expressions in Pascal. There are two major differences, though: type compatibility is even stricter in Modula-2 than in Pascal, and Boolean expressions including AND and OR operators are evaluated differently. The evaluation of a Boolean expression is stopped as soon as the expression value is known: part of the expression might not be evaluated. Thus, it is possible to program:

```
IF (L # NIL) AND (L^.Info # Item) THEN
  L := L^.Next;
END; (* IF *)
```

without any risk of a run time error: if L is NIL, the rest of the expression is not evaluated. Put another way, an AND expression is "short circuited" on the first FALSE condition to return FALSE and an OR expression is "short circuited" on the first TRUE condition to return TRUE.

Standard Procedures and Functions

Arithmetic functions are not standard in Modula-2, they must be imported from standard module MathLib0.

Standard procedure INC and DEC compute fast increments and decrements of variable scalar values, and replace Pascal's PRED and SUCC.

Standard function VAL is the inverse of function ORD.

There is no ROUND function in Modula-2. Pascal's NEW and DISPOSE procedures must be replaced by ALLOCATE and DEALLOCATE, which are imported from module Storage. Both ALLOCATE and DEALLOCATE require two parameters: a variable of pointer type and the amount of space being allocated or deallocated. The latter value is often obtained by using the standard procedure SIZE on the type of object pointed to, as in:

```
TYPE NodePtr = POINTER TO Node;
     Node = RECORD
              Data: CARDINAL;
              Link: NodePtr;
            END;
VAR L : NodePtr;
```

Space is allocated by:

```
ALLOCATE (L, SIZE(Node));
```

Deallocate has the same form. Some Modula-2 compilers support the NEW and DISPOSE operations as they appear in Pascal, but it is still necessary to import the standard procedures ALLOCATE and DEALLOCATE.

The following Modula-2 standard functions and procedures have no equivalent in Pascal.

- Procedure HALT terminates the execution of the program.
- Function CAP capitalizes an alphabetic character.
- Functions MAX and MIN return the largest and the smallest values in a type.
- Procedures INCL and EXCL provide set inclusion and exclusion, while operator / represents set symmetric difference.
- FLOAT is used for explicit conversion from CARDINAL to REAL, as there are no implicit conversions as in Pasal.
- SIZE(x) returns the number of storage units (bytes) assigned to variable or type x.

Module SYSTEM also provides function ADR(x) which returns the address of variable x, and function TSIZE(t) which returns the number of storage units assigned to variables of type t.

Answers to Selected Exercises

Chapter 1

1. Assignment operation.

2. ```
   Int := Grade;      VALID
   Exams[1] := Int;   INVALID
   Exams[3] := Card;  INVALID
   S3[1] := "string processing";   INVALID
   S1 := S2;    VALID
   S2 := S3;    INVALID
   S2[1] := 'A';      VALID
   S1[79] := S3[4];   VALID
   History[1, 1, 2] := black;   VALID
   History[50] := white;  INVALID
   Game[3, 8] := Grade;   INVALID
   History[7] := Game;    VALID
   3200 Square elements
   ```

Chapter 2

1. (a) $200 + 19 = 219$
   (b) $200 + (20 - 10 + 1) * (1 - (-10)) + (15 - 10) = 326$
   (c) $200 + (20 - 0 + 1) * (10 - 0) + (20 - 0) = 430$
   (d) $200 + (20 - 0 + 1) * (6 - 0) + (0 - 0) = 326$
   (e) $200 + (20 - 0 + 1) * (0 - 0) + (20 - 0) = 220$

3. The mapping function is:

   ```
   Address of A[i, j, k] = 200 + address relative to A[0, 1, -2];
       0 <= i <= 4,   1 <= j <= 3,   -2 <= k <= 0;

   Address of A[i, j, k] = 200 + i*9 + (j-1)*3 + k + 2
                         = 3 * (j - 1) * (3 * i + 1)
   ```

4. NewFormula = NewFormula base address + offset * SizeOfElement

6. Suppose the matrix is $N \times N$
   $$\text{Address}(M[i,j]) = \text{Address}(M[1,1]) + N * (N + 1)/2 - (N - i) * (N - i + 1)/2 - (N - j + 1).$$

9. To represent the bit map, we need $m * n / b$ words. P nonzero elements occupy P words. In total $m * n / b + P$ words.

A63
   ```

Chapter 3

1. (a) $O(n)$
   (b) $O(n^2)$
   (c) $O(2^y)$

5. True. If an algorithm only moves an element one position at a time, in the worst case, there may be $(n - 1) + (n - 2) + \cdots + 1$ moves, i.e., $((n - 1) * n / 2)$ moves. That is $O(n^2)$.

7. To compare S against another string, the complexity requirement is $O(length(S))$. Using binary search, the complexity is therefore $O(length(S) * n * log(n))$.

9. $O(n^2)$

11. $O(n^2)$

Chapter 4

4.
```
TYPE ComNum = RECORD
       real: REAL;
       imp : REAL;
     END; (* COMPLEX *)

     ComType = POINTER TO ComNum;

PROCEDURE ComAdd(ComX, ComY: ComType) : ComType;
PROCEDURE ComSub(ComX, ComY: ComType) : ComType;
PROCEDURE ComMul(ComX, ComY: ComType) : ComType;
PROCEDURE Create(RealPart, VirtPart: REAL) : ComType;
PROCEDURE Dispose(C: ComType);
PROCEDURE GetRealPart(C: ComType) : REAL;
PROCEDURE GetVirtPart(C: ComType) : REAL;
```

6.
```
TYPE Sequence = POINTER TO SequenceType;

PROCEDURE GetElement(n : CARDINAL) : Sequence;
PROCEDURE SeqLength(S : Sequence) : CARDINAL;
PROCEDURE EmptySeq(S : Sequence) : BOOLEAN;
PROCEDURE GetFirst(S : Sequence) : Sequence;
PROCEDURE GetLast(S : Sequence) : Sequence;
PROCEDURE AddFirst(VAR S : Sequence);
PROCEDURE DeleteFirst(VAR S : Sequence);
PROCEDURE AddLast(VAR S : Sequence);
PROCEDURE DeleteLast(VAR S : Sequence);
```

Chapter 5

1. Assume the linear list is implemented as an array, A[1] through A[n]:

   ```
   Reverse
       For i := 1 to (n div 2) Do
           Swap A[i] And A[n-i+1]
       End for
   End Reverse
   ```

2. Supposed the linear list structure is implemented dynamically:

   ```
   Concat(L1, L2)
     Set P to L1
     While P^.next is not NULL Do
         Set P to P^.next
     End while
     Set P^.next to L2
   End Concat
   ```

7. Assume the implementation is dynamic:

   ```
   AssignAndAdvance(T1, T2)
       Allocate T1^.next
       Set T1 to T1^.next
       Set T1^.Element to T2^.Element
       Set T2 to T2^.next
   End AssignAndAdvance

   Merge(A, B, C)
       Set A1 to A and B1 to B
       Allocate C and Assign element of A1
       Set A1 to A1^.next
       While A1 <> nil OR B1 <> NIL Do
           If A1 <> NIL AND B1 <> NIL Then
               AssignAndAdvance(C, B1)
               AssignAndAdvance(C, A1)
           Elsif A1 <> nil Then
               AssignAndAdvance(C, A1)
           Else
               AssignAndAdvance(C, B1)
           End if
       End while
       Set C^.next to nil
   End Merge
   ```

8. Here is an abstract algorithm:

   Find element P
   Insert E after P
   Swap E and P

10. Considering more general cases, assuming that the circular list is C, the given element is e and does exist and is not the head of the list, there is more than one element in the list:

```
DivideCircular(C, P1, P2)
    Set P1 and T to C
    Set P2 to C^.next
    While P2^.Element < > e Do
        Set T to P2
        Set P2 to P2^.next
    End while
    Set T^.next to P1
    Set T to P2
    While T^.next < > C Do
        Set T to T^.next
    End while
    Set T^.next to P2
End DivideCircular
```

15. Headers: 300 + 300 = 600 (words)
    Nodes: 5 * (300 * 5) = 7500 (words)
    Total: 600 + 7500 = 8100 (words)

16. Assume the array is n × m:

```
PrintArray
    For i := 1 to n Do
        get a new row pointer
        get first node
        For j := to m Do
            If column number is j Then
                print node content
                get next node
            Else
                print 0
            End if
        End for
    End for
End PrintArray
```

27. EqualSparseMatrix(M1, M2)
       If M1.Rows is not the same as M2.Rows OR
           M1.Columns is not the same as M2.Columns Then
           Return FALSE
       Else
           Compare each link list in each bucket in M1.Row and M2.Rows
           (not necessary to compare Columns)
           Return the result
       End if
    End EqualSparseMatrix

Chapter 6

1. To avoid popping from an empty stack:
   Start with an empty stack, the number of pops should be < or = the number of pushes at any time and when finished, the number of pops should equal the number of pushes.

2. We can use an index to indicate the status of the stack:

   index = 0;
   . . .
   NewPush(item)
      If index = StackSize Then
        report stack full
      Else
        increase index by 1
        push(item)
      End if
   End NewPush

   NewPop
      If index = 0 Then
        report stack empty
      Else
        pop
        decrease index by 1
      End if
   End NewPush

5. Assuming that top1 and top2 are the tops of stack:

   Push1(item)
      If top1 + 1 = top2 Then
        report stack 1 full
      Else
        top1 = top1 + 1
        Stack[top1] = item
      End if
   End Push1

   Pop1(item)
      If top1 = 0 Then
        report stack 1 empty
      Else
        item = Stack[top1]
        top1 = top1 − 1
      End if
   End Pop1

```
Push2(item)
    If top2 − 1 − top1 Then
        report stack 2 full
    Else
        top2 = top2 − 1
        Stack[top2] = item
    End if
End Push2

Pop2(item)
    If top2 = StackSize Then
        report stack 2 empty
    Else
        item = Stack[top2]
        top2 = top2 + 1
    End if
End Pop2
```

Advantages:
    Share space.

Disadvantages:
    Potential stack collision

6. CheckBalance
```
    GetToken
    While NOT end of the expression Do
        If token = '(' Then
            Push it into stack
        Elseif token = ')' Then
            If Empty(stack) Then
                report too many ')'
            Else
                Pop stack
            End if
        End if
        GetToken
    End
    If NOT Empty(stack) Then
        report too many '('
    End if
End CheckBalance
```

9. $A + B / C - D \rightarrow A B C / + D -$
$(A + B) * (C - D) + (E * F) / (G - H) \rightarrow A B + C D - * E F * G H - / +$
$(A - B) * C / (D + E) * (F + G) \rightarrow A B - C * D E + / F G + *$

10. Assume the postfix expression is legally formed:

    EvalPostfix
       While there are more token Do
          GetToken(ch)
          IF ch is operand Then
             Push(ch)
          Else
             Pop(opd2)
             Pop(opd1)
             set temp to opd1 character opd2
             Push(temp)
          End if
       End while
       Pop(result)
    End EvalPostfix

17. This procedure computes:
    $0 + 1 + 2 + \cdots + n$

    ```
    PROCEDURE IterativeF(N: CARDINAL): CARDINAL;
    VAR I, Sum : CARDINAL;
    BEGIN
      Sum := 0;
      FOR I = 0 TO N DO
         Sum := Sum + I;
      END; (* FOR *)
      RETURN Sum;
    END IterativeF;
    ```

18. SeriesPrint prints:
    1, 2, 1, 5, 1, 2, 1, 11, 1, 2, 5, 1, 2, 1,

Chapter 7

1. Assume the implementation is dynamic:

    ```
    DisplayQueue
       Set pointer P to head of Queue Q
       While P is not NIL Do
          Print(P^.Element)
          P := P^.next
       End while
    End DisplayQueue
    ```

3. IncrementQueue
```
   Set N to NumberOfElement(queue)
   For I := 1 To N Do
      DeQueue(queue, E)
      Set E to E + 1
      EnQueue(queue, E)
   End for
IncrementQueue
```

4. ReverseQueue
```
   While NOT Empty(queue) Do
      DeQueue(queue, E)
      Push(stack, E)
   End while
   While NOT Empty(stack) Do
      Pop(stack, E)
      EnQueue(queue, E)
   End while
ReverseQueue
```

6. Merge
```
   MergeQueues(queue1, queue2, Q)
      While NOT Empty(queue2) Do
         DeQueue(queue1, e)
         EnQueue(queue, e)
         Dequeue(queue2, e)
         EnQueue(queue, e)
      End while
      While NOT Empty(queue1) Do
         DeQueue(queue1, e)
         EnQueue(queue, e)
      End while
   End MergeQueues

   If Length(Q1) >= Length(Q2) Then
      MergeQueues(Q1, Q2, Q)
   Else
      MergeQueues(Q2, Q1, Q)
   End if
End Merge
```

8. Assume that the queue is implemented as a dynamic linear list and Key does exist in the queue:

Cancel(Key)
  Set pointer K head of the queue
  If K^.Element is Key Then
    Make K^.next head of the queue
  Else
    Set pointer Predecessor to head of the queue
    Set K to K^.next
    While K^.Element is not Key Do
      Set Predecessor to Predecessor^.next
      Set K to K^.next
    End while
    Set Predecessor^.next to K^.next
  End if
  free(Key)
End Cancel

Chapter 8

1. (a) E, N, O, C, K, L, M, I;
   (b) A;
   (c) D;
   (d) G, H, I, K, L, M;
   (e) G, I
   (f) 4
   (g) 2
   (h) A-B-F-J, A-D-G-K, A-D-H-L, A-D-H-M, B-F-J-N, B-F-J-O

2. Preorder: M, I, B, F, K, J, Z, P, N, S, T;

   Inorder: B, F, I, J, K, M, N, P, S, T, Z;

   Postorder: F, B, J, K, I, N, T, S, P, Z, M;

3. (a)

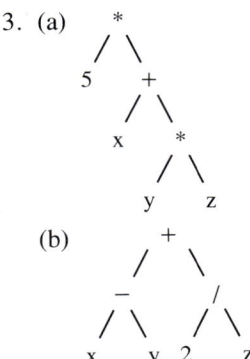

(b)

8. No. The following two trees have the same preorder and postorder traversals:

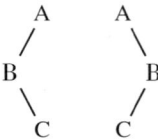

11. Yes.

12. (a) reverse inorder traversal;
    (b) reverse postorder traversal.

13. proof by induction on number of internal nodes:

    Basis: when the number of internal nodes is 0, the tree is a singleton.
    1. The equation holds.

    Assumption:
    when the number of internal nodes is m, the number of external nodes is m + 1;

    Inductive step:
    If we add two children onto an external node, the number of internal node will increase by 1, the number of external node will decrease by 1 because one external node has been turned into internal. That will make the total increase of external node be 1. The equation still holds.

18.

    CountNode(T)

      PreOrder(Tree)
        Set N to N + 1

        If Tree^.Left is not NIL Then
          PreOrder(Tree^.Left)
        End if
        If Tree^.Right is not NIL Then
          PreOrder(Tree^.Right)
        End if
      End PreOrder

      Set N to 0
      PreOrder(T)
      Return N
    End CountNode

```
CountLeaf(T)

    PreOrder(Tree)
        If Tree^.Left and Tree^.Right are both NIL Then
            Set N to N + 1
        End if
        If Tree^.Left is not NIL Then
            PreOrder(Tree^.Left)
        End if
        If Tree^.Right is not NIL Then
            PreOrder(Tree^.Right)
        End if
    End PreOrder

    If T is a singleton tree Then
        Return 1
    Else
        Set N to 0
    End if
    PreOrder(T)
    Return N
End CountNode
```

Chapter 9

1. A binary search tree is an ordered data structure. Any element has its proper position. Therefore no current node is needed in the ADT.

2. To retrieve an element from an ordinary binary tree, the complexity of the operation is $O(n)$. But for a binary search tree, it's $O(\log(n))$. (n is the number of nodes in the tree).

Chapter 10

1. None of them.

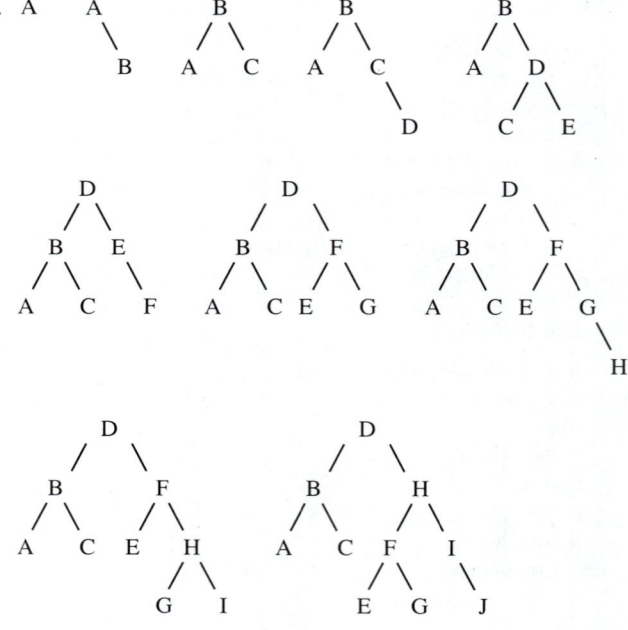

2.

7. Consider a non-leaf node D:
   1. If D's children are leaves, then it is certain that for any element in D, its immediate predecessor and immediate successor are in leaves;
   2. If D's children(child) are(is) not leaves(leaf). Let e be an element in D. Assume that e's immediate predecessor p is not in a leaf but an internal node I. Because of the structure of a B-tree, there must be an element that is greater than p (we can get it by searching along the successor link of e') and smaller than e. This contradicts the assumption that p is e's IMMEDIATE predecessor.
8. Not always. Delete element 8 from B-tree (c) in problem 5 and insert it back, we get a different tree. This depends on the way the deletion is done.

Chapter 12

2. Assuming the table is sorted by keys increasing order, and K1 and K2 are in the table:
   1. Locate K1 by binary search;
   2. Sequentially search through the table until K2 is found.

6. If M is an even number and K is an even number then the result of K MOD M is an even number. This hash function is not good because memory or storage with odd entries are not well utilized when keys are mostly even numbers.

7. (a) Ordered: log(N) to find out (binary search)
   Not ordered: N to find out (linear search)

   (b) Ordered: Less than log(N) (binary search)
   Not ordered: N ÷ 2 on the average

10. Advantages: Simple. Works well when the number of collisions is small;
    Disadvantages: Doesn't work well when the number of collisions is large. One has to search all elements placed in the secondary table, which could become quite big, when a collision happens.

11. Search for a key:

    There is actually no improvement with sorted chain when the key does exist. There is minor improvement when the key is not in the chain. But it still takes linear time to find out. Thus the improvement is not significant.

    Insert a key:

    With the sorted chain, it would take in average (n + 1) / 2 + (time for inserting), which is linear. If the chain is not sorted, it would only take (time for inserting), which is constant.

Chapter 13

1. Assume Match is a procedure that returns the starting position of a match or 0 if no match:

```
NumOccurrences
   Set Count to 0
   CopyText(Text, Temp)
   While more text in Temp Do
      Set N to Match(Pattern, Temp)
      If N = 0 Then
         EXIT
      Else
         Count := Count + 1
         Delete characters from start to position N in Temp
      End if
   End while
End NumOccurrences
```

2. (a) String: ARRAY [1..N] OF CHAR;
   (b) String: ARRAY [1..8] OF CHAR;
   (c) CellPtr = POINTER TO Cell

   TYPE   Cell = RECORD
                    Element : CHAR;
                    next : CellPtr;
                 END; (* RECORD *)
   VAR   String: CellPtr;

5. Assuming the implementation is static:

   Cut(String)
     Set I to 0
     While String[I] is not NULL Do
       Increment I
     End while
     If String [I − 1] is space Then
       Decrement I
       While String[I] is space Do
         Decrement I
       End while
       Set String[I + 1] to NULL
     End if
   End Cut

8. 1. babarbarbados

Mismatch Pos	Match	Backup
1	none	0
2	b	1
3	ba	0
4	bab	1
5	baba	3
6	babar	0
7	babarb	1
8	babarba	3
9	babarbar	0
10	babarbarb	1
11	babarbarba	3
12	babarbarbad	1
13	babarbarbado	1

Chapter 14

3. ```
VerifyList(List)
    Set Count to 0
    While the list is not empty
        GetToken(T)
        Case T
            '(': Set Count to Count + 1
            ')': Set Count to Count - 1
        End case
        If Count < 0 Then
            Output("ill-formed S-expression")
        End if
    End while
    If Count < > 0 Then
        Output("ill-formed S-expression")
    Else
        Output("correct S-expression")
    End if
End VerifyList.
```

5. ```
(DEFUN NEWMEMBER(X STRUCT)
    (COND ((NULL STRUCT) NULL)
          ((ATOM (CAR STRUCT))
              (COND ((EQ X STRUCT) T)
                    (T NEWMEMBER(X (CDR STRUCT))))) 
          ((NEWMEMBER X (CAR STRUCT)) T)
          (T NEWMEMBER(X (CDR STRUCT)))))
```

6. ```
(DEFUN ERASEALL(Y STRUCT)
    (COND ((NULL STRUCT) NIL)
          ((EQ Y (CAR STRUCT)) (ERASEALL Y (CDR STRUCT)))
          (T (CONS (CAR STRUCT)
                   (ERASEALL Y (CDR STRUCT))))))
```

8. ```
(DEFUN REVERSE(LIST)
    (COND ((NULL LIST) NIL)
          ((ATOM LIST) LIST)
          (T (APPEND (REVERSE (CDR LIST))
                     (REVERSE (CAR LIST))))))
```

9. ```
(DEFUN EQUAL(L1 L2)
    (COND ((NULL L1) NIL)
          ((NULL L2) NIL)
          ((ATOM L1)
              (COND ((ATOM L2) (EQ L1 L2))
                    (T NIL)))
          ((EQ (CAR L1) (CAR L2)) (EQUAL (CDR L1) (CDR L2)))
          (T NIL)))
```
```

Chapter 15

1. There is 1 path of length 1 from vertex 1 to vertex 2;
   The result of the square of the adjacency matrix is:

   0 1 1 1
   0 1 0 1   entry [1, 2] = 1
   0 1 2 0   There is 1 path of length 2 from vertex 1 to vertex 2
   0 1 1 1

   The result of the cube of the adjacency matrix is:

   0 2 2 1
   0 1 2 0   entry [1, 2] = 2
   0 2 1 2   There are 2 paths of length 3 from vertex 1 to vertex 2;
   0 2 2 1

2.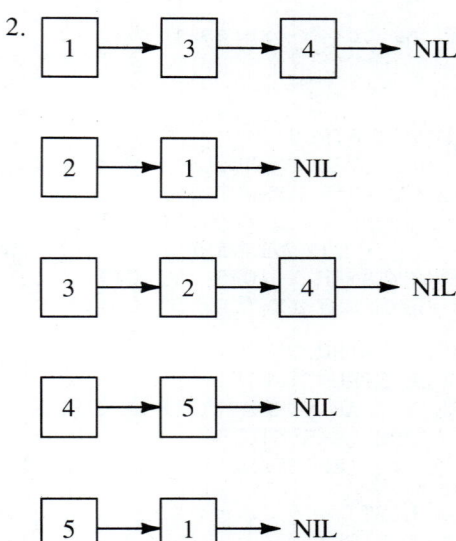

5.

Vertex	Early	Late
1	0	0
2	7	7
3	6	10
4	18	18
5	14	14
6	20	20
7	19	24
8	23	23
9	26	26
10	29	29

The minimum duration of the project is 29.
Activities 1, 2, 4, 5, 6, 8, 9, 10 are critical.
If we speed up activities 2 or 9, we will speed up the whole project.

Chapter 16

1.
   (a) Member(2, X) = TRUE;
   (b) Include(X, 4) = X;
   (c) Exclude(X, 4) = {1,2,3};
   (d) Min(Y) = 3;
   (e) Union(Z, X, Y) → Z = {1,2,3,4,5,6};
   (f) Intersection(Z, X, Y) → Z = {3,4};
   (g) Difference(Z, X, Y) → Z = {1,2};

2. DisplaySet(S)

```
    Set e to Min(S)
    While e <= Max(S) Do
        If Member(e, S) Then
            Display(e)
        End if
        Increment(e)
    End while
End DisplaySet
```

3.
   (a) Set N to a − b + 1; map a to 1, a + 1 to 2, . . . , b to N.
   (b) Set N to 26; map 'a' to 1, 'b' to 2, . . . , 'z' to N.

4.
```
PROCEDURE In(D; Dictionary; e: NameType): BOOLEAN;
VAR I: CARDINAL;
BEGIN
   FOR I:= 1 to D.Last DO
      IF D.Data[I] = e THEN
         RETURN TRUE;
      END (* IF *)
   END (* FOR *)
   RETURN FALSE;
END In;

PROCEDURE Insert(VAR D: Dictionary; e: NameType);
BEGIN
   D.Last := D.Last + 1;
   D.Data[Last] := e;
END Insert;

PROCEDURE Delete(VAR D: Dictionary; e: NameType): BOOLEAN;
(* If successful, return TRUE, FALSE otherwise *)
VAR I, J : CARDINAL;
BEGIN
   I := 1;
   WHILE (D.Data[I] # e) AND (I <= D.Last) DO
      I := I + 1;
   END; (* WHILE *)
   If I > D.Last THEN
      RETURN FALSE;
   ELSE
      FOR J := I TO D.Last - 1 DO
         D.Data[J] := D.Data[J + 1];
      END; (* FOR *)
      D.Last := D.Last - 1;
      RETURN TRUE;
   END; (* IF *)
END Delete;
```

7. ```
PROCEDURE Member(S: Set; e: ElementType): BOOLEAN;
VAR Bucket: BucketType;
    P: POINTER TO Node;
BEGIN
   Bucket := hash(e);
   If S[Bucket] = NIL THEN
      RETURN FALSE;
   ELSE
      P := S[Bucket];
      WHILE P # NIL DO
         IF P^.element = e THEN
             RETURN TRUE
         END; (* IF *)
         P := P^.next;
      END; (* WHILE *)
      RETURN FALSE;
   END; (* IF *)
END Member;
```
```

Index

ABS, 5
Abstract data type, 83, 84, 86, 115, 279, 281, 342, 445, 475, 533–534
Abstraction, 84, A14
Access, 30, 44, 148, 155, 390
Access time, 39, 145
Ackermann, 232–233
Activation record, 211–213
Activity graph, 578, 605
Acyclic graph, 570, 578
Ada, A6
AddFractions procedure, 100, 110
AddIntegers procedure, 125
AddPolynomials procedure, 127
AddTime function, 240
ADDRESS, 207, 264
Address, 33, 38, 46, 144, 147
Adelson-Velskii, 364
Adjacency
 list, 589–590, 595, 598, 601, 603–604, 607
 matrix, 581–582, 585–586, 588–589, 595, 597, 603–604
Adjacent, 389, 566
ADT, 83–85, 87, 92, 94, 98, 108, 116–117, 122, 139, 152, 175, 183, 203, 254, 256, 277, 323, 359, 450, 475, 604, 606, 611, 619, 622, 638
ALGOL, 29, 67
Algorithm, 17, 32, 49–50, 52, 56, 69, 187, 209–210, 238, 292, 309, 325, 344, 349, 360, 376, 395, 398, 400, 409, 416, 434, 451, 454, 465, 477, 530, 550–551, 554, 558–559, 570, 573, 580, 585, 588, 595–596, 604, 615–616, 618, 620, 632, A5–A9, A11–A12, A14, A32

Analysis, 32, 49, 66, 70, 376, 423, A7
Boyer-Moore, 513
Dijkstra's, 595–596, 598, 603, 607
Floyd's, 585, 588, 595, 598, 603, 607
Knuth-Morris-Pratt, 510
Kruskal's, 618–619, 621, 626, 629–630, 632
Prim's, 576–577, 618
Rabin-Karp, 515
Schorr-Waite-Deutsch, 550
Warshall's, 585–586
Alias, 485
All pairs shortest path, 586, 595, 603
ALLOCATE, 97, 177, 200, 201, 305
Allocate procedure, 137–138, 207, 305
AllocateGeneric procedure, 207
AllocateMinorHeader procedure, 171
Allocation, 34, 149
Alphabet, 482
Analysis of algorithms, 32, 49, 66, 70, 376, 423
Ancestor, 394
AND, 6
ARRAY, 4, 26, 30
Array, 7, 29–30, 143, 148, 639
Arrive procedure, 242
ASCII, 5, 291, 459, 482
Assertion, A6–A7, A12, A26, A32
Assign procedure, 87, 95, 483, 497, 507, 613, 625, 639
AssignChar procedure, 88, 484, 501
AssignConst procedure, 87, 483, 498, 506

AssignElement procedure, 451
AssignFraction procedure, 111
Assignment compatible, 13
AssignObject procedure, 207
Associated vector, 147
Atom, 534, 536, 542–543, 550–551, 610
ATOM operator, 537
Atomic, 4, 26
Auxiliary vector, 37
AVL tree, 363–364, 376, 405–406
AVLTree type, 366

B tree, 363, 377–378, 380, 405–406
Background job, 252
Backtrack, 283–284, 287, 551
Backup table, 510
BackwardTraversal procedure, 343, 357
Balance factor, 364–366, 369
Base
 case, 68, 208–209, 230
 type, 6, 9
BASIC, 29, 220
Basic data type, 124
Batch job, 252
Best fit, 151, 176
BestMove procedure, 319
Big-O, 49, 50, 78, A7
Big-omega, 51
Binary
 insertion sort, 64
 search, 42–43, 55, 64, 79, 379, 454, 466, 476
 search tree, 281, 327–328, 330, 334, 359, 364, 395–396, 400, 465, 606, 630, 639
 tree, 281, 284, 323, 364, 431, 451
BinarySearch procedure, 56, 477

Index

BinarySearchTree type, 336, 397, 401
BinaryTree type, 285
BinaryTreeADT module, 285, 297, 326
BinTreeElements module, 315
Bit, 622
  map, 43, 44, 46
  vector, 622, 638
BITSET, 9, 472, 610–611, 616, 622, 626
BOOLEAN, 4, 6, 26
Bottom-up
  development, A10
  testing, A11, A28
Boyer-Moore algorithm, 513
Branch, 280
Breadth first, 284, 288, 572, 574, 576
BreadthFirst procedure, 575
BreadthFirstSearch procedure, 289
BreadthFirstTraversal procedure, 574
Breakpoint, A13
BSTreeADT module, 328, 336
BTree type, 377
Bubble sort, 64, 79
BubbleSort procedure, 65
Bucket, 465, 476
Buddy system, 150, 176
Buffer, 330, 334, 504
Bugs, A20
BuildNodes procedure, 437
BuildTree procedure, 397, 402
BYTE, 204, 205
Byte, 89

C, A6
Caesar's cipher, 492
Call, 219
CAP, 5
CAR operator, 537, 545
CARDINAL, 4, 13, 26, 115, 124, 215, 330, 600
Cardinality function, 613, 616, 625
Cascade sort, 441
CASE tools, A14
CDR operator, 537, 546
Ceiling function, 456

Center procedure, 530
Central memory, 29
CentralStation module, 240, 277–278
Chaining, 464, 476
Change log, A12, A15
ChangeElement procedure, 154, 169
CHAR, 4, 5, 26
Character, 482, 496, 530
  code, 291
  string, 481–482, 496, 529–530
Chart
  modular design, 16, 20, 447
  structure, 16, 72, 99, 224–225, 253, 308–310, 432–433, 527
CheckCPUJobQueues procedure, 266
CheckNewJobs procedure, 254, 266
Child, 281, 293, 345–349, 365–366, 395, 412, 435
CHR, 5
Cipher, 495
Ciphering machine, 495
Circular list, 139, 176
Clear procedure, 568, 583, 591, 620, 638
Clock cycle, 253, 258, 260
Close procedure, 14, 90
Closed hash table, 468
Clustering, 461–463
Coalesced chaining, 466, 468, 470, 474–475
COBOL, 29, 212, 219
Code generation, 187
Coding, A1, A9, A11, A13, A15, A21, A28, A32
Collision, 458, 460, 462–463, 466, 468, 472, 476
Column major order, 34
Combine procedure, 388
ComesBefore procedure, 11
Comment, A11–A12, A26, A29
Communication graph, 618
Compact procedure, 557, 563
Compaction, 550, 557, 561
CompareKeys function, 451
CompareObjects function, 207
ComparePowers function, 126

Comparison function, 60, 229
Compatible, 12
Compilation, 86, 198, 202, 291, 390, 481
Compiler, 445, 450
Complex numbers, 116
Complexity, 49–53, 55, 56, 64, 67, 70, 78, 136–137, 201, 339–340, 376, 392, 412, 415, 418, 423, 431, 440, 465, 503, 510, 513, 517, 530, 549, 551, 554, 558, 562, 578, 586, 588, 597–598, 604, 621, 630, 632–633, A1, A7–A8
  class, 51, 78, A7
Component, 4, 7–9, 13, 30, 618, 632, A10–A11, A18–A19, A26, A29
Composite type, 7
ComputeBackup procedure, 511
ComputeDistribution procedure, 426
ComputeNumberOfLeaves procedure, 436
ComputerSimulation module, 274
ComputerSystem module, 254, 264
ComputeSkip procedure, 514
Concat procedure, 88, 484, 499
Concatenation, 482
Concordance list, 531
COND special form, 538
Configuration, 262
Connected graph, 566, 573–575, 618
CONS operator, 537
ContinuePrinting procedure, 255, 268
Conversion procedure, 188
Copy procedure, 87, 93, 96, 483, 498, 507
CopyItem procedure, 427
CopyList procedure, 563
CopyRest procedure, 22
CopyRun procedure, 427
COUNTATOMS function, 539
CountQueue function, 237, 248
CountWords module, 91, 117
CPM, 578

CPU, 246, 251–253, 256, 258–260, 276
CPUActive function, 254, 266
CPUFinished function, 266
Create procedure, 444, 452, 568, 582, 590
CreateDictionary procedure, 614
CreateFraction procedure, 100, 109
CreateList procedure, 122, 129, 133, 543
CreateNode procedure, 356, 368
CreateQueue procedure, 236, 247, 249
CreateSet procedure, 612, 623, 627
CreateSquare procedure, 494
CreateStack procedure, 183, 199, 201
CreateTree procedure, 285, 297, 328, 336, 342, 353, 437
Critical path, 579
  method, 578
CriticalPath procedure, 579
Cryptography, 491, 527, 531
Current node, 284, 301, 346
Cycle, 566, 606

Dag, 570
Data, 3, 20, 491
  base, 142–143, 445, 481
  encryption, 450, 491
  structure, 4, 7, 116, 154, 156, 181, 226, 276, 279, 343, 412, 415–416, 450, 533, 638, A1, A8–A9, A17
  type, 4, 25, 84
DBMS, 142
DEALLOCATE, 97, 177, 200–201, 305
Deallocate procedure, 137–138, 305
Deallocation, 547
Debugging, A12–A13, A26–A28
DEC, 5
Deciphering, 491
Decision tree, 102
Decode procedure, 531
Decomposition, A2–A4

Definition
  module, 83, 86, 99, A9, A13
  problem, A1–A2, A13, A15, A30, A32
Degenerate binary tree, 339, 364, 391, 395, 405
Degree, 280
Delete procedure, 14, 87, 90, 95, 123, 130, 134, 170, 445, 453, 484, 497, 508, 614, 639
DeleteEdge procedure, 569, 584, 593
DeleteElement procedure, 385
DeleteNode procedure, 285, 300, 329, 337, 342, 357, 360, 371
DeleteTree procedure, 285, 298, 329, 336
DeleteVertex procedure, 568, 583, 592
Deletion, 347–349, 371, 374–376, 384, 405–406, 504
Denominator, 98, 101, 114, 115
Depth, 280
Depth first, 284, 287, 572, 576
DepthFirst procedure, 572
DepthFirstSearch procedure, 288
DepthFirstTraversal procedure, 572
Deque, 277
Dequeue procedure, 237, 248, 250, 392, 394, 406, 575
Dereference, 97
Descendant, 280–281, 301, 316, 324, 337, 354–355, 378
Descriptive vector, 37
Design, 15, 72, 98, 152, 224, 251, 307, 340, 395, 431, 466, 517, 546, 595, 632, A1–A2, A5, A9, A11–A16, A29–A36, A32
Deutsch, Peter, 549
Diagonal matrix, 38–39, 45
Dictionaries module, 614
Dictionary type, 614
Difference, 10, 610, 622
DIFFERENCE operator, 537
Difference procedure, 332, 612, 624
Digraph, 570
Dijkstra, Edsger, 595

Dijkstra procedure, 599
DijkstraAll procedure, 601
Dijkstra's algorithm, 595–596, 598, 603, 607
Direct
  access, 458
  indexing, 458
Directed graph, 566–567, 570–571, 581
Directory, 146
Disk, 252, 260, 276
DiskActive function, 254, 267
DiskFinished function, 267
DispatchJob procedure, 255, 270
DisplayElement procedure, 331
DisplayKeys procedure, 445, 453
DisplayMatrix procedure, 165
DisplayMenu procedure, 351
DisplayNode procedure, 343
DisplaySet procedure, 639
DisplaySquare procedure, 317
DisplayTree procedure, 286, 303, 329, 339, 343, 359, 397, 405
DisplayWord procedure, 331
DISPOSE, 98
DisposeFraction procedure, 100, 110
DisposeMatrix procedure, 153, 167
DisposeQueue procedure, 236, 248, 250
DisposeStack procedure, 184, 200, 202, 204
DisposeString procedure, 88, 96, 485, 498
DisposeTree procedure, 342, 354, 401
Distinct representatives, 615
DistinctReps procedure, 616
Distribution, 390, 424, 426–427, 456, 459, 518
DIV, 4, 209, 418
Divide and conquer, 67, 208, A2, A16
DIVIDE operator, 537
DivideFractions procedure, 100, 110
Division, 459

Documentation, 25, 78, 115, 173, 230, 276, 323, 359, 405, 440, 475, 529, 558, 604, 638, A1, A13–A15, A29, A32
Dotted pair, 536, 540
Double hashing, 463, 479
Double rotation, 364, 366, 376
Doubly linked list, 141, 176
Driver, A10–A11, A29
Dummy run, 425
Dynamic, 37, 122, 132, 136–137, 139–140, 149, 176, 182, 201, 213, 249, 276, 297, 323, 359, 450, 464, 541, 546, 549, 627
   variable, 97

EBCDIC, 5, 291, 459, 482
EBNF, 290
Edge, 566, 581, 589, 592–594, 596, 598–599, 602, 618
Efficiency, 32, 49, 60, 154, 214, 304, 339, 548
Eight queens, 27, A8
Element, 610
Eliminate function, 446, 449
Elimination, 431
Empty function, 184, 200–201, 204, 613, 625
Empty set, 610
EmptyTree function, 342, 353
Enciphering, 491
Encode procedure, 495
Encryption, 450, 491
End of string, 504
Enqueue procedure, 236, 248, 250, 392–393, 406, 575
Enumeration, 6
EOF function, 91
EQ operator, 537
Equal function, 612, 624
EqualElements function, 124
EqualNames function, A23
EqualObjects function, 207
ERASE function, 538
Error, A12, A20, A27–A29
Euclid, 209
Euler, 565
EvaluateSquare procedure, 317
Evaluation, 536
Event, 238–240, 244, 578–579
Event-vertex network, 578–579
ExchangeAndDelete procedure, 372
EXCL, 10, 611
Exclude function, 612, 623, 631, 639
Exclusive or, 466, 495
ExistNode function, 286, 303
ExpandTree procedure, 318
Exponent, 5
Exponential, 52, 78
Expression tree, 289–291
External
   documentation, A13, A30
   fragmentation, 149
   sorting, 409, 418, 440

FACT function, 539
Factorial, 208, 214
   function, 208
False reference, 547
Family tree, 326
FastFibo function, 217
FetchChar function, 88, 484, 501
FetchElement procedure, 154, 169
Fibo function, 217
Fibonacci
   function, 215, 326
   numbers, 231, 424, 425–426
   search, 454
FibonacciSearch function, 455, 477
Field, 4, 8, 121, 160, 194, 249, 293, 343
FIFO, 235
File, 13, 26, 89, 92, 390, 418, 422–423, 425–428, 431, 481
   type, 13, 89
FileCopy procedure, 93, 117
Files module, 89, 92
FileSystem module, 13
Find function, 620, 638
FindMinVertex procedure, 599, 602
FindNode function, 134, 139, 342, 355
FindPredecessor function, 300, 342, 354
FindSuccessor function, 342, 354
FindVertex procedure, 569, 584, 593
First class citizen, 213
First fit, 149, 176
First in/first out, 235, 246, 392
FIRSTATOM function, 538
Fixed size, 151, 176
FlattenTree procedure, 401
FLOAT, 5
Flow of control, A19
Floyd's algorithm, 585, 588, 595, 598, 603, 607
Folding, 459
Forest, 280
Form, 536
Format, A2, A15
FORTRAN, 29, 45, 213, 219–220
ForwardTraversal procedure, 342, 357
Fraction type, 99
Fractions, 98
   module, 99, 108, 117
FractionToReal function, 101
FractionToString procedure, 100, 113
Fragmentation, 149
Free
   list, 151–152
   procedure, 207
   space, 149
FreeGeneric procedure, 207
Frequency, 492, 517, 519
Full binary tree, 296, 324–325, 339, 392
Full function, 199
Function, A26

Game, 279, 307
   tree, 308
Gap, 411–412, 441, 490
Garbage collection, 533, 546, 548, 562
Gathering, 548, 550–551, 557
GCD function, 109, 209, 218
Generalized list, 121, 533, 534
Generate procedure, 241
GenerateSquare procedure, 316
GenerateString procedure, 523
Generation procedure, 190
Generic type, 203–204

GenericStacks module, 204–205
GenericType type, 207
Get procedure, 123, 131, 136, 188
GetAddress procedure, 446, 449
GetAdjacent procedure, 569, 584, 594
GetBooleanResponse procedure, 274
GetChoice function, 107, 164, 351
GetCPUJob procedure, 254, 266
GetCurrentNode procedure, 286
GetDeviceNumbers procedure, 273
GetDiskJob procedure, 255, 267
GetFraction procedure, 107
GetMatrixValues procedure, 154, 169
GetName procedure, 446, 448
GetNumber procedure, 111
GetPhone procedure, 446, 449
GetPrinterJob procedure, 255, 268
GetValidDeviceCount function, 273
GetValue procedure, 207
GetWord procedure, 332, 486
Gilstad, R. L., 423
Global
 data, A12
 rebalancing, 395
Go to, 220, 221
Graph, 566, 578, 582, 588–589, 597–598, 601, 604–605, 618
 theory, 565
 type, 568, 582, 590
Graphs module, 568, 582, 590, 606
GREATERP operator, 537
Greatest common divisor, 104
Greedy, 595, 596

Hanoi procedure, 210
Hash
 function, 458–461, 465, 468, 469, 472, 476–478, 515
 index, 460
 table, 454, 457, 464, 466, 476–477, 631, 639–640
HashCoalesced procedure, 473
HashFunction function, 472
HashRandom procedure, 472
Head, 246, 417

Header, 142, 154–155, 160, 297
Heap, 213, 392–395, 405–406, 412–413
 sort, 412–413, 440–441
HeapSort procedure, 414
Height, 280, 324, 365–366, 373, 378, 380, 390
 balanced tree, 364, 395
Heterogeneous, 8
HIGH, 8, 59
High precision arithmetic, 124, 141, 177
HiredFirst procedure, 11
Hoare, C. A. R., 67
Homogeneous, 8, 31, 44
Huffman, 291–292, 324, 391
HuffmanCodes module, 294

Identifier, 390
IEEE, 5
Iliffe, 143, 176, 177
Implementation, 21, 33, 38, 76, 94, 108, 128, 132, 143, 167, 199, 201, 227, 246, 249, 262, 297, 304, 314, 335, 353, 400, 436, 450, 471, 496, 504, 520, 540, 555, 581, 598, 622, 632, 634, 636, A1, A4, A9, A13–A14, A20–A21, A32
 module, 83, 94
Improper fraction, 98
IN, 610
In function, 614, 639
INC, 5
Incident, 566
INCL, 10, 611
Include procedure, 612, 623, 627, 630–631
Inclusion, 610, 622
Incremental, 395
Indentation, A11, A26, A29
Index, 330
 type, 7, 30
Induction, A6
Infix, 185, 290
InfixToCode module, 188
Information
 hiding, 84, 115–116, 153, 200
 retrieval, 279

InitElement procedure, 451
Initial procedure, 620, 637
Initialization, 94
Initialize procedure, 447
InitializeStandings procedure, A22
InitialRuns procedure, 428
InitJobs procedure, 254, 265
InitMatrix procedure, 153, 167
InitMaze procedure, 196
InitString procedure, 87, 95, 483, 497, 505
Inorder, 284, 289, 324, 343, 360, 396–397, 400
InOrder procedure, 397, 404
InOrderSearch procedure, 302
Input, A2
Input/output, A2, A4, A13, A17
 format, A2
 redirection, 15, 163, 257, A16
InputString procedure, 89, 485, 502
Insert procedure, 88, 123, 130, 134, 140, 170, 403, 445, 452, 484, 499, 508, 614, 639
InsertEdge procedure, 568, 583, 591
InsertElement procedure, 381
Insertion, 369, 370, 376, 378, 380–381, 383, 398, 406, 504
 procedure, 368
 sort, 61, 79–80
InsertionSort procedure, 62
InsertNode procedure, 285, 298, 329, 336, 342, 354, 368
InsertVertex procedure, 568, 583, 591
InsertWord procedure, 332
INTEGER, 4, 13, 26, 115, 124
Interface, A3, A10
Internal
 documentation, A13, A29
 fragmentation, 149
 node, 436, 439
 sorting, 409–410
Interpolation search, 456
InterpolationSearch function, 457
Intersection, 10, 610, 622
 procedure, 612, 624, 628
INTERSECTION function, 539
Intractable, 52, 78

Inverted list, 142
Invocation, 211
IsDigit function, 111
IsUser function, 446, 448
Iteration, 213, 217, 219, 226
IterFactorial function, 214
IterFibonacci function, 216
IterGCD function, 218
IterHanoi procedure, 222, 233
IterQuicksort procedure, 227, 233

Job, 252, 254, 264
JobsActive function, 255, 271
JobsToCPU procedure, 266
JobToDisk procedure, 268
JobToPrinter procedure, 269
Julius Caesar, 492
Justify procedure, 486, 530

Key, 15–17, 53, 56, 330, 337, 345, 359, 392, 399–400, 418, 444, 456–458, 464, 468, 471, 477
Keyed alphabet, 492
Knight's tour, 46
Knuth, D. E., 55, 412
Knuth-Morris-Pratt algorithm, 510
KnuthMorrisPratt function, 511, 528–529
Königsberg bridges, 565
Kruskal procedure, 621
Kruskal's algorithm, 618–619, 621, 626, 629–630, 632

Labeled adjacency matrix, 581
Lambda calculus, 535
Landis, 364
Last in/first out, 182, 194, 230
LDijkstra procedure, 602
Leaf, 280, 324, 345, 347, 356, 377, 380, 383–384, 387, 393, 432, 435, 439–440
LeftBalance procedure, 372
LeftRightRotate procedure, 367
LeftRotate procedure, 367
Length, 566
  function, 87, 95, 483, 497, 505
LESSP operator, 537
LessThan function, 403
Letter sequencing, 396

Level, 280
Lexical analyzer, 390, 450
Lexicographic
  allocation, 34, 37, 45
  order, 34
Liberation, 149, 152
LIFO, 182
Linear
  insertion sort, 61
  list, 121–122, 175, 231, 236, 392, 450, 504, 530, 533, 561, 589, 630–631
  ordering, 570, 610–611
  probing, 461, 466, 474–475
Linked list, 154, 464, 478, 627, 639–640
Lisp, 533, 535, 539–540, 562
List, 121, 542
  adjacency, 589–590, 595, 598, 601, 603–604, 607
  circular, 139, 176
  concordance, 531
  copy, 558
  doubly linked, 141, 176
  free, 151–152
  generalized, 121, 533, 534
  header, 141–142, 146, 542, 544
  inverted, 142
  linear, 121–122, 175, 231, 236, 392, 450, 504, 530, 533, 561, 589, 630–631
  linked, 154, 464, 478, 627, 639–640
  multilinked, 142, 176
  pushdown, 182
  symmetric, 140–141, 176
  type, 122
ListADT module, 122, 129, 133
ListElements module, 124–125
ListError, 124
ListLength function, 123, 135
Local, A12, A26
  module, 244
  procedure, 431, 439
  variable, 211
Logarithm, 52, 78
Logo, 535
LONGCARD, 4, 124
LONGINT, 4, 124
LONGREAL, 4

Lookup procedure, 14
Loop invariant, A6–A7
Low level, 204
Lower triangular matrix, 40

Main memory, 13
Maintenance, 173, A14, A20, A32
MakeEmpty procedure, 613, 625
MakeIndex module, 331, 359, 360
MakeListEmpty procedure, 123, 131, 135
Mapping function, 33, 458
Mark and gather, 548
Mark procedure, 556, 563
Marking, 548–549, 551
Mathematical induction, A6
Matrix, 31, 33
  adjacency, 581–582, 585–586, 588–589, 595, 597, 603–604
  diagonal, 38–39, 45
  labeled adjacency, 581
  lower triangular, 40
  multiplication, 33
  sparse, 38, 41, 42, 45–46, 143, 145, 146, 152–153, 157, 159–160, 162–163, 177
  square, 32
  triangular, 38, 40, 45
  tridiagonal, 38–39, 45
  upper triangular, 40, 45
  weighted adjacency, 581, 586
Matrix type, 153, 167
MatrixMult procedure, 33, 166
MAX, 6
Max procedure, 613, 626
Maze, 193, 230
MCST, 576–577
Mechanical card sorter, 415
Member, 610
  function, 613, 624, 629, 639
MEMBER function, 538
Membership, 10, 610, 622
Memory, 138–139, 143, 145, 149–150, 582, A7
  address, 33, 97
  allocation, 149, 546
  central, 29
  main, 13
  management, 97, 149, 504, 547
Menu, 350

Index A89

Merge, 15, 387, 418, 427
　find set, 620, 632, 640
　procedure, 620, 637
　sort, 72, 81, 418–419, 440, 441
MergeFiles procedure, 22, 27
MergeFilesTest module, 21
MergeInto procedure, 637
MergeRuns procedure, 77, 429
MergeSort procedure, 76, 421
Message, 291
MFSCreate procedure, 620, 637
MFSET type, 620
MFSETs module, 620, 632, 636
Mid square, 459, 476
MIN, 6
Min procedure, 613, 626, 629
Minimax, 310, 313
Minimum cost spanning tree, 576, 578, 618–619
Mismatch, 511, 515
Mixed numbers, 98
MOD, 4, 209, 418
Model, 238
Modular, 202, 223, 296
　design chart, 16, 20, 447, A4, A13, A17, A19, A29
Module, A4, A20
　definition, 83, 86, 99
　implementation, 83, 94
　local, 244
Move procedure, 558
Multidimensional, 7, 30, 148
Multilinked list, 142, 176
MultiplyFractions procedure, 100, 110
Multiway tree, 377, 405
MultMatrix procedure, 174

Name server, 445
NameServer module, 446–447
Natural merge sort, 423
Network, 578, 579
NEW, 97
NewNode procedure, 298
Next fit, 151, 176
NextKey procedure, 403
NextMove procedure, 320
NextNode procedure, 286, 303
NIL, 536
Nim, 326

Node, 133, 159, 201, 280, 289, 297, 310, 324, 328, 330, 334, 337, 341, 344–345, 357–358, 366, 373, 376–378, 380, 382, 384, 387, 435–436, 540, 542–544, 566
　current, 284, 301, 346
　internal, 436, 439
　leaf, 280, 324, 345, 347, 356, 377, 380, 383–384, 387, 393, 432, 435, 439–440
NOT, 6
Null character, 482, 496
NULL operator, 537
Number sequencing, 396
NUMBERP operator, 537
Numerator, 98, 101, 114–115

Octal, 5
ODD, 5
Opaque type, 86, 96–97, 115, 153, 200, 204, 207, 237, 255, 343, 453, 485, 496
Open
　addressing, 461, 476
　array, 59, 204
　procedure, 90
Operating system, 237, 245, 251, 445
Operator
　ATOM, 537
　CAR, 537, 545
　CDR, 537, 546
　CONS, 537
　DIFFERENCE, 537
　DIVIDE, 537
　EQ, 537
　GREATERP, 537
　LESSP, 537
　NULL, 537
　NUMBERP, 537
　PLUS, 537
　PLUS1, 537
　QUOTE, 536
　relational, 10
　SUB1, 537
Optimal search tree, 390–391, 405
Optimization, 291
ORD, 5

Order
　column major, 34
　lexicographic, 34
　row major, 34
　topological, 570
Ordered tree, 280
Output, A2, A15, A19
　procedure, 486
OutputStandings procedure, A25
OutputString procedure, 89, 485, 503
OutputWord procedure, 488
Overflow table, 477
Overhead, 213, 223

Page, 330
PaidMore procedure, 11
Palindrome, 231
Parameter, A12
Parent, 280, 293, 301, 345, 347–348, 365, 380, 390, 394, 435
Partially ordered tree, 392, 405
Partition, 67–68, 224–225, 227
Pascal, A1, A6
Pass, 58, 63–64, 70–72, 411, 412, 422, 431, 554
Path, 193–194, 198, 230, 280, 373, 440, 566, 586, 597, 634–635, 640
　all pairs shortest, 586, 595, 603
　critical, 579
　search, 340, 377, 405
　shortest, 587, 595, 596
　simple, 566
　weighted, 390
Pattern, 511, 513–515, 518–519, 524–525, 528
　matching, 509, 511, 513, 517, 520, 525, 528, 531
PatternMatches module, 520
Perfect hash function, 460
Perfectly balanced tree, 364, 405
Performance, 529
Permutation, 467
PERT, 578
Pivot, 67, 71
Place procedure, 381
PLUS operator, 537
PLUS1 operator, 537

Pointer, 10, 96–97, 138, 142, 144–146, 154–156, 160, 200–201, 212, 249, 297, 338, 341, 354–358, 379, 417, 468, 541–543, 548, 550–551, 557, 559, 561
Polyalphabetic substitution, 493
Polynomial, 62, 177
  arithmetic, 126
Polyphase sort, 423–425, 427, 431, 440
PolyphaseSort procedure, 428
Pop procedure, 182, 184, 200, 202, 204–205, 230, 231
Portable, 204
Pos function, 88, 484, 501
Possible procedure, 315
Post-condition, 85–86
Postfix, 185–186, 231, 290
Postorder, 284, 289, 324, 360
Postponed obligations, 224–225
Precedence, 186
Pre-condition, 85–86
Predecessor, 140, 326, 341, 344, 347, 354, 358, 387
Preface, A11, A26, A29
Prefix, 290
Preorder, 284, 289, 324, 360, 572
Prim procedure, 577
Prim's algorithm, 576–577, 618
Primary clustering, 461–462
PrintCode procedure, 190
PrintComparison procedure, 11
Printer, 252–253, 260, 276
PrinterActive function, 255, 268
PrinterFinished function, 255, 268
PrintExplanation procedure, 272
PrintJobStats procedure, 269
PrintMaze procedure, 196
PrintMove procedure, 222
PrintNum procedure, 209
PrintPath procedure, 588
PrintTree procedure, 338, 359, 404
Priority, 252
Priority queue, 235, 246, 279, 363, 392–395, 405, 598, 602, 607, 638
Probe, 463, 467, 469, 471

Probing
  linear, 461, 466, 474–475
  function, 460
  pseudorandom, 462, 466, 469, 474, 475
  quadratic, 463, 479
Problem solving, A1–A2
Procedure
  type, 10, 286, 329
  variable, 11
Process, 245–246
ProcessLine procedure, 91
Processor, 245
Program
  evaluation review technique, 578
  formatting, A29
  testing, A12
  verification, A6
Programming style, A11
Proof of correctness, A6
Prototyping, A3
Pseudo address, 42
Pseudocode, 17, 21, 58, 61, 64, 69, 73–74, 101, 106, 114, 149, 160, 174, 185, 188, 193, 208, 220–221, 225–227, 229, 255–257, 259, 273, 309, 311, 343–345, 347, 350, 384, 397–398, 400, 413, 416, 419–420, 434, 436, 439, 470, 519, 597, 615, A5–A6, A9, A11–A14, A17, A19, A21, A27
PseudoRandom module, 240, 244, 521
Pseudorandom probing, 462, 466, 469, 474, 475
Public key, 495
Push procedure, 182, 184, 199, 201, 204–205, 230–231
Pushdown list, 182
Put procedure, 123, 131, 136
PutValue procedure, 207

Quadratic, 78
  probing, 463, 479
Queue, 235–236, 240, 244, 246, 251, 253, 258, 276, 289, 330, 575–576
  type, 236, 247, 249
QueueADT module, 236, 247, 249
QueueElements module, 244
QueueError, 236
QueueHead procedure, 237, 248, 251
Queuing theory, 237
Quick sort, 67, 80, 81, 224, 340
QuickSort procedure, 69, 79
Quit procedure, 242
QUOTE operator, 536

Rabin-Karp algorithm, 515
RabinKarp function, 516, 528–529
Radius, 606
Radix, 459
  sorting, 415, 418, 440–441
Random, 518–519, 524, 527
  function, 240, 521
RandomInt function, 521
RandomLetter function, 522
RandomWord procedure, 523
Range error, A27
Rank, 31
  function, A23
ReadByte procedure, 90
ReadChar procedure, 15
ReadjustTree procedure, 438
ReadLine procedure, 89, 485, 503
ReadMatrix procedure, 165
ReadRecord procedure, 21
ReadWord procedure, 14, 90
REAL, 4, 5, 26
ReBalance procedure, 397, 401
Rebalancing module, 397, 401
ReBuild function, 402
RECORD, 4, 26, 281
Record, 7, 8, 16, 17, 194, 359, 423, 443–444, 453, 582, 599, A8, A17
RecordPath procedure, 197
Recurse procedure, 232
Recursion, 55, 67–68, 106, 181, 208–209, 213–214, 219, 223–224, 226, 230, 356
Recursive, 55, 288, 358, 534, 549, 562
  descent, 291
Redirection, 15, 163

Reduce procedure, 109
Reduction, 98
Reference counter, 547
Referent, 97
Refinement, A1, A4, A9, A17, A32
Relational operators, 10
Remove procedure, 385
Rename procedure, 14, 90
Replace procedure, 385
Representation, 101, 144, 145, 281, 283, 312, 392, 459, 541–543, 561, 590, 595, 604, 609, 632, 634–635, 638
Representatives, 615
ReSeed procedure, 521
Reset procedure, 90
Resource, 245
Restore procedure, 222
RetrieveNode procedure, 286
Return, 219
Right justified, 490
RightBalance procedure, 371
RightLeftRotate procedure, 368
RightRotate procedure, 367
Ripple, 202–203
Root, 280, 336, 341, 348, 377–378, 383, 394–395, 440, 551, 606, 634
Rotation, 406
  single, 364–366, 370, 374
  double, 364, 366, 376
Row major order, 34
Run, 72, 418, 423–427
  time check, 37

S-expression, 535–536, 562
Saddle point, 46
Save procedure, 222
Scalar type, 4, 30
ScheduleCPUs procedure, 274
ScheduleDisks procedure, 275
SchedulePrinters procedure, 275
Schorr, H., 549
Schorr-Waite-Deutsch algorithm, 550
Scramble procedure, 450
Scrambler module, 450
Search
  binary, 42–43, 55, 64, 79, 379,
    454, 466, 476
  Fibonacci, 454
  interpolation, 456
  key, 53, 55, 443, 454
  path, 340, 377, 405
  procedure, 444, 452
  sequential, 42, 53, 61, 79, 454, 475
  simple, 509
  tree, 391
SearchAndInsert procedure, 461
SearchBuckets function, 465
Searching, 49, 53, 142, 279, 287, 359, 378, 380, 443, 454, 475–476, 530–531
SearchInNode function, 380
SearchKey function, 329, 338, 379
SearchList procedure, 123, 131, 135
SearchTree procedure, 285, 302
Secondary
  clustering, 463
  storage, 13
Selection sort, 57, 79, 412
SelectionSort procedure, 59
SelectPattern procedure, 524
Self-documenting code, A29
Semantic
  error, A12
  network, 606
Sentinel, 54
Sequence, 86, 116–117, 121–122, 182, 330, 378, 392, 398, 410, 412, 482, 524, 534
Sequencing
  letter, 396
  number, 396
Sequential search, 42, 53, 61, 79, 454, 475
SequentialSearch procedure, 54
SeriesPrint procedure, 233
SET, 10, 26, 611
Set, 7, 9, 610, 612, 623, 627
  empty, 610
  merge find, 620, 632, 640
SetCurrentNode procedure, 286
SetPar procedure, 223
Sets module, 612, 623, 627
SetsElements module, 611
Shaker sort, 67, 80
Shell, D. L., 410
Shell sort, 410, 440, 441
ShellSort procedure, 411
Shift, 466
Shortest path, 587, 595, 596
ShortestPath procedure, 587
ShowMachineState procedure, 255, 271
Sibling, 281
Side effect, A12, A26–A27
SiftDown procedure, 414
Simple
  path, 566
  search, 509
SimpleBoyerMoore function, 514, 528, 529
SimpleSearch function, 509, 528, 529
Simulation, 237, 243, 245, 251–253, 259–260, 273, 276, 278
Single rotation, 364–366, 370, 374
SIZE, 5
SkipBlanks procedure, 111
Smaller function, 22
Software, A14
  bus, A20
Solution, A2
SolveMaze module, 195, 233
Sort
  binary insertion, 64
  bubble, 64, 79
  cascade, 441
  heap, 412–413, 440–441
  insertion, 61, 79–80
  linear insertion, 61
  merge, 72, 81, 418–419, 440, 441
  natural merge, 423
  polyphase, 423–425, 427, 431, 440
  quick, 67, 80, 81, 224, 340
  radix, 415, 418, 440–441
  selection, 57, 79, 412
  shaker, 67, 80
  Shell, 410, 440, 441
  topological, 570, 578
  tournament, 431, 433, 440–441

Sorting, 49, 56, 72, 227, 279, 409, 423
SortStandings procedure, A25
Space
  complexity, 53, 55, 56, 61, 64, 67, 71, 78, 136, 201, 203, 249, 251, 304, 340, 440, A7
  efficiency, 154, 223
  utilization, 39
Spanning tree, 566–567, 576
Sparse matrix, 38, 41, 42, 45–46, 143, 145, 146, 152–153, 157, 159–160, 162–163, 177
SparseMatrix module, 153, 167
Special form, 538
Specification, A2, A5, A9, A13
Square matrix, 32
Stable, 80
Stack, 71, 181–182, 194, 209, 211, 213, 219, 226, 230, 340, 549, 559, 576
  frame, 211, 212
  type, 183, 199, 201
StackElements module, 183, 194
Stacks module, 183, 199, 201, 230
StackTop procedure, 184, 200, 202, 204–205
StartNewCPUJob procedure, 254, 267
StartNewDiskJob procedure, 255, 268
StartNewPrinterJob procedure, 255, 269
Static, 37, 128–129, 136–139, 145–146, 149, 199, 213, 246, 276, 304–305, 323, 360, 450, 496, 530
Stepwise refinement, A3
StoreAndSplit procedure, 382
StoreNode procedure, 286
String, 481–482, 518
  compression, 530
  constant, 8, 89, 482, 529
  type, 87, 116, 483, 496, 505
StringEqual function, 88, 484, 500
StringGreater function, 88, 484, 500

Strings module, 8, 87, 92, 94, 117, 483, 496, 505, A4
StringToFraction procedure, 100, 111
Strong type checking, 472
Strongly typed, 183
Structural design, A2
Structure chart, 16, 72, 99, 224–225, 253, 308–310, 432–433, 527, A2–A4, A9–A10, A13, A16–A17, A28–A29
Structured type, 7
Stub, A10–A11, A28–A29
Style, A11
SUB1 operator, 537
Subarray, 35, 36
Sublinear, 529
Sublist, 543–545, 559
Subrange, 6
Subscript, 7
Subsequence, 410, 412
Subset, 610, 615, 616
  function, 613, 624
Substitution table, 492
SubtractFractions procedure, 100, 110
Subtree, 280, 328, 365, 373, 391, 398
Successor, 287, 289, 341, 344–345, 347, 355, 357, 360
Superset, 610
Swap procedure, 59, 229, 414
Symbol table, 450, 458, 481
Symbolic debugger, A13
Symmetric
  difference, 10, 610, 622
  list, 140–141, 176
Syntactical error, A26
System
  clock, 252
  job, 252
SYSTEM module, 204, 207

Table, 443–444, 450, 456, 475, 477, 586, 631, A17, A19
  backup, 510
  closed hash, 468

hash, 454, 457, 464, 466, 476–477, 631, 639–640
  overflow, 477
  substitution, 492
  symbol, 450, 458, 481
  type, 444, 451
TableElements module, 451
Tables module, 444, 451
Tag field, 9, 343
Tail, 246, 417, 423
  recursion, 217, 218, 230
Telecommunications, 291, 445
Term procedure, 291
Test cases, A9, A11–A12
Test data, 20, 115, 191, 227, A11, A21
TestFractions module, 106
Testing, A9, A13, A15, A20–A21, A27–A29, A30, A32
  program, A17, A20
  strategy, 19, 74, 106, 162, 227, 260, 314, 350, 400, 435, 471, 520, 555, 598, 636, A9, A11, A13, A20, A32
TestSpMatrix module, 164
TestThreadedBST module, 350
Tetrahedral array, 41, 45
Text
  editor, 486
  formatter, 486
TextJustify module, 486
Thrashing, 548
Thread, 341, 343, 345–349, 354, 355, 357–359
ThreadedBSTree type, 343, 353
ThreadedBSTrees module, 342, 353, 360
Three-gram, 527
Tic-Tac-Toe, 307
TicTacToe module, 315
Time
  complexity, 50, 54, 61, 78–79, 201, 203, 249, 251, 409, 439, 572, 576, A7–A8
  efficiency, 154, 223
TimeDiff function, 241
TimeSearch procedure, 525

Top-down
  design, A2
  testing, A9–A10, A28
Topological
  order, 570
  sort, 570, 578
TopoSort procedure, 571
ToString procedure, 88, 485, 502
Tournament sort, 431, 433, 440–441
TournamentSort procedure, 436
Towers of Hanoi, 210, 214, 232–233
Trace, A12, A27
Transitive closure, 585, 587
Transparent type, 86, 96, 485, 529
Transpose, 32
TransposeMatrix procedure, 32
Traversal, 284, 340, 343–344, 357–360, 398, 572
Traverse procedure, 302
TraverseTree procedure, 285, 302, 329, 338
Tree, 279–280, 304, 323, 354, 364, 534, 561, 606, 631, 634, 639
  AVL, 363–364, 376, 405–406
  B, 363, 377–378, 380, 405–406
  binary, 281, 284, 323, 364, 431, 451
  binary search, 281, 327–328, 330, 334, 359, 364, 395–396, 400, 465, 606, 630, 639
  decision, 102
  degenerate binary, 339, 364, 391, 395, 405
  expression, 289–291
  family, 326
  full binary, 296, 324–325, 339, 392
  game, 308
  height balanced, 364, 395
  minimum cost spanning, 576, 578, 618–619
  multiway, 377, 405
  optimal search, 390–391, 405
  ordered, 280
  partially ordered, 392, 405
  perfectly balanced, 364, 405
  search, 391
  spanning, 566–567, 576
TreeError, 285
TreeInsertionSort procedure, 325
TreeSelectionSort procedure, 325
TreeSize function, 286
Triangular matrix, 38, 40, 45
Tri-diagonal matrix, 38–39, 45
TRUNC, 5
Truncation, 459
TryMove procedure, 197
Two-gram, 527
Two-tiered array, 155
TYPE, 7, 26
Type, 86
  abstract data, 83, 84, 86, 115, 279, 281, 342, 445, 475, 533–534
  AVLTree, 366
  base, 6, 9
  basic data, 124
  BinarySearchTree, 336, 397, 401
  BinaryTree, 285
  BTree, 377
  checking, 12, 203
  composite, 7
  data, 4, 25, 84
  Dictionary, 614
  file, 13, 89
  Fraction, 99
  generic, 203–204
  Graph, 568, 582, 590
  index, 7, 30
  List, 122
  Matrix, 153, 167
  MFSet, 620
  opaque, 86, 96–97, 115, 153, 200, 204, 207, 237, 255, 343, 453, 485, 496
  procedure, 10, 286, 329
  Queue, 236, 247, 249
  scalar, 4, 30
  Stack, 183, 199, 201
  String, 87, 116, 483, 496, 505
  structured, 7
  Table, 444, 451
  ThreadedBSTree, 343, 353
  transparent, 86, 96, 485, 529

Undirected graph, 566, 581
Union, 10, 610, 622
UNION function, 539
Union procedure, 612, 623
UpdateStandings procedure, A23
UpdateVertex procedure, 569, 584, 593
Upper triangular matrix, 40, 45
User's manual, 25, A31
Utility routines, A4, A11

VAL, 5
ValidPassword function, 446, 448
Variable
  dynamic, 97
  local, 211
  procedure, 11
Variant, 9, 183, 343
Vector, 31, 33, 36, 37, 147
Verification, A6
VerifyAbsence function, 524
Vertex, 566, 568, 571–572, 593–594, 596–599, 602, 606
VertexCount function, 568, 583, 591
Vigenère square, 493, 494, 531
Virtual element, 144, 148

Waite, W. M., 549
Warshall, S., 585
Warshall procedure, 586, 605
Warshall's algorithm, 585–586
Weight, 390, 589
Weight function, 569, 584, 594
Weighted
  adjacency matrix, 581, 586
  graph, 566–567, 586
  path length, 390
While procedure, 214
WHLStandings module, A22
Williams, J., 412
Win function, 320
Wirth, Niklaus, A1
WORD, 204
Word, 89, 91, 330, 622
Worst fit, 151, 176
WPL, 390–391
WriteByte procedure, 90
WriteChar procedure, 15
WriteElement procedure, 124

WriteMatrix procedure, 165
WriteRecord procedure, 22
WriteWord procedure, 14, 90

XOR, 466, 472

Zero based, 482, 496
Zipf's distribution, 54

Procedures from Abstract Data Types (continued)

Procedures	Modules
Get	ListADT
GetAdjacent	Graphs
GetCurrentNode	BinaryTreeADT
Include	Sets
Initial	MFSETs
InitString	Strings
InputString	Strings
Insert	Strings, ListADT, Tables
InsertEdge	Graphs
InsertElement	BTreeADT
Insertion	AVLTreeADT
InsertNode	BinaryTreeADT, BSTreeADT, AVLTreeADT
InsertVertex	Graphs
Intersection	Sets
LeftBalance	AVLTreeADT
LeftRightRotate	AVLTreeADT
LeftRotate	AVLTreeADT
Length	Strings
ListLength	ListADT
Lookup	FileSystem
MakeEmpty	Sets
MakeListEmpty	ListADT
Max	Sets
Member	Sets
Merge	MFSETs
MFSCreate	MFSETs
Min	Sets
NextNode	BinaryTreeADT
Open	Files
OutputString	Strings
Place	BTreeADT
Pop	Stacks
Pos	Strings
Push	Stacks
Put	ListADT
QueueHead	QueueADT

Procedures from Abstract Data Types (continued)

Procedures	Modules
ReadByte	Files
ReadChar	FileSystem
ReadLine	Strings
ReadWord	FileSystem, Files
Remove	BTreeADT
Rename	FileSystem, Files
Replace	BTreeADT
Reset	Files
RetrieveNode	BinaryTreeADT
RightBalance	AVLTreeADT
RightLeftRotate	AVLTreeADT
RightRotate	AVLTreeADT
Search	Tables
SearchKey	BSTreeADT, BTreeADT
SearchInNode	BTreeADT
SearchList	ListADT
SearchTree	BinaryTreeADT
SetCurrentNode	BinaryTreeADT
StackTop	Stacks
StoreAndSplit	BTreeADT
StoreNode	BinaryTreeADT
StringEqual	Strings
StringGreater	Strings
Subset	Sets
ToString	Strings
TraverseTree	BinaryTreeADT, BSTreeADT
TreeSize	BinaryTreeADT
Union	Sets
UpdateVertex	Graphs
VertexCount	Graphs
Weight	Graphs
WriteByte	Files
WriteChar	FileSystem
WriteElement	ListElements
WriteWord	FileSystem Files